MEDIA ESSENTIALS

LaunchPad for *Media Essentials* goes beyond the printed textbook.

Media Essentials emphasizes convergence and practices it, too. LaunchPad for *Media Essentials*, Macmillan Learning's online course space, includes a number of key features.

Video Clips

Callouts in the boxes and margins throughout the book direct students to a wealth of video clips, which are now divided into two distinct types:

- **Web Clips**, which suggest an easily accessible third-party video clip and provide a related discussion question; links are included in LaunchPad.
- **LaunchPad video quizzes**, where students can view a video directly on LaunchPad, respond to accompanying critical thinking questions, and have their answers recorded in the gradebook.

We've included clips from movies, TV shows, online sources, and other media texts, in addition to insightful interviews with media experts and newsmakers. For a complete list of available clips, see the last book page.

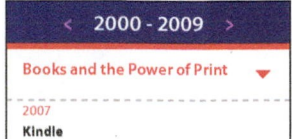

Digital Timeline

A brand new digital timeline feature will help students dive into the history of mass communication and see how one event or advancement led to the next.

LearningCurve

LearningCurve is a gamelike adaptive quizzing system designed to help students review. Each chapter's LearningCurve uses a wealth of review questions and adaptive technology that analyzes student answers, helping them to figure out what they already know and master the concepts they still need to learn.

LaunchPad for *Media Essentials* can be packaged with the book or purchased on its own. To learn more, see the inside back cover or visit launchpadworks.com.

For more information about *Media Essentials*, please visit macmillanlearning.com/communication.

MEDIA ESSENTIALS

A Brief Introduction

Fourth Edition

Richard Campbell
MIAMI UNIVERSITY

Christopher R. Martin
UNIVERSITY OF NORTHERN IOWA

Bettina Fabos
UNIVERSITY OF NORTHERN IOWA

with

Shawn Harmsen
COE COLLEGE

bedford/st.martin's
Macmillan Learning
Boston | New York

For Bedford/St. Martin's

Vice President, Editorial, Macmillan Learning Humanities: Edwin Hill
Senior Program Director for Communication and College Success: Erika Gutierrez
Senior Development Manager: Susan McLaughlin
Senior Developmental Editor: Christina Lembo
Senior Content Project Manager: Kerri A. Cardone
Media Project Manager: Sarah O'Connor Kepes
Senior Workflow Project Manager: Jennifer Wetzel
Production Assistant: Brianna Lester
Marketing Manager: Kayti Corfield
Copy Editor: Jamie Thaman
Indexer: Julie Grady
Photo Researcher: Terri Wright
Director of Rights and Permissions: Hilary Newman
Senior Art Director: Anna Palchik
Text Design: Rick Korab
Cover Design: William Boardman
Cover Photo: Linghe Zhao/Getty Images
Composition: Lumina Datamatics, Inc.
Printing and Binding: King Printing Co., Inc.

Manufactured in the United States of America.

2 1 0 9
f e d c b

For information, write: Bedford/St. Martin's, 75 Arlington Street, Boston, MA 02116
  (617-399-4000)

ISBN 978-1-319-05947-7
ISBN 978-1-319-07781-5 (Loose-leaf Edition)

About the Authors

Richard Campbell, chair of the Department of Media, Journalism, and Film at Miami University, is the author of *"60 Minutes" and the News: A Mythology for Middle America* (1991) and coauthor of *Cracked Coverage: Television News, the Anti-Cocaine Crusade, and the Reagan Legacy* (1994). Campbell has written for numerous publications, including *Columbia Journalism Review, Critical Studies in Mass Communication, Journal of Communication,* and *TV Quarterly*. He also serves on the board of directors for Cincinnati Public Radio. He holds a PhD from Northwestern University.

Dianna Campbell

Christopher R. Martin is a professor of digital journalism at the University of Northern Iowa and author of *Framed! Labor and the Corporate Media* (2003). He has written articles and reviews on journalism, televised sports, the Internet, and labor for several publications, including *Communication Research, Journal of Communication, Journal of Communication Inquiry, Labor Studies Journal,* and *Culture, Sport, and Society*. He is also on the editorial board of the *Journal of Communication Inquiry*. Martin holds a PhD from the University of Michigan and has also taught at Miami University.

Bettina Fabos

Bettina Fabos, an award-winning video maker and former print reporter, is an associate professor of visual communication and interactive media studies at the University of Northern Iowa. She is the author of *Wrong Turn on the Information Superhighway: Education and the Commercialized Internet* (2003). Her areas of expertise include critical media literacy, Internet commercialization and education, and media representations of popular culture. Her work has been published in *Library Trends, Review of Educational Research,* and *Harvard Educational Review*. Fabos has a PhD from the University of Iowa.

Christopher Martin

Shawn Harmsen teaches courses in journalism, digital and broadcast media production, and critical media studies at Coe College in Cedar Rapids, Iowa. Before entering academics, Harmsen worked in radio and television news for over a decade. He did almost every job in the newsroom, from reporter, photographer, and anchor to producer and news director. Harmsen made the transition to scholarly work, earning an MA at the University of Northern Iowa and a PhD at the University of Iowa. While at Iowa, he edited the *Journal of Communication Inquiry* and coauthored work published in *Journalism Practice* and *Journalism and Mass Communication Quarterly*. His research interests include the sociology of news, political reporting, social media, and social movements.

Paul W. Jensen

Brief Contents

Preface

THE DIGITAL FUTURE OF MASS MEDIA HAS ARRIVED, and we're experiencing it firsthand. Not only has there been a fundamental change in the ways we use and consume media, but also in the many ways that media messages saturate our lives. As media industries continue to evolve and converge, we want students to have the critical tools they need to understand the media-saturated world around them. These tools, and an understanding of the fundamentals of media studies, are exactly what we had in mind when we wrote *Media Essentials*.

Media Essentials distills media industries and major concepts like digital convergence and legal controls down to their essence. Each chapter offers incisive historical context, frames key concepts up front, and uses pivotal examples to tell the broader story of how different forms of media have developed, how they work, and how they connect to us today. For example, Chapter 5, "Sound Recording and Popular Music," explores the roots of sound recording, tracing its evolution from cylinders and flat disks to classic vinyl, tape, and, eventually, a number of digital formats. The chapter goes on to describe how popular music—first in the form of rock and roll in the 1950s—shook up American (and global) culture, and continued to do so with folk, country, soul, punk, and hip-hop genres. It then follows the money through an in depth section on the economics of sound recording, explaining how digital formats of recorded music have completely upended the music industry, leaving music fans more likely to stream music on their smartphones than assemble a collection of music, like previous generations of fans might have done. The chapter concludes with a discussion of music's role in a democratic society.

In addition to a wealth of content offered in every chapter, *Media Essentials* continues to be substantially briefer than competing books. Throughout the book, our coverage is succinct, accessible, and peppered with memorable examples, and the book's unique approach—distilling media information to its core—gives instructors the space to add in personal research or social perspectives. This **fourth edition has been further streamlined** to focus on the most essential information and the most relevant examples, and a bright, updated design with more than 80 new photos keeps students engaged as they read.

In this fourth edition, we've also **emphasized the importance of the digital turn**, a shift in media use and consumption resulting from the emergence of the Internet as a mass medium. Characterized by lightning fast Internet and ever-more-powerful personal devices, the digital turn has enabled an array of media to converge and be easily shared, bringing both disruption and innovation to every traditional mass media industry. A new section in Chapter 1 introduces this crucial development right up front, and we've renamed our Converging Media boxes to reflect this increased emphasis; now called The Digital Turn Case Studies, these boxes go in depth on timely issues related to all facets of the digital turn, with new topics that include Fear of Missing Out (FOMO), Netflix's predictive algorithm, "sexting" and pornography, and using online marketing to attract a movie audience in this digital age.

The fourth edition also includes **revised and reorganized economics sections in each industry chapter**, which spotlight the latest economic developments across the media landscape, particularly since the digital turn. For example, Chapter 3 explores the continued impact of convergence on the newspaper business model; Chapter 5 spotlights how making, selling, and profiting from music has changed in this age of streaming; and Chapter 9 focuses on the five leading digital media companies that seek to control the Internet.

Because the book also practices convergence, *Media Essentials* has an online video program accessible in LaunchPad, with clips that offer students firsthand experience with important (and attention-grabbing) media texts, covering everything from groundbreaking films like *12 Years a Slave* to streaming TV hits like *Stranger Things*. **Half of the suggested video clips** accompanying the text's case studies are new to this edition. LaunchPad also includes access to LearningCurve, an adaptive quizzing system that helps students figure out what they know — and what material they need to review. LaunchPad for *Media Essentials* can be packaged with the book at a significant discount.

Hallmark Features of *Media Essentials*

Clear, streamlined, and accessible. Significantly briefer than competing texts, *Media Essentials* addresses all the topics typically covered in introductory mass communication books. From the media industries to legal controls, it offers just the right amount of detail, ensuring that students have enough information to make connections and develop media literacy.

An organization that supports learning. *Media Essentials* offers a chronological table of contents and consistent organization. Each chapter includes a brief history of the topic, a discussion of the evolution of the medium, a look at media economics, and coverage of the medium's relationship to democracy, media literacy, and convergence enabled by the digital turn. This consistent organization and focus helps students make their way through the material while they grasp themes both big and small. Under each major heading, a preview paragraph highlights key ideas and contextualizes them, guiding students through the material.

Learning tools help students master the material. Each chapter opens with an outline highlighting what topics will be covered, while The Digital Turn and Media

Literacy Case Study boxes address relevant topics in greater detail and help students think critically about them. Finally, each chapter concludes with Chapter Essentials, a useful study guide that helps students review material and prepares them for quizzes and exams.

New to This Fourth Edition

Print and media that converge with LaunchPad. LaunchPad for *Media Essentials*, Fourth Edition, Macmillan Learning's online course space, meets students where they love to be – online. Available to be purchased on its own or packaged with the text at a significant discount, LaunchPad for the fourth edition includes the following new features:

- **A brand new digital timeline** feature will help students dive into the history of mass communication and see how one event or advancement led to the next.
- **Media Literacy Practice activities**, which encourage students to apply and practice their media literacy skills, have gone digital. An online activity is included for each chapter.
- **Half of the video clips** accompanying the text's case studies are new to this edition, and the clips throughout the text are now divided into two distinct types:
  - **Web Clips**, which suggest an easily accessible third-party video clip and provide a related discussion question; links are included in LaunchPad
  - **LaunchPad video quizzes**, where students can view a video directly on LaunchPad, respond to accompanying critical thinking questions, and have their answers recorded in the gradebook.

We've included clips from movies, TV shows, online sources, and other media texts like *Stranger Things*, *Black-ish*, and *Spotlight*, in addition to insightful interviews with media experts and newsmakers. For a complete list of available clips, see the inside back cover.

Expanded coverage of the digital turn. Characterized by lightning fast Internet and ever-more-powerful personal devices, the digital turn has enabled an array of media to converge and be easily shared. A new section in Chapter 1 introduces this crucial development right up front, and Converging Media boxes have been renamed to reflect this increased emphasis; now called The Digital Turn Case Studies, these boxes go in depth on a variety of timely issues related to the digital turn. New topics include Fear of Missing Out (FOMO) and using online marketing to attract a movie audience in this digital age.

Revised and reorganized economics sections in each industry chapter. These sections spotlight the latest economic developments across the media landscape, particularly since the digital turn. For example, Chapter 3 explores the continued impact of convergence on the newspaper business model, while Chapter 9 focuses on the five leading digital media companies that seek to control the Internet.

A more streamlined text with an updated design. The text has been further streamlined to focus on the most essential information and the most relevant examples, and a bright, updated design with more than 80 new photos keeps students engaged and energized as they read.

Updated coverage of all the latest developments in the world of mass media.

- New chapter openers bring students into the stories of the media with current and attention-grabbing coverage of recent events, including hashtag activism, the popularity of young-adult fiction, *Stranger Things* and streaming TV, Let's Play gaming videos, WikiLeaks, Snapchat marketing, and President Trump's relationship with the media.
- New and expanded coverage includes developments during and after the 2016 presidential election; a fully updated look at the evolution of the Internet, including the development of commercialization, social media, and the Semantic Web; and more robust coverage of social media and mobile advertising.
- Cutting edge examples discuss *Spotlight*, *Fun Home*, Chance the Rapper, Nintendo Switch, *Black-ish*, Deadpool, and DJ Khaled among others.
- Fully updated figures, tables, and graphs incorporate the latest in industry data.

Student Resources

For more information on student resources or to learn about package options, please visit the online catalog at **macmillanlearning.com**.

LaunchPad: Where Students Learn

Digital tools for *Media Essentials*, Fourth Edition, are available on LaunchPad, a dynamic online platform that combines a curated collection of videos, homework assignments, e-Book content, and the LearningCurve adaptive quizzing program, organized for easy assignability, in a simple user interface. LaunchPad for *Media Essentials* features:

- **A fully interactive e-Book.** Every LaunchPad e-Book comes with powerful study tools, multimedia content, and easy customization tools for instructors. Students can search, highlight, and bookmark, making studying easier and more efficient.
- **LearningCurve adaptive quizzing.** In every chapter, call-outs prompt students to tackle the game-like LearningCurve quizzes to test their knowledge and reinforce learning of the material.

- **Integrated video clips that extend and complement the book.** A rich library of LaunchPad videos and suggested Web clips offers easy access to clips from movies, TV shows, interviews, and more.
- **Video assignment tools.** LaunchPad's video assignment tools provide an easy way for instructors and students to upload, embed, and assess video assignments.
- **The newest edition of our *Media Career Guide*.** LaunchPad includes a digital version of this practical, student-friendly guide to media jobs, featuring tips and career guidance for students considering a major in the media industries.

To learn more about LaunchPad for *Media Essentials* or to purchase access, go to **launchpadworks.com**.

Your e-Book. Your way.

A variety of e-Book formats are available for use on computers, tablets, and e-readers, featuring portability, customization options, and affordable prices. For more information, visit **macmillanlearning.com/ebooks**.

Media Career Guide: Preparing for Jobs in the 21st Century, Eleventh Edition

Sherri Hope Culver; ISBN 978-1-319-12646-9
Practical, student-friendly, and revised to address recent statistics on the job market, this guide includes a comprehensive directory of media jobs, practical tips, and career guidance for students considering a major in the media industries. The *Media Career Guide* can also be packaged at a significant discount with the print text. An electronic version comes integrated in LaunchPad for *Media Essentials*.

Instructor Resources

For more information or to order or download the instructor resources, please visit the online catalog at **macmillanlearning.com**.

LaunchPad for *Media Essentials*, Fourth Edition

At Bedford/St. Martin's, we are committed to providing online resources that meet the needs of instructors and students in powerful yet simple ways. We've taken what we've learned from both instructors and students to create a new generation of technology featuring LaunchPad. With its student-friendly approach, LaunchPad offers our trusted content—organized for easy assignability in a simple user interface. Access to LaunchPad can be packaged with *Media Essentials* at a significant discount or purchased separately.

- **An easy-to-use interface.** Ready-made interactive LaunchPad units give you the building blocks to assign instantly as is, or customize to fit your course. A unit's worth of work can be assigned in seconds, significantly decreasing the amount of time it takes for you to get your course up and running.
- **Intuitive and useful analytics.** The gradebook quickly and easily allows you to gauge performance for your whole class, for individual students, and for individual assignments, making class prep time as well as time spent with students more productive.
- **A fully interactive e-Book.** Every LaunchPad e-Book comes with powerful study tools, multimedia content, and easy customization tools for instructors. Students can search, highlight, and bookmark, making studying easier and more efficient.
- **LearningCurve adaptive quizzing.** In every chapter, call-outs prompt students to tackle the game-like LearningCurve quizzes to test their knowledge and reinforce learning of the material. Based on research as to how students learn, LearningCurve motivates students to engage with course materials, while the reporting tools let you see what content students have mastered, allowing you to adapt your teaching plan to their needs.
- **Integrated video clips that extend and complement the book.** A rich library of LaunchPad videos and suggested Web clips offers easy access to clips from movies, TV shows, interviews, and more.
- **Video assignment tools.** LaunchPad's video assignment tools provide an easy way for instructors and students to upload, embed, and assess video assignments. This flexible functionality lets you use video however you want in a secure setting.
- **Instructor resources.** The Instructor's Resource Manual, test bank, and lecture slides, as well as two 20-question review quizzes for each chapter, are all available in the LaunchPad for *Media Essentials*, Fourth Edition.

Find out more at **www.launchpadworks.com** or contact your Bedford/ St. Martin's sales representative for more details.

Instructor's Resource Manual

This downloadable manual provides instructors with a comprehensive teaching tool for the introduction to mass communication course. Every chapter offers teaching tips and activities culled from dozens of instructors who teach thousands of students. In addition, this extensive resource provides a range of teaching approaches, tips for facilitating in-class discussions, writing assignments, outlines, lecture topics, lecture spin-offs, critical-process exercises, classroom media resources, and an annotated list of more than two hundred video resources.

Lecture Slides

Slide presentations to help guide each chapter's lecture are available for download.

Test Bank

Available formatted for Windows and Mac, the Test Bank includes multiple choice, fill-in-the-blank, and essay questions for every chapter in *Media Essentials*.

Acknowledgments

We wish every textbook author could have the kind of experience we've had while working on *Media Essentials* and would like to thank everyone at Bedford/St. Martin's who supported this project through its editions and stages, including Vice President Edwin Hill, Senior Program Director Erika Gutierrez, Senior Development Manager Susan McLaughlin, Marketing Manager Kayti Corfield, and Senior Editor Christina Lembo, who helped us develop this edition. We also appreciate the tireless work of Senior Content Project Manager Kerri Cardone, who kept the book on schedule while making sure all details were in place; Senior Workflow Manager Jennifer Wetzel; Senior Media Editor Tom Kane; and Editorial Assistant Kathy McInerney. We are also grateful to our research assistant, Susan Coffin. We extend particular and heartfelt thanks to our collaborator and contributor Shawn Harmsen, for all of his invaluable ideas, expertise, and excellent writing, as well as past contributor Jimmie Reeves, particularly for his knowledge in the world of digital gaming.

We also want to thank the many fine and thoughtful reviewers who contributed ideas to earlier editions of *Media Essentials*: Aje-Ori Agbese, *University of Texas Pan American*; Julie Andsager, *University of Iowa*; Vince Benigni, *College of Charleston*; Michael Bowman, *Arkansas State University*; Scott Brown, *California State University, Northridge*; Ted Carlin, *Shippensburg University of Pennsylvania*; Cheryl Casey, *Champlain College*; Jerome D. DeNuccio, *Graceland University*; Barbara Eisenstock, *California State University, Northridge*; Jennifer Fleming, *California State University–Long Beach*; Doug Ferguson, *College of Charleston*; David Flex, *College of DuPage*; Katie Foss, *Middle Tennessee State University*; Nathaniel Frederick, *Winthrop University*; Peter Galarneau Jr., *West Virginia Wesleyan College*; Mary-Lou Galician, *Arizona State University*; Neil Goldstein, *Montgomery Country Community College*; August Grant, *University of South Carolina*; Jennifer Greer, *University of Alabama*; Jodie Hallsten, *Illinois State University*; Allison Hartcock, *Butler University*; Kirk Hazlett, *Curry College*; Amani E. Ismail, *California State University, Northridge*; Kate Joeckel, *Bellevue University*; Sharon Mazzarella, *James Madison University*; Daniel G. McDonald, *Ohio State University*; Gary Metzker, *California State University–Long Beach*; James E. Mueller, *University of North Texas*; Robert M. Ogles, *Purdue University*;

Ileana Oroza, *University of Miami*; Lawrence Overlan, *Wentworth Institute of Technology*; Daniel A. Panici, *University of Southern Maine*; Kenneth Payne, *Western Kentucky University*; Zengjun Peng, *St. Cloud State University*; Samantha Phillips, *University of Miami*; Selene Phillips, *University of Louisville*; David Pierson, *University of Southern Maine*; Jennifer Proffitt, *Florida State University*; D. Matthew Ramsey, *Salve Regina University*; Arthur A. Raney, *Florida State University*; Chadwick Lee Roberts, *University of North Carolina, Wilmington*; Steve H. Sohn, *University of Louisville*; Martin David Sommerness, *Northern Arizona University*; Mark Steensland, *Pennsylvania State–Erie*; Carl Sessions Stepp, *University of Maryland*; Melvin Sunin, *Pennsylvania State–Erie*; Mike Trice, *Florida Southern College*; Matthew Turner, *Radford University*; Richard West, *University of Texas at San Antonio*; Mark J. P. Wolf, *Concordia University Wisconsin*; and Yanjun Zhao, *Morrisville State College.*

We'd also like to thank the excellent reviewers who gave us feedback as we prepared the fourth edition: Barbara Barnett, *University of Kansas*; Ted Carlin, *Shippensburg University of Pennsylvania*; Cheryl Casey, *Champlain College*; Don Diefenbach, *University of North Carolina at Asheville*; Scott Dunn, *Radford University*; Barbara Eisenstock, *California State University, Northridge*; Doug Ferguson, *College of Charleston*; Harvey Jassem, *University of Hartford*; Kate Joeckel, *Bellevue University*; Steven Keeler, *Cayuga Community College*; Jodi Hallsten Lyczak, *Illinois State University*; Mark Raduziner, *Johnson County Community College*; D. Matthew Ramsey, *Salve Regina University*; Martin David Sommerness, *Northern Arizona University*; Jeff South, *Virginia Commonwealth University*; Andris Straumanis, *University of Wisconsin - River Falls*; Erin Szabo, *College of St. Benedict/ St. John's University*; and Matthew Turner, *Radford University.*

Special thanks from Richard Campbell: I am grateful to all my former students at the University of Wisconsin–Milwaukee, Mount Mary College, the University of Michigan, and Middle Tennessee State University, as well as to my current students at Miami University. Some of my students have contributed directly to this text, and thousands have endured my courses over the years—and made them better. My all-time favorite former students, Chris Martin and Bettina Fabos, are coauthors, as well as the creators of our book's Instructor's Manual and Test Bank. I am grateful for all their work, ideas, and energy.

Special thanks from Christopher Martin and Bettina Fabos: We would like to thank Richard Campbell, with whom it is a delight working on this project, as well as Shawn Harmsen, one of Bettina's former students. We also appreciate the great devotion, creativity, and talent that everyone at Bedford/St. Martin's brings to the book. We would like to thank reviewers and our own journalism and media students for their input and for creating a community of sorts around the theme of critical perspectives on the media. Most of all, we'd like to thank our daughters, Olivia and Sabine, who bring us joy and laughter every day, and a sense of mission to better understand the world of media in which they live.

Contents

DANIEL LEAL-OLIVAS/Getty Images

LaunchPad   For videos, review quizzing, and more, visit **launchpadworks.com**

Gustavo Caballero/Getty Images

The Granger Collection

4   Magazines in the Age of Specialization   105

Santi Visalli/Getty Images

5 Sound Recording and Popular Music 133

Splash News/Newscom/Splash News/
Los Angeles/USA

John Shearer/Getty Images

Everett Collection, Inc.

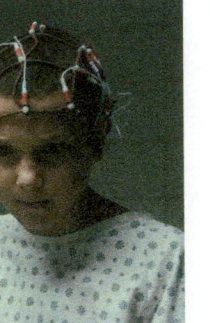

9 The Internet and New Technologies:
The Media Converge 263

Carl Court/Getty Images

Bloomberg/Getty Images

10 Digital Gaming and the Media Playground 293

Gabe Ginsberg/Getty Images

Photo by Matt Sayles/Invision/AP

MEDIA EXPRESSIONS

KENA BETANCUR/Getty Images

14 Media Economics and the Global Marketplace 415

Chesnot/Getty Images

BRENDAN SMIALOWSKI/Getty Images

MEDIA ESSENTIALS

Mass Communication: A Critical Approach

"Black people, I love you. I love us. Our lives matter." After a jury acquitted George Zimmerman in the shooting death of unarmed black teen Trayvon Martin on July 13, 2013, Alicia Garza used these words in a Facebook post describing her anger and heartbreak. When Garza's friend Patrisse Cullors saw the post and shared it along with the hashtag #BlackLivesMatter, these same words inspired a new chapter in civil rights activism: Garza and Cullors brought in friend Opal Tometi and the three women, all in their late twenties or early thirties, cofounded the Black Lives Matter movement.[1]

The organization built an online presence using the hashtag #BlackLivesMatter on social media sites such as Twitter and Tumblr as a way to connect people and share information (including videos) about violence against black men and women—especially by police. Following the shooting death of Michael Brown in Ferguson, Missouri, in 2014, the "hashtag activism" of the Black Lives Matter movement moved offline as more than five hundred people descended on Ferguson to protest the shooting. By the close of 2016, there were thirty-eight Black Lives Matter local chapters.

◀ **#BlackLivesMatter grew from a social media hashtag into an international movement that emphasizes both online and in-person activism.** DANIEL LEAL-OLIVAS/Getty Images

Hashtag activism—so called because of the use of the symbol # before a word or phrase on Twitter that quickly communicates a larger idea or event—offers a compelling illustration of just how powerful social media can be when it is channeled toward a cause. Supporters point to the ability of tools like hashtags to open up new conversations and raise awareness about social issues. In addition to #BlackLivesMatter, for example, #YesAllWomen spurred a flood of posts about the sexism, harassment, and violence experienced by women at the hands of men as a universal characteristic of life as a woman. And online participation can—and does—translate to real-world engagement.

But hashtag activism also captures another aspect of our relationship with social media: that it's complicated. Critics say using hashtags in a social media post can give a false sense of accomplishment with little effort, distracting from the much harder and longer work of creating actual policy change. They also worry that hashtag activism tends to elicit knee-jerk reactions to complex events.

In this way, hashtag activism and other forms of online engagement defy simple evaluations of either "good" or "bad"; rather, they can be both at the same time. As an example, women can share their experiences with sexual harassment on platforms like Twitter, but these platforms also give misogynistic trolls an opportunity to levy more harassment. As Alicia Garza explains, social media has benefits, but social media alone does not effect change: "Twitter is not going to save us. Twitter can be a vehicle that connects us and helps bring us together to strategize around how . . . to transform the world we live in."[2]

Nuanced though it may be, social media's impact on our lives is powerful, and it is here to stay. In this age of smartphones, lightning-fast Internet speeds, and ever-changing technology, it's hard to imagine any successful effort to capture the public's attention that wouldn't make savvy use of social media, be it a marketing campaign for consumer goods, a political campaign, or a social movement. Hashtag activism illustrates just one of the many ways that mass media—including social media—are more integrated into our lives now than ever before.

THE NEED TO COMMUNICATE WITH OTHERS—to tell stories, to persuade, to entertain and be entertained, to share values and ideas—is a defining feature of what it means to be human. Understanding how we use media to facilitate this communication with one another, how our use of media has changed over time, and what these changes might mean for the present and future are all ideas that we consider in mass communication research.

Thinking about these ideas can generate many compelling questions. For example, how do media both reflect and shape society? Who owns and controls the different parts of the mass media? What responsibilities do the owners of mass media corporations have to the public? What responsibilities do we, as members of the public, have in the way we use mass media? Do digital developments like social media and online streaming of music and video represent uncharted media territory, an extension of existing media forms, or both? In this book, we take up these questions and many more by examining the history and business of mass media as well as scholarly research into how media and people interact.

At their best, media try to help us understand the events and trends affecting us. At their worst, they can erode the quality of our lives. For one thing, media's appetite for telling and selling stories can lead them to misrepresent those events or exploit them (and the people they most affect) for profit. Many critics disapprove of how media—particularly TV, cable, and Web sites—seem to hurtle from one event to another, often dwelling on trivial, celebrity-driven content rather than on meaningful analysis of more important events. Critics also fault media for failing to fulfill their responsibility as a watchdog for democracy—which sometimes calls for challenging our leaders and questioning their actions. Finally, the formation and growth of media industries, commercial culture, and new technologies—smartphones, laptops, digital television—have some critics worrying that we now spend more time consuming media than interacting with one another.

Like anything else, mass media have their good sides and bad sides, their useful effects and destructive ones. And that's why it is so important for us to acquire **media literacy**—an understanding of the media that are powerfully shaping our world (and being shaped by it). Only by being media literate we can have a say in the roles that media play around us.

In this chapter, we will take steps to strengthen that literacy by:

- **tracing the evolution of mass communication—from oral and written forms to print and electronic incarnations**

- **examining mass media and the process of communication, including the steps a new medium travels on its journey to mass medium status, and the role that mass media play in our everyday lives**

- **considering two main models of media literacy—cultural and social scientific—which reflect different approaches to understanding how mass communication works and how media affect us**

- **taking a closer look at cultural approaches to media literacy**

- **taking a closer look at social scientific approaches to media literacy**

- **exploring ways of critiquing the mass media and reflecting on the importance of doing so**

launchpadworks.com

Use **LearningCurve** to review concepts from this chapter.

The Evolution of Mass Communication

The mass media surrounding us have their roots in mass communication. **Mass media** are the industries that create and distribute songs, novels, newspapers, movies, Internet services, TV shows, magazines, and other products to large numbers of people. The word *media* is a Latin plural form of the singular noun *medium*, meaning an intervening material or substance through which something else is conveyed or distributed.

We can trace the historical development of media through several eras, all of which still operate to varying degrees. These eras are oral, written, print, electronic, and digital. In the first two eras (oral and written), media existed only in tribal or feudal communities and agricultural economies. In the last three eras (print, electronic, and digital), media became vehicles for **mass communication**: the creation and use of symbols (e.g., languages, Morse code, motion pictures, and binary computer codes) that convey information and meaning to large and diverse audiences through all manner of channels.

Although the telegraph meant that by the middle of the 1800s reporters could almost instantly send a report to their newspaper across the country, getting that news out to a mass audience still required the printing and delivery of a physical object. But with the start of the electronic age in the early twentieth century, radio and then television made mass communication even more widely—and instantly—accessible. If a person was in range of a transmitter, news and entertainment now came at the flick of a switch. By the end of the twentieth century, the Internet revolutionized the entire field of mass communication. We call this profound change in mass media the "digital turn," and this change is still happening today.

Consider, for example, that a smartphone that fits into the palm of a person's hand offers every earlier form of communication anywhere there is a Wi-Fi or cellular signal. One could use the phone to initiate a call or video chat (oral communication), send a text or an e-mail (written communication), read a book (print communication), watch a television program on a service like Hulu (electronic communication), and then send a tweet about the program (digital communication). As shown throughout this book, older forms of communication don't go away but are adapted and converged, or joined together, with newer forms and technologies.

The Oral and Written Eras

In most early societies, information and knowledge first circulated slowly through oral (spoken) traditions passed on by poets, teachers, and tribal storytellers. However, as alphabets and the written word emerged, a manuscript (written) culture developed and eventually overshadowed oral communication. Painstakingly documented and transcribed by philosophers, monks, and stenographers, manuscripts were commissioned by members of the ruling classes, who used them to record religious works and prayers, literature, and personal chronicles. Working people, most of whom were illiterate, rarely saw manuscripts. The shift from oral to written communication created a wide gap between rulers and the ruled in terms of the two groups' education levels and economic welfare.

These trends in oral and written communication unfolded slowly over many centuries. Although exact time frames are disputed, historians generally date the oral and written eras as ranging from 1000 BCE to the mid-fifteenth century. Moreover, the transition from oral to written communication wasn't necessarily smooth. For example, some philosophers saw oral traditions (including exploration of questions and answers through dialogue between teachers and students) as superior. They feared that the written word would hamper conversation between people.

The Print Era

What we recognize as modern printing—the wide dissemination of many copies of particular manuscripts—became practical in Europe around the middle of the fifteenth century. At this time, Johannes Gutenberg's invention of movable metallic type and the printing press in Germany ushered in the modern print era. Printing presses—and the publications they produced—spread rapidly across Europe in the late 1400s and early 1500s. But early on, many books were large, elaborate, and expensive. It took months to illustrate and publish these volumes, which were typically purchased by wealthy aristocrats, royal families, church leaders, prominent merchants, and powerful politicians.

▲ Before the invention of the printing press, books were copied by hand in a labor-intensive process. This beautifully illuminated page is from an Italian Bible from the early 1300s. Bibliotheque Nationale, Paris/Scala-Art Resource, NY

In the following centuries, printers reduced the size and cost of books, making them available and affordable to more people. Books were then being mass-produced, making them the first mass-marketed products in history. This development spurred four significant changes: an increasing resistance to authority, the rise of new socioeconomic classes, the spread of literacy, and a focus on individualism.

Resistance to Authority

Since mass-produced printed materials could spread information and ideas faster and farther than ever before, writers could use print to disseminate views that challenged traditional civic doctrine and religious authority. This paved the way for major social and cultural changes, such as the Protestant Reformation and the rise of modern nationalism. People who read contradictory views began resisting traditional clerical authority. With easier access to information about events in nearby places, people also began seeing themselves not merely as members of families, isolated communities, or tribes but as participants in larger social units—nation-states—whose interests were broader than local or regional concerns.

New Socioeconomic Classes

Eventually, mass production of books inspired mass production of other goods. This development led to the Industrial Revolution and modern capitalism in the mid-nineteenth century. The nineteenth and twentieth centuries saw the rise of a consumer culture, which encouraged mass consumption to match the output of mass production. The revolution in industry also sparked the emergence of a middle class. This class was composed of people who were neither poor laborers nor wealthy political or religious leaders but who made modest livings as merchants, artisans, and service professionals such as lawyers and doctors.

In addition to a middle class, the Industrial Revolution gave rise to an elite class of business owners and managers who acquired the kind of influence once held by only the nobility or the clergy. These groups soon discovered that they could use print media to distribute information and maintain social order.

Spreading Literacy

Although print media secured authority figures' power, the mass publication of pamphlets, magazines, and books also began democratizing knowledge—making it available to more and more people. Literacy rates rose among the working and middle classes, and some rulers fought back. In England, for instance, the monarchy controlled printing press licenses until the early nineteenth century to constrain literacy and therefore sustain the Crown's power over the populace. Even today, governments in many countries control presses, access to paper, and advertising and distribution channels for the same reason. In most industrialized countries, such efforts at control have met with only limited success. After all, building an industrialized economy requires a more educated workforce, and printed literature and textbooks support that education.

Focus on Individualism

The print revolution also nourished the idea of individualism. People came to rely less on their local community and their commercial, religious, and political leaders for guidance on how to live their lives. Instead, they read various ideas and arguments and came up with their own answers to life's great questions. By the mid-nineteenth century, individualism had spread into the realm of commerce. There, it took the form of increased resistance to government interference in the affairs of self-reliant entrepreneurs. Over the next century, individualism became a fundamental value in American society.

The Electronic and Digital Eras

In Europe and America, the rise of industry completely transformed everyday life, with factories replacing farms as the main centers of work and production. During the 1880s, roughly 80 percent of Americans lived on farms and in small towns; by the 1920s and 1930s, most had moved to urban areas, where new industries and economic opportunities beckoned. This shift set the stage for the final two eras in mass communication: the electronic era (whose key innovations included the telegraph, radio, and television) and the digital era (whose flagship invention is the Internet).

The Electronic Era

In America, the gradual transformation from an industrial, print-based society to one fueled by electronic innovation began with the development of the telegraph in the 1840s. Featuring dot-dash electronic signals, the telegraph made media messages instantaneous, no longer reliant on stagecoaches, ships, or the pony express. It also enabled military, business, and political leaders to coordinate commercial and military operations more easily than ever. And it laid the groundwork for future technological developments, such as wireless telegraphy, the fax machine, and the cell phone (all of which ultimately led to the telegraph's demise).

COMMON SENSE;

ADDRESSED TO THE

INHABITANTS

OF

AMERICA,

On the following interesting

SUBJECTS.

I. Of the Origin and Design of Government in general, with concise Remarks on the English Constitution.

II. Of Monarchy and Hereditary Succession.

III. Thoughts on the present State of American Affairs.

IV. Of the present Ability of America, with some miscellaneous Reflections.

Man knows no Master save creating HEAVEN, Or those whom choice and common good ordain.

THOMSON.

PHILADELPHIA;

Printed, and Sold, by R. BELL, in Third-Street.

MDCCLXXVI.

▲ Published in January 1776, Thomas Paine's pamphlet *Common Sense* not only made a case for American independence, but made it in plain and simple language considered accessible to the broader colonial audience. The popular publication is often credited with helping build support for the break with Great Britain. Stock Montage, Inc./Alamy

▲ Beginning in the 1930s, radio and later television sets—encased in decorative wood and sold as stylish furniture—occupied a central place in many American homes. Classicstock/The Image Works

The development of film at the start of the twentieth century and radio in the 1920s were important milestones, but the electronic era really took off in the 1950s and 1960s with the arrival of television—a medium that powerfully reshaped American life.

The Digital Era

With the arrival of cutting-edge communication gadgetry—ever-smaller personal computers, cable TV, e-mail, DVDs, DVRs, direct broadcast satellites, cell phones—the electronic era gave way to the digital era. In **digital communication,** images, texts, and sounds are converted (encoded) into electronic signals (represented as combinations of ones and zeros) that are then reassembled (decoded) as a precise reproduction of, say, a TV picture, a magazine article, a song, or a voice at the other end of a phone. On the Internet, various images, text, and sounds are digitally reproduced and transmitted globally.

As we will see in future chapters, each new form of mass media, from books to television, has led to powerful changes in how people consume information and entertainment. But more recently, we have experienced a **digital turn**—a change that is characterized by its speed and by the way it dismantled the once-clear boundaries between different forms of media. An early medium like radio could take decades to fully emerge (see "The Evolution of a New Mass Medium" on page 12), while today a Web site or app can reach similar audience thresholds in a matter of years or even days. And though electronic media have been around for a long time, it was the emergence of the Internet as a mass medium that allowed an array of media—text, photo, audio, video, and interactive games—to come together in one space and be easily shared. Thus while the foundations for this digital turn were laid in the 1990s, it is the ever-quicker download speeds and more portable and powerful devices of the last decade that have fundamentally changed the ways in which we access and consume media.

The digital turn has made us more fragmented even as it has made us more connected (see also "The Digital Turn Case Study: FOMO in a Digital World" on page 13). We might not be able to count on our friends all watching the same television show, but Facebook, Twitter, and even interactive games like *Pokémon Go* have made it easier for us to connect with friends—and strangers—and tell them what we watched, listened to, and read.

Media Convergence

Although it has its roots in the electronic era, the phenomenon of **media convergence** is one of the defining characteristics of the digital turn. This term has two very different meanings. According to one meaning, media convergence is the technological merging of content across different media channels. For example, magazine articles and radio programs are also accessible on the Internet; and songs, TV shows, and movies are now available on computers, iPods, and cell phones.

Such technological convergence is not entirely new. For instance, in the late 1920s, the Radio Corporation of America (RCA) purchased the Victor Talking Machine Company and introduced machines that could play both radio and recorded music. However, contemporary media convergence is much broader because it involves digital content across a wider array of media.

The term *media convergence* can also be used to describe a particular business model in which a company consolidates various media holdings—such as cable connections, phone services, television transmissions, and Internet access—under one corporate umbrella. The goal of such consolidation is not necessarily to offer consumers more choices in their media but to better manage resources, lower costs, and maximize profits. For example, a company that owns TV stations, radio outlets, and newspapers in multiple markets—as well as in the same cities—can deploy one reporter or producer to create three or four versions of the same story for various media outlets. Thus, the company can employ fewer people than if it owned only one media outlet.

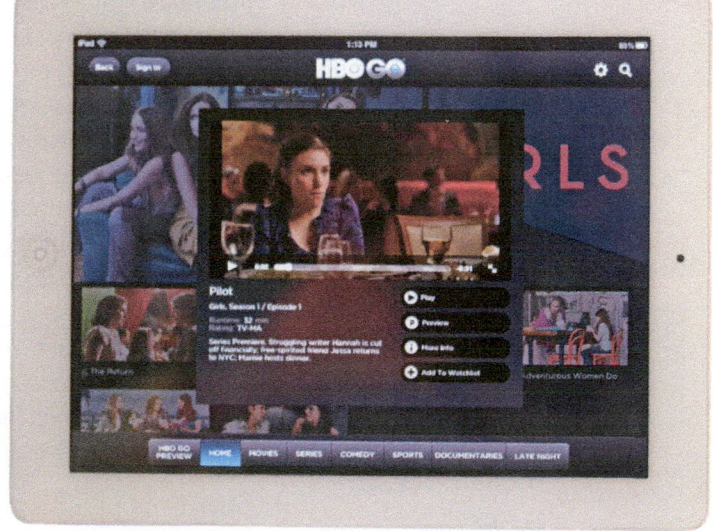

▲ The convergence of online media into one simple device is still a new media concept for many people—an enormous shift from the multiple single-purpose devices most Americans grew up with.
TONY CENICOLA/The New York Times/Redux Pictures

Although it's easy to see how a converged business model benefits media owners—more profits to those companies that downsize their workforce while increasing their media holdings in a variety of markets—this model presents some disadvantages for society. For one thing, it limits the range of perspectives from which messages are delivered, as media content becomes concentrated in fewer hands.

In every chapter in this book, we will discuss how both kinds of convergence have changed the way mass media work and how we use each medium. For example, in later chapters we will see that the music industry is still coming to grips with digital downloading, streaming music services, and online radio;

that convergence and other factors of the digital turn played a key role in damaging the business model of traditional news media, resulting in massive newsroom cuts across the country; and that online piracy and copyright infringement remain major challenges for large music and movie companies.

Mass Media and the Process of Communication

To understand how mass media shape the communication process, let's look at the stages a medium goes through on its journey to becoming a mass medium. Then let's examine the ways in which the media have affected everyday life.

The Evolution of a New Mass Medium

A new medium emerges not just from the work of inventors, such as Thomas Edison, but also from social, cultural, political, and economic changes. For instance, the Internet arose to meet people's desire to transport messages and share information more rapidly in an increasingly mobile and interconnected global population.

Typically, each media industry goes through three stages in its evolution. First is the *development stage* (sometimes referred to as the novelty stage). During this stage, inventors and technicians try to solve a particular problem, such as making pictures move, transmitting messages between ships and shore, or sending mail electronically.

Second is the *entrepreneurial stage*, in which inventors and investors determine a practical and marketable use for the new device. For example, the Internet has some roots in scientists' desire for a communication system that could enable their colleagues across the country to share time on a few rare supercomputers.

Third is the *mass medium stage*. At this point, businesses figure out how to market the new device as a *consumer product*. To illustrate, Pentagon and government researchers developed the prototype for the Internet, but commercial interests extended the medium's usefulness to individuals and businesses.

Debating Media's Role in Everyday Life

Even as far back as ancient times, human beings have discussed and debated the media's merits and dangers. The earliest recorded debates in Western society about the impact of the written word on daily life date back to the ancient Greeks—in particular, to Socrates, Euripides, and Plato. These men argued over whether theatrical plays would corrupt young people by exposing them to messages that conflicted with those promulgated by their teachers.

launchpadworks.com

Agenda-Setting and Gatekeeping

Experts discuss how the media exert influence over public discourse.

Discussion: How might the rise of the Internet cancel out or reduce the agenda-setting effect in media?

The Digital Turn

FOMO in a Digital World

For at least some of us, the social mediated version of ourselves becomes the predominant way we experience the world. As *Time* magazine noted, "Experiences don't feel fully real" until we have "tweeted them or tumbled them or YouTubed them—and the world has congratulated you for doing so."[1] But the flip side of promoting our own experiences on social media as *the most awesome happenings ever (and too bad you aren't here)* is the social anxiety associated with reading about other people's experiences and realizing that you are not actually there.

The problem is called Fear of Missing Out (FOMO), and one report defines it as "the uneasy and sometimes all-consuming feeling that you're missing out—that your peers are doing, in the know about or in possession of more or something better than you."[2] There are plenty of platforms for posting about ourselves and anxiously creeping on others—Facebook, Twitter, Tumblr, LinkedIn, Pinterest, Google+, and Instagram are just a few of the sites that can feed our FOMO problem.

FOMO has been around long before social media was invented. Bragging, photos, postcards, and those holiday letters have usually put the most positive spin on people's lives. But social media, mobile technology, and other conveniences of the digital turn make being exposed to the interactions you missed a 24/7 phenomenon. There is potentially *always* something better you could have/should have been doing.

People with FOMO tend to tether themselves to social media, tracking "friends" and sacrificing time that might be spent having in-person, unmediated experiences.[3] Yet all this time on social media may not equal happiness. According to one study, the more a group of college students used Facebook, the more two components of well-being declined: how people feel moment-to-moment and how satisfied they are with their lives.[4]

Studies about happiness routinely conclude that the best path to subjective well-being and life satisfaction is having a community of close personal relationships. Social psychologists Ed Diener and Robert Biswas-Diener acknowledge that the high use of mobile phones, text messaging, and social media is evidence that people want to connect. But they also explain that "we don't just need relationships: we need close ones." They conclude, "The close relationships that produce the most happiness are those characterized by mutual understanding, caring, and validation of the other person as worthwhile."[5] Thus, frequent contact isn't enough to produce the kinds of relationships that produce the most happiness.

Ironically, there has never been a medium better than the Internet and its social media platforms to bring people together. After all, how many people do you know who met online and went on to have successful friendships and relationships? Still, according to Diener and Biswas-Diener, maintaining close relationships may require a "vacation" from social media from time to time, experiencing something together with a friend or friends. Of course (and we hate to say it), you will still need to text, e-mail, or call to arrange that date.

 **Web Clip**

YouTube.com has many videos about the Fear of Missing Out. One good option to search for: 'Do You Have FOMO?' by Soapboxing and Refinery29. Do you think an audience watching this same video in five years will still relate to feelings of FOMO? In ten years? Why or why not?

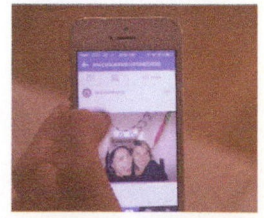

We still debate these sorts of questions. At the turn of the twentieth century, for example, newly arrived immigrants to the United States who spoke little English gravitated toward vaudeville shows and silent films, which they could enjoy without having to understand English. These popular events occasionally became a flash point for some groups. For example, the Daughters of the American Revolution, local politicians, religious leaders, and police vice squads feared that these "low" cultural forms would undermine what they saw as traditional American values.

Today, with the reach of print, electronic, and digital communications and the amount of time people spend consuming them (see Figure 1.1), mass media now play an even more controversial role in society. For instance, some people are frustrated by the overwhelming amount of information available. Others decry what they view as mass media's overly commercial and sensationalistic quality. In their view, too many talk shows exploit personal problems for commercial gain, and too many TV shows and video games feature graphic violence.

People also keep grappling with the dual question: To what extent do mass media shape our values and behaviors and to what extent do our values and behaviors shape the media? Researchers have continued searching for answers

FIGURE 1.1 // DAILY MEDIA CONSUMPTION BY PLATFORM, 2016

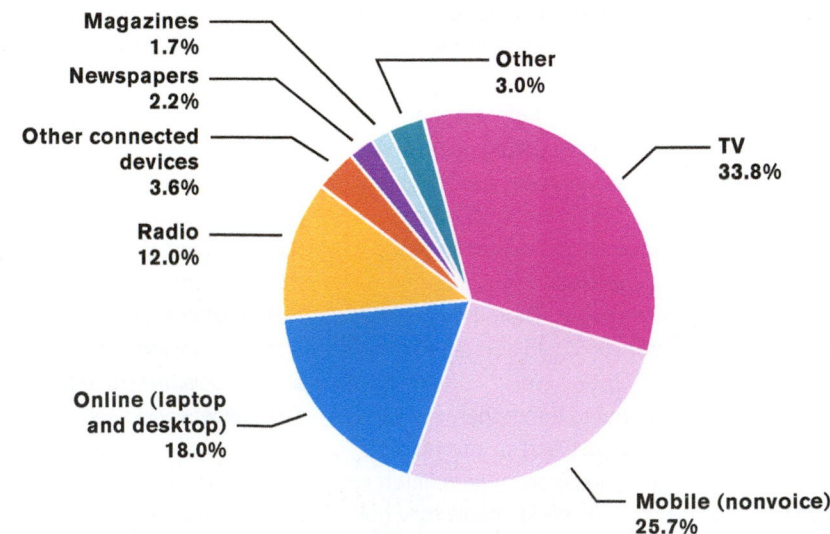

Magazines 1.7%
Newspapers 2.2%
Other connected devices 3.6%
Radio 12.0%
Online (laptop and desktop) 18.0%
Other 3.0%
TV 33.8%
Mobile (nonvoice) 25.7%

Data from: "Average Time Spent with Major Media per Day in the United States as of April 2016 (in Minutes)," http://www.statista.com/statistics/276683/media-use-in-the-us/.

to this question. For example, some have designed studies to determine whether watching violent TV shows makes viewers more likely to commit violent acts. Others argue that violent TV shows don't cause violent behavior in viewers; rather, people who have violent tendencies are drawn to violent TV shows. Still others suggest that certain variables—such as age, upbringing, or genetic predisposition—might be the root cause of violence. Research into such questions of media and violence hasn't yielded conclusive answers, but it does encourage us to keep asking questions and to examine the approaches we use to analyze the media's role in our lives.

▲ Mass media play a significant role in capturing important historical and controversial events. This Pulitzer Prize–winning photo by Stanley Forman, "The Soiling of Old Glory," shows a white teenager attacking an African American lawyer with a flagpole bearing the American flag at a protest over court-ordered busing to desegregate schools in Boston on April 5, 1976. Pulitzer Prize, www.stanleyformanphotos.com

Finally, people have expressed concern about the financial power of mass media industries. In the United States, these industries earn more than $200 billion annually, then reinvest those revenues to research how we choose our media content, what we do with that content, and how they can better serve our needs and influence our behaviors (from shopping to voting) so that they can make more money.

Like the air we breathe, the mass media surround us, and we often take its impact, like that of the air, for granted. And if we don't take it for granted, we frequently can't agree on its quality. To monitor the media's "air quality" more proactively and productively, we must become media literate. We can begin by examining several models for understanding media's nature and impact.

How We Study the Media

Experts have used a variety of approaches to understand how the various media work and what influence they have on our lives. These approaches to mass communication include the linear model (which focused on the communication process), the cultural model (which views mass communication as a cultural characteristic and uses anecdotal evidence to interpret media), and the social scientific model (which uses numerical data-gathering and statistical analysis). We can use our understanding of these models to strengthen our media literacy.

The Linear Model

The linear model was an early attempt to explain how messages were sent and received through mass communication channels. This model, which most scholars now see as outdated, assumed that mass communication was a linear process by which media producers delivered messages to large audiences. Senders (authors, producers, organizations) transmitted messages (programs, texts, images, sounds, ads) through mass media channels (newspapers, books, magazines, radio, television, the Internet) to large groups of receivers (readers, viewers, consumers). In the process, gatekeepers (news editors, executive producers of TV shows and movies) filtered those messages by making decisions about which messages got produced for which audiences. The process also allowed for feedback, in which citizens and consumers could return messages to senders or gatekeepers through letters, phone calls, e-mails, Web postings, tweets, or talk shows.

But the problem with the linear model was that in reality, media messages do not usually move smoothly from a sender at point A to a receiver at point Z. Media messages and stories are encoded and sent in written and visual forms, but senders often have very little control over how their intended messages are decoded or whether the messages are ignored or misread by readers and viewers. The cultural and social scientific models have since developed more sophisticated approaches to media study that improve on the limitations of the linear model.

The Cultural Model

The cultural model of media literacy views media content as a part of culture. Culture consists of the ways in which people live and represent themselves at particular historical times, as manifested in things like fashion, sports, architecture, education, religion, science, and media.

As cultural forms, the media help us make sense of daily life and articulate our values. When we listen to music, read a book, watch television, or scan the Internet, we assign meaning to that song, book, TV program, or Web site. And different people often assign different meanings to the same media content. Take the Harry Potter book series. Some readers see the series as an innocent coming-of-age children's story. Others interpret it as more adult literature, containing pointed metaphors about good and evil that parallel current political events. Still others construe the series as a tool for luring children into a life of witchcraft. And there are others who use the books as a form of creative entertainment, inventing Harry Potter parodies in almost every imaginable media form.

We describe this model for understanding media content as cultural because it recognizes that individuals assign diverse meanings to messages depending on personal characteristics, such as gender, age, educational level, ethnicity, occupation, and religious beliefs. According to this model, audiences actively affirm, interpret, refashion, select, or reject the messages flowing through various media channels. One manifestation of this active audience in the digital

▲ Often, popular stories and characters evolve in our culture over time, acquiring new meaning. Consider the classic 1931 film *Frankenstein* (*top*) and the 1974 parody *Young Frankenstein* (*bottom*). How does each story reflect changes in cultural attitudes? Photofest (top); © 20th Century Fox/ Photofest (bottom)

▲ By analyzing news coverage of such tragedies as the mass shooting in an Orlando nightclub in 2016, the cultural model shows how media content shapes attitudes and beliefs. These in turn play a role in the ongoing political debate over issues such as gun control. Spencer Platt/Getty Images

age is the Internet meme. Coined by British evolutionary biologist Richard Dawkins, the term *meme* has come to mean a digital experience—a video, a sound recording, even just a catchphrase—that is passed electronically from one consumer to another—sometimes with new variations (remakes, remixes, mash-ups, and so forth)—often very quickly. This widespread, rapid transmission is frequently referred to as *viral* and includes brief cultural touchstones, such as an image of actor Sean Bean from the HBO series *Game of Thrones* paired with the catchphrase "Brace Yourself, Winter Is Coming," modified by users in literally hundreds of ways. Unlike network celebrities and corporate brands, the meme is a product of an interactive culture in dialogue with itself.

The cultural approach to studying the media critically analyzes media content, the ways in which audiences interpret that content, and the circumstances of how the media produce such content. This form of research also considers the role of power in mass media. For example, it might evaluate which groups have more or less ability to get their messages heard and seen, and how that translates into financial, political, and cultural rewards.

The Social Scientific Model

The social scientific model also asks important questions about the media, but it is informed by an approach that tests hypotheses with measurable data. The model has its roots in the natural sciences' pursuit of objective research. However, as researchers in this field well know, applying rigorous social scientific methods to the study of human behavior is much less reliable than applying such methods to a highly controlled chemistry or physics laboratory environment.

Nevertheless, social scientific research has provided valuable insight into questions about how the media affect us and has become more sophisticated with the rise of electronic and digital media in the twentieth century. Early research looked at the effects of movies, using electric mechanisms attached to viewers' skin to detect heightened responses to frightening or romantic scenes. More recent research has continued to test hypotheses about media effects, using controlled laboratory experiments. For example, researchers might set out to chart the relationship between stereotypical magazine representations of women of color and readers' occupational expectations for women of color in general.

Politics and public opinion have long attracted the interest of media researchers, beginning with the rise of **survey research** in the twentieth century. Today, media researchers—working for universities, news organizations, the government, and political parties—conduct regular national and regional surveys to take snapshots of the public's opinions on all manner of issues. They also use that information as a basis for action. For example, public opinion researchers (usually working as consultants for political parties or campaigns) test words, ideas, and images on small focus groups to see how different ways of framing a topic—such as "global warming" versus "climate change"—affect voters' decisions.

Just as media research can help political candidates formulate their campaign strategies, it can also help businesses develop and market their products. For instance, consumer product companies use quantitative methods to track the effectiveness of their advertisements; Hollywood studios regularly screen-test movies to figure out which ending works best for viewers; and ratings services track audience numbers for radio, television, and Web sites, compiling immense stores of data that companies use to gauge the effectiveness of their ad spending.

The goal of social scientific media research, then, is to develop testable hypotheses (or predictions) about the media, gather relevant data, and determine whether the data verifies the hypotheses.

A Closer Look at the Cultural Model: Surveying the Cultural Landscape

In the pages that follow, we examine the cultural model of media literacy, which provides many ways to study media content through the lens of culture. We discuss two metaphors researchers use to describe the way people judge media content and present ways to trace changes in our cultural values as media adapt and change.

The "Culture as Skyscraper" Metaphor

Throughout the twentieth century, many Americans envisioned our nation's culture as consisting of ascending levels of superiority—like floors in a sky-scraper. They identified **high culture** (the top floors of the building) with good taste, higher education, and fine art supported by wealthy patrons and corporate donors, and they associated **low** or **popular culture** (the bottom floors) with the questionable tastes of the masses, who lapped up the commercial junk circulated by the mass media, such as reality TV shows, celebrity gossip Web sites, and action films.

Some cultural researchers have pointed out that this high–low hierarchy has become so entrenched that it powerfully influences how we view and discuss culture today.[3] For example, people who subscribe to the hierarchy metaphor believe that low culture prevents people (students in particular) from appreciating fine art, exploits high culture by transforming classic works into simplistic forms, and promotes a throwaway ethic. These same critics accuse low culture of driving out higher forms of culture. They also argue that it inhibits political discourse and social change by making people so addicted to mass-produced media that they lose their ability to see and challenge social inequities (also referred to as the Big Mac Theory).[4]

◀The television program *Veep* chronicles the personal and political fortunes of Washington insider Selina Meyer (Julia Louis-Dreyfus). A combination of raunchy dialogue (low culture) and sharp political satire (high culture) have earned the HBO program a loyal following and many Emmy Awards. HBO/Photofest

The "Culture as Map" Metaphor

Other researchers think of culture as a map. In this metaphor, culture—rather than being a vertically organized structure—is an ongoing process that accommodates diverse tastes. Cultural phenomena, including media—printed materials we read, movies and TV programs we watch, songs and podcasts we listen to—can take us to places that are conventional, recognizable, stable, and comforting. However, they can also take us to places that are innovative, unfamiliar, unstable, and challenging. Rather than elevating one type of media over another, the map metaphor flattens out the hierarchy and emphasizes the ways that ideas connect, like roads connecting towns and cities on a map.

Human beings are attracted to both consistency and change, and cultural media researchers have pointed out that most media can satisfy both of those desires. For example, a movie can contain elements that are familiar to us (such as particular plots) as well as elements that are completely new and strange (such as a cinematic technique we've never seen before).

Tracing Changes in Values

In addition to examining metaphors of culture that we use to understand media's role in our lives, cultural researchers examine the ways in which our values have changed along with changes in mass media. Researchers have been particularly interested in how values have shifted during the modern era and the postmodern period.

The Modern Era

From the Industrial Revolution to the mid-twentieth century—which historians call the **modern era**—four values came into sharp focus across the American cultural landscape. These values were influenced by developments that unfolded during the era and the media's responses to those developments:

- **Working efficiently.** As businesses used new technology to create efficient manufacturing centers and produce inexpensive products more cheaply and profitably, advertisers spread the word about new gadgets that could save Americans time and labor.
- **Celebrating the individual.** With access to novel ideas in the form of scientific discoveries communicated by the media, people began celebrating their power as individuals to pick and choose from ideas instead of merely following what religious and political leaders told them.
- **Believing in a rational order.** Being modern also meant valuing logic and reason and viewing the world as a rational place. In this orderly place, the

printed mass media—particularly newspapers—served to educate the citizenry, helping to build and maintain an organized society.[5] This belief in reason and scientific progress also lent itself to greater trust in experts and various institutions in society, from journalism to the government.

- **Rejecting tradition and embracing progress.** Within the modern era was a shorter phenomenon: the **Progressive Era**. This period of political and social reform lasted roughly from the 1890s to the 1920s and inspired many Americans—and mass media—to break with tradition and embrace change.

The Postmodern Period

In the **postmodern period**—from roughly the mid-twentieth century to today—cultural values changed shape once more, influenced again by developments in American society and the media's responses to those developments. Cultural researchers have identified the following dominant values in today's postmodern period:

- **Celebrating populism.** As a political idea, **populism** tries to appeal to ordinary people by setting up a conflict between "the people" and "the elite." For example, populist politicians often run ads criticizing big corporations and political favoritism. And many famous film actors champion oppressed groups, even though their work makes them wealthy global icons of consumerist culture.

- **Questioning authority.** Related to populism, a defining characteristic of the postmodern perspective is the questioning of the authority figures and institutions that were more widely trusted during the modern era. On the one hand, this may be helping to advance social change, as women and minorities challenge existing power structures. On the other hand, the distrust of experts has fed climate change denial and anti-vaccination campaigns. This questioning of authority may also explain the popularity of movies like *Deadpool* and *Suicide Squad*, which feature gritty antiheroes as protagonists.

- **Embracing technology.** Even as some people question certain kinds of scientific knowledge, there seem to be fewer qualms about using the latest technology, such as computers and smartphones.

▲ Jessica Jones, a lesser-known hero from the Marvel comic books and title character of a show adapted for television by streaming service Netflix, is an example of the kind of morally ambiguous antihero typified in the postmodern era. Everett Collection, Inc.

A Closer Look at the Social Scientific Model: Gathering Data

The social scientific model of media literacy differs in key ways from the cultural model. In this section, we compare analyses of two studies to examine the differences between the two models, and we look more closely at how social scientific researchers gather data to analyze the content of media messages and consumers' responses to those messages.

Comparing Analyses of News Coverage

Cultural and social scientific media researchers often study the same topics, but they ask different types of questions about those topics. For example, two studies recently analyzed news coverage of cancer. The study informed by the cultural approach, titled "Constructing Breast Cancer in the News: Betty Ford and the Evolution of the Breast Cancer Patient," explored a historical turning point in how the media and consumers interpret breast cancer. The study centered on how the news media covered First Lady Betty Ford's mastectomy operation in 1974. The author of the study concluded that coverage of Ford's mastectomy still influences contemporary news coverage of breast cancer. Specifically, many stories on this topic emphasize "the need for breast cancer patients to maintain their femininity."[6]

Research by social scientists asked a question about cancer news coverage that was perhaps less expansive but more measurable. In an article titled "A Comprehensive Analysis of Breast Cancer News Coverage in Leading Media Outlets Focusing on Environmental Risks and Prevention," researchers analyzed the contents of newspaper, television, and magazine accounts of the topic over a two-year span. The researchers didn't interpret the meanings of the news stories (as cultural researchers might have). Instead, they focused on the data they gathered, describing their analysis in more objective terms. For example, the authors noted that "about one-third of the stories included prevention content, primarily focusing narrowly on the use of pharmaceutical products. Little information described risk reduction via other individual preventive behaviors (e.g., diet, exercise, and smoking), parental protective measures, or collective actions to combat contamination sites."[7]

Gathering and Analyzing Data

The social scientists analyzing cancer news coverage used a technique called **content analysis** to gather data. Through content analysis, researchers code and count the content of various types of media. For instance, they total up the number of news stories that contain specific types of information regarding the topic in question (such as how to prevent cancer), count song lyrics containing references to a topic (e.g., sex), or total up the number of occurrences of certain behaviors (e.g., violent acts) shown in a set of movies.

But content analysis is only one way to gather data using the social science approach. Researchers also conduct **experiments** using randomly assigned subjects (college students are popular test subjects) to test people's self-reported recall of or reactions to media content. To illustrate, experimenters might use devices such as eye trackers to record what part of a page or screen each viewer is watching.[8] As noted earlier in the chapter, social science researchers can also gather data through surveys they've designed or use data from the many surveys the federal government funds and makes available.

Critiquing Media

To acquire media literacy, we can read the findings of cultural and social science researchers who have studied various aspects of the media. However, both models have their limits; thus, it's important to view their conclusions with a critical eye. We can also learn to critique media content ourselves in a methodical, disciplined way. Whatever approach we use to develop media literacy, it's helpful to always keep in mind the benefits of a critical perspective.

Evaluating Cultural and Social Scientific Research

Examining the findings of both cultural and social scientific research on media can help us follow a **critical process** that consists of describing, analyzing, interpreting, evaluating, and engaging with mass media. However, the two models have strengths and weaknesses that are important to keep in mind. The cultural model is best at recognizing the complexity of media culture and providing analyses that draw on descriptive, critical, historical, ethnographic, political, and economic traditions. Yet this model has a downside: Although cultural studies can help us see media from new perspectives, the conclusions laid out in a particular study may simply be the author's interpretation. Thus, they may

▲ One way to critique the media is to analyze the highly stylized advertisements and information that appear before us. In trailers and advertisements for the 2016 film *Star Trek Beyond*, what is being sold and what does it reveal about American audiences? Everett Collection, Inc.

not necessarily explain cause-and-effect connections in situations other than those the author examined.

The social scientific model seeks to develop and test theories about how the media affect individuals and society in measurable ways. This approach produces conclusions based on hard numbers, which policy makers often find comforting. It may suggest a clear chain of cause and effect or at least a statistical relationship between the media and an effect.

But like the cultural model, the social scientific model has limits. For example, the options provided in a multiple-choice survey question might not cover all the possible responses that participants could give. As a result, researchers obtain an incomplete picture of how people respond to particular media. Also, definitions of what is being measured may confuse things. To illustrate, researchers might count a bonk on the head shown in a movie as an act of violence, even though the event could be purposeful, accidental, deserved, or part of a character's fantasy. Researchers can thus neglect to ask more nuanced questions, such as whether accidental incidents of violence have a different effect on movie viewers than do purposeful acts of violence. Finally, many social scientific studies are limited to questions that their funding sources—the government, media industry associations, or granting agencies—ask them to study. This situation further constrains the scope of their research.

Ultimately, though, the quality of any media research—cultural or social scientific—depends on the nature of the questions asked and the rigor of the method used. Often, "triangulating" with two or more approaches to test a question makes for much stronger conclusions. For those of us seeking to strengthen our media literacy by consulting research, the best approach may be to balance findings on a particular question from both the cultural and the social scientific models.

Conducting Our Own Critiques

If we want to conduct our own critiques of specific media, we'll need a working knowledge of the particular medium being addressed—whether it's a book, a TV show, a song, a movie, a video game, a magazine, a radio program, or some other form. For example, suppose our goal is to develop a meaningful critique of the TV show *American Horror Story*, Rush Limbaugh's conservative radio program, or weekly magazines' obsession with what celebrities look like at the beach. In each case, we will need to thoroughly familiarize ourselves with the show, program, or magazines in question and start thinking about what messages they seem to be conveying. As we begin this process, we will also need to transcend our own preferences and biases. For instance, we may like or dislike hip-hop, R&B, pop music, or country, but if we want to criticize the messages in one or more of these musical genres intelligently, we need to understand what they have to say and consider why their messages appeal to particular audiences.

Familiarization and a certain amount of self-conscious detachment, then, are the preliminaries of a rigorous process that moves beyond matters of taste or, worse, a cynical, wholesale dismissal of culturally significant experiences. Becoming truly media literate requires mastering this critical process and applying it to everyday encounters with the communication media. The process encompasses five steps: Description, Analysis, Interpretation, Evaluation, and Engagement (see "The Critical Process Behind Media Literacy" on page 28).

▲ Powerful celebrities like Oprah Winfrey have a profound influence on popular opinion and belief. Developing an informed critical perspective on the media allows individuals to engage in discussions about their impact on the world. Paras Griffin/Getty Images

Benefits of a Critical Perspective

Developing an informed critical perspective on the media enables us to participate in a debate about media's impact on our democracy and culture. For instance, on the one hand, the media can be a force for strengthening our democracy and making the world a better place. Consider the role of television in documenting racism and injustice in the 1960s—coverage that encouraged the Civil Rights movement. Or consider how talk-show host Ellen DeGeneres's decision to publicly come out as a lesbian influenced the fight for LGBTQ equality.

On the other hand, media portrayals can have a negative impact. For example, consider how mass media portrayals of people of color might reinforce negative stereotypes and have real-world negative consequences. Or consider how mass media's portrayal of "ideal" male and female behavior might have problematic results for society (see "Media Literacy Case Study: Masculinity and the Media" on pages 26–27). Also consider that the media have helped create a powerful commercial culture in our nation—a culture in which fewer and fewer multinational corporations dominate our economy and generate more and more of the media messages we consume. A society in which only a few voices are telling us stories about what's important, what our values should be, and how we should behave is hardly a healthy democracy.

Because the media constitute forces for both good and ill, it's that much more important for each of us to think carefully about which media we consume; what messages we draw from those media; and how those

Media Literacy

CASE STUDY

Masculinity and the Media

There have been at least eighty-four mass shootings in the United States since 1982 (a number that is still climbing), and more than half of them have occurred since 2006.[1] What are the reasons? Our news media respond with a number of usual suspects: the easy availability of guns in the United States; influential movies, television shows, and video games; mental illness; bad parenting. But educator, author, and filmmaker Jackson Katz sees another major factor. The least talked about commonality in all the shootings is the one so obvious most of us miss it: Nearly all the mass murderers are male (and usually white).

"If a woman were the shooter," Katz says, "you can bet there would be all sorts of commentary about shifting cultural notions of femininity and how they might have contributed to her act."[2] But women were involved in only three of the eighty-four mass shootings; all the others had a man (or men) behind the trigger. "Because men represent the dominant gender, their gender is rendered invisible in the discourse about violence," Katz says.[3]

In fact, the dominance of masculinity is the norm in our mainstream mass media. Dramatic content is often about the performance of heroic, powerful masculinity (e.g., many action films, digital games, and sports). Similarly, humorous content often derives from calling into question the standards of masculinity (e.g., a man trying to cook, clean, or take care of a child). The same principles apply for the advertising that supports the content. How many automobile, beer, shaving cream, and food commercials peddle products that offer men a chance to maintain or regain their rightful masculinity?

Sociologists Rachel Kalish and Michael Kimmel analyzed the problem of mass shootings that usually end in suicide. In their research, they found that males and females generally have similar rates of suicide attempts. "Feeling aggrieved, wronged by the world—these are typical adolescent feelings, common to many boys and girls," they report. How these feelings play out, though, differs by gender. Female suicide behaviors are more

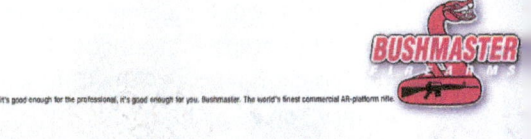

> ⊙ **Visit LaunchPad** to watch a clip from a documentary featuring Jackson Katz. According to Katz, what is the relationship between media, masculinity, and violence? Do you agree with his assessment of this relationship?

launchpadworks.com

▲ AR-15-style rifles, like this Bushmaster model, were used in some of the biggest and bloodiest mass shootings in the United States, including those in Aurora, Colorado, Newtown, Connecticut, San Bernardino, California, and Roseburg, Oregon. A similar weapon was also used in the Orlando, Florida Pulse nightclub shooting. According to the *New York Times*, there are several million AR-15s in circulation in the United States.

likely to be a cry for help. Male suicide behaviors, informed by social norms of masculinity, often result in "aggrieved entitlement." Kalish and Kimmel define this as "a gendered emotion, a fusion of that humiliating loss of manhood and the moral obligation and entitlement to get it back. And its gender is masculine."[4]

There is some evidence that the gun industry understands this sense of masculine entitlement but uses that knowledge to sell guns, not to consider how they might be misused. A marketing campaign begun in 2010 for the Bushmaster .223-caliber semi-automatic rifle showed an image of the rifle with the large tagline "Consider Your Man Card Reissued." The Bushmaster was the same civilian assault rifle used by the shooter who massacred twenty-eight people at the Newtown elementary school in 2012.

How do we find a way out of this cultural cycle? "Make gender—specifically the idea that men are gendered beings—a central part of the national conversation about rampage killings," Katz says. "It means looking carefully at how our culture defines manhood, how boys are socialized, and how pressure to stay in the 'man box' not only constrains boys' and men's emotional and relational development, but also their range of choices when faced with life crises."[5]

APPLYING THE CRITICAL PROCESS

Investigate the way masculinity is portrayed in popular culture by reviewing a list of movies for men compiled by a top-selling men's magazine. For example, *Men's Journal* created a list of what they call the "Best Guy Movies"—a list that includes *Dirty Harry* (1972), *The Godfather* (1972), *Scarface* (1983), *Die Hard* (1988), and *The Terminator* (1984). (See http://www.filmsite.org/guyfilms.html.) Watch one of the movies from this or a similar list.

DESCRIPTION Describe the main hero (or heroes) of the movie, his attributes, and the way he interacts with other characters.

ANALYSIS What patterns emerge in the way the hero talks and acts throughout the movie? What emotions does the hero show, and how often? Does the hero use a weapon, and if so, under what circumstances? How are women represented in this movie, and how does the hero treat them?

INTERPRETATION Does your analysis of the hero's behavior support or contradict the idea that masculinity is defined in the ways described in this case study?

EVALUATION Lists of top "guy movies" tend to reflect the characteristics of what an ideal manly hero should look and act like. What does this suggest about how the lists' creators define what it means to be masculine? Is there much variation in how masculinity is portrayed from movie to movie (to the extent that you are familiar with these movies or can look up plot summaries online)? What might the portrayal of women in "guy movies" tell us about how the ideal manly type is "supposed" to interact with women?

ENGAGEMENT Write a letter to the editor of a men's magazine (or another magazine that compiles such movie lists), and suggest creating an alternative list of movies with more nuanced and three-dimensional portrayals of masculinity.

THE CRITICAL PROCESS BEHIND MEDIA LITERACY

Becoming literate about communication media involves striking a balance between taking a critical stand (developing knowledgeable interpretations and judgments) and being tolerant of diverse forms of expression (appreciating the distinctive variety of cultural products and processes). Finding this balance in a media-literate critical perspective involves completing five overlapping stages that build on one another.

Stage One: Description

Develop descriptive skills associated with breaking down a story into character types and plot structure. Focus on how music, dialogue, camerawork, and editing come together in a way that encourages audience engagement. Master the terms and understand the techniques of telling stories in a particular medium.

Examples
- Describe how the conventions of the documentary are used in sitcoms like *Modern Family* and *Parks and Recreation*.
- Describe the use of gritty or graphic content in a network show like *NCIS* and a cable series like *The Walking Dead*.

Stage Two: Analysis

Focus on and discuss the significant patterns that emerge during the Description stage. Make connections. How does this song or story connect with other items of popular culture?

Examples
- How does the satirical approach of *Last Week Tonight* compare to that of *The Daily Show*?
- What are the similarities and differences between *Fox & Friends* and NBC's *Today*?

Stage Three: Interpretation

Interpret findings. Ask yourself, What does it mean? If there is a distinct pattern, what is the cause or reason? Consider whether comedy, irony, and satire complicate this stage of the critical process.

Examples
- What does the presence of criminal protagonists mean for shows like *Orange Is the New Black*, *Better Call Saul*, and *Breaking Bad*?
- What does it mean when Jeff Dunham fashions a comedy act around Achmed, the Dead Terrorist? Why do Dunham's fans find the "I keel you" line so funny?

Stage Four: Evaluation

Arrive at a critical judgment that goes beyond your personal tastes. Does the media product under analysis cause harm? Does it inspire thought? Does it perpetuate a dehumanizing view of a group? Does it promote active citizenship or passive consumerism?

Examples
- The postapocalyptic action movie *Mad Max: Fury Road* features a very tough female character played by Charlize Theron. Should the movie be celebrated for challenging the normal roles of women in action films?
- *Captain America: Civil War* pits heroes against each other in a clash between the desire for freedom and the need for security. Is this film antigovernment propaganda?

Stage Five: Engagement

Make your voice heard. Take action that connects your critical perspective to your role as a citizen. Become involved in doing your part to challenge media institutions and make them accountable.

Examples
- Write letters to media editors about blind spots in news coverage.
- Contact companies that perpetuate harmful images of women in their advertising and recommend more socially responsible ways of selling their products.

messages affect our actions, the quality of our lives, and the health of our democracy. We also need to ask questions, such as the following:

• Why might some people continue clinging to either/or thinking about media (such as high-brow versus low-brow books or movies) when so many boundaries in our society have blurred? Does this either/or thinking reflect a desire to keep people in their "proper" socioeconomic class?

• What does it mean that public debate and news about everyday life now seem more likely to come from Facebook, John Oliver, or bloggers than from the *New York Times* or the *NBC Nightly News*?[9] Can we no longer distinguish real news from entertainment? If so, does this affect how well informed we are?

• How can we hone our awareness of the economic interests fueling the messages delivered through the media we consume? For example, do you listen to a talk show on a radio station that survives on advertising revenue? If so, ask yourself how the host might distort information (e.g., deliberately inciting conflict between guests) to attract more listeners and therefore bring in more advertising revenue. (Advertisers only want to spend money on ads that will reach as many people as possible.) If such distortion is taking place, how reliable is the information you're consuming by listening to the show?

Unfortunately, we can't rely on professional media critics or watchdog organizations to do all the work of critiquing the media for us and analyzing their effects on our lives. Each of us is responsible for doing some of that work ourselves. As you read through the chapters in this book, you'll learn more about each type of media—and you'll hone your ability to examine each with a critical eye.

CHAPTER ESSENTIALS

Review

- **Media literacy** is the attempt to understand how the media work and what impact they have on our lives. It is important to acquire media literacy so that we have a say in the roles that media play around us.

- The mass media have their roots in mass communication. **Mass media** are the industries that create and distribute songs, novels, newspapers, movies, Internet services, TV shows, magazines, and other products to large numbers of people. **Mass communication** is the creation and use of symbols (such as languages, motion pictures, and computer codes) that convey information and meaning to large and diverse audiences through all manner of channels.

- We can trace the historical development of media through several eras: the oral and written eras (1000 BCE to the mid-fifteenth century), the print era (beginning in the mid-fifteenth century), and the electronic and digital eras (from the late nineteenth century to today).

- **Media convergence** can refer to the technological merging of media content across different media channels (such as the availability of a magazine article in print and online form) or to a business model used by media companies that consolidate media holdings to reduce costs and maximize profits. This convergence, as well as the speed of communication made possible by ever-faster Internet and more powerful personal devices, is an important characteristic of the **digital turn**.

- A new medium goes through three stages on its journey toward mass medium status: the development (or novelty) stage (inventors and technicians try to solve a particular problem), the entrepreneurial stage (inventors and investors find a marketable use for the new device), and the mass medium stage (businesses figure out how to market the new device as a consumer product).

- Experts have used a variety of approaches to understand how the media work and what impact they have on our lives, including the linear model (which most scholars now see as outdated), the cultural model, and the social scientific model.

- Cultural researchers trace changes in values that accompany changes in mass media. The **modern era** saw the rise of four values: efficient work, celebration of the individual, belief in a rational order, and rejection of tradition and an embracing of progress. The **postmodern period** witnessed the emergence of its own values: celebration of **populism**, a questioning of authority, and an embracing of technology.

- Social scientists use **content analysis** to gather data—they code and count the content of various types of media. They also conduct **experiments** to generate data and gather data through surveys.

- Citizens can examine the findings of cultural and social scientific research on media to follow a **critical process**, which consists of describing, analyzing, interpreting, evaluating, and engaging with mass media.

Key Terms

media literacy, p. 5

mass media, p. 6

mass communication, p. 6

digital communication, p. 10

digital turn, p. 10

media convergence, p. 11

survey research, p. 18

high culture, p. 19

low (popular) culture, p. 19

modern era, p. 20

Progressive Era, p. 21

postmodern period, p. 21

populism, p. 21

content analysis, p. 22

experiments, p. 23

critical process, p. 23

Study Questions

1. Explain the interrelationship between *mass communication* and *mass media*.

2. What are the stages a medium goes through before becoming a mass medium?

3. What are the hallmarks of the digital turn and what makes it different from earlier stages of mass media development?

4. What are the strengths and weaknesses of the skyscraper and map models of culture?

5. How might we tell whether a piece of media research comes from someone working under the cultural or the social scientific model?

6. What are the steps of the critical process behind media literacy and why are they important?

2

Books and the Power of Print

Usually when we think of crowds of screaming teenage fans, we envision appearances by popular young music stars and heartthrob film and television actors. But what about book authors? It turns out that even in our digital age, the authors of young-adult (YA) fiction sometimes enjoy intensely devoted fan bases—just like those of celebrated singers and performers. In fact, the convergence of the modern mediascape may even boost and broaden the pop culture appeal of books and the people who write them.

In the photo that opens this chapter, *Paper Towns* and *The Fault in Our Stars* author John Green is surrounded by his teenage fans, many of them young women. Green and fellow YA author Veronica Roth, who wrote the popular Divergent trilogy, are just two authors who attract these kinds of crowds at BookCon, a fan event inspired by the annual comic conventions and trade shows around the world. BookCon was launched in 2014 to highlight "where storytelling and pop culture collide" as part of the otherwise staid BookExpo America, the largest book industry trade show in North America.[1]

As it turns out, storytelling and pop culture tend to collide frequently in the flourishing young-adult book segment of the publishing industry. Think of some of the biggest film franchises in recent years: Harry Potter, Twilight, The Hunger Games, and Divergent. In addition, John Green's books aren't a series, but Hollywood has noticed that they connect with a lot of teens, particularly young women.

◄ John Green and other successful authors who write for the young-adult audience boost reading among young people from middle school through college. They also enjoy the type of fan adoration that's often associated with pop music performers.
Gustavo Caballero/Getty Images

As for what makes a book a "young-adult" book, YA author Seth Fishman argues, "YA really just means a teen protagonist. Oftentimes we see first person or settings based on 'reality' (high school, death match arenas) but just as often we see abnormal (high school with vampires, death match arenas with vampires). In other words, just like adult books."[2]

Young-adult books appear frequently on book industry best-seller lists. Of the six print books to sell more than one million copies in the United States in 2014, four of them were young-adult books, led by *The Fault in Our Stars* and Veronica Roth's series installations: *Divergent, Insurgent,* and *Allegiant.*[3] While YA book sales slowed a bit in 2015, dropping 3 percent from the previous year, the genre remains a prominent player in the publishing mix.[4]

There is a certain irony to the fact that young-adult books are among the biggest sellers. As a writer for the *Huffington Post* noted, "Young people are often criticized for their supposed short attention span and general fickle-mindedness—and yet YA literature is one of the most buoyant segments in publishing."[5] Like all mass media, the book-publishing world is undergoing digital changes, but its ability to attract and obsess young audiences is a reminder that books can be as powerful as ever.

FOR HUNDREDS OF YEARS —before newspapers, radio, and film, let alone television and the Internet—books were the only mass medium. Books have fueled major developments throughout human history, from revolutions and the rise of democracies to new forms of art (including poetry and fiction) and the spread of various religions. When cheaper printing technologies laid the groundwork for books to become more widely available and more quickly disseminated, people gained access to knowledge and ideas that were previously reserved for the privileged few.

With the emergence of new types of mass media, some critics claimed that books would cease to exist. So far, however, that's not happening. In 1950, U.S. publishers introduced more than 11,000 new book titles; by 2014, that number had reached more than 200,000 (see Figure 2.1 on page 36). Though books have adapted to technology and cultural change (witness the advent of e-books), our oldest mass medium still plays a large role in our lives. Books remain the primary repository of history and everyday experience, passing along stories, knowledge, and wisdom from generation to generation.

In this chapter, we will trace the history of this enduring medium and examine its impact on our lives today by:

- assessing books' early roots—including the inventions of papyrus (the first writing surface) and the printing press, as well as the birth of the publishing industry in colonial America

- exploring the unique characteristics of modern publishing, such as how publishing houses are structured

- taking stock of the many types of books that are available today, from the variety of print books to both electronic and digital books

- examining the economics of the book industry, including how players in the industry make money and what they spend it on to fulfill their mission

- considering the role of books in our democracy today, as this mass medium confronts several challenges

The Early History of Books: From Papyrus to Paperbacks

LaunchPad
launchpadworks.com

Use **LearningCurve** to review concepts from this chapter.

Books have traveled a unique path in their journey to mass medium status. They developed out of early innovations, including papyrus (scrolls made from plant reeds), parchment (treated animal skin), and codex (sheets of parchment sewn together along the edge and then bound and covered). They then entered an entrepreneurial stage, during which people explored new ways of clarifying or illustrating text and experimented with printing techniques, such as block printing, movable type, and the printing press. The invention of the printing press set the stage for books to become a mass medium, complete with the rise of a new industry: publishing.

Papyrus, Parchment, and Codex: The Development Stage of Books

The ancient Egyptians, Greeks, Chinese, and Romans all produced innovations that led up to what looked roughly like what we think of today as a book. It all began some five thousand years ago, in ancient Sumeria (Mesopotamia) and Egypt, where people first experimented with pictorial symbols called *hiero-glyphics* or early alphabets. Initially, this writing was placed on wood strips or stones, or pressed into clay tablets. Eventually, these objects were tied or

FIGURE 2.1 // ANNUAL NUMBERS OF NEW BOOK TITLES PUBLISHED, SELECTED YEARS

As each new mass medium was introduced, from film to the Internet, there were fears that it would result in the death of book publishing. As this graph shows, not only did book publishing survive each new major technological advance, but the number of books published has risen over time, most steeply in the last twenty-five years.

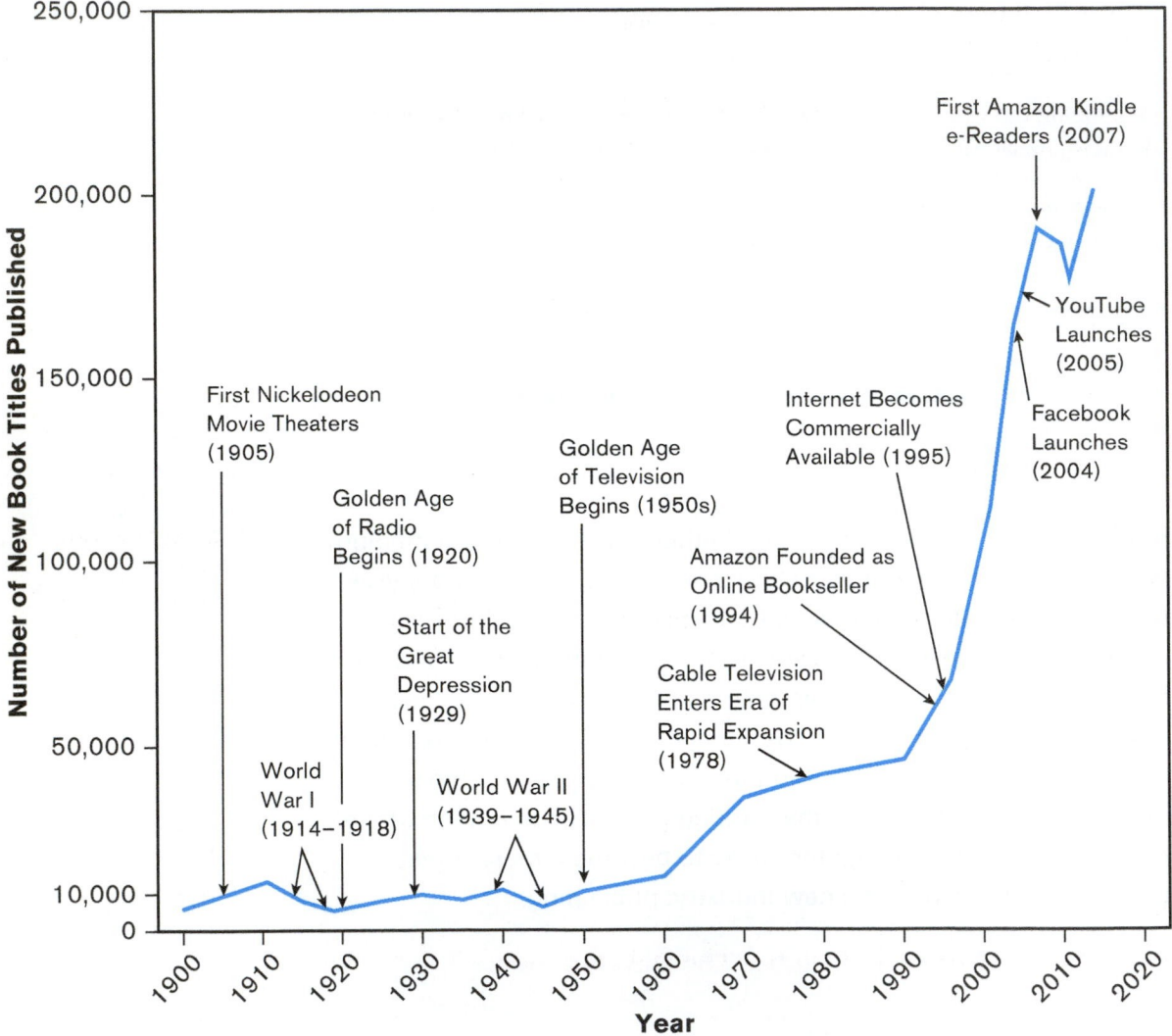

Note: Changes in the Almanac's *methodology in 1997 and for the years 2004–07 resulted in additional publications being assigned ISBNs and included in the count.*

Figures through 1945 from John Tebbel, A History of Book Publishing in the United States, *4 vols. (New York: R. R. Bowker, 1972–81); figures after 1945 from various editions of the* Library and Book Trade Almanac *(formerly* The Bowker Annual *[Information Today, Inc.]) and Bowker press releases.*

stacked together to form the first "books." Around 1000 BCE, the Chinese were using strips of wood and bamboo with writing on them, tied together to make a booklike object.

Then, in 2400 BCE, the Egyptians began turning plants found along the Nile River into a material they could write on called **papyrus** (from which the word *paper* is derived). Between 650 and 300 BCE, the Greeks and Romans adopted the use of papyrus scrolls. Gradually, **parchment**—treated animal skin—replaced papyrus in Europe. Parchment was stronger, smoother, more durable, and less expensive than papyrus. Around 105 CE, the Chinese began making paper from cotton and linen, though paper did not replace parchment in Europe until the thirteenth century.

The first protomodern book was most likely produced in the fourth century by the Romans, who created the **codex**—sheets of parchment sewn together along one edge, then bound with thin pieces of wood and covered with leather. Whereas scrolls had to be rolled and unrolled for use, a codex could be opened to any page, and people could write on both sides of a page.

Writing and Printing Innovations: Books Enter the Entrepreneurial Stage

Books entered the entrepreneurial stage with the emergence of **manuscript culture**. In this stage, new rules about written language and book design were codified—books were elaborately lettered, decorated, and bound by hand. Inventors also began experimenting with printing as an alternative to hand lettering and a way to speed up the production and binding of manuscript copies.

Manuscript Culture
During Europe's Middle Ages (400 to 1500 CE), Christian priests and monks transcribed the philosophical tracts and religious texts of the period, especially versions of the Bible. These **illuminated manuscripts** featured decorative, colorful illustrations on each page and were often made for churches or wealthy clients. These early publishers developed certain standards for their works, creating rules of punctuation, making distinctions between small and capital letters, and leaving space between words to make reading easier. Some elements of this manuscript culture remain alive today in the form of design flourishes, such as the drop capitals occasionally used for the first letter in each chapter of a book.

▲ Illuminated manuscripts were handwritten by scribes and illustrated with colorful and decorative images and designs. Erich Lessing/Art Resource, NY

Block Printing

If manuscript culture involved advances in written language and book design, it also involved hard work: Every manuscript was painstakingly copied one book at a time. From as early as the third century, Chinese printers came up with an innovation that made mass production possible.

These Chinese innovators developed **block printing**. Using this technique, printers applied sheets of paper to large blocks of inked wood into which they had hand-carved a page's worth of characters and illustrations. The oldest dated block-printed book still in existence is China's *Diamond Sutra*, a collection of Buddhist scriptures printed by Wang Chieh in 868 CE.

Movable Type

The next significant step in printing came with the invention of movable type in China around the year 1000. This was a major improvement (in terms of speed) over block printing because rather than carving each new page on one block, printers carved commonly used combinations of characters from the Chinese language into smaller, reusable wood (and later ceramic) blocks. They then put together the pieces needed to represent a desired page of text, inked the small blocks, and applied the sheets of paper. This method enabled them to create pages of text much more quickly than before.

The Printing Press and the Publishing Industry: Books Become a Mass Medium

Books moved from the entrepreneurial stage to mass medium status with the invention of the printing press (which made books widely available for the first time) and the rise of the publishing industry (which arose to satisfy people's growing hunger for books).

The Printing Press

The **printing press** was invented by Johannes Gutenberg in Germany between 1453 and 1456. Drawing on the principles of movable type and adding a device adapted from the design of a wine press, Gutenberg's staff of printers produced the first so-called modern books, including two hundred copies of a Latin Bible—twenty-one of which still exist. The Gutenberg Bible (as it's now known) was printed on a fine calfskin-based parchment called **vellum**.

Printing presses spread rapidly across Europe in the late 1400s and early 1500s. Many of the early books being printed were large, elaborate, and expensive. But printers gradually reduced the size of books and developed less-expensive grades of paper. These changes made books cheaper to produce, so printers could sell them for less, making the books affordable to many more people.

The spread of printing presses and books sparked a major change in the way people learned. Previously, people followed the traditions and ideas framed by local authorities—the ruling class, clergy, and community leaders. But as books became more broadly available, people gained access to knowledge and viewpoints far beyond those of their immediate surroundings and familiar authorities, leading some of them to begin challenging the traditional wisdom and customs of their tribes and leaders.[6] This interest in debating ideas would ultimately encourage the rise of democratic societies in which all citizens had a voice.

The Publishing Industry

In the two centuries following the invention of the printing press, publishing—the establishment of printing shops to serve the public's growing demand for books—took off in Europe, eventually spreading to England and finally to the American colonies. In the late 1630s, English locksmith Stephen Daye set up the first colonial print shop in Cambridge, Massachusetts. By the mid-1760s, all thirteen colonies had printing shops. Some publishers, such as Benjamin Franklin, grew quite wealthy in this profession.

However, in the early 1800s, U.S. publishers had to find ways to lower the cost of producing books to meet the exploding demand. By the 1830s, machine-made paper replaced the more expensive handmade varieties, cloth covers supplanted costlier leather ones, and **paperback books** were made with cheaper paper covers (introduced in Europe), all of which helped to make books even more accessible to the masses. Further reducing the cost of books, publishers introduced paperback **dime novels** (so called because they sold for five or ten cents) in 1860. By 1885, one-third of all books published in the United States consisted of popular paperbacks and **pulp fiction** (a reference to the cheap, machine-made pulp paper that dime novels were printed on).

Meanwhile, the printing process itself also advanced. In the 1880s, the introduction of **linotype** machines enabled printers to save time by setting type mechanically using a typewriter-style keyboard. The introduction of steam-powered and high-speed rotary presses also permitted the production of even more books at lower costs. With the development of **offset lithography** in the early 1900s, publishers could print books from photographic plates rather than from metal casts. This greatly reduced the cost of color illustrations and accelerated the production process, enabling publishers to satisfy Americans' steadily increasing demand for books.

▲ The weekly paperback series *Tip Top Weekly*, which was published between 1896 and 1912, featured the most popular dime novel hero of the day, Yale football star and heroic adventurer Frank Merriwell.
The New York Public Library/Art Resource, NY

The Evolution of Modern Publishing

As demand for books skyrocketed, the publishing industry morphed to satisfy it. Companies that participated in this industry, often called publishing houses, were initially small and focused on offering the works of quality authors. Over time, major corporations with ties to international media conglomerates snapped up these companies. However, regardless of what subject matter they focus on or who owns them, publishing houses are structured in similar ways to carry out the process of attracting authors, developing manuscripts, and marketing published books.

Early Publishing Houses

The modern book industry in the United States developed gradually in the 1800s with the formation of "prestigious" publishing houses: companies that identified and produced the works of respected writers.[7] The oldest American houses include J. B. Lippincott (1792); Harper & Bros. (1817), which became Harper & Row in 1962 and HarperCollins in 1990; Houghton Mifflin (1832); Little, Brown (1837); G. P. Putnam (1838); Scribner's (1842); E. P. Dutton (1852); Rand McNally (1856); and Macmillan (1869).

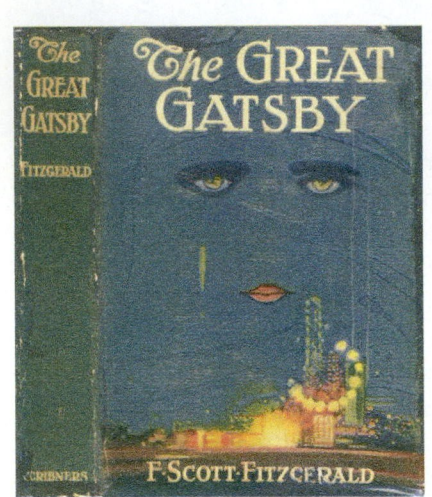

Between 1880 and 1920, as more people moved from rural areas to cities and learned to read, Americans became interested in reading all kinds of books—novels, historical accounts, reference materials, instructional resources. This caught the attention of entrepreneurs eager to profit by satisfying this demand. Thus, a savvy breed of publishing house—focused on marketing—was born. These firms included Doubleday & McClure Company (1897), McGraw-Hill Book Company (1909), Prentice Hall (1913), Alfred A. Knopf (1915), Simon & Schuster (1924), and Random House (1925).

▲ Scribner's—known more for its magazine in the late 1800s than for its books—became the most prestigious literary house of the 1920s and 1930s, publishing F. Scott Fitzgerald (*The Great Gatsby*, 1925) and Ernest Hemingway (*The Sun Also Rises*, 1926). Photo by Princeton University Library. Rare Books Division. Department of Rare Books and Special Collections. Princeton University Library.

The Conglomerates

Book publishing sputtered from the 1910s into the 1940s, as the two world wars and the Great Depression turned Americans' attention away from books. But as the U.S. economy recovered during the 1950s and 1960s, the industry bounced back. Major corporations and international media conglomerates began acquiring the smaller houses to expand their markets and take advantage of the **synergy** (the promotion and sale of different versions of a media product across the various subsidiaries of a conglomerate) between books and other media types.

TABLE 2.1 // WORLD'S TEN LARGEST BOOK PUBLISHERS (REVENUE IN BILLIONS OF DOLLARS), 2016

Rank/Publishing Company (Group or Division)	Home Country	Revenue in $ Billions
1 Pearson	U.K.	$6.625
2 Thomson Reuters	Canada	$5.776
3 RELX Group	U.K./NL/U.S.	$5.209
4 Wolters Kluwer	NL	$4.592
5 Penguin Random House (Bertelsmann & Pearson)	Germany/U.K.	$4.056
6 China South Publishing & Media Group	China	$2.811
7 Phoenix Publishing and Media Company	China	$2.755
8 Hachette Livre (Lagardère)	France	$2.407
9 McGraw-Hill Education	U.S.	$1.835
10 Grupo Planeta	Spain	$1.809

Data from: "The World's 52 Largest Book Publishers, 2016," Publishers Weekly, August 26, 2016, http://www.publishersweekly.com/pw/by-topic/international/international-book-news/article/71268-the-world-s-52-largest-book-publishers-2016.html.

Nowadays book publishing is dominated by a handful of giant corporations. Looking globally and at all kinds of publishing (see Table 2.1), the top five book publishers in terms of revenue are Pearson (textbooks, educational materials), Thomson Reuters (professional books), RELX Group (professional books), Wolters Kluwer (professional books), and Penguin Random House (trade books).

In the United States, the leading publishers of trade books (popular general audience books) may have started out as American companies, but most are now divisions of larger companies based in other countries. Sometimes called "the Big Five," these companies are Penguin Random House (jointly owned since 2013 by German-based Bertelsmann and British-owned Pearson, though in 2017 Pearson announced that it would sell its stake in PRH), Simon & Schuster (owned by CBS), Hachette (owned by Lagardère, based in France), HarperCollins (owned by multinational News Corp.), and Macmillan (owned by German-based Holtzbrinck).

The consolidation of the book industry has raised concerns among observers who mourn the loss of the older houses' distinctive styles and their associations with renowned literary figures, like Mark Twain and Nathaniel Hawthorne. Moreover, the large corporations that now define the industry's direction have huge marketing budgets and can buy needed resources (such as paper, printing, and binding services) at a discount and thus charge less for their product. Few independent publishers have been able to compete against them.

The Structure of Publishing Houses

Regardless of their size or the types of books they publish, publishing houses are structured similarly. For example, they have teams or divisions responsible for acquisitions and manuscript development; copyediting, design, and production; marketing and sales; and administration. And unlike daily newspapers but similar to magazines, most publishing houses pay independent printers to produce their books.

The majority of publishers employ **acquisitions editors** to seek out authors and offer them contracts to publish specific titles. For fiction, this might mean discovering talented writers through book agents or reading unsolicited manuscripts. For nonfiction, editors might examine unsolicited manuscripts and letters of inquiry or match a known writer to a project (such as a celebrity biography). Acquisitions editors also handle **subsidiary rights** for an author—that is, selling the rights to a book for use in other media, such as a mass market paperback, or as the basis for a screenplay.

After a contract is signed, the acquisitions editor may turn the book over to a **developmental editor**, who helps the author draft and revise the manuscript by providing feedback and soliciting advice from reviewers. If a book is to contain illustrations, editors work with photo researchers to select photographs or find artists to produce the needed drawings or other graphics. At this point, the production staff enters the picture. While **copy editors** fix any spelling, punctuation, grammar, or style problems in the manuscript, **design managers** determine the look and feel of the book, making decisions about type styles, paper, cover design, and layout of page spreads.

Simultaneously, the publishing house determines a marketing strategy for the book, including identifying which readers will be most interested in the title, deciding how many copies to print and what price to charge, and selecting advertising channels for reaching the target customers. Marketing budgets usually make up a large part of a publishing company's expenses, and marketing managers are often fairly high up in the organization.

Types of Books: Tradition Meets Technology

Until fairly recently, books of all kinds took printed form: pages bound together through various devices (such as glue or spiral wire) and enclosed by a cover (cardboard, leather, paper). But with the rise of electronic and digital publishing, book formats have expanded beyond print to include audio books (available as CDs or MP3 downloads) and e-books (accessed on the Internet and read on a computer or a handheld device). Regardless of the format, however, books are still highly diverse in terms of their subject matter.

Print Books

Today, the publishing industry produces titles that fall into a wide variety of categories—everything from trade books and textbooks to mass market paperbacks and reference books. These categories have been formally defined by various trade organizations, such as the Association of American Publishers (AAP), the Book Industry Study Group (BISG), and the American Booksellers Association (ABA). While these organizations tend to classify e-books separately to help them keep track of business trends, in practice, ongoing digital convergence means that a book in any of these categories likely has an e-book counterpart. Keeping that in mind, we will discuss e-books and their unique place in book publishing later in this section.

Trade

One of the most lucrative markets in the industry, **trade books** include hardbound and paperback books aimed at general readers and sold at commercial retail outlets. The industry distinguishes among adult trade, juvenile trade, and comics and graphic novels (which contain pictures rather than type). Adult trade books include hardbound and paperback fiction; current nonfiction and biographies; literary classics; books on hobbies, art, and travel; popular science, technology, and computer publications; self-help books; and cookbooks. Juvenile trade categories range from preschool picture books to young-adult or young-reader books, such as the Dr. Seuss books, the Lemony Snicket series, and the Harry Potter series.

Professional

Professional books target various occupational groups, not the general consumer market. This area of publishing capitalizes on the growth of professional specialization that has characterized the U.S. job market, particularly since the 1960s. Traditionally, the industry has subdivided professional books into the areas of law, business, medicine, and technology-science. These books are sold mostly through mail order, the Internet, or sales representatives knowledgeable about the various subject areas.

Textbooks

Textbooks are divided into elementary through high school (el-hi) texts, college texts, and vocational texts. In about half the states in the country, local school districts determine which el-hi textbooks are appropriate for their students. The remaining states, including Texas and California, have statewide

FIGURE 2.2 // STUDENT BUYING BEHAVIORS: PREFERRED TEXTBOOK FORMAT

According to a survey by the National Association of College Stores, the number of students who prefer digital course materials is slowly growing. While 46 percent of students preferred using print textbooks in the 2014–2015 academic year, only 40 percent preferred print in the 2015–2016 academic year (shown below). In addition, six out of ten students used at least one digital textbook or access code during fall 2015.

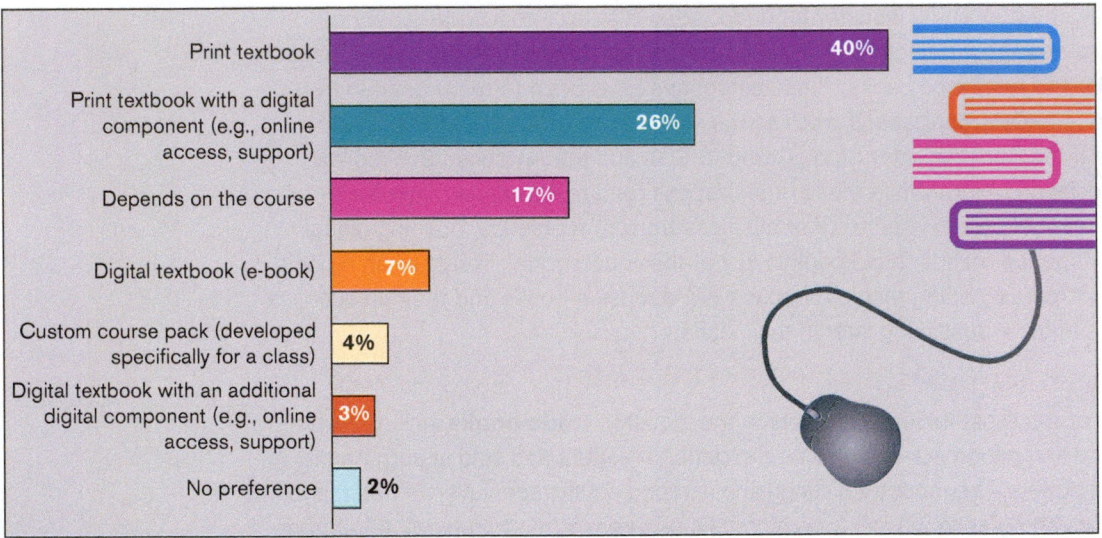

Print textbook — **40%**
Print textbook with a digital component (e.g., online access, support) — **26%**
Depends on the course — **17%**
Digital textbook (e-book) — **7%**
Custom course pack (developed specifically for a class) — **4%**
Digital textbook with an additional digital component (e.g., online access, support) — **3%**
No preference — **2%**

Data from: National Association of College Stores, "Key Findings Report: Student Watch 2015–16 Academic Year," http://www.nacs.org/research /studentwatchfindings.aspx.

adoption policies governing which texts can be used. Unlike el-hi texts, which are subsidized by various states and school districts, college texts are paid for by students (or their parents) and are sold primarily through college bookstores. The high cost of textbooks has led some students to trade, resell, or rent textbooks, or to download less expensive e-book versions. Surveys indicate that college students spent an average of $602 in the 2015–16 academic year on required course materials.[8] (For more on textbook habits, see Figure 2.2.)

Mass Market Paperbacks

Unlike the larger-size trade paperbacks, which are sold mostly in bookstores, **mass market paperbacks** are sold on racks in drugstores, supermarkets, and airports, as well as in bookstores. Contemporary mass market paperbacks are paperback versions of hard cover trade books by blockbuster authors such as Stephen King and Veronica Roth, and are generally priced low (under $10).

Paperbacks first became popular back in the 1870s, when middle- and working-class readers popularized dime novels.

Religious

The best-selling book of all time is the Bible, in all its diverse versions. Over the years, the success of Bible sales has created a large industry for religious books, and many religious-book publishers have extended their offerings to include secular titles on such topics as war and peace, race, poverty, gender, and civic responsibility. Although sales revenue from religious books has been on a slow decline, these books still account for about a half-billion dollars in sales in the United States ($535 million in 2015).[9]

Reference

Reference books include dictionaries, encyclopedias, atlases, almanacs, and volumes related to particular professions or trades, such as legal casebooks and medical manuals. Encyclopedias and dictionaries have traditionally accounted for the largest portion of reference sales. But these reference works have moved mostly to online formats since the 1990s in response to competition from companies offering different formats. These rival formats include free online or built-in word-processing software dictionaries, search engines such as Google, and online resources like Wikipedia.

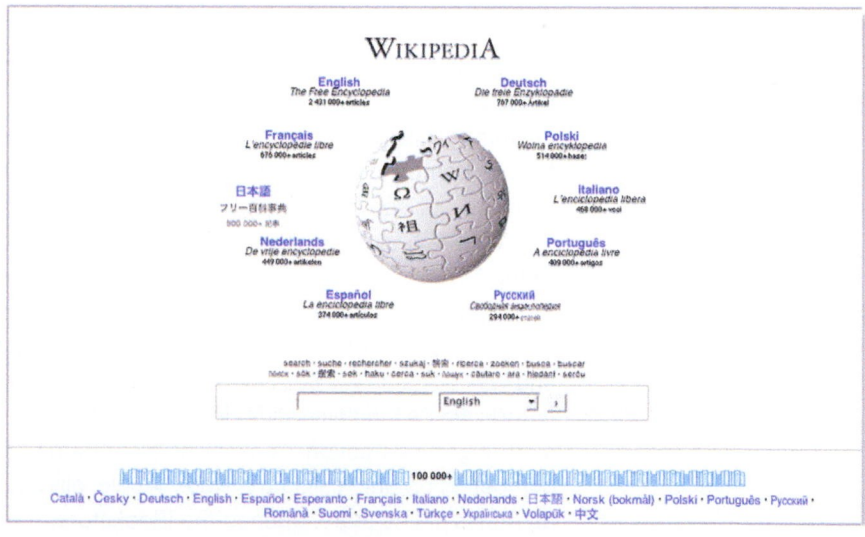

University Press

The smallest market in the printed-book industry is the nonprofit **university press**, which publishes scholarly works for small groups of readers interested in specialized areas, such as literary theory and criticism, art movements, and contemporary philosophy. Some of these presses are small, publishing only a few books a year, but the largest, Oxford University Press, publishes over six thousand titles annually. Whereas large commercial trade houses are often criticized for publishing only high-selling, mainstream books, university presses often suffer the opposite criticism—that they produce mostly obscure books that only a handful of scholars read.

▲ Since its launch in 2001, Wikipedia has grown to include more than forty million entries in more than 250 languages. Despite controversies about bias, inconsistency, and incorrect information, the site is one of the most popular on the Web for general information. Wikipedia

Electronic and Digital Publishing

Within the formal categories previously discussed, publishers are continually experimenting with alternatives to the printed-book format to remain competitive and to leverage the advantages of technologies now available in the digital age. Examples of these alternatives include audio books and e-books.

Audio Books

Audio books (once known as "books on tape," though they are now available primarily on CD or as MP3 downloads) became popular in the 1990s and early 2000s and generally feature actors or authors reading versions of popular fiction and nonfiction trade books. Indispensable to many sightless readers and older readers with diminishing vision, audio books are also popular among readers who have long commutes by car or train, or who want to listen to a book while doing something else, like exercising. By the early 2000s, audio books were readily available on the Internet for downloading to iPods and other portable devices. More recently, audio-book sales have been an area of strong growth in the publishing industry, nearly doubling from about $300 million in 2012 to over $550 million in 2015.[10]

E-Books

The development of the **e-book**—a digital book read on a computer or a digital reading device—has been greatly affected by two defining elements of the digital turn: convergence and speed, made possible by advances in technology. In fact, by comparing early failures to popularize e-books with recent successes at doing so, we see the impact these changes have had in just a few short years.

While efforts to digitize and share books via computer can be traced back to the 1970s, the first attempts to market something recognizable as a forerunner of today's e-readers came from RCA and Sony in the early 1990s. Those early e-readers were heavy, offered few choices, had difficult-to-read screens, and were expensive. But when Amazon, already the largest online bookseller, introduced its Kindle e-reader in 2007, the long-predicted digital book market started gaining traction. Bookselling giant Barnes & Noble soon followed with a competing product called the Nook. Apple, already experiencing success with its iTunes online store, opened the iBookstore.

Since the first Kindle and Nook models were introduced, companies have delivered a steady stream of increasingly more versatile, powerful, and portable electronic devices that allow users to access the Web and run a variety of reading and book-purchasing apps. Apple launched the first of several iPad tablet versions in 2010. Amazon responded by morphing its e-reader into a tablet, releasing the Kindle Fire in 2011, Kindle Fire HDX in 2013, Kindle Voyage in 2014, and Kindle Oasis in 2016. Meanwhile, e-books have been fully adapted to smartphones.

These changes have happened rapidly, with speed playing a significant role in e-books' growing popularity with consumers: With the ability to connect multiple devices to a single account and to buy reading material with nothing more than an Internet connection, an avid reader is only mere moments away from a new book at any given time.

This convergence of technology has motivated publishing houses to make digital copies of their old and new titles, which has led to rapid growth in the electronic side of book publishing, going from a tiny percentage of sales in 2008, following the introduction of the Kindle, to just over a fifth of trade book sales in the United States by 2013.[11] Trade e-book sales went as high as $3.24 billion in 2013, before sliding to $2.84 billion in 2015.[12]

E-books are demonstrating how digital technology can help the oldest mass medium adapt and survive. Distributors, publishers, and bookstores also use digital technology to print books on demand, reviving books that would otherwise go out of print and avoiding the inconveniences of carrying unsold books. But perhaps the most exciting aspect of e-books is their potential for reimagining what a book can be. Computers or tablet touchscreens, such as an iPad, can host e-books with embedded video, hyperlinks, and dynamic content, enabling a professor, for example, to reorganize, add to, or delete the content of an e-textbook in order to tailor it to the needs of a specific class. E-books have also made the distribution of long-form journalism and novellas easier with products like the inexpensive Kindle Singles.

The Economics of the Book Industry

To serve customers profitably, the book business (like other mass media industries) must bring in money while also investing in needed resources. Publishers make money by selling books through specific channels (such as brick-and-mortar stores and online stores) and by selling television and movie rights; publishers spend money on essential activities, such as author advances and book production, distribution, and marketing.

Selling Books

Compared with other mass media industries, book publishing has seen only a relatively modest increase in revenues over the decades. From the mid-1980s to 2015, total revenues went from $9 billion to about $28 billion (see Figure 2.3), but the industry continues to seek new and bigger sources of growth. Publishers bring in money through a variety of channels. The most obvious source of revenue for

FIGURE 2.3 // ESTIMATED U.S. BOOK REVENUE, 2015

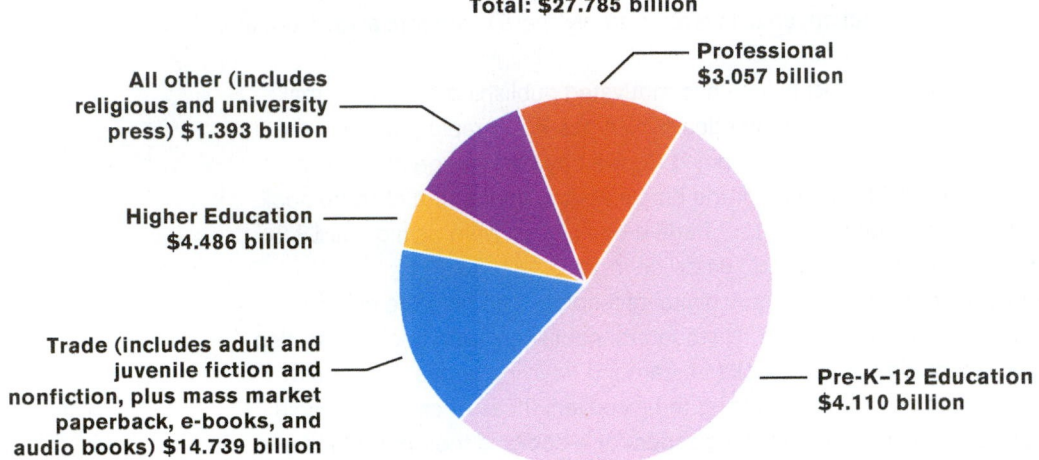

Total: $27.785 billion

Professional
$3.057 billion

All other (includes
religious and university
press) $1.393 billion

Higher Education
$4.486 billion

Trade (includes adult and
juvenile fiction and
nonfiction, plus mass market
paperback, e-books, and
audio books) $14.739 billion

Pre-K–12 Education
$4.110 billion

Data from: Association of American Publishers. For more, see Jim Milliot, "Publishing Sales Dipped in 2015," Publishers Weekly, June 11, 2016, www
.publishersweekly.com/pw/by-topic/industry-news/financial-reporting/article/70881-publishing-sales-dipped-in-2015.html, and American Association of
Publishers, "U.S. Publishing Industry's Annual Survey Reveals Nearly $28 Billion in Revenue in 2015," July 11, 2016, http://newsroom.publishers.org
/us-publishing-industrys-annual-survey-reveals-nearly-28-billion-in-revenue-in-2015/.

publishers is sales of the books themselves—whether they're in print, audio, or
e-book form. There are several main outlets for selling books.

Brick-and-Mortar Stores and Traditional Bookselling

Brick-and-mortar stores include traditional bookstores, department stores, drugstores, used-book stores, and toy stores. Barnes & Noble now dominates book
sales (Borders went bankrupt in 2011) and operates 640 superstores. The rise
of these superstores—along with online competition—has severely cut into
independent bookstores' business, dropping their number from 5,100 in 1991
to only about 2,000 today.

Selling Books Online

Since the late 1990s, online booksellers have created an entirely new book-
distribution system, in which consumers use Web sites to find and buy books.
The strength of online sellers lies in their convenience and low prices, especially their ability to offer backlist titles and the works of less famous authors
that even superstores don't carry on their shelves. The trailblazer is Amazon
.com, established in 1995 by then thirty-year-old Jeff Bezos. In 1997, Barnes &
Noble, the leading retail store bookseller, launched its own heavily invested
and carefully researched bn.com site. In 1999, the ABA launched BookSense
.com to help more than a thousand independent bookstores establish an online
presence.

The shift from buying printed books in brick-and-mortar stores to ordering them online was only part of the way the digital turn changed book publishing's business model. Amazon's bigger objective for the book industry was to transform the entire industry itself, from one based on bound paper volumes to one based on digital files. Amazon quickly grew to control 90 percent of the e-book market, which it used as leverage to force book publishers to comply with its low prices or risk getting dropped from Amazon's bookstore (something that has happened to several independent book publishers who complained).[13]

▲ Amazon's warehouses go far beyond the stockrooms of typical brick-and-mortar stores, housing more than one hundred employees in each location, of which there are dozens across the United States and throughout the world. Bloomberg / Getty Images

Amazon's price slashing caused most of the major trade book publishing corporations to endorse Apple's agency-model pricing, in which publishers would set the e-book prices and digital booksellers would receive a 30 percent commission. When the U.S. Department of Justice ruled in 2013 that Apple and the major publishers had colluded to set book prices (thus denying consumers the lower prices that Amazon's deep discounts might offer), the booksellers responded that government investigators should be more concerned about Amazon.

Of particular concern to publishers is that Amazon has been expanding into the domain of traditional publishers with the establishment of Amazon Publishing, which has grown rapidly since 2009. With a publishing arm that can sign authors to book contracts, the distribution system of the Amazon store, and the potential to put millions of Kindle devices in the hands of readers, Amazon is becoming a vertically integrated company — and a too-powerful entity, traditional publishers fear. Amazon ultimately agreed with the five major book publishers in 2014 and let them set e-book prices. At the same time, Amazon began undercutting the major publishers' e-books (often costing $12.99 to $14.99) with e-books from independent publishers or from its own in-house publishing business, which typically cost from $2.99 to $5.99.

With about 74 percent of the e-book market (see Figure 2.4),[14] at least 25 percent of all *new* trade print books, and about 66 percent of all trade print books, which includes millions of older titles,[15] Amazon's domination is unparalleled. Moreover, in late 2015, Amazon opened its first brick-and-mortar store in Seattle, and by early 2017 it had opened a total of five stores across the country (with more on the way).

FIGURE 2.4 // AMAZON CORNERS THE E-BOOK MARKET

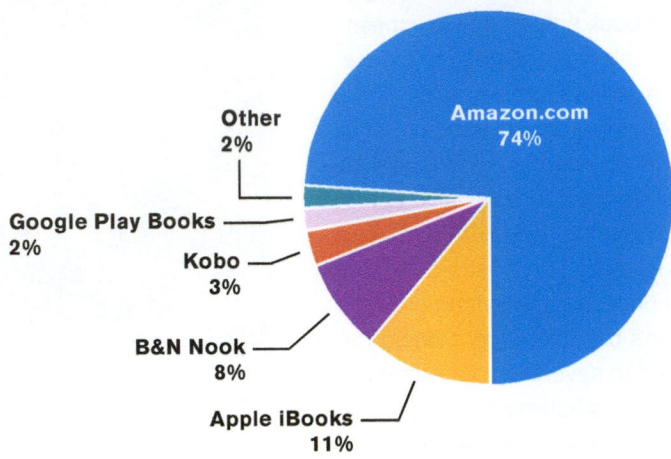

Other 2%

Google Play Books 2%

Kobo 3%

B&N Nook 8%

Apple iBooks 11%

Amazon.com 74%

Data from: "October 2015—Apple, B&N, Kobo, and Google: A Look at the Rest of the eBook Market," October 2015, http://authorearnings.com/report/october-2015-apple-bn-kobo-and-google-a-look-at-the-rest-of-the-ebook-market/.

Influences of Television and Film in the Digital Age

Regardless of what channel a publisher sells its books through, trade publishers are constantly on the hunt for the next *best-seller*—dating back to the huge success of Harriet Beecher Stowe's abolitionist novel *Uncle Tom's Cabin*, which sold fifteen thousand copies in just fifteen days in 1852. Today that hunt is often closely tied to—or even relies on—convergence with both small and large screens.

There are two major facets in the relationship among books, television, and film: how TV and film can help sell books and how books serve as ideas for TV shows and movies. TV exposure for books and authors on talk shows can boost sales, sometimes considerably. One of the most influential forces for promoting books on television was Oprah Winfrey. Each selection for Oprah's Book Club became an immediate best-seller, generating tremendous excitement within the book industry. *The Oprah Winfrey Show* ended in 2011, but the book club was revived online in 2012.

When a book becomes a movie or a television program, book sales soar. Publishers and authors also benefit by selling the rights to adapt a story from page to screen. But the real synergy happens when television and film adaptations spur interest in books and authors, which in turn can generate more interest in movies. This has proven exceptionally true—and exceptionally profitable—in the case of blockbuster book/film crossovers like the Harry Potter series of films. The subgenre of comic books and graphic novels has also led to countless films, including several top box-office hits, like the Dark Knight trilogy and Marvel's interconnected series of superhero films. Other examples

LaunchPad

launchpadworks.com

Tom Perrotta

Based On: Making Books into Movies

Writers and producers discuss the process that brings a book to the big screen.

Discussion: How is the creative process of writing a novel different from that of making a movie? Which would you rather do, and why?

▲ According to reports, HBO pays author George R. R. Martin as much as $15 million a year for the rights to *Game of Thrones*. HBO/Photofest

of movies that have been adapted from books include Veronica Roth's *Allegiant* (2013), Roald Dahl's *The BFG* (1982), and Ransom Riggs's *Miss Peregrine's Home for Peculiar Children* (2011), all of which hit the big screen in 2016.

One of the biggest book-to-TV success stories in the last few years has been HBO's *Game of Thrones*, based on the Song of Ice and Fire series by George R. R. Martin. Other television programs adapted from books include *Pretty Little Liars* on Freeform (formerly ABC Family), based on the series of the same name by Sara Shepard; *Lemony Snicket's A Series of Unfortunate Events* on Netflix, based on the series by Daniel Handler; and *11.22.63* on Hulu, based on the novel by Stephen King. Comic books are also enjoying recent popular and even critical success on the small screen. *Arrow* and *The Flash* are top performers for the CW Television network, while Netflix original series like *Daredevil*, *Jessica Jones*, and *Luke Cage* have had the most success in this subgenre.

Notably, many of these programs are not being produced for traditional television or even cable television. Streaming video services like Netflix and Hulu are just one way that the oldest form of mass media is seizing opportunities available only since the digital turn.

The Cost of Doing Business

Authors need to be compensated for their work, and the author's success, as well as that of the publisher, is driven by sales. To generate sales, publishers must spend money on producing books, distributing their products, and promoting or marketing newly launched titles.

How Authors Get Paid

Authors get paid based on a percentage of sales, historically between 5 and 15 percent of the net price of a book. However, the digital turn means that here, too, things are changing. The amount of the price of a book that goes to the author's royalty is different for printed books, e-books, and self-published e-books (see Figure 2.5).

Also, as part of their contracts, authors sometimes require that publishers pay them *advance money*, an up-front payment that's subtracted from royalties

FIGURE 2.5 // HOW A BOOK'S REVENUE IS DIVIDED

E-books are changing the nature of business expenses, profits, and costs to consumers. Here's where the money goes on a $26 printed trade book, a $12.99 e-book, and a $5.99 self-published e-book.

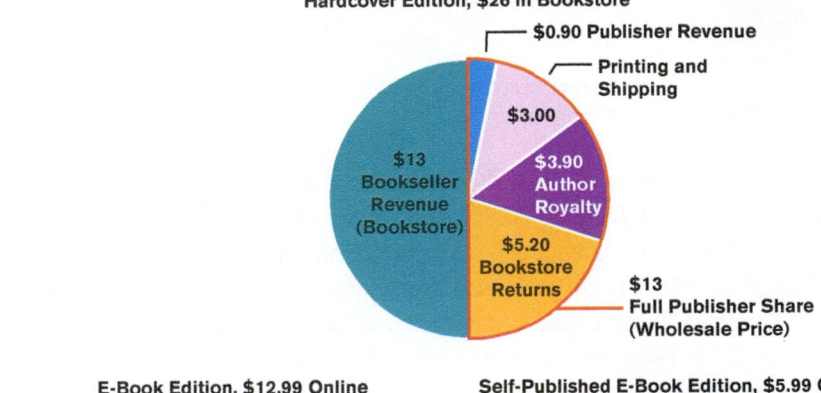
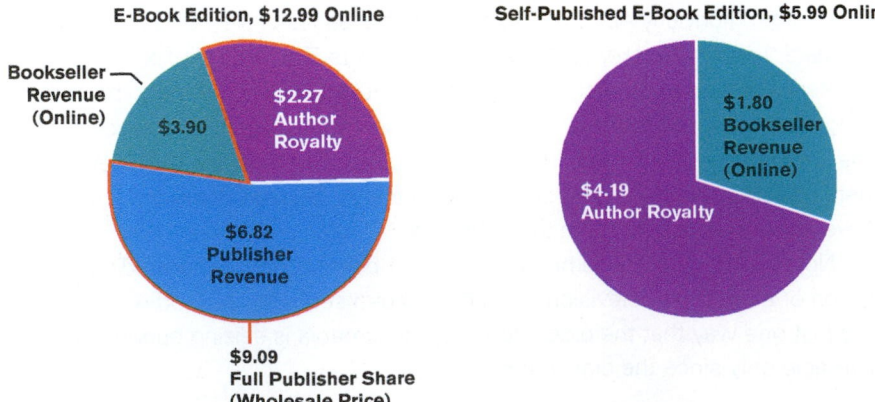

Note: Publishers and booksellers must pay other expenses, such as employees and office/retail space, from their revenue share.

Data from: Ken Auletta, "Publish or Perish: Can the iPad Topple the Kindle, and Save the Book Business?" New Yorker, April 26, 2010, pp. 24–31. Also, Laura Owen, "In Amazon/Hachette Deal, eBook Agency Pricing Is a Winner," GigaOm, November 14, 2014, https://gigaom.com/2014/11/14/in-amazonhachette-deal-ebookagency-pricing-is-a-winner/.

later earned from book sales. New authors may receive little or no advance from a publisher, but commercially successful authors can receive millions.

The Cost of Production, Distribution, and Promotion

In addition to paying authors, publishing houses have certain expenditures, such as overhead (including salaries for employees who edit and design the books), as well as paper, printing, and binding. Once the books are printed, they must be distributed. Distribution costs include maintaining the inventory of books to be sold and fulfilling orders (shipping books to commercial outlets or college bookstores). Publishers monitor their warehouse inventories to ensure that enough copies of a book will be available to meet demand. Publishers don't want to get caught short if a book is popular, but they also don't want to get stuck with copies of a book that doesn't sell.

E-publishing reduces much of this production and distribution overhead because there is no printing, storage, or shipping involved. This in turn has made it far easier for authors to self-publish without using a publishing house (see "The Digital Turn Case Study: Self-Publishing Redefined" on page 54). However, one advantage of traditional publishing houses over self-publishers is that they have the money and expertise to market books. For trade books and some scholarly books, publishing houses may send advance copies of a book to appropriate magazines and newspapers with the hope of receiving positive reviews. A house may also send well-known authors on book-signing tours and arrange radio and TV talk-show interviews, buy shelf space from major chains to assure prominent locations, and buy advertising across the spectrum of traditional and online media. Traditional publishers also have editors and other staff members who can make huge contributions to the quality of a finished book.

Books in a Democratic Society

Books have played a vital role in our democracy — not only by spreading the notion of democracy itself but also by disseminating ideas that inspire people to drive change. For example, Harriet Beecher Stowe's *Uncle Tom's Cabin* sparked outrage over slavery, helping to end the institution in the 1860s. Rachel Carson's *Silent Spring* exposed the perils of the pesticide industry in the 1960s, prompting the American public to demand reform. And Michael Pollan's *The Omnivore's Dilemma* has people thinking about the ethical and nutritional issues connected with factory farming and buying more locally raised meats and vegetables. Books have enabled

The Digital Turn

Self-Publishing Redefined

"I got on the *Twilight* bandwagon. I read *Fifty Shades*. And I just started reading a lot more romance. At some point, I stopped and I thought to myself, 'I think I can do this.'"[1] This is how successful self-published author Meredith Wild (not her real name) described her motivation to transition from running a small software company to writing erotic romance novels. Her Hacker series went to the top of the *New York Times* best-seller list, leading Grand Central Publishing to offer the then thirty-two-year-old author more than $6 million in advance money for the fifth book in the series. Despite the deal with Grand Central, Wild is self-publishing her new Bridge series with Waterhouse Press, an imprint she founded.

 **Web Clip**

YouTube.com has many video interviews with self-published authors. For example, do a quick search for 'Kindle Love Stories: Queen of Hearts — Meredith Wild' posted by Meredith Wild herself. In this interview, does Wild make a compelling argument for the benefits of self-publishing?

Once considered a vain enterprise (hence the term *vanity press*), self-publishing has been equated with amateurism and work that is not worthy of the considerable expenses and promotional resources associated with the big publishing houses. But the commercial success of some authors who have self-published their own e-books (an undertaking that is easier and cheaper than ever since the digital turn) is something big publishers can't ignore. What's more, Wild and other top self-publishing authors are branching out into print, contracting with book printers and distributors to allow them to sell printed copies to bookstores.

Self-published authors are also upsetting the established business model because they need not pay 10 percent to a literary agency, and if they go through Amazon, they receive between 35 and 70 percent of the e-book purchase price rather than the typical 5–15 percent royalty of paper-based book authors.[2] According to a 2016 industry report, the market share of self-published e-books on Amazon grew from just over 25 percent to nearly 45 percent in two years, while the market share of e-books from the top five publishers fell from nearly 40 percent to less than 25 percent.[3] But new opportunities exist for traditional publishers as well: They can carefully watch the ranks of self-publishing authors to recruit new talent, and they have the resources to offer sizable advances and handle the work of promotion, printing, and distribution.

In a somewhat ironic twist, however, Meredith Wild's nascent publishing company, Waterhouse, recently signed two other self-published romance authors,[4] thereby using new digital technologies to branch into the kinds of promotional, distribution, and even printing roles normally associated with traditional publishers. Whether this becomes part of a larger trend remains to be seen, but one thing is for certain: Authors and publishers of all kinds will be watching closely.

people to share ideas freely, discuss those ideas' merits and flaws, and make informed choices — all key elements in any democracy. Indeed, the ability to write whatever one wants has its very roots in our founding documents: Amendment I of the U.S. Constitution's Bill of Rights guarantees freedom of the press.

Though books have long played this crucial role and will continue to do so, they face challenges that threaten to dilute their impact. These challenges include the loss of old books to physical deterioration and the persistence of censorship.

Physical Deterioration

Many older books, especially those from the nineteenth century printed on acid-based paper, gradually deteriorate. To prevent loss of the knowledge in these books, research libraries have built climate-controlled depositories for older books that have permanent research value.

The Google Books Library Project represents a different kind of effort. Begun in 2004, the project features partnerships with the New York Public Library and several major university research libraries to scan millions of books and make them available online and searchable through Google. The Authors Guild and the Association of American Publishers initially resisted having Google digitize books without permission. Google responded that displaying only a limited portion of the books was legal under "fair use" rules. After years of legal battles, a U.S. court of appeals sided with Google's fair-use argument in 2013 and dismissed the lawsuit. The Authors Guild appealed, but in April 2016, the U.S. Supreme Court refused to hear the appeal, so the lower court ruling stands.

Censorship

Throughout human history, rulers intent on maintaining their power have censored or banned books to prevent people from learning about alternative ideas and ways of living. For example, in various parts of the world, some versions of the Bible, Karl Marx's *Das Kapital* (1867), *The Autobiography of Malcolm X* (1965), and Salman Rushdie's *The Satanic Verses* (1989) have all been banned at one time or another. (For more on banned books, see "Media Literacy Case Study: Banned Books and 'Family Values'" on pages 56–57.)

In the United States, censorship and book banning are illegal. But citizens can sometimes force the removal of a particular book from public or school libraries if enough people file a formal complaint—a **book challenge**—about subject matter they find objectionable. The American Library Association (ALA)

Media Literacy

Banned Books and "Family Values"

Fun Home by Alison Bechdel is an autobiographical graphic novel (and now a Broadway musical) about the author's experience with a closeted gay father who took his own life, and her own coming out as a lesbian. The College of Charleston assigned the book to all students as part of a campus-wide reading program. But South Carolina lawmakers took offense to the college's selection of Bechdel's work, citing concerns about the book's discussion of homosexuality, and withdrew funds.[1]

Despite the Constitutional guarantees regarding freedom of speech, there is a long history of books facing censorship in the United States, often in the name of protecting children and a community's "family values." *Ulysses* by James Joyce, *The Scarlet Letter* by Nathaniel Hawthorne, *Leaves of Grass* by Walt Whitman, *The Diary of a Young Girl* by Anne Frank, *Lolita* by Vladimir Nabokov, and *To Kill a Mockingbird* by Harper Lee have all been banned by a U.S. community, school, or library at one time or another. In fact, the most censored book in U.S. history is Mark Twain's *The Adventures of Huckleberry Finn,* the 1884 classic that still sells tens of thousands of copies every year.

The American Library Association tracks challenges that are made against books, and in 2015, *Fun Home* was the seventh most challenged book in schools and libraries across the United States (see also Figure 2.6). Often these challenges come from an individual or a group in a community, but in the example of South Carolina, an entire legislature used its power over the state's purse strings to suppress a book a majority of members didn't like. Equally noteworthy: The group of people they were looking to "protect" weren't children at all but adults attending college.

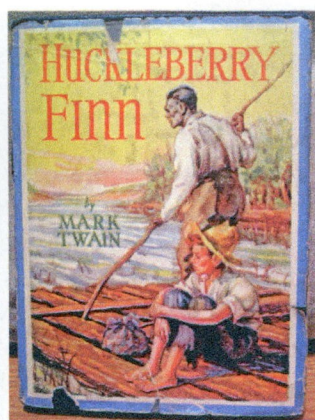

Uschi Gerschner/Newscom /Uschi Gerschner Photography/Salt Lake City UT, USA

▲ Alison Bechdel's *Fun Home* was one of the country's most challenged books in 2015, and Mark Twain's *Huckleberry Finn* is the most censored book in U.S. history.

LaunchPad

⊙ **Visit LaunchPad** to watch a clip from a film adaptation of *Huckleberry Finn.* What audience does it seem to be aimed at?

launchpadworks.com

FIGURE 2.6 // TOP TEN MOST CHALLENGED BOOKS OF 2015

1. *Looking for Alaska* by John Green
   Reasons: Offensive language, sexually explicit, and unsuited to age group
2. *Fifty Shades of Grey* by E. L. James
   Reasons: Sexually explicit, unsuited to age group, and other ("poorly
   written," "concerns that a group of teenagers will want to try it")
3. *I Am Jazz* by Jessica Herthel and Jazz Jennings Reasons: Inaccurate,
   homosexuality, sex education, religious viewpoint,
   and unsuited to age group
4. *Beyond Magenta: Transgender Teens Speak Out* by Susan Kuklin Reasons:
   Anti-family, offensive language, homosexuality, sex education, political
   viewpoint, religious viewpoint, unsuited to age group, and other
   ("wants to remove from collection to ward off complaints")
5. *The Curious Incident of the Dog in the Night-Time* by Mark Haddon Reasons:
   Offensive language, religious viewpoint, unsuited to age group, and other
   ("profanity and atheism")
6. *The Holy Bible* Reasons: Religious viewpoint
7. *Fun Home* by Alison Bechdel Reasons: Violence and other ("graphic images")
8. *Habibi* by Craig Thompson Reasons: Nudity, sexually explicit,
   and unsuited to age group
9. *Nasreen's Secret School: A True Story from Afghanistan* by Jeanette Winter
   Reasons: Religious viewpoint, unsuited to age group, and violence
10. *Two Boys Kissing* by David Levithan Reasons: Homosexuality and other
    ("condones public displays of affection")

Data from: American Library Association, www.ala.org/bbooks/.

APPLYING THE CRITICAL PROCESS

DESCRIPTION Identify two contemporary books that have been challenged or banned in two separate communities. (Check the American Library Association Web site—www.ala.org—for information on the most frequently challenged and banned books or use the LexisNexis database.) Describe the two communities involved and what sparked the challenges or bans.

ANALYSIS Look at the patterns that emerge: the main arguments for censoring these books and for defending these books, and any middle-ground positions or unusual viewpoints brought up in the book controversies.

INTERPRETATION Why did these issues arise, and what do you think are the actual reasons why people would challenge or ban a book? For example, does it seem as though people are genuinely concerned about protecting young readers, or do they just seem personally offended by particular books?

EVALUATION In your opinion, who is right and wrong in these controversies? How are First Amendment protections of printed materials significant here?

ENGAGEMENT Contact your local library and ask what policies are in place to respond to book challenges, and whether it observes the ALA's annual Banned Books Week each September.

▶Banned Books Week is an event sponsored by the American Library Association to raise awareness of challenges to reader freedoms and attempts to ban books. Used with permission from the American Library Association

compiles a list of the most challenged books in the United States. Common reasons for challenges include sexually explicit passages, offensive language, occult themes, violence, homosexual themes, promotion of a religious viewpoint, nudity, and racism. The ALA defends the right of libraries to offer material with a wide range of views and does not support removing books on the basis of partisan or doctrinal disapproval.

This tension between citizens' desire to suppress printed materials they find objectionable and the desire to uphold freedoms guaranteed by the Constitution has long characterized our democracy—and will likely continue to do so.

Resiliency of Reading

The physical deterioration of books and censorship present challenges to books as a mass medium essential to our democracy. But the good news is that books and their readers seem to be adapting quite well to new technology. Americans are still reading books at roughly the same rate as they were in previous years—just not always the same way. A Pew Research Center study found that 73 percent of Americans age eighteen and older had read at least one book in the past year, with the average American reading twelve books per year. Moreover, these readers experienced books across several formats: 65 percent read a book in print, 28 percent read an e-book, and 14 percent listened to an audiobook.[16] The ultimate value of books is their ability to encourage the exchange and exploration of ideas among a broad audience. Clearly, despite the challenges and changes that have reshaped this oldest form of media, they are still serving this purpose.

CHAPTER ESSENTIALS

Review

- Books first developed due to innovations made by the Egyptians, Greeks, Chinese, and Romans. Egyptians created **papyrus** in 2400 BCE. Gradually, people began writing on **parchment** because of its durability and cheaper cost; by the fourth century CE, Romans had created the first protomodern book with the **codex**.

- Books entered the entrepreneurial stage in the Middle Ages, at which time people explored new ways of writing. This led to the emergence of **manuscript culture**, whereby priests and monks advanced the art of bookmaking with **illuminated manuscripts**. At the same time, inventors experimented with new printing techniques, such as **block printing** and movable type.

- The invention of the **printing press** by Gutenberg between 1453 and 1456 allowed for the mass production of books, such as the Bible. This advancement marked books' move to the mass medium stage, complete with the rise of the publishing industry two centuries later.

- Initially, publishing houses were small and focused on offering the works of prestigious authors, but by the 1950s and 1960s, they were snapped up by major corporations with ties to international media conglomerates.

- Regardless of their size or the types of books they publish, all publishing houses are structured similarly. Positions include **acquisitions editors**, **developmental editors**, **copy editors**, **design managers**, and marketing managers.

- Until recently, books of all kinds took only printed form. Some of the categories include **trade books, professional books, textbooks**, **mass market paperbacks,** religious books, **reference books,** and **university press** books. With the rise of electronic and digital publishing, book formats have expanded beyond print to include audio books and **e-books**.

- The book business makes money by selling books—whether through brick-and-mortar stores or online stores—and also by selling TV and movie rights. The book business spends money on essential activities, such as author payments, book production, distribution, and marketing.

- Books have played a vital role in democracy by spreading its very notion and disseminating ideas that have inspired people to drive change. Despite the crucial role of books, they face certain challenges. For example, censorship, which has played a role in book distibution throughout human history, prevents people from learning about alternative ideas or ways of living. In addition, the physical deterioration of books means that some works could be lost.

Key Terms

Study Questions

1. Why was the printing press such an important and revolutionary invention?

2. What does a publishing house do?

3. What are the main ways in which digital technologies have changed the publishing industry?

4. What are the main sources of revenue in book publishing?

5. How do books play a vital role in our society?

3

Newspapers to Digital Frontiers: Journalism's Journey

In 1887, a young reporter left her job at the *Pittsburgh Dispatch* to seek her fortune in New York City. Only twenty-three years old, Elizabeth "Pink" Cochrane had grown tired of writing for the society pages and answering letters to the editor; she wanted to be on the front page. At that time, it was considered "unladylike" for women journalists to use their real names, so the *Dispatch* editors, borrowing from a Stephen Foster song, had dubbed her "Nellie Bly."

After four months of persistent job hunting and freelance writing, Nellie Bly earned a tryout at Joseph Pulitzer's *New York World*, the nation's largest paper. Her assignment: to investigate conditions at the Women's Lunatic Asylum on Blackwell's Island. Her method: to get herself committed to the asylum. After practicing the look of a disheveled lunatic in front of a mirror, she wandered city streets unwashed and seemingly dazed and acted strangely around her fellow boarders in a New York rooming house.[1] Her tactics worked: Doctors declared her mentally deranged and had her committed.

◀ Journalist Nellie Bly—real name Elizabeth Jane Cochrane—laid the groundwork for what we know today as investigative journalism. Her first undercover assignment exposed a need for reform in the care of the mentally ill. The Granger Collection

Ten days later, an attorney from the *World* went in to get her out. Her two-part story appeared in October 1887 and caused a sensation. Nellie Bly's dramatic first-person account documented harsh, cold baths; attendants who abused and taunted patients; and newly arrived immigrant women, completely sane, who had been dragged to the asylum simply because no one could understand them. Bly became famous. Pulitzer gave her a permanent job, and New York City committed $1 million toward improving its asylums. Through her courageous work, Bly pioneered what was then called *detective* or *stunt* journalism—a model that would pave the way toward the twentieth-century practice of investigative journalism.

JOURNALISM IS THE ONLY MEDIA ENTERPRISE that democracy absolutely requires—and is the only media practice and business specifically protected by the U.S. Constitution. However, with the decline in traditional news audiences, mounting criticism of "celebrity" journalists, the growth of partisanship in politics, and the rise of highly opinionated twenty-four-hour cable news and Internet news blogs, mainstream journalists have begun losing their credibility with the public. To understand where journalism and all its current print and electronic forms are today, it's useful to explore the often partisan and sensationalistic history of newspapers—the legacy form of journalism that still represents the bulk of local news coverage in many communities. Yet it's also important to look beyond the printed page to see how journalists took this craft and adapted it to the big screen, to the airwaves, and to the Internet.

In this chapter, we will look at how the profession of journalism, the technology of gathering and sharing the news, and the economics of the news business have shaped one another over the last three hundred years by:

- **exploring journalism's early history, including the rise of the political-commercial press, penny papers, and yellow journalism**

- **assessing the modern era of print journalism, including the tensions between objective and interpretive journalism**

- **considering how journalism has evolved across media, including radio, television, and the Internet**

- **looking at the culture of news and rituals of reporting, including changing definitions of "news," the evolution of journalism's values, and journalistic ethics**

- examining the economics behind print journalism, including the economic impact of the digital turn

- taking stock of the challenges facing journalism today, such as the digitization of content and the proliferation of "fake" news

- considering how journalism's current struggles may affect the strength of our democracy

The Early History of American Journalism

Human beings have always valued **news** — the process by which people gather information and create narrative reports to help one another make sense of events happening around them. The earliest news was passed along *orally* — from family to family and from tribe to tribe — by community leaders and oral historians. Soon after moving from oral to written form, the news shifted from an information source accessible only to elites and local leaders to a mass medium that satisfied a growing audience's hunger for information. In the earliest days of American newspapers (the late 1600s through the 1800s), written news took on a number of formats — political analyses printed on expensive, handmade paper; cheaper accounts printed on machine-made paper; and sensationalist and investigative reports. Each of these formats fulfilled Americans' "need to know" — whether they wanted coverage of the political scene, exposés of corruption in business, or even humorous or entertaining perspectives on current events.

Colonial Newspapers and the Partisan Press

Inspired by the introduction of the printing press in Europe, American colonists began producing their first newspapers in the late seventeenth century. Two main types of early papers developed: the **partisan press** and commercial shipping news. The partisan press got its name because unlike the business models we are familiar with today, these papers were increasingly being sponsored by political parties, politicians, and other partisan groups. They served a vital function before, during, and after the Revolutionary period, critiquing government and disseminating the views of political parties. Other papers were more focused on markets and news about ships that were coming in and out

LaunchPad
launchpadworks.com

Use **LearningCurve** to review concepts from this chapter.

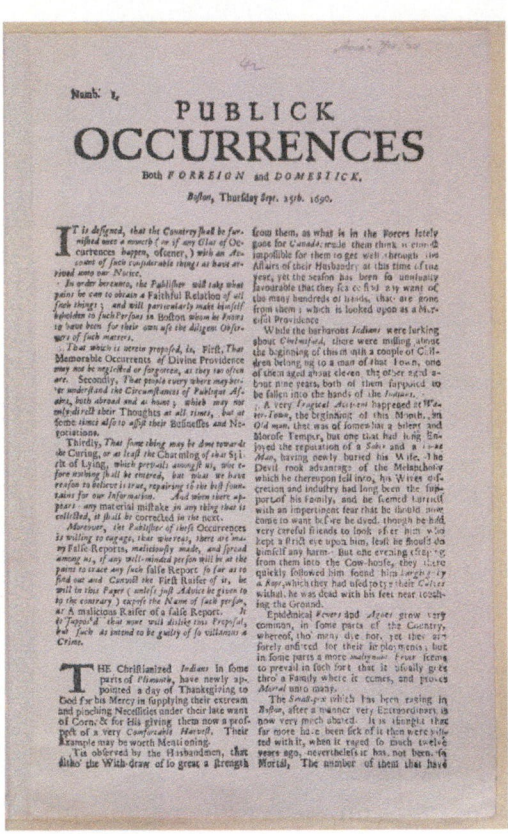

of colonial ports, or they reprinted news (several weeks or months old) from European magazines and newspapers brought on board those ships. In the partisan press, one can see a forerunner to today's editorial pages as well as partisan cable news channels and Web sites. In the commercial papers, one can see the ancestor of today's business sections, as well as numerous papers, cable news programs, and Web sites focused on business news.

The first newspaper, *Publick Occurrences, Both Foreign and Domestick*, was published on September 25, 1690, by Boston printer Benjamin Harris, but it was banned after just one issue for its negative view of British rule. In the early 1700s, other papers cropped up, including Benjamin Franklin's *Pennsylvania Gazette*—which many historians regard as the best of the colonial papers. The *Gazette* was also one of the first papers to make money by printing advertisements alongside news.

One significant colonial paper, the *New-York Weekly Journal*, was founded in 1733 by the Popular Party, a political group that opposed British rule. *Journal* articles included attacks on the royal governor of New York. The party had installed John Peter Zenger as printer of the paper, and in 1734 he was arrested for *seditious libel* when one of his writers defamed a public official's character in print. Championed by famed Philadelphia lawyer Andrew Hamilton, Zenger won his case the following year. The Zenger decision helped lay a foundation—the right of a democratic press to criticize public officials—for the First Amendment to the Constitution, adopted as part of the Bill of Rights in 1791.

▲ The first colonial newspaper, *Publick Occurrences, Both Foreign and Domestick,* was published in 1690 and banned after one issue for its negative portrayal of British rule.
Mary Evans/National Archives/The Image Works

By 1765, the American colonies boasted about thirty newspapers, all of them published weekly or monthly. In 1784, the first daily paper began operations. But even the largest of these papers rarely reached a circulation of fifteen hundred. Readership was largely confined to educated or wealthy men who controlled local politics and commerce (and who could afford newspaper subscriptions).

The Penny Press: Becoming a Mass Medium

During the 1830s, a number of forces transformed newspapers into an information source available to, valued by, and affordable for all—a true mass medium. For example, thanks to the Industrial Revolution, factories could make cheap, machine-made paper to replace the expensive handmade paper previously in use. At the same time, the rise of the middle class, enabled by the growth of literacy, set the stage for a more popular and inclusive press. And with steam-powered presses replacing mechanical presses, publishers could crank out as many as four thousand copies of their newspapers every hour, which dramatically lowered their cost. Popular **penny papers** soon began outselling the six-cent elite publications previously available. The success of penny papers would change not only who was reading newspapers but also how those papers were written.

The First Penny Papers

In 1833, printer Benjamin Day founded the *New York Sun*, lowered the price of his newspaper to one penny, and eliminated subscriptions. The *Sun* (whose slogan was "It shines for all") highlighted local events, scandals, and police reports. It also ran fabricated and serialized stories, making legends of frontiersmen Davy Crockett and Daniel Boone and blazing the trail for Americans' enthusiasm for celebrity news. Within six months, the *Sun* had a circulation of eight thousand—twice that of its nearest competitor. The *Sun*'s success unleashed a barrage of penny papers that favored **human-interest stories**: news accounts that focused on the daily trials and triumphs of the human condition, often featuring ordinary individuals who had faced down extraordinary challenges.

In 1835, James Gordon Bennett founded another daily penny paper, the *New York Morning Herald*. Considered the first U.S. press baron, Bennett—not any one political party—completely controlled his paper's content, establishing an independent publication that served middle- and working-class readers. The *Herald* carried political essays and reports of scandals, business stories, a letters section, fashion notes, moral reflections, religious news, society gossip, colloquial tales and jokes, sports stories, and, later, reports from the Civil War fronts. By 1860, the *Herald* had nearly eighty thousand readers, making it the world's largest daily paper.

Changing Business Models, Changing Journalism

As ad revenues and circulation skyrocketed, the newspaper industry expanded overall. In 1830, about 650 weekly and 65 daily papers operated in the United States, reaching a circulation of 80,000. Just ten years later, the nation had a total of 1,140 weeklies and 140 dailies, attracting more than 300,000 readers.

▲ Andrew Hamilton defends John Peter Zenger, a New York printer arrested for seditious libel in 1734. Zenger eventually won his case, which established the precedent that today allows U.S. journalists and citizens to criticize public officials.

▲ Founded by Benjamin Day in 1833, the *New York Sun* helped usher in the penny press era, bringing news to the working and emerging middle class. North Wind Picture Archives/Almay Stock Photo

As they proliferated and gained new readers, penny papers shifted not just their business models but also the way the news was presented—and, in the process, changed the practice of journalism. Previously, papers had been funded primarily by the political parties that sponsored them, and their content emphasized overt political views. But as they expanded, owners realized they could derive even more revenues from the market—by selling space for advertisements and by hawking newspapers on the streets and through newsstands. Editors began putting their daily reporting on the front page, moving overt political viewpoints to the editorial page. In other words, as the business model relied more on selling to a mass audience, there was a financial incentive to appeal to customers with a wider range of political beliefs. This trend toward an "objective" style as a result of commercial pressures would also be supported by services that provided content for several different newspapers.

The First News Wire Service

In 1848, the enormous expansion of the newspaper industry led six New York newspapers to form a cooperative arrangement and found the Associated Press (AP), the first major news wire service. **Wire services** began as commercial and cooperative organizations that relayed news stories and information around the country and the world using telegraph lines (and, later, radio waves and digital transmissions). In the case of the AP, which functioned as a kind of news co-op, the founding New York papers provided access to their own stories and those from other newspapers.

Such companies enabled news to travel rapidly from coast to coast, setting the stage for modern journalism in the United States. And because the papers still cost only a penny, more people than ever now had access to a widening array of news. Clearly, newspapers had moved from the entrepreneurial stage to the status of mass media.

As individual newspapers, which certainly still retained elements of political ideology, became aware of the financial rewards of not alienating those with differing political viewpoints, wire services saw the need to offer material that as many newspapers as possible would buy. Based on both this economic need and the chance that unreliable telegraph lines might cut off the last part of a report, a journalistic style of writing called the **inverted pyramid** was developed.

Developed by Civil War correspondents working for individual papers or wire services,[2] inverted-pyramid reports were often stripped of adverbs and adjectives, and began—as they do today—with the most dramatic or newsworthy information. They answered the questions who, what, where, when—and, less frequently, why and how—at the top of the story and then narrowed the account down to its less significant details. This approach offered an important advantage: If wars or natural disasters disrupted the telegraph transmissions of these dispatches, at least readers would get the crucial information. Still a staple of introductory news writing courses, this form tends to emphasize immediate events and facts over deeper discussions of context or partisan debate.

But a move away from overt political partisanship on the front page wasn't the only way the economic desire for increasingly larger audiences changed the way journalism was practiced.

Yellow Journalism

Following the tradition established by the *New York Sun* and the *New York Morning Herald*, a new brand of paper arose in the late 1800s. These publications ushered in the era of **yellow journalism**, which emphasized exciting human-interest stories, crime news, large headlines, and easy-to-digest copy. Generally regarded as the direct forerunner of today's tabloid papers, reality TV, and celebrity-obsessed Web sites like TMZ, yellow journalism featured two major characteristics:

1. Overly dramatic—or sensational—stories about crime, celebrities, disasters, scandals, and intrigue
2. News reports exposing corruption, particularly in business and government—the foundation for *investigative journalism*

▲ Generally considered America's first comic-strip character, the Yellow Kid was created in the mid-1890s by cartoonist R. F. Outcault. The cartoon was so popular that newspaper barons Joseph Pulitzer and William Randolph Hearst fought over Outcault's services, giving yellow journalism its name.

THE BIG TYPE WAR OF THE YELLOW KIDS.

ARE THEY NECESSARY EVILS?   They are amusing cusses. War news comes in and they both claim to have seen it first.

The term *yellow journalism* has its roots in the press war that pitted Joseph Pulitzer's *New York World* against William Randolph Hearst's *New York Journal*. During their furious fight to win readers, the two papers ultimately took turns hosting the first popular cartoon strip, *The Yellow Kid*, created in 1895 by artist R. F. Outcault. Pulitzer, a Jewish Hungarian immigrant, had bought the *New York World* in 1883 for $346,000. Aimed at immigrant and working-class readers, the *World* crusaded for improved urban housing, better treatment of women, and equitable labor laws, while railing against big business. It also manufactured news events and printed sensationalized stories on crime and sex. By 1887, its Sunday circulation had soared to more than 250,000—the largest anywhere.

The *World* faced its fiercest competition when William Randolph Hearst in 1895 bought the *New York Journal* (a penny paper founded by Pulitzer's brother Albert) and then raided Joseph Pulitzer's paper for editors, writers, and cartoonists. Hearst focused on lurid, sensational stories and appealed to immigrant readers by using large headlines and bold layout designs. To boost circulation, the *Journal* invented interviews, faked pictures, and provoked conflicts that might result in eye-catching stories. In 1896, its daily circulation reached 450,000. A year later, the circulation of the paper's Sunday edition rivaled the *World*'s 600,000.

Yellow journalism has been vilified for its sensationalism and aggressive tactics to snatch readers from competitors by appealing to their low-brow interests, but this unique era gave birth to several newspaper elements still valued by many readers today, including advice columns and feature stories. It even laid the foundation for the prestigious Pulitzer Prizes, which today recognize quality writing, reporting, and research in such categories as poetry, history, international reporting, editorial cartooning, public service, and explanatory reporting.

The Evolution of Newspaper Journalism: Competing Models and the Rise of Professionalism

In the late 1800s, as newspapers pushed to expand circulation even further, two distinct types of journalism emerged: the story-driven model, which dramatized important events and characterized the penny papers and the yellow press, and "the facts" model, an approach that seemed more impartial and was favored by the six-cent papers.[3] Provocative questions arose: Could news accounts be entirely objective? Should reporters actively interpret the meaning of particular events for readers? In response to these questions, the 1920s saw the rise of *interpretive journalism*, which aimed to explain events and place them in context.

"Objectivity" and Professionalization in Modern Journalism

Throughout the mid-1800s, the more a newspaper appeared not to take sides on its front pages, the more readers it could attract. Also at this time, wire service organizations were serving a variety of newspaper clients in different regions of the country. To satisfy all their clients, newspapers strived for the appearance of impartiality—presenting "the facts" and leaving it up to readers to interpret the implications for their own lives. At the same time, the more sensational aspects of yellow journalism created an image problem for newspapers and their style of journalism, with journalists seen at best as low-status tradesmen and at worst as disreputable. But with the approach of the twentieth century, newspapers and journalism were about to start changing.

Adolph Ochs and the New York Times
The ideal of an impartial, or purely informational, news model was reinvented by Adolph Ochs, who bought the *New York Times* in 1896. Through wise hiring, Ochs and his editors rebuilt the paper around substantial news coverage and provocative editorial pages. To distance the *Times* from the yellow press, the editors also downplayed sensational stories, favoring the documentation of major events or issues, and developed a powerful marketing message touting the *Times* as the higher-brow choice.

▲ Known for getting information and presenting news in a straightforward way—without the opinion of the reporter—the *New York Times* was the first truly modern newspaper. It established itself as the official paper of record by the 1920s and maintains a venerable reputation today. Bloomberg/Getty Images

With the Hearst and Pulitzer papers capturing the bulk of working- and middle-class readers, managers at the *Times* initially tried to use their straightforward, "no frills" reporting to appeal to more affluent and educated readers. In 1898, Ochs also lowered the paper's price to a penny. Soon middle-class readers gravitated to the paper as a status marker for the educated and well informed. Between 1898 and 1899, circulation soared from 25,000 to 75,000. By 1921, the *Times* had a daily circulation of 330,000 and a Sunday circulation of 500,000.

"Just the Facts, Please": Journalism Gets Professional

Early in the twentieth century, with reporters adopting a more "scientific" attitude to news- and fact-gathering, the ideal of objectivity took a firmer hold in journalism. In **objective journalism**, which distinguishes factual reports from opinion columns, reporters ideally strive to maintain a neutral attitude toward the issue or event they cover. They also search out competing points of view among the sources for a story in an effort to provide balanced coverage.

The early twentieth century was also a time when even the most notorious yellow journalists wanted to boost the respectability of the news business. That, combined with a broader cultural trend that favored a more "scientific" approach to the world, pushed the training of new journalists away from apprenticeships and toward universities. Early in the century, Joseph Pulitzer approached Columbia University in New York about setting up the first journalism school. He wanted to see the status of journalists rise to that of other professionals, such as lawyers and doctors. But the reputation of journalism was such that it took several years for the directors of the school to accept the millions Pulitzer offered, finally founding the school in 1912. (In addition to offering graduate degrees, the school began awarding the coveted Pulitzer Prizes in journalism in 1917 and continues to do so to this day.) But the distinction of being the first journalism school in the United States goes to a different Columbia: the School of Journalism at the University of Missouri in Columbia, Missouri, founded in 1908.[4]

Interpretive Journalism

By the 1920s, people began wondering whether the impartial approach to news reporting was sufficient for helping readers understand complex national and global developments. As one news scholar contended, it was partly as a result of "drab, factual, objective reporting" that "the American people were utterly amazed when [World War I] broke out in August 1914, as they had no understanding of the foreign scene to prepare them for it."[5] Such concerns triggered the rise of **interpretive journalism**, which aims to explain the ramifications of key issues or events and place them in a broader historical or social context.

Editor and columnist Walter Lippmann insisted that although objectivity should serve as journalism's foundation, the press should do more. He ranked three press responsibilities: (1) "to make a current record"; (2) "to make a running analysis of it"; and (3) "on the basis of both, to suggest plans."[6]

The rise of radio in the 1930s intensified tensions between the objective and interpretive models of print journalism. As radio gained in popularity, broadcasters increasingly took their news directly from papers and wire services. Seeking to maintain their dominion over "the facts," some newspaper editors and lobbyists argued that radio should provide only interpretive commentary. Other print journalists argued that it was interpretive stories, not objective reports, which could best help newspapers compete against radio. However, most U.S. dailies continued relegating interpretive content to a few editorial and opinion pages.

It wasn't until the 1950s—with the outbreak of the Korean War, the development of atomic power, the deepening of the Cold War, and the U.S. anticommunist movement—that newspapers began providing more interpretive journalism. They did so in part to compete with the latest news medium: television. And their interpretive material often took the form of an "op-ed" page—which appeared opposite the traditional editorial page. The op-ed page offered a wider variety of columns, news analyses, and letters to the editor.

Journalism Evolves across Media

The rise of radio and the coming of television would give way to new forms of journalism. Nearly every new mass medium has eventually found a home for journalism of some kind, from radio and television in the first half of the twentieth century, to the addition of cable television in the 1980s, to the emergence and convergence of the Internet in the 1990s through the present day. Many mass media have coexisted with traditional print journalism, but the converged media offered by the Internet has been the catalyst for some of the biggest changes in the journalism world since its early days.

Investigative Journalism: In the "Spotlight"

When the *Boston Globe* ran a series of stories in the early 2000s, the paper's investigative reporters did more than challenge one of the most powerful institutions in Boston—they took on one of the most powerful institutions in the world. The *Globe's* Spotlight team investigated the Roman Catholic Church, uncovering decades of sexual abuse of children by Catholic priests in and around Boston, as well as cover-ups by top church officials that allowed the abuse to continue. This reporting by the country's "oldest continually operating newspaper investigative unit" prompted criminal investigations and promises of church reform, which are still ongoing.[1] In addition, the behind-the-scenes story of the investigation was later made into a movie, *Spotlight*, which won the 2015 Academy Award for best picture.

The Spotlight team's church investigation is indeed impressive, and it represents one small part of a much bigger story: that of investigative journalism's role in society and its function as watchdog, digging up and exposing wrongdoing by the powerful—from local government officials to private corporations to religious institutions. Modern investigative journalism can trace its roots to the beginning of the twentieth century, when journalists like Nellie Bly (see chapter

▲ *Washington Post* reporters Bob Woodward and Carl Bernstein investigated a plot to bug the Democratic National Committee headquarters at the Watergate building, unraveling a story that implicated President Richard Nixon and led him to resign. AP Images

opener) exposed scandals and prompted reforms. And it was in the 1970s when another formative journalistic event occurred, influencing future generations of investigative reporters: *Washington Post* reporters Bob Woodward and Carl Bernstein started researching after five men were arrested for breaking into Democratic National Committee headquarters at the Watergate office complex in Washington, D.C., on June 17, 1972. By the time they were done, Woodward and Bernstein had uncovered information that connected the break-in and a number of other illegal activities to President Richard Nixon and his staff. The House of Representatives started investigating, Nixon ultimately resigned, and the word *Watergate* became synonymous with the exposure of official misconduct and scandal.

Investigative reporting is vital for a functioning democracy. At the same time, it is a time- and labor-intensive enterprise, and it can take multiple reporters months—or even years—to uncover the secrets that powerful men and women work

⊕ Visit LaunchPad
to watch a clip from the movie *Spotlight*. If fewer news organizations are willing to invest in the type of investigative reporting depicted in this clip, what will the implications be for society?

launchpadworks.com

hard to keep hidden. That makes it an expensive undertaking, and though some smaller local newspapers and even television stations have reporters who do this type of reporting, an investigative effort like that of the Spotlight team is something fewer papers can afford. Even so, communities still need journalists who can act as watchdogs.

One organization that promotes and supports this kind of journalistic work is the nonprofit Investigative Reporters and Editors (IRE). IRE was formed in 1975 and provides training, resources, and a community for investigative journalists. The group works to promote ethical reporting and protect the rights of investigative reporters. The acronym of the organization, IRE, was intentional because, as one founder put it, "What most characterizes the investigative reporter is a 'sense of outrage.'"[2]

With the efforts of organizations like IRE, professionals are taking action to ensure that investigative journalism lives on despite the costs and complications that come with reporting in a digital age. Journalists and media critics will be watching to see how reporting at papers like the *Boston Globe* survives this climate of newsroom cuts, but so, too, should everyday citizens — and the many communities across the country that benefit from this kind of work.

APPLYING THE CRITICAL PROCESS

DESCRIPTION Choose a newspaper, preferably one local to your school or your hometown. Search the newspaper's Web site looking for evidence of reporters or units within the paper who specialize in investigative work. Alternatively, use search engines to seek out stories from the paper that are promoted as investigative.

ANALYSIS How does the newspaper characterize its investigative-reporting efforts? Are there indications it has reporters or teams of reporters dedicated to investigative work? What kinds of investigative stories, if any, are featured on the paper's Web site?

INTERPRETATION Write a two- to three-paragraph critical interpretation of the information you've found. What do your findings suggests about the resources the paper dedicates to investigative reporting. Are there many such reports? Do they seem complicated? If the paper you are examining has investigative coverage on its Web site, does it feature stories only, or does it include online interactive features as well?

EVALUATION Based on what you've discovered, in what ways does this paper seem to serve (or *not* to serve) a watchdog function for the surrounding community? Explain what that might mean for the community's ability to make decisions about local issues and politics.

ENGAGEMENT Contact an editor from the paper you examined and conduct further research into how the paper handles investigative reporting. Ask if the paper's approach to investigative reporting has changed over time, as many newspapers have cut newsroom staff (some quite dramatically).

▲ The rules and rituals governing American journalism began shifting in the 1950s. In the early days, the most influential and respected news program was CBS's *See It Now*, coproduced by Edward R. Morrow and Fred Friendly. The show practiced a kind of TV journalism lodged between the neutral and the narrative traditions. CBS Photo Archive/Getty Images

Journalism on the Airwaves

By the time America plunged into the Great Depression, the unique abilities of broadcasting were becoming apparent. For example, President Franklin Delano Roosevelt tapped this potential during his now-famous "fireside chats." Later, news icon Edward R. Murrow made a name for himself and CBS News during World War II by broadcasting from rooftops during the bombing of London and by taking a recorder with him as he flew on B-17 bombing missions over Germany, taping commentary for later broadcast. By the 1950s, the rules and rituals surrounding journalism would shift with the popularity of the newest medium, television, to which many radio news icons, such as Murrow, would switch. In 1951, his radio program *Hear It Now* was retitled *See It Now*, and it went on to challenge Senator Joseph McCarthy for his reckless abuse of power and disregard for evidence in the name of labeling others as communists in the United States. It was also among the first to warn of the dangers of smoking tobacco. However, as much as Murrow and his work on radio and television are held in high esteem to this day by broadcast journalists (one of the industry's highest awards is named after him), it's worth noting that his coverage of controversial subjects and the accompanying offense taken by advertisers often brought Murrow into conflict with CBS owner William S. Paley and ultimately doomed the program.

The Power of Visual Language

The shift from a print-dominated culture to an electronic-digital culture brings up the question of how the power of visual imagery compares with the power of the printed word. For the second half of the twentieth century, TV news dramatized America's key events visually. Civil Rights activists, for instance, acknowledge that the movement benefited enormously from televised news that documented the plight of southern blacks in the 1960s in evocative moving images. Many people find visual images far more compelling and memorable than written descriptions of events or individuals. If listening to President Roosevelt on the radio was part of creating a national shared experience, the effect was amplified as a nation watched and celebrated together shared milestones, from the first man to walk on the moon to the inauguration of the first African American U.S. president.

But just as sound and moving pictures provide powerful communication tools, the technical requirements and styles that have developed also bring along some shortcomings. TV news reporters share many values and conventions with their print counterparts, yet they also differ from them in significant ways. First, whereas print editors fit stories around ads on the printed page, TV news directors have to time stories to fit between commercials, which can make the ads seem more intrusive to viewers. Second, whereas newspapers can increase or decrease their page counts, time is a finite commodity. This has often led commercial news operations to place strict limits on the length of individual news stories (from twenty to ninety seconds in many cases) in the twenty or so minutes remaining in a half-hour newscast after time is taken for commercials. Of that twenty minutes, around half is typically used for local weather and sports. Third, TV news reporters gain credibility from providing live, on-the-spot reporting; believable imagery; and an earnest, personable demeanor that makes them seem more approachable—even more trustworthy—than detached, faceless print reporters. As TV news reporting evolved, it developed a style of its own—one defined by attractive, congenial newscasters skilled at perky banter (sometimes called "happy talk"), and short, seven- to eight-second quotes (or "sound bites") from interview subjects. Print and TV reporters must also compete with Internet-only outlets, which combine elements of both television and print journalism.

Cable News Enters the Field

The transformation of TV news by cable—with the arrival of CNN in 1980—led to dramatic changes in TV news delivery at the national level. Prior to cable news (and the Internet), most people tuned to their local and national news late in the afternoon or evening on a typical weekday, with each program lasting just thirty minutes. But today, the 24/7 news cycle means that we can get TV news anytime, day or night, and the constant need for new content (sometimes called "feeding the beast" by insiders) has led to major changes in what is considered news. Because it is expensive to dispatch reporters to document stories or to maintain foreign news bureaus, the much less expensive "talking head" pundit has become a standard for cable news channels. Such a programming strategy requires few resources beyond the studio and a few guests.

Today's main cable channels have built their evening programs along partisan lines and follow the model of journalism as opinion and assertion: Fox News goes right with pundit stars like Bill O'Reilly (the ratings king of cable news) and Sean Hannity; MSNBC leans left with Rachel Maddow and Lawrence O'Donnell; and CNN stakes out the middle with hosts who try to strike a more neutral pose, like Anderson Cooper. CNN, the originator of cable news, does much more original reporting than Fox News and MSNBC and does

▲ The popularity of 24/7 cable news has led to increased screen time for news anchors and television personalities. CNN's Christiane Amanpour, who was first hired as a desk assistant in the early 1980s, currently hosts a global affairs interview show and serves as Chief International Correspondent for the cable network. Michael Kovac/ Getty Images

better in nonpresidential election years, as well as when reporting on natural disasters and crime tragedies.

Broadcast and cable news organizations play an important role in society with their (somewhat) traditional approach to television programming. But it's nearly impossible to define or describe the current state of journalism, from whatever source, without discussing its convergence with the Internet.

Internet Convergence Accelerates Changes to Journalism

For mainstream print and TV reporters and editors, online news has added new dimensions to journalism. Both print and TV news can continually update breaking stories online, and many reporters now post their online stories first and then work on traditional versions. This means that readers and viewers no longer have to wait until the next day for the morning paper or for the local evening newscast for important stories. To enhance the online reports, which do not have the time or space constraints of television or print, newspaper reporters are increasingly required to provide video or audio for their stories. This allows readers and viewers to see full interviews rather than just selected print quotes in the paper or short sound bites on the TV report. Journalists might augment stories with interactive tools (like maps plotting reports of crimes in a city over time) or a song recording added to the end of an interview with a musician.

However, in the wake of the digital turn, online news comes with a special set of problems. For example, rather than leaving the office to question a subject in person, print reporters can now do e-mail interviews. Many editors discourage this practice because they think relying on e-mail gives interviewees too much control over shaping their answers. Although some might argue that this provides more thoughtful answers, journalists say it takes the elements of surprise and spontaneity out of the traditional news interview, during which a subject might accidentally reveal important information—something less likely to occur in an online setting.

Another problem for journalists is, ironically, the wide-ranging resources of the Internet, including access to versions of stories from other papers and broadcast stations. The mountain of information available on the Internet has made it all too easy for journalists to—unwittingly or intentionally—copy other journalists' work. In addition, access to databases and other informational sites can keep reporters at their computers rather than out tracking down new kinds of information, cultivating sources, and staying in touch with their communities.

Most notable, however, for journalists in the digital age are the demands that convergence has made on their reporting and writing. Print journalists at newspapers (and magazines) are expected to carry digital cameras so that they can post video along with the print versions of their stories, and TV reporters are expected to write print-style news reports for their station's Web site to supplement the streaming video of their original TV stories. In addition, journalists today are increasingly expected to tweet and blog.

▲ Major newspapers like the *Washington Post* take convergence with digital storytelling and social media very seriously. In 2016, the *Post* inaugurated a new Washington, D.C., headquarters complete with a state-of-the-art multimedia suite, where reporters and producers can shoot, edit, and post videos. Chip Somodevilla/ Getty Images

The Culture of News and Rituals of Reporting

Throughout the twentieth century, sets of beliefs and practices came to define what was accepted as news and what it meant to be a journalist reporting that news. Despite the technical and inherent stylistic differences among print, radio, and television, mainstream journalists in all media shared a similar mission, encountered similar ethical issues, and developed methods designed to get and share information. These concepts have proven invaluable for news operations trying to do the never-ending job of providing the information the public needs to make informed and intelligent decisions. They also provide a framework within which journalists say they are adhering to principles of unbiased truth-seeking and from which they derive a great portion of their authority. Critics suggest that these practices are just as likely to create biases, derail honest discussions about those biases, and paint a picture that distorts reality. But before one can discuss what is a useful tool and what is a potential pitfall, it's helpful to understand more about news culture and the common customs of gathering the news, beginning with the most basic question of journalism: What is news?

What Is News?

As discussed in the beginning of this chapter, news is the process of gathering information and making reports that use a narrative framework; in other words, news reports tell stories. But which stories do they tell? The first task of journalism is to decide what information is **newsworthy**—what merits transformation into a news story. The traditional criteria used to determine newsworthiness (criteria that help shape the culture of newsrooms) are timeliness, proximity, conflict, prominence, human interest, consequence, usefulness, novelty, and deviance:[7]

- Most issues and events that journalists cover are *timely* or *new*. Reporters, for instance, cover speeches, meetings, crimes, and court cases that have just happened.
- The bulk of these events usually occur close by, or in *proximity* to, the readers and viewers who will consume the news stories.
- In developing news narratives, reporters often seek contentious quotes from those with opposing or *conflicting* views. In theory, this helps create balance. In practice, it can lead to seeking the most extreme positions, rather than a range of positions, to create drama.
- Surveys indicate that most people identify more closely with an individual than with an abstract issue. Therefore, the news media tend to report stories that feature *prominent*, powerful, or influential people.
- However, reporters also look for the *human-interest* story: extraordinary incidents that happen to "ordinary" people. In fact, reporters often relate a story about a complicated issue (such as unemployment, health care, or homelessness) by illustrating its impact on an "average" person or a "typical" family.
- Many editors and reporters believe that some news must also be of *consequence* to a majority of their readers or viewers. For example, they might include stories about new business regulations that affect credit cards or home mortgages.
- Likewise, many people look for *useful* stories: for instance, those offering hints on how to buy a used car or choose a college.
- When events happen that are outside the routine of daily life—that is, they are *novel*—they will likely generate news coverage. Examples might include a seven-year-old girl who tries to pilot a plane across the country or a bear that somehow got into a parked car.
- Reporters also cover events that appear to *deviate* from social norms, including murders, rapes, fatal car or plane crashes, fires, political scandals, and wars.

In producing news stories that meet many of these criteria, journalists influence our interpretations of what is going on around us and thus the decisions we make. For example, if we read a story in the newspaper emphasizing the consequences of failing to save for retirement, we may conclude that such saving is important—and that we'd better do more of it. If we see a lot of stories about crime and violence, even as fewer and fewer violent crimes are actually being committed, we might conclude that the world is a more dangerous place than the facts actually suggest.

Values in American Journalism

In addition to telling us how journalists define news, newsworthiness criteria begin to paint a picture of the values that came to define American journalism by the 1960s and 1970s. This was a time some refer to as the "golden age" of journalism, when newspapers enjoyed consistent profitability and the Big Three TV networks (NBC, CBS, and ABC) hadn't yet encountered the competition from cable and online news. It was also a time when the journalism profession was enjoying a boost in prestige and popularity in the wake of big stories about the Watergate scandal and the Pentagon Papers (see "Media Literacy Case Study: Investigative Journalism: In the 'Spotlight'" on pages 74–75). It was from this time that researchers started identifying and critiquing the values—not always recognized by the journalists themselves at the time—that influenced how stories were covered (or not).

Putting It in Neutral

Perhaps the most prominent and obvious of these values is neutrality, or the apparent lack of bias—a quality that remains prized even in a more polarized environment that has given rise to more opinionated forms of news. Many professional journalists believe strongly that their job is to gather and then present facts without judging them. Conventions such as the inverted-pyramid news lead (starting reports with the most important information), the careful attribution of sources (favoring quoted interview subjects rather than the reporter's analysis), the minimal use of adverbs and adjectives (getting rid of ornate, flowery language in order to look "factual"), and the detached third-person point of view (using the omniscient, or all-knowing, authorial point of view favored by many novelists) help reporters present their findings in a supposedly neutral way.

Journalists argue that this dedication to neutrality (and related concepts of fairness, balance, independence, objectivity, and so on) boosts their credibility and is an important part of what separates news from propaganda. Generations of journalists have spent careers trying to live up to these ideals as part of what they see as their mission to serve their audiences and communities. At its best, a commitment by individual journalists to these traditional news values has helped them get the news, hold the powerful to account, and resist manipulation by those who would deceive the public.

Tampa Bay Times | **Herald-Tribune**

Insane.
Invisible.
In danger.

Florida cut $100 million from its mental hospitals. Chaos quickly followed.

FLORIDA'S STATE-FUNDED MENTAL HOSPITALS are supposed to be safe places to care for people who are a danger to themselves or others. But years of neglect and deep budget cuts transformed them into treacherous warehouses where violent patients roam the halls with no supervision and workers are left on their own to oversee dozens of people. Now, no one is safe inside.

▲ The *Tampa Bay Times*, like many modern newspapers, claims to present news in a straightforward way—without the opinion of the reporter. *Times* journalists Leonora LaPeter Anton and Anthony Cormier, together with Michael Braga of the *Sarasota Herald-Tribune*, jointly received the 2016 Pulitzer Prize for investigative reporting for their harrowing exposé of Florida's mental hospitals. Using thoroughly researched statistics and first-hand testimony, they revealed that facilities had fallen into disrepair after state budget cuts.

However, critics in and out of the profession say this approach also brings problems. In practice, total neutrality is itself an impossible goal. In deciding which stories to cover with limited resources, news operations make judgments about what is worthy of attention (or not) by the public. Merely by deciding which information and whose experience to include in a news story, journalists cannot help but present a point of view on the story's topic. And although the pursuit of personal detachment might have become part of a well-intentioned set of standards, it is still true that the origins of the shift from partisan to objective journalism in the 1800s had at least as much to do with economics as with ethics.

Another problem with the concept of "neutrality" for journalism might be the way in which believing one's judgment to be neutral can create dangerous blind spots, which ultimately undermine the ethical intentions of journalists. Assumptions about what is normal or "natural" are often involved when trying to find the neutral position, especially when dealing with social issues. Take, for example, the experience of the *New York Times* during the 1970s and 1980s and the way it covered—or, rather, often ignored—gay rights and the AIDS epidemic. The antigay positions of the paper's management and owners at the time (including Ochs's daughter, Iphigene Ochs Sulzberger) became a target for critics, who said the silence of this "objective" newspaper slowed public attention and public support for the fight against AIDS, contributing to the ultimate death toll from the disease. (The *Times* changed its policies in the late 1980s.)[8]

Diversity in the Newsroom

An important part of the critique of the ability of newsrooms to achieve neutrality or objectivity involves the ways in which the demographics of a newsroom reflect the demographics of the community it covers. For much of the twentieth century, mainstream news operations were dominated by white men and, as such, lacked the perspective that comes with the different lived experiences of other groups in society. This hurts the ability of a newsroom to question what it considers "normal" or "neutral," which is really based on a very non-neutral worldview.

Beginning in the 1970s, there was a push to make newsrooms more diverse. The good news is that from 1977 to 1994, the number of minority reporters in newspaper newsrooms nearly tripled, from 4 percent to 11 percent, and that number has slowly continued to climb.[9] The bad news is that white men are still disproportionally represented in newsrooms today. As of 2016, minority journalists made up about 17 percent of the total workforce at newspapers and digital-only newsrooms, and just over a third of employees were women.[10] Results were similar for leadership positions: 13 percent of newsroom leaders were minorities, and just over 37 percent were women.[11] The problem is that according to the U.S. Census Bureau, this isn't what America looks like: just over 38 percent of all Americans are minorities, and just under 51 percent are women.[12]

Television newsrooms seem to be faring somewhat better than their newspaper counterparts. In 2016, minority journalists made up 23 percent of television newsroom staff and 17 percent of news directors. Women, while still underrepresented, are making gains: In 2016, women made up 44 percent of television newsroom staff and 33 percent of news directors, both of which were record numbers. Radio fared the worst: 9 percent of newsroom staff were minorities, while just under 32 percent of newsroom staff were women.[13]

▲ In June 2015, *NBC Nightly News* permanently promoted Lester Holt to the job of anchor, making him the first African American to be a solo anchor on a nightly network news program. D Dipasupil/Getty Images

Getting a Good Story

According to Don Hewitt, the creator and longtime executive producer of *60 Minutes*, "There's a very simple formula if you're in Hollywood, Broadway, opera, publishing, broadcasting, newspapering. It's four very simple words—tell me a story."[14] For most journalists, the bottom line is "Get the story"—an edict that overrides most other concerns. This is the standard against which many reporters measure themselves and their profession. At its best, it can provide inspiration to keep digging in order to gather perspectives that might be difficult to get or to uncover important information that someone might be trying to hide from public view. At its worst, it can lead to a variety of unethical and even criminal behaviors. It has also occasionally led journalists to make up stories, such as in the early

1980s, when former *Washington Post* reporter Janet Cooke won a Pulitzer Prize for a story she made up about a mother who contributed to the heroin addiction of her eight-year-old son (the prize was later revoked). Or in the early 2000s, when it came to light that *New York Times* reporter Jayson Blair had frequently plagiarized and fabricated stories. These more extreme cases are typically career ending and draw condemnation from the journalistic community.

Getting a Story First

In addition to getting a good story, one of the most valued achievements for a reporter is getting the story first. It is a badge of honor to be a reporter who can *scoop* the competition—that is, uncover and report a story before anyone else. Again, this creates a double-edged sword: It provides motivation for carrying out the necessary and sometimes difficult news-gathering tasks of reporting, but it also applies pressure that too often results in poorly researched stories, rampant misinformation, little or no fact-checking, and all-around sloppy reporting.

What's not always clear is how the public is better served by a journalist's claim to have gotten a story first. What *is* clear is that the problems that have always existed because of the pressure to get the story first have only intensified since the advent of 24/7 cable news channels, the Internet, and competition from bloggers. We discuss this further later in the chapter, when we look more closely at how the entire journalism profession is changing and being challenged in the digital era.

Getting a Story "Right"

Although journalists certainly value being the first ones to uncover an interesting story and tell it in a compelling way, it would be a mistake to ignore the importance to professional journalists of getting the facts correct. Traditionally, serious journalists pride themselves on the results of careful news-gathering, ideally using multiple sources to confirm controversial information and allegations made in news stories. From the lessons learned in journalism schools to the awarding of top prizes for reporting, getting accurate information is the gold standard. More than just a professional standard, getting the truth also carries legal responsibilities. Journalists are taught that the best defense against a libel lawsuit is to be able to show that the report is factually true. However, critics are quick to point out that in practice, the gold standard isn't always met. Reasons for this can range from an honest mistake (journalists are human, after all), to deadline and workload pressures preventing adequate fact-checking, to outright lying or omission of important information due to a desire for self-promotion by sources—and sometimes journalists themselves. In addition, journalists often face the task of sifting through information provided by public relations practitioners, who are paid (on average, at a rate of 50 percent more than their journalistic counterparts) to make their clients look good to the public. As of 2014, U.S. labor statistics indicated that there were 4.4 public relations practitioners for every journalist.[15]

Other Values in Journalism

Some sociologists—including Herbert Gans, who studied the newsroom cultures of CBS, NBC, *Newsweek*, and *Time* in the 1970s—generalize that several basic "enduring values" have been shared by most American reporters and editors. These values include **ethnocentrism** (viewing other cultures through an American "lens"), **responsible capitalism** (the assumption that the main goal of business is to enhance prosperity for everyone), **small-town pastoralism** (favoring small, rural communities over big cities), and a major emphasis on **individualism** and personal stories over the operations of large institutions or organizations.[16] Many of these beliefs are still prevalent in today's more fragmented news culture, though they are undergoing shifts along with the rest of the industry.

When Values Collide: Ethics and the News Media

Up to this point, we have been talking about some of the common practices, values, and goals by which professional journalists tend to define who they are and what they do. As you might have already noticed, these values can sometimes conflict with one another and with the realities of gathering the news (deadlines, shrinking newsroom staffs, bigger demands on limited resources).

Journalists regularly face many such conflicts and ethical dilemmas. For example, they must decide when to protect government secrets and when to reveal those secrets to the public. They must consider whether it is ethically acceptable to use deception or to invade someone's privacy to get information the public deserves to know, and they must guard against accepting gifts or favors in return for producing a news story or presenting a story's subject in a favorable light.

▼ Brian Williams lost his coveted spot as network anchor after he lied about coming under fire while covering the Iraq War, one of several instances in which Williams had been accused of exaggerating the truth. While this was a grave violation of journalistic ethics, NBC didn't fire him; instead, the network moved him to cable news channel MSNBC. Stephanie Klein-Davis/ AP Images

Professional Codes of Ethics

So how do journalists decide what to do in these cases? One way is to refer to sets of ethical guidelines produced by professional journalistic groups, like the Society of Professional Journalists (SPJ), the Radio Television Digital News Association (RTDNA, formerly the Radio-Television News Directors Association), and the National Press Photographers Association (NPPA). Although each has a slightly different focus, all three instruct journalists to seek the truth, hold the powerful accountable, maintain integrity, and consider the consequences of each news report, especially on people who appear in the news. Journalism education programs typically contain stand-alone ethics courses or attempt to integrate ethics into other classes—or both. Each newsroom might have its own printed code of ethical guidelines or, more likely, might rely on veteran reporters and editors to pass along to newer journalists what's considered acceptable in that particular news department. It's also worth noting that these printed codes of ethical conduct are not etched in stone. All of these groups periodically review and update their ethics—especially now, with the new ethical dilemmas that have come with the Internet and social media.

Applying Ethics and Values Inside the Job

Codes of ethics can be helpful, but they would be impossibly long if they were to cover every possible situation a reporter might find. There are times when parts of a given code will come in conflict with one another. What's more, these dilemmas mostly happen when reporters are facing the crush of deadlines and daily duties. Many times the necessity for making a quick decision means answering these questions in a way that has become established professional practice—that is, the way things have always been done. Although relying on the experience of the individual or the organization can be helpful and save time, it can also undermine careful critical examination of a given situation.

In addition to guidelines designed specifically for the profession, a journalist might also borrow from other philosophical approaches to ethics when confronted with an ethical quandary. Although this isn't intended to be a complete list of those approaches, the next few paragraphs attempt to offer some useful examples.

The Greek philosopher Aristotle offered an early ethical concept, the "golden mean," as a guideline for seeking balance between competing positions. For Aristotle, the golden mean referred to the desirable middle ground between extreme positions. For example, Aristotle saw ambition as the golden mean between sloth and greed.

Another ethical principle entails the "categorical imperative," developed by German philosopher Immanuel Kant (1724–1804). This idea suggests that a society must adhere to moral codes that are universal and unconditional, applicable in all situations at all times. For example, the ideal to always tell the truth might lead a Kantian to argue that it's never okay to use deception to get a news story.

British philosophers Jeremy Bentham (1748–1832) and John Stuart Mill (1806–1873) promoted a general ethics principle derived from "the greatest good for the greatest number." This principle directs us "to distribute a good consequence to more people rather than to fewer, whenever we have a choice."[17]

Applying Ethics and Values Outside the Job

Although the Internet, bloggers, social media, and partisan cable stations and Web sites have blurred the lines between journalist and nonjournalist, most mainstream news organizations have ethical expectations of their journalists that extend beyond the hours spent on the job. Journalism's code of ethics also warns reporters and editors not to place themselves in positions that create a **conflict of interest**—that is, situations in which journalists may stand to benefit personally from producing a story or from presenting the subject in a certain light. "Journalists should refuse gifts, favors, fees, free travel and special treatment," the code states, "and avoid political and other activities that may compromise integrity or impartiality, or may damage credibility."[18]

Many news outlets attempt to protect journalists from getting into compromising positions. For instance, in most cities, journalists do not actively participate in politics or support social causes. Some journalists will not reveal their political affiliations, and some have even declined to vote. If a journalist has a tie to any organization, and that organization is later suspected of involvement in shady or criminal activity, the reporter's ability to report fairly on the organization will be compromised—along with the credibility of the news outlet for which he or she works. Conversely, other journalists believe that not participating in politics or social causes means abandoning one's civic obligations.

The Economics of Journalism in the Twenty-First Century

Ask almost any veteran reporter to list the challenges facing the profession of journalism, and either at or near the top will be a concern about rapidly shrinking numbers of reporters, editors, and photographers in the newsroom. Although the business models for broadcasters (see Chapters 6 and 8 for more specifics on the radio and TV broadcasting industries) are not quite the same as that for print newsrooms, they do share this common concern: Budget cuts, for whatever reason, mean cuts to newsroom staff. A 2011 Federal

Communications Commission report expressed concern that layoffs, cutbacks, and ownership consolidation were leaving too few broadcast reporters to adequately serve as watchdogs over the government and businesses in their local communities. For newspapers, the situation is even more troubling, with full-time U.S. professional newsroom employment down from a peak of 56,900 in 1990 to less than 33,000 in 2015, the last year that the American Society of News Editors collected these numbers. Almost all of this drop (well over one-third of total newspaper reporters) happened since the economy began its recession in 2007.[19] Because newspapers are the legacy format for journalism and still represent the lion's share of reporting in most communities, it's important to spend some time in this chapter examining the business side of newspapers and considering what recent developments are doing to the ability of newspapers to fulfill their journalistic missions.

A Business Model in Transition

At the most basic level, the traditional business model for a commercial news enterprise looks like this: The business attracts an audience with its content (such as news) and, in turn, sells that audience's attention to advertisers, who pay for the chance to attract paying customers. If a newspaper can say it has a certain number of readers, or a broadcaster can say it has a certain number of viewers or listeners, it can attach a value to that audience. The bigger that number, the more the business providing the content can charge for an advertisement.

Although some newspapers also earn revenue by charging subscription fees, it became clear by the end of the nineteenth century that keeping subscription prices relatively low helped increase audience size (or *circulation*) and that the real money came in selling that larger audience to advertisers. The majority of large daily papers today devote as much as one-half to two-thirds of their pages to advertisements. What remains after the advertising department places the ads in the paper is called the **newshole**. This space is devoted to front-page news reports, special regional or topical sections, horoscopes, advice columns, crossword puzzles, and letters to the editor.

Although there were some ups and downs, this advertising-centered approach (supplemented with income from subscription fees and classified ads) worked well for newspaper businesses through the twentieth century. Around the year 2000, however, newspaper revenue began to weaken in conjunction with the digital turn: audiences were seeking out free versions of news articles

FIGURE 3.1 // U.S. NEWSPAPER ADVERTISING REVENUE

While online newspaper revenue continues to grow, it can't make up for the huge drop in traditional print revenue.

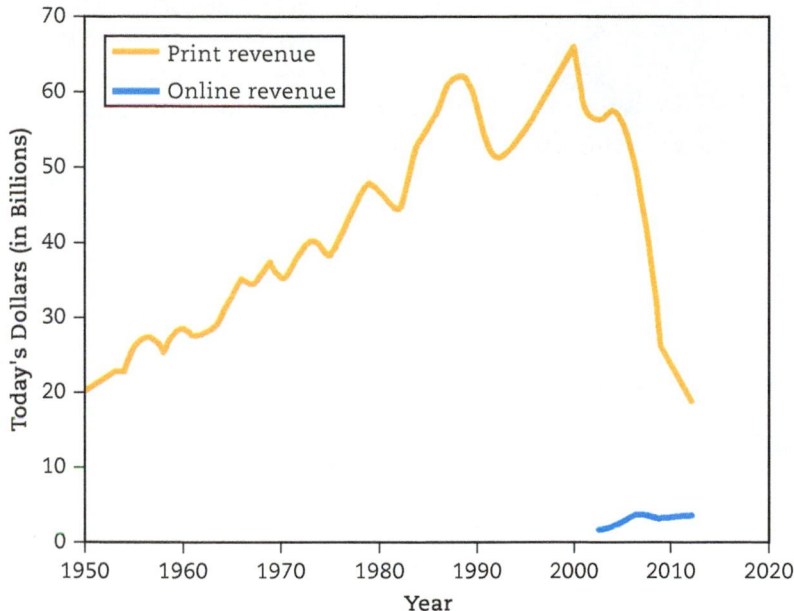

online, and people could place ads for free on sites like craigslist, rather than paying newspapers to run classified ads. Then, when the Great Recession hit in 2007, the advertising revenue bottom really fell out, as major advertisers cut back their ad spending (see Figure 3.1). Since then, the numbers have continued to fall: From 2014 to 2015, for example, advertising revenue dropped more in a single year than it had since 2009.[20]

While the digital turn has created significant challenges for the news industry, newspapers and other traditional news media are attempting to find ways to generate revenue online. Though still a far cry from replacing the lost traditional advertising dollars, digital revenue is increasing as a percentage of newspaper revenue (although that increase is due more to the precipitous fall of print ads rather than to a huge jump in online revenue). According to Pew Research, among newspapers owned by publicly traded companies—which are required to publish revenue data—a full quarter of their advertising revenue came from their digital operations by 2015.[21]

In addition to online advertising, some news sites are trying to make money by using a **paywall**, a subscription fee that allows access to articles. Paywalls can be controversial and unpopular with potential readers who are used to getting free content online. To balance this, the *New York Times* and other newspaper operations (like major chain Gannett) have gone to a hybrid model. A person might access a limited number of articles for free each month (typically ten to twenty), but access to additional articles or other premium products—such as online newspaper archives—requires a paid subscription.

News companies are also finding ways to cater to readers' increasingly digital lifestyles, developing material for new digital platforms like the touchscreen tablet or smartphone. In some cases, digital subscription rates are also tailored, depending on the device (and particular app) the reader is going to use.

Newspaper Operations

Like any other enterprise, a newspaper has to spend money to fulfill its mission. Its costs include salaries and wages and any investments in wire services or feature syndication required to offer content for readers.

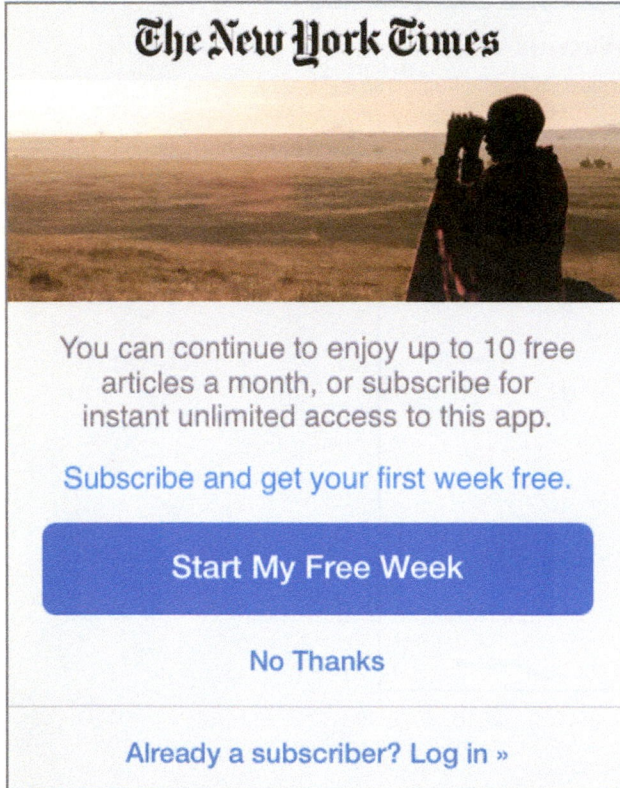

▲ The *New York Times* is one of the papers trying to balance the need to generate income with not angering readers who are now accustomed to free content on the Internet. It has a hybrid paywall model in which a user can read up to ten articles a month for free online, after which he or she has to buy a subscription. By mid-2016, the *Times* reported it had 1.6 million digital-only subscriptions for its news products.

Salaries, Wages, and Shareholder Concerns

A major expense for most newspapers comes in the form of salaries and wages paid to the various editors and reporters working for the paper—although in the last fifteen years, newspapers have shrunk not only their newshole but the size of their reporting staffs. Traditionally, most large papers have a publisher and an owner, an editor in chief, and a managing editor in charge of the daily news-gathering and writing processes, and assistant editors and news managers running different news divisions. These key divisions include features, sports, photos, local news, state news, and a wire service containing much of the day's national and international news reports.

Reporters work for editors. *General assignment reporters* handle all sorts of stories that might emerge—or break—in a given day. *Specialty reporters* are assigned to particular beats (police, courts, schools, local and national government) or topics (education, religion, health, environment, technology). On large dailies, *bureau reporters* file reports from other major cities. In addition, large daily papers feature columnists and critics who cover various aspects of culture, such as books, television, movies, and food. Since 2000, some newspapers have added staff solely responsible for online operations, although newsroom cuts have increasingly led to the shifting of these duties to the remaining reporters and editors.

In addition to paying the salaries and wages of employees, publicly traded companies have to consider how they pay dividends to keep shareholders happy, as well as how they compensate top executives. This can cause some troubling headlines for these companies. For example, newspaper powerhouse Gannett has repeatedly been the target of criticism for giving millions—or even tens of millions—in executive and CEO bonus and pay packages after laying off thousands of reporters over the last decade.

Wire Services and Feature Syndication

To provide adequate coverage of important events from other places, many newspapers rely on wire services and syndicated feature services to supplement local coverage by their own reporters and writers. A few major dailies, such as the *New York Times*, run their own wire services, selling their stories to other papers to reprint. Other agencies, such as the Associated Press (AP), United Press International (UPI), and Reuters (based in London), have hundreds of staffers stationed throughout major U.S. cities and world capitals. These agencies submit stories, photos, and videos each day for distribution to newspapers, newscasts, and online sites across the country and sometimes internationally.

Daily papers generally pay monthly fees for access to all wire stories. Although they use only a fraction of what's available over the wires, editors carefully monitor wire services each day for important stories and ideas for local angles.

In addition, newspapers may contract with **feature syndicates**, such as Universal Uclick (formerly United Features) and Tribune Media Services, to provide work from the nation's best political writers, editorial cartoonists, comic-strip artists, and self-help columnists. These companies serve as brokers, distributing horoscopes and crossword puzzles as well as the columns and comic strips that appeal to a wide audience.

Consolidation and a Crash

As we saw earlier in this section, the 2007 economic crash had a serious impact on the newspaper industry's ability to raise ad revenue. But the recession also had another key impact on the industry—specifically, on the financial health of the country's newspaper chains.

Newspaper chains—newspapers in different cities owned by the same person or company—have been around since the late 1800s. By the 1980s, more than 130 chains owned an average of nine papers each, with the twelve largest chains accounting for 40 percent of total circulation in the United States. This trend continued to pick up steam through the end of the

twentieth century, and by the early 2000s, the top ten chains controlled over half the nation's total newspaper circulation. Gannett, the nation's largest chain, owns over 115 daily papers in thirty-five states, as well as the national newspaper *USA Today.*

As large media corporations were adding up the numbers of newspapers (and often radio and television stations) they owned, they were also adding up the amount of money they were borrowing to make those purchases. Through the 1990s and the first few years of the 2000s, newspapers typically made enough money to make payments on these *leveraged* purchases. And then the economy started to tank in 2007.

As newspaper revenues from ads and subscriptions began to drop dramatically, large chains went from *leveraged* to *overleveraged*, no longer able to keep up with loan payments. In some cases, this meant filing bankruptcy; in other cases, it meant being forced to sell off newspapers; and in still other cases, it meant shutting down altogether. Although some smaller newspaper owners avoided being overleveraged, they still had to deal with the reality of shrinking revenues. Thus, the industry-wide reaction has been to cut costs by laying off huge numbers of editors, reporters, and photographers, and closing bureaus at the national and state capitols.

More than just bad news for the workers who lost their jobs, this trend raises concerns for the communities they are meant to serve. The newspaper industry as a whole lacks competition nationwide, as almost all the cities that once had multiple competing dailies have lost all but one of those daily papers. Critics and journalists worry about the ability of the remaining journalists to meet the information needs of local communities (see "Media Literacy Case Study: Investigative Journalism: In the 'Spotlight'" on pages 74–75). Additionally, the coverage of national and state politics has dropped precipitously, as bureaus at the national and state capitols were among the first victims of budget cuts.

Changes and Challenges for Journalism in the Information Age

In modern America, journalism's highest role has been to provide information that enables citizens to make intelligent decisions. Today, this guiding principle has been partially derailed. Why? First, the media may be producing too much information through too many communication channels, making it harder to confirm facts and engage in thoughtful discussion about them. Second, the information the media now provide has apparently not improved the quality of public and political life — a core mission of journalism. For example, many people feel disconnected from the stories about the major institutions and political processes that serve as the foundation of democratic society.

Earlier in this chapter, we discussed some of the ways in which the Internet has changed how professional journalists do their jobs — many of which are internal in nature. But there are also external changes, happening outside professional newsrooms, affecting the ways in which audiences consume and understand news — and sometimes even the manner in which journalists are expected to report.

Social Media

One of the fastest-growing areas of research among those who study journalism has been trying to determine what the rise of social media sites means to journalism and journalists. Although it's simply too soon to know what all the changes will mean long term, it is possible to make some observations.

Social Networking

The vast majority of news operations use social networking sites like Facebook, Twitter, and Instagram to promote their work, hoping readers will share articles and stories. Often, journalists, reporters, anchors, and editors are required to have accounts at these sites for use as part of their reporting duties (some have separate accounts for just friends and family), from sharing work to finding sources for stories. Some media organizations have also created social media policies to act as ethical guidelines in the digital context.

Social media is also changing the way some people consume the news. For example, a person on Facebook might get a combination of news from dozens of sources based on what friends share or post as well as on what is posted by the news outlets they follow. And those sources aren't limited to whatever lineup might appear on the local airwaves or cable.

Another way consuming news on social media is different is the immediacy and variety of sources in a breaking-news event. For example, a person on Twitter the night of the first demonstrations in Ferguson, Missouri, in August 2014 might have been able to watch the events unfold in 140-character tweets, pictures, and video several hours before even the 24-hour cable news channels began covering the events. In addition, by tweeting and retweeting from their feeds, news consumers became conduits for—and often commentators on—information on those same events. At the same time, however, that

The *Huffington Post:* News Aggregation Aggravates Legacy News

Whether it's an "improbable, insatiable content machine," as the *New York Times Magazine* called it in 2015,[1] or a "parasite," as former *Washington Post* executive editor Len Downie described it in 2010,[2] the *Huffington Post* is undeniably a popular source of online news. A child of the digital turn, the *Huffington Post* was cofounded in 2005 by Arianna Huffington as a way to provide a left-leaning alternative to the *Drudge Report*—a site that presents links to news reports, opinion pieces, and blogs with a generally conservative bent. In a little over a decade, helped along by a savvy approach to providing content that's easy to read on mobile devices and share on social media, the company reported that 200 million people were visiting the *Huffington Post* Web site each month.

The *Huffington Post*, or *HuffPo*, does have its own reporters, but it has long relied on unpaid contributors and *news aggregation*, which is a type of content convergence. With news aggregation, a site packages news summaries, usually providing links to the sources from which it draws (such as online versions of a newspaper, magazine, or wire service). This approach isn't always popular with the journalists who produce those original stories. In a lecture, Len Downie condemned news aggregation as thievery.[3] Arianna Huffington dismissed his concerns: "Once again, some in the old media have decided that the best way to save, if not journalism, at least themselves, is by pointing fingers and calling names."[4]

As the feuding suggests, media convergence often arouses passion and arrogance on both sides of the new/old media divide. But we don't have to pick sides to recognize the paradox of news aggregation, which relies on traditional media to provide content. If fewer and fewer organizations pay newsroom salaries—even though they still use the content these newsrooms produce—news aggregation could help hasten the demise of businesses that do actually pay reporters. Eventually, if there's no one to report and write up the news, there will be nothing for the aggregators to aggregate.

Meanwhile, over at *Huffpo*, there are changes afoot. While the company still relies heavily on news aggregation and unpaid bloggers, it has answered its critics somewhat by hiring paid journalists who have won prestigious reporting awards. The site also has new owners (AOL purchased the site for $315 million in 2011, and Verizon bought AOL in 2015) and, in a surprise move, new leadership: In 2016, Arianna Huffington announced she was stepping down as editor in chief to start a new site focusing on health and wellness.[5] While *HuffPo* maintained its left-leaning editorial perspective following Huffington's departure, it remains to be seen how the site will evolve without Huffington at the helm of the enterprise that bears her name.

▶ Web Clip

YouTube.com has many videos of Arianna Huffington. One good option to search for: 'INBOUND 2013—Arianna Huffington Keynote' posted by HubSpot. How might Huffington's thoughts on businesses reflect the *Huffington Post's* place in the media landscape?

immediacy removes the chance for fact-checking and other benefits that come from thorough reporting. For that matter, the Twitter accounts of prominent people often serve as their own form of breaking news, and their tweets get covered as news stories. For example, President Donald Trump often uses his tweets to stir controversy and capture headlines.

Blogging

Another digital-turn development for journalism is the rise of the blog. A form of social media, blogging derives its name from a combination of *web* and *log*, and started out as a practice of writing a kind of journal that anyone could share online. But what began in the late 1990s and early 2000s as amateur, sideline journalism has now become a major source of news, calling media outlets' authority into question. Widely read blogs like *Daily Kos*, the *Huffington Post*, Andrew Sullivan's the *Dish*, the *Drudge Report*, and *Politico* have moved this Internet feature into the realm of traditional journalism. In fact, many reporters now write a blog in addition to their regular newspaper, television, or radio work. And some big-name newspapers, such as the *Washington Post* and the *New York Times*, even hire journalists to blog exclusively for their Web sites.

Traditional journalists often complain that bloggers aren't held to the same standards of fact checking. A blogger merely has to post his or her opinion about an issue or an event, yet many readers swallow this content whether or not it has been backed by rigorous reporting practices. On the other hand, some blogs have won respect as viable information sources. In 2008, the *Talking Points Memo* blog, headed by Joshua Micah Marshall, won a George Polk Award for legal reporting. Today, some blog sites stand alongside mainstream media as trusted, authoritative sources of news (see "The Digital Turn Case Study: The *Huffington Post*: News Aggregation Aggravates Legacy News" on page 94).

▼ Award-winning blog *TPM* (*Talking Points Memo*) has a staff of about two dozen employees, ranging from reporters and news writers to sales and technical staff.

Citizen Journalism

Through **citizen journalism**, people who are not professional journalists—such as activists concerned about a specific issue—use the Internet to disseminate information and opinions about their favorite issues. Social media and smartphones have made it easier than ever for average people to engage in citizen journalism, since anyone can take photos or record video if something newsworthy happens nearby. Sometimes these pictures and videos are shared first with traditional media

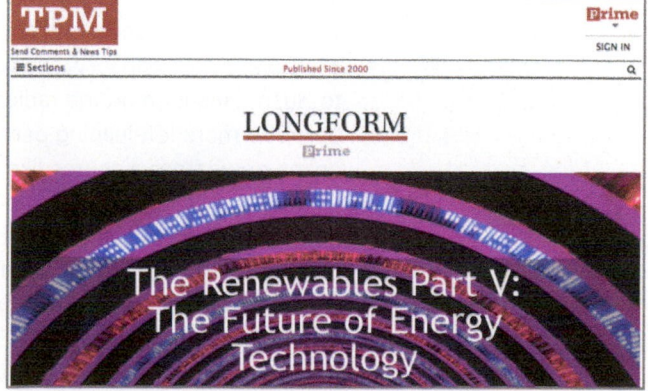

▲One way technology has allowed citizens to become involved in the reporting of news is through smartphone photos and videos. Witnesses can now pass on what they have captured to mainstream news sources. Kaveh Kazemi/ Getty Images

outlets, who then disseminate them to the public. Other times the person who shot the video will upload it directly to social media, where it may go viral.

Some of the most notable videos of this kind document interactions between police officers and members of the public, who are often African American, as in the cases of Eric Garner, Sandra Bland, and Walter Scott. In all these cases, the smartphone videos created a different narrative than what was documented in police reports, and in Scott's case, the officer who shot and killed him was arrested and charged with murder.

With steep declines in newsroom staffs, numerous news media organizations—like CNN (iReport) and many regional newspapers—are increasingly drawing on citizen journalists' work to make up for the loss of professional journalists through newsroom downsizing. But there is also a fear that over utilization of members of the public who lack the education, training, and experience of professional journalists results in a news product that ultimately undermines the news organization's credibility.

The Echo Chamber

The "echo chamber" refers to the idea that as cable news channels, Web sites, and other media consciously cater to the ideological and political viewpoints of a portion of society, those people will seek out only those sources with which they agree and avoid any news that might challenge their worldview. For example, a very conservative person might only watch Fox News on TV, listen to Rush Limbaugh on the radio, and visit Breitbart.com and the *Drudge Report* online. A more left-leaning person might only watch MSNBC on TV and read online news from a source like *Daily Kos*.

One problem with this approach is that the information from these sources might not just be biased toward a particular worldview; in fact, researchers are increasingly discovering that information from these sources is inaccurate and wrong at a much higher rate than that from other sources, like CNN, National Public Radio, or the *New York Times*. Several attempts have been made to determine which of these networks are the most—and least—accurate. One such study in 2012 found that viewers of Fox News are the least informed (in some studies, even less informed than people who don't watch any news).[22] The same study found that listeners to NPR scored the best on questions of national and international news. A more recent effort by fact-checking site PolitiFact.com attempted to rate the truthfulness of fact claims made by pundits and on-air personalities for TV networks. On the scorecard released in 2015, 23 percent of claims made on CNN got rated mostly false, false, or "pants on fire"; for Fox and FoxNews Channel, that number jumps to 58 percent.[23]

The full implications of these findings become clearer when one realizes that according to television ratings agency Nielsen, Fox News has been the most watched cable news network for over a decade. Not only does that call into question the core reason for journalism in a democracy — to inform the public, who will then make public policy decisions based on that information — but it also creates pressure on other networks eager to capture higher ratings (and more ad dollars) to copy the approach of the Rupert Murdoch–owned Fox News.[24]

Satiric Journalism

The winner of the 2016 Television Critics Award for News and Information beat out some stiff competition, including *CBS Sunday Morning*, a CNN series on race on America, and PBS documentarian Ken Burns — and she isn't even a journalist. But when comedian Samantha Bee accepted the award for her work on her TBS satirical show *Full Frontal*, she continued a recent tradition of satirists and their comedy programs being recognized for doing their part to keep the public informed.

While the tradition of regularly satirizing news goes back at least to the mid-1970s with the sketch comedy program *Saturday Night Live*, more recently we've entered what journalist, historian, and author Malcolm Gladwell calls "the Golden Age of satire."[25] In America, this "golden age" hit its stride with the work of Jon Stewart on *The Daily Show with Jon Stewart* (now *The Daily Show with Trevor Noah* since Noah took over in 2015). Using humor to criticize news conventions and the political system, *The Daily Show* employs a combination of monologue, reports from comedians acting as correspondents, and interviews (occasionally even with past and present U.S. presidents). The show is also remarkable for having launched numerous variations on the theme of news satire, as well as the careers of the biggest names in this genre. Stephen Colbert (*The Colbert Report* and now *The Late Show with Stephen Colbert*), John Oliver (*Last Week Tonight*), Samantha Bee (*Full Frontal*), and Noah himself are all past writers and "correspondents" who worked on the program.

These comedians repeatedly reject the label of "journalist," and as news court jesters, they display more amazement, irony, outrage, laughter, and skepticism than would be acceptable for real anchors. Still, they keep winning journalistic awards

▲ Satirical news has become something of a cottage industry in recent years, stemming from *Saturday Night Live*'s Weekend Update segment and *The Daily Show*. After a successful stint as a *Daily Show* "correspondent," Samantha Bee has captured critical and popular praise for her solo effort *Full Frontal with Samantha Bee*. Everett Collection, Inc.

and garnering "serious" attention for their work. For example, studies in 2007 and 2012 found that in addition to regular listeners of National Public Radio, one of the other best-informed audiences was the group that got its news from *The Daily Show*. And John Oliver—who uses a combination of humor and some traditional investigative reporting to make longer stories about complicated topics both funny and broadly understandable—has repeatedly inspired his audience to take action on political and social issues. For example, after one episode in which Oliver called for people to comment on the Federal Communications Commission's Web site in favor of net neutrality (see more on this issue on pages 278–279), the response was so overwhelming it crashed the FCC Web site.

This isn't to say that satirical news could, or even should, be considered a replacement for solid journalism. As Gladwell points out, satire can also undermine its own biting commentary through the laughs it generates. Media researchers such as Heather LaMarre of Temple University have also noted that audiences can, and sometimes do, interpret satire in the opposite way than it was intended. For example, she and colleagues found that when Stephen Colbert was pretending to be an over-the-top right-wing talk-show host on the *Colbert Report* as a way to mock conservative narratives, some conservative audiences thought he was really poking fun at the left side of the political spectrum.[26]

The New "Fake" News: Sites Designed to Deceive

"Fake" news sources like *The Daily Show* or *Full Frontal* aren't inherently designed to deceive: Their audiences are largely in on the joke and appreciate the programs' satirical messages. But another kind of fake news has a much darker purpose: to intentionally mislead audiences for political or financial gain. A growing problem for many years, this new type of fake news exploded into global consciousness during the 2016 U.S. Presidential race. Countless online fake news articles attacking Democratic candidate Hillary Clinton were shared over social media sites like Facebook—articles that got hundreds of millions of views, leading to accusations that they played a role in tipping the election toward Republican candidate Donald Trump. These articles came from sites across the globe: More than one hundred pro-Trump sites were tracked to a single town in Macedonia, for example, while others were tracked to American sources intent on exploiting gullible readers to get advertising dollars.[27]

One such source, Jestin Coler, spoke with National Public Radio. He told reporters that he makes money from advertisers—between $10,000 and $30,000 a month—by getting people to click on and share his sites' invented stories (including one about Hillary Clinton having her political opponents murdered). Coler purposely targeted a conservative audience, claiming that readers on the liberal end of the political spectrum debunked his fake news more quickly, leaving him with fewer clicks and less income.[28]

In addition to speculation that they influenced the presidential election, there have been other frightening consequences from the deluge of fake news and bogus conspiracy theories. On December 4, 2016, 28-year-old Edgar Maddison Welch entered a Washington, D.C., restaurant and opened fire with an assault rifle. (Luckily no one was hit and Welch was arrested.) He did so because he believed a false conspiracy theory, referred to as "Pizzagate," which accused Hillary Clinton of running a child sex ring out of the pizzeria.[29]

In the wake of the election and incidents like the D.C. shooting, news organizations and academics have begun efforts to expose malicious fake news sites and help educate consumers about how to debunk fake news on their own. The *Columbia Journalism Review* argues that part of the battle may be naming it exactly what it is: "Let's retire the dreaded [fake news] moniker in favor of more precise choices: misinformation, deception, lies."[30]

Journalism in a Democratic Society

Journalism is central to democracy: Both citizens and the media must have access to the information needed to make important decisions. Conventional journalists will fight ferociously for the principles that underpin journalism's basic tenets — questioning the government, freedom of the press, the public's right to know, and two sides to every story. These are mostly worthy ideals, but they do have limitations. For example, they do not generally acknowledge any moral or ethical duty for journalists to improve the quality of daily life. Rather, conventional journalism values its news-gathering capabilities and the well-constructed news narrative, leaving the improvement of civic life to political groups, nonprofit organizations, business philanthropists, individual citizens, and practitioners of Internet activism.

Social Responsibility

Although reporters have traditionally thought of themselves first and foremost as observers and recorders, some journalists have acknowledged a social responsibility. Among them was James Agee in the 1930s. In his book *Let Us Now Praise Famous Men*, which was accompanied by the Depression-era photography of Walker Evans, Agee regarded conventional journalism as dishonest, partly because the act of observing intruded on people and turned them into story characters that newspapers and magazines exploited for profit.

Agee also worried that readers would retreat into the comfort of his writing—his narrative—instead of confronting what for many families was the horror of the Great Depression. For Agee, the question of responsibility extended not only to journalism and to himself but to the readers of his stories as well.

Professional conflicts over the ethical way to practice journalism remain. On one end of the spectrum, some journalists refuse to even vote in elections, lest it hurt their ability to remain detached from the politics they cover. These journalists value giving equal time to both sides of a controversial issue, and they argue that failing to remain vigilant against bias and partisanship will set journalism on a slippery slope that begins with sloppy reporting and ends with blatant lies and propaganda.

On the other end of the spectrum, there are those who believe that in addition to providing information, journalists should evaluate that information for the audience and put it into proper historical context. Those belonging to this second school of thought have increasingly voiced concern over what they call "false equivalency" in the news. False equivalency is the idea that in order to remain balanced and unbiased, opposing viewpoints should be presented as if they carry the same relative weight of supporting evidence or scientific consensus. For example, for decades most mainstream media covering climate change gave equal time to those who warned of the dangers of global warming and those who claimed it was a hoax. The problem isn't that news stories acknowledged climate change deniers but that their point of view was presented in a fashion that would lead the audience to believe it was equally valid—despite the fact that more than 95 percent of all climate experts say human behavior is causing the earth to warm at an alarming rate.[31]

As this example illustrates, reporters face challenges in informing the public about issues that may have enormous consequences for generations to come. Because citizens vote for political leaders who set public policy on issues like climate change, the importance of journalists getting the story right is clear.

The Troubled Future of Journalism and Journalism's First Home

While pondering the future of journalism—and of our democracy—we must recognize that a free press isn't free, nor is its survival certain.

As newsroom cutbacks accelerate; as state, national, and foreign bureaus close down; and as industry consolidation continues apace, we must ask ourselves where we will get the thorough reporting we need to make informed choices and present well-considered viewpoints—two hallmarks of a vibrant democracy. A host of current developments in print journalism undermine the newspaper's role as a bulwark of democracy. Many cities now have just one newspaper, which tends to cover only issues and events of interest to middle- and upper-middle-class readers. The experiences and events affecting poorer and working-class citizens get short shrift, and with the rise of newspaper chains, the chances that mainstream daily papers will publish a diversity of opinions, ideas, and information will likely decrease. Moreover, chain ownership—often concerned first about the bottom line and saving money—has tended to discourage watchdog journalism, the most expensive type of reporting. And ownership issues have raised questions about editorial autonomy, as evidenced in 2016, when casino magnate and Republican megadonor Sheldon Adelson bought the *Las Vegas Review-Journal*; reporters and columnists left in protest after they were forbidden from investigating and reporting on Adelson's business interests and partners.[32] This means that we, as citizens, must remain ever mindful of our news sources and not only consider the motivations and interests concealed behind the news we're receiving but also ask ourselves why we're receiving it.

As news increasingly reaches us through a wide range of digital distribution channels, print journalism is losing readers and advertisers and may eventually cease to exist. Editor John Carroll described the situation in no uncertain terms. Having presided over thirteen Pulitzer Prize–winning reports at the *Los Angeles Times* as editor from 2000 to 2005, Carroll left the paper to protest deep corporate cuts to the newsroom. He lamented the apparently imminent demise of newspapers, proclaiming: "Newspapers are doing the reporting in this country. Google and Yahoo! and those people aren't putting reporters on the street in any numbers at all. Blogs can't afford it. Network television is taking reporters off the street. . . . Newspapers are the last ones standing, and newspapers are threatened. . . . Reporting is absolutely an essential thing for democratic self-government. Who's going to do it? Who's going to pay for the news? If newspapers fall by the wayside, what will we know?"[33]

CHAPTER ESSENTIALS

Review

- The social impact of **news**—the process by which people gather information and create narrative reports to make sense of events surrounding them—accelerated with the invention of the printing press, eventually making possible a **partisan press** in the American colonies, which helped spread different political ideas.

- An industrial revolution and a rising middle class helped transform American newspapers through the nineteenth century. **Penny papers** helped boost circulation, enabling papers to become a mass medium, and **wire services** like the Associated Press used telegraph lines to relay information to multiple newspapers around the country and the world.

- As newspapers and their audiences grew larger from the nineteenth into the twentieth century, various styles of journalism emerged, including sensationalist **yellow journalism** and the **inverted pyramid** style of **objective journalism**. As the twentieth century progressed, some looked to **interpretive journalism** to help explain the complexities of an increasingly global society.

- Throughout the twentieth century and into the twenty-first, as radio, television, and later the Internet entered the scene, the practice of journalism moved into each new realm, drawing on and adapting previous practices for new platforms.

- Journalism has developed a professional culture and set of practices that help journalists decide what is **newsworthy** and should fill the **newshole** in their papers or programs. This culture comes with certain values, which include neutrality; newsroom diversity; and the drive to get a good story, to get the story first, and to get the story right. This culture also comes with ethical standards, such as the need to avoid **conflicts of interest**.

- Journalism, while a vital part of a functioning democracy, faces serious challenges in today's media landscape. One of the biggest challenges is the steady reduction in newsroom staffs, due in part to loss of revenue from traditional advertising. Some companies are using online **paywalls** to regain some of this income.

- Other changes and challenges for journalism in the information age include the development of social media sites, citizen journalism, an ever-more-polarized political sphere, and the proliferation of satirical and "fake" news.

- As the fate of print journalism is called into question, we must ask ourselves where we will get the best information, based on strong reporting, that we need to make informed choices and receive multiple points of view.

Key Terms

news, p. 65

partisan press, p. 65

penny papers, p. 67

human-interest stories, p. 67

wire services, p. 68

inverted pyramid, p. 69

yellow journalism, p. 69

objective journalism, p. 72

interpretive journalism, p. 73

newsworthy, p. 80

ethnocentrism, p. 85

responsible capitalism, p. 85

small-town pastoralism, p. 85

individualism, p. 85

conflict of interest, p. 87

newshole, p. 88

paywall, p. 89

feature syndicates, p. 91

newspaper chains, p. 91

citizen journalism, p. 95

Study Questions

1. How did newspapers emerge as a mass medium during the penny press era? How did content changes make this happen?

2. What different forms of journalism developed? What are their characteristics? What are their strengths and limitations?

3. What are some of the differences between the practices of print and broadcast journalism? How might the changes to journalism as it entered the broadcasting age be similar to or different from the changes currently happening to journalism in the Information Age?

4. Describe and discuss some of the business challenges faced by newspapers today.

5. How might satirical and "fake" news be changing the way the public views—and uses—the news?

6. What is journalism's role in a democracy?

4

Magazines in the Age of Specialization

Considering that since the 1960s *Cosmopolitan* has been effectively marketing itself to single women ages eighteen to thirty-four, it shouldn't be surprising that even in the digital age, the publication is one of the most popular magazines among undergraduate college women. What might be surprising is that a college student reading today's *Cosmopolitan*, currently famous for revealing cover photographs and headlines like "67 New Sex Tricks," might have a subscription to the same magazine that her great-great-great grandmother subscribed to. Of course, other than the title, these two magazines don't have much in common.

The 1886 version of *Cosmopolitan* was also targeted at women—but more often married women, with articles on cooking, child care, and household decoration. When it did feature fashion, it was of the high-collared Victorian-era variety.[1] The magazine struggled until it was rescued by journalist and entrepreneur John Brisben Walker, who turned it into an illustrated literary and journalistic magazine.

The magazine grew in prestige and earnings until it was sold at a profit in 1905 to competitor and powerful newspaper publisher William Randolph

◀ Helen Gurley Brown was the editor-in-chief of *Cosmopolitan* magazine for over thirty years, starting in 1965. Her vision—to create a magazine for young, single, professional women—helped make the publication an international success. Santi Visalli/Getty Images

Hearst. The new owner turned *Cosmopolitan* into a muckraking magazine focused on digging up dirt against big business and corrupt politicians. Although this work didn't boost Hearst's political ambitions in the way that he'd hoped, it did help the magazine continue to grow and thrive. Despite this success, the magazine continued to change alongside the tastes of its readership. After 1912, *Cosmopolitan* returned to its literary past, featuring short stories and serialized novels largely targeted toward a female audience. This worked for a while, but by the 1960s, this format seemed dated and was losing interest among subscribers.

In 1965, the Hearst Corporation hired Helen Gurley Brown, who had recently written the best-selling book *Sex and the Single Girl*. Brown modeled the magazine on the book's vision of strong, sexually liberated women. The new *Cosmopolitan*, following this fifth makeover, helped spark a sexual revolution and was marketed to the "Cosmo Girl": women ages eighteen to thirty-four with an interest in love, sex, fashion, and their careers.[2]

Brown's vision of *Cosmo* lives on in the magazine's "fun, fearless female" slogan. Today, it's the top-selling women's fashion magazine — surpassing competitors like *Glamour*, *InStyle*, and *Vogue*. It also maintains a popular Web site and a mobile version for reading on smartphones. *Cosmopolitan*'s ability to reinvent itself repeatedly for over 130 years testifies to the remarkable power of magazines as a mass medium to both adapt to and shape American society and culture.

SINCE THE 1740s, magazines have played a key role in America, becoming a national mass medium even before newspapers, which at the time were mainly local and regional in scope. Magazines provided venues for political leaders and thinkers to offer their views on the broad issues and events of the day, including public education, abolition, women's suffrage, and the Civil War. Many leading literary figures also used magazines to gain public exposure for their essays or stories. Readers consumed the articles and fictional accounts offered in magazines, and snapped up the products and services advertised in each issue, hastening the rise of a consumer society. As consumerism grew, magazines themselves changed, with the most popular titles often focusing less on news and essays, and more on fashion, celebrities, advice, and entertainment.

Today, more than twenty thousand magazines are published in the United States annually. And just like newspapers, these magazines — including *Cosmopolitan* — have met the digital turn by taking increasingly more content online and adapting that content for use on mobile devices.

In this chapter, we will track the shifting role of magazines in the United States by:

- **tracing the early history of magazines, including their highly politicized purpose in colonial and early America and their transformation into the country's first national medium**

- **examining turning points in the evolution of modern American magazines, such as the emergence of muckraking as a magazine-reporting style and the rise and fall of general-interest magazines**

- **taking stock of the many types of magazines specialized for particular audiences (including men, women, sports fans, young people, and minorities)**

- **discovering how magazines are organized and how they operate economically, including how they make money**

- **considering how magazines today are affecting the health of our democratic society**

The Early History of Magazines

Magazines have changed extensively during their journey to mass medium status. They started out in Europe as infrequently published periodicals that looked like newspapers and contained mostly political commentary. They caught on slowly in colonial America and served mostly as vehicles for politicians (such as John Adams and Thomas Jefferson) and thinkers (including Thomas Paine) to convey their views. It wasn't until the nineteenth century that magazines really took off in America. During the 1800s, magazines took the form of specialized and general-interest periodicals that appealed to an increasingly literate populace, that could be published quickly through improved printing technologies, and that boasted arresting illustrations.

Today, the word **magazine** broadly refers to any collection of articles, stories, and advertisements published on a nondaily cycle (such as weekly or monthly) in the smaller tabloid style rather than the larger broadsheet newspaper style.

LaunchPad
launchpadworks.com

Use **LearningCurve** to review concepts from this chapter.

The first issue of Benjamin Franklin's *General Magazine, and Historical Chronicle* appeared in 1741. Although it lasted only six months, Franklin found success in other publications, like his annual *Poor Richard's Almanack*, which appeared in 1732 and lasted twenty-five years. Library of Congress, Prints & Photographs Division, Reproduction number LC-USZ62-58140 (b& w film copy neg.)

The First Magazines: European Origins

The first magazines appeared in seventeenth-century France in the form of bookseller catalogues and notices that book publishers inserted in newspapers. (In fact, the word *magazine* derives from the French term *magasin*, meaning "storehouse.") In Europe, magazines then became channels for political commentary and argument. They looked like newspapers of the time, but they were published less frequently. The first political magazine, called the *Review*, appeared in London in 1704 and was printed sporadically until 1713.

Regularly published magazines or pamphlets, such as the *Tatler* and the *Spectator*, also appeared in England around this time. Offering poetry, politics, and philosophy for London's elite, they served small readerships of a few thousand. The first publication to use the term *magazine* was *Gentleman's Magazine*, which appeared in London in 1731 and consisted of articles reprinted from newspapers, books, and political pamphlets.

Magazines in Eighteenth-Century America: The Voices of Revolution

Without a substantial middle class, widespread literacy, or advanced printing technology, magazines took root slowly in America. Like the partisan newspapers of the time, colonial magazines served politicians, the educated, and the merchant class. However, they also served the wider purpose of conveying colonial leaders' thoughts about the big questions percolating during the era—such as how taxation should work, how much self-rule the colonies should have, how Indians should be treated, and who should have access to public education. Magazines thus gave voice to the people who ultimately decided to break away from England and create a new, independent nation.

The first colonial magazines appeared in Philadelphia in 1741, about fifty years after the earliest newspapers. Andrew Bradford started it all with *American Magazine, or A Monthly View of the Political State of the British Colonies*. Three days later, Benjamin Franklin launched his *General Magazine, and Historical Chronicle*.

Though neither of these experiments was successful, they inspired other publishers to launch magazines in the remaining colonies, beginning in Boston in the 1740s. The most successful of these periodicals simply reprinted articles from leading London newspapers to keep readers abreast of European events.

Magazines in Nineteenth-Century America: Specialization and General Interest

As the nineteenth century dawned, the magazine industry remained somewhat unstable in the newly created United States. During 1800–1825, about five hundred periodicals had cropped up and then withered. However, as the century progressed, the idea of specialized magazines devoted to certain categories of readers gained momentum—leading to the creation of religious magazines, literary periodicals publishing the works of important writers of the day, and magazines devoted to professions such as law and medicine.

▲ Colorful illustrations first became popular in the fashion sections of women's magazines in the mid-1800s. The color for this fashion image from *Godey's* was added to the illustration by hand. NorthWind Picture Archives

The nineteenth century also saw the birth of the first general-interest magazine aimed at a large national audience: the *Saturday Evening Post*, launched in 1821. Like most magazines of the day, the early *Post* included a few original essays but reprinted many pieces from other sources. Eventually, however, the *Post* grew to incorporate news, poetry, essays, play reviews, and the writings of popular authors such as Nathaniel Hawthorne and Harriet Beecher Stowe.

The *Post* was also the first major magazine to appeal directly to women through its "Lady's Friend" advice column. This new device may have served as an inspiration; in 1828, Sarah Josepha Hale started the first magazine directed exclusively to a female audience: *Ladies' Magazine*. In addition to general-interest pieces, such as essays and criticism, the periodical advocated for women's education, work, and property rights. Other women's magazines—including the hugely successful *Godey's Lady's Book*—would soon follow.

Going National as the Twentieth Century Approaches

Thanks to increases in literacy and public education, the development of faster printing technologies, and improvements in mail delivery (through rail transportation), demand for national (versus local) magazines soared. Whereas in 1825 a mere one hundred magazines struggled for survival, by 1850 nearly six hundred magazines were being published regularly, many of them with national readerships. Magazines were on their way to becoming a mass medium. Significant national magazines of this era included *Graham's Magazine* (1840–1858), *Knickerbocker* (1833–1864), the *Nation* (1865–present), and *Youth's Companion* (1826–1929).

The advent of illustration further moved magazines toward mass medium status. By the mid-1850s, drawings, engravings, woodcuts, and other forms of illustration had become a major feature of magazines and greatly heightened their appeal for readers. During the 1890s, magazines (and newspapers) also began including photographs with printed articles, helping to launch an entirely new profession: photojournalism.

The Evolution of Modern American Magazines

As the sun set on the nineteenth century, decreases in postage costs made it cheaper for publishers to distribute magazines, and improvements in production technologies lowered the costs of printing them. Now accessible and affordable to ever-larger audiences, magazines became a true mass medium. They also began reflecting the social, demographic, and technological changes unfolding within the nation as the twentieth century progressed. For example, a new interest in social reform sparked the rise of muckraking or investigative journalism designed to expose wrongdoing. The growth of the middle class initially heightened receptivity to general-interest magazines aimed at broad audiences, but then television's rising popularity put many general-interest magazines out of business. Some magazines struck back by focusing their content on topics not covered by TV programmers and by featuring short articles heavily illustrated with photos.

Distribution and Production Costs Plummet

In 1870, about twelve hundred magazines were being produced in the United States; by 1890, that number had reached forty-five hundred. By 1905, the nation boasted more than six thousand magazines. Part of this surge in titles and readership was facilitated by the Postal Act of 1879, which assigned magazines lower postage rates—putting them on an equal footing with newspapers delivered by mail. This change vastly reduced distribution costs. Meanwhile, advances in mass-production printing, conveyor systems, assembly lines, and printing press speeds lowered production costs and made large-circulation national magazines possible.

This combination of reduced distribution and production costs enabled publishers to slash magazine prices. As prices dropped from thirty-five cents to fifteen cents to ten cents, people of modest means began subscribing to national publications. Magazine circulation skyrocketed, attracting new waves of advertising revenue. Even though publishers had dropped the price of an issue below the actual cost to produce a single copy, they recouped the loss through ad revenue—guaranteeing large readerships to advertisers eager to reach more customers. By the turn of the twentieth century, advertisers increasingly used national magazines to capture consumers' attention and build a national marketplace.

Muckrakers Expose Social Ills

The rise in magazine circulation coincided with major changes in American society in the early 1900s. Americans were moving from the country to the city in search of industrial jobs, and millions were immigrating to the United States hoping for new opportunities. Many newspaper reporters interested in writing about these and other social changes turned to magazines, for which they could write longer, more analytical pieces on such topics as corruption in big business and government, urban problems faced by immigrants, labor conflicts, and race relations. Some of these writers built their careers on crusading for social reform on behalf of the public good—often criticizing long-standing American institutions.

In 1906, President Theodore Roosevelt dubbed these investigative reporters **muckrakers**, because they were willing to crawl through society's muck to uncover a story. Although Roosevelt wasn't always a fan, muckraking journalism led to some much-needed reforms. For example, influenced in part by exposés in *Ladies' Home Journal* and *Collier's* magazines, Congress in 1906 passed the Pure Food and Drug Act and the Meat Inspection Act. Reports in *Cosmopolitan*, *McClure's*, and other magazines led to laws calling for increased government oversight of business, a progressive income tax, and the direct election of U.S. senators.

General-Interest Magazines Hit Their Stride

The heyday of the muckraking era lasted into the mid-1910s, when America was drawn into World War I. During the next few decades and even through the 1950s, **general-interest magazines** gained further prominence. These publications covered a wide variety of topics aimed at a broad national audience—such as recent developments in government, medicine, or society. A key aspect of these magazines was **photojournalism**—the use of photographs to augment editorial content (see "Media Literacy Case Study: The Evolution of Photojournalism" on pages 112–113). High-quality photos gave general-interest magazines a visual advantage over radio, which was the most popular medium of the day. In 1920, about fifty-five magazines fit the general-interest category; by 1946, more than a hundred such magazines competed with radio networks for the national audience. Four giants dominated this magazine genre: the *Saturday Evening Post*, *Reader's Digest*, *Time*, and *Life*.

▲ Muckraking magazines like *McClure's* were the first to publish investigative stories on American institutions. Granger, NYC—All rights reserved.

Media Literacy

The Evolution of Photojournalism

By Christopher R. Harris

What we now recognize as photojournalism started with the assignment of photographer Roger Fenton, of the *Sunday Times* of London, to document the Crimean War in 1856. Since then—from the earliest woodcut technology to halftone reproduction to the flexible-film camera—photojournalism's impact has been felt worldwide, capturing many historic moments and playing important political and social roles. For example, Jimmy Hare's photoreportage on the sinking of the battleship *Maine* in 1898 near Havana, Cuba, fed into growing popular support for Cuban independence from Spain and eventual U.S. involvement in the Spanish-American War; and the documentary photography of Jacob Riis and Lewis Hine at the turn of the twentieth century captured the harsh working and living conditions of the nation's many child laborers. Reaction to these shockingly honest photographs resulted in public outcry and new laws against the exploitation of children. In addition, *Time* magazine's coverage of the Roaring Twenties to the Great Depression and *Life*'s images from World War II and the Korean War changed the way people viewed the world.

With the advent of television, photojournalism continued to take on a significant role, bringing to the public live coverage of the assassination of President John F. Kennedy in 1963 and its aftermath, as well as visual documentation of the turbulent 1960s, including aggressive photographic coverage of the Vietnam War and shocking images of the Civil Rights movement.

Into the 1970s and onward, the emergence of computer technologies has raised new ethical concerns about photojournalism. These new concerns deal primarily with the ability of photographers and photo editors to change or digitally alter the documentary aspects of a news photograph. By the late 1980s, computers could transform images into digital form, easily manipulated by sophisticated software programs. In addition, any photographer can now send images around the world almost instantaneously through digital transmission, and the Internet allows publication of virtually any image without censorship. Because of the absence of physical film, there is a resulting loss of proof, or veracity, of the authenticity of images. Digital images can be easily altered, but such alteration can be very difficult to detect.

A stark example of tampering with a famous image involved an Orthodox Jewish newspaper in Brooklyn that deleted then secretary of state Hillary Clinton and counterterrorism director Audrey Tomason from a photograph of President Barack Obama and other White House staff monitoring the Navy Seals raid that killed

 Web Clip

YouTube.com features a number of videos about photojournalism. For example, search for 'Power of Photojournalism 1/2' posted by the Reynolds Journalism Institute. How does the video define photojournalism as distinct from both regular photography and journalism in general?

Christopher R. Harris is a professor in the Department of Electronic Media Communication at Middle Tennessee State University.

Case Study: *The Evolution of Photojournalism* by Christopher R. Harris. Reprinted by permission of Christopher R. Harris.

▲ Eddie Adams's Pulitzer Prize–winning photo of a general executing a suspected Vietcong terrorist during the Vietnam War is said to have turned some Americans against the war. Adams (1933–2004) later regretted the notoriety the image brought to the general, as the man he shot had just murdered eight people (including six children). Eddie Adams/AP Images

Osama bin Laden. The paper does not publish images of women in accordance with Orthodox Jewish rules about modesty and ignored White House conditions that the supplied photo not be altered. The paper issued an apology shortly thereafter.

Have photo editors gone too far? Photojournalists and news sources are now confronted with unprecedented concerns over truth-telling. In the past, trust in documentary photojournalism rested solely on the verifiability of images as they were used in the media. Now, news sources have a variety of guidelines in place regarding image manipulation, ranging from vague requirements that the image not be changed in a misleading way to specific lists of acceptable Photoshop tools. Just as we must evaluate the words we read, at the start of a new century we must also view with a more critical eye those images that mean so much to so many.

APPLYING THE CRITICAL PROCESS

DESCRIPTION   Select three types of magazines (e.g., national, political, and alternative) that contain photojournalistic images. Look through these magazines, taking note of what you see.

ANALYSIS   Document the patterns in each magazine. What kinds of images are included? What kinds of topics are discussed? Do certain stories or articles have more images than others? Are the subjects generally recognizable, or do they introduce readers to new people or places? Do the images accompany an article or are they stand-alone, with or without a caption?

INTERPRETATION   What do these patterns mean? Talk about what you think the orientation is of each magazine based on the images. How do the photos work to achieve this view? Do the images help the magazine in terms of verification or truth-telling, or are the images mainly to attract attention? Can images do both?

EVALUATION   Do you find the motives of each magazine to be clear? Can you see any examples in which an image may have been framed or digitally altered to convey a specific point of view? What are the dangers in this? Explain.

ENGAGEMENT   If you find evidence that a photo has been altered or has framed the subject in a manner that makes it less accurate, e-mail the magazine's editor and explain why you think this is a problem.

Saturday Evening Post

Although the *Post* had been around since 1821, it didn't become the first widely popular general-interest magazine until 1897. The *Post* printed popular fiction and romanticized American virtues through words and pictures. During the 1920s, it also featured articles celebrating the business boom of the decade. This reversed the journalistic direction of the muckraking era, in which magazines focused on exposing corruption in business. By the 1920s, the *Post* had reached two million in circulation, the first magazine to hit that mark.

Reader's Digest

Reader's Digest championed one of the earliest functions of magazines: printing condensed versions of selected articles from other magazines. With its inexpensive production costs, low price, and popular pocket-size format, the magazine saw its circulation climb to more than one million even during the depths of the Great Depression. By 1946, it was the nation's most popular magazine. By the mid-1980s, it was the most popular magazine in the world.

Time

During the general-interest era, national newsmagazines such as *Time* also scored major commercial success. Begun in 1923, *Time* developed a magazine brand of interpretive journalism, assigning reporter-researcher teams to cover newsworthy events, after which a rewrite editor would shape the teams' findings into articles presenting a point of view on the events covered. Newsmagazines took over photojournalism's role in news reporting, visually documenting both national and international events. Today, *Time*'s circulation stands at about three million.

Life

More than any other magazine of its day, *Life*, an oversized pictorial weekly, struck back at radio's popularity by advancing photojournalism. Launched in 1936, *Life* satisfied the public's fascination with images (invigorated by the movie industry) by featuring extensive photo spreads with its researched articles, lavish advertisements, and even fashion photography. By the end of the 1930s, *Life* had a **pass-along readership**—the total number of people who come into contact with a single copy of a magazine—of more than seventeen million. This rivaled the ratings of even the most popular national radio programs.

▲ Margaret Bourke-White was a photojournalist of many firsts: first female photographer for *Life* magazine, first Western photographer allowed into the Soviet Union, and first female war correspondent. Bourke-White was well known for her photos of World War II, including pictures of Nazi concentration camps, but she also captured images reflecting the economic realities of her time. Margaret Bourke-White/Time Life Pictures/Getty Images

General-Interest Magazines Decline

In the 1950s, weekly general-interest magazines began to lose circulation after dominating the industry for thirty years. Following years of struggle, the *Saturday Evening Post* finally folded in 1969; *Look* (another oversized pictorial weekly), in 1971; and *Life*, in 1972. Oddly, all three at the time were in the Top 10 in paid circulation. Although some critics attributed the problem to poor management, general-interest magazines were victims of several forces: high production costs, increased postal rates, and—most damaging—television. As families began spending more time gathered around their TVs instead of reading magazines, advertisers began spending more money on TV spots, which were less expensive than magazine ads and reached a larger audience.

TV Guide

Launched in 1953 to exploit the nation's growing fascination with television, *TV Guide*, which published TV program listings, took its cue from the pocket-size format of *Reader's Digest* and the supermarket sales strategy used by women's magazines. By filling a need (many newspapers were not yet listing TV programs), the magazine by 1962 had become the first weekly to reach a circulation of eight million. At that time, it had seventy regional editions. (See Table 4.1 for the circulation figures of the Top 10 U.S. magazines.)

When local newspapers began listing TV program schedules, they undermined *TV Guide*'s regional editions, and the magazine saw its circulation decline. In response, the magazine transformed itself to survive. Today, *TV Guide* is a full-size, single-edition, national magazine that focuses on entertainment and lifestyle news and carries only limited listings of cable and network TV schedules. The brand name also lives on at TVGuide.com.

People

People (launched by Time Inc. in March 1974) capitalized on the celebrity-crazed culture that accompanied the rise of television. And, like *TV Guide*, it crafted a distribution strategy emphasizing supermarket sales. These moves helped it become the first successful mass market magazine to be introduced in decades. With an abundance of celebrity profiles and human-interest stories, *People* showed a profit in just two years and reached a circulation of more than two million within

▲ With large pages, beautiful photographs, and compelling stories on celebrities, *Look* entertained millions of readers from 1939 to 1971, emphasizing photojournalism to compete with radio. By the late 1960s, however, TV had lured away national advertisers, postal rates had increased, and production costs had risen, forcing *Look* to fold despite a readership of more than eight million. The Advertising Archives

TABLE 4.1 // THE TOP 10 MAGAZINES (RANKED BY PAID U.S. CIRCULATION AND SINGLE-COPY SALES, 1972 VS. 2016)

1972		2016	
Rank/Publication	**Circulation**	**Rank/Publication**	**Circulation**
1 *Reader's Digest*	17,825,661	1 *AARP The Magazine*	23,144,225
2 *TV Guide*	16,410,858	2 *AARP Bulletin*	22,700,945
3 *Woman's Day*	8,191,731	3 *Better Homes and Gardens*	7,645,364
4 *Better Homes and Gardens*	7,996,050	4 *Game Informer*	6,353,075
5 *Family Circle*	7,889,587	5 *AAA Living*	4,898,168
6 *McCall's*	7,516,960	6 *Good Housekeeping*	4,315,026
7 *National Geographic*	7,260,179	7 *Family Circle*	4,056,156
8 *Ladies' Home Journal*	7,014,251	8 *National Geographic*	3,780,044
9 *Playboy*	6,400,573	9 *People*	3,418,555
10 *Good Housekeeping*	5,801,446	10 *Woman's Day*	3,275,962

Data from: Alliance for Audited Media, http://abcas3.auditedmedia.com/ecirc/magtitlesearch.asp.

five years. Instead of using a bulky oversized format and relying on subscriptions, *People* downsized and generated most of its circulation revenue from newsstand and supermarket sales. To this day, it uses plenty of photos, and its articles are about one-third the length of those in a typical newsmagazine. *People*'s success has inspired the launching of similar magazines specializing in celebrities, human-interest stories, and fashion, such as *InStyle* and *Hello*, and has influenced competing Webzines like *TMZ* and *Wonderwall*.

Types of Magazines: Domination of Specialization

As television has commanded more of Americans' attention, magazines have had to switch tactics to remain viable. General-interest publications have given way to highly specialized magazines appealing to narrower audiences that can be guaranteed to advertisers seeking to tap into niche markets. These narrow groups of readers might be defined by profession (*CIO, Progressive Grocer*), lifestyle (*Dakota Farmer, Game Informer*), gender (*Men's Health, Woman's Day*), age (*AARP The Magazine, Highlights for Children*), or ethnic group (*Ebony, Latina*). There are even specialty magazines appealing to fans of specific interests and hobbies — such as hand-spinning, private piloting, antique gun restoration, and poetry. These niche markets can be categorized in a few broader areas of specialization.

Men's and Women's Magazines

One way the magazine industry competed with television was to reach niche audiences who were not being served by TV, including those interested in sexually explicit subject matter. *Playboy*, started in 1953 by Hugh Hefner, was the first magazine to address this audience by emphasizing previously taboo topics and featuring pornographic photos. Newer men's magazines have broadened their focus to include health (*Men's Health*) and lifestyle (*Details* and *Maxim*) in addition to titillating photos and stories.

Women's magazines had long demonstrated that targeting readers by gender was highly effective. Yet as the magazine industry grew more specialized, publishers stepped up their efforts to capture even more of this enormous market. *Better Homes and Gardens*, *Good Housekeeping*, *Ladies' Home Journal*, and *Woman's Day* focused on cultivating the image of women as homemakers and consumers in the conservative 1950s and early 1960s. As the women's movement advanced in the late 1960s and into the 1970s, such magazines began including articles on sexuality, careers, and politics—topics magazine editors previously associated primarily with men.

Entertainment, Leisure, and Sports Magazines

In addition to *TV Guide*, the television age spawned a number of specialized entertainment, leisure, and sports magazines. Executives have developed multiple magazines for fans of everything from soap operas, running, tennis, golf, and hunting, to quilting, antiquing, surfing, and gaming. Within categories, magazines specialize further, targeting older or younger runners, men or women golfers, duck hunters or bird-watchers, and midwestern or southern antique collectors.

The most popular sports and leisure magazine is *Sports Illustrated*, which took its name from a failed 1935 publication. Launched in 1954 by Henry Luce's Time Inc., *Sports Illustrated*'s circulation held fairly steady in 2016 at about three million. It is now the most successful general sports magazine in history.

launchpadworks.com

Magazine Specialization Today

Editors discuss motivations for magazine specialization and how the Internet is changing the industry.

Discussion: How have the types of magazines you read changed over the past ten years? Have their formats changed, too?

► Specialized magazines target a wide range of interests, from mainstream sports to such hobbies as making model airplanes. Some of the more successful specialized magazines include *Rolling Stone* and *National Geographic*.

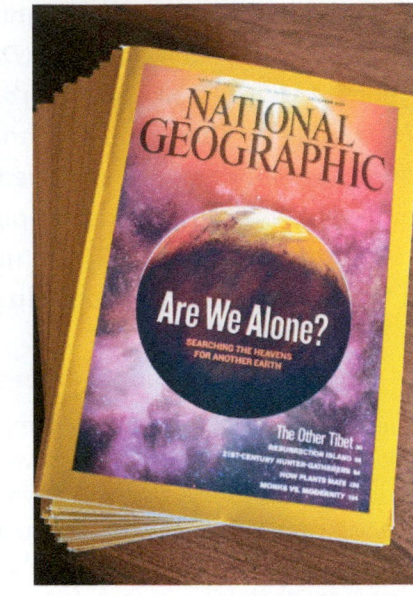

Another popular magazine type that fits loosely into this category comprises magazines devoted to music. The all-time circulation champ in this category is *Rolling Stone*, begun in 1967. Once considered an alternative magazine, by 1982 *Rolling Stone* had become mainstream, with a circulation approaching 800,000. By 2016, that number had expanded to almost 1.5 million.

National Geographic is another successful publication in this category. Founded in 1888, it promoted "humanized geography" and began featuring color photography in 1910. *National Geographic*'s circulation reached one million in 1935 and ten million in the 1970s. Beginning in the late 1990s, its circulation of paid subscriptions began sliding, down to less than four million in 2016 (with an additional half million in international distribution). Still, many of *National Geographic*'s televised specials on nature and culture, which began airing back in 1965, rank among the most popular programs in the history of public TV.

Age-Specific Magazines

Magazines have sliced their target markets even more finely by appealing to ever-narrower age groups often ignored by mainstream television. For example, magazines such as *Boys' Life* (the Boy Scouts' national publication since 1912), *Highlights for Children*, and *Ranger Rick* have successfully targeted preschool and elementary-school children. The ad-free and subscription-only *Highlights for Children* boasts a circulation of more than two million.

Leading female teen magazines have also shown substantial growth; the top magazine for thirteen- to nineteen-year-olds is *Seventeen*, with a circulation of two million in 2016.

Magazines that have had the most success with targeting audiences by age have set their sights on readers over fifty, America's fastest-growing age demographic. These publications have tried to meet the interests of older Americans, whom mainstream culture has historically ignored. By 2016, *AARP The Magazine*—established in 1958 as *Modern Maturity*—had a circulation of more than 23 million, far surpassing that of any other magazine besides its sister publication, *AARP Bulletin*, which has nearly as many subscribers (see Table 4.1 on page 116). *AARP The Magazine* articles cover a range of topics related to lifestyle, travel, money, health, and entertainment, such as the effects of Viagra on relationships, secrets for spectacular vacations, and how playing poker can sharpen your mind.

Elite Magazines

Although they had long existed, *elite magazines* gained popularity as magazines began specializing. Elite magazines are characterized by their combination of literature, criticism, humor, and journalism and by their appeal to highly educated audiences, often living in urban areas. The most widely circulated elite magazine is the *New Yorker*. Launched in 1925 by Harold Ross, the *New Yorker* became the first city magazine aimed at a national upscale audience. Over the years, it featured many prominent biographers, writers, reporters, and humorists and introduced some of the finest literary journalism of the century. By the mid-1960s, the *New Yorker*'s circulation hovered around 500,000; by 2016, it stood at one million print-version subscribers.

Minority Magazines

Minority-targeted magazines have existed since before the Civil War. One of the most influential early African American magazines, the *Crisis*, was founded by W. E. B. Du Bois in 1910 and is the official magazine of the National Association for the Advancement of Colored People (NAACP).

Since then, the major magazine publisher for African Americans has been John H. Johnson, a former Chicago insurance salesman. Johnson started *Negro Digest* in 1942, *Ebony* in 1945 (a picture-text magazine modeled on *Life* but serving black readers), and *Jet* in 1951 (*Jet* announced in 2014 it would switch to a digital-only format). *Essence*, the first major magazine geared toward

▲ *Selecta* is an upscale fashion magazine targeted at Hispanic women. The magazine is published in Spanish, although it maintains Twitter and Instagram feeds in English. Other popular magazines aimed at this audience include *Latina* and *People en Espanol.* Courtesy of Selecta Magazine

African American women, debuted in 1969, and by 2016 it had a circulation of more than one million.

Other magazines have served additional minority groups. For example, the *Advocate*, founded in 1967 as a twelve-page newsletter, was the first major magazine to address issues of interest to gay men and lesbians. Since its founding, it has published some of the best journalism on topics not covered by the mainstream press.

Magazines appealing to Spanish-speaking readers have proliferated since the 1980s, reflecting the growth of Hispanic populations in the United States. Some are Spanish-language versions of existing titles, and others were specifically created to serve a Hispanic audience. Today, *People en Español*, *Latina*, and *Vanidades* rank as the top three Hispanic magazines by ad revenue.

Although national magazines aimed at other minority groups were slow to arrive, there are now magazines targeting virtually every race, culture, and ethnicity, including *Asian Week*, *Native Peoples*, and *Tikkun* (published for Jewish readers).

Trade Magazines

▼ *Variety,* a trade magazine covering the entertainment industry, was founded in 1933 and remains a widely read source of news and reviews. © 2016 Variety Media, LLC

Trade and professional magazines represent one of the most stable segments in the magazine industry. **Trade publications**—specialty magazines aimed at narrowly defined audiences—supply news; spot trends; share data; and disseminate expert insights relevant to specific manufacturing trades, professional fields, and business sectors. The trade press includes such diverse magazines as *Organic Matters* for organic farmers, *Packaging Machinery Technology* for packaging engineers, and *Coach and Bus Week*. Media industries, too, have relied on trade magazines like *Advertising Age* and *Variety*. In addition to narrowly targeted advertising content, trade publications provide an invaluable venue for job notices related to the specific field.

Alternative Magazines

Only eighty-five of the twenty thousand American magazines now in existence have circulations that top one million. This means that most magazines serve relatively small groups of readers. Of these, many are alternative magazines. However, what constitutes an alternative magazine has broadened over time to include just about any publication considered "outside the mainstream," ranging from environmental magazines to alternative lifestyle magazines to punk zines—the magazine world's answer to punk rock. (**Zines**, pronounced "zeens," is a term used to describe self-published magazines.) Numerous alternative magazines have defined themselves in terms of politics—published by either the Left (the *Progressive*, *In These Times*, the *Nation*) or the Right (the *National Review*, *American Spectator*, the *Weekly Standard*). Though their circulations may be relatively small, they often exert significant influence on politics by stimulating public debate and affecting citizens' political choices.

Supermarket Tabloids

With headlines like "Bat Child Escapes," "Extraterrestrials Follow the Teachings of Oprah Winfrey," and "Al-Qaeda Breeding Killer Mosquitoes," **supermarket tabloids** push the limits of credibility. Although they are published on newsprint, the Alliance for Audited Media (formerly the Audit Bureau of Circulations)—which checks newspaper and magazine circulation figures to determine advertising rates—counts weekly tabloids as magazines. Tabloids have their historical roots in newspapers' use of graphics and pictorial layouts in the 1860s and 1870s. But the modern U.S. tabloid began with the founding of the *National Enquirer* by William Randolph Hearst in 1926. Its popularity inspired the founding of other tabloids, like *Globe* (1954) and *Star* (1974), as well as the adoption of a tabloid style by some general-interest magazines, such as *People* and *Us Weekly*. Today, tabloid magazine sales are down from their peak in the 1980s. One of the more far-fetched of these supermarket tabloids, *Weekly World News*, ended its print version in 2007 but still exists online.

Online Magazines

At first observers viewed the Internet as the death knell for print magazines, but now the industry embraces it. Given the costs of paper, printing, and postage, the flexibility of the Web and mobile devices, and the ability to reach new and larger audiences, many magazines are being distributed in both print and digital formats. For example, *Wired* magazine has a print circulation of about 886,000. On its Web (Wired.com) and tablet (app) editions, *Wired* gets an average of twenty-four million unique visitors per month. Links through social media are another way magazine content reaches an audience, and *Wired* reports sixteen million readers through social media like Facebook, Twitter, Google+, Instagram, and Pinterest.

▼ Online magazines like *Slate* (*pictured*) have made the Web their exclusive home. Since launching in 1996, *Slate* has won many awards, such as the National Magazine Award for General Excellence for Digital Media.

(For more on magazines and social media, see "The Digital Turn Case Study: The Digital Pass-Along: Magazine Readers on Social Media" on page 125.)

The Web and app formats give magazines unlimited space—which is at a premium in their printed versions—and the opportunity to do things that print cannot do. Many online magazines now include blogs, original video and audio podcasts, social networks, games, virtual fitting rooms, and 3-D "augmented reality" components that could never work in print. Additionally, many digital magazines (including *Lucky, Seventeen, GQ, Teen Vogue, Brides, Popular Science,* and *Maxim*) offer mobile-specific scanning apps that enable 3-D involvement on every page, not just those pages with a QR code (the square scannable bar codes that link to video and Web pages).

In addition to print magazines that publish digital versions and magazines that have moved from print to online only, other magazines—called **Webzines**—have always been online only. Respected Webzines *Slate* and *Salon*, for example, have made the Web a legitimate arena for reporting breaking news and encouraging public debate about culture and politics.

The Organization and Economics of Magazines

Whatever their circulation size, specialty, or format (print or online), magazines must invest money to staff the departments and carry out the business practices that are essential to their operations — including editorial and production, advertising and sales, and circulation and distribution. Magazines must also bring in money (e.g., from advertising revenues and subscription fees) to fulfill their mission and compete with other media. For instance, to combat loss of ad dollars to TV, many magazines began publishing special editions, which guaranteed advertisers access to their target markets. These competitive strategies fueled the massive growth of magazines despite competition from television, but now magazines face new challenges from Web sites, blogs, and social media, all competing for audiences and ad dollars. To extend their reach, lower their costs, and beef up their budgets, many magazines have merged into large chains, often backed financially by major media conglomerates. Even large chains, however, are not immune to the economic reality that many well-known magazine titles continue to cease production entirely.

Magazine Departments and Duties

Unlike a broadcast station or a daily newspaper, a small newsletter or magazine can begin cheaply via computer-based **desktop publishing**, which enables an aspiring publisher-editor to write, design, lay out, and print or post online a modest publication. For larger operations, however, the work is divided into departments.

Editorial and Production

The lifeblood of any magazine is the *editorial department*, which produces its content, excluding advertisements. Like newspapers, most magazines have a chain of command that begins with a publisher and extends down to the editor in chief, the managing editor, and a variety of subeditors. These subeditors oversee such editorial functions as photography, illustrations, reporting and writing, and copyediting. Magazine writers generally include contributing staff writers, who are specialists in certain fields, and *freelance writers*—self-employed professionals assigned to cover particular stories or regions. Unlike newspapers, some magazines also rely on unsolicited manuscripts to fill their pages.

The *production and technology department* maintains the computer and printing hardware necessary to produce the magazine, though most of the actual printing is often outsourced. Large national magazines will transmit digital copy to regional printers, who can insert local ads and distribute the finished product more quickly.

Advertising and Sales

Consumer magazines rely heavily on advertising revenue brought in by their *advertising and sales department*. The more successful the magazine (that is, the higher its circulation), the more it can charge for ad space. A top-rated consumer magazine might charge more than $357,000 for a full-page color ad and about $115,000 for a one-third-page, black-and-white ad. The average magazine contains about 45 percent ad copy and 55 percent editorial content, a ratio that has remained fairly constant for the past decade.

In some cases, advertisers can strongly influence editorial content. For example, some companies have canceled their ads after a magazine printed articles that were unflattering toward or critical of the firm or its industry.[3] For editors, the specter of a major advertiser bringing its business elsewhere can present a dilemma: Should the magazine shift its editorial point of view to avoid offending advertisers and thus retain much-needed ad revenue? Or should it

▲ *Ms.* magazine, founded in 1972 as the first magazine to take the feminist movement seriously, made another bold move when it stopped carrying advertisements in 1990—except for ads from nonprofit and cause-related organizations. Although that choice has allowed the magazine to publish more thought-provoking articles, it has unfortunately led to continued financial instability.

continue publishing the same types of articles, hoping that if some advertisers are driven away, others that agree with the magazine's viewpoint will come in and take their place?

In addition to grappling with this dilemma, magazines have developed innovative strategies for retaining advertisers. For instance, as television stations began generating more national ad revenues in the 1950s, magazines started introducing different editions to guarantee advertisers a specific audience—and thus win them back. There are several types of special editions:

- **Regional editions** are national magazines whose content is tailored to the interests of specific geographic areas. For example, *Sports Illustrated* often prints several regional versions of its College Football Preview and March Madness Preview editions, picturing a different local star on each of the covers.
- In **split-run editions**, the editorial content remains the same, but the magazines include a few pages of ads purchased by local or regional companies. Most editions of *Time* and *Sports Illustrated*, for instance, contain a number of pages reserved for regional ads.
- **Demographic editions** target particular groups of consumers. In this case, market researchers identify subscribers primarily by occupation, class, and zip code. Time Inc., for example, developed special editions of *Time* magazine for top management, high-income zip-code areas, and ultrahigh-income professional/managerial households.

Circulation and Distribution

Selling magazines (both paper and digital) to an audience is the focus of the *circulation and distribution department*. Currently, about 90 percent of magazines are sold through subscriptions rather than other means, such as single-copy sales by retailers.

One tactic used by magazine circulation departments to increase subscription revenue is to encourage consumers to renew well in advance of their actual renewal dates. Magazines can thus invest and earn interest on early renewal money as a hedge against consumers who drop their subscriptions. Other strategies include **evergreen subscriptions**—those that automatically renew on a credit card account unless subscribers request that the automatic renewal be stopped—and *controlled circulations*, which provide readers with a magazine at no charge by targeting captive audiences, such as airline passengers or association members. These magazines' financial support comes solely from advertising and corporate sponsorship.

The Digital Pass-Along: Magazine Readers on Social Media

For a long time now, magazine publishers have been aware of pass-along readership, the practice of sharing a magazine with someone else when the reader is done with it. Since the digital turn, the idea of sharing magazine content has become even more important in courting online readers, especially those eighteen to thirty-four years of age.

National magazine trade organization MPA (formerly the Magazine Publishers of America, now the Association of Magazine Media) conducted a survey in 2012 of traditional print-magazine readers who are also on social media. What they discovered about this age group reveals not only that there are multiple varieties of convergence but also that readers, especially avid readers, *like* this convergence.[1]

The MPA survey paints a picture of readers who are far from abandoning magazines, with the vast majority of respondents (93%) having read either a print or a digital magazine article in the past sixty days. Over half of these people "Follow" a magazine on Twitter or "Like" its page on Facebook. Part of the survey also focused on those who said they were avid magazine readers. Of that group, almost two-thirds use Twitter or Facebook to follow at least one magazine. In addition, a more recent (2016) MPA survey shows that online readership is shifting from desktop and laptop viewing to mobile devices. But it's not just a one-to-one switch: The MPA report indicates that for every laptop user who went away in 2016, nine mobile users took his or her place.[2]

Avid magazine readers are doing a lot more than just reading articles via social media. According to the earlier survey, over 60 percent of these readers share magazine articles on Facebook or tweet links to articles, reminiscent of the way readers would pass along printed copies of magazines to friends and family. What's more, readers say it's important to them to be able to follow a magazine in a social media environment and then share it quickly. In addition to the Facebook and Twitter platforms, Pinterest has been a popular way for readers to interact with magazines, following and repinning their content.

But the convergence of print and online doesn't stop with methods of sharing articles. Readers in the survey use social media to talk back to the magazines they read or to the columnists they follow. This involves leaving comments in response to articles, uploading their own content (recipes, for example), or posting photographs for possible use in future issues. The ability to engage with favorite magazines—and in some cases the staff of those magazines—is *important* to these readers. This underscores the idea that successful convergence will be a key to success, if not survival, for the magazine industry.

LaunchPad

⊙ **Visit LaunchPad** to watch a clip from *13 Going on 30* set in a magazine office. What has changed in the decade or so since this movie's release?

launchpadworks.com

FIGURE 4.1 // MAGAZINE BRAND AUDIENCE BY DISTRIBUTION FORMAT, 2015

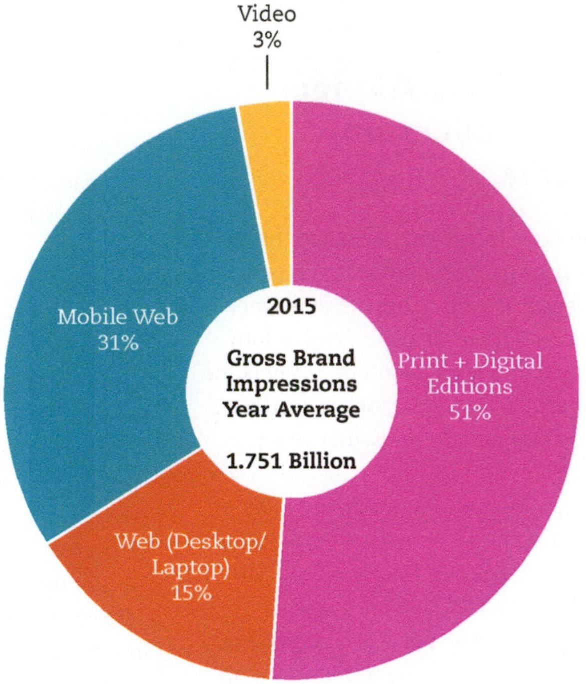

Data from: Magazine Media Factbook 2016/17, *Association of Magazine Media, www.magazine.org/sites/default /files/MPA-FACTbook201617-ff.pdf.*

The biggest trend in magazine sales is the migration to digital distribution (see Figure 4.1). By 2015, combined print and digital editions accounted for about 51 percent of the magazine audience. Mobile editions (usually via apps) attract about 31 percent of the industry's audience, while Web versions of magazines (via desktops and laptops) account for 15 percent.[4] Other models for magazine distribution, such as the Texture app, offer a Netflix-like plan, with more than 170 titles accessible for a monthly fee.

Major Magazine Chains

To survive in an increasingly competitive marketplace, many magazines have merged into large, powerful chains, often backed by deep-pocketed media conglomerates. This strategy provides more funding for magazines and enables them to lower their costs—for example, by centralizing basic functions such as content development or production.

In the commercial magazine industry, large companies or chains have come to dominate the business. Condé Nast is one example. A division of Advance

Publications, which operates the Newhouse newspaper chain, the Condé Nast group controls several upscale consumer magazines, including *Vanity Fair*, *GQ*, and *Vogue*. Time Inc., which spun off from Time Warner in 2014, is the largest magazine publisher in the United States, boasting titles like *People* and *Sports Illustrated*.

Many large publishers—including the Hearst Corporation, the Meredith Corporation, Time Inc., and Rodale Press—have generated additional revenue by creating custom-publishing divisions that produce limited-distribution publications for client companies. These publications, sometimes called **magalogs**, combine the style of glossy magazines with the sales pitch of retail catalogues. For example, a large international corporation might pay a publisher to produce a magalog for its employees on how to manage their 401(k).

A number of major magazines (*Reader's Digest*, *Cosmopolitan*, and *Time* are good examples) have further boosted revenues by launching international editions in several languages. However, most U.S. magazines are local, regional, or specialized and therefore aren't readily exportable to other countries. Of the approximately twenty thousand magazines now published in the United States, only about two hundred circulate routinely in the world market. Moreover, even the best-known and most-circulated magazines, backed by the largest companies, may not survive in the marketplace. For example, Condé Nast shut down its popular *Gourmet* and *Modern Bride* magazines at the end of 2009, though the *Gourmet* brand name continues to be used for occasional online and print publications.

▲ Originally launched in the United States in 1914 by Condé Nast, *Vanity Fair* featured top writers such as Dorothy Parker and P. G. Wodehouse. Known for its mix of social and political commentary, celebrity profiles, fiction, and arts coverage, *Vanity Fair* today includes contributions by noted photographer Annie Leibovitz and writers James Wolcott and Bethany McLean. Pierre L. Rigal/ Conde Nast Collection/Getty Images

Magazines in a Democratic Society

In the early days of the industry, individual magazines had a powerful national voice and united separate communities around important political and social issues, such as abolition and suffrage. Muckrackers promoted social reform in the pages of general-interest magazines. Today, with so many specialized magazines appealing to ever-narrower groups of consumers, magazines no longer foster such a strong sense of national identity.

To be sure, contemporary commercial magazines still provide essential information about politics, society, and culture. Thus, they help us form opinions about the big issues of the day and make decisions—key activities in any democracy. However, owing to their increasing dependence on advertising revenue, some publications view their readers as consumers first (viewers of displayed products and purchasers of material goods) and citizens second. To keep advertising dollars flowing in, editorial staffs may decide to keep controversial content out of their magazine's pages, which constrains debate and thus hurts the democratic process.

There may also be legal ramifications when a magazine publishes unflattering or embarrassing content about powerful people or groups, as tabloid Web site *Gawker* found out firsthand. *Gawker*'s problems began when the site publicly outed PayPal cofounder Peter Thiel as gay in 2007, then posted a sex tape of Terry Bollea (otherwise known as wrestler Hulk Hogan) with his friend's wife in 2012. Thiel secretly bankrolled Bollea's lawsuit against *Gawker*, and in 2016 Bollea was awarded $140 million after a jury agreed *Gawker* had invaded his privacy. *Gawker* filed for bankruptcy, went broke, shut down, and was ultimately sold to Univision, which decided not to resurrect the site but continued running the other Web sites that had been part of the Gawker media group. In a final twist, it was revealed that Thiel had been secretly bankrolling other lawsuits against *Gawker* for years. Some media watchers fear the fallout from this decision could affect more than just *Gawker* if Thiel's tactics encourage others—particularly those who are subjected to legitimate investigative journalism—to use a similar method of revenge by proxy.[5]

Despite these kinds of challenges, however, magazines have arguably had more freedom than other media to encourage and participate in democratic debate. More magazines circulate in the marketplace than do broadcast or cable television channels. And many new magazines are uniting dispersed groups of readers—for example, by giving cultural minorities or newly arrived immigrants a sense of membership in a broader community.

In addition, because most magazines are distributed weekly, monthly, or bimonthly, their publishers are less restricted by deadline pressure than are newspaper publishers and radio and television broadcasters. Journalists writing for magazines can thus take time to offer more rigorous and thoughtful analyses of the topics they cover. The biweekly *Rolling Stone*, for example, often mounts more detailed, comprehensive political pieces than you might find in a daily news source. However, this is changing in some cases, as online publications attempt to cover breaking news and face the kinds of constant deadline pressure that used to be associated only with daily newspapers and broadcasters.

Amid today's swirl of images, magazines and their advertisements certainly contribute to the commotion. But good magazines—especially those offering carefully researched, thoughtful, or entertaining articles and photos—have continued to inspire lively discussion among readers. And if they're also well designed, they maintain readers' connection to words—no small feat in today's increasingly image-driven world.

CHAPTER ESSENTIALS

Review

- The first **magazines**—collections of articles, stories, and advertisements published on a nondaily cycle in a smaller tabloid style—were influenced by seventeenth-century European newspapers. In the American colonies and during the Revolutionary period, magazines provided an important space for sharing ideas about politics and society. By the mid-nineteenth century, increases in literacy, faster printing technology, and improvements in mail delivery helped move magazines toward mass medium status.

- Like newspapers, by the twentieth century some magazines became sources of investigative journalism aimed at social reform and exposing wrongdoings. These investigative reporters were called "**muckrakers**."

- The growth of the middle class created a market for **general-interest magazines**, which covered a wide variety of topics aimed at a broad national audience. A key aspect of these magazines was **photojournalism**.

- General-interest magazines have now given way to highly specialized magazines appealing to narrower audiences and niche markets.

- Following the digital turn, most magazines developed online versions and their own specific apps. Some magazines are published in both print and online versions; others have moved to online-only formats; and still others, **Webzines**, started up online and have remained there.

- Small independent magazines that use **desktop publishing** can be run by one or two people, but larger operations can require hundreds of workers in various departments, including *editorial and production*, which are responsible for nonadvertising content and maintaining hardware; *advertising and sales*, which sells advertising; and *circulation and distribution*, which sells subscriptions and works with retailers for off-the-rack sales.

- National magazines sometimes run multiple versions of the same issue to target specific audiences and guarantee advertising revenue. Versions may include **regional editions**, whose content is tailored to the interests of different geographic areas; **split-run editions**, which contain the same editorial content but have some regionally targeted ads; and **demographic editions**, which target specific groups of consumers.

- Early magazines had a powerful national voice and united separate communities around significant political and social issues. Today, with so much specialization, magazines no longer foster a strong sense of national identity, though they continue to have a strong influence on society.

Key Terms

magazine, p. 107

muckrakers, p. 111

general-interest magazines, p. 111

photojournalism, p. 111

pass-along readership, p. 114

trade publications, p. 120

zines, p. 121

supermarket tabloids, p. 121

Webzines, p. 122

desktop publishing, p. 123

regional editions, p. 124

split-run editions, p. 124

demographic editions, p. 124

evergreen subscriptions, p. 124

magalogs, p. 127

Study Questions

1. How did magazines become national in scope?

2. What role did magazines play in social reform at the turn of the twentieth century?

3. What triggered the move toward magazine specialization?

4. How have the Internet and the digital turn changed the magazine industry? How have they changed magazine consumers?

5. How do magazines serve a democratic society?

5

Sound Recording and Popular Music

Two musical artists, born just a year apart in the United Kingdom and the United States, have dominated the U.S. music industry for the past decade. They are among the top recording stars of their generation, and both have reshaped the industry by signing early in their careers with independent music labels. Whereas stars of an earlier generation might have signed big contracts with one of the major music corporations as soon as they had their first hit, Adele and Taylor Swift stayed with their independent labels and demonstrated that artists can create successful careers without the help of a major corporation.

Adele Laurie Blue Adkins was born in 1988 in North London. Adele's biggest passion was singing, and she was admitted into the London-area BRIT School for Performing Arts & Technology. After a friend posted Adele's three-song demo from a class project to Myspace, the songs impressed executives from XL Recordings, a British independent label that is home to artists like Beck, Radiohead, and M.I.A. The label signed her to a recording contract at the age of eighteen, and Adele's three albums have all been named after the age at which she did the main work of writing and recording: *19* (2008), *21* (2011), and *25* (2015).

◄ Taylor Swift is a global superstar who has never been afraid of doing things her own way. Soon after moving to Nashville with her family at the age of fourteen, Swift launched a successful career without the influence of a major music corporation. The rest, as they say, is history. Splash News/Newscom/Splash News/Los Angeles/USA

Born in 1989, Taylor Swift moved to Nashville, Tennessee, with her family at the age of fourteen to pursue a career in country music. Major record companies were already interested in the young Swift as a long-term development project, but Swift was interested in getting her career started. After seeing her play, veteran music executive Scott Borchetta signed Swift to a contract in 2005 with Big Machine—an independent label he was starting, which now includes Tim McGraw and Rascal Flatts. Her debut album *Taylor Swift* (2006) was released when she was sixteen, and it immediately became a country hit. Her next albums—*Fearless* (2008), *Speak Now* (2010), *Red* (2012), and *1989* (2014)—were even bigger, and moved her into the realm of mainstream pop.

Adele and Taylor Swift have dominated popular music as its best-selling singer-songwriters. With the exception of 2013, Adele or Swift had a Top 10 album every year from 2007 to 2016; sometimes it was the two of them. Both of these artists have won armfuls of Grammy Awards as well.

Adele and Swift have become pioneers in how to be music stars in their own way, maintaining control over their music and their lives. In 2014, for example, Swift removed her music from the streaming site Spotify because she was dissatisfied with the company's low compensation for music creators. Meanwhile, Adele produces albums on her own schedule. After *21*, Adele took a long hiatus, formed a serious relationship, and had a baby.

Aided in part by the success of artists like Adele and Swift, the rise of independent labels is one of the most significant developments in the music industry in the past two decades. The old route to success for musical artists was highly dependent on signing with a major label, which handled all the promotion to sell records. Now, with so many distribution forms for music—traditional CDs and vinyl; digital downloads and streaming; social media; music licensed for use in advertising, television, and film; and (lest we forget) live, in-person concerts—there are multiple paths for talented artists to find an audience, whether with an independent label or on their own.

THE INVENTION OF SOUND RECORDING TECHNOLOGY

transformed our relationship with popular music and made sound recording a mass medium. Before recording, people had one way to listen to music: attend a live performance. With the advent of sound recording, people could also buy recordings and listen to their favorite music as often as they wanted in their own homes. As technological advances made it cheaper and easier for everyone to gain access to sound recordings, music began reshaping society and culture. But the recording industry itself has also changed with the times. Consider what happened in the 1950s after TV began capturing a bigger share of Americans' attention and time: Record labels and radio stations—previously adversaries—joined forces to create Top 40 (or "hit song") programming to attract more listeners and stimulate music sales. Many years later, the industry was forced to shift again in the face of technology, as the MP3 format made recorded music more accessible (and easier to duplicate) than ever. And just as the music industry began integrating digital music downloads into its business model, the digital turn brought a new wrinkle: streaming music.

In this chapter, we assess the full impact of sound recording and popular music on our lives by:

- **examining the early history and evolution of sound recording, including the shift from analog to digital technology and the changing relationship between record labels and radio stations**

- **shining a spotlight on the rise of popular music (including jazz and rock) in the United States**

- **tracing the changes in the American popular-music scene, such as rock's move into the mainstream and the proliferation of rock alternatives (including folk and grunge)**

- **analyzing the economics of the sound recording industry, including how music labels, artists, and other participants make and spend money in an age when paying to *own* music is rapidly transforming into paying to *access* music**

- **considering sound recording's impact on our democratic society today by exploring such questions as whether the recording industry is broadening participation in democracy or constraining it**

The Early History and Evolution of Sound Recording

Early inventors' work helped make sound recording a mass medium and a product that enterprising businesspeople could sell. The product's format changed with additional technological advances (e.g., moving from records and tapes to CDs, and then to online

LaunchPad
launchpadworks.com

Use **LearningCurve** to review concepts from this chapter.

downloads and digital music streaming). Technology also enhanced the product's quality; for example, many people praised the digital clarity of CDs over "scratchy" analog recordings. However, the latest technology — online downloading and streaming of music — has drastically reduced sales of CDs and other physical formats, forcing industry players to look for other ways to survive.

From Cylinders to Disks: Sound Recording Becomes a Mass Medium

In the development stage of sound recording, inventors experimented with sound technology; and in the entrepreneurial stage, people sought to make money from the technology. Sound recording finally reached the mass medium stage when entrepreneurs figured out how to quickly and cheaply produce and distribute multiple copies of recordings.

The Development Stage

In the 1850s, French printer Édouard-Léon Scott de Martinville conducted the first experiments with sound recording. Using a hog's-hair bristle as a needle, he tied one end to a thin membrane stretched over the narrow part of a funnel. When he spoke into the wide part of the funnel, the membrane vibrated, and the bristle's free end made grooves on a revolving cylinder coated with a thick liquid. Although de Martinville never figured out how to play back the sound, his experiments ushered in the *development stage* of sound recording.

The Entrepreneurial Stage

In 1877, Thomas Edison helped move sound recording into its *entrepreneurial stage* by first determining how to play back sound, then marketing the machine that did it. He recorded his own voice by concocting a machine that played foil cylinders, known as the *phonograph* (derived from the Greek terms for "sound" and "writing"). Edison then patented his phonograph in 1878 as a kind of answering machine. In 1886, Chichester Bell and Charles Sumner Tainter patented an improvement on the phonograph, known as the *graphophone*, which played more durable wax cylinders.[1] Both Edison's phonograph and Bell and Tainter's graphophone had only marginal success as a voice-recording office machine. Yet these inventions laid the foundation for others to develop more viable sound recording technologies.

The Mass Medium Stage

Adapting ideas from previous inventors, Emile Berliner, a German engineer who had immigrated to America, made sound recording into a *mass medium*. Berliner developed a turntable machine that played flat disks, or "records," made of shellac. He called this device a *gramophone* and patented it in 1887.

He also discovered how to mass-produce his records by making a master recording from which many copies could be easily duplicated. In addition, Berliner's records could be stamped in the center with labels indicating song title, performer, and songwriter.

By the early 1900s, record-playing phonographs were widely available for home use. Early record players, known as Victrolas, were mechanical and had to be primed with a crank handle. Electric record players, first available in 1925, gradually replaced Victrolas as more homes were wired for electricity.

Recorded music initially had limited appeal, owing to the loud scratches and pops that interrupted the music, and each record contained only three to four minutes of music. However, in the early 1940s, when shellac was needed for World War II munitions, the record industry began manufacturing records made of polyvinyl plastic. These vinyl records (called 78s because they turned at seventy-eight revolutions per minute, or rpms) were less noisy and more durable than shellac records. Enthusiastic about these new advantages, people began buying more records.

▲ A graphophone and a collection of prerecorded wax cylinders. Russell Knight/Getty Images

In 1948, CBS Records introduced the $33\frac{1}{3}$-rpm *long-playing record* (LP), which contained about twenty minutes of music on each side. This created a market for multisong albums and classical music, which was written primarily for ballet, opera, ensemble, or symphony, and continues to have a significant fan base worldwide. The next year, RCA developed a competing 45-rpm record, featuring a quarter-size hole in the middle that made these records ideal for playing in jukeboxes. The two new recording configurations could not be played on each other's machines; thus, a marketing battle erupted. In 1953, CBS and RCA compromised. The LP became the standard for long-playing albums, the 45 became the standard for singles, and record players were designed to accommodate both formats (as well as 78s, at least for a while).

From Records to Tapes to CDs: Analog Goes Digital

The advent of magnetic **audiotape** and tape players in the 1940s paved the way for major innovations, such as cassettes, stereophonic sound, and—most significantly—digital recording. Audiotape's lightweight magnetized strands made possible sound editing and multiple-track mixing, in which instrumentals or vocals could be recorded at one location and later mixed onto a master recording in a studio. This vastly improved studio recordings' quality and boosted sales, though recordings continued to be sold primarily in vinyl format until the late 1970s.

By the mid-1960s, engineers had placed miniaturized (reel-to-reel) audiotape inside small plastic cases and developed portable cassette players. Listeners could now bring recorded music anywhere, which created a market for pre-recorded cassettes. Audiotape also permitted home dubbing, which began eroding record sales.

Some people thought audiotape's portability, superior sound, and recording capabilities would mean the demise of records. However, vinyl's popularity continued, due in part to the improved fidelity that came with stereophonic sound. Invented in 1931 by Alan Blumlein, but not put to commercial use until 1958, **stereo** permitted the recording of two separate channels, or tracks, of sound. Using audiotape, recording-studio engineers could now record many instrumental or vocal tracks, which they would then "mix down" to two stereo tracks, creating a more natural sound.

The biggest recording advancement came in the 1970s, when electrical engineer Thomas Stockham made the first digital audio recordings on standard computer equipment. In contrast to **analog recording**, which captures the fluctuations of sound waves and stores those signals in a record's grooves or a tape's continuous stream of magnetized particles, **digital recording** translates sound waves into binary on-off pulses and stores that information in sequences of ones and zeros as numerical code. Drawing on this technology, in 1983 Sony and Philips began selling digitally recorded **compact discs** (CDs), which could be produced more cheaply than vinyl records and even audiocassettes. By 2000, CDs had rendered records and audiocassettes nearly obsolete except among deejays, hip-hop artists (who still used vinyl for scratching and sampling), and some audiophile loyalists. However, vinyl albums, once nearly extinct, have been making a comeback. Still a relatively small part of the overall market in music sales, vinyl sales have jumped so much that many new albums are being pressed on vinyl. Whether this will be a lasting or a brief trend among a new wave of collectors remains to be seen.

From Downloads to Streaming: Sound Recording Goes through the Digital Turn

In 1992, the **MP3** file format was developed as part of the MP4 video compression standard, enabling sound—including music—to be compressed into small, manageable digital files. Combined with the Internet, MP3 revolutionized sound recording. By the mid-1990s, computer users were swapping MP3 music files online. These files could be uploaded and downloaded in a fraction of the time it took to exchange noncompressed music, and they used up less memory.

launchpadworks.com

Recording Music Today

Composer Scott Dugdale discusses technological innovations in music recording.

Discussion: What surprised you the most about song production as shown in the video?

Unfortunately for music companies and artists, this also meant that it was easy to get copies of songs without paying for them, especially as file-sharing sites like Napster grew in popularity. In 2001, the U.S. Court of Appeals sided with the music industry when it decided that free music file-swapping—music piracy—violated music copyrights. The decision led to Napster's quick demise.

The music industry still loses money to piracy and does its best to fight back. At the same time, music companies realize that MP3s are not going away and have embraced the format through legal music downloads. Launching in 2003 to accompany the iPod, Apple's iTunes Store became the first big success story in music downloading. By 2011, the music industry was making more money from digital downloads than from sales of CDs and other physical media. But just as the music industry was adapting to this approach, the digital turn served up another innovation that favored the music industry even more: streaming.

▲ Apple's iPod began a revolution in digital music when it was released in 2001. The company phased out production of its original iPod in 2014 but still manufactures the Touch Justin Sullivan/Getty Images

Today, streaming is quickly becoming the music industry's best means for controlling the music it sells, as music *ownership* has shifted to music *access*.[2] The access model has been driven by the availability of streaming services such as the Sweden-based Spotify, which made its debut in the United States in 2011 and hit forty million worldwide subscribers in 2016. Other services include Apple Music, Tidal (led by Jay Z and a number of other leading artists), Rhapsody, Deezer (outside the United States), Google Play Music, Amazon Music Unlimited, and SoundCloud. With these services, listeners have flexibility: They can pay a subscription fee (typically $5 to $10 per month) and instantly access millions of songs on demand via the Internet. The streaming market also includes ad-supported streaming services—such as YouTube and Vevo—which have wide international use.

Internet radio services like Pandora stream music, too, but they allow listeners to choose only format or style rather than individual songs. The line between music and radio streaming is easily blurred as new companies get involved in music streaming and existing services react to meet the competition. (For more on streaming music services, see "Media Literacy Case Study: Spotify and Online Streaming: Saving or Sinking the Music Industry?" on pages 142–143. For more on streaming radio, see Chapter 6.)

The Music Industry and Radio: A Rocky Relationship

We can't discuss the development of sound recording without also discussing radio (covered in detail in Chapter 6). Though each industry developed independently of the other, radio constituted recorded sound's first rival for listeners' attention. This competition triggered innovations both in sound recording technology and in the business relationship between the two industries.

In the mid-1920s, when the sound recording industry had just introduced electric record players, radio stations began broadcasting recorded music without compensating the music industry. The American Society of Composers, Authors and Publishers (ASCAP), founded in 1914 to collect copyright fees for music publishers and writers, accused radio of hurting sales of records and sheet music. By 1925, ASCAP established music-rights fees for radio, charging stations between $250 and $2,500 a week to play recorded music. Many stations couldn't afford these fees and had to leave the air. Other stations countered by establishing their own live, in-house orchestras, disseminating music free to listeners. Throughout the late 1920s and 1930s, record sales continued plummeting as the Great Depression worsened.

In the early 1950s, television became popular and began pilfering radio's programs, advertising revenue, and audience. Seeking to reinvent itself, radio turned to the record industry. Brokering a deal that gave radio a cheap source of content and record companies greater profits, many radio stations adopted a new hit-song format—dubbed "Top 40," for the number of records a jukebox could store. Now when radio stations aired songs, record sales soared.

In the early 2000s, though, the radio and recorded-music industries were in conflict again. Upset by online radio stations' decision to stream music on the Internet, the recording industry began pushing for high royalty charges, hindering the development of Internet radio. The most popular online streaming services developed separately from traditional radio stations.

U.S. Popular Music and the Rise of Rock

As sound recording became a mass medium, it fueled the growth of popular music, or **pop music**, which appeals to large segments of the general population as well as sizable groups distinguished by age, region, or ethnic background. Pop music today includes numerous genres — rock and roll, jazz, blues, country, Tejano, salsa, reggae, punk, hip-hop, and dance — many of which evolved from a common foundation. For example, rock splintered off from blues (which originated in the American South), and hip-hop grew out of R&B, dance music, and rock. This proliferation of music genres created a broad range of products that industry players could package and sell — targeted to increasingly narrow listener groups.

It would be a mistake to think of the label "pop music" as an insult, somehow referring to music that is frivolous, unimportant, or unartistic. To be sure, some music is indeed just meant to entertain (or to separate consumers from their dollars). But from the folk music protests of Woody Guthrie to the blurring of racial lines in the development of rock music to the antiwar anthem "What's Going On" by Marvin Gaye, popular music has exerted a major influence on society, culture, and even politics.

The Rise of Pop Music

Though technological advancements made sound recording a mass medium and sparked the proliferation of pop music genres, this music had its earliest roots in something far less technical: sheet music. With mass production of sheet music in the nineteenth and early twentieth centuries, pop developed into a business fed by artists who set standards for the different genres—including jazz, rock, blues, and R&B.

Back in the late nineteenth century, a section of Broadway in Manhattan known as Tin Pan Alley began selling sheet music for piano and other instruments. (The name Tin Pan Alley referred to the way these quickly produced tunes supposedly sounded like cheap pans clanging together.) Songwriting along Tin Pan Alley helped transform pop music into big business. At the turn of the twentieth century, improvements in printing technology enabled song publishers to mass-produce sheet music for a growing middle class. Previously a novelty, popular music now became a major enterprise. With the emergence of the phonograph and recorded tunes, interest in and sales of sheet music soared. (These sales would eventually decline with the rise of radio in the 1920s, which turned audiences more into listeners of music than active participants playing instruments to sheet music in their living rooms.)

As sheet music gained popularity and phonograph sales rose, **jazz** developed in New Orleans. An improvisational and mostly instrumental musical form, jazz absorbed and integrated a diverse array of musical styles, including African rhythms, blues, and gospel. Groups led by Louis Armstrong, Tommy Dorsey,

Media Literacy

Spotify and Online Streaming: Saving or Sinking the Music Industry?

"When I look at the future of music, I don't think scarcity is the model anymore," Spotify CEO Daniel Ek explained in a 2015 interview with *Billboard* magazine. "We have to embrace ubiquity —that music is everywhere."[1] With forty million subscribers and climbing, the Spotify music streaming service is clearly helping to usher in new ways of listening. But while Spotify touts its "music ubiquity," not everyone shares Ek's rosy outlook: Artists such as Taylor Swift, Aimee Mann, and Beck are pushing back against a business model they say hurts composers and performers.

With so many competing interests affected by streaming, it's easy to see why relations among the parties aren't always harmonious. Music streaming services like Spotify want to lock users into a one-stop service for accessing music on demand, collecting monthly individual subscriptions. YouTube and Vevo feature endless playlists of music videos to sell ads. Apple offers streaming subscriptions from iCloud, with options to purchase digital files. Recording labels, and of course the composers and musicians who create the music, have independent Web sites. Different parties have different ideas about what is in their best interests.

The artists themselves are split on what streaming means for them. Some, such as Dave Grohl (Foo Fighters) and Bono (U2), have publicly supported Spotify for making music more available to new audiences and boosting concert ticket sales. Others, such as Taylor Swift, accuse Spotify of paying too little to writers and performers. (Swift yanked her catalog off the streaming site in 2014 in protest, though she added it back again in 2017.) There are also musicians who want a more direct hand in the streaming business —such as Jay Z, who launched the Tidal service in 2015. If that's not confusing enough, consider that while these various business and artistic interests push against one another, they also need to work together to reach consumers and stay in business.

▲ Sweden's Daniel Ek founded his first Internet business in 1997, when he was just fourteen years old. Nine years later, Ek started Spotify with Martin Lorentzon (who left the company in 2015). When Ek married longtime partner Sofia Levander in 2016, guests included Facebook's Mark Zuckerberg and musician Bruno Mars. Michael Loccisano/Getty Images

 **Web Clip**

YouTube.com has many videos about Daniel Ek and Spotify. For example, do a quick search for 'Daniel Ek CEO of Spotify' by Charlie Rose. As services like Spotify develop ever more sophisticated song-recommendation algorithms, how will this affect our exposure to new music? Will these algorithms help to expand our listening habits, or keep us isolated in a personal online bubble?

At the core of the streaming music controversy is the debate over free-to-the-consumer services, which rely on ads to make money, versus premium services, which allow subscribers to skip the ads for a monthly fee. Critics say that "freemium" services hurt sales of CDs and digital downloads. In addition, although a percentage of the ad revenue from those free services goes to royalties, critics maintain that the revenue is too low to make it worthwhile (see details in "Dividing the Profits" section on page 159). Supporters like Ek say that free streaming services have dramatically cut music piracy and that, in the long run, the ongoing royalties (which are collected with every stream of a song) will pay more to artists than a one-time sale of CDs or digital downloads.

Right now, all that seems certain is that the battle over music streaming won't end anytime soon. Online music services such as Spotify, Pandora, and SoundCloud not only face questions about who pays and how much; they also face increased competition as major media companies like Apple and Amazon enter the streaming music business and leverage existing customers into subscribers.

However these debates settle out, the online streaming genie is clearly out of its bottle, and there is no going back. According to Spotify's Ek, that's just how it should be: "Now, finally, after years and years of decline, music is growing again, [and] streaming is behind the growth in music."[2]

APPLYING THE CRITICAL PROCESS

DESCRIPTION   Arrange to interview four to eight friends or relatives about how they access music today. Do they buy music, either online through sites like iTunes or by purchasing CDs in a retail store? Do they listen to streaming services such as Spotify? If they stream, do they use "freemium" services, or do they pay for premium? Does hearing a song while streaming ever lead them to a purchase? Devise other questions that prompt them to explain their listening and purchasing habits, and to consider if these habits have changed over time.

ANALYSIS   Chart and organize your results. Do you recognize any patterns emerging from the data? What influences your friends' or relatives' decisions to purchase or stream music?

INTERPRETATION   Based on the patterns you have charted, determine what they mean. Over time, have the changes in buying and streaming been significant? Why or why not? Why do you think people's buying and listening preferences developed as they did?

EVALUATION   Do you think the rise of music streaming helps or hurts musical artists? Do you think it helps or hurts music fans? Why do so many contemporary musical performers differ in their opinions about streaming music?

ENGAGEMENT   To expand on your findings, arrange to speak with a local musician. How does this artist feel about music streaming services? While major artists like Taylor Swift decry services like Spotify, do undiscovered musicians feel differently about them? Speculate about how musicians might navigate a world in which people buy and access music very differently than they did even a few years ago.

▲ Louis Armstrong (1901–1971) transformed jazz with astonishing improvised trumpet solos and scat singing. Tom Copi/Getty Images

and others counted among the most renowned of the "swing" jazz bands, whose rhythmic sound dominated radio, recordings, and dance halls.

The first pop vocalists of the twentieth century came out of vaudeville—stage performances featuring dancing, singing, comedy, and magic shows. By the 1930s, Rudy Vallée and Bing Crosby had established themselves as the first "crooners" singing pop standards. Bing Crosby also popularized Irving Berlin's "White Christmas," which became one of the most recorded songs in history. Meanwhile, the bluesy harmonies of a New Orleans vocal trio, the Boswell Sisters, influenced the Andrews Sisters, whose boogie-woogie style sold more than sixty million records in the late 1930s and 1940s. Helped by radio, pop vocalists like Frank Sinatra in the 1940s were among the first singers to win the hearts of a large national teen audience. Indeed, Sinatra's early performances incited the kinds of audience riots that would later characterize rock-and-roll concerts.

Rock and Roll Arrives

Pop music's expanding appeal paved the way for **rock and roll** to emerge in the mid-1950s. Rock both reflected and shaped powerful societal forces (such as blacks' migration from the South to the North and the growth of youth culture) that had begun transforming American life. Rock also stirred controversy. Like the word *jazz*, the phrase *rock and roll* was a blues slang expression meaning "sex"—which offended those with more conservative musical tastes and made them worry about their children's choice in music. Rock grew out of a blending of numerous musical styles. For instance, early rock combined the vocal and instrumental traditions of pop with the rhythm-and-blues sounds of Memphis and the country twang of Nashville. As rock and roll developed, that fusion of musical styles contributed to both racial progress and fears reflecting the social unease of the 1950s and 1960s.

Blues and R&B Set the Stage for Rock

The migration of southern blacks to northern cities in search of better jobs during the first half of the twentieth century helped disseminate different popular music styles to new places. In particular, **blues** music traveled north. Blues became the foundation of rock and roll and was influenced by African American spirituals, ballads, and work songs from the rural South.

Influential blues artists included Robert Johnson, Ma Rainey, Bessie Smith, Muddy Waters, Howlin' Wolf, and Charley Patton. After the introduction of the electric guitar in the 1930s, blues-based urban black music began to be marketed under the name **rhythm and blues (R&B)**. This new music appealed to young listeners fascinated by the explicit (and forbidden) sexual lyrics in songs like "Annie Had a Baby," "Sexy Ways," and "Wild Wild Young Men." Although banned on some stations, R&B continued gaining popularity into the early 1950s. Still, black and white musical forms were segregated, and trade magazines in the 1950s tracked R&B record sales on "race" charts, separate from the white "pop" charts.

Rock Reflects and Reshapes Racial Politics

As artists began to produce music that borrowed from what main-stream society thought of as "black" and "white" musical traditions, American society as a whole was entering a tumultuous time of social and political change that would help fuel rock's popularity. By the early 1950s, President Truman's 1948 executive order integrating the armed forces was fully in practice, bringing young men from very different ethnic and economic backgrounds together. Then, in 1954, the Supreme Court's *Brown v. Board of Education* decision declared unconstitutional the "separate but equal" laws that had segregated blacks and whites for decades. Mainstream America began to wrestle with the legacy of slavery and the unequal treatment of its African American citizens. And so rock music reflected the complicated changes happening at the time while also helping to influence those changes. On the one hand, the fusion of musical traditions made rock music popular among young people across racial lines and could be understood as "desegregating" in its own right. On the other hand, sometimes the rock-and-roll business of the 1950s and 1960s (and beyond) perpetuated racial inequalities and denied artists of color the fruits of their artistic efforts. White producers would often give cowriting credit to white performers like Elvis Presley (who never wrote songs himself) for the tunes they recorded. Many producers also bought the rights to potential hits from black songwriters, who seldom saw a penny in royalties or received songwriting credit.

By 1955, R&B hits regularly crossed over to the pop charts, but for a time the white **cover music** versions were more popular and profitable. For example, Pat Boone's cover of Fats Domino's "Ain't That a Shame" shot to No. 1 and stayed on the Top 40 pop chart for twenty weeks. Domino's original made it only to No. 10. A turning point, however, came in 1962, when Ray Charles covered "I Can't Stop Loving You," a 1958 country song by the Grand Ole Opry's Don Gibson. This marked the first time that a black artist covering a white artist's song had notched a No. 1 pop hit.

▲ A major influence on early rock and roll, Chuck Berry, (1926–2017), scored big hits between 1955 and 1958, writing "Maybellene," "Roll Over Beethoven," "School Day," "Sweet Little Sixteen," and "Johnny B. Goode." At the time, he was criticized by some black R&B artists for sounding white and by some white conservative critics for his popularity among white teenagers. Berry's experience is another example of the complicated and sometimes contradictory nature of the relationship between race and popular music. Bettmann/Getty Images

Fear Fuels Censorship

Rock's blurring of racial and other lines alarmed enough Americans that performers and producers alike worried that fans would begin defecting. In an attempt to avoid this, they used various tactics to get people to accept the music. Cleveland deejay Alan Freed played original R&B recordings from the race charts and black versions of early rock on his program, while Philadelphia deejay Dick Clark took a different tactic—playing white artists' cover versions of black music. Still, problems persisted that further eroded rock's acceptance.

One particularly difficult battle rock faced was the perception among mainstream adults that the music caused juvenile delinquency. Such delinquency was statistically on the rise in the 1950s, owing to a variety of contributing factors, such as parental neglect, the rising consumer culture, and the burgeoning youth population after World War II. But adults sought an easier culprit to blame. It was far simpler to point the finger at rock—especially artists who blatantly defied rules governing proper behavior. Authorities responded by censoring rock lyrics.

Rattled by this and other developments, the U.S. recording industry decided it needed a makeover. To protect the enormous profits the new music had been generating, record companies began practicing some censorship of their own. In the early 1960s, the industry introduced a new generation of clean-cut white singers, including Frankie Avalon, Connie Francis, Ricky Nelson, Lesley Gore, and Fabian. Rock's explosive violations of racial, class, and other boundaries gave way to simpler generation gap problems, and the music—for a time—developed a milder reputation.

Rock Blurs Additional Boundaries

Although rock and roll was molded by powerful social, cultural, and political forces, it also shaped them in return. As we've seen, rock and roll began by blurring the boundary between black and white, but it broke down additional divisions as well—between high and low culture, masculinity and femininity, country and city, North and South, and the sacred and the secular.

High and Low Culture

Rock challenged the long-standing distinction between high and low culture initially through its lyrics and later through its performance styles. In 1956, Chuck Berry's song "Roll Over Beethoven" merged rock and roll (which many people considered low culture) with high culture through lyrics that included references to classical music: "You know my temperature's risin' / And the jukebox's blowin' a fuse . . . Roll over Beethoven / And tell Tchaikovsky the news." Rock artists also defied norms governing how musicians should behave:

Berry's "duck walk" across the stage, Elvis Presley's tight pants and gyrating hips, and Bo Diddley's use of the guitar as a phallic symbol shocked elite audiences—and inspired additional antics by subsequent artists.

Masculinity and Femininity

Rock and roll was also the first pop music genre to overtly challenge assumptions about sexual identity and orientation. Although early rock and roll largely attracted males as performers, the most fascinating feature of Elvis Presley, according to the Rolling Stones' Mick Jagger, was his androgynous appearance.[3] Little Richard (Penniman) took things even further, sporting a pompadour hairdo, decorative makeup, and feminized costumes during his performances.[4]

Country and City

Rock and roll also blended cultural borders between early-twentieth-century black urban rhythms and white country & western music. Early white rockers such as Buddy Holly and Carl Perkins combined country or hillbilly music, southern gospel, and Mississippi delta blues to create a sound called **rockabilly**. Conversely, rhythm and blues spilled into rock and roll. Many songs first popular on the R&B charts, such as "Rocket 88," crossed over to the pop charts during the mid to late 1950s, though many of these songs were performed by more widely known white artists.

Rock lyrics in the 1950s may not have been especially provocative or overtly political by today's standards, but soaring record sales and the crossover appeal of the music itself represented an enormous threat to long-standing racial and class divisions defined by geography. Distinctions at the time between traditionally rural white music and urban black music dissolved, as some black artists (such as Chuck Berry) strived to "sound white" to attract Caucasian fans, and some white artists (such as Elvis Presley) were encouraged by record producers to "sound black."

North and South

Not only did rock and roll blur the line between urban and rural, but it also mixed northern and southern influences together. As many blacks migrated north during the early twentieth century, they brought their love of blues and R&B with them. Meanwhile, musicians and audiences in the North had claimed blues music as their own, forever extending its reach beyond its origins in the rural South. Some white artists from the South—most notably Carl Perkins, Elvis Presley, and Buddy Holly—further carried southern musical styles to northern listeners.

Sacred and Secular

Many mainstream adults in the 1950s complained that rock and roll's sexual overtones and gender bending constituted an offense against God—even

▲ Although his unofficial title, King of Rock and Roll, has been challenged by Little Richard and Chuck Berry, Elvis Presley remains among the most popular solo artists of all time. From 1956 to 1962, he recorded seventeen No. 1 hits, from "Heartbreak Hotel" to "Good Luck Charm." Bettmann/Getty Images

though numerous early rock figures (such as Elvis Presley, Jerry Lee Lewis, and Little Richard) had strong religious upbringings. In the late 1950s, public outrage over rock proved so great that even Little Richard and Jerry Lee Lewis, both sons of southern preachers, became convinced that they were playing "the devil's music." Throughout the rock era and even today, boundaries between the sacred and the secular continue to blur through music. For example, some churches are using rock and roll to appeal to youth, and some Christian-themed rock groups are recording in seemingly incongruous musical styles, such as heavy metal.

The Evolution of Pop Music

As the volatile decade of the 1960s unfolded, pop music (including rock) changed to reflect the social, cultural, and political shifts taking place — while continuing to influence these aspects of American life as well. Authorities made further attempts to "tame" rock, concerned about its influence on teenagers. These attempts sparked resistance from defiant young people, many of whom embraced rock musicians from Great Britain who hadn't toned down their style. As pop music continued to adapt, it spun off into several genres, including soul, folk, and psychedelic, as well as punk, grunge, hip-hop, and country.

The British Are Coming!

Rock and roll proved so powerful that it transformed pop music across national borders. For instance, in England during the late 1950s, the young members of the Rolling Stones covered blues songs by American artists Robert Johnson and Muddy Waters. And the young Beatles imitated Chuck Berry and Little Richard.

Until 1964, rock-and-roll recordings had traveled on a one-way ticket to Europe. Even though American artists regularly reached the tops of charts overseas, no British performers had yet appeared on any Top 10 pop lists in the United States. This changed virtually overnight in 1964, when the Beatles came to America with their mop haircuts and delivered pop interpretations of American blues and rock. Within the next few years, more British bands — the Kinks, the Who, the Yardbirds — produced hits that climbed the American Top

 British rock groups like the Beatles and the Rolling Stones first invaded American pop charts in the 1960s. Although the Beatles broke up in 1970, each member went on to work on solo projects. The Stones are still (mostly) together and touring more than fifty years later. Photo by David Redfern/Getty Images (left); Dave J Hogan/Getty Images (right)

40 charts. Ed Sullivan, who booked the Beatles several times on his TV variety show in the mid-1960s, helped promote the group's early success.

With the British invasion, the rock industry split into two styles of music. The Rolling Stones developed a style emphasizing gritty, chord-driven, high-volume rock, which would influence later bands that created glam rock, hard rock, punk, heavy metal, and grunge. Meanwhile, the Beatles presented a more accessible, melodic, and softer sound, which would eventually inspire new genres, such as pop rock, power pop, new wave, and alternative rock. The British groups' success also demonstrated to the recording industry that older American musical forms, especially blues and R&B, could be repackaged as rock and exported around the world.

Motown: The Home of Soul

As rock attracted more and more devotees, it resurrected interest in the styles of music from which it had originated. Throughout the 1960s, black singers like James Brown, Aretha Franklin, Wilson Pickett, Otis Redding, and Ike and Tina Turner picked up on this interest, transforming the rhythms and melodies of older R&B, pop, and early rock and roll into what would become known as **soul**. These artists attracted large and racially diverse audiences, countering the British invaders with powerful vocal performances.

The most prominent independent label supporting black songwriters' and performers' work was Motown, founded in 1959 by former Detroit autoworker and songwriter Berry Gordy. Motown signed many successful black artists and groups, including the Four Tops ("Baby I Need Your Loving"), the Marvelettes ("Please Mr. Postman"), Marvin Gaye ("What's Going On"), and the Jackson 5 ("I'll Be There"). But the label's most successful group was the Supremes, featuring Diana Ross, which scored twelve No. 1 singles between 1964 and 1969 (including "Where Did Our Love Go" and "Stop! In the Name of Love"). The

Supremes' success showed Motown producers that songs emphasizing romance and featuring a danceable beat won far more young white fans than those trumpeting rebellion and political upheaval.

Folk and Psychedelic: Protest and Drugs

Popular music has always been both a product of and a shaper of its time. So it's not surprising that the social upheavals of the 1960s and early 1970s—over Civil Rights, women's rights, environmental protection, the Vietnam War, and the use of recreational drugs—found their reflections in rock music during these decades. By the late 1960s, many songwriters and performers spoke to their generation's social and political concerns through two music genres: folk and psychedelic rock.

Folk Inspires Protest

The musical genre that most clearly expressed pivotal political events of the time was folk, which had long served as a voice for social activism. **Folk music** exists in all cultures; it's usually performed by untrained musicians and passed down mainly through oral traditions. With its rough edges and amateur quality, folk is considered a democratic and participatory musical form. During the 1930s, the work of Woody Guthrie ("This Land Is Your Land") set a new standard for American folk music. Later, in the 1960s and 1970s, groups such as the Weavers, featuring labor activist and songwriter Pete Seeger, carried on Guthrie's legacy. These newer groups inspired yet another crop of singer-songwriters—Joan Baez; Arlo Guthrie; Peter, Paul, and Mary; Phil Ochs; Bob Dylan—who took a stand against worrisome developments of the day, including industrialization, poverty, racism, and war.

Rock Turns Psychedelic

With the increasing use of recreational drugs by young people and the availability of LSD (not illegal until the mid-1960s), more and more rock musicians experimented with and sang about drugs during rock's *psychedelic* era.

Defining groups and performers of this era included newcomers like Jefferson Airplane, Big Brother and the Holding Company (featuring Janis Joplin), the Jimi Hendrix Experience, the Doors, and the Grateful Dead, as well as established artists like the Beatles and the Rolling Stones. These musicians believed they could enhance their artistic prowess by taking mind-altering drugs. They also saw the use of these drugs as a form of personal expression and an appropriate response to the government's failure to deal with social and political problems, such as racism and America's involvement in the Vietnam War.

After a surge of optimism that culminated in the historic Woodstock concert in August 1969, the sun set on the psychedelic era as some of psychedelic rock's greatest stars died from drug overdoses, including Janis Joplin, Jimi Hendrix, and Jim Morrison of the Doors.

Punk, Grunge, and Alternative Rock: New Genres on the Horizon

As rock and roll moved from the edges of the American music scene into the mainstream, other genres arose to take its place on the fringes. While many people had considered rock a major part of the rebel counterculture in the 1960s, in the 1970s they increasingly viewed it as part of consumer culture. With major musical acts earning huge profits, rock had become just another product for manufacturers and retailers to promote, package, and profit from. According to critic Ken Tucker, this situation produced "faceless rock" performed by bands with "no established individual personalities outside their own large but essentially discrete audiences" of young white males.[5] To Tucker, these "faceless" groups—REO Speedwagon, Styx, Boston, Journey, Kansas—filled stadiums and entertained the maximum number of people while stirring up the minimum amount of controversy. It was only a matter of time before new types of music—punk, grunge, and alternative rock—arose to challenge rock's mainstream once more. Concurrently, an older genre—country music—rose to greater prominence, crossing over to gain more mainstream acceptance.

Punk Revives Rock's Rebellious Spirit

Punk rock arose in the late 1970s to defy the orthodoxy and commercialism of the record business. Punk attempted to revive rock's basic defining characteristics: simple chord structures that anyone with a few guitar lessons could master, catchy melodies, and politically or socially defiant lyrics. Emerging in New York City around bands such as the Ramones, Blondie, and Talking

▲ Born Robert Allen Zimmerman in Minnesota, Bob Dylan took his stage name from Welsh poet Dylan Thomas. He led a folk music movement in the early 1960s with engaging, socially provocative lyrics, but later infused folk with the electric sounds of rock. He continues recording and touring today, typically spending most of April through November on the road. He was awarded the Nobel Prize in Literature in 2016. Andrew DeLory

▲ Joan Jett, of the punk-rock group the Runaways and later Joan Jett and the Blackhearts, was influential in breaking down the boys' club mentality of rock and roll. She was inducted into the Rock and Roll Hall of Fame in 2015. Mark Metcalfe/Getty Images

Heads, punk quickly spread to England, where a soaring unemployment rate and growing class inequality ensured the success of socially critical rock. Groups like the Sex Pistols, the Clash, the Buzzcocks, and Siouxsie and the Banshees sprang up and even scored Top 40 hits on the U.K. charts. Despite their popularity, the Sex Pistols—one of the most controversial groups in rock history—was eventually banned for offending British decorum.

Punk didn't succeed commercially in the United States, in part because it was so hostile toward the commercialization of the mainstream music industry. However, it did help to break down the boys' club mentality of rock, launching unapologetic and unadorned front women like Patti Smith, Joan Jett, Debbie Harry, and Chrissie Hynde. It also introduced all-women bands whose members not only wrote but also performed their own music. Many of these female groups made it into the mainstream. Through these and other innovations, punk reopened the door to experimentation at a time when the industry had turned music into a purely commercial enterprise.

Grunge and Alternative Reinterpret Rock

Building on the innovative spirit of punk, the **grunge** genre further transformed rock in the 1990s. Grunge got its name from its often-messy guitar sound and the torn jeans and flannel shirts worn by its musicians and fans. Its lineage traced back to 1980s bands like Sonic Youth, the Minutemen, and Hüsker Dü. In 1992, after years of limited commercial success, this younger cousin of punk finally broke into the American mainstream with the success of Nirvana's "Smells Like Teen Spirit," the hit single from the album *Nevermind*.

Some critics view punk and grunge as subcategories or fringe movements of **alternative rock**, even though grunge was far more commercially successful than punk. This vague label encompasses many types of experimental rock music, which offered departures from the staged extravaganzas of 1970s glam rock. Such music appealed chiefly to college students and twentysomethings and set itself apart from the sounds of Top 40 and commercial FM radio. The same is true of **indie rock**, a broad category of independent-minded rock music usually distributed by smaller record labels. This genre, which can be traced to 1980s punk and post-punk acts, has achieved greater commercial success in recent years.

Hip-Hop Redraws Musical Lines

With the growing segregation of radio formats and the dominance of mainstream rock by white male performers, the place of black artists in the rock world diminished from the late 1970s onward. This trend—combined with the rise of "safe" dance disco by white bands (the Bee Gees), black artists (Donna Summer), and integrated groups (the Village People)—created space for a new sound to emerge beginning in the late 1970s: **hip-hop**, a term for the urban culture that includes *rapping*, *cutting* (or *sampling*) by deejays, breakdancing, street clothing, poetry slams, and graffiti art.

Similar to punk's opposition to commercial rock, hip-hop music stood in direct opposition to the polished, professional, and often less political world of soul. Its combination of social politics, swagger, and confrontational lyrics carried forward long-standing traditions in blues, R&B, soul, and rock and roll.

Initially, the music industry saw it as a novelty destined to go nowhere. But by 1985, hip-hop had become a popular genre with the commercial successes of groups and artists like Run-DMC, the Fat Boys, LL Cool J, and Queen Latifah. Soon, white groups like the Beastie Boys and Linkin Park were combining hip-hop and hard rock, while some white artists (such as Eminem, Iggy Azalea, and Macklemore) were attracting huge followings by emulating black rap artists. This has not been without controversy, however, as some critics worry about a repeat of the appropriation of urban musical forms by white artists, robbing those original artists of both opportunities and their artistic voice. These concerns over race and cultural appropriation will likely continue to be a source of controversy.

Although hip-hop encompasses many different styles, its most controversial subgenre is probably **gangster rap**. In seeking to describe gang violence in America, gangster rap has been accused of inciting violence through its lyrics and the illegal activities of some of its performers. Gangster rap drew widespread condemnation in 1996 with the shooting death of Tupac Shakur, a rapper and convicted sex offender. Criticism mounted in 1997 after a drive-by shooter killed the Notorious B.I.G., who had dealt drugs before becoming a rapper. Under pressure, the hip-hop industry softened its hard edges. Most prominently, artist Sean "Diddy" Combs developed a more danceable hip-hop that combined singing and rapping with musical elements of rock and soul. Today,

▲ Nirvana front man Kurt Cobain's vocal style, as well as a decidedly unglamorous look quite different from the much more theatrical "hair bands" of the 1980s, helped define the grunge genre in the early 1990s. The release of Nirvana's *Nevermind* in September 1991 bumped Michael Jackson's *Dangerous* from the top of the charts and signaled a new direction in popular music. Other grunge bands soon made their way to the charts, including Pearl Jam, Alice in Chains, Stone Temple Pilots, and Soundgarden. Pycha/DAPR/Zuma Press. Copyright 1993 by DAPR

▲ Chance the Rapper (real name Chancelor Bennett) made history in 2016 when his album *Coloring Book* became the first streaming-exclusive album to hit the Billboard 200. The album also garnered several Grammy nominations. Working without a label, Chance distributes his music using word of mouth and SoundCloud. Christopher Polk/Getty Images

hip-hop's stars include artists such as Vince Staples, who revisits the gangster genre, and artists like Kendrick Lamar, Chance the Rapper, Future, and Run the Jewels, who bring an old-school social consciousness to their performances.

From its origins in an urban American subculture, hip-hop has become a major part of mainstream global culture. Today, it's big business, and its most successful practitioners have diversified from record labels to clothing lines, restaurants, and movie production companies.

The Country Road

Country music has attracted enough loyal listeners in its various forms to survive as a profitable sector of the recording industry since the early days of pop music. Though the many styles of **country** represent significant variations in the development of this musical form, they all share one element: the country voice, inflected by a twang or a drawl. In the late 1950s, the wilder honky-tonk sounds of country were tamed by a smoother style, inspired by the mellower songs of Elvis Presley. Replacing the fiddles, electric guitars, and nasal vocals of honky-tonk with symphonic strings, pitch-perfect background vocalists, and crooning stars like Jim Reeves and Patsy Cline, the emergent style would become known as the "Nashville sound." This laid-back and toned-down form of country music reigned throughout the 1960s.[6] In the 1970s, some singers and producers aimed for more mainstream acceptance. Lynn Anderson, Charlie Pride, and Marie Osmond belted out hits that made the country idiom well liked in suburban America.[7] By the 1970s, country music saw two emerging trends: pop country, typified by artists like Glen Campbell, Dolly Parton, and Kenny Rogers, who appealed to a wider audience; and the edgier outlaw country, performed by artists like Waylon Jennings, Johnny Cash, Kris Kristofferson, and Willie Nelson. The mainstreaming of country music hit its stride in the 1990s, with Garth Brooks, Shania Twain, and other major crossover stars helping to boost the popularity of the genre. More recently, Taylor Swift found early success in country music before becoming a pop superstar. Today's top country artists include Luke Bryan, Carrie Underwood, and the Zac Brown Band.

▲ "I feel like one of the things that sets country music apart from other types of music is the storyteller aspect," Grammy Award–winning singer-songwriter Carrie Underwood writes on her official Web site. "I want three-and-a-half-minute movies on the radio. You can follow the characters, and you can see it all playing out in your head." Jason Merritt/Getty Images

The Economics of Sound Recording

Sound recording is a complex business, with many participants playing many different roles and controlling numerous dimensions of the industry. Songwriters, singers, and musicians create the sounds. Producers and record labels sign up artists to create music and often own the artists' work. Promoters market artists' work, managers handle bands' touring schedules, and agents seek the best royalty deals for their artist-clients.

Ever since sound recording became a mass medium, there's been a lot of money to be had from the industry — primarily through sales of records and CDs. But with the increasing amount of music available digitally, the traditional business model has broken down. The business has also changed through consolidation. Only three major labels remain (Universal Music Group, Sony Music Entertainment, and Warner Music Group), and they control about 65 percent of the recording-industry market in the United States. But despite the oligopoly (few owners exerting great control over an industry), the biggest changes in the music industry — both of which developed as a result of the digital turn — are the rise of independent music labels and online music streaming.

A Shifting Power Structure

Over the years, the U.S. recording industry has experienced dramatic shifts in its power structure. From the 1950s through the 1980s, the industry consisted of numerous competing major labels as well as independent production houses, or **indies**. Over time, the major labels began swallowing up the indies and then buying each other. By 1998, only six big labels remained: Universal, Warner, Sony, BMG, EMI, and Polygram. That year, Universal acquired Polygram; in 2003, BMG and Sony merged; and in late 2011, EMI was auctioned off to Universal. Today, only three major music corporations exist: Universal Music Group, Sony Music Entertainment, and Warner Music Group. With their stables of stars, financial resources, and huge libraries of music to sell, these firms exert a great deal of control, at one time capturing about 85 percent of the market in the United States. Critics, consumers, and artists alike complain that this consolidation of power in the hands of a few resists new sounds in music that may not have traditional commercial appeal and supports only those major artists and styles that have large mainstream appeal. In 2015, the big three labels' control of the U.S. market had slipped to around 65 percent. And although this is still a major portion of the market, the bigger news is that this comes as a result of recent growth in independent labels (see Figure 5.1).

The Indies Grow with Digital Music

The rise of rock and roll in the 1950s and early 1960s showcased a rich diversity of independent labels—including Sun, Stax, Chess, and Motown—all vying for a share of the new music. That tradition lives on today. In contrast to the three global players, some five thousand large and small independent production houses (indies) record music that appears to be less commercial. Often struggling enterprises,

FIGURE 5.1 // U.S. MARKET SHARE OF THE MAJOR LABELS IN THE RECORDING INDUSTRY, 2015

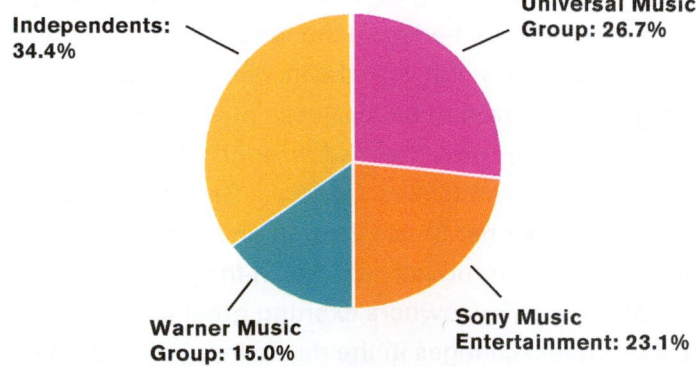

Independents: 34.4%

Universal Music Group: 26.7%

Warner Music Group: 15.0%

Sony Music Entertainment: 23.1%

Data from: Nielsen Music, 2016, and *Billboard.* Figures are rounded.

indies require only a handful of people to operate them. For years, indies accounted for 10 to 15 percent of all music releases. But with the advent of downloads and streaming, the enormous diversity of independent-label music became much more accessible, and the market share of indies more than doubled in size. Indies often still depend on wholesale distributors to promote and sell their music, or enter into deals with one of the three major labels to gain wider distribution for their artists (similar to independent filmmakers using major studios for film distribution). Independent labels have produced some of the best-selling artists of recent years: Big Machine Records (Taylor Swift, Rascal Flatts), Dualtone Records (the Lumineers), XL Recordings (Adele, Vampire Weekend), and Cash Money Records (Drake, Nicki Minaj).

Making, Selling, and Profiting from Music

Like most mass media, the music business is divided into several areas, each working in a different capacity. These areas are making the music, selling the music, and dividing the profits. All these areas are essential to the industry, yet there has always been a certain amount of conflict between business concerns and artistic concerns.

Making the Music

For major labels and indies, the process of music producing begins with **A&R (artist and repertoire) agents**, the talent scouts of the industry who discover, develop, and sometimes manage artists. A&R executives at the labels scout new talent and listen to demonstration recordings, or *demos*, from new artists, deciding what music to reject, whom to sign, and which songs to record.

Recording is complex and expensive. A typical recording session involves the artist, the producer, the session engineer, and audio technicians. In charge of the overall recording process, the producer handles most nontechnical elements of the session, including reserving studio space, hiring session musicians if necessary, and making final decisions about the recording's quality. The session engineer oversees the technical aspects of the recording session—everything from choosing recording equipment to managing the audio technicians.

Once the music is made, it has to be distributed. Digital distribution has eased the production and distribution costs involved with producing, storing, and shipping physical recordings, such as CDs and vinyl (which has seen a minor resurgence), yet it comes with its own challenges, as the music industry tries to turn music into money.

Selling the Music

In the recording industry, the product that generates revenue is the music itself. However, selling music is more challenging now than ever before. As recently as 2011, physical recordings (CDs and some vinyl) accounted for

▲ Often many of the year's most acclaimed albums are released by artists on independent labels. Kishi Bashi is the stage name of singer, songwriter, and multi-instrumentalist Kaoru Ishibashi. A member of several indie bands—including Jupiter One and Of Montreal—Ishibashi has performed at major festivals, including SXSW and Austin City Limits. Scott Dudelson/Getty Images

about 50 percent of U.S. music sales. But CD sales declined and now constitute about 22 percent of the U.S. market, while vinyl sales equal about 6 percent (see Figure 5.2). Digital sales—which include digital downloads from online retailers (like iTunes and Amazon), subscription streaming services (like Rhapsody and the paid version of Spotify), free streaming services (like the ad-supported Spotify, YouTube, and Vevo), streaming radio services (like Pandora

FIGURE 5.2 // THE EVOLUTION OF DIGITAL SOUND RECORDING SALES

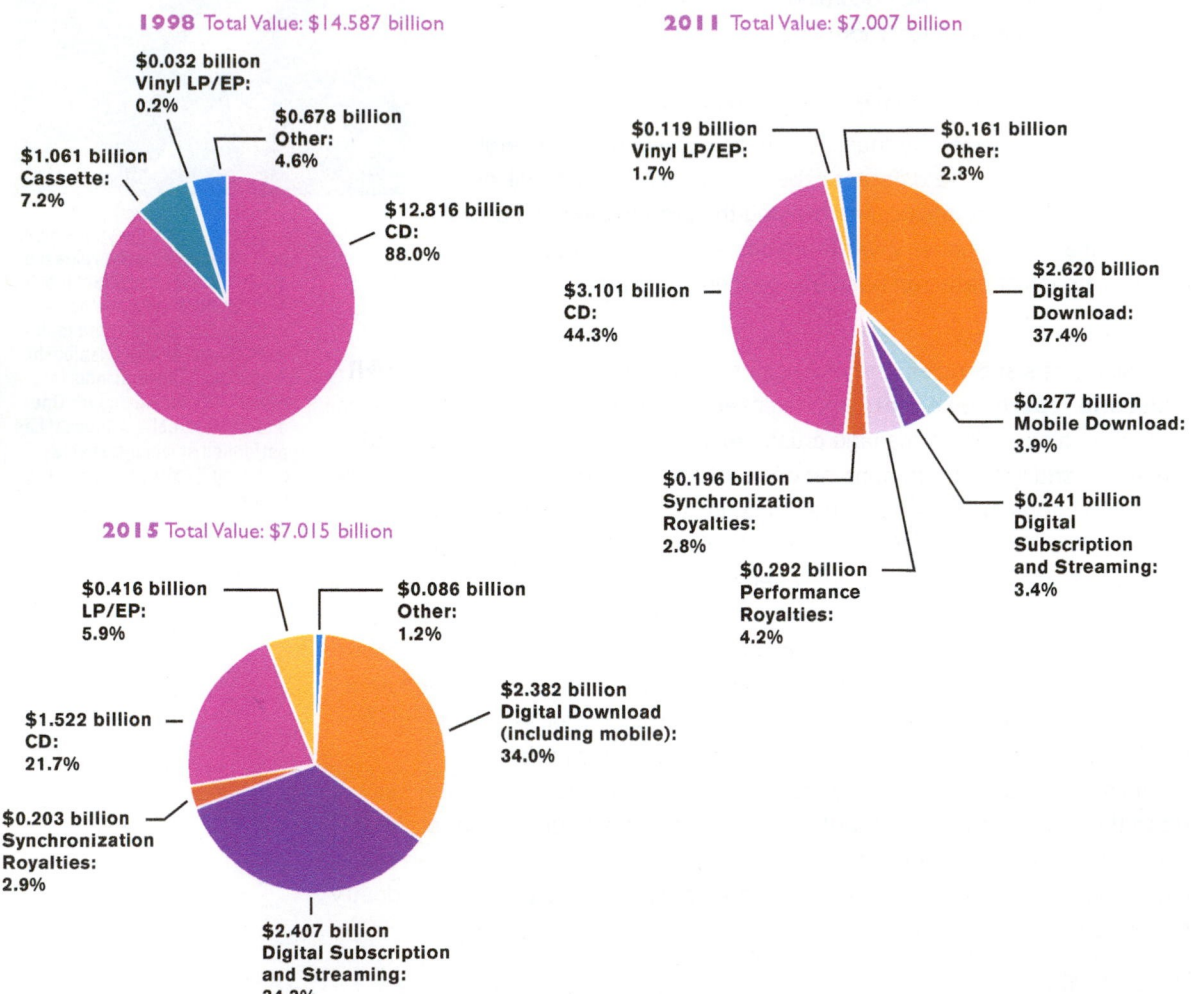

1998 Total Value: $14.587 billion

$0.032 billion Vinyl LP/EP: 0.2%
$0.678 billion Other: 4.6%
$1.061 billion Cassette: 7.2%
$12.816 billion CD: 88.0%

2011 Total Value: $7.007 billion

$0.119 billion Vinyl LP/EP: 1.7%
$0.161 billion Other: 2.3%
$3.101 billion CD: 44.3%
$2.620 billion Digital Download: 37.4%
$0.277 billion Mobile Download: 3.9%
$0.196 billion Synchronization Royalties: 2.8%
$0.292 billion Performance Royalties: 4.2%
$0.241 billion Digital Subscription and Streaming: 3.4%

2015 Total Value: $7.015 billion

$0.416 billion LP/EP: 5.9%
$0.086 billion Other: 1.2%
$1.522 billion CD: 21.7%
$0.203 billion Synchronization Royalties: 2.9%
$2.382 billion Digital Download (including mobile): 34.0%
$2.407 billion Digital Subscription and Streaming: 34.3%

Data from: Recording Industry Association of America, Annual Year-End Statistics, www.riaa.com/wp-content/uploads/2016/03/RIAA-2015-Year-End-shipments-memo.pdf. Figures are rounded.

Note: 1998 is the year before Napster arrived and the peak year of industry revenue. In 2011, digital product revenue surpassed physical product revenue for the first time. Synchronization royalties are those from music being licensed for use in television, movies, and advertisements.

and iHeartRadio), ringtones, and synchronization fees (payments for use of music in various media, such as film, TV, and advertising)—have grown to capture over 70 percent of the U.S. market.

In previous decades, the primary sales outlets for music were direct-retail music stores (independents or chains) and general retail outlets like Walmart, Best Buy, and Target. But after more than fifteen years of declining CD sales in the United States, direct-retail music stores largely disappeared, and big retailers now typically opt for stocking only top-selling CDs rather than offering a variety of choices.

Total U.S. music sales hit a peak of $14.6 billion in 1998, but revenue started shrinking in 2000 as file-sharing began undercutting CD sales. Within about a decade, annual music industry revenue was only half what it had been, dropping to $7 billion by 2011, where it has hovered ever since.

The international recording industry is a major proponent of music streaming services because they are a new revenue source. (For more on other revenue sources, see "The Digital Turn Case Study: 360 Degrees of Music" on page 160.) Although **online piracy**—unauthorized online file-sharing—still exists, the advent of advertising-supported music streaming services has satisfied consumer demand for free music and weakened interest in illegal file-swapping. There are now almost four hundred licensed online music services worldwide.[8]

Dividing the Profits

The complex relationship between artists and businesspeople in the recording industry (including label executives and retailers) becomes especially obvious in the struggle over who gets how much money. To see how this works, let's consider the costs and profits from a typical $1.29 iTunes digital download. iTunes gets 30 percent of every song sale, which equals about $0.40 per song. A standard $0.09 royalty for the song publisher and writer leaves about $0.60 for the record company. Artists at a typical royalty rate of about 15 percent would get $0.20 from the song download.

Another venue for digital music is streaming services. Spotify reports that, similar to Apple's iTunes, it pays out about 70 percent of its revenue to music-rights holders (divided between the label, performers, and songwriters), retaining about 30 percent for itself. Spotify uses a formula (see Figure 5.3) to pay

FIGURE 5.3 // SPOTIFY ROYALTY SYSTEM

Spotify Monthly Revenue × (Artist's Spotify Streams / Total Spotify Streams) × Approx. 70% to Music Labels/Owners × Artist's Royalty Rate = Artist Earnings

Data from: www.spotifyartists.com/spotify-explained/, accessed October 17, 2016.

The Digital Turn

360 Degrees of Music

It used to be that recording labels made most or all of their money by receiving a percentage of the money generated by the sale of physical media, such as CDs and records. But the arrival of the digital turn saw sales revenue cut in half in little over a decade; in response, the recording industry is turning to 360-degree agreements. Defined by legal scholar Sara Karubian as "a legal contract between a musical artist and one company incorporating components of an artist's career that have traditionally been handled by separate contracts with different companies," the 360-degree deal gives a single corporation control over everything, from merchandising and publishing to endorsements and touring.[1]

This means that in addition to the money a record company would make from sales of recordings, the company would also get a cut of money from concert tours, publishing (if the artist is also the songwriter), merchandise, endorsements, even television and movie appearances, for the length of the contract. In theory, the record company would help organize, market, and cover the up-front costs of concert tours, merchandise production, and so on. The recording industry describes these deals as mutually beneficial, centralizing and maximizing revenue for the artist and the label at a time when both are suffering from the drop in music recording sales.

But in practice, critics worry that there may be downsides to these arrangements. Depending on the negotiated deal, a 360-degree arrangement might allow a record label to take a chunk of the profit from a concert tour or song sales even if the label didn't help fund or promote it. These deals also shift power back to conglomerates at a time when more indie labels have gained traction in the industry.

As an alternative to signing a 360-degree agreement, some artists are content to become "touring bands," making a little money off albums and singles but using them primarily to promote their live shows and accompanying merchandise. Musical acts with large enough fan bases may also follow the lead of British alternative rock group Radiohead, which handles its career without contracted-label backing. But while few big artists can maintain a label-free career, many more are offering fans the option of buying their music directly through the artist's or the label's Web site, often selling exclusive packages that may include digital downloads, vinyl albums, T-shirts, limited edition releases, and concert tickets. In these cases, artists are allowing multiple media to converge into their own hands. Whether through 360-degree deals, touring careers, or a self-releasing strategy, convergence is changing the way many musicians make money.

....

⊙ **Visit Launchpad** to watch a clip showing Katy Perry on tour. How might an expensive tour bring in additional money for an artist like Perry?

launchpadworks.com

the music labels, which then pay the artists based on how much Spotify earns and how many times a song is played compared to all other songs played in a given month. On average, each stream is worth between $0.006 and $0.0084. Depending on the popularity of the song, that could add up to a little or a lot of money—though even a play count of one million would still only net between $6,000 and $8,400 dollars.[9]

Songs played on Internet radio, like Pandora, Slacker, or iHeartRadio, have yet another formula for determining royalties. In 2003, the nonprofit group SoundExchange was established to collect royalties for Internet radio. SoundExchange charges fees of $0.0022 per stream for subscription (premium) services, and $0.0017 per stream for nonsubscription (free) services.

Finally, video services like YouTube and Vevo generate advertising revenue through music videos, which can attract tens of millions of views. There aren't standard formulas for sharing ad revenue from music videos, but there is movement in that direction. In 2012, Universal Music Group and the National Music Publishers' Association agreed that music publishers would be paid 15 percent of advertising revenues generated by music videos licensed for use on YouTube and Vevo.

In addition to sales royalties, there are also performance and mechanical royalties that go to various participants in the industry. A *performance royalty* is paid to artists and music publishers whenever a song they created or own is played in any money-making medium or venue—such as on the radio, on television, in a film, or in a restaurant. Performance royalties are collected and paid out by the three major music performance rights organizations: ASCAP; the

◄ Solomon Linda (on far left, pictured with his singing group, the Original Evening Birds), the writer of the frequently covered hit song "The Lion Sleeps Tonight," signed over the copyright for the song for 10 shillings—the equivalent of 87 cents today—in 1952. After Linda's death in 1962, with only $22 to his name, his family fought for the royalties he should have received, resulting in a successful financial settlement for the family in **2006.** Naashon Falk/Full Frame

Society of European Stage Authors and Composers (SESAC); and Broadcast Music, Inc. (BMI). Songwriters also receive a *mechanical royalty* each time a recording of their song is sold. The mechanical royalty is usually split between the music publisher and the songwriter. However, songwriters sometimes sell their copyrights to publishers to make a short-term profit. In these cases, they forgo the long-term royalties they would have received by retaining the copyright.

Sound Recording in a Democratic Society

Of all the developments that have unfolded since sound recording became a mass medium, controversies sparked by some forms of popular music have raised the most provocative questions about music's role in our democracy. Battles over what artists should be allowed to say in a song and how they should behave on stage or in a video speak to the heart of democratic expression. Are songs that express violent intent toward gay people, women, or ethnic or racial groups hate crimes? Are songs protected as free speech under the First Amendment of the U.S. Constitution? Moreover, will the ongoing consolidation of the industry by a few powerful music labels encourage them to "approve" lyrics and other forms of musical expression only if doing so will earn them maximum profits? Will the Internet and the shift to digital downloads and music streaming continue to create more spaces for independent music to grow and for alternative voices to be heard? Popular musical forms that push at cultural boundaries face a dilemma: how to uphold the right to free expression while resisting control by companies bent on maximizing profits. Since the 1950s, forms of rock music have arisen to break through boundaries, then have been reined in to create a successful commercial product, then have reemerged as new agents of rebellion—and on and on, repeating the cycle.

Still, this dynamic between popular music's innovation and capitalism's profit motive seems like an ongoing dance that has sustained—at least until the age of the Internet—the economic structure of the music industry. The major labels need indies to identify and develop new and fresh talent. And talent is fresh only if it seems alternative or less commercial and comes from nonmainstream origins, such as ethnic communities, backyard garages, dance parties, and neighborhood clubs. For a long time, it was taken as a given that musicians need the major labels if they want to distribute their work widely, become famous, and reach large audiences. But examination of major label practices, in terms of both business and artist relations, may not reinforce this belief any longer, especially given the considerable success of several musical acts that have never been on a major label. A major component of media literacy as related to popular music involves evaluating the usefulness and pitfalls of the conglomerates that attempt to lead the industry. It also involves considering the ways in which the digital turn has changed this dynamic—and what is staying the same. The interdependence of artists and businesses presents alluring opportunities (and potential trade-offs) for participants in the industry as well as those who watch and analyze it.

CHAPTER ESSENTIALS

Review

- In the development stage of sound recording, inventors experimented with sound technology; in the entrepreneurial stage, people sought to make money from the developing technology; finally, in the mass medium stage, entrepreneurs figured out how to cheaply produce and distribute multiple copies of recordings.

- The introduction of **audiotape** in the 1940s paved the way for commercial **stereo** recording.

- Records and tapes are examples of **analog recording**. **Digital recording**, which got its start in the 1970s, enabled the creation of **compact discs** and later the **MP3** file format, which would revolutionize sound recording and lead the way to digital downloading and music streaming.

- As sound recording became a mass medium, it fueled the growth of **pop music**, with numerous genres evolving from a common foundation (the first of which were **blues** and **jazz**). Pop

led to the creation of major genres in modern American music, including **rock and roll, rhythm and blues (R&B), soul, folk music, punk rock, grunge, alternative rock, indie rock, hip-hop, gangster rap**, and **country**.

- Rock and roll broke down many racial divisions in American culture, giving rise to genres like **rockabilly**. Yet the early rock and roll industry also promoted white **cover music** versions of black artists' songs, undermining black songwriters and performers.

- Over the years, the recording industry has gone from numerous competing labels and independent production houses, or **indies**, to a few major labels swallowing up the indies and buying each other out. Recently, however, indies have been growing again.

- The process of sound recording often starts with **A&R (artist and repertoire) agents**, who find new talent for record companies to recruit. From there, artists work with their record labels to record music, promote their music, and go on tour.

- In the recording industry, artists and businesspeople divide profits in a variety of ways, depending on how the money is generated. Revenue is earned through the sales of digital downloads and recordings on CD and vinyl, as well as through fees and royalties paid by online music streaming services, online radio stations, and third parties who want to use a song in other media, like films. The ease of music streaming has helped to weaken interest in **online piracy**.

- Some forms of popular music have raised questions about music's role in our democracy, such as what artists should be allowed to say in a song and whether or not they are protected under the First Amendment. The challenge becomes how to support freedom of expression while resisting powerful control by companies whose profit motives are usually paramount.

Key Terms

audiotape, p. 137

stereo, p. 138

analog recording, p. 138

digital recording, p. 138

compact discs, p. 138

MP3, p. 138

pop music, p. 140

jazz, p. 141

rock and roll, p. 144

blues, p. 144

rhythm and blues (R&B), p. 145

cover music, p. 145

rockabilly, p. 147

soul, p. 149

folk music, p. 150

punk rock, p. 151

grunge, p. 152

alternative rock, p. 152

indie rock, p. 152

hip-hop, p. 153

gangster rap, p. 153

country, p. 154

indies, p. 156

A&R (artist and repertoire) agents, p. 157

online piracy, p. 159

Study Questions

1. How did sound recording survive the advent of radio and the Great Depression?

2. How did rock and roll significantly influence two mass media industries?

3. Why did hip-hop and punk rock emerge as significant musical forms in the late 1970s and 1980s? What do their developments have in common, and how are they different?

4. What are some of the major changes the recording industry experienced as a result of the digital turn? What have these changes meant for artists? For record labels? For consumers?

5. How does popular music push the boundaries of the First Amendment? Why might music be worthy of those constitutional guarantees of free speech?

Popular Radio and the Origins of Broadcasting

"You can't stop technology, nor can you control it. The only winning strategy is to embrace it—and embrace it as early as you can."[1] So says Bob Pittman, the media executive who founded MTV in the 1980s and who became an executive at Clear Channel Communications, the largest radio corporation in the United States, in 2010.

Long before Pittman was hired, a profit-minded Clear Channel embraced technology by making drastic cuts to news and programming staffs at its local radio stations across the country and simulcasting much of the same programming (including prerecorded announcers playing as if live) across multiple distant cities. This is how Clear Channel became the poster child for the success—and the excess—of media consolidation following the Telecommunications Act of 1996.

Not only a radio giant, the company has long been one of the biggest live-music-event promoters and outdoor billboard owners, among its other media and entertainment enterprises. But the technologies of station consolidation and automation were not entirely a winning strategy for Clear

◄ iHeartRadio has gone from a radio giant to a thoroughly converged media powerhouse. The company—still the largest owner of terrestrial radio stations in the United States—is also investing in online media, billboards, concerts, and other live performances. Here, hip-hop star Drake performs at the iHeart Radio Music Festival in Las Vegas. John Shearer/Getty Images

Channel. From owning more than 1,200 stations at its peak in 2005, it sold off hundreds of stations a decade later, settling at about 860 stations. During that time, it earned a reputation as the company that killed much of local radio news, stifled deejays' individuality and passion for music, and lost sight of the public's interest.

Under Pittman, part of embracing technology is an attempt to create a new reputation for Clear Channel. So in 2014, Clear Channel Communications became iHeartMedia, named to reflect the brand of its new streaming radio network, iHeartRadio. Although the majority of profits at iHeartMedia still come from its terrestrial AM and FM radio stations, iHeartMedia is banking on its 1,900 live-broadcast and digital-only streaming radio stations (along with its new on-demand streaming service) for the future.[2]

Whereas Clear Channel was distant and corporate, iHeartMedia is throwing its promotional energy into a number of national music events, including the iHeartRadio Music Festival, the iHeartRadio Ultimate Pool Party, the iHeartRadio Jingle Ball Concert Tour, the iHeartRadio Country Festival, the iHeartRadio Ultimate Valentine's Escape, and the iHeartRadio Fiesta Latina. True to its word, the company's professed strategy is "delivering entertaining and informative content across multiple platforms, including broadcast, mobile, and digital as well as events," and then delivering its audiences to "advertisers, business partners, music labels, and artists."[3]

Is this the future of radio? Other radio corporations and stations around the world are also part of the trend toward streaming audio. But does streaming mean that the radio industry is running itself out of the local radio business? Pittman doesn't think so. "In the most simple terms, what we added were more radios. We've always had radios in the car, radios by the bed, and radios at work, and now we also have what are new radios to the consumer—digital devices—at workstations and in everyone's hands," Pittman says. "More ways to listen to the radio means more occasions for our listeners to connect to our legendary brands and our one of a kind personalities—and it's a very good thing for us, our listeners, our advertisers, and the music industry."[4]

THE STORY OF RADIO—from its invention in the late nineteenth century to its current incarnation as a multitechnology mass medium—is one of the most remarkable in media history. In the United States, the early days of network radio gave Americans "a national identity" and "a chance to share in a common experience."[5] Even with the arrival of television in the 1950s, the recent "corporatization" of broadcasting, and the demographic segmentation of radio today, this medium has continued to play a powerful role in our lives.

Likewise, the ways in which legislators a century ago wrote the first laws governing radio set the stage for later laws written to cover all forms of electronic mass media, from television to cable to the Internet. For people throughout the nation, the music and talk emanating every day from their radios, PCs, and handheld devices powerfully shape their political opinions, social mores, and (owing to advertisements) purchasing decisions. In this chapter, we will explore these themes by:

- **examining radio's early history, including how its evolution from one-to-one to one-to-many communication led to new regulations and innovations in programming**

- **looking at how technological advances such as transistors and FM sparked the rise of format radio**

- **familiarizing ourselves with the array of characteristics defining radio today, such as format specialization, nonprofit business models, and digital radio technologies**

- **exploring the economics behind modern radio, including advertising and consolidation of ownership over the public airwaves**

- **considering radio's influence on American culture in an age when control of the public airwaves lies in fewer hands than ever**

The Early History of Radio

Radio did not emerge as a full-blown mass medium until the 1920s, though its development can be traced back to the introduction of the telegraph in the 1840s. As with most media, inventors tinkered in these earliest years with the technologies of the day to address practical needs. The telegraph and early experiments with wireless transmission set the stage for radio as a communication medium.

Inventors Paving the Way: Morse, Maxwell, and Hertz

The **telegraph**—the precursor of radio technology—was invented in the United States in the 1840s and was the first technology to enable messages to move faster than human travel. This meant that news and other messages

LaunchPad
launchpadworks.com

Use **LearningCurve** to review concepts from this chapter.

could be transmitted from coast to coast within minutes, rather than the days required to physically carry information from place to place. American artist and inventor Samuel Morse initially developed this practical system of sending electrical impulses from a transmitter through a cable to a reception device. Telegraph operators used what became known as **Morse code**—a series of dots and dashes that stood for letters of the alphabet and interrupted the electrical current along a wire cable. By 1844, Morse had set up the first telegraph line, which linked Washington, D.C., and Baltimore, Maryland. By 1861, telegraph lines stretched from coast to coast. Just five years later, the first transatlantic cable, capable of transmitting about six words a minute, ran between Newfoundland and Ireland along the ocean floor.

Though revolutionary, the telegraph had significant limitations. For one thing, it couldn't transmit the human voice. Moreover, because it depended on wires, it was useless for anyone seeking to communicate with ships at sea. The world needed a telegraph *without* wires. In the mid-1860s, Scottish physicist James Maxwell theorized the existence of **radio waves**, which could be harnessed to send signals from one place to another without wires. In the 1880s, German physicist Heinrich Hertz tested Maxwell's theory by using electrical sparks that emitted **electromagnetic waves**, invisible electronic impulses similar to light. The experiment was the first recorded transmission and reception of radio waves, and it would dramatically advance the development of wireless communication.

Innovators in Wireless: Marconi, Fessenden, and De Forest

As the nineteenth century unfolded, inventors building on the earlier technologies continued improving wireless communication. New developments took wireless from **narrowcasting** (person-to-person or point-to-point transmission of messages) to **broadcasting** (transmission from one point to multiple listeners; also known as one-to-many communication).

Marconi: The Father of Wireless Telegraphy

In 1894, a twenty-year-old, self-educated Italian engineer named Guglielmo Marconi read Hertz's work. He quickly realized that developing a way to send high-speed messages over great distances would transform communication, commercial shipping, and the military. The young engineer set out to make wireless technology practical. After successfully figuring out how to build a wireless communication device that could send Morse code from a transmitter to a receiver, Marconi traveled to England in 1896. There, he received a patent on **wireless telegraphy**, a form of voiceless *point-to-point communication*.

▼ Guglielmo Marconi (1874–1937) transmitted the first radio signal across the Atlantic Ocean in 1901. He shared the 1909 Nobel Prize in Physics for his contributions to wireless telegraphy, soon required on all seagoing ships and credited with saving more than seven hundred lives when the *Titanic* sank in 1912. SSPL/The Images Works

In London the following year, the Italian inventor formed the Marconi Wireless Telegraph Company, later known as British Marconi. He began installing wireless technology on British naval and private commercial ships. This left other innovators to explore the wireless transmission of voice and music, later known as **wireless telephony** and eventually **radio**. In 1899, Marconi opened a branch in the United States, commonly referred to as American Marconi. That same year, he sent the first wireless Morse code signal across the English Channel to France. In 1901, he relayed the first wireless signal from Cornwall, England, across the Atlantic Ocean to St. John's, Newfoundland. History often cites Marconi as the "father of radio," but Russian scientist Alexander Popov accomplished similar feats in St. Petersburg at the same time, and Nikola Tesla, a Serbian Croatian inventor who had immigrated to the United States, invented a wireless electrical device in 1892.

Fessenden: The First Voice Broadcast

Marconi had taken major steps in London and the United States. But it was Canadian engineer Reginald Fessenden who transformed wireless telegraphy into *one-to-many communication.* Fessenden is credited with providing the first voice broadcast. Formerly a chief chemist for Thomas Edison, he went to work for the U.S. Navy and eventually for General Electric (GE), where he focused on improving the frequency of wireless signals. Both the navy and GE were interested in the potential for voice transmission. On Christmas Eve in 1906, using a powerful transmitter built by GE, Fessenden gave his first public demonstration, sending his violin performance of "O Holy Night" and a reading of a Bible passage through the airwaves from his station at Brant Rock, Massachusetts, to an unknown number of shipboard operators off the Atlantic Coast.

De Forest: Birthing Modern Electronics

American inventor Lee De Forest improved the usefulness of broadcasting by greatly increasing listeners' ability to hear dots and dashes, and later speech and music, on a receiver. In 1906, he developed the Audion vacuum tube, which detected and amplified radio signals. The device was essential to the development of voice transmission, long-distance radio, and (eventually) television. Although De Forest had the patent for the Audion, he was accused in court and by fellow engineers of stealing others' ideas, even when the court ruled in his favor.[6] Many historians consider the Audion—which powered radios until the arrival of transistors and solid-state circuits in the 1950s—the origin of modern electronics.

In 1907, De Forest demonstrated his invention's power and practical value by broadcasting a performance

▼ Inventor Lee De Forest's (1873–1961) lengthy radio career was marked by incredible innovations, missed opportunities, and poor business practices. In the end, De Forest was upset that radio content had stooped, in his opinion, to such low standards. With a passion for opera, he had hoped radio would be a tool for elite culture. Everett Collection, Inc.

by Metropolitan opera tenor Enrico Caruso to his friends in New York. The next year, he and his wife, Nora, played records into a microphone from atop the Eiffel Tower in Paris; the signals were picked up by receivers up to five hundred miles away.

Early Regulation of Wireless/Radio

By the turn of the twentieth century, radio had become a new force in American life. Recognizing radio's power to shape political opinion, economic dynamics, and military strategy and tactics, U.S. lawmakers moved to ensure U.S. control over the fledgling industry. With this goal in mind, legislators first defined radio as a shared resource for the public good. They then passed laws regulating how the public airwaves could be used and in what manner private businesses could take part in the industry.

Providing Public Safety

Because radio waves crossed state and national borders, legislators determined that broadcasting constituted a "natural resource" — a kind of interstate commerce — that should be regulated on the public's behalf in the public's best interests. Therefore, radio waves could not be owned, just licensed for use for a set period of time.

The first public safety rule came in 1910, when Congress passed the **Wireless Ship Act**. The law mandated that all major U.S. seagoing ships carrying more than fifty passengers and traveling more than two hundred miles off either coast be equipped with wireless equipment with a one-hundred-mile range. The importance of this act was underscored by the *Titanic* disaster in 1912, when over seven hundred passengers were saved by nearby ships responding to the passenger liner's radio distress signals. In the wake of the *Titanic* tragedy, Congress passed the **Radio Act of 1912**. It required all radio stations on land or at sea to be licensed and assigned special call letters. The act helped bring some order to the airwaves, which had been increasingly jammed with amateur radio operators. This act also formally adopted the SOS Morse-code distress signal.

Ensuring National Security

By 1915, more than twenty American companies sold wireless point-to-point communication systems, primarily for use in ship-to-shore communication. American Marconi (a subsidiary of British Marconi) was the biggest of these companies. But with World War I erupting in Europe, the U.S. Navy questioned the wisdom of allowing a foreign-controlled company to wield so much power over communication. When the United States entered the war in 1917, the government closed down all amateur radio operations, took control of key radio transmitters, and blocked British Marconi from purchasing radio equipment from General Electric. These moves addressed concerns about national security. They also enabled the United States to reduce Britain's influence over communication and tightened U.S. control over the emerging wireless infrastructure.

RCA: The Formation of an American Radio Monopoly

Some members of Congress, along with some business leaders, opposed federal legislation granting the government or the navy a radio monopoly. To secure a place in the fast-evolving industry, GE proposed a plan by which it would create a *private-sector monopoly*—a privately owned company that would have the government's approval to dominate the radio industry. In 1919, the plan was accepted by the powers that be at both GE and the U.S. Navy—the government branch most prominently fighting for control of the radio industry in America. GE founded the **Radio Corporation of America (RCA)** to purchase and pool patents from the navy, AT&T, GE, the former American Marconi, and other companies to ensure U.S. control over the manufacture of radio transmitters and receivers. Under the various agreements, AT&T made most of the transmitters; GE (and later Westinghouse) made radio receivers; and RCA administered patents, collected royalties, and redistributed them to the others.[7]

KDKA: The First Commercial Radio Station

With the advent of the United States' global dominance in mass communication, many people became intrigued by radio's potential. Amateur stations popped up in places like San Jose, California; Medford, Massachusetts; New York; Detroit; and Pierre, South Dakota. The best-known early station was begun by an engineer named Frank Conrad, who worked for GE's rival, Westinghouse Electric Company. In 1916, he set up a radio studio above his Pittsburgh garage by placing a microphone in front of a phonograph. Conrad broadcast music and news to his friends (whom he supplied with receivers) two evenings a week on experimental station 8XK. When a Westinghouse executive got wind of Conrad's activities in 1920, he established KDKA, generally regarded as the first commercial (profit-based) broadcast station. The following year, the U.S. Commerce Department officially licensed five radio stations for operation; by early 1923, more than six hundred commercial and noncommercial stations were operating. Just two years later, a whopping 5.5 million radio sets were in use across America—made by companies such as GE and Westinghouse and costing about $55 ($664 in today's dollars). Radio was officially a mass medium.

▲ Westinghouse engineer Frank Conrad transformed his hobby into Pittsburgh's KDKA. Although this station is widely celebrated as the first broadcasting outlet, one can't underestimate the influence Westinghouse had in promoting this "historical first." Westinghouse saw the celebration of Conrad's garage studio as a way to market the company's radio equipment. The resulting legacy has thus overshadowed other individuals who also experimented with radio broadcasting. Bettmann/Getty Images

The Networks

With the establishment of the private sector's involvement in radio, the groundwork was laid for radio to take off as a business, which would enable commercial station owners (and the advertisers that funded them) to reach more listeners more efficiently than ever. The radio **network** arose: a cost-saving operation that links a group of affiliate or subsidiary broadcast stations that share programming produced at a central location. (At that time, stations were linked through special phone lines; today, they're linked through satellite relays.)

The network system enabled stations to control program costs and avoid unnecessary duplication of content creation. Simply put, it was cheaper to produce programs at one station and broadcast them simultaneously over multiple owned or affiliated stations than for each station to generate its own programs. Networks thus brought the best musical, dramatic, and comedic talent to one place, where programs could be produced and then distributed all over the country. This new business model concentrated control of radio in the hands of a few corporate players, all of whom jockeyed for additional power.

AT&T: Making a Power Grab

The shift toward networks began in 1922, when RCA's partnership with AT&T began to unravel. In a major power grab, AT&T, which already had a government-sanctioned monopoly in the telephone business, decided to break its RCA agreements in an attempt to monopolize radio. Identifying the new medium as the "wireless telephone," AT&T argued that broadcasting was merely an extension of its control over the telephone. The corporate giant complained that RCA had gained too much power. In violation of its early agreements with RCA, AT&T began making and selling its own radio receivers.

That same year, AT&T started WEAF (now WNBC) in New York, the first radio station to regularly sell commercial time to advertisers. Advertising, company executives reasoned, would ensure profits long after radio-set sales had saturated the consumer market. AT&T claimed that under the RCA agreements, it had the exclusive right to sell ads, which AT&T called *toll broadcasting*. Most people in radio at the time recoiled at the idea of using the medium for advertising, viewing the medium instead as a public information service. But executives remained riveted by the potential of radio ads to enhance profits.

Still, the initial motivation behind AT&T's toll broadcasting idea was to dominate radio. Through its agreements with RCA, AT&T retained the rights to interconnect the signals between two or more radio stations via telephone wires. By the end of 1924, AT&T had interconnected twenty-two stations in a network to air a talk by President Calvin Coolidge. Some of these stations were owned by AT&T, but most simply consented to become AT&T "affiliates," agreeing to air the phone company's programs.

Seeing AT&T's success, GE, Westinghouse, and RCA launched a competing network. AT&T promptly denied them access to its telephone wires, so the new network used inferior telegraph lines to connect its stations. In 1925, the Justice Department, irritated by AT&T's power grab, redefined patent agreements. AT&T received a monopoly on providing the wires, known as *long lines*, to interconnect stations nationwide. In exchange, AT&T agreed to sell its network to RCA for $1 million and promised not to reenter broadcasting for eight years.

▲ David Sarnoff, creator of NBC and network radio, demonstrated calculated ambition in the radio industry, which can easily be compared to Bill Gates's more recent drive to control the computer software and Internet industries.
Topham/The Image Works

NBC: RCA Forms a Network

The commercial rewards of the network and affiliate system continued to excite executives' imaginations. For example, in September 1926, after RCA bought AT&T's telephone line–based radio network, David Sarnoff, RCA's general manager, created a new subsidiary called the National Broadcasting Company (NBC). NBC's ownership was shared by RCA (50%), General Electric (30%), and Westinghouse (20%). The former group of AT&T stations became known as NBC-Red. The network RCA, GE, and Westinghouse had already been building became NBC-Blue. By 1933, NBC-Red would have twenty-eight affiliates; NBC-Blue, twenty-four.

CBS: A Rival Network Challenges NBC

The network and affiliate system under RCA/NBC thrived throughout most of the 1920s and brought Americans together as never before to participate in the big events of the day. For example, when aviator Charles Lindbergh returned from the first solo transatlantic flight in 1927, an estimated twenty-five to thirty million people listened to his welcome-home party on the six million radio sets then in use. At the time, it was the largest shared audience experience in the history of any mass medium.

During this decade, competition stiffened further within the industry. For instance, in 1928, William Paley, the twenty-seven-year-old son of a Philadelphia cigar company owner, bought the Columbia Phonograph Company and built it into a network later renamed the Columbia Broadcasting System (CBS). Unlike NBC, which actually charged its affiliates up to $96 a week for the privilege of carrying its programming, CBS paid affiliates as much as $50 an hour to carry its programs. By 1933, Paley's efforts had netted CBS more than ninety affiliates, many of which had defected from NBC. Paley also concentrated on developing news programs and entertainment shows, particularly soap operas and comedy-variety series. To that end, CBS raided NBC not just

▲ William S. Paley (*shown standing*), president of Columbia Broadcasting System for more than fifty years, activates the world's largest hookup of radio stations at that time in 1928. Known for his early support of quality programming and network news, Paley was also criticized for undermining his news division to sidestep controversy or increase profits.
Bettmann/Getty Images

for affiliates but also for top talent, such as comedian Jack Benny and singer Frank Sinatra. In 1949, CBS finally surpassed NBC as the highest-rated network on radio.

The Radio Act of 1927

The growing concentration of power in the network and affiliate system raised a red flag for government leaders. Throughout the 1920s to early 1940s, lawmakers would enact many regulations aimed at regaining control over the industry. In particular, by the late 1920s, the government had become alarmed by RCA/NBC's growing influence over radio content. Moreover, as radio moved from narrowcasting to broadcasting, battles among various players over such issues as more frequency space and less channel interference heated up. Manufacturers, engineers, station operators, network executives, and the listening public demanded action to address their conflicting interests. Many wanted more sweeping regulation than the simple licensing function granted under the Radio Act of 1912, which gave the Commerce Department little power to deny a license or unclog the airwaves.

To restore order, Congress passed the **Radio Act of 1927**, which introduced a pivotal new principle: Licensees did not *own* their channels but could use them as long as they operated to serve the "public interest, convenience, or necessity." To oversee licenses and negotiate channel problems, such as too many stations trying to air on too few frequencies, the 1927 act created the **Federal Radio Commission (FRC)**, whose members were appointed by the president.

Although the FRC was intended as a temporary committee, it grew into a powerful regulatory agency. With passage of the **Federal Communications Act of 1934**, the FRC became the **Federal Communications Commission (FCC)**. Its jurisdiction covered not only radio but also the telephone and the telegraph (and later television, cable, and the Internet). More significantly, by this time Congress and the president had sided with the already-powerful radio networks and acceded to a system of advertising-supported commercial broadcasting as best serving the "public interest, convenience, or necessity," overriding the concerns of educational, labor, religious, and citizen broadcasting advocates.

In 1941, an activist FCC set out to break up what it saw as overly large and powerful networks, which led to a Supreme Court ruling forcing RCA to sell NBC-Blue. The divested enterprise became the American Broadcasting Company (ABC). Such government crackdowns brought long-overdue reforms to the radio industry. However, they came too late to prevent considerable damage to noncommercial radio.

The Golden Age of Radio

From the late 1920s to the 1940s, radio basked in a golden age marked by a proliferation of informative and entertaining programs (such as weather forecasts, farm reports, news, music, dramas, quiz shows, variety shows, and comedies). This diversity of programming shaped—and was shaped by—American culture. It also paved the way for programs that Americans would later enjoy on television, as NBC, CBS, and ABC created television networks in the late 1940s and 1950s.

▲ This giant bank of radio network microphones makes us wonder today how President Franklin D. Roosevelt managed to project such an intimate and reassuring tone in his famous fireside chats. Conceived originally to promote FDR's New Deal policies amid the Great Depression, these chats were delivered between 1933 and 1944 and touched on national topics. Roosevelt was the first president to effectively use broadcasting to communicate with citizens. Bettmann/Getty Images

Early Radio Programming

In the early days of radio, only a handful of stations operated in most large radio markets. Through the networks they were affiliated with, these stations broadcast a variety of programs into listeners' homes (and in some cases, their cars). People had favorite evening programs, usually fifteen minutes long. After dinner, families would gather around the radio to hear comedies, dramas, public service announcements, and more. Popular programs included *Amos 'n' Andy* (a serial situation comedy), *The Shadow* (a mystery drama), *The Lone Ranger* (a western), *The Green Hornet* (a crime drama), and *Fibber McGee and Molly* (a comedy), as well as the "fireside chats" regularly presented by President Franklin D. Roosevelt.

Variety shows featuring musical performances and comedy skits planted the seeds for popular TV variety shows that would come later, such as the *Ed Sullivan Show*. *Quiz shows* (including *The Old Time Spelling Bee*) introduced Americans to the thrill of competition. These radio programs set the stage for later competition-based TV shows, ranging from *The Price Is Right* and *Who Wants to Be a Millionaire* to reality-based shows such as *Survivor*, *Project Runway*, and *Top Chef*.

Dramatic programs, mostly radio plays broadcast live from theaters, would inspire later TV dramas, including "soap operas." (The term came into use after Colgate-Palmolive began selling its soap products on dramas it sponsored.) Another type of program, the *serial*, introduced the idea of continuing story lines from one day to the next—a format soon adopted by soap operas and some comedy programs.

Radio as Cultural Mirror

Radio programs powerfully reflected shifts in American culture, including attitudes about race and levels of tolerance for stereotypes. For example, the situation comedy *Amos 'n' Andy* was based on the conventions of the nineteenth-century minstrel show and featured black characters stereotyped as shiftless and stupid. Created as a blackface stage act by two white comedians, Charles Correll and Freeman Gosden, the program was criticized as racist by some at the time; however, NBC and the program's producers claimed that *Amos 'n' Andy* was as popular among black audiences as it was among white listeners.[8]

Early radio research estimated that the program aired in more than half of all radio homes in the nation during the 1930–31 season, making it the most popular radio series in history. In 1951, *Amos 'n' Andy* made a brief transition to television, after Correll and Gosden sold the rights to CBS for $1 million. It became the first TV series to have an all-black cast. But amid a strengthening Civil Rights movement and a formal protest by the National Association for the Advancement of Colored People (NAACP), which argued that "every character is either a clown or a crook," CBS canceled the program in 1953.[9]

The Authority of Radio

In addition to reflecting evolving cultural beliefs, radio increasingly shaped them—in part by being perceived by listeners as the voice of authority. The adaptation of science-fiction author H. G. Wells's *War of the Worlds* (1898) on the radio series *Mercury Theatre on the Air* provides the most notable example of this. Considered the most famous single radio broadcast of all time, *War of*

▲ On Halloween eve in 1938, Orson Welles's radio dramatization of *War of the Worlds* (*left*) created a panic up and down the East Coast, especially in Grover's Mill, New Jersey—the setting for the fictional Martian invasion, which many listeners assumed was real. A seventy-six-year-old Grover's Mill resident (*right*) guarded a warehouse against alien invaders. Hulton Archive/Getty Images (left); Bettmann/Getty Images (right)

the Worlds was produced and hosted by Orson Welles, who also narrated it. On Halloween eve in 1938, the twenty-three-year-old Welles aired the Martian-invasion story in the style of a contemporary radio news bulletin. For people who missed the opening disclaimer, the program sounded like an authentic news report, with apparently eyewitness accounts of battles between Martian invaders and the U.S. Army.

The program triggered a panic among some listeners. In New Jersey, some people walked through the streets with wet towels wrapped around their heads for protection against deadly Martian heat rays. In New York, young men reported to their National Guard headquarters to prepare for battle. Across the nation, calls from terrified citizens jammed police switchboards. The FCC called for stricter warnings both before and during programs imitating the style of radio news.

The Evolution of Radio

In the 1950s, a new form of mass media — television — came on the scene. TV snatched radio's advertisers, program genres, major celebrities, and large evening audiences. The TV set even physically displaced the radio as the living room centerpiece around which families gathered. To survive, players in the radio industry transformed their business model so that they could provide new forms of value for listeners.

Transistors: Making Radio Portable

The portability of radio proved to be a major advantage in the medium's struggle for survival. In the late 1920s, car radios had existed but were considered a luxury. But when Bell Laboratories invented the transistor in 1947, radios became more accessible than ever before—and portable. **Transistors** were small electrical devices that, like vacuum tubes, could receive and amplify radio signals. However, they used less power and gave off less heat than vacuum tubes and were more durable and less expensive. Best of all, they were tiny. The development of transistors let radio go where television could not—to the beach, to the office, into bedrooms and bathrooms, and into nearly all new cars.

The FM Revolution

To replace the shows radio had lost to TV, many people in radio switched the medium's emphasis to music, turning to the recording industry for content. However, making music sound better on radio would require some technological innovation. Until then, radio technology had centered on **AM** (amplitude modulation). This type of modulation was sufficient for radio content such as talk, but it wasn't ideal for music. For that, radio needed **FM** (frequency modulation), which provided greater clarity as well as static-free radio reception.

FM radio had existed for decades. American inventor Edwin Armstrong had discovered and developed it during the 1920s and early 1930s. Between 1930 and 1933, Armstrong filed five patents on FM. The number of FM stations grew to 700 but then fell to 560 by the 1950s, as Armstrong was pulled into legal skirmishes over patents with such heavy hitters as RCA executive David Sarnoff, who had initially supported Armstrong's explorations into FM but then opted to throw his weight behind the development of TV. In 1954, weary from years of legal battles, Armstrong wrote a note apologizing to his wife, removed the air conditioner from his thirteenth-story New York apartment, and jumped to his death. It wasn't until the early 1960s, when the FCC opened up more spectrum space for the superior sound of FM, that FM began to grow into the preferred radio band for music.

The Rise of Format Radio

Once radio became portable and FM was introduced, music began to dominate the medium more than ever. This eventually led to the creation of **format radio**, in which station managers (rather than disc jockeys) controlled the station's hour-by-hour music programming. Of course, in the late 1930s, music had been radio's single biggest staple, accounting for 48 percent of all programming. However, most music was live, which many people considered superior to recorded music. The first disc jockeys demonstrated that recorded music could attract just as many listeners as live music.

As early as 1949, station owner Todd Storz and his program manager in Omaha, Nebraska, noticed that bar patrons and waitresses repeatedly played certain favorite songs from the forty records available in a jukebox. Drawing from jukebox culture, Storz hit on the idea of **rotation**: playing the top songs many times during the day. By the mid-1950s, the **Top 40 format** was born. Although the term *Top 40* derived from the number of records stored in a jukebox, this format came to refer to the forty most popular hits in a given week as measured by record sales.

As format radio grew, program managers combined rapid deejay chatter with the best-selling songs of the day and occasional oldies—popular songs from a few months earlier. Managers created a program log for deejays to follow and sectioned off blocks of roughly four hours throughout the day and night. Each block was designed to appeal to listeners' interests and thus attract more advertising dollars. For instance, a Top 40 station would feature its best deejays in the morning and afternoon periods, during listeners' commutes to and from school or work. Management also made savvy use of research. For example, if statistics showed that teenagers tended to listen to the radio mostly during evening hours and preferred music to news, then stations marketing to teens avoided scheduling news breaks during those hours.

The expansion of FM in the mid-1960s created room for stations to experiment, particularly with classical music, jazz, blues, and non–Top 40 rock songs. Many noncommercial stations broadcast from college campuses, where student deejays and managers rejected the commercialism associated with Top 40 tunes and began playing lesser-known alternative music and longer album cuts.

The Characteristics of Contemporary Radio

Contemporary radio differs markedly from its predecessor. In contrast to the few stations per market in the 1930s, most large markets today include more than forty stations that vie for listener loyalty. With the exception of national network-sponsored news segments and nationally syndicated programs, most programming is locally produced (or made to sound like it) and heavily dependent on the music industry for content. In short, stations today are more specialized. Listeners are loyal to favorite stations, music formats, and even radio personalities, rather than to specific shows, and they generally listen to only four or five stations. More than fifteen thousand radio stations now operate in the United States.

Format Specialization

Radio stations today use a variety of formats to serve diverse groups of listeners (see Figure 6.1). To please advertisers, who want to know exactly who is listening, formats usually target audiences according to their age, income, gender, or race/ethnicity. Radio's specialization enables advertisers to reach smaller target audiences at costs much lower than those for television. The most popular formats include the following:

- **Country.** The most popular format in the nation (except during morning drive time, when news/talk is number one), country is traditionally the default format for small communities with only one radio station. Country music has old roots in radio, starting in 1925 with the influential Grand Ole Opry program on WSM in Nashville.
- **News and talk radio.** As the second most popular format in the nation, news and talk radio has been buoyed by the popularity of personalities like Howard Stern, Tavis Smiley, and Rush Limbaugh. This format tends to cater to adults

FIGURE 6.1 // THE MOST POPULAR RADIO FORMATS IN THE UNITED STATES AMONG PERSONS AGE TWELVE AND OLDER

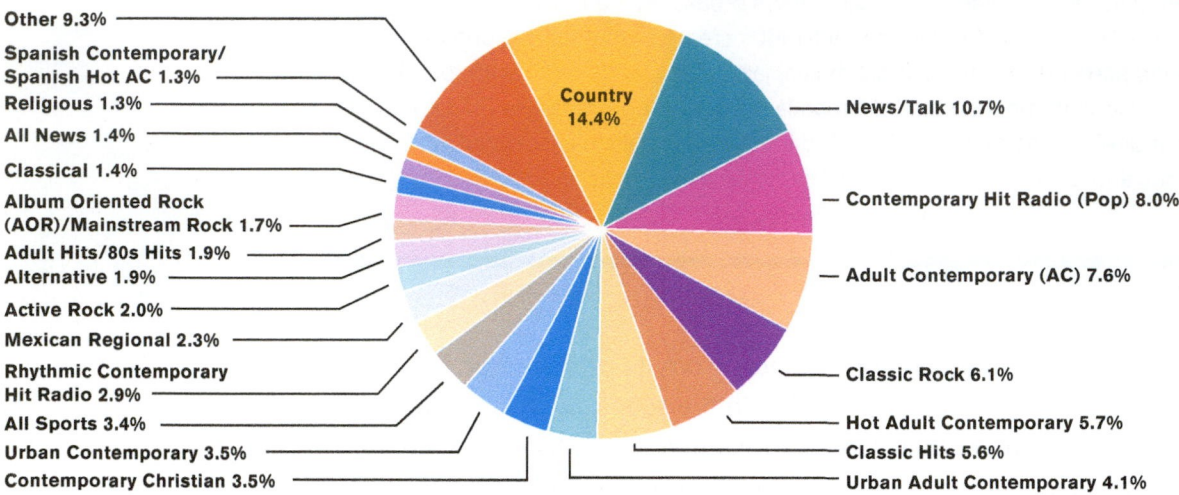

Other 9.3%
Spanish Contemporary/
Spanish Hot AC 1.3%
Religious 1.3%
All News 1.4%
Classical 1.4%
Album Oriented Rock
(AOR)/Mainstream Rock 1.7%
Adult Hits/80s Hits 1.9%
Alternative 1.9%
Active Rock 2.0%
Mexican Regional 2.3%
Rhythmic Contemporary
Hit Radio 2.9%
All Sports 3.4%
Urban Contemporary 3.5%
Contemporary Christian 3.5%

Country 14.4%

News/Talk 10.7%
Contemporary Hit Radio (Pop) 8.0%
Adult Contemporary (AC) 7.6%
Classic Rock 6.1%
Hot Adult Contemporary 5.7%
Classic Hits 5.6%
Urban Adult Contemporary 4.1%

Data from: Nielsen report: "State of the Media: Audio Today 2016, How America Listens," February 25, 2016, http://vhet337bl8816t3lw2ltlf5f.wpengine .netdna-cdn.com/StateofThe%20MediaQ12016.pdf.

over age thirty-five (except for sports talk programs, which draw mostly male sports fans of all ages). Though more expensive to produce than a music format, it appeals to advertisers seeking to target working and middle-class adult consumers (see "Media Literacy Case Study: Host: The Origins of Talk Radio" on pages 184–185).

- **Contemporary hit radio (CHR).** Also called Top 40 radio, CHR encompasses everything from rap to pop rock and appeals to many teens and young adults. Since the mid-1980s, however, these stations have lost ground steadily, as younger generations turned first to MTV and then to online sources for their music, rather than to radio.

- **Adult contemporary (AC).** This format, also known as middle of the road, or MOR, is among radio's oldest and most popular formats. It reaches about 7.6 percent of all listeners, most of them over the age of forty, with an eclectic mix of news, talk, oldies, and soft rock music.

- **Urban contemporary.** In 1947, WDIA in Memphis was the first station to program exclusively for black listeners. This format targets a wide variety of African American listeners, primarily in large cities. Urban contemporary typically plays popular dance, rap, R&B, and hip-hop music.

- **Spanish-language radio.** One of radio's fastest growing, this format is concentrated mostly in large Hispanic markets, such as Miami, New York, Chicago,

Las Vegas, California, Arizona, New Mexico, and Texas. Besides talk shows and news segments in Spanish, this format features a variety of Spanish, Caribbean, and Latin American musical styles.

In addition, today there are other formats that are spin-offs of **album-oriented rock (AOR)**, a format that hit its stride in the 1970s playing both popular and deeper cuts from albums by such artists as Pink Floyd, AC/DC, and Queen. Classic rock serves up rock favorites from the mid-1960s through the 1990s to the baby-boom generation and other listeners who have outgrown Top 40. The oldies format originally served adults who grew up on 1950s and early 1960s rock and roll. As that audience has aged, oldies formats now target younger audiences with the classic hits format, featuring songs from the 1970s, 1980s, and 1990s. The alternative music format recaptures some of the experimental approach of the FM stations of the 1960s, although with much more controlled playlists, and has helped to introduce artists such as Twenty One Pilots and Cage the Elephant.

Research indicates that most people identify closely with the music they listened to as adolescents and young adults. This tendency partially explains why classic hits and classic rock stations combined have surpassed Top 40 stations today. It also helps explain the recent nostalgia for music from the 1980s and 1990s.

Nonprofit Radio and NPR

Although commercial radio dominates the radio spectrum, nonprofit radio maintains a voice. Two government rulings, both in 1948, aided nonprofit radio. Through the first ruling, the government began authorizing noncommercial licenses to stations not affiliated with labor, religion, education, or civic groups. The first license went to Lewis Kimball Hill, a radio reporter and pacifist during World War II who started the **Pacifica Foundation** to run experimental public stations. Pacifica stations have often challenged the status quo in both radio and government. In the second ruling, the FCC approved 10-watt FM stations. Before 1948, radio stations had to have at least 250 watts to get licensed. A 10-watt station with a broadcast range of only about seven miles took very little capital to operate, so the ruling enabled many more people to participate in radio. Many of these tiny stations became training sites for students interested in a broadcasting career.

During the 1960s, nonprofit broadcasting found a new friend in Congress, which proved sympathetic to an old idea: using radio and television as educational tools. In 1967, Congress created the first noncommercial networks: **National Public Radio (NPR)** and the **Public Broadcasting Service (PBS)**. Under the provisions of the **Public Broadcasting Act of 1967** and the **Corporation for Public Broadcasting (CPB)**, NPR and PBS

Host: The Origins of Talk Radio
By David Foster Wallace

The origins of contemporary political talk radio can be traced to three phenomena of the 1980s. The first of these involved AM music stations getting absolutely murdered by FM, which could broadcast music in stereo and allowed for much better fidelity on high and low notes. The human voice, on the other hand, is midrange and doesn't require high fidelity. The eighties' proliferation of talk formats on the AM band also provided new careers for some music deejays—Don Imus, Morton Downey Jr.—whose chatty personas didn't fit well with FM's all-about-the-music ethos.

The second big factor was the repeal, late in Ronald Reagan's second term, of what was known as the Fairness Doctrine. This was a 1949 FCC rule designed to minimize any possible restrictions on free speech caused by limited access to broadcasting outlets. The idea was that, as one of the conditions for receiving an FCC broadcast license, a station had to "devote reasonable attention to the coverage of controversial issues of public importance" and consequently had to provide "reasonable, although not necessarily equal," opportunities for opposing sides to express their views. Because of the Fairness Doctrine, talk stations had to hire and program symmetrically: If you had a

▲ After the Fairness Doctrine was repealed in the mid-1980s, stations were free to air hours of partisan political programming—including that offered by talk show host Rush Limbaugh—without being required to give equal time to opposing viewpoints. Since the 1990s radio stations have found Limbaugh's style of over-the-top conservative programming lucrative, though his attacks on women and minorities have resulted in some backlash against him, his advertisers, and the stations that carry him. shepard sherbell/Getty Images

three-hour program whose host's politics were on one side of the ideological spectrum, you had to have another long-form program whose host more or less spoke for the other side. Weirdly enough, up through the mid-eighties it was usually the U.S. Right that benefited most from the doctrine. Pioneer talk syndicator Ed McLaughlin, who managed San Francisco's KGO in the 1960s, recalls that "I had more liberals on the air than I had conservatives or even moderates for that matter, and I had a hell of a time finding the other voice."

The Fairness Doctrine's repeal was part of the sweeping deregulations of the Reagan era, which aimed to liberate all sorts of industries from government interference and allow them to compete freely in the marketplace. The old, Rooseveltian logic of the doctrine had been that since the

Excerpted from David Foster Wallace, "Host: The Origins of Talk Radio," Atlantic, April 2005, 66–68.

▶ Web Clip

YouTube.com has many clips of talk radio hosts on television. For example, do a quick search for 'ROUND 2: Michael Moore on The Sean Hannity Show, Friday, October 9th, 2009' posted by mmflint. How might a talk radio host vary his or her broadcasting routine for a different medium?

airwaves belonged to everyone, a license to profit from those airwaves conferred on the broadcast industry some special obligation to serve the public interest. Commercial radio broadcasting was not, in other words, originally conceived as just another for-profit industry; it was supposed to meet a higher standard of social responsibility. After 1987, though, just another industry is pretty much what radio became, and its only real responsibility now is to attract and retain listeners in order to generate revenue.

More or less on the heels of the Fairness Doctrine's repeal came the West Coast and then national syndication of *The Rush Limbaugh Show* through Mr. McLaughlin's EFM Media. Limbaugh is the third great progenitor of today's political talk radio partly because he's a host of extraordinary, once-in-a-generation talent and charisma — bright, loquacious, witty, complexly authoritative — whose show's blend of news, entertainment, and partisan analysis became the model for legions of imitators. But he was also the first great promulgator of the Mainstream Media's Liberal Bias idea. This turned out to be a brilliantly effective rhetorical move, since the MMLB concept functioned simultaneously as a standard around which Rush's audience could rally, as an articulation of the need for right-wing (that is, unbiased) media, and as a mechanism by which any criticism or refutation of conservative ideas could be dismissed (either as biased or as the product of indoctrination by biased media). Boiled way down, the MMLB thesis is able both to exploit and to perpetuate many conservatives' dissatisfaction with extant media sources — and it's this dissatisfaction that cements political talk radio's large and loyal audience.

APPLYING THE CRITICAL PROCESS

DESCRIPTION Check your local listings to find a typical morning or late-afternoon hour of a popular right-wing talk-news radio station and an hour of a typical left-wing talk-news radio station from the same time period. Listen to each program over a two- to three-day period. Keep a log of what topics are covered and what news stories are reported.

ANALYSIS Look for patterns. What kinds of stories are covered? What kinds of topics are discussed? Create a chart to categorize the stories. How much time is given to *reporting* (clearly verified information) compared to time devoted to *opinion*? What kinds of interview sources are used?

INTERPRETATION What do these patterns mean? Is there a balance between reporting and opinion? Do you detect any bias, and if so, how did you determine this?

EVALUATION Do you agree with the 1949–1987 Fairness Doctrine rule that broadcasting should provide "reasonable, although not necessarily equal," attention to "controversial issues of public importance"? Why or why not? From which station did you learn the most, and which station did you find most entertaining? Explain. What did you like and dislike about each station?

ENGAGEMENT Contact the local general manager, program director, or news director at the stations you analyzed. Ask them what their goals are for their daily talk-news programming and what audience they are trying to reach. Incorporate their comments into a report on your findings. Finally, offer suggestions on how to make the programming at each station better.

▲ National Public Radio has created a variety of well-received podcasts, ranging from entertainment stories to hard news, to exist alongside its radio programming. The NPR Politics Podcast team (shown here) typically records a show once a week. Because podcasts aren't part of the set broadcasting schedule, however, the team can also record more frequently — as it did in the weeks leading up to the 2016 election. NPR

were mandated to provide alternatives to commercial broadcasting. With almost one thousand member stations, NPR draws over thirty-six million listeners each week to popular news and interview programs like *Morning Edition*, *All Things Considered*, and *Fresh Air*. In addition to traditional radio listeners, almost four million people download NPR podcasts each week.[10] NPR and PBS stations rely on a blend of private donations, corporate sponsorship, and a small amount of public funding.

Radio and Convergence

Like every other mass medium, radio has made the digital turn by converging with the Internet. Interestingly, this digital turn is taking radio back to its roots in some ways. Internet radio allows for much more variety, which is reminiscent of radio's earliest years, when nearly any individual or group with some technical skill could start a radio station. Moreover, podcasts have brought back such content as storytelling, instructional programs, and local topics of interest, which have largely been missing in corporate radio. And the portability of smartphones hark back to the compact transportability that first came with the popularization of transistor radios in the 1950s. When we talk about these kinds of convergence, we are talking about the blurring of lines between categories. Even so, it's still possible to identify four particular ways radio is converging with digital technologies:

- **Internet radio.** Emerging in the 1990s with the popularity of the Web, Internet radio stations come in two types. The first involves an existing AM, FM, satellite, or HD station "streaming" a simulcast version of its on-air signal over the Web. More than twelve thousand radio stations stream their programming over the Web today.[11] iHeartRadio is one of the major streaming sites for broadcast and custom digital stations. The second kind of online radio station is one that has been created exclusively for the Internet. Pandora, 8tracks, and Slacker are some of the leading Internet radio services. In fact, services like Pandora allow users to have more control over their listening experience and the selections that are played. Listeners can create individualized stations based on a specific artist or song that they request (see "The Digital Turn Case Study: Streaming Radio Becomes Mainstream" on page 188).

- **Podcasting and portable listening.** Developed in 2004, podcasting (the term marries *iPod* and *broadcasting*) refers to the practice of making audio files available on the Internet so that listeners can download and listen to them on their smartphones, iPods, tablets, or computers. This popular distribution method quickly became mainstream as mass media companies created commercial podcasts to promote and extend existing content, such as news and reality TV, while independent producers kept pace with their own podcasts on niche topics like knitting, fly-fishing, and learning Russian. By 2016, one in five Americans were listening to podcasts at least once a month.[12]

  For the broadcast radio industry, portability used to mean listening on a transistor or car radio. But with the digital turn to iPods and mobile phones, broadcasters haven't been as easily available on today's primary portable audio devices. Smartphones today come equipped with a chip that makes them able to receive FM radio signals, something that is used quite frequently in developing countries. In the United States, however, these chips have mostly been deactivated by cellular and smartphone companies that make money by charging customers for streamed data or streaming music services. Although some companies have started activating the chip—including Sprint, AT&T, and T-Mobile—Verizon and Apple were still refusing to do so as of 2016.[13] Meanwhile, the National Association of Broadcasters continues pushing for FM chip activation, arguing that when cellular towers get overwhelmed in times of emergency, phones that can access FM radio signals would still get vital updates.[14] In addition, the chip would help commercial radio stations by putting them on the same digital devices as their competitors, like Pandora.

- **Satellite radio.** Another alternative radio technology added a third band—satellite radio—to AM and FM. Two companies, XM and Sirius, completed their national introduction by 2002 and merged into a single provider in 2008. The merger was precipitated by their struggles to make a profit after building competing satellite systems and battling for listeners. SiriusXM offers about 165 digital music, news, and talk channels to the continental United States, with monthly prices ranging from $11 to $20 and satellite radio receivers costing from $50 to $200. SiriusXM access is also available on

LaunchPad
launchpadworks.com

Going Visual: Video, Radio, and the Web
This video looks at how radio adapted to the Internet by providing multimedia on its Web sites to attract online listeners.

Discussion: If video is now important to radio, what might that mean for journalism and broadcasting students who are considering a job in radio?

▲ Howard Stern's broadcast radio show holds the record for FCC indecency fines, a fact that he and his cohost, Robin Quivers, used for material on the show. Stern avoided further indecency fines when he moved to satellite radio in 2006.
Getty Images/Getty Images

The Digital Turn

Streaming Radio Becomes Mainstream

For the past sixty years, a big part of the traditional radio business model has been playing recorded music that draws in an audience while selling targeted ad spots to advertisers. A by-product of this arrangement is that listeners discover new music and go out and buy it. With the digital turn, however, online music streaming services are challenging this long-standing relationship between audience and product. First there are the on-demand services like Spotify, which allow users to pick and play specific songs and artists (see Chapter 5). The other kind of service is the online radio station, like Pandora, which puts a digital spin on the usual listener–radio station interaction.

Pandora Radio, launched in 2000, provides an experience similar to that of broadcast and satellite radio but without a human deejay. Pandora selects songs based on an analysis of up to four hundred attributes that company employees index and categorize. Listeners can create personalized stations by entering key words (Alternative Coffee House Rock), artist or band names (Foo Fighters), or even song titles ("Heathens"). After creating the station, Pandora streams music with characteristics that match the station's name. Unlike terrestrial radio stations, Pandora pays song licensing fees to the music rights organization SoundExchange, which

was set up specifically for online and satellite radio stations. With almost seventy-eight million active listeners, Pandora is one of the largest online radio services operating in the United States.[1] It is also continuing to branch out, readying to launch its own on-demand streaming service as it gets more and more competition from both traditional radio and other Internet sites.[2]

For example, leading radio corporation Clear Channel Communications (now iHeartMedia) unveiled its iHeartRadio service (www.iheart.com) in 2008, putting more than 850 of its stations from across the country on an ad-supported streaming service. In 2017, the company added an on-demand music streaming service that works in conjunction with its radio stations, incorporating options to skip songs and listen offline.[3] Apple, which changed the music industry with music downloads, began seeing a decline in its iTunes music store sales, so it started a music streaming option. Apple Music is a subscription-based service with a number of streams, including the popular live Beats 1 station.

But even with competition from the Internet, traditional radio does enjoy a few advantages over sites like Pandora. Radio remains the most local of broadcast media, allowing deejays to break into the playlist to provide live traffic, weather, and news updates, or broadcast live from a community event. At the same time, online streaming means a local radio station can have global reach. For example, KQNY 91.9 FM—Plumas Community Radio in Quincy, California—has listeners from Japan, Germany, the United Kingdom, and Mexico, who enjoy hearing the eclectic mix of programming from its mostly volunteer staff.[4]

▶ Web Clip

YouTube.com features music videos from a wide variety of artists. For example, you can search for 'Taylor Swift—Bad Blood ft. Kendrick Lamar' posted by TaylorSwiftVEVO. Besides YouTube, what are some of the many ways a listener might seek out this track?

mobile devices via an app. U.S. automakers (investors in the satellite radio companies) now equip most new cars with a satellite band, in addition to AM and FM. SiriusXM had about thirty million subscribers by 2016.

- **HD radio.** Approved by the FCC in 2002, HD radio is a digital technology that enables AM and FM radio broadcasters to multicast two to three additional compressed digital signals within their traditional analog frequency. For example, KNOW, a public radio station at 91.1 FM in Minneapolis–St. Paul, runs its National Public Radio news format on 91.1 HD1, Radio Heartland (acoustic and Americana music) on 91.1 HD2, and the BBC news service on 91.1 HD3. About twenty-two hundred radio stations now broadcast in digital HD.

The Economics of Commercial Radio

Radio today remains one of the most used mass media, reaching 93 percent of all Americans age twelve or older every week.[15] Because of this continued broad reach, the airwaves are still desirable real estate for advertisers and content programmers, who want to target people in and out of their homes; for record labels, who want their artists' songs played; and for radio station owners, who want to attract large groups of diverse listeners to dominate multiple markets.

Selling Ads and Paying for Programming

About 10 percent of all U.S. spending on media advertising goes to radio stations. Like newspapers, radio generates its largest profits by selling local and regional ads. Thirty-second radio ads range from $1,500 in large markets to just a few dollars in the smallest markets. Today, gross advertising receipts for radio are about $17.3 billion (about 75 percent of the revenues are from local ad sales, with the remainder in national spot ads, network, and digital radio sales), up from about $16 billion in 2009 but down from an industry peak of $21.7 billion in 2006.[16] Nevertheless, the number of stations keeps growing, now totaling more than 2,000 broadcasting in HD and 15,508 broadcasting in analog. Of those analog stations, 4,671 are AM, 6,737 are FM commercial, and 4,100 are FM educational.[17]

Traditionally, local radio stations have received much of their content free from the recording industry: Only about 20 percent of a typical broadcast radio station's budget goes toward covering programming costs. This is because radio broadcasters have long paid mechanical royalties to songwriters and music publishers but no royalties to the performing artists or record companies,

arguing that artists and record labels get their payout from the increased album sales driven by radio airplay. Satellite and Internet radio, on the other hand, pay royalties to performers and labels through the performance rights organization SoundExchange. Since 2009, performers and the music industry have been pushing for terrestrial radio to begin paying performers and labels like their satellite and Internet counterparts. So far, the National Association of Broadcasters has successfully resisted this push.

When radio stations do want to purchase programming, they often turn to radio networks like Westwood One, which provides syndicated programs ranging from talk and news to entertainment and music. Stations can pay for this programming with money, receive the programming in exchange for time slots for national ads, or combine the two. In addition, some stations spend money on local programming. Although corporate consolidation and drastic local cutbacks have taken a toll on radio stations, some still hire staff to provide locally produced content—news, sports, weather, community affairs talk shows—and to play music.

Manipulating Playlists with Payola

Payola, the practice by which record promoters pay deejays to play particular records, continues to require ongoing government oversight to expose illegal playlist manipulation. The practice was rampant during the 1950s, as record companies sought to guarantee record sales. In response, management took control of programming, arguing that if individual deejays had less control over which records would be played, the deejays would be less susceptible to bribery.

Despite congressional hearings and new regulations, payola persisted. Record promoters showered their favors on a few influential, high-profile deejays, whose backing could make or break a record nationally, or on key program managers in charge of Top 40 formats in large urban markets.

With the growth of streaming music and streaming radio services, the practice of payola has again surfaced. But because streaming services aren't broadcasting, they fall outside the FCC's oversight. *Billboard* magazine reports that music promoters have been paying to influence playlists at services like Spotify, Deezer, and Apple Music. Playlists, used by hundreds of thousands of subscribers as a way to discover music, are created by the streaming services, influential individuals, or the music labels themselves. Spotify announced in 2015 that it would prohibit any playlists that had been influenced by money or other compensation. Yet the three major music labels continue to influence streaming music: Universal Music Group features its music playlists on Digster, Sony showcases its music on Filtr, and Warner Music Group promotes its playlists on Topsify.[18]

Radio Ownership: From Diversity to Consolidation

From the 1950s through the 1980s, the FCC tried to encourage diversity in broadcast ownership—and thus programming—by limiting the number of stations a media company could own. The **Telecommunications Act of 1996** introduced a new age of consolidation in the industry, as the FCC eliminated most ownership restrictions on radio. As a result, some twenty-one hundred stations and $15 billion changed hands that year alone. From 1995 to 2005, the number of radio station owners declined by one-third, from sixty-six hundred to about forty-four hundred.[19]

The 1996 act allows individuals and companies to acquire as many radio stations as they want, with relaxed restrictions on the number of stations a single broadcaster may own in the same city. The larger the market or area, the more stations a company may own within that market.

This has reshaped the radio industry. Take, for example, the former Clear Channel Communications. It was formed in 1972 with one San Antonio station; in 1998, it swallowed up Jacor Communications, the fifth-largest radio chain, and became the nation's second-largest group, with 454 stations in 101 cities. Clear Channel continued its rapid expansion into the nation's largest radio owner, hitting a peak of 1,205 stations in 2005. As mentioned previously, Clear Channel changed its name to iHeartMedia in 2014, a rebranding the company says better reflects its diverse media businesses, especially those involving the Internet. Today, it owns 860 radio stations (still the largest) and has branched out into other areas, owning about 750,000 billboard and outdoor displays in over forty countries across five continents, including 950 digital displays across thirty-seven U.S. markets. iHeartMedia also distributes many of the leading syndicated programs, including *The Rush Limbaugh Show*, *The Glenn Beck Program*, *On Air with Ryan Seacrest*, and *Delilah*. iHeartMedia is also an Internet radio source with its iHeartRadio, which has more than ninety million registered users.

Combined, the top three commercial radio groups—iHeartMedia, Cumulus, and Townsquare Media—own over sixteen hundred stations (about 10% of all U.S. stations), dominate the fifty largest markets in the United States, and control at least one-third of the entire radio industry's $17.3 billion revenue.

When large corporations regained control of America's radio airwaves in the 1990s, activists in hundreds of communities across the United States protested by starting up their own noncommercial "pirate" radio stations, capable of broadcasting over a few miles with low-power FM signals of 1 to 10 watts. The major complaint of pirate radio station operators was that the FCC had long since ceased licensing low-power community radio stations. In 2000, the FCC responded to tens of thousands of inquiries about the development of a new local radio broadcasting service: It approved a

▲ Though much mainstream radio programming is now managed by corporations, with many more specific voices opting to produce podcasts rather than traditional radio shows, local college and community stations can keep broadcasting locally. Luisa Porter/AP Images

new noncommercial **low-power FM (LPFM)** class of 10- and 100-watt stations to give voice to local groups lacking access to the public airwaves. LPFM station licensees included mostly religious groups but also high schools, colleges and universities, Native American tribes, labor groups, and museums. Then FCC chairman William E. Kennard, who fostered the LPFM initiative, explained: "This is about the haves—the broadcast industry—trying to prevent many have-nots—small community and educational organizations—from having just a little piece of the pie. Just a little piece of the airwaves which belong to all of the people."[20]

Radio in a Democratic Society

As the first national electronic mass medium, radio has powerfully molded American culture. It gave us soap operas, situation comedies, and broadcast news, and it helped popularize rock and roll, car culture, and the politics of talk radio. Yet for all its national influence and recent move toward consolidation, broadcast radio is still a supremely local medium. For decades, listeners have tuned in to hear the familiar voices of their community's deejays and talk-show hosts, and to enjoy music popular in their cultural heritage.

The early debates over how radio should be used produced one of the most important and enduring ideas in communication policy for any democracy: a requirement to operate in the service of "public interest, convenience, or necessity." But as we've seen, the broadcasting industry has long chafed at this policy. Executives have maintained that because radio corporations invest heavily in technology, they should have more control over the radio frequencies on which they operate—as well as own as many stations as they want. Deregulation in the past few decades has moved the industry closer to that corporate vision. Today, nearly every radio market in the nation is dominated by a few owners, and those owners are required to renew their broadcasting licenses only every eight years.

This trend has begun moving radio away from its localism, as radio groups often manage hundreds of stations from afar. Given broadcasters' reluctance to openly discuss their own economic arrangements, public debate regarding radio as a natural resource has dwindled. Looking to the future, we face a big question: With a few large broadcast companies now permitted to dominate radio ownership nationwide, how much will the number and kinds of voices permitted to speak over the public airwaves be restricted? And if restrictions occur, what will happen to the democracy we live in, which is defined by local communities' having a say in how they're governed? To ensure that mass media, including radio, continue to serve democracy, we—the public—must play a role in developing the answers to these questions.

CHAPTER ESSENTIALS

Review

- With the invention of the **telegraph** in the 1840s, operators used **Morse code** to send electrical signals over wires. Then, experiments involving **radio waves** and **electromagnetic waves** dramatically advanced the development of wireless communication. As the nineteenth century unfolded, new developments—including inventions from Marconi, Fessenden, and De Forest—took wireless from **narrowcasting** (point-to-point communication) to **broadcasting** (one-to-many communication).

- A sharp increase in the number of radio stations and the growth of the radio **network**, such as NBC in 1926, prompted government to pass the **Radio Act of 1927**, which created the **Federal Radio Commission (FRC)** to oversee licenses and negotiate channel problems. The **Federal Communications Act of 1934** replaced the FRC with the **Federal Communications Commission (FCC)**, the agency that still oversees radio stations.

- The late 1920s to the 1940s constituted a golden age of radio, but the massive popularity of television in the 1950s led to its decline—until **transistors** made radios portable and music-intensive **format radio** introduced the idea of **rotation** into its programming. The addition of better-sounding **FM** radio to the existing **AM** radio also served to strengthen the industry through the latter half of the twentieth century and into the twenty-first.

- Currently, commercial radio stations stick to a variety of formats, including **country**, **news and talk radio**, **contemporary hit radio (CHR)**, **adult contemporary (AC)**, **urban contemporary**, **Spanish-language radio**, and **album-oriented rock (AOR)**.

- Nonprofit radio stations and noncommercial networks, such as **National Public Radio (NPR)** and the **Public Broadcasting Service (PBS)**, were created to provide alternatives to commercial broadcasting. **Low-power FM (LPFM)** stations were also approved in 2000 as an alternative to corporate-controlled radio.

- Since the digital turn, four alternative radio technologies have helped bring more diverse sounds and options for listening to radio audiences: **Internet radio**, **podcasting** and portable listening, **satellite radio**, and **HD radio**.

- Commercial radio stations take in revenue from advertisers and spend money on assets such as content programming, often purchasing programming from national network radio.

- As control of the public airwaves consolidates into fewer and fewer hands, it's important to think about the impact this will have on local communities and the variety of voices that will be heard on those airwaves.

Key Terms

telegraph, p. 169

Morse code, p. 170

radio waves, p. 170

electromagnetic waves, p. 170

narrowcasting, p. 170

broadcasting, p. 170

wireless telegraphy, p. 170

wireless telephony, p. 171

radio, p. 171

Wireless Ship Act, p. 172

Radio Act of 1912, p. 172

Radio Corporation of America (RCA), p. 173

network, p. 174

Radio Act of 1927, p. 176

Federal Radio Commission (FRC), p. 176

Federal Communications Act of 1934, p. 176

Federal Communications Commission (FCC), p. 176

transistors, p. 179

AM, p. 180

FM, p. 180

format radio, p. 180

rotation, p. 180

Top 40 format, p. 180

country, p. 181

news and talk radio, p. 181

contemporary hit radio (CHR), p. 182

adult contemporary (AC), p. 182

urban contemporary, p. 182

Spanish-language radio, p. 182

album-oriented rock (AOR), p. 183

Pacifica Foundation, p. 183

National Public Radio (NPR), p. 183

Public Broadcasting Service (PBS), p. 183

Public Broadcasting Act of 1967, p. 183

Corporation for Public Broadcasting (CPB), p. 183

Internet radio, p. 186

podcasting, p. 187

satellite radio, p. 187

HD radio, p. 189

payola, p. 190

Telecommunications Act of 1996, p. 191

low-power FM (LPFM), p. 192

Study Questions

1. How did broadcasting, unlike print media, come to be federally regulated?

2. What is the significance of the Radio Act of 1927 and the Federal Communications Act of 1934?

3. How did radio adapt to the arrival of television?

4. What has been the main effect of the Telecommunications Act of 1996 on radio station ownership?

5. What changes are currently happening to the radio business as a result of the digital turn?

6. What is the relevance of localism to debates about ownership in radio?

7

Movies and the Impact of Images

In May 1977, a groundbreaking film took audiences to a galaxy far, far away. George Lucas's space epic *Star Wars* targeted young people, a new primary audience for Hollywood, and introduced massive promotion and lucrative merchandising tie-ins—all the now-typical characteristics of a blockbuster. Repeat attendance and positive buzz made the first *Star Wars* the most successful movie of its generation.

Star Wars marked a cultural shift in movies and a technological transformation, with each new film in the series pushing the boundaries of what was possible with special effects. From stop-motion models used in the 1977 movie to the seamless digital effects of *Star Wars: The Force Awakens* (2015) and *Star Wars: The Last Jedi* (2017), the franchise continues to push the envelope of how special effects can make the space fantasy seem ever more real—and audience grabbing. The trajectory of the *Star Wars* franchise is a prime example of how movie storytelling can be enhanced by new technology, a pattern that stretches back into the early days of film.

Another movie about space—made over a century ago with what was then state-of-the-art technology and special effects—also amazed audiences and captured imaginations. Georges Méliès's *A Trip to the*

◀ In its forty-year journey from sci-fi blockbuster to movie industry megalith, the *Star Wars* franchise has been at the forefront of movie-making technology. The franchise has also set the bar for converged financial and cultural success: From prequels to sequels, from toys to theme park rides, from clothing to catchphrases, the box office numbers have always been only part of the *Star Wars* story. Everett Collection, Inc.

Moon, released in 1902, was an early example of how new techniques and technologies led filmmakers to make movies that heralded new eras in film-making. Along with *Star Wars*, Warner Brothers' *The Jazz Singer* in 1927, Orson Welles's *Citizen Kane* in 1941, and James Cameron's *Avatar* in 2009 all mark such changes in the art, craft, and business of filmmaking. Méliès pioneered the use of fantasy in film, Warner Brothers ushered in the sound era, Welles developed deep-focus cinematography and other technical milestones, and Cameron masterfully deployed the innovation of digital performance-capture technology to transform the 3-D movie from gimmick to potential art form. The movies, then, have always been a technological spectacle, a grand illusion that—like a magic act—uses smoke, light, and trickery to make marvelous illusions come to life. Since the early twentieth century, the movies have operated as one of the world's chief storytellers.

These movie narratives create community, too. We attend theaters or watch at home with family and friends. Movies distract us from our daily struggles: They evoke and symbolize universal themes of human experience (childhood, coming of age, family relations, growing older, coping with death); they help us understand and respond to major historical events and tragedies (for instance, the Holocaust and 9/11); and they encourage us to rethink contemporary ideas as the world evolves, particularly in terms of how we think about race, class, spirituality, gender, and sexuality. The best films can untether us from the reality of our daily lives, only to challenge us to try to reconnect with our world in a new way.

Of course, as cultural products, movies are subject to the same economic constraints as are other mass media forms. For example, there is a tendency for the major studios to roll out standardized big-budget blockbusters in hopes of finding the next *The Force Awakens*, while narratives that break the mold can sometimes languish for lack of major studio backing. But in the emerging terrain of digital video and Internet distribution, the ability of moviemakers to find audiences without major studio support is increasing.

GIVEN THE FILM INDUSTRY'S LENGTHY AND COMPLEX ROLE in Americans' lives, along with its steady transformation in response to new technologies, cultural change, and other developments, it's vital to take a closer look at this unique mass medium. We need to ask big questions about what purposes movies serve for us today, compared to the past; how strong an impact the U.S. film industry has on society and culture in our own country and in others; and where the film industry may be headed in the future.

To these ends, we use this chapter to examine the rich legacy and current role of movies by:

- **considering film's early history, including the technological advances that made movies possible**

- **tracing the evolution of the Hollywood studio system, which arose to dominate the global film industry**

- **exploring how narrative styles developed in moviemaking, including the transition from silent film to "talkies" and the emergence of different camera techniques and movie genres**

- **examining the transformation of the Hollywood studio system in response to new forces, such as the birth of television and the rise of home entertainment**

- **analyzing the economics of the movie business — specifically, how it makes money and what it invests in to stay profitable**

- **weighing movies' role in our democracy today and in the diverse world around us**

The Early History of Movies

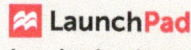

LaunchPad
launchpadworks.com

Use **LearningCurve** to review concepts from this chapter.

Filmmaking has passed through several stages on its way to mass medium status. In the following pages, we trace those stages — including development (when inventors first made pictures move), entrepreneurial (when experimenters conducted movie demonstrations for a small number of paid viewers), and finally true mass medium (when movies became widely accessible and began telling coherent stories with specific meanings for viewers). Throughout these stages, creative and bold innovators have worked together to continually advance the medium, revealing the strongly collaborative nature of this industry.

Advances in Film Technology

The concept of film goes back as early as Leonardo da Vinci, who theorized in the late 1400s that a device could be created to reproduce reality. There were other early precursors to film as well. For example, in the 1600s, the

▲ Eadweard Muybridge's studies of horses in motion, like the one shown, proved that a horse gets all four feet off the ground during a gallop. In his various studies of motion, Muybridge could use twelve cameras at a time. Eadweard Muybridge/Getty Images

magic lantern projected images painted on glass plates using an oil lamp as a light source. In 1824, the *thaumatrope* consisted of a two-sided card whose different images appeared to combine when the card was twirled. And the *zoetrope*, created in 1834, was a cylindrical device with slits cut into it that rapidly spun images on the inside, making it appear to viewers as if the images were moving.

But the true development stage of film-making began when inventors discovered a process for making a series of photographs appear to move while being projected on a screen.

Muybridge and Goodwin Make Pictures Move

Eadweard Muybridge, an English photographer living in America, is credited with being the first person to make images move. He studied motion by using multiple cameras to take successive photographs of humans and animals in motion. By 1880, he had developed a method for projecting the photographic images on a wall for public viewing.

Meanwhile, other inventors were also capturing moving images and projecting them. In 1884, George Eastman (founder of Eastman Kodak) developed the first roll film—a huge improvement over the heavy metal-and-glass plates previously used to make individual photos. Louis Aimé Augustin Le Prince, a Frenchman living in England, invented the first motion-picture camera using roll film. Le Prince, who disappeared mysteriously on a train ride to Paris in 1890, is credited with filming the first motion picture, *Roundhay Garden Scene*, in 1888. Recorded at twelve frames per second, the film depicts several people strolling on a lawn and runs for just a few seconds.

In 1889, a New Jersey minister, Hannibal Goodwin, improved Eastman's roll film by using thin strips of transparent, pliable material called **celluloid**, which could hold a coating of chemicals sensitive to light. Goodwin's breakthrough enabled a strip of film to move through a camera and be photographed in rapid succession, producing a series of pictures.

Edison and the Brothers Lumière Create Motion Pictures

The early developers of film laid the groundwork for the shift to the entrepreneurial stage. During this stage, inventors came up with new projection and distribution technologies, enabling people to come together in a public place to view movies. The action began in the late 1800s, when American inventor and businessman Thomas Edison (with the help of his assistant, William Kennedy

Dickson) combined his incandescent light bulb, Goodwin's celluloid, and Le Prince's camera to create another early movie camera, the **kinetograph**, and a single-person viewing system, the **kinetoscope**. This small projection system required individual viewers to look through a small hole to see images moving on a tiny plate.

Meanwhile in France, brothers Louis and Auguste Lumière developed the *cinematograph*—a combined camera, film development, and projection system. The projection system was particularly important, as it enabled more than one person at a time to see the moving images on a large screen.

▲ Kinetoscopes allowed individuals to view motion pictures through a window in a cabinet that held the film. The first kinetoscope parlor opened in 1894 in New York City and was such a hit that many others quickly followed. Everett Collection, Inc.

With inventors around the world now dabbling in moving pictures, Edison continued innovating in film. He patented several inventions and manufactured a new large-screen system called the **vitascope**, through which longer film-strips could be projected without interruption. This device hinted at the potential of movies as a future mass medium. Staged at a music hall in New York in April 1896, Edison's first public showing of the vitascope featured shots from a boxing match and waves rolling onto a beach. Some members of the audience were so taken with the realism of the images that they stepped back from the screen's crashing waves to avoid getting their feet wet.

At this point, movies consisted of movement recorded by a single continuous camera shot. Early filmmakers had not yet figured out how to move the camera itself or how to edit film shots together. Moreover, movies' content consisted simply of people or objects in motion, without conveying any story. Nonetheless, various innovators had spotted the commercial possibilities of film. By 1900, short movies had become part of the entertainment industry, used as visual novelties in amusement arcades, traveling carnivals, wax museums, and vaudeville theaters.

Telling Stories: The Introduction of Narrative

With the introduction in the late 1890s of **narrative films**—movies that tell stories through the series of actions depicted (later matched with sound)— the industry advanced from the entrepreneurial stage to mass medium status. Film now promised to offer a far richer experience than other storytelling media—specifically, books and radio. Unlike those media, narrative films provided realistic moving images and compelling stories in which viewers became so immersed that they sometimes forgot they were watching a fictional representation.

▲ *The Great Train Robbery* (1903) may have introduced the western genre, but it was actually filmed in New Jersey. The still above shows a famous scene in which a bandit shoots his gun at the audience. Everett Collection, Inc.

Some of the earliest narrative films (which were silent) were produced and directed by French magician and inventor Georges Méliès, who opened the first public movie theater in France in 1896. Méliès began producing short fantasy and fairy-tale films, including *The Vanishing Lady* (1896), *Cinderella* (1899), and *A Trip to the Moon* (1902). He increasingly used editing and unique camera tricks and techniques, such as slow motion and cartoon animation, which would become key ingredients in future narrative filmmaking.

The first American filmmaker to adapt Méliès's innovations to narrative film was Edwin S. Porter. Porter shot narrative scenes out of order (for instance, some in a studio and some outdoors) and reassembled, or edited, them to tell a story. In 1902, he made what is regarded as America's first narrative film, *The Life of an American Fireman*, which included the first recorded close-up. Porter also introduced the western genre and the first chase scene in *The Great Train Robbery* (1903).

The Arrival of Nickelodeons

Another turning point in film's development as a mass medium was the 1907 arrival of **nickelodeons**—a type of movie theater whose name combines the admission price (five cents) with the Greek word for "theater." According to media historian Douglas Gomery, these small and uncomfortable makeshift theaters often consisted of converted storefronts redecorated to mimic vaudeville theaters.[1] Nickelodeons showed silent films, which typically transcended language barriers and provided workers and immigrants with an inexpensive escape from the challenges of urban life. Not surprisingly, nickelodeons flourished during the great European immigration at the dawn of the twentieth century. Between 1907 and 1909, the number of nickelodeons in the United States skyrocketed from five thousand to ten thousand. The craze peaked by 1910, when entrepreneurs began seeking more affluent spectators, attracting them with larger and more lavish movie theaters.

The Evolution of the Hollywood Studio System

By the 1910s, movies had become a major industry, and entrepreneurs developed many tactics for controlling it — including monopolizing patents on film-related technologies and dominating the "three pillars" of the movie business: production (making movies), distribution (getting films into theaters), and exhibition (playing films in theaters). Controlling all the parts of an industry's supply chain achieves **vertical integration**. In the film business, it means managing the entire moviemaking process — from the development of an idea to the screening of the final product before an audience. The resulting concentration of power gave rise to the **studio system**, in which creative talent was firmly controlled by certain powerful studios. Five vertically integrated movie studios, sometimes referred to as the Big Five, made up this new film **oligopoly** (a situation in which an industry is controlled by just a few firms): Paramount, MGM, Warner Brothers, Twentieth Century Fox, and RKO. An additional three studios, sometimes called the Little Three — Columbia, Universal, and United Artists — did not own chains of theaters but held powerful positions in movie production and distribution.

Edison's Attempt to Control the Industry

Among the first to try his hand at dominating the movie business and reaping its profits, Thomas Edison formed the Motion Picture Patents Company, known as the Trust, in 1908. A cartel of major U.S. and French film producers, the company pooled film-technology patents, acquired most major film distributorships, and signed an exclusive deal with George Eastman, who agreed to supply stock film only to Trust-approved theater companies.

However, some independent producers refused to bow to the Trust's terms. These producers abandoned film production centers in New York and New Jersey and moved to Cuba; Florida; and ultimately Hollywood, California. In particular, two Hungarian immigrants — Adolph Zukor (who would eventually run Paramount Pictures) and William Fox (who would found the Fox Film Corporation, later renamed Twentieth Century Fox) — wanted to free their movie operations from the Trust's tyrannical grasp. Zukor's early companies figured out ways to bypass the Trust. A suit by Fox, a nickelodeon operator turned film distributor, resulted in the Trust's breakup for restraint-of-trade violations in 1917.

A Closer Look at the Three Pillars

Ironically, film entrepreneurs like Zukor who fought the Trust realized they could control the film industry themselves through vertical integration. The three pillars of vertical integration occur in a specific sequence: First, movies are produced. Next, copies are distributed to people or companies who get them out to theaters. Finally, the movies are exhibited in theaters. So, while power through vertical integration was becoming concentrated in just a few big studios, other studios were seeking to dominate one or another of the three pillars. This competition sparked tension between the forces of centralization and those of independence.

▲ With legions of fans, Mary Pickford became the first woman ever to make a salary of $1 million in a year and gained the freedom to take artistic risks with her roles. She launched United Artists—a film distribution company—with Douglas Fairbanks, Charlie Chaplin, and D. W. Griffith. No woman since has been as powerful a player in the movie industry. Here she is seen with Buddy Rogers in *My Best Girl.* Everett Collection, Inc.

Production

A major element in the production pillar is the choice of actors for a particular film. This circumstance created an opportunity for some studios to gain control using tactics other than Edison's pooling of patents. Once these companies learned that audiences preferred specific actors to anonymous ones, they signed exclusive contracts with big-name actors. In this way, the studio system began controlling the talent in the industry. For example, Adolph Zukor hired a number of popular actors and formed the Famous Players Film Company in 1912. One Famous Players performer was Mary Pickford, who became known as "America's Sweetheart" for her portrayal of spunky and innocent heroines. Pickford so elevated film actors' status that in 1919, she broke from Zukor to form her own company, United Artists. Actor Douglas Fairbanks (her future husband) joined her, along with comedian-director Charlie Chaplin and director D. W. Griffith.

Although United Artists represented a brief triumph of autonomy for a few powerful actors, by the 1920s the studio system had solidified its control over all creative talent in the industry. Pioneered by director Thomas Ince and his company, Triangle, the system constituted a kind of assembly line for moviemaking talent: Actors, directors, editors, writers, and others all worked under exclusive contracts for the major studios. Ince also designated himself the first studio head, appointing producers to handle hiring, logistics, and finances so that he could more easily supervise many pictures at once. The studio system proved so efficient that major studios were soon producing new feature films every week. Pooling talent, rather than patents, turned out to be a more ingenious tactic for movie studios seeking to dominate film production.

Distribution

Whereas there were two main strategies for controlling the production pillar of moviemaking (pooling patents or pooling talent), studios seeking power in the industry had more options open to them for controlling distribution. One early effort to do so came in 1904, when movie companies provided vaudeville theaters with films and projectors on a *film exchange* system. In return for their short films, shown between live acts in the theaters, movie producers received a small percentage of the vaudeville ticket-gate receipts.

Edison's Trust used another tactic: withholding projection equipment from theater companies not willing to pay the Trust's patent-use fees. However, as with the production of film, independent film companies looked for distribution strategies outside the Trust. Again, Adolph Zukor led the fight, developing **block booking**. Under this system, movie exhibitors who wanted access to popular films with big stars like Mary Pickford had to also rent new or marginal films featuring no stars. Although this practice was eventually outlawed as monopolistic, such contracts enabled the studios to test-market possible up-and-coming stars at little financial risk.

As yet another distribution strategy, some companies marketed American films in Europe. World War I so disrupted film production in Europe that the United States stepped in to fill the gap, eventually becoming the leader in the commercial movie business worldwide. After the war, no other nation's film industry could compete economically with Hollywood. By the mid-1920s, foreign revenue from U.S. films totaled $100 million. Even today, Hollywood dominates the world market for movies.

Exhibition

Companies could gain further control of the movie industry by finding ways to get more people to buy more movie tickets. Innovations in exhibition (such as construction of more inviting theaters) transformed the way people watched films and began attracting more middle- and upper-middle-class viewers.

Initially, Edison's Trust tried to dominate exhibition by controlling the flow of films to theater owners. If theaters wanted to ensure they had films to show their patrons, they had to purchase a license from the Trust and pay whatever price it asked. But after the Trust collapsed, emerging studios in Hollywood came up with their own ideas for controlling exhibition and making certain the movies they produced were shown. When industrious theater owners began forming film cooperatives to compete with block-booking tactics, producers like Zukor conspired to buy up theaters. Zukor and the heads of several major studios understood that they did not have to own all the theaters to ensure that their movies would be shown. Instead, the major studios needed to own only the first-run theaters (about 15% of the nation's theaters). First-run theaters premiered new films in major downtown areas and generated 85 to 95 percent of all film revenue.

The studios quickly realized that to earn revenue from these first-run theaters, they would have to draw members of the middle and upper-middle classes to the movies. With this goal in mind, they built **movie palaces**, full-time single-screen theaters that provided a more enjoyable and comfortable movie-viewing environment. In 1914, the three-thousand-seat Strand Theatre, the first movie palace, opened in New York.

▲ The historic Fox Movie Palace, located in Detroit, was originally built in the late 1920s and restored in 1990. James Marshall/Getty Images

Another major innovation in exhibition was the development of *mid-city movie theaters*. These theaters—built in convenient locations near urban mass-transit stations—attracted city dwellers as well as the initial wave of people who had moved to the outskirts of cities in the 1920s and commuted into work from the suburbs. This strategy is alive and well today, as **multiplexes** and **megaplexes** featuring many screens (often fourteen or more) lure middle-class crowds to interstate highway crossroads.

Hollywood's Golden Age: The Development of Style

Once the Hollywood studio system was established as a profitable business model, studios had the luxury of developing a distinctive moviemaking style that ultimately marked Hollywood's Golden Age. This style began taking shape in 1915, characterized by the use of new narrative techniques (such as close-up camera shots and multiple story lines) in the silent era, the later introduction of sound, and the rise of movie genres. Hollywood's monopolization of this style produced numerous films that have since become treasured classics. Yet during Hollywood's Golden Age, other moviemaking models — including global cinema, documentaries, and independent films — provided alternatives to the classic style and shaped the medium just as powerfully.

Narrative Techniques in the Silent Era

Though telling stories in films occurred early on, moviemaking hit its stride as a viable art form when studios developed innovative narrative techniques, including the use of varied camera distances, close-up shots, multiple story lines, fast-paced editing, and symbolic imagery—even before sound was introduced. As these techniques evolved, making a movie became more than just telling a story; it became about *how* to tell the story. For example, when filmed from different camera angles, the same sequence of events can affect viewers quite differently.

D. W. Griffith, among the earliest "star" directors, used nearly all of these techniques at the same time in *The Birth of a Nation* (1915)—the first *feature-length film* (more than an hour long) produced in America. Although considered a technical masterpiece and an enormous hit, the film glorified the Ku Klux Klan and stereotyped southern blacks. The National Association for the Advancement of Colored People (NAACP) campaigned against the film, and protests and riots broke out at many screenings.

Other popular films created during the silent era were historical and religious epics, including *Napoleon*, *Ben-Hur*, and *The Ten Commandments*. But the era also produced pioneering social dramas, mysteries, comedies, horror films, science-fiction movies, war films, crime dramas, and westerns.

Augmenting Images with Sound

Hollywood's Golden Age also saw the introduction of sound in 1927, which further established a distinctive narrative style and set new commercial standards in the industry. The availability of movies with sound pushed annual movie attendance in the United States from sixty million a week in 1927 to ninety million a week just two years later. By 1931, nearly 85 percent of America's twenty thousand theaters accommodated **talkies** (sound pictures). And by 1935, the rest of the world had adopted talkies as the commercial standard.

Earlier attempts at creating talkies had failed; however, technical breakthroughs in the 1910s at AT&T's research arm, Bell Labs, produced prototypes of loudspeakers and sound amplifiers. Experiments with sound continued during the 1920s, particularly at Warner Brothers. In 1927, the studio produced *The Jazz Singer*, a feature-length silent film interspersed with musical numbers and brief dialogue. Starring Al Jolson, a charismatic and popular vaudeville singer who wore blackface makeup as part of his act, the movie further demonstrated racism's presence in the film industry. Warner Brothers' 1928 release *The Singing Fool*, which also starred Jolson, became the real breakthrough for talkies. Costing $200,000 to make, the film raked in a whopping $5 million and "proved to all doubters that talkies were here to stay."[2]

Warner Brothers was not the only studio exploring sound technology. Five months before *The Jazz Singer* opened, Fox premiered sound-film **newsreels** (weekly ten-minute compilations of news events from around the world). Fox's newsreel company, Movietone, captured the first film footage with sound of the takeoff and return of Charles Lindbergh, who piloted the first solo, nonstop flight across the Atlantic Ocean in May 1927. The Movietone sound system eventually became the industry standard.

Inside the Hollywood System: Setting the Standard for Narrative Style

By the time talkies had transformed the film industry, Hollywood had established firm control over narrative style—the recognizable way in which directors told stories through the movies they made. Hollywood had set the

▲ Al Jolson in *The Singing Fool* (1928). The film was the box-office champ for more than ten years, until it was dethroned by *Gone with the Wind* in 1939.
© Warner Bros./Photofest

LaunchPad
launchpadworks.com

Storytelling in *Gravity*
Visit LaunchPad to view a short clip from the Oscar-winning movie *Gravity*.

Discussion: Based on this clip, how does the movie seem to use advanced technical tools in service of classical studio-system storytelling?

example for most moviemaking style worldwide and continues to dominate American filmmaking style today. The model it developed serves up three ingredients that give Hollywood movies their distinctive flavor: the narrative (story), the genre (type of story), and the author (director). The right blend of these ingredients—combined with timing, marketing, and luck—has enabled Hollywood to create a long string of movie hits, from 1930s and 1940s classics like *Gone with the Wind* and *Casablanca* to recent successes like *Jurassic World* and *Captain America: Civil War*.

Hollywood Narratives

As we've seen, storytelling had long existed in movies, even in the silent era. But it was Hollywood's Golden Age that saw the emergence of a distinctive narrative style that movie viewers soon associated with American filmmaking. *Narrative* always includes a story (what happens to whom) and discourse (how the story is told). Most movies feature a number of stories that play out within the film's larger, overarching narrative. These narratives also present recognizable character types (protagonist, antagonist, romantic interest, sidekick) and have a clear beginning, middle, and end. The plot is usually propelled by the main character's decisions and actions to resolve a conflict by the end of the movie. Nowadays, filmmakers also use computer-generated imagery (CGI) or digital remastering to augment narratives with special effects—providing a powerful experience that satisfies most audiences' appetite for both the familiar and the distinctive.

Hollywood Genres

▼Hollywood genres help us categorize movies. The 1949 film *White Heat* is considered a film noir drama, Rob Reiner's *When Harry Met Sally* (1989) is a romantic comedy, and *Beauty and the Beast* (2017) is a fantasy film. Everett Collection, Inc. (left); Everett Collection, Inc. (middle); MANDEVILLES FILMS/WALT DISNEY PICTURES/Album/Newscom/Album Photo Press (right)

In addition to establishing a unique narrative style in its Golden Age, Hollywood gave birth to movie **genres**, categories in which conventions regarding characters, scenes, and themes recur in combination. Familiar genres include comedy, drama, romance, action/adventure, mystery/suspense, gangster, westerns, horror, fantasy/science fiction, musicals, and film noir (French for "black film")—a genre developed in the United States after World War II that explores unstable characters and the sinister side of human nature.

Grouping films by category enabled the movie industry to achieve both *product standardization* (a set of formulas for producing genres) and *product differentiation* (a diverse set of movie-watching experiences for viewers to choose from).

Hollywood "Authors"

As another defining characteristic of Hollywood's Golden Age, movie directors gained significant status. In commercial filmmaking, the director serves as the main "author" of a film. Sometimes called by the French term, *auteurs*, successful directors develop a particular cinematic style or an interest in specific topics that differentiates their narratives from those of other directors. During Hollywood's Golden Age, notable directors included Alfred Hitchcock, Howard Hughes, Sam Goldwyn, and Busby Berkeley—each famous for his defining moviemaking style. Today, directors are just as distinctive: When you hear that a new movie is a "Spielberg film," a "Tarantino project," or "the latest from the Coen brothers," you have a good idea of what to expect.

As the 1960s and 1970s unfolded, the films of Francis Ford Coppola (*The Godfather*), Brian De Palma (*Carrie*), William Friedkin (*The Exorcist*), George Lucas (*Star Wars*), Martin Scorsese (*Taxi Driver*), and Steven Spielberg (*Jaws*) signaled the start of a period that Scorsese has called "the deification of the director." Through this development, a handful of talented directors gained the kind of economic clout and celebrity standing that had previously belonged only to top movie stars. Though directors lost power in the 1980s and 1990s, the tradition carries on with well-known directors like Tim Burton, Wes Anderson, and Christopher Nolan.

Even today, most well-known film directors are white men. Only four women have ever received an Academy Award nomination for directing a feature film: Lina Wertmüller in 1976 for *Seven Beauties*, Jane Campion in 1994 for *The Piano*, Sofia Coppola in 2004 for *Lost in Translation,* and Kathryn Bigelow in 2010 for *The Hurt Locker* (she won). Directors from other groups have also struggled for recognition in Hollywood—and a few have become successful. Well-regarded African American directors include Ava DuVernay (*13th*, 2016), John Singleton (*Abduction*, 2011), and Spike Lee (*Chi-Raq*, 2015). (For more, see "Media Literacy Case Study: Breaking through Hollywood's Race Barrier" on pages 212–213.) Asian Americans M. Night Shyamalan *(Split*, 2016), Ang Lee (*Billy Lynn's Long Halftime Walk*, 2016), and Wayne Wang (*Snow Flower and the Secret Fan*, 2011) have also built accomplished directing careers.

▲ Women directors have long struggled in Hollywood, but some, like Ava DuVernay, are making a name for themselves. DuVernay, who directed the acclaimed Martin Luther King film *Selma* (2014), will also direct the film version of Madeleine L'Engle's popular novel *A Wrinkle in Time*. With a budget of over $100 million, the film is scheduled for a 2018 release. Everett Collection, Inc.

Outside the Hollywood System: Providing Alternatives

Despite Hollywood's dominance of the film industry, viewers have long had alternatives to the feature-length, hugely attended, big-budget movies offered by the studio system. These alternatives include global cinema, documentaries, and independent films.

Global Cinema

Films made in other countries constitute less than 2 percent of motion pictures seen in the United States today. Yet foreign films did well in 1920s America, especially in diverse neighborhoods in large cities. These films' popularity has waxed and waned since the Great Depression, in response to such developments as assimilation of immigrants, postwar prosperity, and the rise of the home video market.

To be sure, the modern success in the United States of movies like *The Girl with the Dragon Tattoo* (Sweden, 2009), *Instructions Not Included* (Mexico, 2013), and *The Mermaid* (China, 2016) suggests that American audiences are willing to watch subtitled films with non-Hollywood perspectives. But foreign films have continued losing screen space to the expanding independent American film market. Today, the largest foreign-film industry is in India, which aficionados call "Bollywood" (a play on words combining *Bombay*—now Mumbai—and *Hollywood*). Bollywood produces as many as one thousand films every year, most of them romances or adventure musicals displaying a distinct style.

▲ *The Mermaid* (2016) is currently the highest-grossing Chinese film of all time, having made over $550 million at the box office. Everett Collection/Inc.

Documentaries

Documentaries, through which directors interpret reality by recording real people and settings, evolved from several earlier types of nonfictional movies: *interest films* (which contained compiled footage of regional wars, political leaders, industrial workers, and agricultural scenes), *newsreels*, and *travelogues* (depictions of daily life in various communities around the world).

Over time, documentaries developed a unique identity. As educational, noncommercial presentations, they usually required the backing of industry, government, or philanthropy to cover production and other costs. By the late 1950s and early 1960s, the development of portable cameras led to a documentary style known as **cinema verité** (French for "truth film"). Portable cameras enabled documentarians (such as Robert Drew, for *Primary*, 1960) to go where cameras could not go before and record fragments of everyday life unobtrusively.

Perhaps the major contribution of documentaries has been their willingness to tackle controversial subject matter or bring attention to issues about which the public might not be aware. For example, *Blackfish*, a documentary by Gabriela Cowperthwaite released in 2013, examines the controversial practice of training orca whales for entertainment venues like SeaWorld. The movie, which first screened at the Sundance Film Festival, sparked anti-SeaWorld protests across the country. American documentary filmmaker Michael Moore often targets corporations or the government in his films, which include *Fahrenheit 9/11* (2004), a critique of the Bush administration's Middle East policies and the Iraq War, and *Where to Invade Next* (2015), a look at the quality of life in other countries.

Independent Films

The success of some documentary films dovetails with the rise of **indies**, another alternative to the Hollywood system. As opposed to directors who work within the Hollywood system, independent filmmakers typically operate on a shoestring budget and show their movies in campus auditoriums, small film festivals, and—if they're lucky—independent theaters. Successful independents like Kevin Smith (*Clerks*, 1994; *Yoga Hosers*, 2016), Robert Rodriguez (*El Mariachi,* 1992; *Spy Kids* franchise, 2001–2011; *Alita: Battle Angel*, scheduled for 2018), and Sofia Coppola (*Lost in Translation*, 2003; *The Beguiled*, 2017) continue to find substantial audiences in theaters and through online services like Netflix, which promote work produced outside the studio system.

The rise of independent film festivals in the 1990s also helped Hollywood rediscover low-cost independent films as alternatives to the standard big-budget blockbuster types of movies. Big studios looked to these festivals as ways to find new talent, which sometimes led them to purchase independent film companies or set up deals to help with distribution for a cut of the profit. This feeder system has since declined somewhat, but indie films are turning more and more to digital platforms and social media to find audiences (see "The Digital Turn Case Study: Attracting An Audience in a Digital Age" on pages 222–223).

The Transformation of the Hollywood Studio System

Beginning in the late 1940s, a number of forces began reshaping how people viewed movies and what they expected to see when they watched a film. These forces stemmed from new regulations seeking to break up studios' hold over the film industry, social developments (e.g., massive migrations of city dwellers to the suburbs),

Media Literacy

Breaking through Hollywood's Race Barrier

Despite inequities and discrimination, a thriving black cinema existed in New York's Harlem district during the 1930s and 1940s. Usually bankrolled by white business executives who were capitalizing on the black-only theaters fostered by segregation, independent films featuring black casts were supported by African American moviegoers, even during the Depression. But it was a popular Hollywood film — *Imitation of Life* (1934) — that emerged as the highest-grossing film in black theaters during the mid-1930s. The film told the story of the friendship between a white woman and a black woman whose young daughter denied her heritage and passed for white, breaking her mother's heart.

Despite African Americans' long support of the film industry, their moviegoing experience has not been the same as that of whites. From the late 1800s until the passage of Civil Rights legislation in the mid-1960s, many theater owners discriminated against black patrons. In large cities, blacks often had to attend separate theaters, where new movies might not appear until a year or two after white theaters had shown them. In smaller towns and in the South, blacks were often not allowed to patronize local theaters before midnight. In addition, some theater managers required black patrons to sit in less desirable areas of the theater.[1]

Changes took place during and after World War II, however. With the "white flight" from central cities during the suburbanization of the 1950s, many downtown and neighborhood theaters began catering to black customers in order to keep from going out of business. By the late 1960s and early 1970s, these theaters had become major venues for popular commercial films such as *Guess Who's Coming to Dinner?* (1967).

Based on the popularity of these films, black photographer-turned-filmmaker Gordon Parks — who'd directed *The Learning Tree* (1969), adapted from his own novel — started making commercial action/adventure films, including *Shaft* (1971), remade by John Singleton in 2000. Popular in urban theaters, especially among black teenagers, the movies produced by both Parks and his son — Gordon Parks Jr. (*Super Fly*, 1972) — spawned a number of commercial imitators, labeled blaxploitation movies. These films were the subjects of heated cultural debates in the 1970s, both praised for their realistic depictions of black urban life and criticized for glorifying violence. Nevertheless, these films reinvigorated urban movie attendance.

Opportunities for black film directors expanded in the 1980s, 1990s, and 2000s, with work from such notable directors as Spike Lee, Tyler Perry, and Julie Dash, who in 1991 was the first black female director to get a general theatrical film release. But only recently have black filmmakers achieved a measure of mainstream success. Lee Daniels received only the second Academy Award nomination for a black director for *Precious: Based on the Novel "Push" by Sapphire* in 2009 (the first was John Singleton, for *Boyz N the Hood* in 1991). In 2013, *12 Years a Slave*, a film adaptation of Solomon Northup's 1853 memoir by black British director Steve McQueen, won three Academy Awards,

⊙ Visit LaunchPad to watch a clip from a Tyler Perry film. How does Perry establish a clear and distinctive voice in his work?

launchpadworks.com

▲ Spike Lee's many films include *Do the Right Thing* (1989), *Malcolm X* (1992), and *Chi-Raq* (2015). Julie Dash directed *Daughters of the Dust* (1991) and *Travel Notes of a Geechee Girl* (2017), among other films. Everett Collection, Inc. (left); The Washington Post/Getty Images (right)

including best picture, and a best director nomination for McQueen. McQueen became the first black director to win a best picture award. The overall lack of recognition of nonwhite actors, writers, and directors during the 2016 Academy Awards, however, led to a trending #OscarsSoWhite hashtag and an Academy response to diversify its membership. In 2017, African Americans won more Oscars than ever, including Mahershala Ali receiving best actor, and Viola Davis winning best supporting actress.

Beyond industry awards, women and people of color still have few opportunities in being able to make decisions on what stories get told. "It's not about what's being lauded," said acclaimed African American actor Don Cheadle. "It's about what's getting greenlit . . . and who's being developed to be the people who can sit in those chairs to greenlight a film. And that is much more important than who's going to walk across a stage and say thank you."[2]

APPLYING THE CRITICAL PROCESS

DESCRIPTION Consider a list of the all-time highest-grossing movies in the United States, such as the one on Box Office Mojo, www.boxofficemojo.com/alltime/world/.

ANALYSIS Note patterns in the list. For example, of the top fifty or so, pay attention to how many films are from African American directors or have major roles with African American actors. Note what the most popular genres are.

INTERPRETATION What do the patterns mean? Economically, it's clear why Hollywood likes to have successful blockbuster movie franchises. But what kinds of films and representations get left out of the mix?

EVALUATION It is likely that we will continue to see an increase in youth-oriented, animated/action movie franchises that are heavily merchandised and intended for wide international distribution. Indeed, Hollywood does not have a lot of motivation to put out movies that don't fit these categories. Is this a good thing?

ENGAGEMENT Watch a film by an African American director and consider what's missing from most theater marquees. Visit aafca.com or browse imdb.com to find more films that feature African American directors and actors. See if Netflix, Hulu, or your campus libraries carry any of these titles, and request them if they don't. Spread the word on notable African American films by reviewing them online or in a college newspaper.

and competing mass media (namely, the increasing popularity of TV). Together, these changes forced the Hollywood studio system to adapt in an effort to remain viable and profitable, even after national weekly movie attendance peaked in 1946.

The Paramount Decision

An important force reshaping the Hollywood system took form in the wake of the **Paramount decision.** This 1948 court ruling (fueled by the government's discomfort with the movie industry's power) forced the big, vertically integrated studios to break up their ownership of movie production, distribution, and exhibition. As a result, the studios eventually gave up their theater businesses.

The ruling never really changed the oligopoly structure of the Hollywood film industry, because it failed to weaken the industry's control over movie distribution. However, it did open up opportunities in the exhibition pillar of the industry for new players outside Hollywood. For instance, art houses began showing more documentaries and foreign films, and thousands of new drive-in theaters sprang up in farmers' fields—all of which offered alternative fare to moviegoers.

Flight to the Suburbs

After World War II, waves of Americans experienced a severe case of pent-up consumer demand after years of wartime frugality. Thus, they migrated from cities to the suburbs to purchase their own homes and spend their much-increased discretionary income on all manner of newly available luxuries. These changes badly hurt the Hollywood studio system: Suburban neighborhoods were located far from downtown movie theaters, and people's leisure-time preferences had shifted from watching movies to shopping for material goods, such as cars, barbecue grills, and furniture.

To make matters worse for studios, the average age of couples entering marriage dropped from twenty-four to nineteen after the war. Thus, there were significantly fewer young couples going to the movies on dates.

Television

As Hollywood responded to the political, regulatory, and social changes transforming 1940s and 1950s America, it also sought to strike back at the major technological force emerging at that time: television. Studios used several strategies in their efforts to compete with TV.

First, with growing legions of people gathering around their living-room TV sets, studios shifted movie content toward more serious themes—including alcoholism (*The Lost Weekend*, 1945), racism (*Pinky*, 1949), sexuality (*Peyton Place*, 1957; *Butterfield 8*, 1960; and *Lolita*, 1962), and other topics from which television stayed away. Ironically, such films challenged the authority of the

◄When the current ratings system was created in 1967, it did not include the now-popular PG-13 rating. That rating was introduced in 1984, following an outcry over violence in the PG-rated *Indiana Jones and the Temple of Doom* and *Gremlins.* © Amblin/Warner Bros./Photofest

industry's own Motion Picture Production Code, adopted in the early 1930s to restrict film depictions of violence, crime, drug use, and sexual behavior. (For more on the Code, see Chapter 13.) In 1967, the Motion Picture Association of America initiated the current ratings system, which rates films for age appropriateness rather than censoring all adult content.

Second, the film industry introduced a host of technological improvements designed to lure Americans away from their TV sets. These innovations included Technicolor, a series of color film processes that was all the more alluring in a world where TV screens showed only black-and-white images. Movie theaters also began offering wide screens, stereophonic sound, and extra-clear film, which was a huge improvement over previously fuzzy images. But although these developments may have drawn some people back to downtown movie theaters, they weren't enough to surmount the studios' core problem: the middle-class flight to the suburbs, away from downtown movie theaters.

Home Entertainment

Things got even more challenging for the studio system in the 1970s, when the introduction of cable television and the videocassette gave rise to the home-entertainment movement. Despite some worries that this trend would be a blow to the studios, Hollywood managed to adapt, developing a new market for renting and selling movies—first on VHS, then on DVD, and more recently on the Blu-ray format.

Studios and indies alike are looking toward Internet distribution for the future of the video business. Currently, movie fans can download or stream movies and television shows for rent or for purchase from services like Netflix, Amazon, Hulu, Google, and the iTunes store to their television sets through devices like Roku, Apple TV, TiVo Premiere, video game consoles, and Internet-ready TVs. As people invest in wide-screen TVs and sophisticated sound systems, home entertainment is getting bigger and keeping pace with the movie theater experience. Interestingly, home entertainment is also getting smaller—movies are increasingly becoming available to stream and download on portable devices like tablets, laptop computers, and smartphones.

The Economics of the Movie Business

Despite the many changes transforming the movie business, the Hollywood studio system continues to make money. In fact, since 1963, Americans have purchased roughly 1 billion movie tickets each year; in 2016, 1.32 billion tickets were sold. In addition, gross revenues from North American box-office sales have climbed above the $11 billion mark, and global box-office revenues continue to grow.[3]

The growing global market for Hollywood films has helped cushion the industry as it undergoes a significant transformation, brought on by the demise of the video rental business and the rise of video streaming. In order to flourish, the movie industry has had to continually revamp its production, distribution, and exhibition systems and consolidate its ownership.

Making Money on Movies Today

The cost of producing films has risen, and studios have had to find ways to generate more revenue in order to produce movies profitably. On top of that, with 80 to 90 percent of newly released films failing to make money at the domestic box office, studios need a couple of major hits each year to make money through one of the six main revenue sources:

1. **Box-office sales.** Studios get about 40 percent of the theater box-office take in this first "window" for movie exhibition (the theater gets the rest). Studios have recently found that they can often reel in bigger box-office receipts for 3-D films and their higher ticket prices.

2. **DVD/video sales and rentals.** Sales to the home video market (video-on-demand, subscription streaming, Blu-ray, DVD sales and rentals) typically start about three to four months after a theatrical release and generate more revenue than domestic box-office income for major studios.

3. **Cable and television outlets.** This includes premium cable (such as HBO and Showtime), and network and basic cable showings. The syndicated TV market also pays the studios on a negotiated film-by-film basis.

4. **Foreign distribution.** Studios earn revenue from distributing films in foreign markets. In fact, at a record-breaking $27.2 billion in 2016 (about 70 percent of worldwide box office revenues of $38.6 billion), international box-office gross revenues are more than double U.S. and Canadian box-office receipts ($11.4 billion in 2016), and they continue to climb annually, even as other countries produce more of their own films.

5. **Independent-film distribution.** Studios make money by distributing the work of independent producers and filmmakers, who hire the studios to gain wider circulation. Independents pay the studios 30 to 50 percent of the box-office and home video revenue they make from their movies.

6. **Licensing and product placement.** Studios earn revenue from merchandise licensing (for example, licensing sales of action figures representing characters from a particular movie) to retailers. Companies that make cars, snacks, and other products also pay studios to place their products in movies, so that actors and characters will be shown using those products. Famous product placements include Reese's Pieces in *E.T.: The Extra-Terrestrial* (1982), Pepsi-Cola in *Back to the Future II* (1989), and *The Lego Batman Movie* (2017)—an entire movie built around the popular toy line.

Conglomerations and Synergy in the Movie Industry

The current Hollywood commercial film business is ruled primarily by six companies: Warner Brothers, Paramount, Twentieth Century Fox, Universal, Columbia Pictures, and Disney (Buena Vista)—all owned by large parent conglomerates except for Disney (see Figure 7.1). Together, the **Big Six** account for about 87 percent of the revenue generated by commercial films. They also control more than half the movie market in Europe and Asia.

Synergy—the promotion and sale of a product throughout the various subsidiaries of a media conglomerate—provides

▼Though expensive to produce, blockbusters like *Guardians of the Galaxy* (2014) get made not only because of the potential for big audiences and merchandising but also because when they hit it big, studios keep the gravy train rolling with sequels. *Guardians of the Galaxy Vol. 2* was released in 2017. Atlaspix/Alamy

a powerful advantage to large movie studios. Companies like Disney promote the new movies produced by its studio division as well as books, soundtracks, calendars, T-shirts, and toys based on these movies. This synergy also helps explain why a company like Disney has been snapping up other studios, including Pixar (purchased for $7.6 billion in 2006), Marvel (purchased for $3.96 billion in 2009), and Lucasfilm (purchased for $4.06 billion in 2012).[4] Pixar has created some of the most successful animated movies of the past two decades, such as *Up* (2009), *Toy Story 3* (2010), *Cars 2* (2011), *Monsters University* (2013), *Inside Out* (2015), and *Finding Dory* (2016). Marvel appears to have been even more of a bargain. Disney-produced films from the Marvel cinematic universe include *The Avengers* (2012), *Iron Man 3* (2013), *Captain America: The Winter Soldier* (2014), *Avengers: Age of Ultron* (2015), and *Doctor Strange* (2016). After acquiring Lucasfilm, Disney released *Star Wars: Episode VII: The Force Awakens* (2015), which became the highest-earning film in U.S. box-office history, and *Rogue One: A Star Wars Story* (2016). The franchises from all three studios are highly marketable, with characters that have spawned lucrative lines of toys, books, and an array of related products.

FIGURE 7.1 // MARKET SHARE OF U.S. FILM STUDIOS AND DISTRIBUTORS, 2016 (IN MILLIONS)

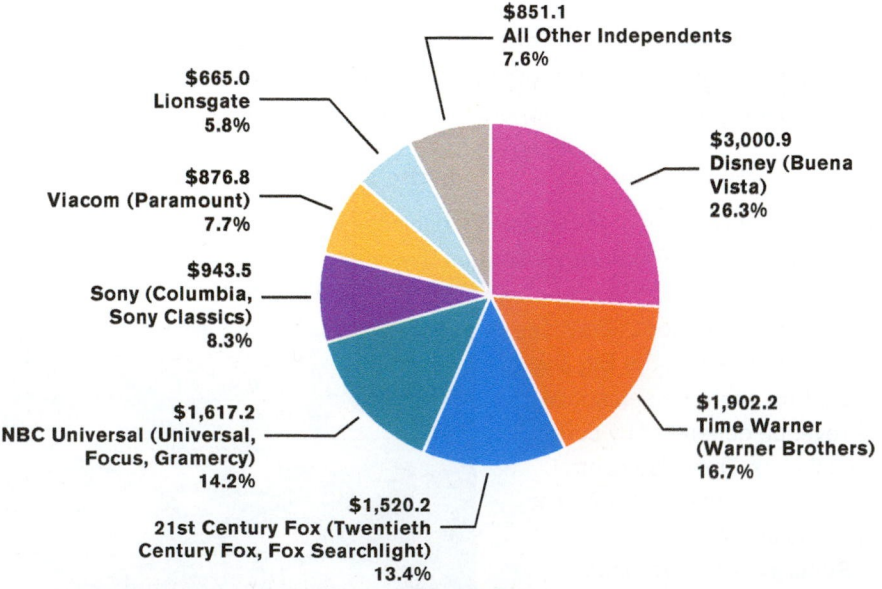

Data from: Box Office Mojo, "Studio Market Share, 2016," www.boxofficemojo.com/studio/?view=company&view2=yearly&yr=2016&p=.htm.

Note: Based on gross box-office revenue, January 1, 2016–December 31, 2016. Overall gross for period: $11.376.9 million.

Convergence: Movies Adjust to the Digital Turn

The biggest challenge the movie industry faces today is the Internet. After witnessing the difficulties that illegal file-sharing brought on the music labels (some of which share the same corporate parent as film studios), the movie industry has more quickly embraced the Internet for movie distribution through outlets like Amazon and Netflix.

The popularity of Netflix's streaming service (added in 2008 to its DVD-rental-by-mail service) opened the door to other similar services (see Figure 7.2). That same year, NBC Universal (Universal Studios), News Corp. (21st Century Fox), and Disney launched Hulu. Since then, others—such as Comcast (Xfinity TV), Google (YouTube), Walmart (Vudu), and Amazon (Amazon Video)—have also gotten into online digital movie distribution. Movies are also increasingly available to stream or download on mobile phones and tablets. Several companies, including Netflix, Hulu, Amazon, Google, and Apple, have developed distribution to mobile devices.

FIGURE 7.2 // ONLINE VIDEO STREAMING MARKET SHARE, MAY 2015 AND MAY 2016

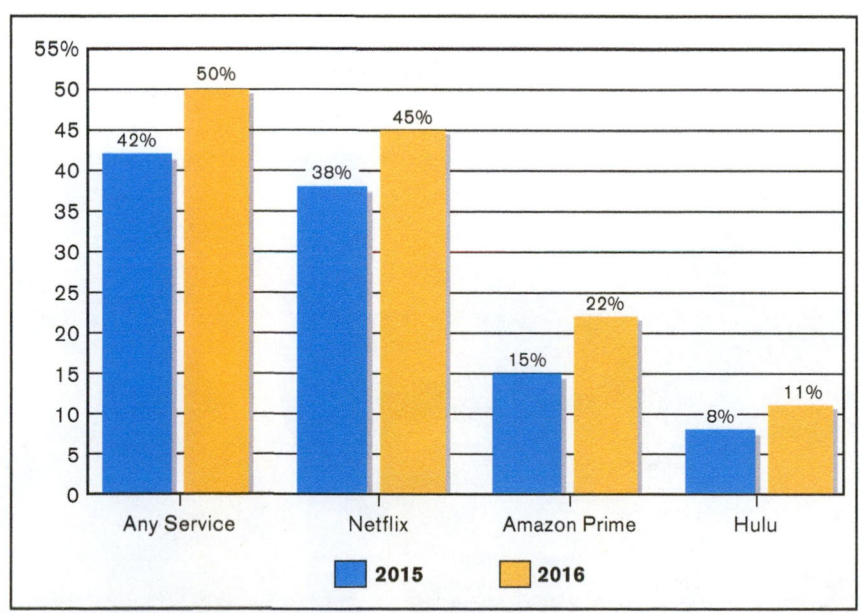

Percentage of U.S. households with a television that subscribe to a paid video streaming service. Note: Some households may subscribe to more than one.

Data from: Christine Wang, "Overwhelming Majority of People Watching Streaming Services Still Choose Netflix," CNBC, July 21, 2016, www.cnbc.com/2016/07/21/overwhelming-majority-of-people-watching-streaming-services -still-choose-netflix.html.

The year 2012 marked a turning point: For the first time, movie fans accessed more movies through digital online media than physical copies, like DVDs or Blu-rays.[5] For the movie industry, this shift to Internet distribution has mixed consequences. On the one hand, the industry needs to offer movies where people want to access them, and digital distribution is a growing market. On the other hand, although streaming is less expensive than producing physical DVDs, the revenue is still much lower compared to DVD sales, which had a larger impact on the major studios that had grown reliant on healthy DVD revenue.

The digital turn creates two long-term paths for Hollywood. One path is that studios and theaters will lean even more heavily toward making and showing big-budget blockbuster film franchises with a lot of special effects, since people will want to watch those on the big screen (especially IMAX and 3-D) for the full effect; plus, they are easy to export for international audiences. The other path features inexpensive digital distribution for lower-budget documentaries and independent films, which likely wouldn't get wide theatrical distribution anyway but could find an audience in those who watch at home.

The Internet has also become an essential tool for movie marketing—one that studios are finding less expensive than traditional methods, like television ads or billboards. Many studios now use a full menu of social media to promote films in advance of their release (see also "The Digital Turn Case Study: Attracting an Audience in a Digital Age" on pages 222–223).

► Digital video is now common in Hollywood films. One of the latest digital cameras, the Red, is considered affordable at $17,500, making digital equipment more accessible to new or lower-budget filmmakers. Everett Collection, Inc.

In addition to distribution and promotion, special effects and digital video have led to dramatic changes in the film industry. Powerful computer-generated imagery (CGI) makes the fantastic seem common, whether it be a superhero fighting aliens or elves fighting orcs. But while top-end CGI can be expensive, filmmakers of the last decade cut costs by switching from expensive and bulky 16-mm and 35-mm film cameras to **digital video**, which eliminates the need to buy and pay to develop film. Between digital video and computer-based desktop editors like Adobe Premiere Pro, it's possible to make movies for a few thousand dollars and post them on venues like YouTube and Vimeo.

The Movies in a Democratic Society

From the earliest days of film, there were questions about how the medium would fit into society and how First Amendment free-speech protections would—or wouldn't—apply to movies. As community and political leaders increasingly realized how powerful movies could be, they became concerned about the power of film to upset existing social norms. But a mid-twentieth-century government crackdown on movies and those who made them would destroy lives and alter Hollywood for decades to come.

In 1947, in the wake of the unfolding Cold War with the Soviet Union, some members of Congress began investigating Hollywood for alleged subversive and communist ties. During the investigations, the House Un-American Activities Committee (HUAC) coerced prominent people from the film industry to declare their patriotism and to give up the names of colleagues suspected of having politically unfriendly tendencies. Upset over labor union strikes and outspoken writers, many film executives were eager to testify and provide names. For instance, Jack L. Warner of Warner Brothers suggested that whenever film writers made fun of the wealthy or America's political system in their work, or if their movies were sympathetic to "Indians and the colored folks,"[6] they were engaging in communist propaganda. Many other prominent actors and directors also "named names," either out of a belief that it was their patriotic duty or out of fear of losing their jobs.

Eventually, HUAC subpoenaed ten unwilling witnesses who were questioned about their memberships in various organizations. The so-called **Hollywood Ten**—nine screenwriters and one director—refused to discuss their memberships or to identify communist sympathizers. Charged with contempt of Congress in November 1947, they were eventually sent to prison. Although jailing the Hollywood Ten clearly violated their free-speech rights, in the atmosphere of the Cold War many people worried that "the American way"

The Digital Turn

Attracting an Audience in a Digital Age

"I bet you're wondering why I'm wearing this red suit," the costumed superhero says, looking straight into the camera while sitting on the edge of a busy highway overpass. "It's so the bad guys don't see me bleed," he continues, and gestures with his head toward some approaching vehicles. "Let's hope these guys are wearing their brown pants." He jumps from his perch, free-falling several stories before plunging through the sunroof of an SUV and attacking the villainous henchmen inside.

These opening lines of leaked test footage for the movie *Deadpool* hint at the fourth-wall-breaking vulgar irreverence that this comic book character is known for. These lines also illustrate screenwriters Rhett Reese and Paul Wernick's understanding of just how well a self-aware, wise-cracking, visually stimulating antihero would appeal to an Internet audience in a post-digital-turn world.

In fact, it was the character's appeal to scores of fans on the Internet that helped the movie get made in the first place. In a 2016 interview with talk-show host Jimmy Fallon, actor Ryan Reynolds explained that the test footage he and three friends created sat on a shelf for four years at Fox Studios. Then someone leaked it to the Internet. "The Deadpool fans freaked out and overwhelmed Fox, and Fox basically had to

▲ Thanks in part to a marketing campaign that played up the character Deadpool's tendency for absurdity, dark humor, and irreverence, the movie broke several box-office records when it opened on Valentine's Day weekend in 2016. Earning over $150 million in just four days, this success quickly ensured a sequel. © Twentieth Century Fox Film Corporation/Photofest

green-light the movie," said Reynolds. "The problem was, this footage was owned by Fox and was sort of illegal, it got leaked. I know that one of us [who made the test footage] did it, but I'm 70 percent sure it wasn't me."[1]

There are many ways digital technology has changed movies, from technical advances in 3-D and high definition to ever-more-powerful computer-generated special effects. But as the story of *Deadpool*'s Internet appeal suggests, the digital turn also presents new ways for studios to fill seats when a film hits the theater. *Deadpool*'s adept use of digital marketing started with the leaked trailer, but it didn't stop there; the movie's digital media blitz included more short videos, a Deadpool Tinder profile, actor Ryan Reynolds's Deadpool-esque tweets, and even Deadpool emojis.

The traditional approach to most marketing efforts is to focus on print and TV ads four to six weeks before a movie is released. But studios

▶ Web Clip

YouTube.com has many video examples of digital marketing. For example, search for 'Team Thor — Official Marvel' posted by Marvel UK to watch a clip from a tongue-in-cheek video with superheroes Thor and the Hulk. How might a clip like this help franchises capture viral video buzz in between theatrical releases?

also invest in a variety of digital strategies before a movie hits theaters. For example, NBC Universal got millions of followers on Facebook for its *Fifty Shades of Grey* and *Fast and Furious* franchises long before the films were released.[2] In addition, marketing across multiple digital platforms helps studios retain a level of buzz about upcoming movies set in increasingly complex cinematic universes, like those of the *X-Men* (Fox); *Star Wars* and *Avengers* (Disney); and Superman, Batman, and the Justice League (Warner Brothers/Time-Warner). These efforts help keep audiences interested as they wait for the next film installment to hit theaters.

And it's not just big film studios that have found success using online marketing. One of the first independent films that turned online buzz into box-office success was 1999's *The Blair Witch Project*, which used now-archaic message boards and newsgroups to help gross over $140 million in ticket sales — despite its tiny budget of just $22,500. These days, indies use an even bigger array of online platforms to help attract an audience, investors, and major studios. For example, a filmmaker might use a site like YouTube or Vimeo to upload all or part of a film, recruit the film's cast and crew to post about the film on social media, and hope to get featured on a site like Gizmodo's io9.com to boost publicity.[3] And unlike film festivals — which have long been used to promote indie films but which can cost hundreds or thousands of dollars in registration fees — this online exposure can reach a large audience at no additional cost to the filmmaker.

At the same time, social media and other digital marketing efforts can be tricky. Most social media sites allow businesses to track follows, likes, and even how much others are talking about a topic on their platform, but it's not always clear how that buzz translates into ticket sales. Studio public relations and marketing teams can also be cautious about online conversations, which by their very nature are unpredictable. For example, when Amber Heard filed for divorce from Johnny Depp, saying the actor had abused her, the hashtag #ImWithAmber went viral along with calls to boycott Depp's *Alice through the Looking Glass*, a sequel to the very successful *Alice in Wonderland*. The negative publicity before the film launched on Memorial Day weekend in 2016 is believed to have contributed to disappointing ticket sales for the Disney film.

Publicity has always been important to movies. But marketing films after the digital turn, and having audiences interact with marketing campaigns in ways that are beyond studio control, might feel a little like jumping off a freeway overpass into heavy traffic — and not being sure where you'll land.

could be sabotaged via unpatriotic messages planted in films. Upon release from jail, the Hollywood Ten found themselves blacklisted, or boycotted, by the major studios, and their careers in the film industry were all but ruined. The national fervor over communism continued to plague Hollywood well into the 1950s.

When HUAC made sure to include the film industry in its communist witch hunts, they were reacting to the way they saw film as a powerful cultural tool that could threaten the status quo. That's because movies function as **consensus narratives**—popular cultural products that provide us with shared experiences. Whether they are dramas, romances, westerns, or mysteries, movies communicate values, hopes, and dreams through accessible language and imagery that can reinforce some cultural norms, challenge others, and even bridge cultural differences. This can be a double-edged sword.

As the American film industry has continued to dominate the movie-watching experience in many other nations, observers have begun questioning this phenomenon. Some have wondered whether American-made films are helping to create a kind of global village, where people around the world share a universal culture. Others have asked whether these films stifle local cultures worldwide.

With the rise of international media conglomerates, public debate over such questions has ebbed. This is worrisome, as movies exert a powerful impact on people's beliefs, values, and even actions. As other nations begin to view the American film industry as an interloper in their people's culture, they may develop a resentment against the United States overall.

Likewise, the continuing power of the movie industry within our own nation raises questions about movies' role in our democracy. It's vital that those of us who consume movies do so with a critical eye and a willingness to debate these larger questions about this mass medium's cultural, political, and social significance. The political significance of film is easy to see in movies that strike a political chord with many members of the audience, such as Michael Moore's *Capitalism: A Love Story* (a director and film that surely would have drawn the wrath of HUAC) or Clint Eastwood's *American Sniper*. But that's not to say that viewers need only watch serious, issue-based films closely or critically. If anything, a consensus narrative is more powerful when audiences accept it without even really knowing that's what they are doing.

For instance, most mainstream audiences see Disney's movies as harmless forms of entertainment. But a critical look at the images of femininity in Disney films, from *Snow White* to *Pirates of the Caribbean*, reveals a consistent view of beauty that hews close to a Barbie-doll ideal. What's more, inner beauty is typically reflected by an attractive outward appearance. Other Disney films (like *The Lion King* and *Pocahontas*) verge on racial stereotyping or xenophobia, as when the heroes of *Aladdin* look less Middle Eastern than the villains. A media-literate viewer, then, must recognize that part of the cultural power of broad entertainments like Disney movies is bound up in packaging potentially questionable messages about gender, race, and class in stories that seem transparently wholesome. Given the expanded viewing options and the increasing access to independent, foreign, and otherwise nonmainstream films, viewers can seek out various alternatives to mass-marketed Hollywood films. With an entity as large as the U.S. film industry producing compelling messages about what we should value, how we should live, and how we should act, it's vital for those of us who consume movies to do so with a critical, media-literate eye—and to seek out other cinematic voices.

CHAPTER ESSENTIALS

Review

- Major advances in film technology took place in the late nineteenth century. Eadweard Muybridge created a method for making images move, and George Eastman developed the first roll film, capable of capturing moving images and projecting them. Soon after, Hannibal Goodwin improved roll film by using strips of transparent, pliable material called **celluloid**, enabling a strip of film to move through a camera and be photographed in rapid succession, producing a series of pictures.

- Film moved to the entrepreneurial stage with the invention of new projection and distribution technologies, such as Thomas Edison's **kinetograph**, **kinetoscope**, and **vitascope**.

- Movies advanced to the mass medium stage in the late 1890s with the introduction of **narrative films** and the arrival of early movie theaters, called **nickelodeons**.

- The "three pillars" of the movie business are production (making movies), distribution (getting films into theaters), and exhibition (playing films in theaters). Controlling these three parts achieved **vertical integration**. The resulting concentration of power gave rise to the **studio system**. Five film studios made up the early twentieth century's film **oligopoly**.

- Once the Hollywood studio system established itself as a profitable business, the Golden Age of Hollywood began to take shape, beginning with the introduction of new narrative techniques in 1915. Over the next decades, the Golden Age would be marked by the introduction of sound pictures (**talkies**) and later sound-film **newsreels**, movie **genres**, and the rise in status of the movie director.

- Outside the Hollywood system, many alternatives to the feature-length film exist, such as global cinema, **documentaries**, and independent films (or **indies**).

- Beginning in the 1940s, a number of political, social, and cultural forces reshaped how people viewed movies, forcing the Hollywood studio system to adapt. For example, the **Paramount decision** in 1948 and the migration of Americans from the cities to the suburbs changed the way movies were consumed.

- Filmmakers make money from box-office sales, DVD/video sales and rentals, cable and television outlets, foreign distribution, independent-film distribution, and licensing and product placement.

- Big media conglomerates like the **Big Six**—Warner Brothers, Paramount, Twentieth Century Fox, Universal, Columbia Pictures, and Disney (Buena Vista)—also make money through **synergy**.

- The dawn of the digital age is forcing studios to rethink their business models. The movie industry has embraced the Internet more quickly than has the music industry, distributing movies online through outlets like Apple's iTunes store and Netflix.

- The continuing power of the movie industry raises questions about movies' role in society—both internationally and within the United States. Therefore, it's vital for those who consume movies to do so with a critical eye.

Key Terms

Study Questions

1. How did film go from the development stage to the mass medium stage?

2. Why did Thomas Edison and the Trust fail to shape and control the film industry, and why did Adolph Zukor of Paramount succeed?

3. Why are genres and directors important to the film industry?

4. What political and cultural forces changed the Hollywood system in the 1950s?

5. What are the various ways in which major movie studios make money in the film business?

6. Do films contribute to a global village in which people throughout the world share a universal culture, or do U.S.-based films overwhelm the development of other cultures worldwide? Discuss.

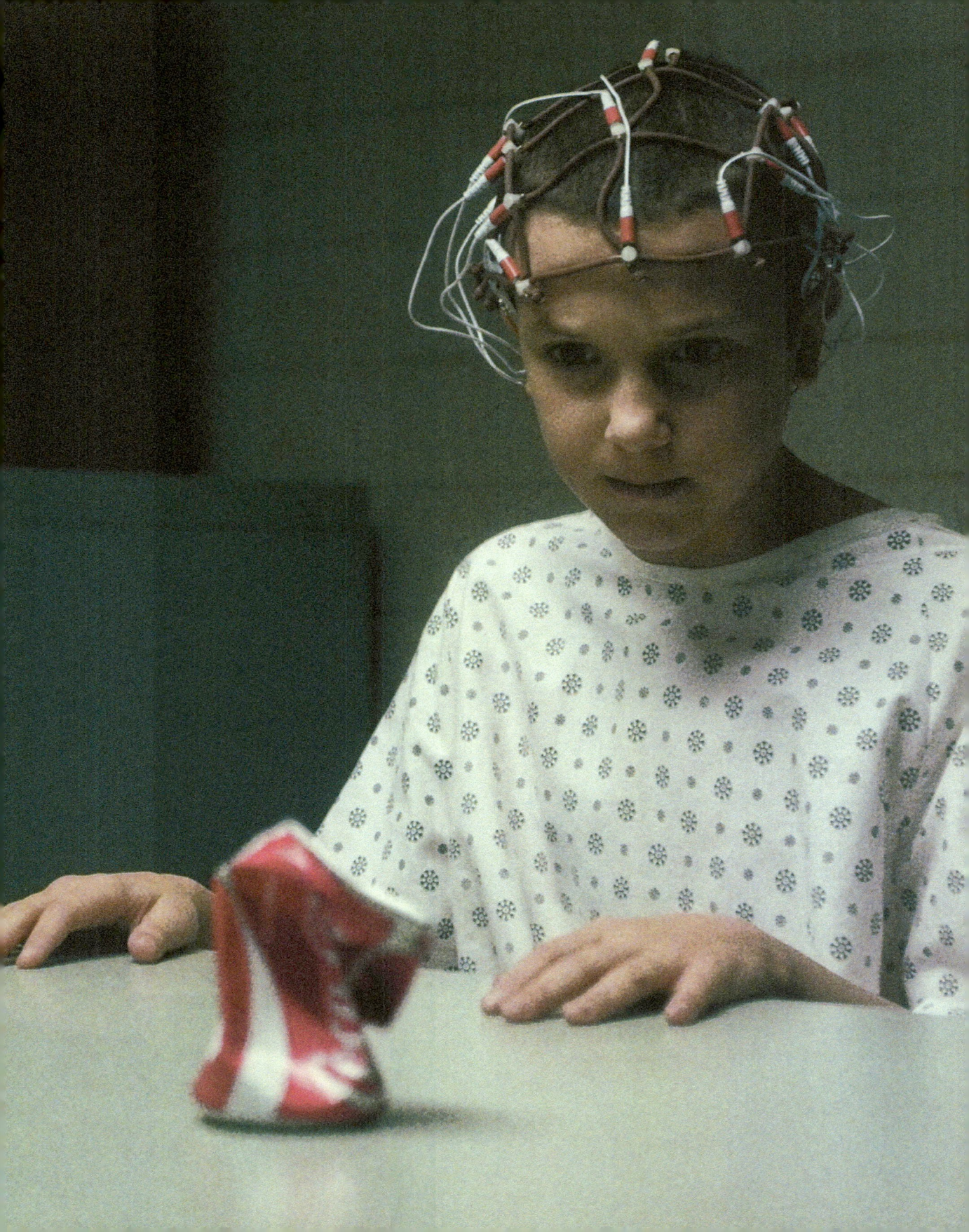

8

Television, Cable, and Specialization in Visual Culture

A panicking man in a lab coat is attacked by an unseen creature in a government building. A group of preteen boys play Dungeons & Dragons—and then one of them disappears after being backed into a garden shed by the still-unrevealed monster. With this intense opening, Netflix's moody, nostalgia-filled *Stranger Things* began its first episode—and struck a chord with audiences. The homage to 1980s horror and science fiction racked up over eight million views in less than three weeks after its eight-episode season was released in July 2016, catapulting it ahead of earlier Netflix original-series hits like *House of Cards*, *Daredevil*, and *Narcos*.[1]

Twin brothers Matt and Ross Duffer created *Stranger Things*, which is set in the early 1980s and has an abundance of suspense and mystery, in addition to strong nostalgic appeal. The Duffers say the show is an homage to some of their favorite films growing up, such as *Jaws* and *E.T.: The Extra-Terrestrial*, as well as the work of Stephen King.[2] Yet while the show itself is set well before the digital turn, its delivery method is decidedly modern: As a Netflix original series, it is available only through Internet streaming—not through network or cable TV.

◀ With its first season running just eight episodes long, Netflix's suspenseful *Stranger Things* appeals to viewers who want to stream and binge-watch their favorite programs on a wide variety of devices. Netflix/Photofest

With the popularity of streaming shows like *Stranger Things*, the Internet is quickly becoming the future of television. Whereas television used to be available only on traditional TV sets, and people mostly watched only the original broadcast networks (ABC, CBS, and NBC), things are different today. Audiences of all ages—even those who remember when watching TV meant using an antenna that picked up a half-dozen channels or less—are moving toward video streaming. And viewers born after the mid-1990s may not even be accustomed to watching a television set at all, having grown up viewing Internet programs almost exclusively on laptops, tablets, and smartphones.

That's not to say that television is dead, although it *is* certainly changing. On the surface, a mutually beneficial relationship has developed among online streaming services and broadcasters and cable providers—Hulu, after all, is jointly owned by Disney (ABC), 21st Century Fox (Fox), Comcast (NBC), and Time Warner (Turner Broadcasting System). Internet streaming services help cable and broadcast networks increase their audiences through *time shifting*, as viewers watch favorite TV shows days, even weeks, after they originally aired. But as original shows like *Stranger Things* have become hits for companies like Netflix, streaming networks also represent increasing competition for audiences' attention—and their dollars. And this means that a battle may be brewing among streaming companies and their broadcast and cable counterparts.

But even as video streaming shakes up the TV landscape, one thing remains unchanged: High-quality stories resonate with enthusiastic audiences. Whether seen through streaming or cable, good shows can still draw a range of viewers, from younger fans who grew up with the Internet to older fans who embrace programs that capture their nostalgia for a time before this technology existed.

FOR A LONG TIME AFTER ITS INCEPTION, television brought millions of American viewers together to share major turning points in U.S. history. For example, people gathered around their sets to watch coverage of Civil Rights struggles, the moon landing, the Watergate scandal, the explosion of a space shuttle, the 9/11 attacks, Hurricane Katrina, and the wars in Iraq and Afghanistan. Television also united people around more enjoyable activities, such as movie, television, and music awards shows (the Oscars, the Emmys, or the CMA Awards), or major sporting events like the Super Bowl. Throughout the country, Americans watched the latest episode of their favorite TV comedy or drama at home, then discussed it with friends and colleagues the next day.

The invention of cable and then satellite television resulted in more channels and programming options than ever to choose from, each of them appealing—like magazines—to narrow niches of viewers. New platforms keep attracting more users as the ways we experience television continue to change. In 1977, only 14 percent of all American homes received cable service (which at that time carried just twelve channels). In 1999, that number had grown to 70 percent (with many times more channels). However, that number has been slipping due to competition from Internet-based streaming and direct broadcast satellite (DBS) services, leading to an increase in "cord-cutting" (the practice of canceling cable and relying on the Internet to access programs). Even traditional cable television customers no longer rely on the same services, with digital cable, DVR, and video-on-demand providing more options for what we watch and how we watch it.

These technologies have changed the way we watch television and modified the role it plays in our lives. It's become easier to watch only what we want—when and where we want. But it's also harder to capture that sense of community that comes from watching a program together in our living rooms and talking about it with others afterward.

In this chapter, we examine television's impact on American life—yesterday, today, and tomorrow—by:

- **considering television's early history, including its foundational technological innovations, the development of program content, and the arrival of cable**

- **tracing turning points in the evolution of network programming, such as the development of daily news broadcasts, the arrival of new entertainment forms (comedy, drama, talk shows, reality television), and the creation of public television**

- **exploring the evolution of cable and satellite programming, including the emergence of basic and premium services**

- **assessing the regulatory challenges network television and cable have faced, such as the government's attempts to decrease networks' control over content and limit cable's growth**

- **examining network television and cable in the digital age, including the impact of home video; the Internet, smartphones, and mobile video; and direct broadcast satellite**

- **analyzing the economics of television by considering how industry players make money and what they spend it on to stay in business**

- **raising questions about television's role in our democratic society, such as whether it is uniting us or fragmenting us and whether it's giving a greater or fewer number of people a voice**

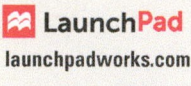
The Early History of Television

In 1948, only 1 percent of American households had a television set. By 1953, more than 50 percent had one, and by the early 1960s, the number had risen past 90 percent. During these early years, several major developments shaped television and helped turn it into a dominant mass medium. Others, especially an infamous scandal over corrupt TV quiz shows, brought its potential and promise into question.

Becoming a Mass Medium

Inspired by the ability to transmit audio signals from one place to another, inventors had long sought to send "tele-visual" images. For example, in the 1880s, German inventor Paul Nipkow developed the *scanning disk*, a large flat metal disk perforated with small holes organized in a spiral pattern. As the disk rotated, it separated pictures into pinpoints of light that could be transmitted as a series of electronic lines. Subsequent inventors improved on this early electronic technology. Their achievements pushed television from the development stage to the entrepreneurial stage and then to the mass medium stage—complete with technical standards, regulation, and further innovation (such as the move from black-and-white to color television).

The Development Stage: Establishing Patents

Television's development and commercialization were fueled by a battle over patents between two independent inventors—Vladimir Zworykin and Philo Farnsworth—each seeking a way to send pictures through the air over long distances. In 1923, after immigrating to America and taking a job at RCA, the Russian-born Zworykin invented the *iconoscope*, the first TV camera tube to convert light rays into electrical signals. He received a patent for his device in 1928.

Around the same time, Farnsworth—an Idaho teenager—transmitted the first electronic TV picture by rotating a straight line scratched on a square of painted glass by 90 degrees. RCA accused Farnsworth of patent violation. But in 1930, after his high school teacher provided evidence of his original

▼ Philo Farnsworth, one of the inventors of television, experiments with an early version of an electronic TV set. Bettmann/Getty Images

drawings from 1922, Farnsworth received a patent for the first electronic television and later licensed his patents to RCA and AT&T, which used them to commercialize the technology. He also conducted the first public demonstration of television at the Franklin Institute in Philadelphia in 1934—five years before RCA's much more famous public demonstration at the 1939 World's Fair.

The Entrepreneurial Stage: Setting Technical Standards

Turning television into a business required creating a coherent set of technical standards for product manufacturers. In the late 1930s, the National Television Systems Committee (NTSC), a group representing engineers, inventors, network executives, and major electronics firms, began outlining industry-wide manufacturing practices and defining technical standards. In 1941, the Federal Communications Commission (FCC) adopted an **analog** standard (a 525-line image) for all U.S. TV sets (which at that time could show only black-and-white images). About thirty countries adopted this system, though most of Europe and Asia eventually adopted a system with slightly better image quality and resolution.

The Mass Medium Stage: Assigning Frequencies and Introducing Color

TV signals are part of the same electromagnetic spectrum that carries light waves and radio signals. In the early days of television, and before the advent of cable, the number of TV stations a city or region could support was limited because airwave frequencies interfered with one another (so you could have a Channel 5 but not a Channel 6 in the same market). In the 1940s, the FCC began assigning certain channels in specific geographic areas to prevent interference. In 1952, after years of licensing freezes due to World War II, the FCC created a national map and tried to distribute all available channels evenly throughout the country. By the mid-1950s, the nation had more than four hundred television stations in operation. Television had become a mass medium.

Television's new status led to additional standards. In 1952, the FCC tentatively approved an experimental color system developed by CBS; however, its signal could not be received by black-and-white sets. In 1954, RCA's color system, which sent TV images in color but allowed older sets to receive the images as black-and-white, became the color standard.

Controlling TV Content

As a mass medium, television had become big business, and broadcast networks began jockeying for increased control over its content. As in radio during the 1930s and 1940s, early television programs were developed, produced, and supported by a single sponsor—often a company, such as Goodyear, Colgate, or Buick. This arrangement gave the companies that controlled brand-name

▲ Shown here on the assembly line, this 1954 RCA CT-100 was the first mass-produced electronic color TV set. Only affluent customers could afford these early sets, priced at $1,000 or more. Anonymous/AP Images

products extensive power over what was shown on television. But then newly emerging broadcast networks wanted more control and, using several strategies, set out to diminish sponsor and ad agency control.

One strategy involved lengthening program times. Sylvester "Pat" Weaver, president of NBC, took the lead. A former advertising executive used to controlling radio content for his clients, Weaver increased TV program length from fifteen minutes (standard for radio programs) to thirty minutes and even longer. This substantially raised program costs for advertisers, discouraging some from sponsoring programs.

In addition, NBC introduced two TV program types to gain more control over content. The first type—the magazine format—featured multiple segments, including news, talk, comedy, and music. These early-1950s programs—*Today* and the *Tonight Show*—are still attracting morning and late-evening audiences. By running daily rather than weekly, they made studio production costs much more prohibitive for a single sponsor. Instead of sponsoring, an advertiser would pay the network for thirty- or sixty-second time slots during the show. The network, not the sponsor, now owned such programs or bought them from independent producers. In the second new program type—the "television spectacular"—networks bought programs on special topics from producers and sold ad spots to multiple advertisers. Early spectaculars (which came to be called "specials") included decades of Bob Hope Christmas shows and the 1955 TV version of *Peter Pan*, which drew over sixty-five million viewers—more than triple the audience for one episode of *American Idol*.

Staining Television's Reputation

In the late 1950s, corruption in an increasingly popular TV program format—quiz shows—tainted television's reputation and further altered the power balance between broadcast networks and program sponsors. Quiz shows had become huge business. They were (and remain) cheap to produce, with inexpensive sets and amateurs as guests. For each show, the corporate sponsor—such as Revlon or Geritol—prominently displayed its name on the set throughout the program.

But as it turned out, many quiz shows were rigged. To heighten the drama and get rid of unappealing guests, sponsors pressured TV executives to give their favorite contestants answers to the quiz questions and allow them to rehearse their responses. The most notorious rigging occurred on *Twenty-One*, a quiz show owned by Geritol, whose profits had climbed by a whopping $4 million a year after it began sponsoring the program in 1956.

When investigations exposed the rigging, the fraud undermined Americans' belief in television's democratic promise—to bring inexpensive, honest information and entertainment into every household. The scandals had magnified the separation between the privileged, powerful few (wealthy companies) and the general public. For the next forty years, the broadcast networks kept quiz shows out of **prime time**—the block of time (7–11 P.M. EST) with large viewer audiences.

▲ In 1957, the most popular contestant on the quiz show *Twenty-One* was college professor Charles Van Doren (*left*). Congressional hearings on rigged quiz shows revealed that Van Doren had been given answers to help him defeat opponents whom the show's producers and sponsors deemed less appealing than Van Doren. The Everett Collection

Introducing Cable

Despite the quiz-show scandals, broadcast television continued to grow in popularity in the late 1950s; however, some communities remained unable to receive traditional over-the-air TV signals, often because of their isolation or because mountains or tall buildings blocked transmission. The first small cable systems—called **CATV**, or community antenna television—originated in Oregon, Pennsylvania, and New York City in the late 1940s as an early attempt to solve this problem. New cable companies ran wires from relay towers that brought in broadcast signals from far away. The cable companies then strung wire from utility poles and sent the signals to individual homes, stimulating demand for TV sets in those communities.

These early systems served only about 10 percent of the country and usually contained only twelve channels because of early technical and regulatory limits. Yet cable offered big advantages. First, it routed each channel in a separate wire, thereby eliminating the over-the-air interference that sometimes happened with broadcast transmissions. Second, it ran signals through *coaxial cable*, a core of aluminum wire encircled by braided wires that provided the option of adding more channels. Initially, many small communities with CATV received twice as many channels as were available over the air in much larger cities. Eventually, the cable industry would pose a major competitive threat to conventional broadcast television. But cable would also encounter new challenges (and opportunities) with the invention of satellite television, which uses large dishes to "downlink" signals from communication satellites in order to transmit cable TV services like HBO and CNN (see Figure 8.1).

FIGURE 8.1 // A BASIC CABLE TELEVISION SYSTEM

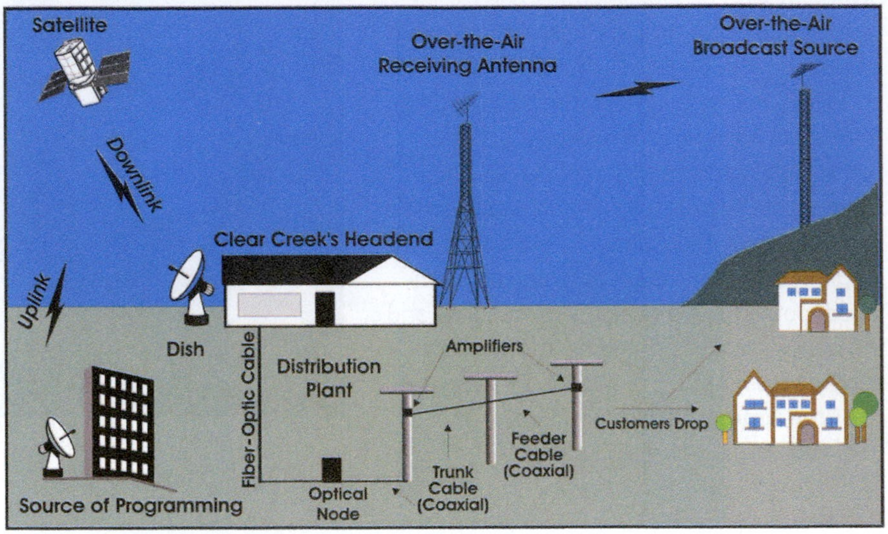

Data from: Clear Creek Telephone & TeleVision.

The Evolution of Network Programming

Even with the emergence of mostly small-town cable operations, broadcast networks still controlled most TV programming in the 1950s. They began specializing in many types of programming (much of it "borrowed" from radio), including early-evening newscasts, variety shows, sitcoms, and soap operas. Eventually, additional genres and services emerged, including talk shows, newsmagazines, reality television, and public television. Television's powerful cultural presence has meant that its portrayals of women, African Americans, and other groups have had profound implications for those groups (see "Media Literacy Case Study: Race, Gender, and Sexual Orientation in TV Programming" on pages 242–243).

Information: Network News

Over time, many Americans abandoned their habit of reading an afternoon newspaper and began following the network evening news to catch coverage of the latest national and international events. By the 1960s, NBC, CBS, and ABC offered their thirty-minute versions of the evening news, dominating national TV news coverage until the emergence of CNN and the 24/7 cable news cycle in the 1980s. The network news divisions have been responsible for a number of milestones. The *CBS-TV News*, which premiered on CBS in May 1948, became in 1956 the first news show videotaped for rebroadcast in central and western time zones on **affiliate stations** (local TV stations that contract with a network to carry its programs; each network has roughly two hundred affiliates around the country), while NBC's weekly *Meet the Press* (1947–) remains the oldest show on television.

As with entertainment programming, the ever-broadening competition from cable and online sources of news has siphoned off network viewers. In 1980, the Big Three evening news programs had a combined audience of more than fifty million on a typical weekday evening. That audience now hovers around twenty-four million.[3] Nonetheless, all three network newscasts often draw more viewers than do many prime-time programs.

Entertainment: Comedy

Originally, many new programs on television were broadcast live and are therefore lost to us today. The networks did sometimes manage to save early 1950s shows through poor-quality **kinescopes**, made by using a film camera to record live TV shows off a studio monitor (which today would be like saving a *Big Bang Theory* episode by shooting the TV screen in our living room with a video camera). However, the producers of *I Love Lucy* decided to preserve their comedy series by filming each episode, like a movie. This produced a high-quality version of each show that could be played back as a rerun. In 1956, videotape was invented, and many early comedies were preserved this way, allowing networks to create a rerun season in late spring and summer, thereby reducing the number of episodes produced each year from thirty-nine live broadcasts to about twenty-four taped programs.

In capturing *I Love Lucy* on film for future generations, the program's producers understood the enduring appeal of comedy. Although a number of comedy programs and ideas were stolen from radio, television eventually developed its own history with comedy, which became a central programming strategy for both the networks and cable. TV comedy has been delivered to audiences through sketch comedy and situation comedy (sitcom).

Sketch Comedy

Most current audiences are familiar with **sketch comedy** thanks to NBC's long-running *Saturday Night Live* (1975–). In the early days of television, variety shows drew heavily from vaudeville-style performers, such as singers, dancers,

▲ In 1968, after the popular CBS news anchor Walter Cronkite visited Vietnam, CBS produced the news special "Report from Vietnam by Walter Cronkite." Most political observers said that Cronkite's opposition to the war—along with his reputation as "the most trusted man in America"—influenced President Lyndon Johnson's decision not to seek reelection. CBS Photo Archive/Getty Images

Some sitcoms focus on character relationships rather than screwball plots, and they often also reflect social and cultural issues of the time in which the show is set. For example, ABC's *Fresh Off the Boat* features an Asian American family adjusting to life in Florida in the late 1990s. ABC/Photofest

acrobats, animal acts, stand-up comics, and ventriloquists. Typically, these shows required new ideas for sketches and other acts each week, along with new characters and new sets. This is still somewhat true of *Saturday Night Live* (many *SNL* alums have written about the all-consuming demands of working on the show), but today other sketch comedy is often pretaped and delivered without variety elements, on shows like *Portlandia* and *Inside Amy Schumer*, which offer more diverse and specific viewpoints than the earlier mass-appeal variety shows.

Situation Comedy

In contrast, **situation comedy (sitcom)** is at least in some ways a simpler story form than sketch comedy. In sitcoms, you have the same characters in the same places from week to week, dealing with an increasingly complicated situation (often at home or at work), which is usually resolved in some way at the end of the half-hour program.[4] From early hits like *I Love Lucy* and *The Honeymooners* to *How I Met Your Mother*, *Modern Family*, and *The Big Bang Theory*, the programs developed more grounded character development. Other shows take this development further, adding more serious elements to create a *dramedy*. *M*A*S*H* was an early example of this form, which has become more common with shows like *Louie* and *Jane the Virgin*.

Entertainment: Drama

Television's drama programs, which also came from radio, developed as another key genre of entertainment programming. Because production of TV entertainment was centered in New York in its early days, many of the sets, technicians, actors, and directors came from the New York theater world. Young stage actors often worked in the new television medium if they couldn't find stage work. The TV dramas that grew from these early influences fit roughly into two categories: anthology dramas and episodic series.

Anthology Drama

Although the subject matter, style, and storytelling are very different, **anthology dramas** share some of the same challenges as sketch comedy. Both essentially start from scratch each week, requiring new stories, new characters, and new sets. And like the variety programs of early television, the anthology dramas of the early 1950s borrowed heavily from live theater, first with stage performances and later with *teleplays* (scripts written for television).

launchpadworks.com

Television Drama: Then and Now

Head to LaunchPad to watch clips from two drama series: one several decades old and one more recent.

Discussion: What kinds of changes in storytelling can you see by comparing and contrasting the two clips?

But by the 1960s, networks were moving away from anthologies. This shift was due not only to the demands of producing a completely new story each week but also to the fact that anthologies mimicked the stage tradition of dealing with heavy, complicated, and controversial topics. This increasingly contrasted with the goal of producing less challenging programming as well as with advertising, which tended to claim products could offer quick and easy fixes to life's problems. These factors combined to make the programs less appealing to advertisers, and thus to networks, regardless of the artistic, cultural, and social contributions anthologies could make. Despite having virtually disappeared from network television, anthology drama's legacy continues on American public television, especially with the imported British program *Masterpiece Theatre* (1971–), now known as *Masterpiece Classic*, *Masterpiece Mystery!*, and *Masterpiece Contemporary*.

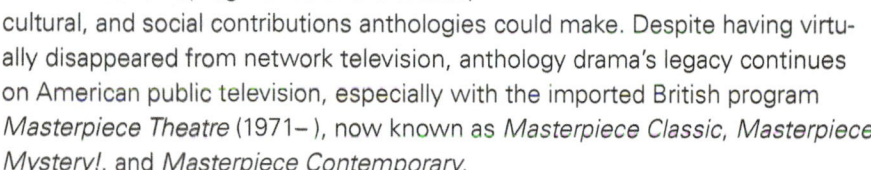

▲ *Empire*—a soapy Fox drama series about the music industry, featuring big-name actors Terrence Howard and Taraji P. Henson—quickly became one of TV's biggest hits after it debuted in 2015. The show has been nominated for numerous awards, and Henson won a best actress Golden Globe in 2016 for her portrayal of Cookie Lyon. Everett Collection, Inc.

Episodic Series

Abandoning anthologies, network producers and writers developed **episodic series**, first used on radio in the late 1920s. In this format, main characters continue from week to week, sets and locales remain the same, and technical crews stay with the program. Story concepts are broad enough to accommodate new adventures each week, establishing ongoing characters with whom viewers can regularly identify. Such episodic series come in two general types: chapter shows and serial programs.

Chapter shows are self-contained stories that feature a problem, a series of conflicts, and a resolution. Often reflecting Americans' hopes, fears, and values, this structure has been used in a wide range of dramatic genres, including network medical dramas like *ER* and *Grey's Anatomy*; police/crime network shows like *CSI: Crime Scene Investigation* and *Lethal Weapon;* family dramas like *The Fosters*; and fantasy/science fiction like *Sleepy Hollow*. **Serial programs** are open-ended episodic shows; that is, most story lines continue from episode to episode. Among the longest-running and most familiar serial programs in TV history are daytime *soap operas*, which typically run five days a week; however, by 2017 just four soap operas remained on network television.

Over the years the lines between traditionally separate chapter and serial approaches have blurred. Although many dramas are written to tell a more-or-less self-contained story in each episode, they also commonly incorporate serial elements, with story arcs that carry over several episodes, or even from season to season. Many dramas today somewhat resemble the television *miniseries*, a form that is less common now but has a notable place in broadcast television history. A miniseries typically ran during prime time over a few nights or perhaps over a week or two and then was over. Perhaps the most famous example was when ABC turned Alex Haley's novel *Roots: The Saga of an American Family* into an award-winning miniseries in 1977. Current shows like HBO's *True Detective* and FX's *Fargo* have positioned themselves as a hybrid of miniseries and serial drama, with one season covering a full serialized story before starting over with a new (if sometimes related) set of characters in subsequent seasons.

Talk Shows and TV Newsmagazines

Many other programming genres have arisen in television's history, both inside and outside prime time. Talk shows like the *Tonight Show* (1954–) emerged to satisfy viewers' curiosity about celebrities and politicians, and to offer satire on politics and business. Variety programs like the *Ed Sullivan Show* (1948–1971) have introduced new comedians as well as music artists, including Elvis Presley and the Beatles. **TV newsmagazines** like CBS's long-running *60 Minutes* usually feature three stories per episode, alternating hard-hitting investigations of corruption or political intrigue with softer feature stories about Hollywood celebrities and cultural trends.

Reality Television

Reality television dominated programming from the late 1990s through much of the first decade of the twenty-first century. Inspired by MTV's longest-running program, *The Real World* (1992–), the genre's biggest success was probably Fox's *American Idol*, which was the nation's top-rated show from 2004 to 2009. The popularity of the genre meant variations showed up on many of the niche channels up and down the broadcast and cable lineups. One could (and largely still can) find offerings ranging from network programs like *The Bachelor* and *Shark Tank* to cooking-based shows like *Hell's Kitchen* to talent contests like *The Voice* and *Dancing with the Stars*.

Featuring non-actors, cheap sets, and limited scripts, reality shows (like quiz shows) are much less expensive to produce than are sitcoms and dramas. For a time, critics worried the combination of popularity with cheap overhead would spell the doom of scripted television programs. However, no reality programs made it into the 2015–16 Top 10 rated shows.[5]

Public Television

In the 1960s, public television was created by Congress to serve viewers whose interests were largely ignored by ad-driven commercial television. Much of this noncommercial television was targeted to children, older Americans, and the well educated. Under President Lyndon Johnson, Congress passed the

Public Broadcasting Act of 1967. The act created the Corporation for Public Broadcasting (CPB), which in 1969 established the Public Broadcasting Service (PBS). The act led to the creation of children's series like *Mister Rogers' Neighborhood*, *Sesame Street*, and *Barney*. Public television also broadcasts more adult fare, such as *Masterpiece Theatre* and other imported British programs.

In the early 2000s, despite the continued success of such staples as *Sesame Street*, government funding of public television was slashed. The Obama administration restored some of it, but with the rise of cable and satellite, people who have long watched PBS now often get their favorite kinds of content from sources other than network and public television. For example, the BBC — historically a major provider of British programs to PBS — also sells its shows to cable channels (including its own BBC America) and to streaming video services, such as Netflix. In 2015, Sesame Workshop reached a deal with cable channel HBO to produce more new episodes of *Sesame Street*, to air exclusively on HBO for six months before being provided to PBS stations for free. Though some were upset by HBO's exclusive window, money from HBO will keep *Sesame Street* on the air (and at a lower cost to PBS stations) for the foreseeable future.

▲ The most influential children's show in TV history, *Sesame Street* (1969–) has been teaching children their letters and numbers for more than forty-five years. © PBS/Photofest

The Evolution of Cable Programming

As network programming evolved, so did cable programming, offering a greater variety of content and services thanks in part to satellite technology. For instance, in 1975, the HBO (originally called Home Box Office) premium cable service began delivering uncut, commercial-free movies and exclusive live coverage of major boxing matches via satellite for a monthly fee. The following year, WTBS — an independent Atlanta broadcast station then owned by future media mogul Ted Turner — was uplinked to a satellite and made available to cable companies, becoming the first cable "superstation." In 1980, Turner, who had become a major player in cable, established CNN (originally the Cable News Network) as a 24/7 news operation. Such efforts gave more people greater and

Race, Gender, and Sexual Orientation in TV Programming

From the first days of television, the America portrayed across all genres of programming was far whiter than the country's actual population. It was rare for actors of color to appear at all, and if they did, it was often in minor roles, like someone holding a door or waiting a table. Members of other minority groups—including lesbians, gays, bisexuals, and transgender individuals—experienced similar marginalization: They were treated largely as if they didn't exist, and when they were represented, the portrayals were often deeply rooted in stereotypes. People of color and members of the LGBTQ community were often cast as villains or clownish caricatures—either objects to be feared or the butt of the joke.[1] For example, *Amos 'n' Andy* drew criticism, first as a radio show and later as a TV program, for representing blacks as lower class and unintelligent. In addition, women were often depicted as mothers, homemakers, or trophies to be won by amorous men, and as overly emotional and weaker or less competent than men.

There was also the problem of assimilated representation: minority characters that were made acceptable because they behaved just like the white characters on white shows. In the 1980s, *The Cosby Show* drew praise for challenging many stereotypical portrayals of African Americans on television and for proving that a show about a black family could be a ratings success. Still, some critics argued that the Huxtable family reflected a version of black success that seemed tied to adopting a white middle-class vision of the American Dream.

As programs like *The Cosby Show* illustrate, a study of race, gender, and sexual orientation representations on television is a complicated undertaking, but it is also an important one. We can critique television's portrayal of various minority groups, but we can also consider ways in which sitcoms, dramas, and news programs have challenged racism, misogyny, and bigotry in society.

For example, African American characters in the 1970s—in sitcoms like *Sanford and Son* and *The Jeffersons* and dramas like the mini-series *Roots*—contrast greatly with current representations in sitcoms and dramas like *Black-ish* and *Empire*. Similarly, the change in what we consider "normal" or "acceptable" roles for women—from the housewives and mothers in programs like *Leave It to Beaver* in the late 1950s to the superhero stars in shows like *Buffy the Vampire Slayer* (1997–2003) and *Jessica Jones* (2015–)—shows huge improvements in gender representation. We can also examine the way gay and lesbian characters (and sometimes the actors who portrayed them) started coming out of the closet in the 1990s on programs like *Ellen*, *Will and Grace*, and *Roseanne*. And we can consider differences and similarities in how actors like Desi Arnaz (*I Love Lucy*) and Gina Rodriguez (*Jane the Virgin*) portrayed members of the Latino community a half-century apart from each other.

Many media scholars have also looked at news programming and what it means for the information industry to be dominated by straight white males. Whereas

▲ *Amos 'n' Andy* (left) began as a radio program, with both characters voiced by white men. When it switched to television in 1951, the show hired African American actors, but it was criticized by the NAACP for promoting negative stereotypes. *Black-ish* (right) tells the story of a successful advertising executive who worries that he and his family have become too assimilated into white culture. CBS Photo Archive/Getty Images (left); ABC/Photofest (right)

newsrooms are more diverse now than they were during the golden age of network TV news (1960s–1980s), scholars argue that problems remain—including a lack of understanding about alternative points of view. According to media scholar and former television journalist Edward Alwood, who has researched how mainstream news covers LGBTQ issues, "For many years, newsrooms have been almost exclusively controlled by white, middle-class, heterosexual men who have relied on a common set of assumptions to guide them in how they reflect the world through their work. Although bias is traditionally regarded as an intentional distortion of the facts, another form of bias results from unwitting ignorance."[2]

Critics worry that the more television programming ignores or misrepresents groups of Americans, the more distorted our understanding of the world around us will be. For this reason, it's especially important to produce programs that preserve cultural and narrative authenticity—and do so without reducing characters to one-dimensional stereotypes.

APPLYING THE CRITICAL PROCESS

DESCRIPTION   Watch an episode of a current television program and one of an older show from a similar genre. For example, you could watch episodes of *The Big Bang Theory* (current) and *Friends* (1990s), both sitcoms

about groups of friends living in a city. Or *Black-ish* (current) and *Sanford and Son* (1970s), both family sitcoms starring black actors. Or *Transcendent* (current) and *Queer Eye for the Straight Guy* (2000s), reality television programs featuring members of the LGBTQ community.

ANALYSIS   Make a list of each show's characters, and describe them in detail. Note which characters play major and minor roles, and how they are portrayed (e.g., as a stereotype, or in a positive or negative light). Jot down three of each character's defining characteristics. Take note of which groups described in this case study do *not* appear in each program.

INTERPRETATION   What do these representations mean? Are the characters fully formed and three-dimensional or shallow and one-dimensional?

EVALUATION   According to popular wisdom, our society—and the TV programming that acts as a mirror of that society—is generally becoming more inclusive. Do the shows you viewed from different eras support this idea? Why or why not?

ENGAGEMENT   Organize a "watch party" with a group of friends to view the two programs you examined for this activity. Discuss how each program portrays men, women, people of color, and members of the LGBTQ community. Consider how these portrayals might be empowering, problematic, or both.

more convenient TV access to movies, news, sports, and other content — presenting a direct challenge to traditional over-the-air broadcast TV.

With the advent of satellite TV, cable companies could excel at **narrowcasting** — the delivery of specialized programming, such as the History Channel or the Food Network, for niche viewer groups — which cut into broadcasting's large mass audience. Narrowcasting gave rise to different types of cable stations offering various content, and cable providers offering various service options: Viewers could choose basic cable services with just a few channels for a modest monthly fee or add more niche channels and premium cable services for a higher monthly or per-use fee.

Basic Cable

Basic cable offers numerous channels appealing to specific audiences' interests that the broadcast networks don't offer — such as ESPN (sports), CNN (news), MTV and VH1 (music), Nickelodeon (new children's programs and older TV series reruns), Lifetime (movies), BET (Black Entertainment Television), the Weather Channel, and QVC (home shopping). Basic cable also traditionally offers **superstations** (independent broadcast TV stations uplinked to a satellite), such as WPIX (New York) and WGN (Chicago), although in 2014 WGN became WGN America, a regular entertainment-based cable channel with higher-profile original programming.

Typically, local cable companies pay each satellite-delivered service between $.06 cents per month per subscriber (for low-cost, low-demand channels like C-SPAN) and over $7 per month per subscriber (for high-cost, high-demand channels like ESPN). That fee is passed along to consumers as part of their basic monthly fee.

In 1992, eighty-seven cable networks were in business. By 2014, that number had grown to over nine hundred.[6] With the advent of high-bandwidth fiber-optic cable and *digital cable* in the late 1990s, cable systems could expand their offerings beyond the basic analog channels. Digital cable typically used set-top cable boxes to offer on-screen program guides and dozens of additional premium, pay-per-view, and audio music channels, increasing total cable capacity to between 150 and 500 channels. Even more than broadcast network programming, cable services evolved far beyond the old limited categories of news information and fictional entertainment. Satisfied with smaller niche audiences, cable became much more specialized than its broadcast counterpart.

Specialized Information: CNN

CNN, the first 24/7 cable TV news channel, quickly mastered continuous coverage of breaking news events and, early on, avoided presenting news anchors as celebrities (like network anchors). With around-the-clock programming, it began delivering up-to-the-minute news in great detail and featuring live, unedited coverage of news conferences, press briefings, and special events. Although it has since cut many of its international bureaus, CNN today dominates international TV news coverage. It operates in more than two hundred territories and countries where many viewers use it to practice their English; more than two billion people have access to a CNN service. Spawning a host of competitors in the United States and worldwide, CNN now battles for viewers with other twenty-four-hour news providers, including the Fox News Channel; MSNBC; CNBC; EuroNews; Britain's Sky Broadcasting; Al Jazeera; and thousands of Web and blog sites, such as *Politico*, the *Huffington Post*, the *Drudge Report*, and *Salon*. (See Chapter 3 for more on cable news, news satire, and "fake news.")

Specialized Entertainment: MTV

Launched in 1981, MTV (originally the Music Television Network) and its global offspring reach more than 400 million homes worldwide. MTV initially played popular music videos from mainstream white artists for white suburban teens; however, the popularity of Michael Jackson's *Thriller* album in late 1982 opened MTV up to black artists and more diverse music forms. Then, in the late 1980s and early 1990s, MTV began providing more original programming with shows like *The Real World* and *Beavis and Butt-head* and more recently *Girl Code* and *The Shannara Chronicles*. Since MTV's inception, critics have worried that much of its programming has encouraged vulgarity and overt sexism. Advocates maintain that MTV (and cable overall) has created a global village by giving people around the world a common language and cultural bond. They also applaud MTV's special programs on important social issues, such as drug addiction, racism, and social/political activism—especially its Rock the Vote campaigns, which encourage young people to participate in national elections.

Premium Cable

Besides basic programming, cable offers special **premium channels,** featuring recent and classic Hollywood movies as well as original movies and popular series—such as HBO's *Girls* and Showtime's *Homeland*—all with no advertising. Premium services have also proved innovative. They include pay-per-view

▲ Anderson Cooper has been the primary anchor of *Anderson Cooper 360°* since 2003. Although the program is mainly taped and broadcast from his New York City studio. Cooper is one of the few talking heads who still report live fairly often from the field for major news stories. Most notably, he has done extensive coverage of the 2010 BP oil spill in the Gulf of Mexico, the February 2011 uprisings in Egypt, and the immigration crisis in Europe in 2015. In 2013, he won a Gay and Lesbian Alliance Against Defamation (GLAAD) Media Award for openly gay media professionals, after coming out the previous year. Lawrence Schwartzwald/Newscom/Polaris Images/Paris/France

▲ *Westworld* is an HBO series about a futuristic amusement park in which rich human guests can act out consequence-free fantasies with lifelike androids. As in the 1973 movie of the same name, on which the series was based, the dream vacations become nightmares when the androids start to malfunction. HBO/Photofest

(PPV) programs; video-on-demand (VOD); and interactive services through which consumers can bank, shop, play games, and access the Internet. Subscribers pay fees in addition to charges for basic cable.

Innovative Content

HBO—the oldest premium cable channel—pioneered original, uncut movies and series on cable. Its most successful and acclaimed shows include *The Sopranos*, *True Detective*, *Curb Your Enthusiasm,* and *Game of Thrones*. Since the late 1990s, HBO has regularly garnered more Emmy nominations each year for its original programs than any of the traditional networks.

Other premium channels have also found success creating their own series. Showtime's most recent successes have been *Homeland* and *Ray Donovan*. Starz's *Ash vs. Evil Dead* and *American Gods* both tap into existing cult followings—one for the *Evil Dead* movie franchise and the other for a popular fantasy novel.

Innovative Viewing Options: Pay-per-View and Video-on-Demand

In addition to presenting fresh types of programming, premium cable has introduced innovative viewing options to customers. **Pay-per-view (PPV)** channels came first. These offered recently released movies or special one-time sporting events (such as a championship boxing match) to subscribers who paid a designated charge to their cable company. In the early 2000s, U.S. cable companies introduced a new pay-per-view option for their digital customers: **video-on-demand (VOD)**. Through VOD, customers choose among hundreds of titles, then download a selection from the cable operator's server onto their cable TV box hard drive either for free (for access to older TV series or movies) or for any amount up to six dollars (for more popular recent movies). They watch the movie the same way they would watch a video, pausing and fast-forwarding when desired. Today, the largest cable companies and DBS services also offer digital video recorders (DVRs) to their customers.

Regulatory Challenges Facing Television and Cable

Though cable cut into broadcast TV's viewership, both types of programming came under scrutiny from the U.S. government. Initially, thanks to extensive lobbying efforts, cable growth was suppressed to ensure that ad-revenue streams of local broadcasters and traditional TV networks were not harmed by the emergence of cable. Later, as cable developed, FCC officials worried that power and profits were growing increasingly concentrated in fewer and fewer industry players' hands. Therefore, the commission set out to mitigate the situation through the implementation of a variety of rules and regulations.

Restricting Broadcast Networks' Control

From the late 1950s to the end of the 1970s—the **network era**—CBS, NBC, and ABC dominated prime-time TV programming. By the late 1960s, the FCC, viewing the three networks as a quasi-monopoly, passed a series of regulations to undercut their power. The Prime Time Access Rule (PTAR), introduced in April 1970, reduced networks' control of prime-time programming from four to three hours in an effort to encourage more local news and public affairs programs, usually slated for the 6–7 P.M. EST time block. However, most stations simply ran thirty minutes of local news at 6 P.M. and then acquired syndicated quiz shows (*Wheel of Fortune*) or **infotainment** programs (*Entertainment Tonight*) to fill up the remaining half hour.

▼ Major merger deals, such as Disney's acquisition of ABC in 1995, have caused many independent companies to argue that a few corporations have too much control over broadcast content. ROBERT SULLIVAN/ Getty Images

In 1970, the FCC also created the Financial Interest and Syndication Rules—called **fin-syn**—which banned the networks from running their own syndication companies and thus reduced their ability to reap profits from syndicating old TV series. Five years later, the Department of Justice limited the networks' production of non-news shows, requiring them to seek most of their programming from independent production companies and film studios.

With the rise of cable and home video in the 1990s, the FCC gradually phased out fin-syn, arguing that by then the TV market had grown more competitive. Beginning in 1995, the networks were once again allowed to syndicate and profit from rerun programs, but only those they had produced in-house.

Buoyed by the spirit of deregulation in the 1980s and 1990s, the elimination of fin-syn and other rules opened the door for major merger deals (such as Disney's acquisition of ABC in 1995) that have constrained independent producers from creating new shows and competing for prime-time slots. Many independent companies and TV critics complain that the corporations that now own the networks—Disney, CBS, 21st Century Fox, and Comcast—have historically exerted too much power and control over broadcast television content.

Reining in Cable's Growth—For a While

Throughout the 1950s and 1960s (before the broadcast networks accumulated extensive power), the FCC blocked cable companies from bringing distant TV stations into cities and towns that had local channels. The National Association of Broadcasters (NAB), the main trade organization for over-the-air television, lobbied Congress to restrict cable's growth so that it would not interfere with broadcast station interests and local TV ad sales. However, by the early 1970s, particularly with the advent of communication satellites, cable had the capacity for more channels and better reception—and the potential to expand beyond small, isolated communities. In 1972, new FCC rules began to allow cable to start expanding while still protecting broadcasters.

Through the **must-carry rules**, the FCC required all cable operators to carry all local TV broadcasts on their systems. This ensured that local network affiliates, independent stations (those not carrying network programs), and public television channels would benefit from cable's clearer reception. The FCC also mandated **access channels** in the nation's top one hundred TV markets, requiring cable systems to provide free nonbroadcast channels for local citizens, educators, and governments to use.

Because the Communications Act of 1934 had not anticipated cable, the industry's regulatory status was unclear at first. As a result, there was uncertainty in the 1970s about whether cable should be treated like print and broadcast media (with cable receiving First Amendment protections of its content choices). Cable operators argued that they should be considered **electronic publishers**, able to choose which channels and content to carry. However, some FCC officials and consumer groups maintained that cable systems were really more like **common carriers**—services, like phone companies, that do not get involved in monitoring channel content. Thus, access to content should be determined by whoever paid the money to lease or use the channel (like a telephone company that does not interfere with the content of a phone call). In 1979, this debate ended in the landmark *Midwest Video* case, in which the U.S. Supreme Court upheld cable companies' right to dictate their own content and defined the industry as a form of electronic publishing.[7] With cable's regulatory future secured, competition to obtain franchises to supply local cable services intensified.

Through the 1980s and early 1990s, Congress approved several cable acts before rewriting the nation's communications laws in the **Telecommunications Act of 1996**, which took away a number of ownership restrictions from radio and television and also brought cable fully under federal oversight, treating the industry like broadcasting. In its most significant move, Congress used the Telecommunications Act to knock down regulatory barriers. By allowing regional phone companies, long-distance carriers, and cable companies to enter one another's markets, lawmakers hoped to spur competition and lower rates for consumers. Instead, cable and phone companies have merged operations in many markets, keeping prices at a premium. In fact, broadcast networks are now bundled together with cable networks under larger corporate ownership, as discussed later in this chapter. The Telecommunications Act laid the legal groundwork necessary for these mergers to happen.

Television in the Digital Age

Thanks to new technologies — home video, the Internet, smartphones, mobile video, and DBS — Americans can now watch the visual content they want (whether it's movies, broadcast TV shows, or cable programming) whenever and wherever they want (on a TV set, on their laptop, on a handheld mobile device). In other words, watching television after the digital turn no longer requires an actual television. What's more, with video streaming on the Internet, we are in the middle of a transformation in how programs are produced, distributed, and watched.

Home Video and Recording

The introduction of videocassettes and **videocassette recorders (VCRs)** in the mid-1970s changed television viewing in two key ways. First, it enabled **time shifting**: Viewers could suddenly tape-record TV programs and play them back later. Even though the recording quality of the new VHS (Video Home System) consumer standard was much lower than watching the TV program in real time, liberation from a time-locked TV schedule was a life changer for many viewers. Starting in 1999, the **digital video recorder (DVR)** rapidly replaced VCRs, and viewers recorded shows on DVDs instead of VHS tapes. Today, with so much content available via streaming at any time, time shifting has switched to online viewing.

Second, home video spurred a booming video rental business. Video rental, formerly the province of walk-in video stores like Blockbuster, has given way

▲ The emergence of home recording technology, such as Sony's Betamax VCR in 1975, changed American viewing habits. The Advertising Archives

to mail services like Netflix (which started as a mail service and later added streaming), movie rental boxes like RedBox, or online services like Netflix, Amazon, and Hulu. Both time shifting and rentals/streaming have threatened the TV industry's advertising-driven business model: when viewers watch DVDs and stream TV shows, they aren't watching the ads that normally accompany network and cable programming.

The Internet, Smartphones, and Mobile Video

The way traditional television has converged across so many digital platforms is perhaps one of the most striking examples of how fast these changes can take place—and how dramatic they can be. The first part of this picture is the Internet, which has fueled convergence with other technologies as high-speed connections and Wi-Fi have become more common.

Many new TV sets are Internet ready out of the box. For those that aren't or for older-model televisions, there are a wide variety of options for consumers who want to connect their TV to the Internet, from laptops and high-end video game consoles to dedicated devices such as the Roku box. The advantage is the ability to watch streaming content on what often has the biggest screen and best sound in a home (see also the Chapter 7 discussion of home entertainment).

On the other end of the screen-size spectrum, consumers can take their TV viewing with them using smartphones and tablets capable of accessing the Internet via Wi-Fi systems or with faster cellular technology commonly called 4G LTE (Long-Term Evolution, which beat out WiMax technology as the common standard for telephone and mobile broadband).

Once consumers have the hardware in place, the next piece of the picture is the service they will use to find whatever show they want to watch. Some programs will stream episodes directly from their Web sites (like Comedy Central's *The Daily Show*) or make segments available via YouTube (like HBO's *Last Week Tonight with John Oliver*). Other programs and networks keep tighter control of their programs and try to earn money by selling them via services like Apple's iTunes Store or on Amazon.com, or through fee-based streaming services such as Hulu or Netflix. And streaming services these days no longer rely solely on showing films and shows created by others: Sites like Netflix, Amazon, and Hulu have started producing their own programs with their own fan bases (see also the opening of this chapter).

The final piece of the convergence puzzle is understanding that the streaming services can also link all of an audience member's devices together. So, for example, using a combination of apps for smartphones and tablets as well as devices like a Roku box at home, a person might use the same Netflix account on any of these devices anywhere there is Internet service (see also "The Digital Turn Case Study: Bingeing Purges Traditional Viewing Habits").

The Digital Turn

CASE STUDY

Bingeing Purges Traditional Viewing Habits

Why settle for just one show at the same time every week when you can watch two episodes any time you want? Or three? Or a dozen? Binge viewing, or bingeing, means watching multiple episodes of a program one after another. Although bingeing has been around since the emergence of DVDs and Blu-ray discs, it wasn't until streaming video services gained a significant foothold that it became a cultural phenomenon.

Binge watching is most common among millennials: In a 2015 survey, almost 90 percent of younger millennials reported binge-watching programs. But it's not just for younger generations. The same survey showed that a third of viewers over the age of sixty-nine sometimes binge-watched their favorite shows.[1]

In addition, a study commissioned by Netflix showed that an increasing number of users will watch an entire season of a TV show within a week. This study also found that almost two-thirds of self-identified binge viewers use their mobile phones (or another second screen) while bingeing, and that this use complements their viewing instead of competing with it.[2] For that matter, smartphones and tablets mean that binge watching can happen practically anywhere, and the ability to stream programs or view them on demand means that it can happen anytime.

But what are the larger implications for television viewing now that bingeing has become so popular? On the business side of television and cable, major media giants like Comcast, which want to charge Web sites more for faster Internet connections, are butting heads with net neutrality advocates and companies like Netflix, which

see the Comcast proposal of a tiered Internet system as nothing more than a shakedown (see also the section on net neutrality in Chapter 9, pages 278–279).

On the creative side of the business, some critics note a positive trend in the number of high-quality dramatic and comedic television programs being produced, which they see as a welcome change after reality television meant less demand for scripted productions.

The social implications of binge viewing will likely be the subject of some debate. Some critics worry that bingeing might lead to loss of productivity or social interaction for students and workers alike, while others argue that the flexibility offered by streaming video (and DVRs) makes it easier to be productive, because being a fan of a particular program doesn't mean having to adjust personal schedules to accommodate TV schedules. Still others point out that simultaneous engagement with social media can encourage conversations that might not have happened in years past. Binge watchers may be watching TV differently than people did in other eras, but they may also be learning to engage with TV more actively than ever before.

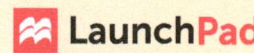

▶ **Visit LaunchPad** to view a clip from the frequently binge-watched program *Stranger Things*. What might the success of this series, which was produced for a streaming video service rather than a broadcast or cable network, mean for the future of television production and consumption?

launchpadworks.com

DBS

Direct broadcast satellite (DBS) has long been the biggest challenger to the cable industry—at least until digital streaming appeared on the scene. In its early days, DBS transmission was especially efficient in regions with rugged terrain or isolated farmland, where it was difficult or cost prohibitive to install cable wiring. DBS differs from cable in that it allows individual consumers to downlink satellite-transmitted signals into their homes without having them relayed through cable companies, which process these same signals and then send them out to homes via wires.

Japanese companies launched the first DBS system in Florida in 1978, but the early receiving dishes, which dotted the rural landscape in the 1980s, were ten to twelve feet in diameter and expensive ($3,000). By 1994, however, full-scale DBS service was available, and consumers could soon buy satellite dishes the size of a large pizza. Today, there are two U.S.-based DBS companies: DirecTV (now owned by AT&T) and Dish (formerly known as Dish Network). These companies offer consumers most of the same channels and tiers of service that cable companies carry, often at a slightly lower monthly cost. While DBS and cable have long competed against each other with prices and bundles of services, both are now facing competition from streaming video.

The Economics of Television and Cable

The economics of TV and cable differ in certain ways, as we'll see in the pages that follow. However, like all other industries, both TV and cable must bring in revenue from specific sources and then invest that money in the business processes that are crucial to their operations.

Shows, Ads, and Subscriptions for Sale

Sources of revenue differ in some respects between TV and cable. Both broadcast network and cable programming make money from syndication and advertising, but only cable makes money from subscriptions—monthly fees charged to consumers for different tiers of service.

Syndication

Syndication—leasing TV stations the exclusive right to air older TV series—is a critical source of revenue for broadcast networks and cable companies. Early each year, executives from thousands of local TV stations gather at the world's largest "TV supermarket" convention, the National Association of Television

Program Executives (NATPE), to acquire programs that broadcast networks (and, more recently, cable channels) have put up for syndication. Networks might make cash deals—selling shows to the highest-bidding local station—or give a program to a local station in exchange for a split in the advertising revenue—usually called a **barter** deal, as no money changes hands. Through this process, the stations obtain the exclusive local market rights, usually for two- or three-year periods, to network-created game shows, talk shows, and **evergreens**—popular reruns, such as *The Big Bang Theory, Modern Family*, or *Seinfeld*. Buying syndicated programs is usually cheaper for local TV stations than producing their own programs, and it provides a familiar lead-in show to the local news.

▲ *The Walking Dead* has been enormously successful for AMC, the cable channel that produces and airs the hit zombie-apocalypse program. The show's high ratings mean AMC can charge advertisers a premium rate. An edited-for-broadcast-TV version of the show entered syndication in 2014, and AMC also has agreements with streaming services like Netflix. AMC/Photofest

Many local stations show syndicated programs during **fringe time**—immediately before the evening's prime-time schedule and following the local evening news or the network's late-night talk show. Syndicated shows filling these slots are either "off-network" or "first-run." In **off-network syndication**, older programs that have had long runs during network prime time, such as *Everybody Loves Raymond*, are made available as reruns to local stations, cable operators, online services, and foreign markets. **First-run syndication** is any non-network program specifically produced for sale only into syndication markets, such as *Ellen* or *Wheel of Fortune*.

Advertising

Advertising is another major source of revenue for the industry. TV shows live or die based on how satisfied advertisers are with the quantity and quality of the viewing audience. Since 1950, the major organization tracking and rating prime-time viewing has been Nielsen, which estimates what viewers are watching in the nation's major markets. Ratings services provide advertisers, networks, and local stations with considerable detail about viewers—from race and gender to age, occupation, and educational background.

In TV measurement, a **rating** is a statistical estimate based on a random sample, expressed as the percentage of households tuned to a program in the total market being sampled. Another audience measure is the **share**, which gauges the percent of homes tuned to a program compared with those actually using their sets at the time of the sample. Prime-time advertisers want to reach relatively affluent eighteen- to forty-nine-year-old viewers, who account for most consumer spending. If a show is attracting those viewers, advertisers will compete to buy time during that program. (See Figure 8.2 for costs for a

FIGURE 8.2 // PRIME-TIME NETWORK TV PRICING

Average costs are shown for a thirty-second commercial during prime-time programs on Monday and Thursday nights in 2016.

Monday

	8:00 P.M.	8:30 P.M.	9:00 P.M.	9:30 P.M.	10:00 P.M.
ABC	*Dancing with the Stars* ($125,260)				*Conviction* ($109,662)
CBS	*The Big Bang Theory* ($289,136)	*Man with a Plan* ($126,490)	*2 Broke Girls* ($138,203)	*The Odd Couple* ($108,438)	*Scorpion* ($109,988)
NBC	*The Voice* ($214,079)				*Timeless* ($188,046)
FOX	*Gotham* ($130,674)		*Lucifer* ($126,798)		No network programming

Thursday

	8:00 P.M.	8:30 P.M.	9:00 P.M.	9:30 P.M.	10:00 P.M.
ABC	*Grey's Anatomy* ($193,210)		*Notorious* ($144,274)		*How to Get Away with Murder* ($178,339)
CBS	*NFL Thursday Night Football* ($522,910)				*Pure Genius* ($87,584)
NBC	*Superstore* ($87,707)	*The Good Place* ($93,992)	*Chicago Med* ($135,535)		*The Blacklist* ($145,122)
FOX	*Rosewood* ($83,430)		*Pitch* ($93,554)		No network programming

Data from: "Cost for a 30-Second Commercial," Advertising Age: Marketing Fact Pack, *2017 edition, pp. 18–19.*

thirty-second commercial during prime-time programs.) Traditionally, shows that did not reach enough of the "right" viewers wouldn't attract advertising dollars and thus risked being canceled. But in the age of niche markets and Internet competition, smaller audience ratings and shares are tolerated, especially in cable programming.

Advertising also brings in money for cable. Most basic cable channels block out time for local and regional ads from, for example, restaurants, clothing stores, or car dealerships in the area. These ads are cheaply produced compared with national network ads, and they reach a smaller audience.

Subscriptions

In addition to making money from syndication and from selling local ads, cable companies also earn revenue through monthly subscriptions for basic service, pay-per-view programming, and premium movie channels. Cable companies charge the customer a monthly fee—an average of $103 a month in 2016[8]—and then pay cable channels a fee per customer per month for their basic cable programming. A premium channel like HBO charges the cable company a higher fee than most other channels or cuts out the cable company altogether with a streaming service like HBO Now. Consumers also buy subscriptions to streaming sites like Netflix, which must negotiate with whomever holds the rights to the programs in order to offer them in their catalogues.

Making Programs and Getting in Front of an Audience

For both TV and cable, primary costs include production (creation of programming). TV networks also invest heavily in distribution (airing of the programs they've created) by paying affiliate stations a fee to show their content. Cable operators distribute their programs most often by downlinking them from communication satellites and transmitting them to their various communities.

Production

Key players in the TV and cable industry—networks, cable stations, producers, and film studios—spend fortunes creating programs that they hope will keep viewers captivated for a long time. Roughly 40 percent of a new program's production budget goes to "below-the-line" costs, such as equipment, special effects, cameras and crews, sets and designers, carpenters, electricians, art directors, wardrobe, lighting, and transportation. The remaining 60 percent covers the creative talent—or "above-the-line" costs—such as actors, writers, producers, editors, and directors. In highly successful long-running series, actors' salary demands can drive these above-the-line costs from 60 percent to more than 90 percent.

Many prime-time programs today are developed by independent production companies owned or backed by a major film studio, such as Sony or Disney. In addition to providing and renting production facilities, these studios serve as a bank, offering enough capital to carry producers through one or more seasons. After a network agrees to carry a program, it's kept on the air through **deficit financing**: The production company leases the show to a network for a license fee that is less than the cost of production, assuming it will recoup this loss later in lucrative rerun syndication.

To save money and control content, many networks and cable stations create their own programs, including TV newsmagazines and reality programs. For example, NBC's *Dateline* requires only about half the outlay (between $700,000 and $900,000 per episode) demanded by a new hour-long drama. In addition, by producing projects in-house, the networks avoid paying license fees to independent producers.

Distribution

Whereas cable companies rely on subscriptions to fund distribution of content, the broadcast networks must pay their affiliate stations a fee to show the programs the networks have either created or licensed from independent production companies. In return for this fee, networks have the right to sell the bulk of advertising time (and run promotions of its own programs) during the shows—which helps them recoup their investments in these programs. Through this arrangement, local stations not only receive income but also get national programs that attract large local audiences to the local ad slots they retain as part of their affiliation contracts with the networks.

The networks themselves don't usually own their affiliated stations, except in major markets like New York, Los Angeles, and Chicago. Instead, they sign contracts with local stations (one each from the two-hundred-plus top regional TV markets) to rent time on these stations to air their network programs.

Ownership and Consolidation

Despite their declining reach and the rise of cable, the traditional networks have remained attractive business investments. In 1985, General Electric, which once helped establish RCA/NBC, bought back NBC. In 1995, Disney bought ABC for $19 billion; in 1999, Viacom acquired CBS for $37 billion (Viacom and CBS split in 2005, but Viacom's CEO remains CBS's main stockholder). And in 2013, Comcast completed its purchase of NBC Universal from GE—a deal valued at $30 billion.

In the late 1990s, cable became a coveted investment, not so much for its ability to carry TV programming as for its access to households connected with high-bandwidth wires. Today, there are about 5,000 U.S. cable systems, down from 11,200 in 1994. Since the 1990s, thousands of cable systems have been bought by large **multiple-system operators (MSOs)**, corporations like Comcast and Charter that own many cable systems. The industry now uses the term **video subscription services** to collectively refer to cable operators, DBS services, and streaming services like Netflix and Hulu (see Table 8.1).

Comcast and Charter
In cable, the industry behemoth today is Comcast, especially after its takeover of NBC and move into network broadcasting. Back in 2001, AT&T had merged its cable and broadband industry in a $72 billion deal with Comcast, then the third-largest MSO. The new Comcast instantly became the cable industry leader. In addition to offering cable, Internet, and other services under the Xfinity brand, Comcast owns numerous cable channels, such as E!, Bravo, and USA, as well as all the NBC news, sports, and television stations and cable channels. The mega corporation also owns Universal's movie production studios and theme parks, and is one of the main partners (with Fox, Disney, and Time Warner) behind Hulu. Along with Comcast, the other large MSO is Charter, which became the nation's second largest cable company with its 2016 acquisition of Time Warner Cable for $78 billion, and the additional purchase of Bright House Networks for $10.4 billion.

TABLE 8.1 // TOP 10 VIDEO SUBSCRIPTION SERVICES

Rank	Video Subscription Service	Subscribers (in millions)
1	Netflix	47.0
2	AT&T/DirecTV	25.3
3	Comcast	22.4
4	Charter Communications	17.5
5	Dish	13.9
6	Hulu	12.0
7	Verizon FiOS	4.7
8	Altice	4.6
9	Cox Communications	4.0
10	Frontier Communications	1.7

Data from: NCTA—The Internet & Television Association, www.ncta.com/industry-data.

Dish and DirecTV

In the DBS market, Dish and DirecTV control virtually all the DBS service in the continental United States. Dish began operations as a satellite television provider in 1996 as a unit of EchoStar Communications, a satellite equipment company. Today, Dish remains independently owned. DirecTV was founded in 1994. Since 2015, it has been owned by AT&T, a boost to the telephone giant's existing TV, voice, and Internet services. In 2016, AT&T moved to further expand its video services by agreeing to buy Time Warner for more than $85 billion. Time Warner's greatest value to AT&T is as a media provider (especially its film and TV content) for DirecTV and AT&T wireless and Internet services.

Television in a Democratic Society

The development of cable, VCRs and DVD players, DVRs, the Internet, and smartphone services has fragmented television's audience by appealing to viewers' individual and special needs. And by providing more specialized and individual choices, these changes have altered television's former role as a national unifying cultural force, potentially de-emphasizing the idea that we are all citizens who share the culture of a larger nation and world. Moreover, many cable channels have survived mostly by offering live sports or recycling old television shows and movies. Although cable and on-demand services like Netflix are creating more and more original quality programming, they rarely reach even the diminished audience numbers commanded by the traditional broadcast networks. In fact, given that the television networks and many leading cable channels are now owned by the same media conglomerates, cable has evolved into something of an extension of the networks. And even though cable audiences are growing and network viewership is contracting, the division between the two is blurring. New generations that grow up on cable and the Internet rarely make a distinction between a broadcast network, a cable service, and an on-demand program. In addition, tablets, smartphones, and Internet services that now offer or create our favorite programs are breaking down the distinctions between mobile devices and TV screens. Today, the promise that cable once offered as a place for alternative programming and noncommercial voices is being usurped by the Internet, where all kinds of TV experiments are under way.

The bottom line is that television, despite the audience fragmentation, still provides a gathering place for friends and family at the same time that it provides access anywhere to a favorite show. Like all media forms before it, television is adapting to changing technology and shifting economics. As the technology becomes more portable and personal, television-related industries continue to search for less expensive ways to produce stories and more channels on which to deliver them. But what will remain common ground on this

▶ "Keep Portland Weird" is a promotional slogan for the Oregon city (borrowed from Austin). It's fitting, then, that the show *Portandia* is defined by its quirky characters and stories that play up this weirdness. The show has developed a relatively small but devoted fan base thanks to niche cable channel IFC and online streaming. IFC/Photofest

shifting terrain is that television will continue as our nation's chief storyteller, whether those stories come in the form of news bulletins, sporting events, cable dramas, network sitcoms, or YouTube vignettes.

TV's future will be about serving smaller rather than larger audiences. As sites like YouTube develop original programming and as niche cable services like the Weather Channel produce reality TV series about storms, no audience seems too small and no subject matter too narrow for today's TV world. For example, in 2013, *Duck Dynasty* had become a hit series on A&E—a program about an eccentric Louisiana family that got rich making products for duck hunters. The program averaged a cable-record 12.4 million viewers in 2012–13, but then lost 75 percent of its audience by 2015, as many viewers grew weary of the series. An overwhelming number of programming choices like this now exist for big and small TV screens alike. How might this converged TV landscape, with its volatile ups and downs in viewer numbers, change how audiences watch—and pay for—television? With hundreds of shows available, will we adopt à la carte viewing habits, in which we download or stream only the shows that interest us, rather than pay for cable (or DBS) packages with hundreds of channels we don't watch?

CHAPTER ESSENTIALS

Review

- In the development stage of television, early inventors (Zworykin and Farnsworth) competed to establish a patent for the first electronic television. In the entrepreneurial stage, television developed technical standards and turned into a business, and the FCC adopted **analog** (broadcast signals made of radio waves) for all U.S. TV sets. In the mass medium stage, the FCC began assigning channels throughout the country and later introduced the color standard.

- The introduction of cable provided access for communities that couldn't receive over-the-air broadcast signals, but it also posed a major competitive threat to broadcast television. The first small cable systems originated in the late 1940s.

- Beginning in the 1950s, broadcast networks began specializing in different types of programming, ranging from news to entertainment in such genres as **situation comedy (sitcom)** and drama.

- With the advent of satellite TV, cable companies could excel at **narrowcasting**—delivering specialized programming on **basic cable, premium channels, pay-per-view (PPV), video-on-demand (VOD)**, and later streaming video.

- During the **network era**—from the late 1950s to the end of the 1970s—CBS, NBC, and ABC dominated prime-time TV programming. To undercut the networks' power, the FCC passed a series of regulations, such as one that banned the networks from running their own syndication companies. These rules have since been eliminated.

- The FCC and cable operators went back and forth for many years about how much legal authority the federal agency had to regulate the industry. The **Telecommunications Act of 1996** eventually brought cable fully under federal jurisdiction.

- Home video technologies challenged traditional television, beginning with the introduction of **videocassette recorders (VCRs)** in the mid-1970s. **Digital video recorders (DVRs)** started replacing VCRs in 1999, and today, **time shifting** has switched to online viewing.

- Traditional and cable television have converged across multiple platforms and joined with video streaming services to make content available via many sources, including the Internet, TV sets, and smartphones.

- **Direct broadcast satellite (DBS)** allows individual consumers to downlink hundreds of satellite channels and services for a monthly fee.

- Both broadcast networks and cable programmers make money from **syndication** and advertising; cable providers and video streaming services also collect subscription fees.

- Networks and programmers spend money on production and distribution of programs.

- Cable systems have been bought up by **multiple-system operators (MSOs)**; this trend suggests a move toward oligopoly, in which a handful of megafirms control programming. Cable systems are now classified as **video subscription services**, which also include streaming services like Netflix.

- Even with niche programming and increasingly fragmented audiences, television provides a forum where people gather to participate in cultural or sociological events—like the Super Bowl—which can have both positive and negative effects on broadcasting and society.

Key Terms

Study Questions

1. What were the major factors that shaped the early history of television?

2. Why did cable and its programming pose a challenge to broadcasting?

3. What role has the FCC taken in regulating networks and cable?

4. What are the technological challenges that network television and cable face?

5. How has television served as a national cultural center or reference point?

9

The Internet and New Technologies: The Media Converge

"I will not discuss any issue that has become public solely on the basis of WikiLeaks. As our intelligence agencies have said, these leaks are an effort by a foreign government to interfere with our electoral process, and I will not indulge it."[1] This statement from Florida senator Marco Rubio, delivered in October 2016, came after the controversial Web site released a series of private e-mails from Hillary Clinton's allies to the public. As Rubio's words illustrate, WikiLeaks is viewed by many people—both inside and outside the government—with suspicion. It is also a fitting example of the contradictory and complicated nature of the Internet after the digital turn.

First launched in 2006, the site gained notoriety as a place where wannabe whistle-blowers could take secret information from a government or major corporation and release it online to the public. WikiLeaks and its founder, Julian Assange, earned the ire of the U.S. government after posting classified documents and aiding Edward Snowden—a

◀ WikiLeaks founder Julian Assange is a lightning rod for controversy. Beginning in 2012, he sought asylum at the Ecuadoran embassy in London to avoid extradition—both to the United States for prosecution over secret diplomatic cables leaked by his site and to Sweden over a sexual assault charge. Five years later Sweden dropped the rape investigation, but, he is still living in the embassy. Carl Court/Getty Images

former computer contractor for the U.S. National Security Agency who leaked details of the U.S. government's online spying program at home and abroad. Then, in 2016, the site made public thousands of e-mails from Clinton campaign chairman John Podesta's private Gmail account—e-mails multiple U.S. intelligence agencies say were stolen by hackers working for Russian intelligence agencies. These actions have raised important questions about issues of freedom of speech, privacy, and security on the Internet.

When President Bill Clinton's administration announced in the mid-1990s that a computer network primarily used by government agencies and universities was about to open up into a public information superhighway, no one could have foreseen the way the Internet would connect and change the world. (Certainly no one would have guessed that a Web site it spawned would help undermine Hillary Clinton's bid for the presidency two decades later.) The Internet has revolutionized and encompassed all forms of mass communication—not replacing them but converging them. It connects people across great distances almost instantly, and offers access to boundless information, entertainment, and more.

But as the example of WikiLeaks demonstrates, this interconnectivity comes with risks, and there is controversy over what is good or bad, what is acceptable or unsafe, and which people are villains and which are heroes. Some argue that Assange and his Web site are pulling back the curtain on secrets that should not be withheld from the public. Others contend that the WikiLeaks agenda isn't really about "the public's right to know." They say Assange and the site have their own biases against the United States and a disturbing history with the Russian government[2] and that what they are doing isn't whistle-blowing meant to expose wrongdoing by the powerful but a form of propaganda meant to advance an agenda.[3]

As you consider these issues, think about the ways in which you balance convenience and connectivity with privacy and security as you go online—and the ways that governments, politicians, or corporations may do the same. Ask yourself the following questions: Are there limits to the public's right to know? Under what conditions do secrecy and confidentiality serve the public interest? And what, ultimately, is accomplished by releasing sensitive information?

THE INTERNET—the vast network of telephone and cable lines, wireless connections, and satellite systems that link and carry computer information worldwide—was described early on as the *information superhighway.* This description suggests that people envisioned a new system for conveying information that would replace the old one (books, newspapers, television, and radio). Created in the 1950s, the Internet was a government-sponsored technology enabling military and academic researchers in different locations to share information and findings by computer. Drawing on the technology used to build the first computer (the ENIAC, invented in 1946), the Internet exploited the power of digitization. Through **digitization**, information in analog form (such as text or pictures) is translated into binary code—a series of ones and zeros that can be encoded in software and transmitted between computers.

In many ways, the original description of the Internet has turned out to be accurate. This medium has expanded dramatically from its initial incarnation to a vast entity that encompasses all other media today (video and audio content in addition to text). Since becoming a mass medium in the mid-1990s, the Internet has transformed the way we do business, communicate, socialize, entertain ourselves, and get information—in short, it has profoundly touched the way most of us interact with media across all aspects of our lives.

Unlike other mass media, the Internet seems to have no limits. More and more content is being made accessible on it, more and more people are gaining access to it, and more and more types of media are converging on it. But one thing *is* certain: As governments, corporations, and public and private interests vie to shape the Internet so that it suits their needs, the questions of who will have access to it and who will control it are taking on more urgency.

In this chapter, we explore these questions, along with the Internet's impact on various aspects of our lives, by:

- **examining the early history of the Internet, including its initial uses as a military-government communication tool**

- **tracing the evolution of the Internet to a mass medium with multimedia capability**

- **analyzing the economics of the Internet, including the new business models it has inspired and the noncommercial entities that use it**

- **considering concerns that have arisen regarding the security of personal information on the Internet and the appropriateness of content now accessible through this medium**

- **weighing the negative and positive implications of the Internet for our democratic society**

The Early History of the Internet

After World War II, the United States entered the Cold War against the Soviet Union, pitting the two great powers in a decades-long battle of military and economic superiority. The space race was a symbolic part of the Cold War, and when the Soviet spacecraft *Sputnik* became the first to orbit the earth in 1957, the United States was shocked at being beaten. The event ushered in a new era of U.S. government spending on technological, scientific, and military developments. The United States would later make its first successful rocket launch with *Explorer* in 1958, but perhaps more important to our world today was the creation that same year of a new U.S. Defense Department research agency that would eventually develop the Internet. In the decades that followed, new technology like microprocessors and fiber-optic cable increased the commercial viability of data transmission, paving the way for the Internet to become a mass medium.

Military Functions, Civic Roots

Created in 1958, the U.S. Defense Department's Advanced Research Projects Agency (ARPA) assembled a team of computer scientists around the country to develop and test technological innovations. Computers were relatively new at this time, and there were only a few expensive mainframe computers, each big enough to fill an entire room. Yet the scientists working on ARPA projects wanted access to these computers. A solution to the problem was proposed: First, share computer-processing time by creating a wired network system in which users from multiple locations could log onto a computer whenever they needed it. Second, to prevent logjams in data communication, the network used a system called packet switching, which broke down messages into smaller pieces to easily route through the network, and reassembled them on the other end. This system provided multiple paths linking computers to one another, thereby allowing communication to continue if one of the paths got clogged or disrupted—much like the national highway system supported by President Dwight Eisenhower. This computer network became the original

▲ Unveiled on April 7, 1964, the IBM 360 was considered one of the most influential computer rollouts. Programmers could use the special typewriter to talk to the mainframe. Van D Bucher/Getty Images

FIGURE 9.1 // **DISTRIBUTED NETWORKS**

Paul Baran, a computer scientist at the Rand Corporation during the Cold War era, worked on developing a national communications system. Centralized networks (*a*) lead all the paths to a single nerve center. Decentralized networks (*b*) contain several main nerve centers. In a distributed network (*c*), which resembles a net, there are no nerve centers; if any connection is severed, information can be immediately rerouted and delivered to its destination. But is there a downside to distributed networks when it comes to the circulation of network viruses?

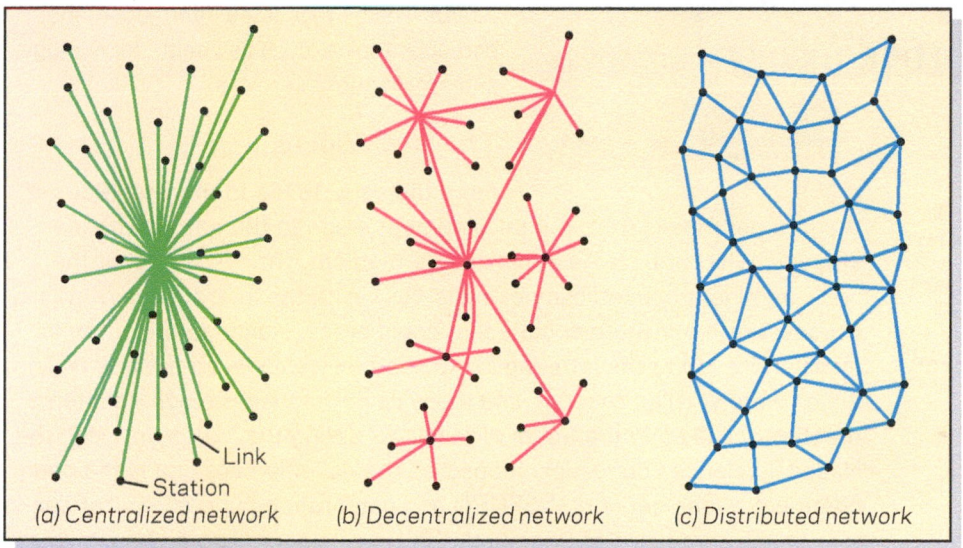

Data from: Katie Hafner and Matthew Lyon, Where Wizards Stay Up Late *(New York: Simon & Schuster, 1996)*

Internet—called **ARPAnet** and nicknamed the Net—and it enabled military and academic researchers to communicate on a distributed network system (see Figure 9.1).

With only a few large, powerful research computers in the country, many computer scientists were suddenly able to access massive (for that time) amounts of computer power. The first Net messages ever were sent in 1969, when ARPAnet connections linked four universities: the University of California–Los Angeles, the University of California–Santa Barbara, Stanford, and the University of Utah. By 1970, another terminal was in place in Cambridge, Massachusetts, at the computer research firm Bolt, Beranek and Newman (BBN), and by late 1971, there were twenty-three Internet hosts at university and government research centers across the United States. That same year, Ray Tomlinson of BBN came up with an essential innovation to help researchers communicate—**e-mail**—and decided to use the "@" sign to separate the user's name from the computer name, a convention that has been used ever since.

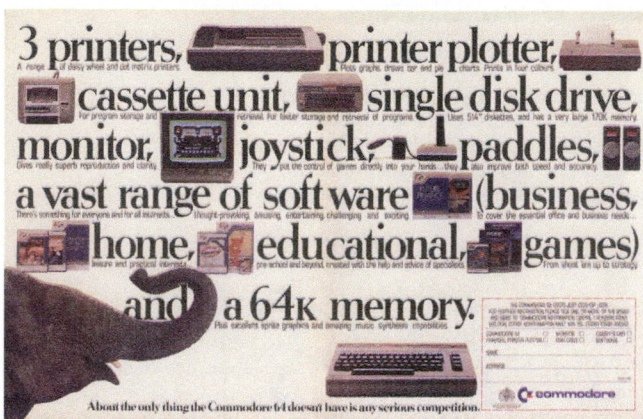

▲ This advertisement for the Commodore 64, one of the first home PCs, touts the features of the computer. The Commodore was heralded in its time, but today's PCs far exceed its abilities. The Advertising Archives

During this development stage, the Internet (still called ARPAnet at this time) was used primarily by universities, government research labs, and corporations involved in computer software and other high-tech products. These users exchanged e-mail and posted information on computer *bulletin boards*—sites that listed information about particular topics, such as health, technology, and employment services.

The Net Widens

From the early 1970s to the late 1980s, the Internet moved from the development stage to the entrepreneurial stage, in which it became a marketable medium. The first signal of the Net's imminent marketability came in 1971 with the introduction of **microprocessors**—miniature circuits that could process and store electronic signals. This led to the introduction of the first *personal computers* (*PCs*), which were smaller, cheaper, and more powerful than the bulky systems that had occupied entire floors of buildings during the 1960s. In 1986, the National Science Foundation sponsored the development of a high-speed communications network (NSFNET) and established supercomputer centers on the campuses of Princeton, the University of Illinois, the University of California–San Diego, and Cornell, and a fifth in Pittsburgh—jointly operated by Carnegie Mellon, the University of Pittsburgh, and Westinghouse—which were designed to speed up access to research data and encourage private investment in the Net. This government investment triggered a dramatic rise in Internet use and opened the door to additional commercial possibilities.

Also in the mid-1980s, **fiber-optic cable**—thin bundles of glass capable of transmitting thousands of messages simultaneously (via laser light)—became the standard for conveying communication data speedily, making the commercial use of computers even more viable than before. Today, thanks to this increased speed, the amount of information that digital technology can transport is nearly limitless.

In 1990, ARPAnet officially ended; and in 1991, the NSF opened its network fully to commercial use. By this time, a growing community of researchers, computer programmers, amateur hackers, and commercial interests had already tapped into the Internet. These tens of thousands of participants in the network became the initial audience for the Internet's emergence as a mass medium.

The Evolution of the Internet: Going Commercial, Getting Social, Making Meaning

During the 1990s and early 2000s, the Internet's primary applications were e-mail (one-to-one communication) and Web page display (one-to-many communication). By 2005, it had evolved into a far more powerful commercial and social network. In other words, the Web became a many-to-many tool, as an increasing number of applications led to the creation of new content and navigational possibilities for users. While doing so, it continued to change our relationship with the Internet. Today, users can make purchases; engage in real-time conversations with others; write, read, and comment on blogs and wikis; share photos and videos; and interact within virtual 3-D environments. And as the Internet gets more commercial and more social, the next phase of Web development is already starting. This so-called Semantic Web takes connectivity beyond people and Web sites to other machines — from cars to refrigerators.

The Commercialization of the Internet

The introduction of the World Wide Web and the first Web browsers in the 1990s helped transform the Internet into a mass medium. Soon after these developments, the Internet quickly became commercialized, leading to battles between corporations vying to attract the most users and those who wished to preserve the public, nonprofit nature of the Net.

The World Begins to Browse

Internet use before the 1990s consisted mostly of people transferring files, accessing computer databases from remote locations, and sending e-mails through an unwieldy interface. The **World Wide Web** (or the Web) changed all of that. Developed in the late 1980s by software engineer Tim Berners-Lee at the CERN particle physics lab in Switzerland to help scientists better collaborate, the Web enabled users to access texts through clickable links rather than through difficult computer code. Known as *hypertext*, the system allowed computer-accessed information to associate with, or link to, other information on the Internet—no matter where it was located. **HTML (hypertext markup language)**, the written code that creates Web pages and links, can be read by all computers. Thus, computers with different operating systems (Windows, Macintosh, Linux) can communicate easily through hypertext. After CERN

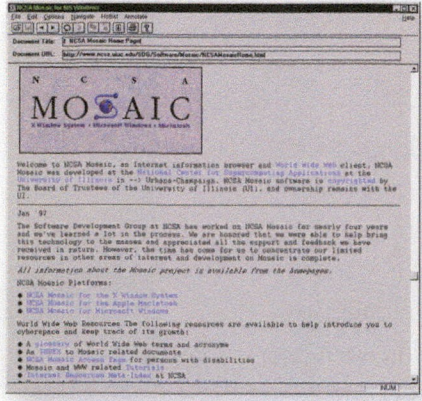

▲ The GUI (graphical user interface) of the World Wide Web changed overnight with the release of Mosaic in 1993. As the first popular Web browser, Mosaic unleashed the multimedia potential of the Internet. Mosaic was the inspiration for the commercial browser Netscape, which was released in 1994. Courtesy of the National Center for Supercomputing Applications and the Board of Trustees of the University of Illinois

released the World Wide Web source code into the public domain in 1993, many people began to build software to further enhance the Internet's versatility.

The release of **Web browsers**—software applications that help users navigate the Web—brought the Web to mass audiences for the first time. Computer programmers led by Marc Andreessen at the University of Illinois (a supercomputer center that was part of NSFNET) released Mosaic in 1993, the first user-friendly browser to load text and graphics together in a magazine-like layout. With its attractive fonts and easy-to-use navigation buttons, Mosaic was a huge improvement over previous technology. In 1994, Andreessen joined investors in California's Silicon Valley to introduce another major advance—a commercial browser called Netscape. Together, the World Wide Web, Mosaic, and Netscape gave the Internet basic multimedia capability, enabling users to transmit pictures, sound, and video.

As the Web became the most popular part of the Internet, many thought that the key to commercial success on the Net would be through a Web browser. In 1995, Microsoft released its own Web browser, Internet Explorer, which overtook Netscape as the most popular Web browser. Today, Internet Explorer has been replaced by Microsoft's Edge, and Google Chrome and Firefox are the top browsers.

Users Link in through Telephone and Cable Wires

In the first decades of the Internet, most people connected to "cyberspace" through telephone wires. In 1985, AOL began connecting home users to its proprietary Web system through dial-up access, and quickly became the United States' top **Internet service provider (ISP)**. AOL's success was so great that by 2001, the Internet start-up bought the world's largest media company, Time Warner—a deal that shocked the industry and signaled the Internet's economic significance as a vehicle for media content. As **broadband** connections—which can quickly download multimedia content—became more available, users moved away from the slower telephone dial-up service to high-speed service from cable, telephone, and satellite companies.[4] By 2007, both AT&T (offering DSL and cable broadband) and Comcast (offering cable broadband) surpassed AOL in numbers of customers. Today, other major ISPs include Verizon, Charter Communications, and Cox.

People Embrace E-Mail and IM

E-mail was one of the earliest services of the Internet, and people typically used the e-mail services connected to their ISPs before major Web corporations such as Google, Microsoft (Hotmail), and Yahoo! began to offer free Web-based e-mail accounts to draw users to their sites. Today, all the top e-mail services include advertisements in their users' e-mail messages, one of the costs of the "free" e-mail accounts. Google's Gmail goes one step further by scanning messages to dynamically match a relevant ad to the text each time an e-mail message is opened. Such targeted advertising has become a hallmark feature of the Internet.

Although e-mail remains a standard for business-related text communications in the digital era, it has been surpassed in popularity by **instant messaging (IM)**, which enables less formal typed conversations in real time. Major IM services include Google Chat, Facebook Chat, Microsoft's Skype, AOL Instant Messenger (AIM), Yahoo! Messenger, and Apple's Messages. IM has evolved and expanded with mobile texting, embracing smartphone apps like Snapchat, a photo messaging service that thrives on the cultural popularity of sending selfies and captions to friends. Other apps, like Phhhoto and Instagram Stories, offer variations of some of the features of Snapchat for sharing photos and videos.

Search Engines Organize the Web

As the number of Web sites on the Internet quickly expanded, companies seized the opportunity to provide ways to navigate this vast amount of information by providing directories and search engines. One of the more popular search engines, Yahoo!, began as a directory. In 1994, Stanford University graduate students Jerry Yang and David Filo created a Web page to organize their favorite Web sites, first into categories, then into more and more subcategories as the Web grew.

Eventually, though, cataloging individual Web sites became impractical. **Search engines** offer a more automated route to finding content by allowing users to enter key words or queries to locate related Web pages. Search engines are built on mathematical algorithms. Google, released in 1998, became a major success because it introduced a new algorithm that ranked a page's "popularity" on the basis of how many other pages linked to it. Google later moved to maintain its search dominance with its Google Voice Search and Google Goggles apps, which allow smartphone users to conduct searches by voicing search terms or by taking a photo. By the end of 2016, Google's global market share accounted for more than 76 percent of searches, while Microsoft's Bing claimed 8.2 percent, China's Baidu reached 7.2 percent, and Yahoo! claimed 6.6 percent.[5]

The Web Gets Social

As the Internet has developed, it has focused more intently on *media convergence*: different types of content (video, text, audio) created by all sorts of sources (users, corporations, nonprofit organizations) coming

▲ Instagram Stories, launched in 2016, is an unapologetic attempt to compete with Snapchat. Like Snapchat, Instagram Stories lets users post photos or short videos that are only available for a day.

together and accessed on a variety of devices (personal computers, smartphones, tablets). Whereas the early Internet was primarily a medium for computer-savvy users to deliver text-and-graphic content, it has since been transformed into a place where people can access and share all manner of media content. And whereas the signature products of the early Internet were increased content access and accompanying dot-com consumerism, the iconic achievement of the Web in more recent years has been social networking.

In a little over a decade, a number of different types of social media have evolved, with multiple platforms for the creation of user-generated content. European researchers Andreas M. Kaplan and Michael Haenlein identify six categories of social media on the Internet: social networking sites, blogs, collaborative projects, content communities, virtual game worlds, and virtual social worlds.[6]

Social Networking Sites

Social networking sites—including Facebook, Twitter, Google+, Tumblr, and Pinterest—have become among the most popular places on the Internet. The largest of these sites, Facebook, started at Harvard in 2004 as an online substitute to the printed facebooks the school created for incoming first-year students. Today, it has become a global phenomenon, with nearly two billion active users and available in more than one hundred languages. Facebook empowers users to create personal profiles, upload photos and videos, stream live video, and share articles and memes, all while connecting with old friends and meeting new ones.

The popularity of social media and social networking sites, combined with the explosion in mobile devices, has altered our relationship with the Internet. In the world in which the small screens of smartphones are becoming the preferred medium for linking to the Internet, we don't typically get the full open Internet, one represented by the vast searches brought to us by Google. Instead, we get a more managed Internet—what some

▲ Etsy is principally a commerce site, but the way it connects crafters with potential buyers has a social component, creating a sense of community even in the business of buying and selling goods.

call a closed Internet or a walled garden[7]—brought to us by apps or platforms that carry out specific functions via the Internet. Are you looking for a nearby restaurant? Don't search online—use this app especially designed for that purpose. The distributors of these apps act as gatekeepers; Apple has more than 1.5 million apps in its App Store, and Apple approves every one of them.

The competing Android app stores on Google Play and Amazon have a similar number of apps (with many fewer apps in the Windows Store), but Google and Amazon exercise less control over approval of apps than Apple does.

Blogs

Years before there were status updates or Facebook, **blogs** (short for Weblogs) enabled people to easily post their ideas to a Web site. Popularized with the release of Blogger (now owned by Google) in 1999, blogs contain articles or posts in chronological journal-like form, often with reader comments and links to other sites. Blogs can be personal or corporate multimedia sites, sometimes with photos, graphics, podcasts, and video. Some blogs have developed into popular news and culture sites, such as the *Huffington Post*, *TechCrunch*, *Mashable*, *HotAir*, *ThinkProgress*, and *TPM (Talking Points Memo)*.

Some blogs are simply an individual's online journal or personal musings. Others provide information, analysis, or commentary that isn't presented in the more traditional news media. Although some are written by journalists, the vast majority of the Web's blogs are written by individuals who don't use established editorial practices to check their facts.

Some of the leading platforms for blogging include Blogger, WordPress, Tumblr, Weebly, and Wix. But by 2017, the most popular form of blogging was microblogging, with about 313 million active users on Twitter.[8]

Collaborative Projects

Probably the most common examples of projects in which users build something together, often with anyone being able to edit or add information, are Web sites called **wikis** (*wiki* means "quick" in Hawaiian). These include Wikitravel (a global travel guide); WikiLeaks (see beginning of this chapter); and, of course, *Wikipedia*, the online encyclopedia that is constantly being updated by interested volunteers.

Although *Wikipedia* has become one of the most popular resources on the Web, some people have expressed concern that its open editing model compromises its accuracy.[9] When accessing any wiki, the user may not know for certain who has contributed which parts of the information found there, who is changing the content, and what the contributors' motives are. This worry has led *Wikipedia* to lock down topic pages that are especially contested, which has inevitably led to user protests about information control. At the same time, *Wikipedia* generally offers a vibrant forum where information unfolds, debates happen, and controversy over topics can be documented. And just like a good term paper, the best *Wikipedia* entries carefully list their sources, allowing a user to dig deeper and have some way of judging the quality of information in a given listing.

But wikis aren't the only way in which Internet users collaborate. Kickstarter is a popular fund-raising tool for creative projects such as books, recordings,

LaunchPad
launchpadworks.com

....

The Rise of Social Media

Media experts discuss how social media are changing traditional media.

Discussion: Some consider the new social media an extension of the very old oral form of communication. Do you agree or disagree with this view? Why?

You Tube   crazy honey badger

▲ YouTube remains the most popular Web site for watching videos online. Some videos blur the lines between amateur and professional content. For example, one famous YouTube video about honey badgers combines preexisting *National Geographic* footage with commentary by an enthusiastic amateur narrator. The video, which was uploaded in January 2011, has garnered over eighty-two million views.

and films. InnoCentive is a crowd-sourcing community that offers award payments for people who can solve business and scientific problems. And Change.org lets people create and circulate online petitions. Sometimes this leads to change—such as a 2011 petition started by a Massachusetts fourth-grade class that got Universal Studios to include more environmental messaging on its Web site for its animated film *The Lorax*. Other efforts, however, aren't so successful. For example, a Change.org petition asking members of the electoral college to make Hillary Clinton president instead of Donald Trump failed to sway electors despite having the site's largest response ever: nearly 5 million signatures.[10]

Content Communities

Content communities are the best examples of the many-to-many ethic of social media. **Content communities** exist for the sharing of all types of content, from text (Fanfiction.net) to photos (Flickr, Photobucket) and videos (YouTube, Vimeo). YouTube, created in 2005 and bought by Google in 2006, is the most well-known content community, with over a billion users around the world uploading and watching amateur and professional videos. YouTube gave rise to the viral video—a video that becomes immediately popular as a result of millions sharing it through social media platforms. According to the site, users watch four million videos per day and upload three hundred hours of video every minute.

Virtual Game Worlds and Virtual Social Worlds

Virtual game worlds (covered in greater detail in Chapter 10) and virtual social worlds invite users to role-play in rich 3-D environments, in real time, with players throughout the world. In virtual game worlds (also known as massively multiplayer online role-playing games, or MMORPGs) such as *World of Warcraft* and *Elder Scrolls Online*, players can customize their online identity, or avatar, and work with others through a game's challenges. Community forums for members extend discussion and shared play outside the game. Virtual social worlds, like *Second Life*, enable players to take their avatars through simulated environments and even make transactions with virtual money.

The Next Era: The Semantic Web

Many Internet visionaries talk about the next generation of the Internet as the *Semantic Web*, a term that gained prominence after hypertext inventor Tim Berners-Lee and two coauthors published an influential article in a 2001 issue

LaunchPad

launchpadworks.com

The Internet in 1995

In a clip from the 1995 thriller *The Net*, Sandra Bullock's character communicates using her computer.

Discussion: How does this movie from over two decades ago portray online communication? What does it get right, and what seems outdated now?

of *Scientific American*.[11] Semantics is the study of meaning, so a Semantic Web refers to a more meaningful—or organized—Web. Essentially, the future promises a layered, connected database of information that software will sift through and process automatically for us. Whereas the search engines of today generate relevant Web pages for us to read, the software of the Semantic Web will make our lives even easier as it places the basic information of the Web into meaningful categories and makes significant connections for us.

One early example of the Semantic Web is Apple's voice recognition assistant, Siri, which first shipped with its iPhone 4S in 2011. Siri uses conversational voice recognition to answer questions, find locations, and interact with various iPhone functionalities, such as the calendar, reminders, the weather app, the music player, the Web browser, and the maps function.

The next generation of this trend is already launching with what is called the "Internet of things." This refers to the increasing number of "dumb" home appliances and controls that are getting "smart" by connecting to the Internet. Appliances, lights, air-conditioning, heating, window shades, and home entertainment systems can now be controlled via wireless (**Wi-Fi**) home networks and synced to smartphones via apps. In addition, a new breed of devices boasting voice-control capabilities—including Google Home, Amazon Echo, and Microsoft's Home Hub—can control home devices connected to this Internet of things.

While they come with many conveniences, it's important to note that devices on the Internet of things may also have a downside. For example, these devices currently lack the security software used on computers, smartphones, and tablets. In October 2016, hackers exploited this weakness to launch attacks on major Web sites, including Netflix, Twitter, Amazon, and Spotify, using Web-connected DVRs, routers, and Internet-controlled security cameras.[12] In addition, privacy experts point out that voice activation works only when our devices are listening to us. Because these devices are also connected to the Internet, we are potentially opening the door for hackers, corporations, and even governments to eavesdrop on us in the privacy of our own homes.

▼ This high-tech refrigerator uses a combination of cameras, a tablet-style interface, and wireless Internet to help its owner keep track of grocery needs even when away from home. Some security experts have noted that devices like these lack the firewalls and anti-virus protection of most computers, smartphones, and tablets. Bloomberg/Getty Images

The Economics of the Internet

One of the unique things about the Internet is that no one owns it. But that hasn't stopped some corporations from trying to control it. Companies have realized the potential of dominating the Internet business through access to phone and broadband wires, search engines, software, social networking, and providing access to content, all in order to sell the essential devices that display the content or to amass users who become an audience for advertising. However, there remain those who want to keep the spirit of the Internet's independent early days alive, and alternative voices still have a home on the noncommercial Web.

Ownership: Controlling the Internet

By the end of the 1990s, four companies—AOL, Yahoo!, Microsoft, and Google—had emerged as the leading forces on the Internet, each with a different business angle. AOL attempted to dominate the Internet as the top ISP, connecting millions of home users to its proprietary Web system through dial-up access. (For more on ISPs, see "Media Literacy Case Study: Net Neutrality" on pages 278–279.) Yahoo!'s method was to make itself an all-purpose entry point—or **portal**—to the Internet. Computer software behemoth Microsoft's approach began by integrating its Windows software with its Internet Explorer Web browser, drawing users to its MSN.com site and other Microsoft applications. Finally, Google made its play to seize the Internet with a more elegant, robust search engine to help users find Web sites.

Since the end of the 1990s, the digital turn toward convergence has changed the Internet and the fortunes of its original leading companies. AOL's technological shortcomings in broadband contributed to its devaluation and eventual spin-off from Time Warner in 2009, and Yahoo! was eclipsed by Google in the search engine business. In today's converged world, in which mobile access to digital content prevails, Microsoft and Google still remain powerful. Those two, along with Apple, Amazon, and Facebook, constitute the leading companies of digital media's rapidly changing world.

Microsoft

Microsoft, the oldest of the dominant digital firms (established by Bill Gates and Paul Allen in 1975), is an enormously wealthy software company that struggled for years to develop an Internet strategy. As its software business declined, its flourishing digital game business (Xbox) helped it continue to innovate and find a different path to a future in digital media. The company finally found moderate success on the Internet with its search engine Bing in 2009. With the 2012 release of the Windows Phone 8 mobile operating system and the Surface tablet, Microsoft made headway in the mobile media business. In 2014, Microsoft brought its venerable office software to mobile devices, with Office for iPad and Office Mobile for iPhones and Android phones, all of which work with OneDrive, Microsoft's cloud service.

Google

Google, established in 1998, had instant success with its algorithmic search engine and now controls over 76 percent of the global search market, generating billions of dollars of revenue yearly through the pay-per-click advertisements that accompany key-word searches. The company has branched out into a number of other Internet offerings, including Google Shopping, Google Maps, Gmail, Blogger, the Chrome browser, YouTube, and the Chromecast streaming device. Google has also challenged Microsoft's Office programs with Google Apps, a cloud-based bundle of word-processing, spreadsheet, calendar, IM, and e-mail software. Google competes against Apple's iTunes with Google Play, an online media store, and challenges Facebook with the social networking tool Google+. To compete in the device market with Apple, Amazon, and Microsoft, Google also has its own line of Pixel mobile phones and a tablet, plus the inexpensive Chromebook laptop computers, which are extremely popular in K–12 schools.

As the Internet goes wireless, Google has acquired other companies in its quest to replicate its online success in the wireless world. Beginning in 2005, Google bought the Android operating system and mobile phone ad placement company AdMob. Google's biggest challenge is the "closed Web": companies like Facebook and Apple that steer users to online experiences that are walled off from search engines and threaten Google's reign as the Internet's biggest advertising conglomerate.

Apple

Apple, Inc., was founded by Steve Jobs and Steve Wozniak in 1976 as a home computer company and is today among the most valuable companies in the world (often moving in and out of the number one spot alongside companies like ExxonMobil and Google).[13] Apple had been only moderately successful and was near bankruptcy in 1997, when Jobs, having been forced out of the company for a decade, returned. Apple introduced the iPod and iTunes in 2001, two innovations that led the company to become the number one music retailer in the United States. Then, in 2007, Jobs introduced the iPhone, transforming the mobile phone industry. The company further redefined portable computing with the iPad in 2010.

▲ Google has grown from a popular search engine to a major digital conglomerate, with a variety of holdings and over sixty thousand full-time employees. The company has toyed with the idea of opening a retail store akin to Apple's high-traffic storefronts, taking a step in that direction by opening a temporary pop-up store in New York City in October 2016. JEWEL SAMAD/Getty Images

Media Literacy

Net Neutrality

For more than a decade, the debate over net neutrality has framed the potential future of the Internet. Far from being any closer to a final resolution, the debate has become even more heated recently and has begun to expand into areas that include the overall Internet speed and access being provided by the infrastructure owned by various Internet service providers (ISPs). **Net neutrality** refers to the principle that every Web site and every user—whether a multinational corporation or a private citizen—has the right to the same Internet network speed and access. The idea of an open and neutral network has existed since the origins of the Internet, but there had never been a legal formal policy until 2015, when the Federal Communications Commission reclassified broadband Internet service and approved net neutrality rules. Still, as we will see, this battle is far from over.

The opposition to net neutrality is dominated by some of the biggest communications corporations. These major telephone and cable companies— including Comcast, AT&T, Charter, Verizon, and Cox—control 98 percent of broadband access in the United States through DSL and cable modem service. These companies want to offer faster connections and priority to clients willing to pay higher rates, and provide preferential service for their own content or for content providers who make special deals with them—in other words, to

▲ Without a net neutrality policy, ISPs may make the Internet into a two-tiered system: a fast lane reserved for the companies able to afford it, and a slow lane for all others. Steve Sack, The Minneapolis Star Tribune

eliminate net neutrality. For example, tiered Internet access might mean that these companies would charge customers more for data-heavy services like Netflix, YouTube, Hulu, or iTunes. These companies argue that the profits they could make with tiered Internet access would allow them to build expensive new networks, benefiting everyone.

But supporters of net neutrality—mostly bloggers, video gamers, educators, religious groups, unions, and small businesses—argue that the cable and telephone giants actually have incentive to rig their services and cause net congestion in order to force customers to pay a premium for higher-speed connections. They claim that an Internet without net neutrality would hurt small businesses, nonprofits, and Internet innovators, who might be stuck in the "slow lane" and not be able to afford the fast connections that large corporations can afford. Large Internet corporations like Google, Amazon, eBay, Microsoft, Skype, and Facebook also support net neutrality because their

businesses depend on their millions of customers having equal access to the Web.

The FCC's attempts to adopt net neutrality rules were twice rejected by federal courts with the argument that because broadband Internet service had been defined by the FCC as an information service in 2002 rather than a telecommunications service (like telephones or cable TV services), the FCC did not have the authority to impose net neutrality regulations. This reflected an older way of looking at the Internet, which today consists of so much more than it did in the early days.

The FCC finally made net neutrality stick in 2015, when it reclassified broadband Internet service as a telecommunications service and put net neutrality rules into place.[1] Specifically, the FCC has rules that disallow **blocking** (broadband providers prohibiting access to legal content and services), **throttling** (intentionally impairing or degrading Internet performance based on content or source), and **paid prioritization** (favoring some Internet traffic over other lawful traffic in exchange for payment, thereby creating "fast lanes").[2]

Supporters of the FCC's regulations say that the large private ISPs, which largely operate as monopolies in their areas, have been more focused on profits than customer service and technological advancement, making intervention necessary. They argue that the overall Internet speed in the United States is too slow, based in part on a number of studies that showed the U.S. system lagging far behind systems in other countries. For example, customers in South Korea, Japan, and most of Europe are paying less for much faster service.[3] Companies like Comcast say that paid prioritization would help pay for a faster Internet, but some studies on Internet service find that the U.S. communities with the fastest service are those that have systems owned and operated by local governments without a tiered fee structure,

found in places like Chattanooga, Tennessee, and Cedar Falls, Iowa.[4]

Despite the 2015 FCC rules, it's clear that this issue isn't settled. The fight will continue in the court system as well as in the political arena. FCC members are appointed by the sitting president and confirmed by the Senate for five-year terms. The vote that approved the new rules in 2015 was 3–2 along party lines, with Democrats in favor of net neutrality rules and Republicans opposed to them. Now that Republican Donald Trump is president and Republicans have control of both the House and the Senate, we may see the pendulum swing once again.

APPLYING THE CRITICAL PROCESS

DESCRIPTION Interview a sample of people about their views on net neutrality. Would they be willing to pay higher rates for faster connections? Do they think every Web site should have the same network speed and access?

ANALYSIS What sorts of patterns emerge from your interviews? Are there common views on the way the Internet should be accessed? Do your interviewees seem to be concerned or unconcerned about the issue of net neutrality? Do your questions make them think about this issue for the first time?

INTERPRETATION What do these patterns mean? Is the idea of net neutrality better or worse for democracy? Would eliminating net neutrality undercut the usefulness and accessibility of the medium?

EVALUATION Is net neutrality a benefit of the Internet? What should the standards of speed and access to it be? How should they be enforced?

ENGAGEMENT Learn about and take action for or against net neutrality. Share your knowledge with your peers.

With the iPhone and iPad now at the core of Apple's business, the company began providing content—music, television shows, movies, games, newspapers, magazines—to sell its media devices. The next wave of Apple innovations was the iCloud, a storage and syncing service that enables users to access media content anywhere (with a wireless connection) on its mobile devices. The iCloud also helps ensure that customers purchase their media content through Apple's iTunes store, further tethering users to its media systems. In addition, in early 2017, Apple announced plans to begin creating original television programs and movies for the first time.[14]

Amazon

Amazon started its business in 1995 in Seattle, selling the world's oldest mass medium (books) online. Amazon has since developed into the world's largest e-commerce store, selling not only books but also electronics, garden tools, clothing, appliances, and toys. Yet by 2007, with the introduction of its Kindle e-reader, Amazon was following Apple's model of using content to sell devices. The Kindle became the first widely successful e-reader, and by 2010, e-books were outselling hardcovers and paperbacks at Amazon. In 2011, in response to Apple's iPad, Amazon released its own color touchscreen tablet, the Kindle Fire, giving Amazon a device that can play all the media it sells online and in its Appstore. Like Apple, Amazon has a Cloud Player for making media content portable, as well as a streaming music service. Amazon is now also competing with television, cable networks, and Netflix by producing Amazon Original television series for its streaming service and even branching into feature films. By early 2017, the Amazon-produced film *Manchester by the Sea* was pulling in major awards, including a Golden Globe and two Oscars.

Facebook

Facebook's immense, socially dynamic audience (about two-thirds of the U.S. population and nearly two billion users across the globe) is its biggest resource. Like Google, it has become a data processor as much as a social media service, collecting every tidbit of information about its users—what we "like," where we live, what we read, and what we want—and selling this information to advertisers. Because Facebook users reveal so much about themselves in their profiles and the messages they share with others, Facebook can offer advertisers exceptionally tailored ads: A user who recently got engaged gets ads like "Impress Your Valentine" and "Vacation in Hawaii," while a teenage girl sees ads for prom dresses and sweet-sixteen party venues.

As a young company, Facebook has suffered growing pains while trying to balance its corporate interests (capitalizing on its millions of users) with its users' interest in controlling the privacy of their information. In 2012, Facebook had the third-largest public offering in U.S. history, behind General Motors and Visa, with the company valued at $104 billion. Facebook's valuation is a reflection of investors' hopes of what the company can do with almost two billion active users rather than evidence of the company's financial success so far. In recent years, Facebook has focused on moving its main interface from the computer screen to mobile phones. Its purchase of Instagram in 2012 for $1 billion was part of that strategy. Facebook continues to make investments to expand beyond its core services, with purchases in 2014 of WhatsApp, an instant messaging service, and Oculus VR, a virtual reality technology company.

Advertising

In 2015, Internet advertising revenue in the United States totaled almost $60 billion.[15] But it wasn't always so lucrative. In the early years of the Web, advertising consisted of traditional display ads placed on pages. These reached small general audiences and thus weren't very profitable. In the late 1990s, Web advertising began shifting to search engines. Paid links now appear as "sponsored links" at the top, bottom, and side of a search engine result list. Every time a user clicks on a sponsored link, the advertiser pays the search engine for the click-through. However, even though search engines insist on the relevance of their search results, the increasingly commercial nature of the Web and the ability of commercial sites to buy advertisements on popular sites (thus making more links) mean that search engine results are biased toward commercial sites. Today, a site like Google is making billions of dollars in revenue from these pay-per-click advertisements.

More than just attaching ads to searches for certain key words, Google has become a model of how to generate dollars through **targeted advertising**, or ads targeted to a consumer based on information the various Web sites have gathered about that individual. For example, Google's e-mail program, Gmail, has an automatic search function that "reads" e-mails and then, based on the key words it finds, selects ads to show users. This is one example of **data mining**, a system of collecting information about consumers, of which consumers are largely unaware. Millions of people have embraced the ease of **e-commerce**; the buying and selling of products and services on the Internet. What many people don't know is that their personal information may be used without their knowledge for commercial purposes, such as this targeted advertising.

Another common method that commercial interests use to track the browsing habits of computer users is **cookies**, or information profiles that are automatically collected and transferred between computer servers whenever users access Web sites.[16] The legitimate purpose of a cookie is to verify that a user has

▲ This kiosk at the Denver International Airport lets travelers try out Facebook's Oculus VR system — an opportunity clearly aimed at generating interest in the product. Andy Cross/Getty Images

been cleared for access to a particular Web site, such as a library database that is open to university faculty and students only. However, cookies can also be used to create marketing profiles of Web users to target them for advertising. Many Web sites require the user to accept cookies in order to gain access to the site.

Facebook is another site that has had success with targeted advertising, though it has gotten itself into some trouble as a result of aggressive data-mining efforts. Because typical Facebook users reveal so much about themselves in their profiles and messages, Facebook can offer advertisers exceptionally tailored ads. But in 2011, the Federal Trade Commission (FTC) accused Facebook of taking information it had told users would be private and sharing it with advertisers and third-party applications. Facebook CEO Mark Zuckerberg ended up settling with the FTC, admitting to "a bunch of mistakes," and agreeing to submit to privacy audits.[17]

In addition, the rise in smartphone use has contributed to extraordinary growth in mobile advertising, which jumped from $3.4 billion in 2012 to $20.7 billion in 2015, accounting for 35 percent of all Internet advertising income for the year.[18]

The Noncommercial Web

Despite powerful commercial forces dictating much of the content we access online, the pioneering spirit of the Internet's independent early days endures; the Internet continues to be a participatory medium where anyone can be involved. Two of the most prominent areas in which alternative voices continue to flourish are in open-source software and digital archiving.

▼ Linus Torvalds, the Finnish software developer, holds a license plate bearing the name of his invention, the Linux computer operating system. Since Torvalds's first version of Linux in 1991, hundreds of other developers around the world have contributed improvements to this open-source software rival of Microsoft's Windows. AP Photo/Paul Sakuma

Open-Source Software

Microsoft has long dominated the software industry—requiring users to pay for both its applications and its upgrades, and keeping its proprietary code protected from changes by outsiders. Yet independent software creators persist in making alternatives through **open-source software**, in which code can be updated by anyone interested in modifying it. One example is the open-source operating system Linux, introduced in 1991 by Linus Torvalds and shared with computer programmers and hobbyists around the world, who have avidly participated to improve it. Today, even Microsoft acknowledges that Linux is a credible alternative to expensive commercial programs.

Digital Archiving

Librarians have worked tirelessly to build digital archives that exist outside of any commercial system. One of the biggest and most impressive digital-preservation initiatives is the Internet Archive (www.archive.org), established in 1996. The Internet Archive aims to ensure that researchers, historians, scholars, and all U.S. citizens have access to digitized content. This content comprises all the text, moving images, audio, software, and more than 279 billion archived Web pages reaching back to the earliest days of the Internet.

The Internet Archive has also partnered with the Open Content Alliance to digitize every book in the public domain (generally, those published before 1922). This book-scanning effort is the nonprofit alternative to Google's Library Project, which has the colossal goal of digitizing every book ever printed. Working with the Boston Public Library, several university and international libraries, and a few corporate sponsors, the Open Content Alliance aims to keep as much online information as possible in the "commons"—a term that refers to the collective ownership of certain public resources, such as the broadcast airwaves, the Internet, and public parks. The alliance's concern is that online content like digital books might otherwise become solely the property of commercial entities.

Security and Appropriateness on the Internet

When we watch television, listen to the radio, read a book, or go to a movie, we don't need to provide personal information to get access to the media content we're consuming. However, when we use the Internet—whether it's to sign up for an e-mail account, comment on a blog, or shop online—we give away personal information, even if we don't mean to. This has raised concerns about the security of information, personal safety, and the appropriateness of content available on the Web.

Information Security: What's Private?

Government surveillance, online fraud, unethical data-gathering methods, and malicious programs have become common, making the Internet a potentially treacherous place.

- *Government Surveillance.* Since the inception of the Internet, government agencies around the world have obtained communication logs, Web browser histories, and the online records of users who thought their Internet activities were private. In the United States, for example, the USA PATRIOT Act (which became law about a month after the September 11 attacks in 2001 and was renewed in 2006, with several provisions later extended further) grants sweeping powers to law-enforcement agencies to intercept individuals' online communications, including e-mail messages and browsing records. The act was intended to allow the government to more easily uncover and track potential terrorists and terrorist organizations, but many now argue that it is too vaguely worded, allowing the government to unconstitutionally probe the personal records of citizens without probable cause and for reasons other than preventing terrorism. Moreover, searches of the Internet permit law-enforcement agencies to gather huge amounts of data, including the communications of people who are not the targets of an investigation. Documents leaked to the news media in 2013 by former CIA employee and former National Security Agency (NSA) contractor Edward Snowden (see chapter opening) revealed that the NSA had continued its domestic spying program for more than a decade, collecting bulk Internet and mobile phone data on millions of Americans.

- *Online Fraud.* The Internet has increasingly become a conduit for online robbery and *identity theft*, the illegal obtaining of someone's credit and identity information to fraudulently spend his or her money. One particularly costly form of Internet identity theft is **phishing**. Through this tactic, scammers send phony e-mail messages that appear to be from official Web sites e.g., eBay, PayPal, Chase—asking customers to enter or update their credit card details and other personal information (such as bank account numbers). Once scammers have this information, they can go on a shopping spree using the victim's credit card or siphon funds out of the victim's bank account.

- *Unethical Data Gathering.* As discussed in the earlier section about the business of the Internet, companies use cookies to collect information and tailor marketing messages. Even more frustrating is **spyware**, information-gathering software that is often secretly bundled with free downloaded software and that sends pop-up ads to users' computer screens.

- *Malicious Programs.* Spyware is just one kind of **malware** (malicious software) that hackers sneak onto computers, tablets, smartphones, and high-tech household appliances. Other types of malware, such as worms and Trojan horses, can do more than just spy on a device: they actually take control. For example, malware can tell infected computers and devices to contact a particular Web site at a preprogrammed time, overwhelming and crashing the site in a distributed denial-of-service (DDoS) attack.

▼ The hacking of The Democratic National Committee and Clinton adviser John Podesta's e-mails by Russian Intelligence — and their steady release via WikiLeaks — was a big story during and after the 2016 U.S. presidential election. Brooks Kraft/Getty Images

(For more on hacking see "The Digital Turn Case Study: Activism, Hacktivism, and Anonymous" on pages 288–289.)

In 1998, the FTC developed fair information principles to combat the unauthorized collection of personal data online. Unfortunately, the FTC has no power to enforce these principles, and most Web sites either don't self-enforce them or say they do when they really don't.[19] Consumer and privacy advocates are calling for stronger regulations, such as requiring Web sites to adopt opt-in policies. **Opt-in policies** require a Web site to obtain explicit permission from consumers before it can collect their browsing-history data.

Personal Safety: Online Predators, Spreading Hate, and Deciding What's Appropriate

In addition to the various kinds of scams and malware that target electronic devices, predators also use the Internet to cause harm. One predatory behavior is called **catfishing**, which is the practice of pretending to be another person, even a person of a different gender, to trick someone into having an online relationship. One of the scariest forms of catfishing happens when a child molester poses as a friendly person on social networking sites, with the goal of forming relationships with naïve young people. Once a relationship takes root online, the predator suggests a face-to-face meeting, with the intent of exploiting the young person sexually. These incidents have provoked an outcry from parents and demands for better mechanisms for protecting Internet users' safety.

There are also concerns about controversial online content that can be harmful to users or to society, such as sites that cultivate hate, sexually explicit content, and instructions on making weapons or drugs. Because of their controversial nature, sites that carry potentially dangerous information (such as bomb-building instructions and hate speech) have also incited calls for Internet censorship. The terrorist attacks of September 11, 2001, along with tragic incidents such as mass shootings in schools and churches, have intensified debate about whether such information should be available on the Net. The Southern Poverty Law Center, which identifies and tracks white supremacists and other hate groups, warns that some Web sites, including 4chan and Reddit, can be used to spread bigotry and recruit new members to these groups.

Public objection to indecent and obscene Internet content has led to various legislative efforts to tame the Web. For example, the Children's Internet Protection Act of 2000 was passed and upheld in 2003. This act requires schools and libraries that receive federal funding for Internet access to use software that filters out any visual content deemed obscene, pornographic, or harmful to minors, unless disabled at the request of adult users. Yet regardless of laws, pornography continues to flourish on commercial sites, individuals' blogs, and social networking pages.

The Internet in a Democratic Society

Despite concerns over some online content, many tout the Internet as the most democratic social network ever conceived. But this same medium has also presented threats to our democracy—in the form of a division between people who can afford to use the Internet and those who can't, and the Internet's increasing commercialization.

Access: Closing the Digital Divide

Coined to echo the term *economic divide* (the disparity of wealth between the rich and the poor), the term **digital divide** refers to the contrast between the information haves (those who can afford to pay for Internet services) and the information have-nots (those who can't).

In the early 2000s, the digital divide was a fairly straightforward concept: affluent, white, educated city dwellers had access to dial-up Internet at two or three times the rate of other citizens. But since the digital turn, the concept has gotten more nuanced even as the Internet has become more tightly woven into aspects of daily life—including opportunities for education and employment.

As Web sites became more complicated and streaming audio and video more common, Internet speed has become increasingly important. Typically, broadband connections are capable of the best downloading and uploading speeds, a key factor in the usability of the Internet. At the same time, the rise of smartphones and other Internet-capable wireless phones and devices—as well as Wi-Fi hotspots—have enabled more users to connect to the Internet wherever they are.

In general, the overall digital divide has narrowed in the United States since 2000. For example, there is a smaller gap between the percentage of low-income households and affluent households that have Internet access, and the gap between whites, blacks, and Hispanics who have access is lower than it used to be. However, when measuring access by level of education and dial-up versus broadband, there is still a significant divide (see Figure 9.2).

Globally, though, the have-nots face an even greater obstacle in crossing the digital divide. Although the Web claims to be worldwide, the most economically powerful countries—such as the United States, Sweden, Japan, South Korea, Australia, and the United Kingdom—account for much of its activity and content. In nations such as Jordan, Saudi Arabia, Syria, and Myanmar (Burma), the government permits limited or no access to the Web. In other countries, an inadequate telecommunications infrastructure hampers access to the Internet. However, as mobile phones become more popular in the developing world, they could provide one remedy to the global digital divide.

Ownership and Customization

Some people have argued that the biggest threat to democracy on the Internet is its increasing commercialization. Similar to what happened with radio and television, the growth of commercial channels on the Internet has far outpaced the emergence of viable nonprofit channels, as a few corporations have gained more control over this medium. Although there was much buzz about lucrative Internet start-ups in the 1990s, it was the largest corporations (such as Microsoft, Google, Apple, and Amazon) that weathered the crash of the dot-coms in the early 2000s and maintained their dominance.

FIGURE 9.2 // DIGITAL DIVIDE BASED ON DEMOGRAPHICS AND INTERNET SPEED

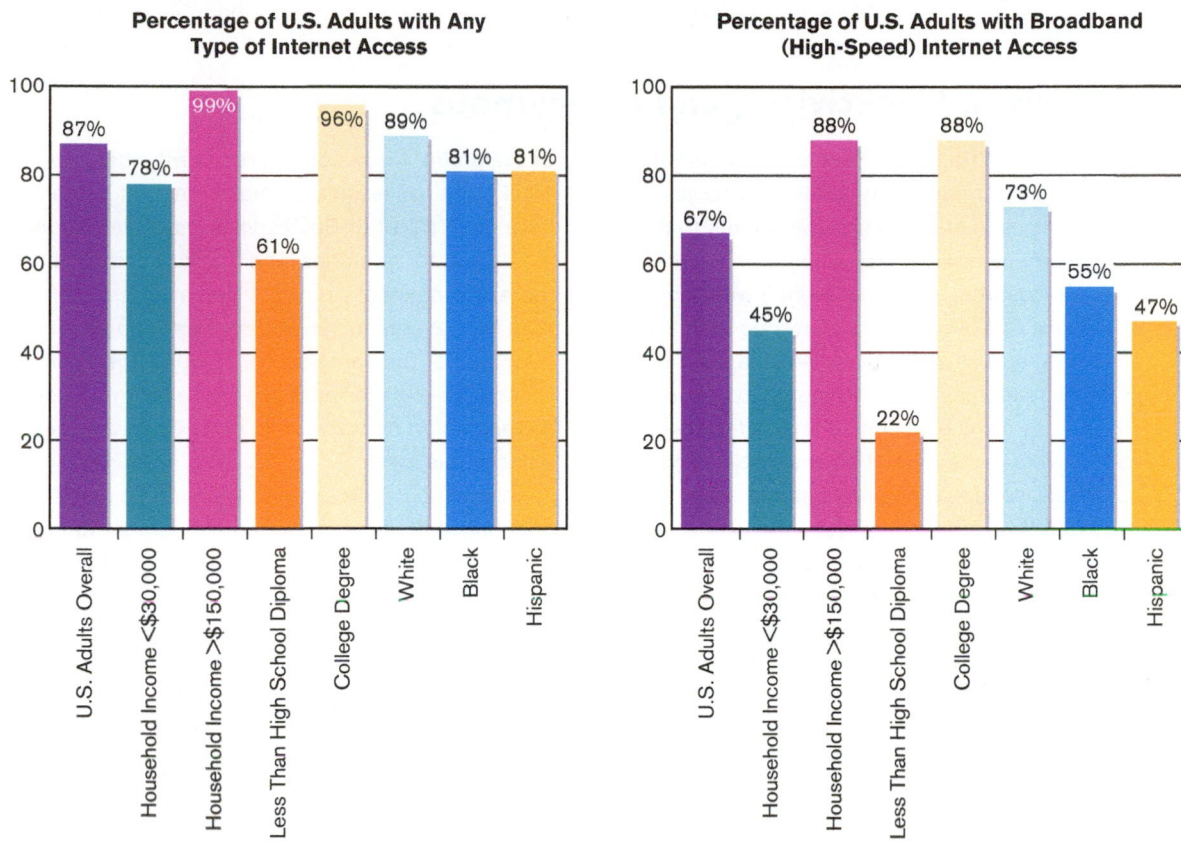

Data from: Lee Rainie, "Digital Divides 2016," Pew Research Center, July 14, 2016, www.pewinternet.org/2016/07/14/digital-divides-2016/.

As we've seen, the Internet's booming popularity has tempted commercial interests to gain even more control over the medium. It has also sparked debate between defenders of the digital age and those who want to regulate the Net. Defenders argue that newer media forms—digital music files, online streaming of films and TV shows, blogs—have made life more satisfying and enjoyable for Americans than has any other medium. Further, they maintain that **mass customization**, whereby individual consumers can tailor a Web page or other media form, has enabled us to express our creativity more easily and conveniently than ever. For example, if we use a service like Facebook or WordPress, we get the benefits of creating our own personal Web space without having to write the underlying code. On the other hand (dissenters point out), we're limited to the options, templates, and other platform features provided by the media company. So (the dissenters ask), how free are we, really, to express our true creative selves? And how much are we being controlled by the big Internet firms?

The Digital Turn

CASE STUDY

Activism, Hacktivism, and Anonymous

In the fall of 2016, when Kentucky computer hacker Deric Lostutter pled guilty to federal charges of conspiracy and making false statements to the FBI, he found himself facing up to ten years in prison.[1] Lostutter, who was aligned with the hacker collective Anonymous, had conspired with another hacker to access a Steubenville, Ohio, high school football team fan site. Their intent? To obtain social media posts and a video that implicated two football players in the rape of an unconscious girl. The Steubenville rape case drew national attention, and Trent Mays, seventeen, and Ma'lik Richmond, sixteen, were ultimately convicted using scores of texts and photos from teens who shared details of the victim's assault on social media—details Lostutter claimed were covered up to protect the town's star football players.[2]

To some, Lostutter was a hero, who kept a vile crime from being swept under the rug. To others, especially federal law enforcement, Lostutter was just another criminal—an online vigilante. To better understand this controversy, as well as the confusing dichotomy of good and bad that hackers often represent, it helps to understand Anonymous. Even if you aren't very familiar with this loosely organized group of *hacktivists*, who hack computer systems in the name of being activists for a cause, you may be familiar with the stylized Guy Fawkes mask often used as a symbol of the group. Masks of Fawkes (a member of a 1605 plot to assassinate King James I of England) have been a part of Guy Fawkes Day celebrations in England for centuries. The mask became even more internationally recognizable as a result of the Alan Moore graphic novel *V for Vendetta* and the 2006 film of the same name, in which the main character—part terrorist or part freedom fighter, depending on how you view him—is never seen without this mask.

Anonymous first came to widespread public attention in 2008, after a video of a fervent Tom Cruise, meant for only internal promotional use by the Church of Scientology, was leaked to the Web site *Gawker*. The church tried to suppress the video through copyright claims, and Anonymous retaliated. It launched a DDoS attack on the Scientology Web site, inundated the church with prank calls and faxes, and "doxed" the church by stealing and then publishing sensitive internal documents. Since then, targets of Anonymous have ranged from the Indian government (protesting plans to block certain Web sites) to Monsanto (protesting malicious lawsuits and dominance of the food industry) to KKK members (revealing member identities and taking over the KKK's Twitter account because of threats of violence against protesters in Ferguson, Missouri) to jihadists (crashing Web sites in the wake of the attack at the *Charlie Hebdo* magazine in Paris that left twelve dead).

Anonymity is part of the ethos of Anonymous. The group has a general agenda of sorts (distrust of governments, protection of a free and open Internet, opposition to child pornography, and a distaste for corporate conglomerates) and has championed causes both online and with live

⊙ Visit LaunchPad to watch a portion of *We Are Legion: The Story of the Hacktivists*. How does this film seem to portray the practice of hacktivism?

launchpadworks.com

▲ Protesters and activists around the world have adopted a stylized mask of Guy Fawkes, a British man who plotted to blow up the English Parliament in 1605. The mask has come to signify opposition to oppressive governments and corporate institutions. Attila Volgyi/Polaris/Newscom

demonstrations. But otherwise, there isn't much organization to the group. Rather, it is made up of individual hackers who act independently without expecting recognition. A reporter from the *Baltimore City Paper* aptly characterized Anonymous as "a group, in the sense that a flock of birds is a group. How do you know they're a group? Because they're traveling in the same direction. At any given moment, more birds could join, leave, peel off in another direction entirely."[3]

It can often be easy to find the good in the activities of hacktivists. But it's also true that Anonymous members are violating a number of laws when they hack into private systems, cause those systems to crash, and expose the information on those systems. Certainly hackers have caused serious harm through activities like identity theft and the stealing of personal information.

When Deric Lostutter was discovered and arrested, this ethical quandary became a matter for the courts, not just a source of moral debate. While Lostutter was ultimately sentenced to two years in prison in March of 2017, he could have received up to five years for each of the two charges against him — which, as *Rolling Stone* pointed out, meant that he was "facing more jail time than the convicted rapists."[4] (One rapist received a minimum sentence of one year; the other got two years.)

And so this leaves us with some profound questions: Is Anonymous just another dark corner of the Internet where those with less-than-pure intentions can carry out their plans? Or do we need groups like Anonymous to serve as a kind of conscience over the Internet, because governments, corporations, and others in power sometimes can't be trusted?

CHAPTER ESSENTIALS

Review

- The **Internet**—the vast central network of telephone and cable lines, wireless connections, and satellite systems designed to link and carry computer information worldwide—was created in the late 1960s as the U.S. Defense Department's **ARPAnet** and used as a military-government communication tool. **E-mail** enabled researchers to communicate from separate locations.

- Innovations in the 1970s and 1980s took the Internet from the development stage to the entrepreneurial stage. **Microprocessors** led to the introduction of the first personal computers (PCs), and **fiber-optic cable** helped make the commercial use of computers even more viable.

- The introduction of the **World Wide Web** and the first **Web browsers** in the 1990s helped transform the Internet into a mass medium. Soon after these developments, the Internet quickly became commercialized. Key features of the commercial Internet include **Internet service providers (ISPs)**, which bring Web access to customers; e-mail and instant messaging services; and **search engines**, which are capable of searching and retrieving information and linking to Web sites based on a few key words.

- The Internet has become more converged and more social. People use the Web for a variety of social media, of which six categories have been identified: **social networking sites**, **blogs**, collaborative projects (including **wikis**), **content communities,** virtual game worlds, and virtual social worlds.

- The Web's next phase centers around a Semantic Web, which takes connectivity beyond people and Web sites to other machines—from cars to refrigerators.

- Although no one owns the Internet, a number of corporations have tried to control it. Microsoft, Google, Apple, Amazon, and Facebook are currently the leading Internet companies.

- Advertising is big business, and companies like Google have become models of how to generate dollars through **targeted advertising**, or ads targeted to a consumer based on information the various Web sites have gathered about that individual.

- Noncommercial entities on the Web do not make a profit from the Internet. **Open-source software** is shared freely and developed collectively, whereas digital archiving aims to ensure that data is stored and preserved digitally, so that all people have access to it.

- Government surveillance; online fraud, such as **phishing;** unethical data gathering, such as **spyware;** and the use of **malware** have raised questions about information security on the Web and what should be considered private. At the same time, the issues of protecting people from online predators and figuring out what constitutes appropriate content on the Web—particularly regarding sexually explicit material—have sparked public concern.

- The Internet has made it easier for more people to voice opinions and become involved in a wide range of topics, but it has also revealed a **digital divide** regarding those who have access to information and those who do not.

Key Terms

digitization, p. 265
ARPAnet, p. 267
e-mail, p. 267
microprocessors, p. 268
fiber-optic cable, p. 268
World Wide Web, p. 269
HTML (hypertext markup language), p. 269

Web browsers, p. 270
Internet service provider (ISP), p. 270
broadband, p. 270
instant messaging (IM), p. 271
search engines, p. 271

social networking sites p. 272
blogs p. 273
wikis p. 273
content communities p. 274
Wi-Fi p. 275
portal p. 276
net neutrality p. 278
blocking p. 279
throttling p. 279
paid prioritization p. 279
targeted advertising p. 281

data mining p. 281
e-commerce p. 281
cookies p. 281
open-source software p. 282
phishing p. 284
spyware p. 284
malware p. 284
opt-in policies p. 284
catfishing p. 285
digital divide p. 286
mass customization p. 287

Study Questions

1. How did the Internet originate? What does its development have in common with earlier mass media?

2. Trace the evolution of the Internet from early Web browsers to today's increasingly Semantic Web. What are the key differences between the phases of Internet growth?

3. How have major companies tried to control the Internet? Which failed, and why?

4. What are the central concerns about the Internet regarding security and appropriateness?

5. What is the digital divide? In modern society, what are the implications of being on the "have-not" side of that divide?

10

Digital Gaming and the Media Playground

In 2016, Felix Kjellberg made an estimated $15 million.[1] With over fifty million subscribers to his YouTube channel, one might assume that Kjellberg is a musician or a celebrated director, but he is neither of those things: The Swedish YouTube star is a gamer. He makes videos of himself playing video games, he posts them online, and the money comes rolling in. "I just want to make entertaining videos," says Kjellberg, who goes by the handle PewDiePie. "[People think I sit] and just yell at the screen over here, which is true! But there's so much more to it than that."[2]

PewDiePie is just one of the top gamers who post Let's Play videos — videos in which individuals record themselves playing games (*Minecraft* is particularly popular) while delivering a running monologue. This phenomenon is clearly enabled by convergence: Gamers play using digital devices, record videos of themselves on *other* digital devices, and use an online streaming service to upload the videos, which are then watched by millions of viewers on *their* digital devices. This creates a fan base that allows gamers to sell advertising on their channels, endorse games and other products, and even sign book deals. (PewDiePie's online

◀ Using kitschy, throwback 8-bit graphics, *Minecraft* has become both a gaming phenomenon and something of a spectator sport. Many fans enjoy watching Let's Play videos of other enthusiasts playing the game — and providing tips and tricks that viewers can try at home. Bloomberg/Getty Images

celebrity also recently brought attention to his other activities, including encouraging anti-Semitic speech, which resulted in lost sponsorships and partnerships for him.)

These days, digital gaming is a global industry worth billions of dollars, thanks to the wide range of games available on a variety of devices. But gaming is more than just a business venture; it is a growing part of daily life for many Americans. Roughly half of the adults in the United States play video games (split almost evenly between men and women), with 10 percent identifying themselves as "gamers."[3] Games can be solitary or they can be social, and players can interact with the outside world (*Pokémon Go*) or be immersed in a different world altogether (virtual reality). And as Let's Play videos illustrate, gamers also enjoy other gaming-related media—media that further promote the games themselves.

With more people playing games in more places, scholars and critics have begun to look more closely at the role of digital games in society and culture. Recognition of the cultural and economic importance of digital games has meant more press coverage (see "Media Literacy Case Study: Writing about Games" on pages 316–317), as well as a growing critique on what the games say about women and minorities. There are also questions about the impact of games and gaming culture on children—a particularly relevant issue for Let's Play videos, since their audience skews toward teens, tweens, and even younger children. Some have a reputation for being kid friendly, like PopularMMOS (Patrick Brown). Others, like PewDiePie, have a reputation for using stronger language than some parents might like.

As society grapples with these issues, one thing is clear: Gaming has become an everyday form of entertainment, rather than simply the niche pursuit of hard-core enthusiasts. From casual smartphone games to involved computer strategy games to multiplayer games accessed with a console, today's digital games are more than a distraction—they are a mass medium in their own right.

DIGITAL GAMES offer play, entertainment, and social interaction. Like the Internet, they combine text, audio, and moving images. But they go even further than the Internet by enabling players to interact with aspects of the medium in the context of the game—from deciding when an on-screen character jumps or punches to controlling the direction of the story in games such as *World of Warcraft*. This creates an experience so compelling that vibrant communities of fans have cropped up around the globe. And the games have powerfully shaped the everyday lives of millions of people worldwide.

Players can now choose from a massive range of games designed to satisfy almost any taste. Today, digital gaming and the media playground encompass classic video games like *Super Mario Bros.*, virtual sports-management games like ESPN's *Fantasy Football,* and more physically interactive games like those found on *Wii Fit*—to say nothing of massively multiplayer online role-playing games and casual games like *Angry Birds.* Indeed, for players around the world, digital gaming has become a social medium—as compelling and distracting as other social media. The U.S. Supreme Court has even granted digital gaming First Amendment freedom of speech rights, ensuring its place as a mass medium.

In this chapter, we take a look at the evolving mass medium of digital gaming by:

- **examining the early history of digital gaming, including its roots in penny arcades**

- **tracing the evolution of digital gaming from arcades and bars to living rooms and hands**

- **discussing the rise of gaming as a social medium that forms communities of play**

- **analyzing the economics of gaming, including the industry's various revenue streams**

- **raising questions about the role of digital gaming in our democratic society**

The Early History of Digital Gaming

When the Industrial Revolution swept Western civilization two centuries ago, the technological advances involved weren't simply about mass production. They also promoted mass consumption and the emergence of *leisure time* — both of which created moneymaking opportunities for media makers. By the late nineteenth century, the availability of leisure time sparked the creation of mechanical games like pinball. Technology continued to grow, and by the 1950s, computer science students in the United States had developed early versions of the video games we know today.

Mechanical Gaming

In the 1880s, the seeds of the modern entertainment industry were planted via a series of coin-operated contraptions devoted to cashing in on idleness. First appearing in train depots, hotel lobbies, bars, and restaurants, these leisure

▲ The modern pinball machine with flipper bumpers. Ken Reid/ Getty Images

machines (also called "counter machines") would find a permanent home in the first thoroughly modern indoor playground: the **penny arcade**.[4]

Arcades were like nurseries for fledgling forms of amusement, which would mature into mass entertainment industries during the twentieth century. They offered fun even as they began shaping future media technology. For example, automated phonographs used in arcade machines evolved into the jukebox, and the kinetoscope (see Chapter 7) set the stage for the coming wonders of the movies. But the machines most relevant to today's digital gaming were more interactive and primitive than the phonograph and kinetoscope. Some were strength testers, which dared young men to show off their muscles by punching a boxing bag or arm-wrestling a robotlike Uncle Sam. Others required more refined skills and sustained play, such as those that simulated bowling, horse racing, and football.[5]

Another arcade game, the bagatelle, spawned the **pinball machine**, the most prominent of the mechanical games. In pinball, players score points by manipulating the path of a metal ball on a play field enclosed in a glass case. In the 1930s and 1940s, players could control only the launch of the ball. For this reason, pinball was considered a sinister game of chance, which—like the slot machine—fed the coffers of the gambling underworld. As a result, pinball was banned in most American cities, including New York, Chicago, and Los Angeles.[6] However, pinball gained mainstream acceptance and popularity after World War II with the addition of the **flipper bumper**, which enables players to careen the ball back up the play table. This innovation transformed pinball into a challenging game of skill, touch, and timing—all of which would become vital abilities for video game players years later.

The First Video Games

The postwar popularity of pinball set the stage for the emergence of video games; the first video game patent was issued on December 14, 1948. It went to Thomas T. Goldsmith and Estle Ray Mann for what they described as a "Cathode-Ray Tube Amusement Device." The invention, which was never marketed or sold, featured the key component of the first video games: the **cathode ray tube (CRT)**.

CRT-type screens provided the images for analog television and for early computer displays, on which the first video games appeared a few years later. Computer science students developed these games as novelties in the 1950s and 1960s, but because computers consisted of massive mainframes at the time, the games were not readily available to the general public.

However, more and more people owned televisions, and this development provided a platform for video games. Ralph Baer, a German immigrant and television engineer, developed the first home television gaming console, a system called Odyssey. Released by Magnavox in 1972 and sold for a whopping $100. Odyssey used player controllers that moved dots of light around the screen in a twelve-game inventory of simple aiming and sports games. From 1972 until Odyssey's replacement by a simpler model (the Odyssey 100) in 1975, Magnavox sold roughly 330,000 of the consoles.[7]

In the next decade, a ripped-off version of one of the Odyssey games brought the delights of video gaming into modern **arcades**, establishments gathering multiple coin-operated games together in a newer version of the penny arcade. The same year that Magnavox released the Odyssey console, a young American computer engineer named Nolan Bushnell and a friend formed a video game development company called **Atari**. The enterprise's first creation was *Pong*, a simple two-dimensional tennis-style game with two vertical paddles that bounced a white dot back and forth. Unlike the Odyssey version, *Pong* made blip noises when the ball hit the paddles or bounced off the sides of the court. *Pong* quickly became the first video game to hit it big in arcades.

In 1975, Atari began successfully marketing a home version of *Pong* through an exclusive deal with Sears. The arrangement established the home video game market. Just two years later, Bushnell (who also started the Chuck E. Cheese pizza-arcade restaurant chain) sold Atari to Warner Communications for an astounding $28 million. Although Atari folded in 1984, plenty of companies — including Nintendo, Sony, and Microsoft — followed its early lead, transforming the video game business into a full-fledged industry.

▲ A later model of the Odyssey console, the Odyssey,[2] was released in 1978 and featured a full keyboard that could be used for educational games.
The Advertising Archives

The Evolution of Digital Gaming

In their most basic form, digital games involve users in an interactive computerized environment where they strive to achieve a desired outcome. These days, most digital games go beyond a simple competition like *Pong*; they often entail sweeping narratives and offer imaginative and exciting adventures, sophisticated problem-solving opportunities, and multiple possible outcomes.

But the boundaries were not always so varied. Digital games evolved from their simplest forms in the arcade into four major formats: television, handheld devices, computers, and finally the Internet. As these formats evolved and graphics advanced, distinctive types of games emerged and became popular. These included classically structured games played in arcades and on consoles and mobile devices, online role-playing games, computerized versions of card games, fantasy sports leagues, and virtual social environments. Together, these varied formats constitute an industry that now generates $100 billion in annual revenues worldwide — and that has become a socially driven mass medium.

Arcades and Classic Games

By the late 1970s and early 1980s, games like *Asteroids*, *Pac-Man*, and *Donkey Kong* filled arcades and bars, competing with traditional pinball machines. In a way, arcades signaled digital gaming's potential as a social medium because many games allowed players to compete with or against each other, standing side by side. To be sure, arcade gaming has been superseded by the console and computer. But the industry still attracts fun-seekers to amusement parks, malls, and casinos, as well as to businesses like Dave & Buster's—a gaming–restaurant chain operating in more than fifty locations.

To play the classic arcade games, as well as many of today's popular console games, players use controllers like joysticks and buttons to interact with graphical elements on a video screen. With a few notable exceptions (puzzle games like *Tetris*, for instance), these types of video games require players to identify with a position on the screen. In *Pong*, this position is represented by an electronic paddle; in *Space Invaders*, it's an earthbound shooting position. After *Pac-Man*, the **avatar** (a graphic interactive "character" situated within the world of the game) became the most common figure of player control and position identification. In the United States, the most popular video games today assume a first-person perspective, in which the player "sees" the virtual environment through the eyes of an avatar. In contrast, players in South Korea often favor real-time strategy games with an elevated three-quarters perspective, which affords

▼ Though home consoles have become widespread, some gaming fans still enjoy playing in arcades, which have evolved from their earliest counterparts and provide a different social experience from today's Internet-enabled home systems. Marilyn K Yee/The New York Times/Redux Pictures

a grander and more strategic vantage point on the field of play. (See Table 10.1 for examples of these and other major video game conventions.)

Consoles Power Up

Today, many digital games are played on home **consoles**, devices people use specifically to play video games. These systems have become increasingly more powerful since the appearance of the early Atari consoles in the 1970s. One way of charting the evolution of consoles is to track the number of bits (binary digits) they can process at one time. The bit rating of a console is a measure of its power at rendering computer graphics. The higher the bit rating, the more detailed and sophisticated the graphics. The Atari 2600, released in 1977, used an 8-bit processor, as did the wildly popular Nintendo Entertainment System, first released in Japan in 1983. Sega Genesis, the first 16-bit console, appeared in 1989. In 1992, 32-bit computers appeared on the market; the following year, 64 bits became the new standard. The 128-bit era dawned with the marketing of Sega Dreamcast in 1999. With the current generation of consoles, 256-bit processors are the standard.

▼ These images trace gaming graphics from 8 bits (*Space Invaders*) to 16 bits (*Super Mario World*) to 64 bits (*Mario Kart 64*) to a modern 256-bit entry in the *Tomb Raider* series. The Advertising Archives; Jamaway/Alamy; Jamaway/Alamy; KRT/Newscom

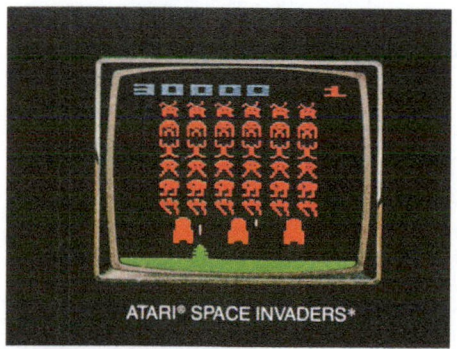

TABLE 10.1 // MAJOR VIDEO GAME CONVENTIONS

Innovation	Description	Examples	Visual Representation
Avatars	On-screen figures of player identification	Pac-Man (right), the Mario Bros., Sonic the Hedgehog, Link from *Legend of Zelda*	 Kevin Britland/Alamy
Bosses	Powerful enemy characters that represent the final challenge in a stage or the entire game	Bowser from the *Mario* series, Hitler in *Castle Wolfenstein*, *Donkey Kong* (right)	 Jamaway/Alamy
Vertical and Side Scrolling	As opposed to a fixed screen, scrolling that follows the action as it moves up, down, or sideways in what is called a "tracking shot" in the cinema	Platform games like *Jump Bug*, *Jungle King*, and *Super Mario Bros.*; also integrated into the design of *Angry Birds* (right)	 lifestyleUK/Alamy
Isometric Perspective (also called Three-Quarters Perspective)	An elevated and angled perspective that enhances the sense of three-dimensionality by allowing players to see the tops and sides of objects	*Zaxxon* (right), real-time strategy games like *StarCraft*, god games like *Civilization* and *Populous*	 ArcadeImages/Alamy
First-Person Perspective	Presents the gameplay through the eyes of your avatar	First-person shooter (FPS) games like *Castle Wolfenstein*, *Doom* (right), *Halo*, and *Call of Duty*	 Bloomberg/Getty Images

(continued)

TABLE 10.1 // (CONTINUED)

Innovation	Description	Examples	Visual Representation
Third-Person Perspective (or Over-the-Shoulders Perspective)	Enables you to view your heroic avatar in action from an external viewpoint	*Tomb Raider* (right), *Assassin's Creed*, and the default viewpoint in *World of Warcraft*	ZCHE/Newscom/WENN/
Cut Scenes (also called In-Game Cinematic or In-Game Movie)	Narrative respite from gameplay, providing cinematic scenes that advance the story; often appear at the beginning of games and between levels	Well-known early example appears in *Maniac Mansion* (1987); cut scenes from games like the *Grand Theft Auto* series (right) have become increasingly vivid and complex	The Advertising Archives

But more detailed graphics have not always replaced simpler games. Nintendo, for example, offers many of its older, classic games for download onto its newest consoles even as updated versions are released, for nostalgic gamers as well as new fans. Perhaps the best example of enduring games is the *Super Mario Bros.* series. Created by Nintendo mainstay Shigeru Miyamoto in 1983, the original *Mario Bros.* game began in arcades. The 1985 sequel—*Super Mario Bros.*, developed for the 8-bit Nintendo Entertainment System—became the best-selling video game of all time. It held this title until as recently as 2009, when it was unseated by Nintendo's *Wii Sports*. Graphical elements from the *Mario Bros.* games, like the "1-Up" mushroom that gives players an extra life, remain instantly recognizable to gamers of all ages.

The Big Three: Nintendo, Sony, and Microsoft

Through decades of ups and downs in the digital gaming industry (Atari closing down, Sega no longer making video consoles), three major home console makers emerged: Nintendo, Sony, and Microsoft. Nintendo has been making consoles since the 1980s; Sony and Microsoft came later, but both companies were already major media conglomerates and thus well positioned to support and promote their interests in the video game market. Sony introduced its PlayStation series in 1994, and its current console is the PlayStation 4 (PS4). There are currently more than sixty million active PlayStation users, about one-third of which are paid online subscribers.[8] Microsoft's first foray into video game consoles was the Xbox, released in 2001 and linked to the Xbox LIVE online service in 2002. Xbox LIVE allows its nearly fifty million subscribers to play online and enables users to download new content directly to the console—the Xbox One.

Nintendo released a new kind of console, the Wii, in 2006. The device supported traditional video games like the *New Super Mario Bros.* However, its unique wireless motion-sensing controller also took the often-sedentary nature out of video gameplay. Games like *Wii Sports* require the user to mimic the full-body motion of bowling or playing tennis, while *Wii Fit* uses a wireless balance board for interactive yoga, strength, aerobic, and balance games. In 2012, Nintendo released the more powerful Wii U, a high-definition-capable console that pairs with a Wii U GamePad and is compatible with all earlier Wii games and controllers. Then, in 2017, Nintendo started selling the Switch—a hybrid of a television console, traditional game controllers, and a tablet.

Since 2014, Sony's PlayStation 4 has been the most popular of the new generation of consoles; as of June 2016, PlayStation 4 had nearly doubled Xbox One in sales and more than tripled the sales of Wii U.[9]

Console Convergence: More Than Just a Game

In the earlier days of video games, the most prominent media crossovers came when a movie or a TV cartoon was derived from a popular game. Now, with the newest generation of video game consoles, the consoles themselves are powerful entertainment centers, with multiple forms of media converging in a single device. In addition to their impressive graphics and other gaming functions, these consoles can play DVD and Blu-ray discs and manage cable, broadcast, and Internet streaming video signals, all with high-definition video and multichannel surround sound audio. Users can also use them to surf the Internet and access social media, take videos, and use video chat functions both inside of games and out. The game consoles also interact with other electronic devices, like smartphones and tablets. And the Xbox One (Microsoft) can stream to a user's Windows 10 PC.

Portable Consoles Compete with Smartphones and Tablets

Advances in graphics and gameplay have also enhanced smaller handheld devices dedicated to playing video games. Nintendo's Game Boy was an early success, launching in 1989 and beating out the competing Sega Game Gear and Atari Lynx. These early handhelds gave way to later generations of devices offering increasingly converged portable gaming experiences. For example, the Nintendo DS, released in 2004, and PlayStation Portable (PSP), released in 2005, allowed owners to link up with other players on the Internet via built-in Wi-Fi capabilities.

In 2011, Nintendo released the 3DS as a successor to the DS. When Nintendo released the Wii U console the following year, it came with the GamePad controller, which is a hybrid of a console controller and a portable game device. The company took the concept a step further in 2017 with the Switch, which features a hybrid console that incorporates a touchscreen tablet.

Portable players are big business, with each upgrade spurring new sales. For example, globally, Nintendo has sold 118 million Game Boys, more than 81 million Game Boy Advances, 154 million DS players, and almost 60 million 3DS players.[10] Sony sold over 76 million PSPs before the device was discontinued in 2014.[11] The company also launched the PlayStation Vita portable in 2012, though sales have been sluggish outside Japan.[12]

▲ Nintendo Switch players have a choice: They can use the Switch as a tablet (shown here), or they can plug the device into the TV, using it like a traditional game console. Chesnot/ Getty Images

One of the biggest challenges to these portable game consoles is the widespread use of smartphones and touchscreen tablets. These devices are not typically designed principally for games, but their capabilities bring casual gaming to customers who might not have been interested in the handheld consoles of the past. Even people who wouldn't identify themselves as gamers may kill time by playing *Candy Crush* on their phones.

Manufacturers of tablets and smartphones have caught on to converged gaming potential: After years of relatively little interest in video games, Apple introduced Game Center in 2010, which was designed to help gamers join one another for group play, communicate, and keep track of friends' high scores. (Apple discontinued the app in 2016 but kept the functionality intact.) Google responded in 2013 with Google Play Games for phones and tablets, which runs on the Android system. Both allow users to download new games, invite friends or find others for multiplayer gaming, track their scores, and view high scores on a leader board. With annual sales of smartphones topping a billion units worldwide, the market for gaming on Apple and Android devices is enormous and growing every year.[13]

Computer Gaming

Early home computer games, like the early console games, often mimicked (and sometimes ripped off) popular arcade games like *Frogger*, *Centipede*, *Pac-Man*, and *Space Invaders*. But for a time in the late 1980s and much of the 1990s, personal computers held some clear advantages over console gaming. The versatility of keyboards, compared with the relatively simple early console controllers, allowed for ambitious puzzle-solving games like *Myst*. Moreover, faster processing speeds gave some computer games richer, more detailed three-dimensional (3-D) graphics. Many of the most popular, early first-person shooter games (like *Doom* and *Quake*) were developed for home computers rather than traditional video game consoles. As consoles caught up with greater processing speeds and disc-based games in the late 1990s, elaborate computer games attracted less attention.

But computer-based gaming survives in the form of certain genres not often seen on consoles. Examples include the digitization of card and board games and strategy games like *Civilization*. There are also PC versions of multiplatform games like *Minecraft*.

The Internet and Social Gaming

With the introduction of the Sega Dreamcast in 1999—the first console to feature a built-in modem—game playing emerged as an online, multiplayer social activity. The Dreamcast didn't last, but online connections are now a normal part of console video games. Internet-connected players oppose one another in combat, fight together against a common enemy, or team up to achieve a common goal (like sustain a medieval community). With multiple players joining in digital games via the Internet, this form of gaming has become a contemporary social medium.

Some of the biggest social gaming titles have been first-person shooter games like *Counter-Strike*, an online spin-off of the popular *Half-Life* console game. Each player views the game from the first-person perspective but also plays on a team, as either a terrorist or a counterterrorist. The ability to play online has added a new dimension to other, less combat-oriented games, too. For example, football and music enthusiasts playing already-popular console games like *Madden NFL* and *Rock Band* can now engage with others in live, online, multiplayer play. And young and old alike can compete against teams in other locations in Internet-based bowling tournaments using the Wii.

The increasingly social nature of video games has made them a natural fit for social networking sites. Many online games—like *Lexulous* (inspired by the board game *Scrabble*) and *Farmville*—are now embedded in these sites. **Online fantasy sports** games also reach a mass audience with a major social component. Players—real-life friends, virtual acquaintances, or a mix of both—assemble teams and use actual sports results to determine scores in their online games. But rather than experiencing the visceral thrills of, say, *Madden NFL 17*, fantasy football participants take a more detached, managerial perspective on the game—a departure from the classic video game experience. Fantasy sports' managerial angle makes it even more fun to watch almost any televised game. That's because players focus more on making strategic investments in individual performances scattered across the various professional teams than they do in rooting for local teams. In the process, players become statistically savvy aficionados of the game overall, rather than rabid fans of a particular team. According to the Fantasy Sports Trade Association, in 2015, over fifty-seven million Americans and Canadians played fantasy sports.[14]

This kind of online community building has also enabled a fairly recent form of gaming: **massively multiplayer online role-playing games (MMORPGs)**. These games are set in virtual worlds that require users to play through an avatar of their own design. The fantasy adventure game *World of Warcraft* made a big splash when it launched just in time for the 2004 holiday season, growing steadily until membership peaked at around 12 million active subscribers globally in 2010, before those numbers dropped to around 5.5 million by the end of 2015.[15] Users can select from ten different types of avatars, including dwarves, gnomes, night elves, orcs, trolls, and humans. To succeed, many players join with other players to form guilds or tribes, working together toward in-game goals that can be achieved only through teams. Other top MMORPGs include *Final Fantasy XIV: A Realm Reborn*, *Star Wars: Old Republic*, and *Guild Wars 2*.

Simulations like *Second Life* represent a different kind of social gaming experience. Rather than featuring combat, conflict, or some kind of quest, *Second Life* lets players build human avatars and then use real money to buy virtual land and trade in virtual goods and services.

Second Life and MMORPGs like *World of Warcraft* are aimed at teenagers and adults. But one of the biggest areas in online gaming is the children's market. Club Penguin, a moderated virtual world purchased by Disney, enables kids to play games and chat as colorful penguins. Similarly, the toy maker Ganz developed the online Webkinz World to revive its stuffed animal sales. Each Webkinz stuffed animal comes with a code that lets players access the online world, play games, and care for the virtual version of their plush pets.

Online games have further fostered media convergence. *World of Warcraft*, for instance, is now a comic-book series, a quarterly magazine, and a feature film. The "massively multiplayer" aspect of MMORPGs also indicates that digital games—once designed for solo or small-group play—have expanded to reach large groups, similar to traditional mass media.

Fighting the Dark Side of Gaming Culture: Anita Sarkeesian and Feminist Frequency

Anita Sarkeesian has a well-documented love of playing video games, from *Mario Kart* to *Half-Life 2*. But that hasn't stopped her from becoming one of the most outspoken, and targeted, critics of how video games depict and treat women. In 2012, a successful Kickstarter campaign helped her launch the *Tropes vs Women in Video Games* video series on her Feminist Frequency YouTube channel. As Sarkeesian explains, she was moved to examine video games because she saw, as a girl growing up and playing the games, that so many troubling stereotypes about women were enmeshed in games and gaming culture.

"The games often reinforce a similar message, overwhelmingly casting men as heroes and relegating women to the roles of damsels, victims or hypersexualized playthings," Sarkeesian explains in a 2014 *New York Times* op-ed. "The notion that gaming was not for women rippled out into society, until we heard it not just from the games industry, but from our families, teachers and friends. As a consequence, I, like many women, had a complicated, love-hate relationship with gaming culture."[1]

"Love-hate" is probably also a good way to describe the reaction to Sarkeesian's critique of games. On the one hand, she has gained critical acclaim and visibility for her videos and writing, appearing in the *New York Times*, *Businessweek*, and *Rolling Stone*. On the other hand, since she began releasing her videos on digital games, she has been the target of incredibly graphic and violent threats of rape, torture, and murder on social media. This ongoing online harassment reached a new low in the fall of 2014, when another of her Feminist Frequency video releases coincided with the #GamerGate controversy.

The story surrounding the event that ostensibly touched off the #GamerGate firestorm started when a computer programmer, Eron Gjoni, had a bad breakup with game designer Zoe Quinn. Gjoni then went online with their breakup, claiming that Quinn had had an affair with a writer at Kotaku, an influential gamers' Web site that had given her newest game a positive review. Gjoni's supporters pointed to this as indicative of a larger trend of shady journalistic ethics in the gaming press, and they organized their criticisms under the hashtag #GamerGate. Very quickly, however, the attacks on journalistic ethics were overshadowed by those focused on "slut-shaming" Quinn, as well as anonymous threats of rape, torture, and death.[2]

It was at this point that Sarkeesian (and other critics) spoke up and pointed out that the deeply disturbing threats that many female gamers and critics were experiencing proved her point about a deeper problem in the gaming culture, which in turn reflected broader cultural misogyny. Soon Sarkeesian and others found themselves victims of vicious harassment. In one instance, before

Feminist Frequency ✓
@femfreq

With great gameplay & a rich world filled with female characters, Dishonored 2 is a terrific sequel. Anita's review:

Dishonored 2 Review
Please watch: "The Courageous Life of Ida B. Wells #OrdinaryWomen" https://www.youtube.com/watch?v=7lp-SEYwRTA ~~~~~~~~~~~ Subscribe to our YouTube chann...
youtube.com

RETWEETS 25   LIKES 73

3:30 PM - 21 Nov 2016

▲Feminist Frequency maintains an active Twitter presence, using its tweets to share video game reviews, link to commentary, and promote the *Ordinary Women* video series.

a speech Sarkeesian was scheduled to deliver at Utah State University, an anonymous person threatened to carry out the biggest school shooting ever if the video game critic spoke. Sarkeesian canceled her speech after campus police said Utah's gun laws prohibited them from turning away any audience member who showed up with a gun.

Misogyny and threats against women are not unique to our digital age, but the particular harassment faced by Sarkeesian and Quinn is a phenomenon enabled by the digital turn. Digital game players learn of criticism by reading it from any number of print or online sources, or by watching it on YouTube. Then, they discuss and coalesce as a community (and build anger) on Reddit, or in 4chan or 8chan discussion boards, before lashing out again on social media. Some gamers take it even

further, making death threats and using various computer hacking techniques to attack the targets of their anger (see also the discussion of hacktivism in the previous chapter).

However, the women who find themselves targets of this harassment can also use the elements of convergence to tell their story—and change the narrative. While the flood of harassment has profoundly affected Sarkeesian's daily life, the attacks have brought many supporters her way as well, helping her reach a bigger audience and expand her efforts. When Sarkeesian started, she made her videos with the help of a friend and a DSLR camera. Now Feminist Frequency is a nonprofit entity with a staff and the ability to take on bigger projects.

One such project announced in 2016 was a video series called *Ordinary Women: Daring to Defy History*. These videos tell the stories of important women in history who are often overlooked, from African American journalist Ida B. Wells to Chinese pirate Ching Shih, who commanded forty thousand men in the early nineteenth century. One goal of this effort is to demonstrate how easy it is for creative types to find compelling stories about exciting women instead of relegating women to the roles dictated by sexist tropes.

And as Sarkeesian explained in a 2016 interview in the Daily Beast, taking action is what helps to create change: "In the *Tropes* episodes we're identifying patterns—we're not saying your one game is *the* problem. . . . We all have the responsibility . . . to start *changing* those patterns and not reinforcing them."[3]

Gaming Communities, Immersion, and Addiction

To fully explore the larger media playground, we need to look beyond digital gaming's technical aspects and consider the human faces of gaming. The attractions of this interactive playground validate digital gaming's status as one of today's most powerful social media. Players can interact socially within the games themselves; they can also participate in communities outside the games, organized around gaming-related interests. At the same time, the compelling nature of the gaming experience leads some players to become immersed in virtual worlds — and others to become addicted to gameplay.

Communities of Play: Inside the Game

Virtual communities often crop up around online video games and fantasy sports leagues. Indeed, players may get to know one another through games without ever meeting in person, interacting in two basic types of groups: PUGs and guilds or clans. PUGs (short for "Pick-Up Groups") are temporary teams usually assembled by matchmaking programs integrated into the game. The members of a PUG may range from elite players to noobs (clueless beginners) and may be geographically and generationally diverse. PUGs are notorious for harboring ninjas and trolls—two universally despised player types (not to be confused with ninja or troll avatars). Ninjas are players who snatch loot out of turn and then leave the group; trolls are players who delight in intentionally spoiling the gaming experience for others.

Because of the frustration of dealing with noobs, ninjas, and trolls, most experienced players join organized groups called guilds or clans. These groups can be small and easygoing or large and demanding. Guild members can usually avoid PUGs and team up with guildmates to complete difficult challenges requiring coordinated group activity. As the terms *ninja*, *troll*, and *noob* suggest, online communication is often encoded in gamespeak—a language filled with jargon, abbreviations, and acronyms relevant to gameplay. The typical codes of text messaging (OMG, LOL, ROFL, and so forth) form the bedrock of this language system.

Players communicate in two forms of in-game chat—voice and text. Xbox LIVE, for example, uses three types of voice chat that allow players to socialize and strategize, either in groups or one-on-one. Other in-game chat systems, like that in *World of Warcraft*, are text-based, with chat channels for trading in-game goods or coordinating missions within a guild. These methods of communicating with fellow players who may or may not know one another outside the game create a sense of community around the game's story. Some players have formed lasting friendships or romantic relationships through game playing. Avid gamers have even held in-game ceremonies, like weddings or funerals—sometimes for game-only characters, sometimes for real-life events.

Communities of Play: Outside the Game

Communities also form outside games, through Web sites and even face-to-face gatherings dedicated to digital gaming in its many forms. This is similar to when online and in-person groups form to discuss other mass media, such as movies, TV shows, and books. These communities extend beyond gameplay, enhancing the social experience gained through the game. Sites that cater to communities of play fit into three categories. Some collect and share user-generated **collective intelligence** on gameplay.[16] Others are independent sites that operate as community organizers for gamers. Still others are maintained by the industry and focus on distributing promotional material provided by hardware manufacturers and game publishers.

▲ The first *Warcraft* game was released in 1994; the first MMORPG version, *World of Warcraft*, followed in 2004. In this version, players can compete and cooperate within an online game; they can also participate in text-based chatting. A film version arrived in 2016, though the game was surpassed in popularity by *League of Legends* in 2012. Sean Gallup/Getty Images

Collective Intelligence

Gamers looking for tips and cheats provided by fellow players need only Google what they want. Many collective intelligence sites have popped up for games ranging from *Assassin's Creed* and *Grand Theft Auto* to *Halo* and *God of War*.

Independent Sites

Penny-arcade.com is perhaps the best known of the independent community-building sites. Founded by Jerry Holkins and Mike Krahulik, the site started out as a Web comic focused on video game culture. It has since expanded to include forums and a Webcast called PATV, which documents behind-the-scenes work at Penny Arcade. Penny Arcade organizes a live festival for gamers called the Penny Arcade Expo (PAX)—a celebration of gamer culture—and a children's charity called Child's Play.

Industry Sites

GameSpot.com and IGN.com are apt examples of the giant industry sites. GameSpot serves all the major gaming platforms and provides reviews, news, videos, cheats, and forums. It also has a culture section that features interviews with game designers and other creative artists. IGN.com has most of the same services, as well as its *Daily Fix*—a regular Webcast about games.

Immersion and Addiction

As games and their communities have grown more elaborate and alluring, many players have spent an increasing amount of time immersed in them—a situation that can feed addictive behavior in some people. These deep levels of involvement are not always considered negative, especially within the media playground, but they are nonetheless issues to consider as gaming continues to evolve.

Immersion

For better or worse, gaming technology of the future promises experiences that will be more immersive, more portable, and more inclusive. As gaming matures as a mass medium, the industry will use its potential for immersion to attract different audiences seeking diverse experiences, and it will do so in a variety of ways.

For example, some games involve a player's entire body in the gameplay rather than just a few fingers on a control pad. The Nintendo Wii system successfully harnessed user-friendly motion-control technology in handheld controllers and, for some games, a balance board, in order to open up gaming to nontraditional players—women, senior citizens, and technophobes of all ages. Microsoft's Kinect system uses sensor cameras and microphones to translate a player's movements and commands into actions by on-screen avatars. Used with Xbox LIVE, players can interact in full video or avatar form with friends online.

Some game systems aim to transport players to new worlds from the comfort of their homes, using various combinations of special goggles, helmets, vests, and gloves embedded with visual and audio functions, haptic feedback capabilities, and sensors. Examples of these types of virtual reality (VR) devices include the Oculus Rift, Sony PlayStation VR, HTC Vive VR, and Samsung Gear VR. And in a combination of low and high tech, Google Cardboard turns a smartphone into an old-fashioned stereoscope or View-Master through a cardboard viewer and accompanying app.

There are other new approaches to immersion as well. A company called the VOID is creating a virtual reality play park, where a VR game is played out like laser tag in a real space: 60-by-60-foot rooms with digital overlays that feature different types of scenes, such as haunted castles, futuristic battlefields, and backdrops based on the 2016 *Ghostbusters* movie. Participants can "feel" laser and creature attacks through the interactive VR gear that they wear during the experience. And enhanced reality games like *Pokémon Go* take immersion in a different direction, moving the gaming experience out of living rooms and arcades and into the world. Using smartphones screens to reveal "hidden" characters and rewards, the game requires players to walk around outside in order to participate.

But digital gaming technologies aren't just for entertainment. Games get used in workforce training, in military recruiting, for social causes, in classrooms, and as part of multimedia journalism. For instance, to accompany related news stories, the *New York Times* developed an interactive game called *Gauging Your Distraction.* The game demonstrates how distractions like cell phones affect a person's driving ability. All of these developments continue to make games an ever-larger part of our media experiences — even for people who may not consider themselves avid gamers.

▲ In the summer of 2016, *Pokémon Go* captured the attention of gamers around the globe. For several weeks, players were out pursuing Pokémon at locations of all kinds, from public parks to shopping malls. While that intense level of excitement has since faded, the game continues to be popular. LILLIAN SUWANRUMPHA/ Getty Images

Addiction

No serious — and honest — gamer can deny the addictive qualities of digital gaming. In a 2011 study of more than three thousand third through eighth graders in Singapore, one in ten were considered pathological gamers, meaning that their gaming addiction was jeopardizing multiple areas of their lives, including school, social and family relations, and psychological well-being. Children with stronger addictions were more prone to depression, social phobias, and increased anxiety, which led to poorer grades in school. Singapore's high percentage of pathological youth gamers is in line with studies from other countries, including the United States (8.5%), China (10.3%), and Germany (11.9%).[17] Gender is a factor in game addiction: A 2013 study found that males are much more susceptible. This makes sense, given that the most popular games — action and shooter games — are heavily geared toward males.[18]

These findings are not entirely surprising, given that many digital games are not addictive by accident but rather by design. Just as "habit formation" is a primary goal of virtually every commercial form of digital media, from newspapers to television to radio, cultivating obsessive play is the aim of most game designs. From recognizing high scores to offering a variety of difficulty settings (encouraging players to try easy, medium, and hard versions) to embedding levels that gradually increase in difficulty, designers provide constant in-game incentives for obsessive play. This is especially true of multiplayer online games — such as *Halo*, *Call of Duty*, and *World of Warcraft* — which make money from long-term engagement by selling expansion packs or charging monthly subscription fees. These games have elaborate achievement systems with hard-to-resist rewards, including military ranks like "General" or fanciful titles like "King Slayer," as well as special armor, weapons, and mounts (creatures your avatar can ride, including bears, wolves, and even dragons), all aimed at turning casual players into habitual ones.

This strategy of promoting habit formation may not differ from the cultivation of other media obsessions, like watching televised sporting events. Even so, real-life stories, such as that of the South Korean couple whose three-month-old daughter died of malnutrition while the negligent parents spent ten-hour overnight sessions in an Internet café raising a virtual daughter, bring up serious questions about video games and addiction. South Korea, one of the world's most Internet-connected countries, is already sponsoring efforts to battle Internet addiction.[19] Meanwhile, industry executives and others cite the positive impact of digital games, such as the learning benefits of *SimCity* and the health benefits of *Wii Fit*.

The Economics of Digital Gaming

The Entertainment Software Association (ESA) reports that 65 percent of U.S. households own a device used to play video games, and about the same number of households has at least one member who plays games for three or more hours per week.[20] The entire U.S. video game market, including portable and console hardware and accessories, adds up to about $23.5 billion annually and $100 billion globally.[21] Thanks largely to the introduction of the Wii and mobile games, today's audience for games extends beyond the young-male gamer stereotype.

Digital gaming companies can make money selling not just consoles and games but also online subscriptions, companion books, and movie rights. In addition to the costs of production, shipping, and marketing, digital gaming companies also pay writers, artists, and programmers to create the games.

Selling Digital Games

Traditionally, the primary source of revenue in the digital gaming industry is the sale of games and the consoles on which they can be played. But just as the digital turn has altered the distribution relationships between other mass media and their audiences, it has also transformed the selling of electronic games. Although the selling of $60 AAA (top of the line) console games at retail stores is an enduring model, many games are now free (with opportunities for hooked players to pay for additional play features), and digital stores are making access to games almost immediate.

Pay Models
There are three main pay models in the electronic game industry: the boxed game/retail model, the subscription model, and the free-to-play model. Of these, the

boxed game/retail model is the most traditional, dating back to the days of cartridges on Atari, Sega, and Nintendo console systems. By the 1990s, games began to be released on CD-ROMs and later DVDs, to better handle the richer game files. Many boxed games are now sold with offers of additional downloadable content.

Some of the most popular games are also sold via the *subscription model*, in which gamers pay a monthly fee to play. Notable subscription games include *World of Warcraft* and *Star Wars: The Old Republic.* Subscriptions can generate enormous revenue for game publishers. At its height of popularity, *World of Warcraft* earned more than $1 billion a year for Activision Blizzard.[22] Players first buy the game and then pay a subscription from $12.99 to $14.99 a month.

Free-to-play (sometimes called *freemium*) is the latest pay model and is common with casual and online games, such as *100 Balls*. Free-to-play games are offered online or downloadable for free to gain or retain a large audience. These games make money by selling extras (like power boosters to aid in gameplay) or in-game subscriptions for upgraded play. In addition to free casual games (e.g., *Angry Birds Seasons*, *Clash of Clans*, and *Temple Run*), popular MMORPG games—like Sony Online Entertainment's *EverQuest* and *DC Universe Online*—also offer free-to-play versions.

Video Game Stores vs. Digital Distribution

Several brick-and-mortar stores sell boxed game titles (Walmart, Best Buy, Target), but there is only one major video game store chain—GameStop, which operates more than 7,100 stores in fourteen countries. The biggest challenge to gaming stores, regardless of size, is digital distribution. All three major consoles are Wi-Fi capable, and each has its own digital store—Xbox LIVE Marketplace, Wii Shop Channel, and PlayStation Store. Using these platforms, customers can purchase and download games, get extra downloadable content, and buy other media—such as television shows and movies—as the consoles compete to be the sole entertainment center of people's living rooms.

Although the three major console companies control digital downloads to their devices, several companies compete for the download market in PC games. The largest is Steam, which carries more than 7,500 games from a variety of game publishers. Of course, the most ubiquitous digital game distributors are Apple's App Store and Google Play, where users can purchase games on mobile devices. Although Google's Android system has surpassed the iPhone in market penetration, Apple customers are more likely to purchase apps, including games—a situation that has drawn more independent developers to work in the Apple operating system.

Digital Gaming Tie-Ins and Licensing

Beyond the immediate industry, digital games have had a pronounced effect on media culture. Fantasy league sports have spawned a number of draft specials on ESPN as well as a regular podcast, *Fantasy Focus*, on ESPN Radio.

▲ Milla Jovovich stars as Alice in the popular *Resident Evil* film series, including *Resident Evil: Retribution* (2012) and *Resident Evil: The Final Chapter* (2016). However, not all game adaptations have been so successful; film versions of *Super Mario Bros.*, *Doom*, and *Prince of Persia* disappointed at the box office—though gaming companies were still paid for the rights. Everett Collection, Inc.

Like television shows, books, and comics before them, digital games have inspired movies, such as *Lara Croft: Tomb Raider* (2001), *Ratchet and Clank* (2016), *Assassin's Creed* (2016), and the *Resident Evil* series (2002–present). For many Hollywood blockbusters today, a video game spin-off is a must-have item. Recent box-office hits like *Deadpool* (2016) and *Star Wars Rogue One* (2016) have companion video games for consoles and portable players. Japanese manga and anime (comic books and animation) have also inspired video games, such as *Akira*, *Astro Boy*, and *Naruto*.

Whereas game adaptations of other media can serve partly as advertising for a cross-media franchise, some games also include direct advertising. In-game advertisements are ads for companies and products that appear as billboards or logos on products in the game environment or as screen-blocking pop-up ads. In-game ad specialist agency IGA claims to put "hundreds of millions of impressions per week" in video games for clients like McDonald's, T-Mobile, Geico, AT&T, and Red Bull.[23]

Making Digital Games

Development, marketing, and licensing constitute the major expenditures in game publishing, and AAA game titles (games that represent the current standard for technical excellence) can cost even more than a blockbuster film to make and promote.

The **development budget** pays for writers to create the concept and storyline of a game, artists to design characters and scenery, actors to voice characters, and programmers to turn the ideas and images into computer code. Each new generation of gaming platforms doubles the number of people involved in designing, programming, and mixing digitized images and sounds.

But as costly as development can be, big game releases spend even more on marketing. The successful launch of a game involves online promotions, banner ads, magazine print ads, in-store displays, and—the most expensive of all—television ads. In many ways, the marketing blitz associated with introducing a major new franchise title, including cinematic television trailers, resembles the promotional campaigns surrounding the debut of a blockbuster movie.

For example, the most expensive game developed to date is *Destiny*, a $500 million massively multiplayer online first-person shooter game by Activision. About $140 million of that price tag was the cost of game development, with the remaining $360 million going to marketing.[24] Some other video

launchpadworks.com

Video Games at the Movies

Alice, the hero of the game-based *Resident Evil* film series, fights zombies in this clip.

Discussion: In what ways does this clip replicate the experience of gameplay? In what ways are films inherently different?

game titles that have cost more than $100 million to make and market are *Call of Duty 2*, *Grand Theft Auto 5*, *Final Fantasy 7*, and *Star Wars: The Old Republic*.

Independent gamemakers must also deal with two types of licensing. First, they have to pay royalties to console manufacturers (Nintendo, Sony, or Microsoft) for the right to distribute a game using their system. These royalties vary from $3 to $10 per unit sold. The other form of licensing involves **intellectual properties** — stories, characters, personalities, and music that require licensing agreements. In 2005, for instance, John Madden reportedly signed a $150 million deal with EA Sports that allowed the company to use his name and likeness for the following ten years.[25]

▲ Producers of big blockbuster games pay close attention to initial sales, the digital game equivalent of a movie's opening weekend. The game *Destiny* cost $500 million to produce, but it racked up as much in initial global orders when it hit the market in 2014.

Digital Gaming in a Democratic Society

Though many people view gaming as a simple leisure activity, the digital gaming industry has sparked controversy. Parents and politicians have expressed concern about the content of some games, whereas other critics say the portrayal of women and minorities in games is either nonexistent or troubling. Meanwhile, the gaming industry has argued that it qualifies for free-speech protection, and that its ratings and regulations should not necessarily bear the force of law.

Self-Regulation

Back in 1976, an arcade game called *Death Race* prompted the first public outcry over violence in digital gaming. The primitive graphics of the game depicted a blocky car running down stick-figure gremlins that, if struck, turned into grave markers. Described as "sick and morbid" by the National Safety Council, *Death Race* inspired a *60 Minutes* report on the potential psychological damage of playing video games. Since then, violent video games have prompted citizens' groups and politicians to call for government regulation of digital game content.

In 1993, after the violence of *Mortal Kombat* and *Night Trap* attracted the attention of religious and educational organizations, U.S. Senator Joe Lieberman conducted a hearing that proposed federal regulation of the gaming industry. Following a pattern established in the movie and music industries, the gaming industry implemented a self-regulation system enforced by an industry panel.

Media Literacy

Writing about Games

A host of opportunities await talented writers interested in pursuing a career in gaming journalism. Gaming publications provide information on news, games, and peripherals associated with a popular platform. Some, like the *Official Xbox Magazine*, are sanctioned by console manufacturers. Others, like *Edge* and *Game Informer*, report on a broader spectrum of the digital gaming industry. Almost all follow a reveal/preview/review cycle, whereby periodicals announce, promote, and evaluate new consoles and games.

Whereas the origins of gaming journalism were dominated by manufacturer publications and fanzines (magazines written by gamers for other gamers), in recent years the gaming press has grown to include more traditional journalism practices, such as those on online sites like Kotaku, Gamasutra, and Eurogamer. Like other forms of journalism, the relationship between reporter and subject can affect credibility as well as create some complicated ethical situations. For example, some independent gaming artists rely on the site *Patreon* (like a Kickstarter site for patrons of the arts) for financial support, and then release material first to their backers from the site. As some gaming journalism sources create policies preventing writers from donating, others have to balance this principle with the journalistic goal of getting the story first (see also Chapter 3's discussion of journalism values and ethics on pages 81–87).

Another problem some gaming journalists have experienced is pushback from gamers who have seemingly grown used to the more fan-based style of reporting, which was less likely to include any critique of gaming culture. As *Vox* writer Todd VanDerWerff suggests, this has led to a "fundamental disconnect between what those who *read* gaming media believe journalism to be and what it actually is."[1] This disconnect probably helped contribute to the #GamerGate controversy, as some gamers responded to criticism of the treatment of women and minorities in games and gaming culture by launching deeply disturbing attacks on journalists and critics (see also "The Digital Turn Case Study: Fighting the Dark Side of Gaming Culture: Anita Sarkeesian and Feminist Frequency" on pages 306–307).

Another trend in the gaming press is New Games Journalism. An article published in *PC Gamer*, a British magazine, provided the inspiration for the movement. In the piece, Ian Shanahan (who uses the screen name always_black) relates the story of how a random online opponent opened a lightsaber duel with a racial slur because he assumed Shanahan to be a player of color. Shanahan then transports the reader into a fleeting gaming moment when, for him, winning a routine match carried special meaning and significance beyond the fantasy of the game he was playing at the time of the challenge, *Jedi Knight II*.[2]

Kieron Gillen, a fellow British writer, found Shanahan's article so compelling that he wrote a widely read blog post calling for the establishment of New Games Journalism—an intensely personal form of game writing that would embrace the

 **Web Clip**

YouTube.com has many gaming-related videos. For example, you can search for 'Hero Generations — Gamasutra interviews creator Scott Brodie' by Gamasutra. Do you think this video represents a form of New Games Journalism? Why or why not?

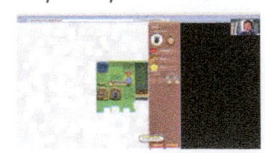

▲ New Games Journalist Kieron Gillen cofounded PC gaming blog Rock, Paper, Shotgun (RPS), which includes game reviews and other commentary. While Gillen is no longer a regular contributor to the site (he is now a comic-book writer), his posts are available via the RPS archive.

human side of gaming. The idea of writing about games in the manner of the New Journalism of the 1960–1970s attracted the attention of game writers on both sides of the Atlantic. Citing the examples of Tom Wolfe, Truman Capote, Norman Mailer, and Hunter S. Thompson, Gillen argued that "the worth of a videogame lies not in the game, but in the gamer." If done correctly, New Games Journalism would resemble travel journalism, but would take readers to imaginary places instead of real ones. "Our job is to describe what it's like to visit a place that doesn't exist outside of the gamer's head," writes Gillen, and to "go to a place, report on its cultures, foibles, distractions and bring it back to entertain your readers."[3]

Video game fans may be prepared to write professional articles that follow the reveal/preview/review rituals of traditional games journalism. However, all media students have something to say about their own experiences with digital gaming and the digital playground. New Games Journalism thus counts as a provocative development. With its focus on the player experience, it gives a voice to anyone who wants to comment on this emergent medium.

APPLYING THE CRITICAL PROCESS

DESCRIPTION Read two game reviews, each from a well-known site—for example, read a review from Kieron Gillen at www.rockpapershotgun.com/author/KieronGillen/ and a review posted on GameSpot or Kotaku.

ANALYSIS Compare the styles of the two reviews that you read. How does each review address you—as a consumer? A citizen? A fellow gamer? What part of the gaming experience does each review emphasize? What type of reader does each seem to be trying to attract?

INTERPRETATION For each review, determine whether its style is closer to that of New Games Journalism (it focuses on what playing the game means to the reviewer as a person) or the traditional approach (it focuses more on the features and descriptions of the game).

EVALUATION Discuss the strengths and weaknesses of each review. Which review appealed to you most? What was it about that review that made it more compelling?

ENGAGEMENT Write your own gaming article. If you choose to write in the style of New Games Journalism, report on a particularly meaningful experience you had with digital gaming, or go to a video arcade on a busy night and record your opinions about what arcade gaming means today. If you choose the traditional approach, focus more fully on the features and descriptions of the game that you are reviewing.

The industry founded the **Entertainment Software Rating Board (ESRB)** to institute a labeling system designed to inform parents of sexual and violent content that might not be suitable for younger players. Currently, the ESRB sorts games into six categories: EC (Early Childhood), E (Everyone), E 10+ (Everyone 10+), T (Teen), M (Mature 17+), and AO (Adults Only 18+).[26]

Free Speech and Video Games

Though 80 percent of retail outlets voluntarily chose to observe the ESRB guidelines and not sell M- and AO-rated games to minors, the ratings did not have the force of law. In 2005, California tried to make renting or selling an M-rated game to a minor an offense enforced by fines. The law was immediately challenged by the industry and struck down by a lower court as unconstitutional. California petitioned the Supreme Court to hear the case. In a landmark decision handed down in 2011, the Supreme Court granted digital games speech protections afforded by the First Amendment. According to the opinion written by Justice Antonin Scalia, video games communicate ideas worthy of such protection:

> Like the protected books, plays, and movies that preceded them, video games communicate ideas—and even social messages—through many familiar literary devices (such as characters, dialogue, plot, and music) and through features distinctive to the medium (such as the player's interaction with the virtual world).[27]

Scalia even mentions *Mortal Kombat* in footnote 4 of the decision:

> Reading Dante is unquestionably more cultured and intellectually edifying than playing *Mortal Kombat*. But these cultural and intellectual differences are not constitutional ones. Crudely violent video games, tawdry TV shows, and cheap novels and magazines are no less forms of speech than *The Divine Comedy*. . . . Even if we can see in them "nothing of any possible value to society" . . . they are as much entitled to the protection of free speech as the best of literature.[28]

However, as in the music, television, and film industries, First Amendment protections will not make the rating system for the gaming industry go away. Parents continue to have legitimate concerns about the games their children play. Game publishers and retailers understand it is still in their best interests to respect those concerns, even though the ratings cannot be enforced by law.

Alternate Voices

While much of the concern over video games has historically focused on portrayals of general violence, in recent years there has been a growing criticism about the portrayals of women and minorities in gaming and gaming culture. This has prompted pointed questions from gaming critics, including avid female gamers: Why aren't more games created to appeal to women? Why don't more heroic female avatars exist? Why are some portrayals of women so deeply disturbing? For example, critics often point out the popular game series *Grand Theft Auto*, which in one of its versions made it so that a character could build up health by having sex with a prostitute, and then get his money back by killing the woman (see also "The Digital Turn Case Study: Fighting the Dark Side of Gaming Culture: Anita Sarkeesian and Feminist Frequency" on pages 306–307).

▲ Games like *Abzu* focus on the artistry of the creators, letting players explore a painstakingly detailed undersea world.

Other critics point to the lack of heroic representations of nonwhite characters.

That's not to say there aren't games being written from other perspectives. Paradoxically, as the costs of the biggest blockbuster games skyrocket into the hundreds of millions of dollars, mobile gaming has provided a new entry point for independent game developers. Online funding sites like Kickstarter and Patreon are also helping independent game artists write and develop their own games. Some examples include *Depression Quest*, a nontraditional game that uses a multiple-choice text adventure to simulate the experience of having depression, or *Gone Home*, which deals with LGBT issues.[29] These games, although nowhere near as well known as top-tier box games or casual games, have received good reviews in the gaming press. In addition, other games have found success by offering a gaming experience that differs from the shoot-`em-up or action-packed fare that tends to dominate the lists of top-selling games. For example, the 2016 game *Abzu* lets players explore beautifully rendered undersea environments rather than engage in combat.

Decades ago, groundbreaking critical cultural scholar Stuart Hall wrote that even though popular television wasn't considered "high culture" by many social critics and academics of the time, it was still very important to study and understand the cultural messages contained in television because so many people spent so much time engaged with it. He argued that when looking at an entire nation, relatively few people in a society had the time or resources required to frequent museums or attend the opera. But they did own and watch televisions.[30]

Perhaps a similar argument can be made about digital games. In one form or another, they are growing in popularity across ages and genders. Gamers both serious and casual spend many hours engaging with these virtual worlds, absorbing what they see and hear. Once considered a distraction, they're now a prominent part of the mass media landscape.

CHAPTER ESSENTIALS

Review

- Coin-operated contraptions first appeared in train depots, hotel lobbies, bars, and restaurants in the 1880s, before finding a permanent home in the **penny arcade.** The most prominent of the mechanical machines, the **pinball machine** gained mainstream acceptance and popularity after World War II with the addition of the **flipper bumper**, which made the game more interactive.

- **Cathode ray tube (CRT)** screens provided the images for analog television as well as the displays for early computers, on which the earliest video games appeared.

- Magnavox released Odyssey, the first home gaming system, in 1972. That same year, computer

engineer Nolan Bushnell formed a video game development company called **Atari**. Atari's first creation was *Pong*, which became the first big **arcade** video game. In 1975, Atari began successfully marketing a home version of *Pong*, thus establishing the home video game market.

- By the late 1970s and early 1980s, games like *Asteroids*, *Pac-Man*, and *Donkey Kong* filled arcades and bars, competing with traditional pinball machines. After *Pac-Man*, the **avatar** became the most popular figure of player control in a video game.

- Through decades of ups and downs in the digital gaming industry, three major **console** makers emerged: Nintendo, Sony, and Microsoft.

- With multiple players joining in digital gaming through the Internet, gaming has become a contemporary social medium. The social dimension of gaming is especially apparent in **online fantasy sports** games and **massively multiplayer online role-playing games (MMORPGs)**.

- Virtual communities crop up around online video games and fantasy sports, and players get to know one another without ever meeting in person. There are also sites that cater to communities of play, including sites that collect and share user-generated **collective intelligence** on gameplay, independent sites that operate as community organizers for gamers, and sites maintained by the industry that are primarily devoted to distributing promotional material.

LaunchPad

Visit LaunchPad for *Media Essentials* at **launchpadworks.com** for additional learning tools:

- **REVIEW WITH LEARNINGCURVE**
  LearningCurve adaptive quizzing helps you master the concepts you need to learn from this chapter.

- **VIDEO: TABLETS, TECHNOLOGY, AND THE CLASSROOM**
  Tech experts discuss the use of handheld electronic devices like tablets in the classroom.

- **MEDIA LITERACY PRACTICE**
  This activity challenges you to develop a critical perspective and apply it to everyday encounters with communication media.

- As games and their communities have grown more elaborate, many players have spent an increasing amount of time immersed in them— a situation that can feed addictive behavior in some people.

- There are three main pay models for the video game industry: the boxed game/retail model, the subscription model, and the free-to-play model.

- Development, marketing, and licensing constitute the major expenditures in game publishing. The marketing costs often equal or exceed the development costs.

- In response to a threat of regulation, the digital game industry founded the **Entertainment Software Rating Board (ESRB)** to institute a labeling system designed to inform parents of sexual and violent content that might not be suitable for younger players.

- In a landmark decision handed down in 2011, the Supreme Court granted digital games First Amendment free-speech protections.

- More critics and gaming journalists are speaking out about the need for improvement in the portrayal of women and minorities in games and gaming culture, which has led to some online backlash against these critics, including threats of violence. However, it has also led to the development of games from other perspectives.

Key Terms

penny arcade, p. 296
pinball machine, p. 296
flipper bumper, p. 296
cathode ray tube (CRT), p. 296
arcade, p. 297
Atari, p. 297
avatar, p. 298
consoles, p. 299
online fantasy sports, p. 304

massively multiplayer online role-playing games (MMORPGs), p. 305
collective intelligence, p. 309
development budget, p. 314
intellectual properties, p. 315
Entertainment Software Rating Board (ESRB), p. 318

Study Questions

1. Why were the first video games developed at major research universities?

2. Why is bit rate useful for charting the evolution of gaming consoles?

3. How does online fantasy football differ from the classic video game?

4. What is an example of a Web site that addresses gamers as citizens of a virtual community?

5. On what grounds did the Supreme Court grant video games First Amendment protections?

Advertising and Commercial Culture

"I didn't even know how to follow people on Snap, I was just learning it." Khaled Mohamed Khaled, known to his fans as DJ Khaled, remembered during a 2017 interview with National Public Radio. "My phone breaks, I go to the Apple store. . . . I snap while I'm inside the store. I realized there's like five thousand to ten thousand people in the store now. And I was like, 'Is Justin Bieber in here? Is the Beatles in here?' Like, they were screaming all my quotes and my music. It was a love that was unbelievable."[1]

DJ Khaled was a local deejay and celebrity in the Miami area when he catapulted to international stardom, thanks in part to his frequent "snapping"—slang for posting videos and photos on the social media platform Snapchat. Widely recognized as the platform's first and biggest star, Khaled is known for documenting his daily thoughts and sharing inspirational messages, catchphrases, and even the birth of his child. At the same time, Khaled uses his brief videos to promote products, including Cîroc vodka and Dove soap. And advertisers are lining up to get a piece of the action. According to a senior vice president at Coca-Cola—one of the biggest

◀ DJ Khaled is considered the first Snapchat star. His successful use of the social media platform to promote himself, his music, and various consumer products helped boost him to international success. Gabe Ginsberg/Getty Images

advertisers on Snapchat—"DJ Khaled has completely cracked the platform. He's the king of Snapchat."[2]

While advertisers have always looked to monetize the love that celebrities like Khaled receive from their fans (stars are popular pitch people for a variety of products), Khaled's story stands out because it doesn't come from a Madison Avenue ad agency—it comes from the world of social media. By harnessing a new medium to market himself, his music, and a variety of consumer products, Khaled has found the recipe for advertising, marketing, and branding success in a post–digital turn world.

From the perspective of advertisers today, capitalizing on the opportunities available through social media—and avoiding its pitfalls (see "The Digital Turn Case Study: Marketing, Social Media, and Epic Fails" on page 347)—is a must for every major brand. In fact, industry experts estimate that in 2017, 35 percent of the nearly $200 billion that will be spent on advertising in the United States will go to Internet marketing.[3]

Building ads into TV shows and movies has long been a standard practice, so the convergence of advertising into the digital realm is not surprising. But as advertising has proliferated and become part of our daily lives, it has come to look very different from how it did in its infancy. In the digital age, advertising is everywhere, from billboards to T-shirt logos to Snapchat snaps.

Regardless of its changing forms, advertising continues to play a leading role in contemporary life. For consumers, ads shape our purchasing decisions. For companies, savvy advertising can drive sales. Advertising has also given rise to whole new industries and lucrative business models—from ad agencies that produce slick campaigns for high-end clients to the most basic classified ads created by individuals on craigslist to the search engine industry led by Google and fueled by online ads. With social media playing such a prominent part in our lives, more and more companies will try to find success through nontraditional marketing channels like Snapchat—and they'll be using personalities like DJ Khaled to get their message out to the public.

ADVERTISING COMES IN MANY FORMS—from classifieds to business-to-business ads to those providing detailed information on specific consumer products. However, in this chapter, we concentrate on the more conspicuous consumer advertisements that shape product images and brand-name identities. So much of consumer advertising intrudes into daily life, causing many people to routinely complain about it. And people are increasingly finding ways to avoid ads—for example, by using digital DVRs to zip through them or by blocking pop-ups with Web browsers. However, because advertising shows up in most media—the Internet, TV, radio, books, newspapers, magazines, movies—it serves as a kind of economic glue holding these industries together. Without consumer advertisements, most media businesses would cease to function in their present forms. The good news for these media businesses is that the advertising industry has been growing for several years, and in 2017, global advertising spending was on track to hit a record-breaking $1 trillion.[4]

In this chapter, we take a close look at advertising's evolving role in our lives by:

- **examining the early history of American advertising, including the rise of ad agencies, brand-name recognition, advertising's power to create new markets and build a consumer culture, and regulation to control that power**

- **tracing the evolution of U.S. advertising, including the shift to emphasizing visual design in ads, specialization and restructuring of advertising agencies, and the impact of the Internet on this medium**

- **assessing persuasive techniques in contemporary advertising, such as using testimonials, playing on people's fears, and placing products on movie sets or on TV shows**

- **considering the nature of "commercial speech" and regulation of such speech—for example, to combat deception in advertising**

- **exploring advertising's impact on our democracy**

The Early History of American Advertising: 1850s to 1950s

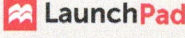
LaunchPad
launchpadworks.com

Use **LearningCurve** to review concepts from this chapter.

Before the Industrial Revolution, most Americans lived in isolated areas and produced much of what they needed — tools, clothes, food — themselves. There were few products for sale, other than by merchants who offered additional goods and services in their own communities, so anything like modern advertising simply wasn't necessary.

All that began changing in the 1850s with the Industrial Revolution and the linking of American villages and towns through railroads, the telegraph, and new print media. Merchants (such as patent medicine makers and cereal producers) wanted to advertise their wares in newspapers and magazines, giving rise to advertising agencies that managed these deals. These first national ads introduced the notion that it was important for sellers to differentiate their product from competing goods — which inspired more and more businesspeople to adopt advertising to drive sales.

Over the coming decades, all this fueled the growth of a consumer culture, in which Americans began desiring specific products and giving their loyalty to particular brands. Critics began decrying advertising's power to seemingly dictate values and create needs in people — triggering the formation of watchdog organizations and careful consumers.

The First Advertising Agencies

The first American advertising agents were newspaper **space brokers**: individuals who purchased space in newspapers and then sold it to various merchants. Newspapers, accustomed to advertisers' not paying their bills (or paying late), welcomed the space brokers, who paid up front. Brokers usually received discounts of 15 to 30 percent, then sold the space to advertisers at the going rate. In 1841, Volney Palmer opened the first ad agency in Philadelphia; for a 25 percent commission from newspaper publishers, he sold space to advertisers.

The first full-service modern ad agency, N. W. Ayer, introduced a different model: Instead of working for newspapers, the agency worked primarily for companies—or clients—that manufactured consumer products. Opening in 1869 in Philadelphia, N. W. Ayer helped develop, write, produce, and place ads in selected newspapers and magazines for its clients. The agency collected a fee from its clients for each ad placed, which covered the price that each media outlet charged for placement of the ad, plus a 15 percent commission. According to this model, the more ads an agency placed, the larger its revenue. Today, while the commission model still dominates, some advertising agencies now work for a flat fee, and some are paid on how well the ads they create drive sales for the client.

▼ Originally called the Joseph A. Campbell Preserve Company back in 1869, the Campbell Soup Co. introduced its classic red-and-white soup can labels in 1897. Today, the label is updated, but Campbell's red-and-white cans remain one of the most recognized brands in the country. © RICHARD B.LEVINE/Newscom/Levine Roberts Photography/NEW YORK/NY/USA

Retail Stores: Giving Birth to Branding

During the mid-1800s, most manufacturers sold their goods directly to retail store owners, who usually set their own prices by purchasing products in large quantities. Stores would then sell these loose goods—from clothing to cereal—in large barrels and bins, so customers had no idea who made them. This arrangement shifted after manufacturers started using newspaper advertising to create brand names — that is, to differentiate their offerings and their company's image from those of their competitors in the minds of consumers and retailers — even if the goods were basically the same. For example, one of the earliest brand names, Quaker Oats (the first cereal company to register a trademark in the 1870s), used the image of William Penn, the Quaker who founded Pennsylvania in 1681, in its ads to project a company image of honesty, decency, and hard work.

Consumers, convinced by the ads, began demanding certain products. And retail stores felt compelled to stock the desired brands. This enabled manufacturers, not the retailers, to begin setting the prices of their goods — confident that they'd prevail over the stores' anonymous bulk items. Indeed, product differentiation in brand-name packaged goods represents advertising's single biggest triumph. Though most ads don't trigger a large jump in sales in the short run, over time they create demand by leading consumers to associate particular brands with qualities and values important to them.

Patent Medicines: Making Outrageous Claims

As the nineteenth century marched on, patent medicine makers, excited by advertising's power to differentiate their products, invested heavily in print ads developed and placed by ad agencies. But many patent medicines (which consisted of mostly water and high concentrations of ethyl alcohol) made outrageous claims about the medical problems they could cure. The misleading ads spawned public cynicism. As a result, advertisers began to police their own ranks and developed industry codes to restore consumers' confidence. Partly to monitor patent medicine claims, Congress passed the Federal Food and Drugs Act in 1906.

Department Stores: Fueling a Consumer Culture

Along with patent medicine makers, department stores began advertising heavily in newspapers and magazines in the late nineteenth century. By the early 1890s, more than 20 percent of ad space in these media was devoted to department stores.

By selling huge volumes of goods and providing little individualized service, department stores saved a lot of money — and passed these savings on to

▲ Unregulated patent medicines, such as the one represented in this ad for Armour's Vigoral, created a bonanza for nineteenth-century print media in search of advertising revenue. After several investigative (or "muckraking") magazine reports about deceptive patent medicine claims, Congress created the Food and Drug Administration (FDA) in 1906. The Advertising Archives

customers in the form of lower prices (as Target and Walmart do today). The department stores thus lured customers away from small local stores, making even more money, which they could reinvest in advertising. This development further fueled the growth of a large-scale consumer culture in the United States.

Transforming American Society

By the dawn of the twentieth century, advertising had become pervasive in the United States. As it gathered force, it began transforming American society. For one thing, by stimulating demand among consumers for more and more products, advertising helped manufacturers create whole new markets. The resulting brisk sales also enabled companies to recover their product-development costs quickly. In addition, advertising made people hungry for technological advances by showing how new machines — vacuum cleaners, washing machines, cars — might make daily life easier or better. All this encouraged economic growth by increasing sales of a wide range of goods.

Advertising also began influencing Americans' values. As just one example, ads for household-related products (mops, cleaning solutions, washing machines) conveyed the message that "good" wives were happy to vanquish dirt from their homes. By the early 1900s, business leaders and ad agencies believed that women, who constituted as much as 70 to 80 percent of newspaper and magazine readerships, controlled most household purchasing decisions. Agencies developed simple ads tailored to supposedly feminine characteristics — ads featuring emotional and even irrational content. For instance, many such ads portrayed cleaning products and household appliances as "heroic" and showed grateful women gushing about how the product "saved" them from the shame of a dirty house or the hard labor of doing laundry by hand.

Early Regulation of Advertising

During the early 1900s, advertising's growing clout — along with revelations of fraudulent advertising claims and practices — catalyzed the formation of the first watchdog organizations. For example, advocates in the business community in 1913 created the nonprofit Better Business Bureau, whose mission included keeping tabs on deceptive advertising. The following year, the government established the Federal Trade Commission (FTC), in part to help monitor advertising abuses. Alarmed by government's willingness to step in, players in the advertising industry urged self-regulation to keep government interference at bay.

At the same time, advertisers recognized that a little self-regulation could benefit them in other ways as well. They especially wanted a formal service that tracked newspaper and magazine readership, guaranteed accurate audience measures, and ensured that newspapers didn't overcharge agencies and their clients. To that end, publishers formed the Audit Bureau of Circulation (ABC) in 1914 to monitor circulation figures. In 2012, the group changed the name of its North American operations to Alliance for Audited Media, a rebranding partly aimed at staying relevant in a time of emerging digital newspaper and magazine business.

But it wasn't until the 1940s that the industry began to deflect the long-standing criticisms that advertisers created needs that consumers never knew they had, dictated values, and had too strong a hand in the economy. To promote a more positive self-image, the ad industry developed the War Advertising Council. This voluntary group of ad agencies and advertisers began organizing war bond sales, blood donor drives, and scarce-goods rationing. Known today by a broader mission and its postwar name, the Ad Council chooses a dozen worthy causes annually and produces pro bono *public service announcements* (PSAs) aimed at combating social problems, such as illiteracy, homelessness, drug addiction, smoking, and AIDS.

With the advent of television in the 1950s, advertisers had a brand-new visual medium for reaching consumers. Critics complained about the increased intrusion of ads into daily family life. They especially decried what was then labeled **subliminal advertising**. Through this tactic, TV ads supposedly used hidden or disguised print and visual messages (often related to sex, like the shape of a woman's body in an ice cube for a vodka ad) that allegedly register only in viewers' subconscious minds, fooling them into buying products they don't need. However, research has reported over the years that subliminal ads are no more powerful than regular ads. Demonstrating a willingness to self-regulate, though, the National Association of Broadcasters banned the use of anything resembling a subliminal-type ad in 1958.

▲ During World War II, government offices around the world engaged the advertising industry to create messages supporting the war effort. Advertisers promoted the sale of war bonds, conservation of natural resources such as tin and gasoline, and even the saving of kitchen waste so that it could be fed to farm animals. Bettmann/Getty Images

The Evolution of U.S. Advertising: 1950s to Today

As the twentieth century progressed, U.S. advertising changed in several ways. Visual design began to play a more prominent role in ads, reflecting people's growing interest in imagery. This trend helped spark the growth of new types of ad agencies, which began dominating the field — large global firms serving a broad range of clients, and small companies working for a select group of clients. Ad agencies of all types developed a distinctive organizational structure, which included specialized departments responsible for such activities as account planning and creative development. But that, too, began changing with the advent of the Internet in the 1990s. The new medium presented fresh possibilities for designing and placing ads, giving rise to entirely new types of players in the advertising sector, including search engine giant Google.

Visual Design Comes to the Fore

Visual design began playing a more central role in advertising during the 1960s and 1970s. This revolution was influenced in part by overseas design schools and European designers — whom agencies hired as art directors and who were not tied to word-driven print and radio advertising. The new emphasis on imagery also drew inspiration from changes in television and cable content. By the early 1970s, agencies had developed teams of writers and visual artists, thus granting equal status to images and words in the creative process. Video-style ads featuring prominent performers (Ray Charles, Michael Jackson, Madonna) soon saturated TV.

Today, thanks to technologies such as mobile phones, tablet computers, and incredibly crisp digital displays, visual design has reached new levels of sophistication. For example, ads on mobile phones feature full-motion 3-D animation and high-quality audio. At the same time, designers have had to simplify the imagery they create so that ads and logos can show up clearly and scroll vertically on small digital screens. Finally, to appeal to the global audience, many ad agencies are hiring graphic designers who can capture a diversity of visual styles from around the world.

New Breeds of Advertising Agencies Are Born

The increasing prominence of visual design in advertising led to the development of two specialized types of advertising agencies: **mega-agencies**, large firms that are formed from the merging of several individual agencies and that maintain worldwide regional offices, and **boutique agencies**, smaller companies that devote their talents to a handful of select clients. Both types of agencies wield great control over the kinds of advertising we see daily.

Mega-Agencies

Mega-agencies provide a full range of services — from handling advertising and public relations to operating their own in-house radio and TV production studios. The five largest mega-agencies are WPP, Omnicom Group, Publicis Groupe, the

FIGURE 11.1 // *GLOBAL REVENUE FOR THE WORLD'S LARGEST AGENCIES IN 2015 (IN BILLIONS OF DOLLARS)*

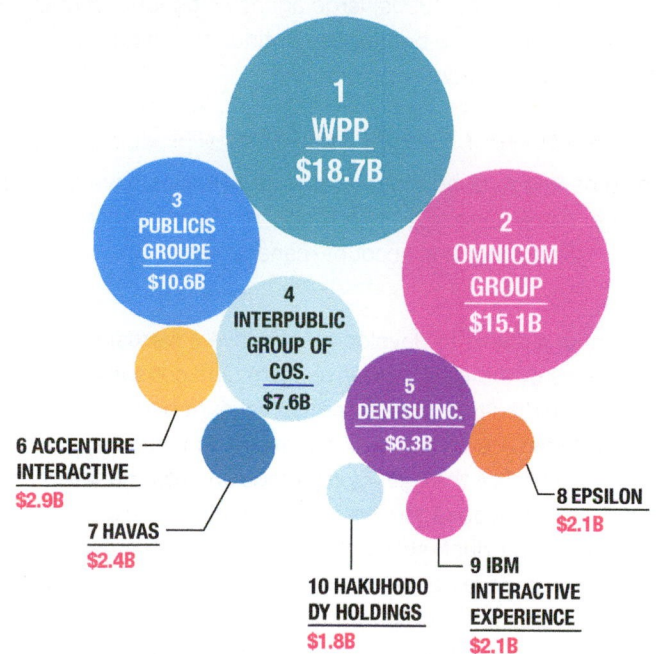

Data from: Advertising Age Marketing Fact Pack 2017, *p. 24.*

Interpublic Group of Companies, and Dentsu, with a combined revenue in 2015 of just over $58 billion (see Figure 11.1).

The mega-agency trend has stirred debate among consumer and media watchdog groups. Some have considered large agencies a threat to the independence of smaller firms, which were slowly bought up in the 1990s. Others warn against having a few firms control much of the distribution of advertising dollars globally. According to these critics, with such concentration of power, the cultural values depicted in U.S. and European ads (such as an obsession with youth or appearance) could unduly influence people in developing countries or regions with markedly different values. Such critics decry the intrusion of American culture into these areas.

Boutique Agencies

The visual revolution in advertising during the 1960s elevated the standing of the creative side of the ad business, particularly the designers, writers, and graphic artists who became closely identified with the look of specific ads. Breaking away from bigger agencies, many of these individuals formed small boutique agencies. Offering more personal services, the boutiques prospered—thanks to the innovative ad campaigns they developed to popularize brands like Nike, ESPN, and Target.

Throughout the 1980s and 1990s, large agencies bought up many of the boutiques. Nevertheless, some boutiques continue to operate as fairly independent subsidiaries of multinational corporations.

Ad Agencies Develop a Distinctive Structure

Regardless of type (mega or boutique), most ad agencies have a similar organizational structure, comprising four main functions: account planning, creative development, media buying, and account management.

Account Planning

The account planner's role is to develop an effective advertising strategy by combining the views of the client, creative team, and consumers. Consumers' views are the most difficult to understand, so account planners coordinate **market research** to assess consumers' behaviors and attitudes concerning particular products long before the agency develops any ads. Researchers might test consumers' preferences regarding a wide range of things—including possible names for a new product, size of text in a possible print ad, and potential features of a product in development.

Agencies have increasingly employed scientific methods to study consumer behavior. The earliest type of market research, **demographics**, mainly documented audience members' age, gender, occupation, ethnicity, education, and income, and then looked for patterns between these characteristics and consumers' purchasing choices. (For example, what types of clothing and skin-care products do high-earning women over forty years of age generally purchase?) Today, demographic data have become even more specific, enabling marketers to identify consumers' economic status and geographic location (usually by zip code) and compare their consumption behaviors, lifestyles, and attitudes.

By the 1960s and 1970s, advertisers and agencies began using **psychographics**, a research approach that attempts to categorize consumers according to their attitudes, beliefs, interests, and motivations. Psychographic analysis often relies on **focus groups**, a small-group interview technique in which a moderator leads a discussion about a product or an issue, usually with six to twelve participants. For instance, a focus group moderator might ask participants what they think of several possible names for a new brand of beer, why they like or dislike particular names proposed, and what role beer plays in their lives.

In 1978, this research grew even more sophisticated when Strategic Business Insights (formerly SRI International) developed its **Values and Lifestyles (VALS)** strategy. Using questionnaires, VALS researchers today divide respondents into eight types—thinkers, innovators, achievers, strivers, survivors, believers, makers, and experiencers—associated with certain behaviors and preferences of interest to clients. For example, an automaker considering which vehicle models to advertise during which types of TV shows might be told that *achievers* watch a lot of sports programs and prefer luxury cars, whereas *thinkers* enjoy TV dramas and documentaries and like minivans and hybrids.

VALS research assumes that not every product suits every consumer and encourages advertisers to pitch various sales slants to particular market niches. Ultimately, VALS (and similar research techniques) provides advertisers with microscopic details suggesting which consumers may be most likely to buy which products, but it also stereotypes people as consumers, reduced to eight manageable categories.

Creative Development

Teams of writers and artists—many of whom regard ads as a commercial art form—make up the nerve center of the advertising business. They outline the rough sketches for print and online ads and then develop the words and graphics. For radio, "creatives" prepare a working script, generating ideas for everything from choosing the narrator's voice to determining background sound effects. For television, they develop a **storyboard**, a roughly drawn comic-strip version showing each scene in the potential ad. For digital media, the creative team may develop Web sites, interactive tools, games, downloads, social media campaigns, and **viral marketing**—short videos or other forms of content that they hope will swiftly capture an ever-widening circle of attention as users share the content with friends online or by word of mouth.

Lemon.

This Volkswagen missed the boat. The chrome strip on the glove compartment is blemished and must be replaced. Chances are you wouldn't have noticed it. Inspector Kurt Kroner did.

There are 3,389 men at our Wolfsburg factory with only one job: to inspect Volkswagens at each stage of production. (3000 Volkswagens are produced daily; there are more inspectors than cars.)

Every shock absorber is tested (spot checking won't do), every windshield is scanned. VWs have been rejected for surface scratches barely visible to the eye.

Final inspection is really something! VW inspectors run each car off the line onto the Funkhronprüfstand (car test stand), tote up 189 check points, gun ahead to the automatic

brake stand, and say "no" to one VW out of fifty.

This preoccupation with detail means the VW lasts longer and requires less maintenance, by and large, than other cars. (It also means a used VW depreciates less than any other car.)

We pluck the lemons; you get the plums.

▲ The New York ad agency Doyle Dane Bernbach created a famous series of print and television ads for Volkswagen beginning in 1959, helping to usher in an era of creative advertising that combined a single-point sales emphasis with bold design, humor, and apparent honesty. The Advertising Archives

Creatives often lock horns with researchers over what will appeal most to consumers and how best to influence target markets. However, both sides acknowledge that they can't predict with absolute certainty which ads will succeed, especially in a competitive economy in which eight out of ten products introduced to market typically fail. Agencies say ads are at their best if they slowly create and then hold brand-name identities by associating certain products over time with quality and reliability in the minds of consumers. Famous brands like Coca-Cola, Budweiser, Toyota, and Microsoft spend millions of dollars each year just to maintain their brand-name aura. However, some economists believe that much of the money

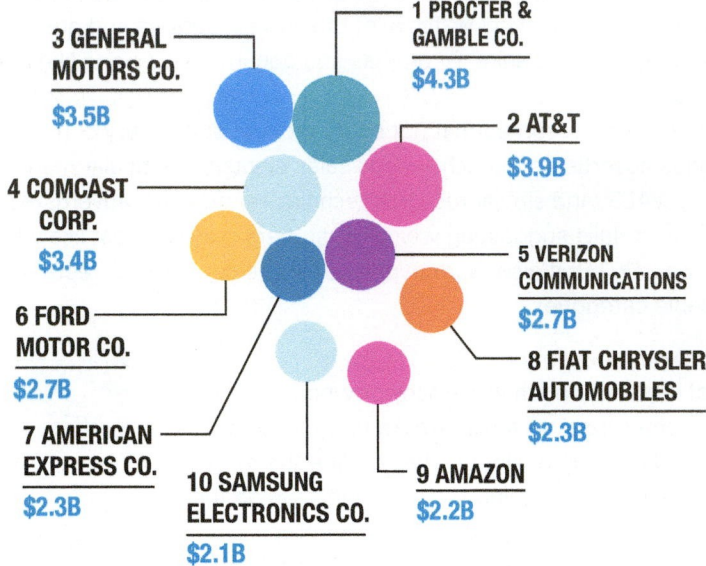

FIGURE 11.2 // **TOP U.S. ADVERTISERS IN 2015 (IN BILLIONS OF DOLLARS)**

3 GENERAL MOTORS CO.
$3.5B

1 PROCTER & GAMBLE CO.
$4.3B

2 AT&T
$3.9B

4 COMCAST CORP.
$3.4B

5 VERIZON COMMUNICATIONS
$2.7B

6 FORD MOTOR CO.
$2.7B

8 FIAT CHRYSLER AUTOMOBILES
$2.3B

7 AMERICAN EXPRESS CO.
$2.3B

10 SAMSUNG ELECTRONICS CO.
$2.1B

9 AMAZON
$2.2B

Data from: Advertising Age Marketing Fact Pack 2017, *p. 8*

spent on advertising, especially to promote new products, is ultimately wasted, since it just encourages consumers to change from one well-known brand name to another (see Figure 11.2).

Media Buying

An ad agency's media coordination department is staffed by media planners and **media buyers**: people who choose and purchase the types of media that are best suited to carry a client's ads and reach the targeted audience. For instance, a company like Procter & Gamble, always among the world's top purchasers of advertising, displays its hundreds of major brands—most of them household products like Crest toothpaste, Ivory soap, and Pampers diapers—on TV shows viewed primarily by women, who still do the majority of household cleaning.

Client companies usually pay an ad agency a commission or fee for its work. But they might also add incentive clauses to their contracts with the agency. For example, they may pay a higher fee if sales reach a specific target after an ad is aired—or pay a lower fee if sales fall short of the target. Incentive clauses can sometimes encourage agencies to conduct repetitive **saturation**

advertising, by which they inundate a variety of media with ads aimed at target audiences. The initial Miller Lite beer campaign ("Tastes great, less filling"), which used humor and retired athletes to reach its male audience, ran from 1973 to 1991 and became one of the most successful saturation campaigns in media history.

Of course, such efforts are expensive. And indeed, the cost of advertising—especially on network television—increases each year. The Super Bowl remains the most expensive program for purchasing television advertising, but running a thirty-second ad during a national prime-time TV show can cost anywhere from just over $14,000 to just under $700,000, depending on the program's popularity and ratings. Cost thus strongly influences where and when media buyers place ads.

Account Management

An agency's **account executives** are responsible for bringing in new business. For example, if a potential new client has requested bids for an upcoming ad campaign, the account executive might coordinate the presentation of a pro-posed campaign, complete with cost estimates. Account executives also man-age relationships with established clients, including overseeing project budgets, market research, creative work, and media planning done on their campaigns. Account executives thus function as liaisons between the client firm and the agency's creative team.

The advertising business is volatile, and account-management departments are especially vulnerable to upheavals. Clients routinely conduct **account reviews**—assessing an existing ad agency's campaign or inviting several new agencies to submit new campaign strategies. If clients are dissatisfied, they may switch agencies, something that has occurred more and more frequently since the late 1980s.[5]

Online and Mobile Advertising Alter the Ad Landscape

When the Internet made its appearance as a new mass medium in the 1990s, it presented a host of new decisions for companies to grapple with—such as what kinds of ads to invest in and where to place them. It also opened the door for new giants (such as Google) to dominate the online-advertising industry. Building on the popularity of smartphones and tablets, mobile advertising is the latest trend in advertising. Experts project that more dollars will soon be spent on Internet advertising than on television ads.[6]

The Rise of Web Advertising

The earliest form of Web advertising showed up in the mid-1990s and fea-tured banner ads, the printlike display ads that load across the top or side of a Web page. Since that time, Web advertising has grown in sophistication.

Other formats have emerged, including pop-up ads, pop-under ads, multimedia ads, and—ironically—the classic thirty-second video ad. Internet advertising now also includes classified ad sites—the most prominent is craigslist—and unsolicited e-mail ads known as **spam**. In fact, a number of companies have emerged in the past few years, several in India, devoted simply to producing spam ads for various clients.

Today, paid search advertising dominates sites such as Google, Yahoo!, and Bing. These search engines have quietly morphed into online advertising companies, selling sponsored links associated with search terms and distributing online ads to affiliated Web pages.[7] This type of advertising is far more precise than the earlier Web ads, enabling companies to reach target customers defined in ever-narrower terms, such as where they live and what key words they use while searching the Web. Some observers claim that clients in the near future will pay only for highly targeted ads and proven results. This targeting is even more precise with mobile advertising, as ads can be tailored to what a person has bought in the past and to where that individual is at any particular moment.

These and other advances in Internet marketing helped boost the stunning growth of online marketing in a very short time. Consider Google's track record. On the cusp of the digital turn in 2001, Google earned roughly $70 million in ad revenue. In five years, that number had jumped to more than $10 billion, and by 2015, Google's ad revenue approached $70 billion.[8] To put that number in perspective, the biggest broadcast network advertising haul in 2015 (by CBS) was $6.7 billion, and the largest ad agency—WPP—made just under $19 billion.[9] Facebook, another Internet giant, reported $17 billion in advertising revenue in the same year.[10]

The future of online advertising looks bright. Top advertising firms predict that from 2015 to 2019 the percentage of ad dollars spent on Internet marketing will go from just under 30 percent to just over 40 percent, continuing to drain away the shares of traditional television, radio, and print advertising. The same experts anticipate that the growth will occur mostly in advertising on mobile platforms, rather than Internet ads aimed at desktop users. While mobile Internet advertising in 2015 represented about a third of all online advertising dollars, it's expected to account for well over half by 2019.[11]

Some of this growth is a result of leading Internet companies aggressively expanding into the advertising market by acquiring smaller Internet advertising agencies. For example, in the past few years Google bought DoubleClick, the biggest online ad server, and AdMob, a mobile advertising company. Amazon.com didn't purchase an ad agency but partnered with San Francisco–based online advertiser Triggit to sell ads to Amazon users based on their browsing history. At the same time, traditional advertising and marketing agencies are striking back by expanding their Internet marketing expertise and capabilities. Traditional broadcast and print media are also investing in ventures centered around Internet convergence to recapture dollars no longer spent on traditional types of ads. For example, a newspaper may use social media to steer Internet users to a story on the paper's Web page, where the sales department can sell banner and pop-up ads to advertisers.

How Online Ads Work

Online ads are generally placed by advertising agencies and served to hundreds of client sites by the agencies' computers. The agencies track **ad impressions** (how often ads are seen) and **click-throughs** (how often users land briefly on a site before clicking through to the next site). They also develop consumer profiles that direct targeted advertisements to Web site visitors. Online agencies gather information about Internet users through "cookies" (code that tracks users' activity on the Web) and online surveys.

Mobile phones and tablets have provided a "third screen" (in addition to TV and personal computers) for online advertisers. These devices present the possibility for advertisers to tailor ads to phone users' specific geographic location. For example, a restaurant chain can display a special promotional ad on the mobile phone of someone driving a car or walking in the area of its nearest location. Google has also developed unique applications for mobile advertising and search. For example, the Google Goggles smartphone app enables users to take a photo of an object—such as a book cover, a landmark, or a logo—and then have Google return related search results. Google's Voice Search app lets users speak their search terms. Such apps are designed to maintain Google's dominant search engine position (which generates most of its profits) on the increasingly important mobile platform.

Advertising on Social Media

Social media, such as Facebook, Twitter, Snapchat, and Instagram, provide a wealth of data for advertisers to mine. These sites and apps create an unprecedented public display of likes, dislikes, locations, and other personal information; advertisers use such information to further refine their ability to send targeted ads. The information users provide goes straight back to advertisers so they can revise their advertising and better engage their viewers. With this better understanding of individual users, companies and organizations can also choose between buying traditional paid advertisements on social media sites and selling ads micro-targeted to those individual users.

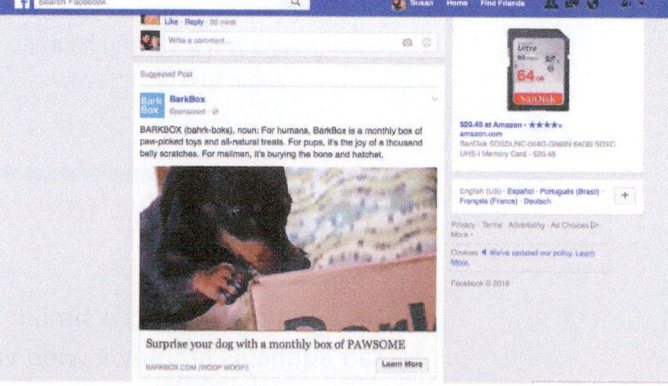

▼Social media advertising is growing rapidly. Sites like Facebook, Twitter, and Instagram gather a huge amount of information from their users every day, allowing advertisers to reach specific users by displaying ads for products related to those users' unique preferences and behaviors.

The type of social media advertising varies by—and is often tailored to—what the site actually does. For example, an ad on Facebook will typically appear as a clickable image next to the newsfeed. On Twitter, a sponsored tweet will usually appear in the feed. On YouTube, a user will most likely have to watch a commercial—or at least the first few seconds of a commercial—before or during a video.

Going Viral: The Internet Gold Standard

According to an old adage in marketing, the most effective form of advertising is word of mouth—a recommendation from a friend or family member. In today's post–digital turn, defined by social media, word-of-mouth recommendations are referred to as "earned media," and they are every bit as valuable.

Earned media can be passive or active on the part of the social media user. Say, for example, that you "Like" a page for a company, product, or person on Facebook, which causes that particular product to pop up on your friend's wall with a notification saying that you're a fan. This is a passive endorsement on your part, because the social media account has done the promotion for you. An active endorsement, on the other hand, occurs when you share a post on Facebook or issue a retweet on Twitter—with or without some kind of personal message that goes along with the repost or retweet.

When reposting and retweeting is repeated thousands—or millions—of times, a post has gone viral. But because a traditional advertisement does not tend to get a lot of shares on social media platforms, marketers have to come up with innovative and visually interesting ways—for example, through videos, memes, and photos—to prompt the viral response. Recent examples of viral videos include one from Apple Music showing hip-hop star Drake secretly lip-syncing and lifting weights to a Taylor Swift song, and one with animals jumping on a trampoline from department store John Lewis.

In addition to viral marketing that users watch, another popular method allows users to take part in creating the content that is shared. For instance, Snapchat users can add branded filters to their digital photos before sharing with friends. A Snapchat filter for the movie *Ghostbusters* made it seem as though users were being haunted by ghosts, while one for Taco Bell turned a user's head into a giant taco.

Persuasive Techniques in Contemporary Advertising

In addition to using a similar organizational structure, most ad agencies employ a wide variety of persuasive techniques in the ad campaigns they create for their clients. Indeed, persuasion — getting consumers to buy one company's products and services and not another's — lies at the core of the advertising industry. Persuasive techniques take numerous forms, ranging from conventional strategies (such as having a famous person endorse a product) to not-so-conventional strategies (for instance, showing video game characters using a product).

▲ Matthew McConaughey has appeared in a series of ads for the Lincoln Motor Company, which began shortly after his Academy Award win for Best Actor in 2014. Nancy Rivera/ACE Pictures/Newscom/Ace Pictures/ New York City/NY/USA

Do these tactics work — that is, do they boost sales? This is a tough question, because it's difficult to distinguish an ad's impact on consumers from the effects of other cultural and social forces. But companies continue investing in advertising on the assumption that without the product and brand awareness that advertising builds, consumers just might go to a competitor.

Using Conventional Persuasive Strategies

Advertisers have long used a number of conventional persuasive strategies.

- **Famous-person testimonial:** A product is endorsed by a well-known person. For example, Serena Williams has become a leading sports spokesperson, having appeared in ads for such companies as Nike, Kraft Foods, and Procter & Gamble.
- **Plain-folks pitch:** A product is associated with simplicity. For instance, General Electric ("Imagination at work") and Microsoft ("Your potential. Our passion") have used straightforward slogans stressing how new technologies fit into the lives of ordinary people.
- **Snob appeal:** An ad attempts to persuade consumers that using a product will maintain or elevate their social status. Advertisers selling jewelry, perfume, clothing, and luxury automobiles often use snob appeal.
- **Bandwagon effect:** The ad claims that "everyone" is using a particular product. Brands that refer to themselves as "America's favorite" or "the best-selling" imply that consumers will be "left behind" if they ignore these products.
- **Hidden-fear appeal:** A campaign plays on consumers' sense of insecurity. Deodorant, mouthwash, and shampoo ads often tap into people's fears of having embarrassing personal hygiene problems if they don't use the suggested product.

- **Irritation advertising:** An ad creates product-name recognition by being annoying or obnoxious. (You may have seen one of these on TV, in the form of a local car salesman loudly touting the "unbelievable bargains!" available at his dealership.)

Associating Products with Values

In addition to the conventional persuasive techniques just described, ad agencies draw on the **association principle** in many campaigns for consumer products. Through this technique, the agency associates a product with a positive cultural value or image—even if that value or image has little connection to the product. For example, many ads displayed visual symbols of American patriotism in the wake of the 9/11 terrorist attacks in an attempt to associate products and companies with national pride.

Yet this technique has also been used to link products with stereotyped caricatures of targeted consumer groups, such as men, women, or specific ethnic groups. For example, many ads have sought to appeal to women by portraying men as idiots who know nothing about how to use a washing machine or how to heat up leftovers for dinner. The assumption is that portraying men as idiots will make women feel better about themselves—and thus be attracted to the advertised product (see "Media Literacy Case Study: Idiots and Objects: Stereotyping in Advertising" on pages 342–343).

Another popular use of the association principle is to claim that products are "real" and "natural"—possibly the most common adjectives used in advertising. For example, Coke sells itself as "the real thing." The cosmetics industry offers synthetic products that make us look "natural." And "green" marketing touts products that are often manufactured and not always environmentally friendly.

In the 1950s and 1960s, Philip Morris used the association principle to transform the image of its Marlboro filtered cigarette brand (considered a product for women in the 1920s) into a product for men. Ad campaigns featured images of active, rugged males, particularly cowboys. (Three of the men who appeared in these ad campaigns eventually died of lung cancer caused by cigarette smoking.) By 2016, the branding consultancy BrandZ listed Marlboro as the world's twelfth most valuable brand (down from the ninth most valuable in 2014), with an estimated worth of $84 billion (Google, Apple, and Microsoft were the top three rated brands; see Table 11.1).

Telling Stories

Many ads also tell stories that contain elements found in myths (narratives that convey a culture's deepest values and social norms). For example, an ad might take the shape of a mini-drama or sitcom, complete with characters, settings,

TABLE 11.1 // THE TOP 10 GLOBAL BRANDS

Rank	Brand	Brand Value ($Billions)	Brand Value Change, 2016 vs. 2015 (%)
1	Google	229.2	32
2	Apple	228.5	−8
3	Microsoft	121.8	5
4	AT&T	107.4	20
5	Facebook	102.6	44
6	Visa	100.8	10
7	Amazon	99.0	59
8	Verizon	93.2	8
9	McDonald's	88.7	9
10	IBM	86.2	−8

Data from: "2016 BrandZ Top 100 Global Brands," Kantar Millward Brown, http://wppbaz.com/admin/uploads/files/BZ_Global_2016_Infographic_A4.pdf.

and plots. Perhaps a character experiences a conflict or problem of some type. The character resolves the situation by the end of the ad, usually by purchasing or using the product. The product and those who use it emerge as the heroes of the story.

But brands can play a variety of roles in commercial storytelling. Besides emerging as the solution to a problem, a brand sometimes *becomes* the character, as in M&M commercials in which animated versions of the candies exhibit their own distinct personalities and find themselves in a number of silly scenarios. In addition, some commercials are one-time stories, while others take the form of a running gag. In a series of Snickers commercials, for example, a cranky person (played by a number of celebrities) transforms into someone who is happy and calm after taking a bite of the candy bar.

Although most of us realize that ads telling stories create a fictional world, we often can't help but get caught up in them. That's because they reinforce our values and assumptions about how the world works. And they reassure us that by using familiar brand names—packaged in comforting mini-stories—we can manage the everyday tensions and problems that confront us.

Media Literacy

Idiots and Objects:
Stereotyping in Advertising

Over the years, critics and consumers alike have complained about stereotyping in mainstream advertising. *Stereotyping* refers to the process of assigning people to abstract groups whose members are assumed to act as a single entity—rather than as individuals with distinct identities—and to display shared characteristics, which often have negative connotations.

Today, particularly in beer ads, men are often stereotyped as inept or stupid, incapable of negotiating a routine day or a normal conversation unless fortified—or dulled—by the heroic product. Throughout advertising history, men have often been portrayed as doofuses and idiots when confronted by ordinary food items or a simple household appliance.

▶ Web Clip

YouTube.com includes many commercials—and commercial parodies. One good option to search for: 'Totino's Super Bowl Commercial' by Saturday Night Live, which parodies football-themed snack ads. What do you think the ad is saying about stereotyping in advertisements?

On the other hand, in the early history of product ads on television, women were often stereotyped as naïve or emotional, needing the experienced voice of a rational male narrator to guide them around their own homes. Ads have also stereotyped women as brainless or helpless or offered them as a man's reward for drinking a particular beer, wearing cool jeans, or smoking the right cigarette. Worst of all, women, or even parts of women—with their heads cut from the frame—have been used as objects, merely associated with a particular product (e.g., a swimsuit model holding a new car muffler or wrapped around a bottle of Scotch). Influenced by the women's movement and critiques of advertising culture, such as Betty Friedan's *The Feminine Mystique* (1963), ads depicting women have changed to some degree. Although many sexist stereotypes still persist in advertising, women today are portrayed in a variety of social roles.

In addition to ads that have stereotyped men and women, there is also invisible stereotyping. This occurs when whole segments of the population are ignored—particularly African, Arab, Asian, Latin, and Native Americans. Advertising—especially in its early history—has often faced criticism that many segments of the varied and multicultural U.S. population have been missing or underrepresented in the ads and images that dominate the landscape.

In the last several years, however, conscious of how diverse the United States has become, some ad campaigns have been making changes. One example of this is a series of ads for the breakfast cereal Cheerios (a brand owned by General Mills). In the summer of 2013, the company released an ad that featured a white mom, an African American father, and a biracial daughter. The ad received praise from some advertising critics but garnered so many racist comments on YouTube (where the company also posted the ad) that it had to disable

UNITED COLORS OF BENETTON.

▲ Like many Benetton ads, this one features a small logo in the corner and no additional information about the company or its products. Why might a clothing company produce an ad that doesn't feature clothing of any kind? Image Courtesy of The Advertising Archives

the commenting function. In early 2014, Cheerios debuted an ad during the Super Bowl featuring the same mother and father telling the little girl she was going to get a little brother; later that year, the company started another ad campaign that included two gay white dads from Quebec talking in a heartfelt way about the adoption of their black daughter. In all these cases, some groups hailed them as progress while others ripped them apart, often with racist or homophobic slurs.[1]

Italian clothing manufacturer Benetton has a long history of tackling controversial topics, ranging from interracial relationships to kissing politicians, in its United Colors of Benetton advertisements. The most famous of these do not actually show any of the clothes the company makes — just a small logo somewhere in the photograph. More than the tame domestic scenes presented in the Cheerios ads, the photos in the Benetton marketing campaigns are much more provocative — and controversial on multiple levels.

In both cases, some media critics have praised the companies for presenting more diversity and social awareness in their advertising while remaining skeptical of the motives behind the ads. After all, they say, the first goal of advertising is to boost sales.

APPLYING THE CRITICAL PROCESS

DESCRIPTION Gather four to six advertisements from various newspapers, magazines, or Internet sites that feature individuals (and not just products).

ANALYSIS Examine the content of each ad: What product is being sold? What are the profiles of the people who appear in the ad, or what are they doing? Note the publication or Web site each ad comes from. What patterns emerge, and what do these patterns suggest to you?

INTERPRETATION What do the patterns mean? How are the people in each ad helping to sell the product? What is the message that each ad is trying to portray? Why did the advertiser choose the specific newspaper, magazine, or Internet site to advertise the product?

EVALUATION Do any of the ads foster existing stereotypes? Explain how they do or do not. Do you think these ads are effective? How might the stereotypes in these ads convey a distorted or mixed message to the consumer?

ENGAGEMENT Choose one ad from your selection to revise. How might you redesign this ad to remove existing stereotypes? Compose a draft. Do you think your ad is more or less effective than the original? Explain your answer.

Placing Products in Media

Product placement—strategically placing ads or buying space in movies, TV shows, comic books, and video games so that they appear as part of a story's set environment—is another persuasive strategy ad agencies use. For example, the film *Get Out* (2017) prominently featured Windows products such as Bing, the Windows Phone, and The Surface Pro in multiple scenes; the TV show *The Biggest Loser*, which is sponsored by Subway, takes contestants on field trips to the sandwich shop; and Instagram recently hired thirty "influencer dudes" to put Axe products in their hair, which they featured in their "Instagroom" videos.

Many critics argue that product placement has gotten out of hand. In 2005, watchdog organization Commercial Alert asked both the FTC and the FCC to mandate that consumers be warned about product placement in television shows. The FTC rejected the petition, and by 2008 the FCC had still made no formal response to the request. Most defenders of product placement argue that there is little or no concrete evidence or research that this practice harms consumers. The 2011 documentary *POM Wonderful Presents: The Greatest Movie Ever Sold* takes a satirical look at product placement—and filmmaker Morgan Spurlock financed the film's entire budget using that very strategy.

Commercial Speech and Regulating Advertising

Advertisements are considered **commercial speech** — defined as any print or broadcast expression for which a fee is charged to organizations and individuals buying time or space in the mass media. Though the First Amendment protects freedom of speech and of the press, it doesn't specify whether advertisers can say anything they want in their commercial speech; thus, the question of whether commercial speech is protected by the Constitution is tricky. In some critics' view, certain forms of advertising can have destructive consequences and should therefore be regulated. These include ads that target children, that tout unhealthy products (such as alcohol and tobacco), that prompt people to adopt dangerous behaviors (such as starving themselves to look like models in magazines), and that hawk prescription medications directly to consumers instead of to doctors.

To be sure, no one has figured out just how much power such ads have to actually influence target consumers. Indeed, studies have suggested that 75 to 90 percent of new consumer products fail because the buying public doesn't embrace them — suggesting that advertising isn't as effective as some critics might think.[12] Nevertheless, serious concerns over the impact of advertising persist.

Targeting Children and Teens

Because children and teenagers may influence billions of dollars each year in family spending—on everything from snacks to cars—advertisers have increasingly targeted them, often viewing young people as "consumers in training." When ads influence youngsters in a good way (for example, by getting them interested in reading books), no one complains about advertising's power. It's when ads influence kids and teens in what is perceived as a dangerous way (such as tempting them with unhealthy foods) that concerns arise.

For years, groups such as Action for Children's Television (ACT) worked to limit advertising aimed at children (especially ads promoting toys associated with a show). In addition, parent groups have pushed to limit the heavy promotion of unhealthy products like sugar-coated cereals during children's TV programs. Congress has responded weakly, hesitant to question the First Amendment's protection of commercial speech and pressured by determined lobbying from the advertising industry. The Children's Television Act of 1990 mandated that networks provide some educational and informational children's programming, but the act has been difficult to enforce and has done little to restrict advertising aimed at kids.

In addition to trying to control TV advertising aimed at young people, critics have complained about advertising that has encroached on school property. The introduction of Channel One into thousands of schools during the 1989–90 school year has been one of the most controversial cases of in-school advertising. The brainchild of advertising firm Whittle Communications, Channel One offers free video and satellite equipment (tuned exclusively to Channel One) in exchange for a twelve-minute package of current events programming that includes two minutes of commercials.

Over the years, the National Dairy Council and other organizations have also used schools to promote products—for example, by providing free filmstrips, posters, magazines, folders, and study guides adorned with member companies' logos. Many teachers, especially in underfunded districts, have been grateful for these free materials. However, many parent and teacher groups have objected to Channel One (which claims to reach five million students), because in their view it requires teens to watch commercial messages in a learning environment.

Another way commercials and marketing reach teens, tweens, and even younger kids is through their mobile devices such as smartphones and tablets.

LaunchPad
launchpadworks.com

Advertising and Effects on Children

Scholars and advertisers analyze the effects of advertising on children.

Discussion: In the video, some argue that using cute, kid-friendly imagery in alcohol ads can lead children to begin drinking; others dispute this claim. What do you think, and why?

▲ Critics argue that toothpick-sized models set unattainable standards that can lead to eating disorders among women. AP Photo/L.M. Otero

With mobile advertising exploding and more and more kids having access to these devices, monitoring the ads children see is becoming even more difficult.

Triggering Anorexia and Overeating

Some critics accuse ads of contributing to anorexia among girls and women; others, of contributing to obesity among young and adult Americans. To be sure, companies have long marketed fashions and cosmetics by showing ultrathin female models using their products. Through such campaigns, advertising strongly shapes standards of beauty in our culture. Many girls and women apparently feel compelled to achieve those standards—even if it means starving themselves or having repeated cosmetic surgeries.

At the same time, advertising has been blamed for the tripling of obesity rates in the United States since the 1980s. Corn-syrup-laden soft drinks, fast food, junk food, and processed food are the staples of media advertising. Critics maintain that advertisements for fattening products have directly contributed to widespread obesity in the United States. The food and restaurant industry has denied this connection. Industry advocates claim that people have the power to decide what they eat—and many individuals are making poor choices, such as eating too much fast food.

Promoting Smoking

One of the most sustained criticisms of advertising is its promotion of tobacco consumption. Each year, an estimated 400,000 Americans die from diseases related to nicotine addiction and poisoning. Still, for a long time tobacco companies kept cranking out ad campaigns designed to win over new customer segments, which often included teenagers.

The government's position regarding the tobacco industry began changing in the mid-1990s. At that time, new reports revealed that tobacco companies had known that nicotine was addictive as far back as the 1950s and had withheld that information from the public. Settlements between the industry and states have put significant limits on advertising and marketing of tobacco products. For example, ads cannot use cartoon characters such as Joe Camel, because such characters appeal to young people. And companies can't show ads on billboards or in subway or commuter trains, where young people might be vulnerable to them. In June 2009, President Obama, himself a professed addicted smoker since his teen years, signed the Family Smoking Prevention and Tobacco Control Act. The act allows the Food and Drug Administration (FDA)

The Digital Turn

Marketing, Social Media, and Epic Fails

One might expect one of the top tech companies in the world to be immune to social media epic fails. Unfortunately for Microsoft, that wasn't the case in 2016, when the company's artificial intelligence ended up looking anything but smart.

Microsoft had developed a software program called Tay and set it up with a Twitter account called "TayTweets," with the idea that the program would "learn" how to interact with others from its online conversations. Learn it did: In just a few short hours, Internet trolls had "taught" Tay to deliver racist and misogynistic Twitter rants—and even to advocate genocide.

Microsoft quickly took the Twitter account offline and deleted the offensive tweets, but not before the company had joined the ranks of famous people and corporations across the globe who have been embarrassed on social media—sometimes because of damage they brought on themselves and sometimes (as with Microsoft) because they were taken advantage of by unscrupulous individuals.

But even though social media promotions can backfire, as this one did, companies continue to seek them out in hopes of harnessing the social power of the Internet.

In addition to using the more traditional method of paid advertising to promote a product, brand, or person online, the holy grail of online marketing is the kind that receives massive and mostly free exposure by going *viral*—that is, marketing that's shared and reshared on social media, spreading across the Internet. If a piece of advertising catches on, it can be a very powerful way to spread a marketing message. But this kind of accessibility can be a double-edged sword; just as social media can amplify a marketing message, it can also amplify a mistake.

Sometimes social media disasters are simply mistakes that are corrected relatively quickly—but not fast enough to outrun the speed of the Internet. An employee at U.S. Airways found this out the hard way after responding to a customer service complaint on Twitter by tweeting back a graphically pornographic picture. An internal investigation later determined it had been unintentional.

Brands can also get into trouble in the social media world with ill-conceived attempts at humor. Cinnabon landed in hot water after actor Carrie Fisher's death when the company tweeted: "RIP Carrie Fisher, you'll always have the best buns in the galaxy" next to an image of her as Princess Leia and a cinnamon roll superimposed over the character's iconic hairstyle.

Experts in marketing and advertising are always watching cases like this and hoping to learn how to get the most positive social media buzz (see also the chapter introduction on DJ Khaled) while avoiding a social media fail. As we've discussed throughout this chapter (and this book), online and social media advertising continues to be a rapidly growing part of the mass media industry. Companies, brands, and ad agencies that learn to successfully navigate the social media waters will have a big advantage.

 **Web Clip**

YouTube.com includes many commercials—and commercial parodies. For example, check out another video from Saturday Night Live called 'Pepboys—SNL,' which parodies reactions to advertisements. How might constructing an effective ad be especially difficult in today's digital world?

to lessen the nicotine in tobacco products and block misleading cigarette-packaging labels that say "low tar" and "light." Despite these restrictions, tobacco companies still spend about $9 billion annually on U.S. advertisements—more than twenty times the amount spent on anti-tobacco public service spots.

Promoting Drinking

In 2014, nearly ninety thousand people in the United States died from alcohol-related or alcohol-induced diseases; another ten thousand lost their lives in car crashes involving drunk drivers. Many of the same complaints regarding tobacco advertising are being leveled at alcohol ads. For example, critics have protested that one of the most popular beer campaigns of the late 1990s—featuring a trio of frogs croaking *Budweis-errrr*—used cartoon-like animal characters to appeal to young viewers. Some alcohol ads, such as Pabst Brewing Company's ads featuring Snoop Dogg for Blast by Colt 45 (a strong flavored malt beverage that the Massachusetts attorney general called "binge-in-a can"), have specifically targeted young minority populations.

▲Budweiser, a heavy spender on ads during the Super Bowl and throughout the year, came under fire in 2015 for advertising on a Bud Light bottle calling it "the perfect beer for removing 'no' from your vocabulary"—a tagline that, as many pointed out, carried connotations of coercion, ignoring consequences of actions, and even sexual assault. Stephen Lovekin/Getty Images

The alcohol industry has also heavily targeted college students with ads, especially for beer. The images and slogans in alcohol ads often associate the products with power, romance, sexual prowess, or athletic skill. In reality, though, alcohol is a depressant: It diminishes athletic ability and sexual performance, triggers addiction in as much as 10 percent of the U.S. population, and factors into many domestic-abuse cases. Thus, many ads present a false impression of what alcohol products can do for consumers.

Hawking Drugs Directly to Consumers

New advertising tactics by the pharmaceutical industry—such as marketing directly to consumers instead of to doctors—have also drawn fire from critics worried about vulnerable groups of consumers. According to a study by the Kaiser Family Foundation, from 1994 to 2007 spending on direct-to-consumer advertising for prescription drugs soared from $266 million to $5.3 billion. By 2016, that number was up to $5.8 billion.[13] About two-thirds of such ads are shown on television, and they've proved effective for the pharmaceutical companies that invest in and use them. A survey found that nearly one in three adults has talked to a doctor about a particular drug after seeing an ad for it on TV, and one in eight subsequently received a prescription.[14] The tremendous growth of prescription drug ads brings with it the potential for misleading or downright false claims. That's because a brief TV advertisement can't effectively communicate all the cautionary information consumers need to know about these medications. Meanwhile, the money spent marketing to patients is dwarfed by the $24 billion drug companies spend to market directly to doctors.[15]

Monitoring the Advertising Industry

Worried about advertising's power over vulnerable consumers, a few nonprofit watchdog and advocacy organizations, such as Commercial Alert and the American Legacy Foundation, have emerged. Such groups strive to compensate for some of the shortcomings of the FTC and other government agencies in monitoring false and deceptive ads and the excesses of commercialism. At the same time, the FTC is still trying to combat the negative impact of advertising, though its effectiveness remains questionable, especially in light of cutbacks at the agency that have been going on since the 1980s.

Commercial Alert

Since 1998, Commercial Alert has worked to "limit excessive commercialism in society." Founded in part with help from longtime consumer advocate Ralph Nader, Commercial Alert became a project of Public Citizen, a nonprofit consumer protection organization based in Washington, D.C. In addition to its efforts to check commercialism, Commercial Alert has challenged specific marketing tactics that allow corporations to intrude into civic life. In 2016, Commercial Alert worked to oppose ads disguised as regular posts on Instagram and proposals for corporate sponsorships in national parks. The organization also advocated to keep hospital obstetrics wards free of ads for infant formula and other products. In constantly questioning the role of advertising in our democracy, Commercial Alert has aimed to strengthen noncommercial culture and limit the amount of corporate influence on publicly elected government officials and organizations.

▲ In 2005, "Truth," the national youth smoking prevention campaign, won an Emmy Award in the National Public Service Announcement category. Courtesy truth®/Legacy

The American Legacy Foundation

Some nonprofit organizations have used innovative advertising of their own to offset the effects of ads for dangerous products. In 2000, the American Legacy Foundation launched an anti-smoking/anti–tobacco industry ad campaign called "Truth." The campaign's mission has been to counteract tobacco marketing and reduce tobacco use among young people. The "Truth" project uses print and television ads that contradict the images that have long been featured in cigarette ads. For example, one of their early spots showed a giant rat expiring on a city sidewalk, clutching a cardboard sign saying that cigarettes contain the same chemical found in rat poison. Many "Truth" spots prominently reference the foundation's Web site, thetruth.com, which offers statistics, discussion forums, and outlets for teen creativity, such as games.

The FTC

Through its truth-in-advertising rules, the FTC has played an investigative role in substantiating the claims of various advertisers. Thus, the organization contributes to some regulation of the ad industry. The FTC usually permits a certain amount of *puffery*—ads featuring hyperbole and exaggeration—particularly when an ad describes a product as "new and improved." However, the FTC defines ads as deceptive when they are likely to mislead reasonable consumers through statements made, images shown, or omission of certain information. (For example, in some Campbell Soup ads once featuring images of a bowl of soup, marbles had been placed in the bottom of the bowl to push bulkier ingredients to the surface. This was deceptive advertising because it made the soup look less watery than it really was.) Moreover, when an advertiser makes comparative claims for a product, such as it's "the best," "the greatest," or "preferred by four out of five doctors," FTC rules require statistical evidence to back up the claims.

When the FTC discovers deception in advertising, it usually requires advertisers to change or remove the ads from circulation. The FTC can also impose monetary civil penalties, which are paid to consumers. And it occasionally requires an advertiser to run spots correcting the deceptive ads.

Advertising in a Democratic Society

Advertising has had both creative and destructive effects on our democratic society. With its ability to "produce" not products but actual consumers, it became the central economic support system for American mass media industries, powerfully fueling our economy. Yet in creating a consumerist society, the ad industry has also widened divisions between those who can afford to buy all the alluring products it promotes and those who cannot (or, alternately, those who go into debt buying the alluring products on credit). When some people can participate in an economy and others are unable to, democracy is undermined. Moreover, advertising's ubiquity intrudes on our privacy and subjects us to corporate efforts to gather our personal information (such as income and spending habits).

Equally worrisome, fewer and fewer large media conglomerates are controlling an increasing amount of commercial speech, especially in mainstream, traditional media. This raises the question of whether we're getting all the

◄ Eye-catching logos and short, simple slogans have long been an important part of selling a candidate to the public. During the 2016 presidential election, the "Make America Great Again" slogan on a hat was an instantly recognizable symbol of then candidate Donald Trump.
Spencer Platt/Getty Images

information we need to make well-reasoned choices — a key characteristic of any democratic society.

Advertising's role in politics offers an apt example. Since the 1950s, political consultants have adopted market-research and advertising techniques to "sell" their candidates to the electorate. **Political advertising**, the use of ad techniques to promote a candidate's image and persuade the public to adopt a particular viewpoint, is the most popular form of this. Many political ads are shown on television in the form of thirty-second spots paid for by candidates from the two main parties or largely unregulated political action committees and Super PACs, made legal by the 2010 Supreme Court case *Citizens United v. Federal Elections Commission*. The *Citizens United* decision is already having a huge impact on political ad spending, which topped $6.28 billion in all races in 2012.[16] In the 2016 campaign, Democratic presidential candidate Hillary Clinton, Republican presidential candidate Donald Trump, and their various affiliated PACs raised $2.3 billion combined.[17] But campaign spending wasn't limited to the top of the ticket. When including outside money groups — groups that are technically unaffiliated with the candidates but have many ties to them in practice — the Center for Responsive Policy estimates that upwards of $6.9 billion was spent on 2016 congressional and presidential races.[18]

One result of this is that only very wealthy candidates, or those with the wealthiest patrons, can typically afford these expensive promotional strategies. Thus, citizens who rely on television for their information don't get a complete picture of the options available and may never learn about obscure but qualified third-party candidates who can't afford to pay for TV spots. The present political environment, in which the most affluent can flood the commercial media with their paid messages, has become a situation in which free speech really isn't free.

Moreover, critics have raised probing questions about the unintended consequences of political ads aired on television. For example, can serious information about complex political issues really be conveyed in a thirty-second spot? If not, viewers aren't getting a full understanding of the issues and can't make informed voting decisions. And do repeated attack ads, which assault another candidate's character, undermine citizens' confidence in the electoral process? If so, people may stop voting entirely—a *really* bad thing for a democracy.

Political ads most often appear during traditional televised commercial breaks, but other forms of advertising can be more subtle, especially in the digital world of promotion-paid Twitter accounts, product placement, and ads woven into search engine results. During the 2016 election, for example, we saw how extensive media coverage—though not advertising in the strictest sense—can still provide free publicity for a candidate's campaign and drive the broader political narrative. During his candidacy, Donald Trump parlayed decades in the public spotlight, his status as a reality TV star, and his growing Twitter following into an unprecedented amount of free media coverage. From his extensively covered role in the "Birther" movement (which questioned the authenticity of then president Obama's birth certificate) to regular appearances on Fox News to attention from a wide range of news sources before he even made a dent in any polls, Trump obtained, by some estimates, billions of dollars worth of free air time and mentions across the media spectrum—in part because his controversial and bombastic rhetoric translated into ratings for the news organizations that covered him so extensively.[19] In early 2016, CBS chairman and CEO Les Moonves said of Donald Trump's place in the election and his network's resulting ratings bump: "It may not be good for America, but it's damn good for CBS."[20]

Despite these and other concerns about advertising's potential negative consequences for our democracy, it maintains its hold on American culture—for several reasons. Without advertising, many mass media industries—television, the Internet, movies—would have to entirely reinvent their business models, as newspapers and magazines are doing right now in the face of losing so much of their ad revenue sources over the last decade. Leaders in these industries continue to embrace advertising as an economic necessity. Consumers themselves hold conflicting views of the ad industry: Some dismiss advertising as trivial and ineffective. These individuals don't typically support strong monitoring of the industry. Others find ads entertaining, decorating their rooms or clothing with their favorite product posters or company logos and happily identifying with the images certain products convey. They, too, remain oblivious to advertising's less-than-positive effects on our society. Advertising can be enjoyable—think of the viewers who watch the Super Bowl to see new ads that are often hyped just as heavily as the products they hawk, or even the game itself—but if we consider it just entertainment, we misunderstand its ultimate purpose.

What does all this mean for advertising's future in the United States? As with any other mass medium, it's important that we remember what advertising's purpose is, understand how it both benefits and costs our society, and "consume" commercial culture and its ads with a critical eye.

Think about it: In what ways are our own behaviors, values, and decisions—in all aspects of our life—affected by advertising? How might we consume and respond to ads more critically? And in what ways could we all participate in efforts to monitor the advertising landscape?

CHAPTER ESSENTIALS

Review

- The first American advertising agents were newspaper **space brokers**. The first modern ad agencies worked mainly for companies that manufactured consumer products.

- As a result of manufacturers using newspaper stories and ads to create brand names, consumers began demanding specific products, and retail stores began stocking desired brands, ushering in product differentiation.

- By the twentieth century, advertising had transformed American society, creating new markets, shaping values, and influencing the rising consumer culture. This influence catalyzed the first watchdog organizations, such as the Better Business Bureau and the Federal Trade Commission (FTC).

- Beginning in the 1960s and 1970s, visual design played a more prominent role in advertising. This trend sparked the growth of new types of advertising agencies: **mega-agencies** and smaller **boutique agencies.**

- Regardless of the type of ad agency, most have similar organizational structures, consisting of departments for account planning (including **market research**), creative development, media buying, and account management.

- The growth of the Internet in the 1990s changed the advertising industry considerably. Internet advertising includes pop-up ads, **spam**, banner ads on Web pages, paid promotions with social media platforms, and content like memes and videos designed to go viral through voluntary sharing by Internet users.

- Ad agencies use a number of persuasive strategies, such as **famous-person testimonials, plain-folks pitches, snob appeals**, the **bandwagon effect, hidden-fear appeals**, and **irritation advertising**.

- In addition, advertisers draw on the **association principle** and tell stories or narratives that convey a culture's deepest values and social norms. They also focus on **product placement**—strategically placing ads or buying space in movies, TV shows, comic books, and video games so that they appear as part of a story's environment.

- Advertisements consist of **commercial speech**, and the question of whether advertisers are fully protected by the First Amendment remains controversial.

- Serious concerns exist over the impact of advertising on children; teens; and those susceptible to eating disorders, smoking, alcoholism, or inappropriate prescription-drug use, leading to the creation of nonprofit watchdog and advocacy organizations such as Commercial Alert and the American Legacy Foundation.

- Advertising has helped fuel the economy while also creating a consumer society with divisions between those who can afford to buy certain products and those who cannot. It has also raised concerns about the impact of a handful of large media conglomerates controlling commercial speech.

- The enormous amount of cash required to pay for **political advertising** raises concerns about who can afford to run for office and who gets to be heard by elected officials.

- Despite these issues, without advertising, many mass media industries would not survive. Given its pervasiveness, it's important for the public to be critical consumers of advertising.

Key Terms

space brokers, p. 326
subliminal advertising, p. 329
mega-agencies, p. 330
boutique agencies, p. 330
market research, p. 332

Study Questions

1. What role did advertising play in transforming the United States into a consumer society?

2. What are the major divisions at most ad agencies? What is the function of each department?

3. How do the common persuasive techniques used in advertising work?

4. What are four serious contemporary issues regarding health and advertising? Why is each issue controversial?

5. What are the effects of advertising on a democratic society?

12

Public Relations and Framing the Message

Traditionally, public relations (PR) professionals try to influence audiences, often by attempting to gain positive coverage in the news media. Social media like Twitter, Facebook, YouTube, Instagram, and Tumblr have shortened the path of communication; now PR pros can communicate directly with their audience—as can many of their famous clients.

Some celebrities have carefully developed incredibly strong followings through social media. Taylor Swift has 74.6 million Facebook "Likes," 84.1 million Twitter followers, and almost 101.6 million Instagram fans. Fellow diva Beyoncé has 64.5 million Facebook "Likes," 14.8 million Twitter followers, and more than 100 million Instagram fans.

And then there's Vin Diesel. Although he doesn't quite have the same standing in traditional media as does Taylor Swift, he qualifies as a superstar on social media. On Facebook, he is the world's third-biggest celebrity, with more than 101.6 million "Likes," trailing only World Cup soccer star Cristiano Ronaldo and singer Shakira. Diesel is new to Twitter, so he has a mere 90.3 thousand followers, but he also has 37.6 million Instagram fans and a popular Web site, vindiesel.com.

◀ With the help of a skilled PR team and due in part to the popularity of *The Fast and the Furious* franchise, Vin Diesel, pictured here, is ranked the third-biggest celebrity on Facebook. Photo by Matt Sayles/Invision/AP

Diesel's social media popularity provides some clues about the incredible popularity of *The Fast and the Furious* movie franchise. The huge success of the seventh installment's opening in April 2015 took many industry watchers by surprise. In just seventeen days, the movie earned more than $1 billion worldwide, a record pace in crossing that mark at the time. The eighth installment, *The Fate of the Furious*, which arrived in theaters in April 2017, crushed box office records with a $532.5 million opening weekend; more than 80 percent of the box office came from international screens outside of the United States and Canada.[1]

To increase demand, the movie studio (Universal) and many stars of the franchise had built a growing community of fans since the first film, *The Fast and the Furious*, in 2001. For example, in addition to No. 3 Vin Diesel, other top Facebook stars affiliated with the franchise include Dwayne Johnson (#21), Jason Statham (#23), and Wiz Khalifa (#41, who performs on several of the soundtracks). Romeo Santos and Tyrese Gibson also have more than 30 million followers each. It is likely that no other film has had a cast with as many top Facebook celebrities. Among movie sites on Facebook, the *Fast and Furious* page ranked No. 2, with more than 61.5 million "Likes."

With such a built-in fan base and long-running characters, it is not surprising that the most recent installments have done so well at the box office.

But it wasn't always an easy journey. Tragedy hit the production of the seventh movie with an off-set car accident in November 2013 that killed star Paul Walker. As the *Guardian* recounted, Walker's death left Universal in a difficult position in terms of finishing the film and also handling his passing with sensitivity. The studio's strategy was to use social media to reach out to fans.

Universal issued three messages via social media during a seven-month period immediately after Walker's death, until *Fast & Furious 7* wrapped in July 2014. The correspondence was respectful and illustrated the uncommon dialogue the studio, Vin Diesel, and other cast members have enjoyed with the films' audience. *Fast and Furious* had built up a cinematic superpower over 14 years, a borderless social media tribe of millions.[2]

Universal didn't build this franchise on a big star; rather, it built it on a big audience, one that it and the movie's cast had been developing for years via social media. With a fan base like that, it's no surprise the studio has plans to release a new sequel in the franchise every other year through 2021.

AS THE STORY OF VIN DIESEL AND *THE FAST AND THE FURIOUS* FRANCHISE REVEALS, the field of public relations continues to grow and change with the media industries it depends on. An effective public relations effort involves numerous activities, including shaping the public image of a product (or a person or an organization), establishing or restoring communication between consumers and companies, and promoting particular individuals or organizations. Broadly defined, **public relations** refers to the total communication strategy conducted by a person, a government, or an organization attempting to reach an audience and persuade it to adopt a point of view.[3] Or, in the brief definition offered by the Public Relations Society of America (PRSA), "Public relations helps an organization and its publics adapt mutually to each other."

Although public relations may sound very similar to advertising, which also seeks to persuade audiences, it differs in important respects. Advertising uses discrete, simple, and fixed messages ("Our appliance is the most efficient and affordable"), transmitted directly to the public through the purchase of ads for specific products or services. Whereas advertising focuses mainly on sales, public relations develops or reshapes an image for a person, an organization, a product, a service, or an issue to make it more marketable, popular, important, compelling, or accessible, among other desired outcomes. In doing so, public relations creates more complex messages that may evolve over time (e.g., a political campaign or a long-term strategy to dispel unfavorable reports about "fatty processed foods"). PR may be transmitted to the public indirectly, often through articles and reports in the news media. Finally, public relations messages often reflect larger trends and ideas that are percolating through society—such as the notion that it is good to recycle or that smoking is bad for you. Even broad ideas like "liberty" or "fairness" often take on connotations based on public relations efforts. PR thus shapes and is shaped by what is going on in society at large.

Since its inception, PR has exerted a huge influence on American society and culture. For example, after the Industrial Revolution, when people began purchasing (rather than making) many of the goods they needed, manufacturers used PR to emphasize how various industries benefited consumers. By helping to drive economic activity, the public relations profession thus contributed to an improvement in standards of living in the United States. PR also set the tone for the corporate image-building that characterized the twentieth century—and for the debates over today's environmental, energy, labor, and other public policy issues. However, PR's most significant impact is probably on the political process: Politicians and organizations hire PR professionals to shape their image in the media, which influences how people vote. No matter what issue you care about, there is undoubtedly someone doing PR on its behalf, on all sides.

Today, there are more than seven thousand PR firms in the United States, plus thousands of PR departments within corporate, government, and non profit organizations.[4] Moreover, since the 1980s, the formal study of public relations has grown significantly at colleges and universities. By 2016, the

Public Relations Student Society of America (PRSSA) boasted more than eleven thousand student members and more than three hundred chapters in colleges and universities.

In this chapter, we examine the workings and the impact of public relations in more detail by:

- **looking at the early days of public relations, including the emergence of press agents and the birth of modern PR**

- **considering how the PR profession has evolved in terms of the structure of public relations firms and the functions that PR practitioners perform (such as formulating messages about their clients and conveying those messages to the public)**

- **exploring the tensions that have arisen between public relations professionals and the press, and the causes behind those tensions**

- **considering the role PR plays in our democratic society by focusing on the impact of public relations on the political process in particular**

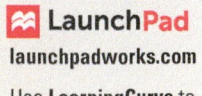

Early History of Public Relations

Public relations traveled an interesting path in its journey toward becoming a profession. The first PR practitioners were **press agents**, people who conveyed favorable messages to the public about their clients, often by staging stunts that reporters described in newspapers. As the United States became industrialized and people began purchasing more goods and services, larger companies — impressed by press agents' power to shape public opinion — began hiring these early practitioners to further their interests. Some PR tactics proved deceitful, but when journalists and citizens complained, PR agencies began policing themselves to foster more ethical practices in the profession.

Age of the Press Agent: P.T. Barnum and Buffalo Bill

The earliest press agents excelled at **publicity**—a type of PR communication that uses various media messages to spread information and interest (or buzz) about a person, a corporation, an issue, or a policy. The most effective publicity efforts not only excited people's imagination but also helped establish enduring national values.

In the 1800s, some publicity tactics could also border on the outrageous. Consider press agent Phineas Taylor (P. T.) Barnum, who used gross exaggeration, fraudulent stories, and staged events to secure newspaper coverage for his clients, for his American Museum, and (later) for his circus, which he dubbed "The Greatest Show on Earth."

William F. Cody was another notorious publicity hound. From 1883 to 1916, Cody, who once killed buffalo for the railroads, used press agents to promote himself and his traveling show: "Buffalo Bill's Wild West and Congress of Rough Riders of the World." The show employed sharpshooter Annie Oakley and Lakota holy man Sitting Bull, whose legends were partially shaped by Cody's press agents. These agents were led by John Burke, one of the first to use an array of media channels to generate publicity. Burke promoted Cody's show through a heady mix of newspaper stories, magazine articles and ads, dime novels, theater marquees, poster art, and early films. Burke and Buffalo Bill fired up Americans' love of rugged individualism and frontier expansion—a national mythology that later showed up in books, radio programs, and Hollywood films about the American West.

▲ Buffalo Bill's Wild West and Congress of Rough Riders of the World" show, depicted here, was internationally popular as a touring show for more than thirty years. Library of Congress Prints & Photographs Division, Reproduction number LC-USZC4-3169 (color film copy transparency) LC-USZ62-24458 (b&w film copy neg.)

Business Adopts Press Agent Methods

The successes enjoyed by P. T. Barnum, Buffalo Bill, John Burke, and others demonstrated that publicity could not only stimulate business but also help any individual or organization (such as not-for-profit groups and government agencies) spread the word about its value and fulfill its mission. For businesses, press agentry became an important mechanism for generating profits and (in some cases) bringing in the government funding needed to achieve their mission. However, in the early days of press agents, some of the tactics used were especially deceptive.

Around 1850, for example, the railroads began hiring press agents to help them obtain federal funds, which hinged on positive public perceptions of the railroads' value. These agents' tactics included bribing reporters to write favorable news stories about the railroads. Agents also engaged in **deadheading**—giving journalists free rail passes with the tacit understanding that they would write glowing reports about traveling by rail. Finally, the larger railroads used **lobbyists**—professionals who seek to influence lawmakers' votes—to gain federal subsidies and establish policies (such as rate reductions) that made it harder for smaller regional lines to compete. Thanks to such efforts, a few large rail companies gained dominance over the industry.

Utility companies such as Chicago Edison and AT&T also used press agent strategies in the late 1800s for similar ends. Again, some of their tactics were deceptive. For instance, they, too, bought votes of key lawmakers, and they hired third-party editorial services to produce written pieces in their favor. For example, these services sent articles touting the utilities to newspapers, produced ghostwritten articles lauding the utilities' value, and influenced textbook authors to write historical accounts that put the utilities in a positive light.[5]

Professional Public Relations Emerges

By the early 1900s, some journalists began investigating and reporting on the questionable promotional practices businesses were using, which helped increase awareness of these tactics among the public. Facing a more informed citizenry, businesses were finding it harder to buy favorable press and use it to mislead people. Two PR pioneers—Ivy Ledbetter Lee and Edward Bernays—realized that public relations needed to be more professional. To that end, they ushered in new approaches that emphasized honesty, directness, and an understanding of psychology and sociology.

Ivy Ledbetter Lee: More Than One Side to Every Story

Press agent Ivy Ledbetter Lee counseled his corporate clients that honesty and directness were better PR devices than the deceptive practices of the 1800s, which had given big business a bad name. Lee opened one of the first PR firms in the early 1900s with George Parker. Following a rail accident in late 1906, the Pennsylvania Railroad hired the firm to help downplay the resulting unfavorable publicity. Lee advised the railroad to admit its mistake, vow to do better, and let newspapers in on the story, rather than trying to cover up the accident or deny responsibility. In 1912, Lee quit the firm to work for the Pennsylvania Railroad.

In 1914, Lee went to work for John D. Rockefeller Jr., who by the 1880s controlled 90 percent of the nation's oil industry. Rockefeller and his Standard Oil Company already had image problems, beginning when journalists published a powerful muckraking series about his business tactics, running from 1902 to 1904. In 1913–14, strikebreakers at one of Rockefeller's mining companies and members of the state militia battled striking coal miners trying to win recognition for their union. Fifty-three workers and their family members were killed in Ludlow, Colorado. The oil magnate hired Lee to contain the damaging publicity fallout. Lee immediately distributed a series of "fact sheets" to the press, telling the company's side of the story and discrediting the tactics of the

◀Ivy Lee, a founding father of public relations, did innovative crisis work with John D. Rockefeller Jr., staging photo opportunities at the Ludlow mines. Bettmann/Getty Images; Rockefeller Archive Center

United Mine Workers, who had organized the strike. Lee clearly recognized that there are several sides to every story and that decisions about which facts to present to the public—and which to leave out—could strongly shape public perceptions. Lee also brought in the press and staged photo opportunities at Rockefeller's company, which helped rehabilitate the Rockefeller family's image. While certainly effective, his efforts earned him the nickname "Poison Ivy" Lee from his enemies.

Edward Bernays: Public Relations Counselor

Edward Bernays was the first person to apply the findings of psychology and sociology to the public relations profession. Bernays, who opened his own PR office in 1919, described the shaping of public opinion through PR as the "engineering of consent." That is, he believed that skilled experts, leaders, and PR professionals could shape messages and ideas in ways people could rally behind.[6]

Indeed, Bernays referred to himself as a "public relations counselor" rather than a "publicity agent." Over the years, his client list included such big-name companies as the American Tobacco Company (now R. J. Reynolds Tobacco), General Electric, and General Motors. Bernays also worked for the Committee on Public Information (CPI) during World War I. In that role, he developed propaganda that supported the U.S. entry into the war and promoted the image of President Woodrow Wilson as a peacemaker.

Bernays also demonstrated that women could work in the PR profession. His business partner and later wife, Doris Fleischman, collaborated with him on many of his campaigns as a researcher and coauthor. PR later became

▶Edward Bernays and his business partner and wife, Doris Fleischman, creatively influenced public opinion. Bernays worked on behalf of a client, the American Tobacco Company (who owned Lucky Strike and other brands), to make smoking socially acceptable for women. Bettman/ Getty Images; Image Courtesy of The Advertising Archives

one of the few professions accessible to women who chose to work outside the home. Today, women outnumber men by more than three to one in the profession.

The Evolution of Public Relations

As the PR profession evolved, two major types of public relations organizations took shape: PR agencies and in-house PR services. Practitioners in this field began excelling at specific functions, such as researching target audiences and formulating messages conveyed to them.

PR Agencies and In-House PR Services

Over seven thousand U.S. companies identify themselves as public relations agencies today. Many of the largest companies are owned by, or are affiliated with, multinational communications holding companies, such as WPP, Omnicom, and Interpublic (see Table 12.1). For example, three of the largest PR agencies—Burson-Marsteller, Hill + Knowlton, and Ogilvy Public Relations—together generated almost 1.2 billion dollars in PR revenue for their parent corporation, the WPP Group, in 2015. Other PR firms are independent. These companies tend to be smaller than the conglomerate-owned ones and have just local or regional operations. New York and Chicago–based Edelman, the largest independent PR agency, is an exception, boasting global operations and clients around the world.

TABLE 12.1 // THE TOP 10 PUBLIC RELATIONS FIRMS, 2015 (BY WORLDWIDE REVENUE IN MILLIONS OF U.S. DOLLARS)

Rank	Agency	Parent Firm	Headquarters	Revenue
1	Edelman	Independent	Chicago & New York	$847
2	Weber Shandwick	Interpublic	New York	$677
3	Fleishman-Hillard	Omnicom	St. Louis	$587
4	Ketchum	Omnicom	New York	$490
5	MSL Group	Publicis	Paris	$473
6	Burson-Marsteller	WPP	New York	$466
7	Hill + Knowlton Strategies	WPP	New York	$375
8	Ogilvy Public Relations	WPP	New York	$316
9	Brunswick Group	Independent	London	$264
10	BlueDigital	BlueFocus Communication Group	Beijing	$215

Data from: "CRM/Direct and Public Relations," Advertising Age, May 2, 2016, p. 21.

Many corporations, professional organizations, and nonprofit entities retain PR agencies to provide a range of services. Large organizations of all types—particularly in the manufacturing and service industries—often have their own in-house PR staffs as well. These departments handle numerous tasks, such as writing press releases, managing journalists' requests for interviews with company personnel, and staging special events.

▲ World War II was a time when the U.S. government used propaganda, such as Uncle Sam, and other PR strategies to drum up support for the war. David Pollack/Getty Images

A Closer Look at Public Relations Functions

Regardless of whether they work at a PR agency or on staff at an organization's in-house PR department, public relations professionals pay careful attention to the needs of their clients and to the perspectives of their targeted audiences. They provide a multitude of services, including developing publicity campaigns and formulating messages about what their clients are doing in such areas as government relations, community outreach, industry relations, diversity initiatives, and product or service development. Some PR professionals also craft **propaganda**. This is communication that is presented as advertising or publicity and that is intended to gain (or undermine) public support for a special issue, program, or policy—such as a nation's war effort (see "The Digital Turn Case Study: Military PR in the Digital Age" on page 367). In addition, PR practitioners might produce employee newsletters, manage client trade shows and conferences, conduct historical tours, appear on news programs, organize damage control after negative publicity, or analyze complex issues and trends affecting a client's future.

Research: Formulating the Message

Like advertising, PR makes use of mail, telephone, and Internet surveys; focus groups; and social media analytics tools—such as Google Analytics, Klear, Keyhole, and Twitter Analytics—to get a fix on an audience's perceptions of an issue, a policy, a program, or a client's image. This research also helps PR firms focus their campaign messages.

The Digital Turn

Military PR in the Digital Age

Public relations has a long connection with the military and wartime communication. After all, one of the founders of modern public relations, Edward Bernays, got his start developing propaganda promoting U.S. military involvement in World War I. Gaining and keeping public support has long been a key to any military endeavor, and public relations and wartime propaganda have played a major role in shaping public opinion.

But as media technology has changed over the last century, so have the PR efforts of governments looking for support for various wars. By the time the United States invaded Afghanistan and Iraq in 2002 and 2003, convergence had begun to alter the military PR game—in ways that were both positive and negative.

On the positive side, troops and their families now use social media to stay in touch with each other, an important way to boost morale. Some of these messages home have even gone viral, including a 2010 YouTube video of soldiers in Afghanistan blowing off steam by dancing to a Lady Gaga song. Military bloggers also helped connect the home front with the front lines in ways that carried more authenticity than any press release.

On the other hand, some of the posts shared by soldiers on social media have had the opposite effect. From pictures and videos of inappropriate or dishonorable behavior while in uniform (including a January 2012 video of four U.S. Marines urinating on Taliban corpses in Afghanistan) to sites that make crude and threatening posts about female soldiers, the military has struggled for years to come up with a useful and enforceable social media policy. Complicating the task even further are social media sites by former military members or civilians, whom the Department of Defense has no control over or ability to punish.[1]

Still another dimension to converged military public relations is that it's a tool that anyone can use—including our enemies. Terrorist groups have taken advantage of the global reach of the Internet to post videos ranging from propaganda statements to executions. This new reality of waging war after the digital turn was the subject of a 2009 report published by the Strategic Studies Institute of the U.S. Army War College. The report argues that "terrorist attacks ought to be understood as consciously crafted *media events*": "Their true target is not that which is blown up—that item or those people—for that is merely a stage prop. The goal, after all, is to have a psychological effect (to terrorize), and it isn't possible to have such an effect on the dead."[2]

The U.S. military's public relations effort, then, must contend with the way converged and viral media makes its job trickier and more difficult to control. Part of fighting a war in an era of converged media involves recognizing that public perceptions matter—and because of this, images matter. And these images are more accessible and easier to disseminate than ever before.

▶ Web Clip

YouTube.com has an array of videos of soldiers dancing to popular songs. For example, search for 'Telephone Remake' posted by malibumelcher. How might videos like this one affect a viewer's thoughts about war and the military?

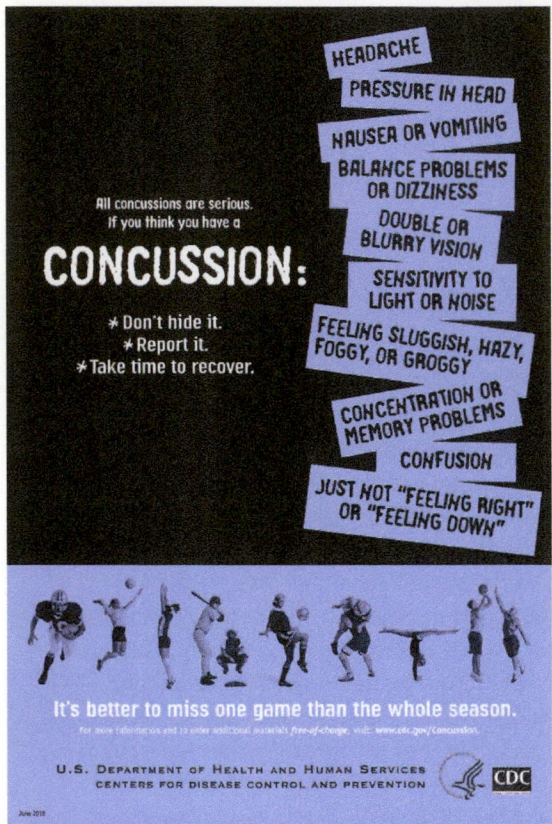

Communication: Conveying the Message

Once a PR group has formulated a message, it conveys that message through a variety of channels. With advances in digital technology, these channels have become predominantly Internet based in recent years. **Press releases**, or news releases, are announcements written in the style of news reports that provide new information about an individual, a company, or an organization, now typically issued via e-mail. In issuing press releases, PR agents hope that journalists will pick up the information and transform it into news reports about the agents' clients.

Since the introduction of portable video equipment in the 1970s, PR agencies and departments have also been issuing **video news releases (VNRs)**— thirty- to ninety-second visual press releases designed to mimic the style of a broadcast news report. Although networks and large TV news stations do not usually broadcast VNRs, news stations in small TV markets regularly use material from these releases, which can also be sent to editors of well-trafficked blogs and other Web sites, or displayed independently online. As with press releases, VNRs give PR firms some control over what constitutes "news" and a chance to influence the public's opinion about an issue, a program, or a policy, although the FCC requires that the source of a VNR be disclosed if video from the VNR is broadcast in a news program.

PR firms can also bring attention to nonprofits by creating **public service announcements (PSAs)**: usually fifteen- to sixty-second audio or video reports that promote government programs, educational projects, volunteer agencies, or social reform.

Public Relations in the Internet Age

Historically, public relations practitioners have tried to earn news media coverage (as opposed to buying advertising) to communicate their clients' messages to the public. Although that is still true, the Internet, with its instant accessibility, offers public relations professionals a number of new routes for communicating with the public.

A company's or an organization's Web site has become the home base of public relations efforts. Companies and organizations can upload and maintain their media kits (including press releases, VNRs, images, executive bios, and organizational profiles), giving the traditional news media access to the information at any time. And because everyone can access these corporate Web sites, the barriers between the organization and the groups that PR professionals ultimately want to reach have been broken down.

The Web also enables PR professionals to have their clients interact with audiences on a more personal, direct basis through social media tools like Facebook, Twitter, YouTube, Instagram, Wikipedia, and blogs. Now people can be "friends" and "followers" of companies and organizations. Corporate executives can share their professional and personal observations and seem downright chummy through a blog (e.g., Whole Foods Market's blog by co-CEO John Mackey). Executives, celebrities, and politicians can seem more accessible and personable through a Twitter feed. But social media's immediacy can also be a problem, especially for those who send messages into the public sphere without considering the ramifications.

Another concern about social media is that sometimes such communications appear without complete disclosure, which is an unethical practice. Some PR firms have edited *Wikipedia* entries for their clients' benefit, a practice *Wikipedia* founder Jimmy Wales has repudiated as a conflict of interest. A growing number of companies also compensate bloggers to subtly promote their products, unbeknownst to most readers. Public relations firms and marketers are particularly keen on working with "mom bloggers," who appear to be an independent voice in discussions about consumer products but may receive gifts in exchange for their opinions. In 2009, the Federal Trade Commission instituted new rules requiring online product endorsers to disclose their connections to companies.

Managing Media Relations

Some PR practitioners specialize in media relations. These specialists promote a client or an organization by securing publicity or favorable coverage in the various news media. In an in-house PR department, media-relations specialists will speak on behalf of their organization or direct reporters to experts inside and outside the company who can provide information about whatever topic the reporter is writing about.

Media-relations specialists may also recommend advertising to their clients when it seems that ads would help focus a complex issue or enhance a client's image. In addition, they cultivate connections with editors, reporters, freelance writers, and broadcast news directors to ensure that their press releases or VNRs are favorably received.

Media Literacy

The NFL's Concussion Crisis

The stylized violence of hard hitting is a favored American football tradition. Broadcasts of games repeat the most violent tackles with instant replay, often using slow motion to enhance the drama of the hit. Over the years, NFL Films has created several video collections featuring hours of player collisions, with titles like *Crunch Course*, *Moment of Impact*, and *NFL's Hardest Hits*.

But this celebration of big hits has begun to seem callous and cruel as decades of professional football popularity have produced retired players in their thirties, forties, fifties, and older who are experiencing the trauma of brain damage. The diagnosis is CTE, chronic traumatic encephalopathy, which can leave its victims with such problems as hearing loss, memory loss, aggression, depression, and overall dementia. The concussion problem for football players is caused not only by the big concussions that knock them unconscious but also by what researchers call "sub-concussions"—the hits to the head that happen many times during a game and that can number in the hundreds and thousands over the course of a career.

CTE can best be confirmed upon death, when the interior of the brain can be examined to show the buildup of a protein that strangles neurons. Several distraught players suffering the symptoms of CTE have committed suicide. Dave Duerson, who played in the NFL in the 1980s and 1990s, killed himself in 2011 at the age of fifty, leaving a message to his family requesting that his brain be studied for CTE; researchers verified that he indeed had the condition. In 2012, just two years after retiring from the field, NFL star Junior Seau committed suicide at age forty-three; as with Duerson, researchers checked his brain and confirmed that he had CTE.

In the 2013 book *League of Denial: The NFL, Concussions, and the Battle for Truth*, ESPN investigative reporters (and brothers) Mark Fainaru-Wada and Steve Fainaru explain that the NFL spent years responding to the crisis of concussions with dubious public relations tactics: first covering it up, then denying it, then generating its own scientific studies to dispute the independent research. (The book inspired the 2015 movie *Concussion*, starring Will Smith.) The NFL's response mirrors the deceptive tactics used by big tobacco companies for decades to deny smoking's link to cancer.

The NFL has a lot to protect. Its business is a $10 billion industry, and the very nature of the game requires hulking players to knock their heads and bodies into other very large players, often running at full speed.[1] As a result, more than four thousand retired players have sued the NFL to cover their head trauma expenses. These stories have begun to change the country's attitude toward the game. News stories about the effects of football concussions are increasingly common, and youth football league participation has dropped nearly 10 percent in the past two years, as parents have grown scared of the impact of the game on their children's health.

More recently, the NFL has responded by trying to change the conversation, acknowledging a

> ⏵ **Visit LaunchPad** to watch a clip from a video about concussions in the NFL. The clip suggests that the NFL has promoted the violent aspects of football. If this is the case, does the league bear some responsibility for player injuries? Why or why not?

launchpadworks.com

Chicago Tribune/Getty Images.

concussion problem but emphasizing that the game has continuously evolved toward more safety in rules and technology (suggesting, perhaps, that it's just a matter of time before this forward march solves the concussion crisis). Indeed, the NFL hired a public relations counsel to help develop the NFLevolution.com site, which was later renamed PlaySmartPlaySafe.com. The NFL's corporate communications department also courted "mommy bloggers" to promote football as a healthy, safe activity for their children.

Yet as players continue to come forward with fears or diagnoses of CTE, and as long as the game (and business) of football continues to be played this way, the NFL's public relations crisis will likely persist. As Fainaru-Wada and Fainaru write, "There has never been anything like this in the history of sports: a public health crisis that emerged from the playing fields of our twenty-first-century pastime."[2]

APPLYING THE CRITICAL PROCESS

DESCRIPTION   Listen to a National Public Radio interview with sportswriter George Dohrmann about the NFL's attempts to repair its image and interest children in football (search for "NFL Targets Kids in Outreach Campaign" from December 4, 2016). Then do a Google search to see if there has been any discussion in your local media sources about CTE and youth, high school, or college football programs.

ANALYSIS   Did you locate any local articles and letters to the editor discussing the risk of CTE related to these local football groups? Are there any patterns in the kinds of arguments being put forward by different sources—for example, local parents, doctors, players, or coaches? Do their arguments seem to echo the NFL's arguments as described in this case study or the Dohrmann interview?

INTERPRETATION   What might these patterns mean? Do certain groups tend to argue particular points more than do other groups? What might be the underlying reason(s) for these patterns?

EVALUATION   Based on what you have read and heard, do the NFL's talking points about CTE appear to have influenced the local discussion/debate about CTE and the safety of football? Although it may be difficult to tell if there is a direct connection—successful PR is often almost invisible or appears to occur naturally in a public debate—similarities in arguments can be noted through observation.

ENGAGEMENT   Write a letter to the editor of a local newspaper describing the results of your investigation. If appropriate, urge caution that some narratives coming from local sources may (even unknowingly) be influenced by PR rather than science.

▶Public relations efforts by governments can be designed to help protect a nation's economy. For example, Brazil launched a massive campaign to both acknowledge the risk of the Zika virus and reassure tourists that they could stay safe—an especially important task given that Brazil was hosting the 2016 Olympic games. Kyodo via AP Images

If a client company has had some negative publicity (for example, one of its products has been shown to be defective or dangerous, or a viral video on the Internet has spread disinformation about the company), media-relations specialists also perform damage control or crisis management (see "Media Literacy Case Study: The NFL's Concussion Crisis" on pages 370–371). In fact, during a crisis, these specialists might be the sole source of information about the situation for the public. How PR professionals perform this part of their job can make or break an organization. The handling of the 2010 BP oil rig explosion and Tylenol tampering deaths in the 1980s offer two contrasting examples.

BP's *Deepwater Horizon* oil rig exploded on April 10, 2010, killing eleven workers. The oil gushed from the ocean floor for months, spreading into a vast area of the Gulf of Mexico and killing wildlife. BP's many public relations missteps included its multiple underestimations of the amount of oil leaking, the chairman's reference to the "small people" of the Gulf region, the CEO's wish that he could "get his life back," and the CEO's attendance at an elite yacht race in England even as the oil leak persisted. BP tried to salvage its reputation by vowing to clean up the damaged areas, establishing a fund to reimburse those economically affected by the spill, and creating a campaign of TV commercials to communicate its efforts. Nevertheless, harsh criticism persisted, and BP's ads were overwhelmed by online parodies and satires of its efforts. In 2016, claims against BP were resolved in a federal court settlement of more than $20 billion, the largest civil penalty for an environmental disaster. Projects to restore the Gulf Coast from Texas to Florida remain in progress.

A decidedly different approach was taken in the 1982 tragedy involving Tylenol pain-relief capsules. Seven people in the Chicago area died after consuming capsules that someone had laced with poison. The parent company, Johnson & Johnson, and its PR representatives discussed whether to pull all Tylenol capsules from store shelves. Some participants in these discussions worried that this move might send the message that corporations could be intimidated by a single deranged person. Nevertheless, Johnson & Johnson's chairman and the company's PR agency, Burson-Marsteller, opted to fully disclose the tragedy to the media and to immediately recall all Tylenol capsules across the nation. The recall cost the company an estimated $100 million and cut its market share in half.

Burson-Marsteller tracked public opinion about the crisis and about its client nightly through telephone surveys. It also organized satellite press conferences to debrief the news media. In addition, it set up emergency phone lines to take calls from consumers and health-care providers who had questions about the crisis. When the company reintroduced Tylenol three months later, it did so with tamper-resistant bottles that almost every major drug manufacturer soon copied. According to Burson-Marsteller, which received PRSA awards for its handling of the crisis, the public thought Johnson & Johnson had responded admirably to the situation and did not hold Tylenol responsible for the deaths.

In fewer than three years, Tylenol had recaptured its dominant share of the market.

Coordinating Special and Pseudo-Events

Another public relations practice involves coordinating *special events* to raise the profile of corporate, organizational, or government clients. Through such events, a corporate sponsor aligns itself with a cause or an organization that has positive stature among the public. For example, John

▼The intense media coverage at awards shows drums up ad revenue for broadcasts and seemingly endless magazine coverage. Can we consider the Oscars or Golden Globes a pseudo-event? Dan MacMedan/ Getty Images

Hancock Financial has been the primary sponsor of the Boston Marathon since 1986 and provides the race's prize money.

In contrast to a special event, a **pseudo-event** is any circumstance created for the sole purpose of gaining coverage in the media. Pseudo-events may take the form of press conferences, TV and radio talk-show appearances, or any other staged activity aimed at drawing public attention and media coverage. Clients and sometimes paid performers participate in these events, and their success is strongly determined by how much media attention the event attracts. For example, during the 1960s, antiwar and Civil Rights activists staged protest events only if news media were assembled.

Fostering Positive Community and Consumer Relations

Another responsibility of PR practitioners is to sustain goodwill between their clients and the public. Many public relations professionals define "the public" as consisting of two distinct audiences: communities and consumers. Thus, they carefully manage relations with both groups.

PR specialists let the public know that their clients are valuable members of the communities in which they operate by designing opportunities for them to demonstrate that they are good citizens. For example, they arrange for client firms to participate in community activities, such as hosting plant tours and open houses, making donations to national and local charities, participating in local parades and festivals, and allowing employees to take part in community fund-raising drives for good causes.

PR strategists also strive to show that their clients care about their customers. For example, a PR campaign might send the message that the business has established product-safety guarantees, or that it will answer all calls and mail from customers promptly. These efforts result in satisfied customers, which translates into repeat business and new business, as customers spread the word about their positive experiences with the organization.

Cultivating Government Relations

PR groups working for or in corporations also cultivate connections with the government agencies that have some say in how companies operate in a particular community, state, or nation. Through such connections, these groups can monitor the regulatory environment and determine new laws' potential implications for the organizations they represent. For example, a new regulation might require companies to provide more comprehensive reporting on their environmental safety practices, which would represent an added responsibility.

Government PR specialists monitor new and existing legislation, look for opportunities to generate favorable publicity, and write press releases and direct-mail letters to inform the public about the pros and cons of new regulations. In many industries, government relations has evolved into **lobbying**: the process of trying to influence lawmakers to support legislation that would serve an organization's or industry's best interests. In seeking favorable legislation, some lobbyists contact government officials on a daily basis. In Washington, D.C., alone, there are more than eleven thousand registered lobbyists, and lobbying expenditures targeting the federal government rose to $3.12 billion in 2016, up from $2.63 billion ten years earlier and $1.57 billion in the year 2000 (see Figure 12.1).[7]

The billions of dollars that lobbyists inject into the political process—treating lawmakers to special events and making campaign contributions in return for legislation that accommodates their clients' interests—is viewed by many as unethical. Another unethical practice is **astroturf lobbying**, which consists of phony grassroots public affairs campaigns engineered by unscrupulous public relations firms. Through this type of lobbying, PR firms deploy blogs, social media campaigns, massive phone banks, and computerized mailing lists to drum up support and create the impression that millions of citizens back their client's side of an issue—even if the number is much lower.

FIGURE 12.1 // TOTAL LOBBYING SPENDING AND NUMBER OF LOBBYISTS* (2000–2016)

Total Lobbying Spending		Number of Lobbyists*	
2000	$1.57 Billion	2000	12,537
2001	$1.64 Billion	2001	11,832
2002	$1.83 Billion	2002	12,114
2003	$2.06 Billion	2003	12,909
2004	$2.19 Billion	2004	13,166
2005	$2.44 Billion	2005	14,072
2006	$2.63 Billion	2006	14,486
2007	$2.87 Billion	2007	14,829
2008	$3.30 Billion	2008	14,171
2009	$3.50 Billion	2009	13,766
2010	$3.52 Billion	2010	12,948
2011	$3.33 Billion	2011	12,627
2012	$3.31 Billion	2012	12,185
2013	$3.24 Billion	2013	12,109
2014	$3.24 Billion	2014	11,800
2015	$3.22 Billion	2015	11,514
2016	$3.12 Billion	2016	11,143

Note: Figures are calculations by the Center for Responsive Politics based on data from the Senate Office of Public Records, accessed February 4, 2017, www.opensecrets.org/lobby.

*The number of unique registered lobbyists who have actively lobbied.

Just as corporations use PR to manage government relations, some governments have used PR to manage their image in the public's mind. For example, following the September 11, 2001, terrorist attacks on the United States, the Saudi Arabian government hired the PR firm Qorvis Communications to help repair its image with American citizens after it was revealed that many of the 9/11 terrorists were from Saudi Arabia.[8]

Tensions between Public Relations and the Press

The relationship between PR and the press has long been antagonistic. This tension has several sources, including the complex interdependence of the two professions as well as the press's skepticism about PR practices. Some of the press's complaints about PR have led public relations practitioners to take steps to enhance their profession's image.

▼ The manipulation of scientific facts by "experts" trying to promote a specific agenda is addressed in a series of books by John Stauber and Sheldon Rampton. *Trust Us, We're Experts! by Sheldon Rampton and John Stauber © 2002*

HOW INDUSTRY MANIPULATES SCIENCE AND GAMBLES WITH YOUR FUTURE

TRUST US, WE'RE EXPERTS!

SHELDON RAMPTON AND JOHN STAUBER

AUTHORS OF TOXIC SLUDGE IS GOOD FOR YOU!

"If you want to know how the world wags, and who's wagging it, here's your answer."—Bill Moyers

Elements of Interdependence

Journalists have historically viewed themselves as independent professionals providing a public service: gathering and delivering the facts about current events to the public. Some have accused PR professionals of distorting the facts to serve their clients' interests. Yet journalists rely heavily on public relations practitioners to provide the information used in creating news reports. Many editors, for instance, admit that more than half of their story ideas each day originate from PR work, such as press releases. In the face of newspaper staff cutbacks and television's growing need to cover local news events, professionals in the news media need PR story ideas more than ever. This doesn't sit comfortably with some journalists.

As another example of the two professions' interdependence, PR firms often raid news media's workforces for new talent. Because most press releases are written in the style of news reports, the PR profession has always sought skilled writers who are well connected to sources and knowledgeable about the news business. But although many reporters move into the PR profession, few public relations practitioners—especially those who started their careers as journalists—move back into journalism.

PR practitioners, for their part, maintain that they make reporters' jobs easier — supplying the kinds of information reporters used to gather themselves. Some members of the news media criticize their own ranks for being lazy. Others, grateful for the help, have hesitated to criticize a particular PR firm's clients — which brings up questions of journalistic ethics.

Journalists' Skepticism about PR Practices

In addition to the uncomfortable interdependence characterizing the journalism and PR professions, several specific complaints about PR from journalists have heightened the tension between the two groups. Specifically, some journalists maintain that PR professionals undermine the facts and block reporters' access to information. Journalism's most prevalent criticism of public relations is that it counters the truths reporters seek to bring to the public by selectively choosing which facts to communicate or by delivering deceptive information. To be sure, outright deception is unethical, and the PR profession has worked to eradicate it in its own ranks. But deciding which facts to present is something that journalists do, too. After all, a reporter cannot say everything about a particular event, so he or she must choose which information to include and which to leave out. Journalists have also accused PR professionals of blocking the press's access to business leaders, political figures, and other newsworthy people. This strategy, reporters explain, attempts to manipulate reporters by giving exclusives to those most likely to write a favorable story, or cutting off a reporter's access to a newsworthy client if the reporter has written unfavorably about that person.

Others dislike the PR field's tendency to present publicity as news, claiming that this practice takes media space and time away from organizations and individuals who do not have the money or sophistication required to attract the public eye. These critics also complain that by presenting client information in a journalistic context, PR gains credibility for its clients that the purchase of advertising does not offer.

The relationship between journalists and PR professionals became even more notably tense as President Donald Trump and his White House staff promoted what they called "alternative facts" and repeatedly called mainstream news organizations "fake news." The Public Relations Society of America issued a statement in early 2017, saying, "PRSA strongly objects to any effort to deliberately misrepresent information. Honest, ethical professionals never spin, mislead or alter facts."[9]

Shaping PR's Image

Questionable PR moves in the past and journalism's hostility toward PR prompted some public relations practitioners to direct their skills toward improving their profession's image. In 1948, the PR industry formed the PRSA, its own professional

LaunchPad
launchpadworks.com

Give and Take: Public Relations and Journalism
This video debates the relationship between public relations and journalism.

Discussion: Are the similarities between public relations and journalism practices a good thing for the public? Why or why not?

TABLE 12.2 // PUBLIC RELATIONS SOCIETY OF AMERICA ETHICS CODE

In 2000, the PRSA approved a completely revised Code of Ethics, which included core principles, guidelines, and examples of improper conduct. Here is one section of the Code.

PRSA MEMBER STATEMENT OF PROFESSIONAL VALUES

This statement presents the core values of PRSA members and, more broadly, of the public relations profession. These values provide the foundation for the Member Code of Ethics and set the industry standard for the professional practice of public relations. These values are the fundamental beliefs that guide our behaviors and decision-making process. We believe our professional values are vital to the integrity of the profession as a whole.

ADVOCACY
We serve the public interest by acting as responsible advocates for those we represent. We provide a voice in the marketplace of ideas, facts, and viewpoints to aid informed public debate.

HONESTY
We adhere to the highest standards of accuracy and truth in advancing the interests of those we represent and in communicating with the public.

EXPERTISE
We acquire and responsibly use specialized knowledge and experience. We advance the profession through continued professional development, research, and education. We build mutual understanding, credibility, and relationships among a wide array of institutions and audiences.

INDEPENDENCE
We provide objective counsel to those we represent. We are accountable for our actions.

LOYALTY
We are faithful to those we represent, while honoring our obligation to serve the public interest.

FAIRNESS
We deal fairly with clients, employers, competitors, peers, vendors, the media, and the general public. We respect all opinions and support the right of free expression.

Data from: The full text of the PRSA Code of Ethics is available at www.prsa.org.

Note: Adherence to the PRSA Code of Ethics is voluntary; there is no enforcement mechanism.

organization. The PRSA functions as an internal watchdog group that accredits PR agents and firms, maintains a code of ethics, and probes its own practices, especially those pertaining to its influence on the news media. In addition to the PRSA, independent organizations devoted to uncovering shady or unethical public relations activities publish their findings in periodicals like *PR Week* and *PR Watch*. In particular, the Center for Media and Democracy's *PR Watch* seeks to serve the public by discussing and investigating PR practices. Indeed, ethical issues have become a major focus of the PR profession (see Table 12.2).

PR practitioners have also begun using different language — such as *strategic communication, institutional relations, corporate communications, crisis communications,* and *news and information services* — to describe

◀ Leslie Ryan (left) and John Wentworth (right) were vice president and executive vice president, respectively, for the communications department of CBS Television Distribution until Wentworth retired in 2017. (Ryan remains with CBS.) In these roles, they essentially work as big-name publicists whose "clients" include syndicated television shows like *Jeopardy!*, *Entertainment Tonight*, and *Judge Judy.* Alexander Tamargo/Getty Images

what they do. Their hope is that the new language will signal a more ethically responsible industry. Public relations' best strategy, however, may be to point out the shortcomings of the journalism profession itself. Journalism organizations only occasionally examine their own practices, and journalists have their own vulnerability to manipulation by public relations. Thus, by not publicly revealing PR's strategies to influence their news stories, many journalists have allowed PR professionals to interpret "facts" to their clients' advantage.

Public Relations in a Democratic Society

PR's most significant impact on our democracy may be its involvement in the political process, especially when organizations hire public relations specialists to favorably shape or reshape a candidate's image. As with military propaganda (see also "The Digital Turn Case Study: Military PR in the Digital Age" on page 367), the history of modern public relations goes hand in hand with political campaigns. In fact, Edward Bernays, who literally wrote the book on propaganda in 1928, is believed to have staged the first presidential publicity stunt: a pancake breakfast for Calvin Coolidge with vaudevillian performers.

The need to handle a candidate's image has become increasingly important, as technology has allowed images of the candidates to be broadcast into America's living rooms. In 1952, President Dwight D. Eisenhower became the first presidential candidate to hire a marketing agency to produce his "Eisenhower Answers America" television commercials, whereas President

John F. Kennedy set the bar for future presidential candidates with his ease and charisma on-screen.[10]

By the end of the twentieth century, no president or major presidential candidate could exist without an immense PR effort. Sometimes that effort takes the shape of a well-crafted traditional PR push, as with the presidential campaign run by David Axelrod in 2008 that put Barack Obama in the White House. Other times, as in the case of Donald Trump's successful 2016 presidential campaign, it involves leveraging social media and a larger-than-life media personality into billions of dollars' worth of media coverage. Trump's social media tool of choice is his Twitter account, which he and his PR team used to obtain publicity and influence the stories that were covered by the news media throughout the campaign.

Political public relations efforts don't end after an election, however. PR is in play when candidates take office, govern, or participate in or react to political movements — like the Tea Party or Occupy Wall Street. Many journalism outlets cover the news in permanent twenty-four-hour cycles, so PR agencies must stay involved with political, social, and media processes.

In addition, as discussed earlier in the chapter, the role of public relations efforts and lobbying is about more than presidential candidates and other politicians. From railroad companies looking for money from federal, state, and local governments to the explosion in the lobbying profession (see Figure 12.1 on page 375), outside groups wanting to influence the government's actions have an enormous and not always easy-to-understand impact on how our democracy functions.

Though public relations often provides political information and story ideas, the PR profession bears only part of the responsibility for "spun" news; after all, it is the job of a PR agency to get favorable news coverage for the individual or group it represents. PR professionals to some extent police their own ranks for unethical or irresponsible practices, but the news media should also monitor the public relations industry, as they do other government and business activities. Journalism also needs to be more conscious of how its own practices play into the hands of spin strategies. As a positive example of change on this front, many major newspapers and TV networks now offer regular assessments of the facts and falsehoods contained in political advertising. This media vigilance should be on behalf of citizens, who are entitled to robust, well-rounded debates on important social and political issues.

Like advertising and other forms of commercial speech, PR campaigns that result in free media exposure raise a number of questions regarding democracy and the expression of ideas. Large companies and PR agencies, like well-financed politicians, have money to invest in figuring out how to obtain favorable publicity. The question is not how to prevent that but how to ensure that other voices — those less well financed and less commercial — also receive an adequate hearing. To that end, journalists need to become less willing conduits in the distribution of publicity. PR agencies, for their part, need to show clients that participating as responsible citizens in the democratic process can serve them well and enhance their image. But in the end, all citizens bear the responsibility of understanding that the public relations industry surrounds us, regardless of what sides of issues we favor. It is a part of the media experience and, as such, part of our daily lives. Therefore, media literacy must also include awareness and knowledge of PR and all the ways it can affect us.

CHAPTER ESSENTIALS

Review

- **Public relations** refers to the total communication strategy conducted by a person, a government, or an organization attempting to reach and persuade its audience to adopt a point of view. The first PR practitioners in the 1800s were **press agents**, who focused on **publicity**.

- In the early days of press agents, some of the tactics used were deceptive. Agents bribed journalists to write favorable stories and engaged in **deadheading**, or giving reporters free rail passes.

- Big companies began using **lobbyists**, professionals who seek to influence lawmakers' votes—a practice which continues to this day.

- By the early 1900s, journalists began investigating some of the questionable PR practices being used, precipitating the professionalization of public relations. This effort was spearheaded by PR pioneers Ivy Ledbetter Lee and Edward Bernays.

- As the PR profession grew, two major types of public relations organizations took shape: PR agencies and in-house PR services.

- Many large PR agencies are owned by or affiliated with multinational holding companies, such as WPP, Omnicom, and Interpublic. Other firms are independent, such as Edelman.

- Both PR agencies and in-house services have many functions. They sometimes craft **propaganda**, and they research, formulate, and issue messages on behalf of clients, often via **press releases**, **video news releases (VNRs)**, or **public service announcements (PSAs)**.

- Some PR practitioners manage media relations, which includes responding to negative images or crisis situations. PR agents may also coordinate special and staged **pseudo-events** in an effort to raise the profile of corporate, organizational, or business clients.

- PR practitioners foster positive community and consumer relations and cultivate government relations, which is sometimes accomplished via **lobbying**. **Astroturf lobbying** is a kind of lobbying that consists of phony grassroots public affairs campaigns engineered by unscrupulous PR firms.

- The tense relationship between PR and the press consists of a complex interdependence of the two professions as well as journalists' skepticism about PR practices. PR practitioners maintain that they make journalists' jobs easier by supplying information, whereas journalists argue that PR agents selectively choose which facts to bring forward.

- The industry formed its own professional organization (the Public Relations Society of America) in 1948, which functions as a watchdog group.

- PR's impact on the political process is significant, as many organizations hire public relations specialists to shape or reshape a candidate's image.

- The fact that most affluent people and corporations can afford the most media exposure through PR raises questions about whether this restricts the expression of ideas from other, less affluent sources.

Study Questions

1. Who were the individuals who conducted the earliest type of public relations in the nineteenth century? How did they contribute to the development of modern public relations in the twentieth century?

2. What are the two organizational structures for a PR firm? What are some of the ways these structures conduct business for their clients?

3. Explain the antagonism between journalism and public relations. Can and should the often hostile relationship between the two be mended? Why or why not?

4. In what ways does the profession of public relations serve the process of election campaigns? In what ways can it impede such campaigns?

Key Terms

public relations, p. 359
press agents, p. 360
publicity, p. 360
deadheading, p. 361
lobbyists, p. 361
propaganda, p. 366
press releases, p. 368
video news releases
   (VNRs), p. 368

public service
   announcements (PSAs),
   p. 368
pseudo-event, p. 374
lobbying, p. 374
astroturf lobbying, p. 375

13
Legal Controls and Freedom of Expression

"You've seen what happened in Paris, and Nice. All over Europe, it's happening," President Donald Trump told an audience of military leaders about two weeks after taking office. "It's gotten to the point where it's not even being reported. And in many cases the very, very dishonest press doesn't want to report it."[1]

The "it" to which Trump was referring was terrorist attacks, which he said the media had been covering up in an attempt to undermine his recent executive order restricting people from seven predominantly Muslim countries from entering the United States. A few days later, when the White House issued a longer list of terrorist events it claimed had been ignored or insufficiently covered, news organizations quickly responded with a flood of evidence from their very public, very accessible archives to demonstrate that the opposite was true: They had covered many terrorist attacks extensively.

The terrorism cover-up accusation was just one of many attacks that the new president launched against the media during his first weeks in office. He accused them of lying about the size of his inauguration crowd when they disputed inflated attendance estimates.[2] He called their reports

◀ Demonstrators supported media outlets like the *New York Times* in the face of a series of attacks on press freedoms by President Donald Trump and his administration. KENA BETANCUR/Getty Images

of Russian attempts to compromise him "fake news."[3] And Trump counselor Kellyanne Conway blamed the media for ignoring a "massacre" in Bowling Green, Kentucky, which had never happened.[4] By the start of Trump's second month in office, his administration was also banning news organizations—such as the *New York Times*, CNN, and the BBC—from press briefings and saying he was going to rewrite the laws for libel.[5]

Presidents have long had a complicated, sometimes contentious relationship with the journalists who cover them. After all, journalists uncovered Richard Nixon's wrongdoing during Watergate, which ultimately caused him to resign the presidency. But according to a number of media critics, the Trump administration's adversarial relationship with the media has gone beyond the "normal" tensions inherent in the office. In fact, some observers view the accusations levied at the media as an attempt to build up resentment toward journalists in order to attack their First Amendment protections—protections written into the Constitution for the express purpose of holding powerful people (including the president) accountable. According to the First Amendment, adopted in 1791, "Congress shall make no law . . . abridging the freedom of speech, or of the press."

News operations, journalism organizations, and First Amendment watchdogs responded to Trump's attacks, pushing back against a president who called the news media "the enemy of the American people."[6] England-based wire service Reuters, in an open memo to its reporters, issued a call to continue investigative reporting in America during Trump's administration.[7] Radio Television Digital News Association (RTDNA) executive director Mike Cavender issued a statement after Trump ordered multiple federal agencies to stop sharing press releases and other content with the public: "RTDNA decries this latest attempt by President Trump to control what we know and when we know it. It is anathema to the freedom of information and the First Amendment rights that America, until now anyway, has been respected for throughout the world."[8]

Statements about the importance of press freedom did not just come from media organizations. Former Republican president George W. Bush—himself no stranger to dust-ups with the news media—spoke on the topic in late February 2017: "I consider the media to be indispensable to democracy. . . . Power can be very addictive and it can be corrosive and it's important for the media to call to account people who abuse their power, whether it be here or elsewhere."[9]

Given the relationship between the news media and those who hold power in government, we must ask ourselves a key question: What can be done to protect the freedom of the press and other freedoms promised under the First Amendment?

DEBATES OVER WHAT CONSTITUTES "freedom of the press" and "free speech" (or "free expression") have intensified as technological advances like Twitter have enabled easy creation of new types of media content, allowed politicians to bypass journalists, and revolutionized the speed and method by which people share information—and misinformation.

New debates have also arisen over how the First Amendment should function in a political system awash in money. For example, in 2010, the U.S. Supreme Court decision in *Citizens United v. Federal Election Commission* removed many of the limits on how much groups can donate to political candidates, with the majority opinion of the court essentially upholding the idea that political contributions are a form of free speech. Critics say that rather than protecting free speech, the court decision sold out the democratic process and reinforced an existing oligarchic tendency in government—that is, that the most wealthy and powerful have controlling influence.

In this chapter, we examine these and other key First Amendment issues in more detail by:

- **exploring the origins of free expression and a free press, taking a closer look at the First Amendment to the U.S. Constitution, identifying four models of free expression, tracing the evolution of censorship, examining five forms of unprotected expression, and comparing the First Amendment with the Sixth Amendment**

- **shining a spotlight on film and its relationship with the First Amendment by taking a look at the social and political pressures that affected moviemaking in its early days, self-regulation in the film industry, and the emergence of the film rating system**

- **taking stock of free expression in the broadcast and online media, including examining the Federal Communications Commission (FCC) regulation of broadcasting, definitions and regulation of indecent speech, laws governing political broadcasts, the impact of the Fairness Doctrine, and communication policy regarding the Internet**

- **considering the First Amendment's role in our democracy today, including such questions as who (journalists? citizens? both?) should fulfill the civic role of watchdog**

The Origins of Free Expression and a Free Press

In the United States, freedom of speech and freedom of the press are protected by the First Amendment in the Bill of Rights, developed for our nation's Constitution. Roughly interpreted, these freedoms suggest that anyone should be able to express his or her views, and that the press should be able to publish whatever it wants, without prohibition from Congress. But there's always been a tension between the notion of "free expression" and the idea that some expression (such as sexually explicit words or images) should be prohibited or censored. Many people have wondered what free expression really means.

In this section, we examine several aspects of free speech and freedom of the press. We explore the roots of the First Amendment and different interpretations of *free expression* that have arisen in modern times. We look at evolving notions of censorship and forms of expression that are not protected by the U.S. Constitution. And we consider ways in which the First Amendment has clashed with the Sixth Amendment, which guarantees accused individuals the right to speedy and public trials by impartial juries.

A Closer Look at the First Amendment

To understand how the idea of free expression has developed in the United States, we must understand how the notion of a free press came about. The story goes back to the 1600s, when various national governments in Europe controlled the circulation of ideas through the press by requiring printers to obtain licenses from them. Their goal was to monitor the ideas published by editors and writers and swiftly suppress subversion. However, in 1644, English poet John Milton published his essay *Areopagitica*, which opposed government licenses for printers and defended a free press. Milton argued that in a democratic society, all sorts of ideas—even false ones—should be allowed to circulate. Eventually, he maintained, the truth would emerge. In 1695, England stopped licensing newspapers, and most of Europe followed suit. In many democracies today, publishing a newspaper, magazine, or newsletter requires no license.

Less than a hundred years later, the writers of the U.S. Constitution were ambivalent about the idea of a free press. Indeed, the version of the Constitution ratified in 1788 did not include such protection. The states took a different tack, however. At that time, nine of the original thirteen states had charters defending freedom of the press. These states pushed to have federal guarantees of free speech and the press approved at the first session of the new Congress. Their efforts paid off: The Bill of Rights, which contained the first ten amendments to the Constitution, won ratification in 1791.

However, commitment to freedom of the press was not yet tested. In 1798, the Federalist Party, which controlled the presidency and the Congress, passed the Sedition Act to silence opposition to an anticipated war against France. The act was signed into law by President John Adams and resulted in the arrest and conviction of several publishers. However, after failing to curb opposition, the Sedition Act expired in 1801, during Thomas Jefferson's presidency. Jefferson, a Democratic-Republican who had challenged the act's constitutionality, pardoned all defendants convicted under it.[10] Ironically, the Sedition Act—the first major attempt to constrain the First Amendment—ended up solidifying American support behind the notion of a free press.

Interpretations of Free Expression

Americans are not alone in debating what constitutes free expression and whether constraining expression is ever appropriate. In the middle of the twentieth century, mass communication researchers living in the midst of the Cold War created four models to describe the different approaches to "free expression."[11] We can think of these as the authoritarian, state, libertarian, and social responsibility models. These models are distinguished by the degree of freedom their proponents advocate, and by the ruling classes' attitudes toward the freedoms granted to average citizens.

The Authoritarian Model

The **authoritarian model** is a form of government characterized by an elite ruling class that curtails the political and press freedoms of the general public. It developed around the time the printing press first arrived in sixteenth-century England. Under this model, criticism of government and public dissent are not tolerated, especially if such speech undermines "the common good"—an ideal defined by elites and rulers. The government actively censors, threatens, or bureaucratically oppresses media outlets it considers oppositional, and rewards those media outlets aligned with its political objectives. Today, this model exists in countries like Russia, Hungary, and Turkey, and many developing countries where journalism's job is deemed to support government and business efforts to foster economic growth, minimize political dissent, promote social stability, and keep the current regime in power.

▲ John Milton's *Areopagitica* is one of the most significant early defenses of freedom of the press. Print Collector/Getty Images

▲ Government control of the press under the state model has led to protests like that of this Burmese monk and others like him.

The State Model

In the authoritarian model, the news is controlled by private enterprise. Under the **state model**, the government controls the press and what it reports. Leaders believe that the press should serve the goals of the state. Although the government tolerates some criticism, it suppresses ideas that challenge the basic premises of state authority. Today, a few countries use this model, including Myanmar (Burma), China, Cuba, and North Korea.

The Libertarian Model

The **libertarian model** is the flip side of both the state and the authoritarian models. This model encourages vigorous criticism of government and supports the highest degree of individual and press freedoms. Proponents of the libertarian model argue that *no* restrictions should be placed on the mass media or on individual speech. In North America and Europe, many alternative newspapers and magazines operate on such a model. They often emphasize the importance of securing rights for sidelined populations and follow an ethic that absolute freedom of expression is the best way to fight injustice and arrive at the truth.

The Social Responsibility Model

The **social responsibility model** captures the ideals of mainstream journalism in the United States and most other democracies. The concepts and assumptions behind this model were outlined in 1947 by the Hutchins Commission, which was formed to examine the press's increasing influence. The commission's report called for the development of press watchdog groups, on the assumption that the mass media had grown too powerful. The report also concluded that the press needed to take more responsibility for improving American society by providing such services as news forums for the exchange of ideas and better coverage of social groups and the complete range of economic classes.

The social responsibility model has roots in revolutionary Europe. This model calls for the press to be privately owned, so that newspapers operate independently of government. By doing so, the press functions as a **Fourth Estate**—an unofficial branch of government that watches for abuses of power by the legislative, judicial, and executive branches. The press supplies information about such abuses to citizens so that they can make informed decisions about political and social issues.

The Evolution of Censorship

In the United States, the First Amendment theoretically prohibits censorship. Over time, Supreme Court decisions have defined censorship as **prior restraint**—meaning that courts and governments cannot block any publication or speech before it actually occurs. The principle behind prior restraint is that a law has not been broken until an illegal act has been committed. However, the Court left open the idea that the judiciary could halt publication of news in exceptional cases—for example, if such publication would threaten national security. In the 1970s, two pivotal court decisions tested the idea of prior restraint.

▲ In 1971, Daniel Ellsberg, a former Pentagon researcher, turned against America's military policy in Vietnam and leaked information to the press. The federal case against him was dropped in 1973 when illegal government-sponsored wiretaps of Ellsberg's psychoanalyst came to light during the Watergate scandal. Bettmann/Getty Images

The Pentagon Papers Decision

In 1971, with the Vietnam War still raging, Daniel Ellsberg, a former Defense Department employee, stole a copy of the forty-seven-volume report "History of U.S. Decision-Making Process on Vietnam Policy." A thorough study of U.S. involvement in Vietnam since World War II, the report was classified by the government as top secret. Ellsberg and a friend leaked the report—nicknamed the Pentagon Papers—to the *New York Times* and the *Washington Post*. In June 1971, the *Times* began publishing excerpts of the report. To block any further publication, the Nixon administration applied for and received a federal court injunction against the *Times* to halt publication of the documents, arguing that it posed "a clear and present danger" to national security by revealing military strategy to the enemy.

In a 6–3 vote, the Supreme Court sided with the newspaper. Justice Hugo Black, in his majority opinion, attacked the government's attempt to suppress publication: "Both the history and language of the First Amendment support the view that the press must be left free to publish news, whatever the source, without censorship, injunctions, or prior restraints."[12] The Pentagon Papers case came back into discussion more recently with the government leak cases of Edward Snowden and Chelsea Manning, both of whom Ellsberg publicly defended.[13]

The Progressive Magazine Decision

The conflict between prior restraint and national security resurfaced in 1979, when the U.S. government issued an injunction to block publication of the *Progressive*, a national left-wing magazine. The editors had planned to publish an article titled "The H-Bomb Secret: How We Got It, Why We're Telling It." The dispute began when the magazine's editor sent a draft to the Department of Energy to verify technical portions of the article. Believing that the article contained sensitive data that might damage U.S. efforts to halt the proliferation of nuclear weapons, the department asked the magazine not to publish it. When the magazine said it would proceed anyway, the government sued the *Progressive* and asked a federal district court to block publication.

In an unprecedented action, Justice Robert Warren sided with the government, deciding that "a mistake in ruling against the United States could pave the way for thermonuclear annihilation for us all. In that event, our right to life is extinguished and the right to publish becomes moot."[14] Warren was seeking to balance the *Progressive*'s First Amendment rights against the possibility that the article, if published, would spread dangerous information and undermine national security. During appeals, several other publications printed their own stories about the H-bomb, and the U.S. government eventually dropped the case. None of the articles, including one ultimately published by the *Progressive*, contained precise details on how to design a nuclear weapon. But Warren's decision represented the first time in American history that a prior-restraint order imposed in the name of national security stopped initial publication of a news report.

Unprotected Forms of Expression

Despite the First Amendment's provision that "Congress shall make no law" restricting speech and the press, the federal government, state laws, and even local ordinances have on occasion curbed some forms of expression. And over the years, the U.S. court system has determined that some kinds of expression do not merit protection under the Constitution. These forms include sedition, copyright infringement, libel, obscenity, and violation of privacy rights.

Sedition

For more than a century after the Sedition Act of 1798, Congress passed no laws prohibiting the articulation or publication of dissenting opinions. But sentiments that fueled the Sedition Act resurfaced in the twentieth century, particularly in times of war. For instance, the Espionage Acts of 1917 and 1918 — enforced during the two world wars — made it a federal crime to utter or publish "seditious" statements, defined as anything expressing opposition to the U.S. war effort.

For example, in the landmark *Schenck v. United States* (1919) appeal case, taking place during World War I, the Supreme Court upheld the conviction of a Socialist Party leader, Charles T. Schenck, for distributing leaflets urging American men to protest the draft. Justices argued that Schenck had violated the recently passed Espionage Act.

In supporting Schenck's sentence—a ten-year prison term—Justice Oliver Wendell Holmes noted that the Socialist leaflets were entitled to First Amendment protection, but only during times of peace. In establishing the "clear and present danger" criterion for expression, the Supreme Court demonstrated the limits of the First Amendment.

Copyright Infringement

Appropriating a writer's or an artist's words, images, or music without consent or payment is also a form of expression not protected by the First Amendment. A **copyright** legally protects the rights of authors and producers to their published or unpublished writing, music, lyrics, TV programs, movies, or graphic art designs. Congress passed the first Copyright Act in 1790, which gave authors the right to control their published works for fourteen years, with the opportunity to renew copyright protection for another fourteen years. After the end of the copyright period, the work would enter the **public domain**, which would give the public free access to the work. (For example, a publisher could reprint a written work that had entered the public domain.) The idea was that a period of copyright control would give authors financial incentive to create original works, and that moving works into the public domain would give others incentive to create works derived from earlier accomplishments.

But in time, artists, as they began to live longer, and corporations, which could also hold copyrights, wanted to prolong the period in which they could profit from creative works. In 1976, Congress extended the copyright period to the life of the author plus fifty years (seventy-five years for a corporate copyright owner). In 1998, as copyrights on works such as Disney's

▼ In a 1994 landmark case, the Supreme Court ruled that the rap group 2 Live Crew's 1989 song "Pretty Woman" was a legitimate parody of the 1964 Roy Orbison song and was thus covered by the fair-use exception to copyright. Janette Beckman/Getty Images

Mickey Mouse were set to expire, Congress again extended the copyright period for an additional twenty years.

Today, nearly every innovation in digital culture creates new questions about copyright law. For example, is a video remix that samples copyrighted sounds and images a copyright violation or a creative accomplishment protected under the concept of *fair use* (the same standard that enables students to legally quote attributed text in their research papers)? One of the laws that tips the debates toward stricter enforcement of copyright is the Digital Millennium Copyright Act of 1998, which outlaws technology or actions that circumvent copyright systems. In other words, it may be illegal merely to create or distribute technology that enables someone to make illegal copies of digital content, such as a movie DVD.

Libel

The biggest legal worry haunting editors and publishers today is the possibility of being sued for libel, a form of expression that, unlike political speech, is not protected under the First Amendment. **Libel** is defamation of someone's character in written or broadcast form. It differs from **slander**, which is spoken defamation. Inherited from British common law, libel is generally defined as a false statement that holds a person up to public ridicule, contempt, or hatred, or that injures a person's business or livelihood. Examples of potentially libelous statements include falsely accusing someone of professional incompetence (such as medical malpractice), falsely accusing a person of a crime (such as drug dealing), falsely stating that someone is mentally ill or engages in unacceptable behavior (such as public drunkenness), and falsely accusing a person of associating with a disreputable organization or cause (such as being a member of the Mafia or a neo-Nazi military group).

Since 1964, *New York Times v. Sullivan* has served as the standard for libel law. The case stems from a 1960 full-page advertisement placed in the *New York Times* by the Committee to Defend Martin Luther King and the Struggle for Freedom in the South. Without naming names, the ad criticized the law-enforcement tactics used in southern cities to break up Civil Rights demonstrations. The city commissioner of Montgomery, Alabama, L. B. Sullivan, sued the *Times* for libel, claiming the ad defamed him indirectly. Alabama civil courts awarded Sullivan $500,000, but the *Times*' lawyers appealed to the Supreme Court. The Court reversed the ruling, holding that Alabama libel law violated the *Times*' First Amendment rights.[15]

Private individuals (such as city sanitation employees, undercover police informants, or nurses) must prove three things to win a libel case: (1) that the public statement about them was false; (2) that damages or actual injury occurred (such as loss of a job or mental anguish); and (3) that the publisher or broadcaster was negligent in failing to determine the truthfulness of the statement.

In the *Sullivan* case, the Supreme Court asked future civil courts to distinguish whether plaintiffs in libel cases are "public officials" or "private individuals." To win libel cases, the Court said, public officials (such as movie or sports stars, political leaders, or lawyers defending a prominent client) are held to a tougher standard and must prove falsehood, damages, negligence, and **actual malice** on the part of the news media. *Actual malice* means that the reporter or editor either knew the statement was false and printed or broadcast it anyway, or acted with a reckless disregard for the truth. Because actual malice against a public official is hard to prove, it is difficult for public figures to win libel suits.

Historically, the best defense against libel in American courts has been the truth. In most cases, if libel defendants can demonstrate that they printed or broadcast true statements, plaintiffs will not recover any damages—even if their reputations were harmed. There are other defenses against libel as well. For example, prosecutors (who would otherwise be vulnerable to accusations of libel) are granted *absolute privilege* in a court of law, so they can freely make accusatory statements toward defendants—a key part of their job. Reporters who print or broadcast statements made in court are also protected against libel.

▲ Melania Trump sued British tabloid the *Daily Mail* for libel in September 2016 over reports (since retracted) that she worked as an escort in the 1990s, stating that her damages amounted to $150 million. (Libel law standards for public figures are easier to apply in the United Kingdom.) She also threatened to sue *People* magazine.
D Dipasupil/Getty Images

Another defense against libel is the rule of **opinion and fair comment**, the notion that libel consists of *intentional* misstatements of factual information, not expressions of opinion. However, the line between fact and opinion is often blurry. For instance, one of the most famous tests of opinion and fair comment came with a case pitting conservative minister and political activist Jerry Falwell against Larry Flynt, publisher of *Hustler*, a pornographic magazine.

The case developed after a spoof ad in the November 1983 issue of *Hustler* suggested that Falwell had had sex with his mother. Falwell sued for libel, demanding $45 million in damages. The jury rejected the libel suit but found that Flynt had intentionally caused Falwell emotional distress—and awarded Falwell $200,000. Flynt's lawyers appealed, and the U.S. Supreme Court overturned the verdict in 1988, explaining that the magazine was entitled to constitutional protection.

Libel laws also protect satire, comedy, and opinions expressed in reviews of books, plays, movies, and restaurants. However, such laws do not protect malicious statements in which plaintiffs can prove that defendants used their free-speech rights to mount an uncalled-for, damaging personal attack.

Obscenity

For most of this nation's history, legislators have argued that **obscenity** is not a form of expression protected by the First Amendment. However, experts have not been able to agree on what constitutes an obscene work, especially as definitions of obscenity have changed over the years. For example, during the 1930s, novels (such as James Joyce's *Ulysses*) were judged obscene if they contained "four-letter words."

The current legal definition of *obscenity*, derived from the 1973 *Miller v. California* case, states that obscene materials meet three criteria: (1) the average person, applying contemporary community standards, finds that the material as a whole appeals to prurient interest (that is, incites lust); (2) the material depicts or describes sexual conduct in a patently offensive way; and (3) the material as a whole lacks serious literary, artistic, political, or scientific value. The *Miller* decision acknowledged that different communities and regions of the country have different standards with which to judge obscenity. It also required that a work be judged *as a whole*. This was designed to keep publishers from simply inserting a political essay or literary poem into pornographic materials to demonstrate that their publication contained redeeming features.

Since the *Miller* decision, major prosecutions of obscenity have been rare (most have been aimed at child pornography), and most battles now concern the Internet, for which the concept of community standards has been eclipsed by the medium's global reach. A new complication in defining pornography has emerged with cases of "sexting," in which minors produce and send sexually graphic images of themselves via cell phones or the Internet (see "The Digital Turn Case Study: Is 'Sexting' Pornography?" on page 397).

The Digital Turn

Is "Sexting" Pornography?

According to U.S. federal and state laws, when someone produces, transmits, or possesses images with graphic sexual depictions of minors, it is considered child pornography. Digital media have made the circulation of child pornography even more pervasive, according to a 2006 study on child pornography on the Internet. About one thousand people are arrested each year in the United States for child pornography, and according to a U.S. Department of Justice guide for police, they have few distinguishing characteristics other than being "likely to be white, male, and between the ages of 26 and 40."[1]

Now a social practice made quick and easy by the technology of the digital turn has challenged the common wisdom of what is obscenity and who are child pornographers: What happens when the people who produce, transmit, and possess images with graphic sexual depictions of minors are minors themselves? The practice in question is "sexting," the sending or receiving of sexual images via mobile phone text messages, social media apps like Snapchat, or the Internet. Sexting occupies a gray area of obscenity law—yes, the images are of minors, but they do not fit the intent of child pornography laws, which are designed to stop the exploitation of children by adults.

While such messages are usually meant to be private—something personal between sender and receiver—technology makes it otherwise. And given the endless archives of the Internet, such images never really go away but can be accessed by anyone with enough skills to find them.

Surveys suggest that about one-third of older teenagers have sent or received sexually suggestive nude or nearly nude images via text messaging.[2] Various cases illustrate how young people engaged in sexting have gotten caught up in a legal system designed to punish pedophiles.

In 2008, eighteen-year-old Florida resident Phillip Alpert sent nude images of his sixteen-year-old girlfriend to friends after they got in an argument. Alpert was convicted of child pornography and thus required by Florida law to be registered as a sex offender for the next twenty-five years. In 2009, three Pennsylvania girls took seminude pictures of themselves and sent the photos to three boys. All six minors were charged with child pornography. A judge later halted the charges in the interest of freedom of speech and parental rights. In Cañon City, Colorado, a 2015 texting scandal involving middle and high school students exchanging hundreds of nude photos resulted in student suspensions, a canceled high school football game, and a criminal investigation. Ultimately, the state district attorney did not bring charges against the students involved, but felony charges were a possibility.

Twenty states have responded with new sexting laws, so that teens involved in sexting will generally face misdemeanor charges rather than be subject to the harsher felony laws against child pornography.[3] In the states without such laws, however, charges are often at the discretion of prosecutors and the courts and could be as harsh as a felony crime, with the accompanying fine, jail time, and permanent criminal record. How do you think sexting should be handled by the law?

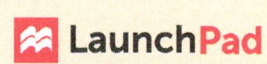

⊙ **Visit LaunchPad** to watch a video clip about sexting. What legal and social consequences did the teenager in this clip face after sharing nude images? Were those consequences fair? Unfair? Why?

launchpadworks.com

Violation of Privacy Rights

Whereas libel laws safeguard a person's character and reputation, the right to privacy protects an individual's peace of mind and personal feelings. In the simplest terms, the **right to privacy** addresses a person's right to be left alone, without his or her name, image, or daily activities becoming public property. The most common forms of privacy invasion are unauthorized tape recording, photographing, or wiretapping of someone; making someone's personal records, such as health and phone records, available to the public; disclosing personal information, such as religious or sexual activities; and appropriating (without authorization) someone's image or name for advertising or other commercial purposes.

In general, the news media have been granted wide protections under the First Amendment to do their work, even if it approaches or constitutes violation of privacy. For instance, journalists can typically use the names and pictures of private individuals and public figures without their consent in their news stories. Still, many local municipalities and states have passed "anti-paparazzi" laws protecting public individuals from unwarranted scrutiny and surveillance on their private property.

In a recent test of the boundaries of privacy for public figures, a Florida jury in 2016 ordered gossip entertainment Web site *Gawker* to pay more than $140 million to Terry G. Bollea, better known as the former professional wrestler Hulk Hogan (see also Chapter 4, page 128). In 2012, *Gawker* posted a brief excerpt of a grainy sex tape that showed Bollea having sex with his best friend's wife. The court decision forced *Gawker* to declare bankruptcy and put itself up for sale. *Gawker* argued that its actions were protected by the First Amendment, and that Bollea was a public figure who had often talked about his sex life in media interviews. But the jury determined that Bollea's privacy had been violated, and it awarded him the huge sum for both emotional and economic distress, and as well as punitive damages.

A number of laws also protect regular citizens' privacy. For example, the Privacy Act of 1974 protects individuals' records from public disclosure unless they give written consent. In some cases, however, private citizens become public figures—for example, rape victims who are covered in the news. In these situations, reporters have been allowed to record these individuals' quotes and use their images without permission.

The Electronic Communications Privacy Act of 1986 extended the law regarding private citizens to include computer-stored data and the Internet, such as employees' e-mails composed and sent through their employer's equipment. However, subsequent court decisions ruled that employees have no privacy rights in electronic communications conducted on their employer's equipment. The USA PATRIOT Act of 2001 further weakened the earlier laws, giving the federal government more latitude in searching private citizens' records and intercepting electronic communications without a court order.

New technology has also created new legal questions. For example, in early 2016, there was a brief but significant standoff between the FBI and Apple over the FBI's getting access to an iPhone. The phone in question was recovered from one of the terrorists in the December 2015 attack in San Bernardino, California. A court ordered Apple to create a software key to allow the FBI to unlock the iPhone. Apple responded that writing such software would make all iPhones subject to FBI scrutiny and could make them more susceptible to other hackers. The day before a court hearing on the matter, the FBI withdrew its case, saying that it had already cracked the code needed to access the iPhone itself. Yet the question remains whether technology companies like Apple should provide customers with the most robust privacy possible or assist law-enforcement agencies in gaining access to their products.

▲ The request by the FBI for Apple's help in hacking iPhones is just one example of privacy and security issues that arise around personal technology. In early 2017, concerns were raised again when U.S. customs agents started asking people to unlock their phones and allow access to their social media accounts as a requirement for entry into the country.   FREDERIC J. BROWN/Getty Images

First Amendment versus Sixth Amendment

First Amendment protections of speech and the press have often clashed with the Sixth Amendment, which guarantees an accused individual in "all criminal prosecutions . . . the right to a speedy and public trial, by an impartial jury." Gag orders, shield laws, and laws governing the use of cameras in a courtroom all put restrictions on speech and other forms of expression for the sake of Sixth Amendment rights.

Gag Orders

In recent criminal cases, some lawyers have used the news media to comment publicly on cases that are pending or in trial. This can make it difficult to assemble an impartial jury, thus threatening individuals' Sixth Amendment rights. In the 1960s, the Supreme Court introduced safeguards for ensuring fair trials in heavily publicized cases. These included placing speech restrictions, or **gag orders**, on lawyers and witnesses. In some countries, courts have issued gag orders to prohibit the press from releasing information or giving commentary that might prejudice jury selection or cause an unfair trial. But in the United States, especially since a Supreme Court review in 1976, gag orders have been struck down as a prior-restraint violation of the First Amendment.

Shield Laws

Shield laws state that reporters do not have to reveal the sources of the information they use in news stories. The news media have argued that protecting sources' confidentiality maintains reporters' credibility, protects sources from possible retaliation, and serves the public interest by providing information

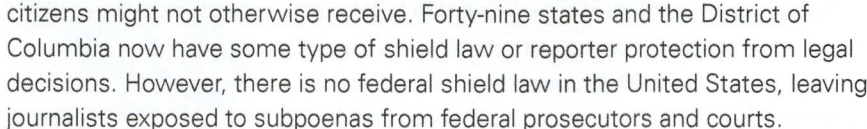
citizens might not otherwise receive. Forty-nine states and the District of Columbia now have some type of shield law or reporter protection from legal decisions. However, there is no federal shield law in the United States, leaving journalists exposed to subpoenas from federal prosecutors and courts.

Laws Governing the Use of Cameras in a Courtroom

Debates over limiting electronic broadcast equipment and photographers in courtrooms date back to the Bruno Hauptmann trial in the mid-1930s. Hauptmann was convicted and executed for the kidnap-murder of the nineteen-month-old son of Anne and Charles Lindbergh (the aviation hero who made the first solo flight across the Atlantic Ocean in 1927). During the trial, Hauptmann and his attorney complained that the circus atmosphere fueled by the presence of radio and flash cameras prejudiced the jury and turned the public against him. After the trial, the American Bar Association amended its professional ethics code, stating that electronic equipment in the courtroom detracted "from the essential dignity of the proceedings." For years after the Hauptmann trial, almost every state banned photographic, radio, and TV equipment from courtrooms.

But as broadcast equipment became more portable and less obtrusive, and as television became the major news source for most Americans, courts gradually reevaluated the bans. In the early 1980s, the Supreme Court ruled that the presence of TV equipment did not make fair trials impossible. The Court then left it up to each state to implement its own system. Today, all states allow television coverage of some cases (some just trial courts, some just appellate courts, some both), though most also allow presiding judges to place certain restrictions on coverage of courtrooms. The state courts are now dealing with questions about the use of other electronic devices, such as smartphones and tablets, and whether or not to allow reporters to tweet or send blog posts live from the courtroom. In some places, the decision about whether to allow

▼ An early 1980s Supreme Court ruling opened the door for the debut of court TV in 1991 and the televised O. J. Simpson trial in 1994 (the most publicized case in history). Vince Bucci/AFP/Getty Images

tweeting and live-blogging is left up to the judge in each particular case.[16] In other circumstances, a judge may sidestep the tweeting problem by simply banning all cell phones and similar electronic devices from the courtroom.[17]

The United States Supreme Court continues to ban TV from its proceedings, although it broke its anti-radio rule in 2000 by permitting delayed broadcasts of the hearings on the Florida vote recount case that determined the winner of the 2000 presidential election.

Film and the First Amendment

Back when the Bill of Rights was ratified, our nation's founders could not have predicted the advent of visual media. Film, which came into existence in the late 1890s, presented new challenges for those seeking to determine whether expression in film should be protected. The First Amendment said nothing explicit about film, so lawmakers, courts, society, and industry began an ongoing struggle over exactly how to apply it. As new communication technologies emerged, so did concerns over the impact of films on the values and morals of the public — especially children. It's useful to understand how these ongoing battles over the limits of free speech have played out over the last century, inasmuch as the model of self-regulation and self-censorship developed in the movie industry is often invoked in discussions of the regulation of video games, the Internet, and similar technologies (see also discussions about regulation in technology-specific chapters).

Citizens and Lawmakers Control the Movies

During the early part of the twentieth century, civic leaders in individual towns and cities formed local *review boards*, which screened movies to determine their moral suitability for the community. By 1920, more than ninety cities in the United States had such boards, which were composed of vice squad officers, politicians, and other citizens. By 1923, twenty-two states had such boards.

Meanwhile, lawmakers seeking to please their constituencies introduced legislation to control films. For example, after African American heavyweight champion Jack Johnson defeated white champion Jim Jeffries in 1910, the federal government outlawed transportation of boxing movies across state lines. The move reflected racist attitudes (a fear of images of a black man defeating a white man) more than a distaste for violent imagery, as legislators pandered to white constituents who saw Johnson as a threat.

The idea of film as free speech took a big hit in 1915, when the Supreme Court decided in

▼ Jack Johnson (1878–1946) was the first black heavyweight boxing champion, from 1908 to 1914. His stunning victory over white champion Jim Jeffries in 1910 resulted in race riots across the country and led to a ban on the interstate transportation of boxing films. Bettmann/Getty Images

the *Mutual v. Ohio* case that films were "a business pure and simple" and thus not protected by the First Amendment. The Court further described the film industry as a circus, a "spectacle" for entertainment with "a special capacity for evil."[18]

The Movie Industry Regulates Itself

In the early 1920s, a series of scandals—including the rape and murder of an aspiring actress at a party thrown by silent-film comedian Fatty Arbuckle—rocked Hollywood and pressured the movie industry to regulate itself before public review boards or the government could force regulations on them (or before audiences were driven away from movie theaters by the scandals). Over the next few decades, the industry set up its own way of policing not only the content of films but also the personal lives of actors, directors, and others involved in the moviemaking process.

The Motion Picture Producers and Distributors of America

In the 1920s, industry leaders hired Will Hays, a former Republican National Committee chair, as president of the Motion Picture Producers and Distributors of America (MPPDA). Under Hays, promising actors or movie extras who had even minor police records were **blacklisted**, meaning they were put on a list of people who would subsequently not be hired by any of the movie studios. Hays also developed a public relations division for the MPPDA, which promptly squelched a national movement to create a federal law censoring movies.

The Motion Picture Production Code

In the early 1930s, the Hays Office established the Motion Picture Production Code. The code stipulated that "no picture shall be produced which will lower the moral standards of those who see it. Hence the sympathy of the audience shall never be thrown to the side of crime, wrong-doing, evil or sin." The code also dictated which phrases, images, and topics producers and directors had to avoid. For example, "excessive and lustful kissing" and "suggestive postures" were not allowed. The code also prohibited negative portrayals of religion or religious figures. Anyone who broke these rules was blacklisted.

Almost every executive in the industry adopted the code, viewing it as better than any regulation that would have come from the government, and it influenced most commercial movies for the next twenty years. And yet the level of self-censorship and control Hays and his organization achieved under this "voluntary" self-censorship and blacklisting was arguably greater than anything the government could have achieved on its own. Not only did it stifle creativity and critique, but it spread with anticommunist hysteria in the mid-twentieth century, when individuals could get blacklisted for the merest suspicion of communist sympathies.

This ideologically based blacklisting, inherently a violation of a citizens First Amendment rights, hit its peak in the 1950s, just as the grip of Hays's motion picture code was about to crumble. In 1952, the Supreme Court decided in *Burstyn v. Wilson* that New York could not ban the Italian film *The Miracle* under state regulations barring "sacrilegious" films. The Court had decided that movies were an important vehicle for public opinion, putting American movies on the same footing as books and newspapers in terms of protection under the First Amendment.

▲ Roberto Rossellini's The *Miracle* (1948), a 40-minute Italian film, is about a peasant woman who mistakenly thinks she has experienced a virgin pregnancy. When it was shown in New York City with two other short films under the group title *The Way of Love,* Catholic groups protested. The attempt to ban the film in New York led to a landmark Supreme Court decision placing movies with books and newspapers in terms of First Amendment protection. Everett Collection, Inc.

The Rating System and Forced Self-Censorship

In the wake of the 1952 *Miracle* case and the demise of the production code, renewed discontent over sexual language and imagery in movies pushed the MPPDA (renamed the Motion Picture Association of America, or MPAA) in the late 1960s to establish a movie-rating system to help concerned viewers avoid offensive material. Eventually, G, PG, R, and X ratings (X isn't used by the MPAA but as a promotional tool by adult filmmakers) emerged as guideposts for films' suitability for various age groups. In 1984, the MPAA added the PG-13 rating to distinguish slightly higher levels of violence or adult themes in movies that might otherwise qualify as PG, and later the NC-17 rating (no children under 17) for films with strong content that aren't deemed pornographic.

Ratings have an important relationship to the ability of a film to make money. An R can sometimes have a negative effect, but an NC-17 in most cases is seen as a kiss of death, not least because several major theater chains refuse to screen films rated NC-17, and many outlets won't run ads for them. Critics have attacked the system for being secretive (in theory, the identities of ratings board members is kept anonymous) and for applying standards arbitrarily and unequally. For example, violence is generally more acceptable than nudity or sexual content, and often similar sex scenes can earn films wildly different ratings, depending on the scene's point of view. Critics say this forces directors and producers to re-edit films in ways that silence the voices of certain groups in order to avoid an NC-17 rating—and probable bankruptcy. This raises important free-speech questions not only for movies but also for the industries that look to the film industry as a model of self-regulation (and self-censorship).

The First Amendment, Broadcasting, and the Internet

As the film industry developed, the lack of clarity regarding the First Amendment's protection of expression in movies prompted the industry to regulate itself. And with the rise of additional new media that our nation's founders could not have envisioned — namely, broadcasting and the Internet — legislators and industry players once again began debating the question of how free these media are under the First Amendment. Different types of protections and levels of regulation developed in broadcast and cyberspace. Whereas film received protections similar to print in the 1952 Supreme Court ruling, broadcast is subject to fewer protections, and the Internet is so new that people are still debating how First Amendment rights might apply to it.

The FCC Regulates Broadcasting

Drawing on the argument that limited broadcast signals constitute a scarce national resource, Congress passed the Communications Act of 1934 (see Chapter 6 on radio). The act mandated that radio broadcasters operate in "the public interest, convenience, or necessity," suggesting that they were not free to air whatever they wanted. Since that time, station owners have challenged the "public interest" statute and argued that because the government is not allowed to dictate newspaper content, it similarly should not be permitted to control licenses or mandate broadcast programming. But the U.S. courts have outlined major differences between broadcast and print, as demonstrated by two precedent-setting cases.

The first case — *Red Lion Broadcasting Co. v. FCC* (1969) — began when WGCB, a small-town radio station in Red Lion, Pennsylvania, refused to give airtime to author Fred Cook. Cook wrote a book criticizing Barry Goldwater, the Republican Party's presidential candidate in 1964. On a syndicated show WGCB aired, a conservative radio preacher and Goldwater fan verbally attacked Cook on the air. Cook asked for response time from the stations that carried the attack. Most complied, but WGCB snubbed him. He appealed to the FCC, which ordered the station to give Cook free time. The station refused, claiming the First Amendment gave it control over its programming content. The Supreme Court sided with the FCC and ordered the station to give Cook airtime, arguing that the public interest — in this case, the airing of differing viewpoints — outweighs a broadcaster's rights.

The second case — *Miami Herald Publishing Co. v. Tornillo* (1974) — centered on the question of whether the newspaper in this case, the *Miami*

Herald, should have been forced to give political candidate Pat Tornillo Jr. space to reply to an editorial opposing his candidacy. In contrast to the *Red Lion* decision, the Supreme Court sided with the paper. The Court argued that forcing a newspaper to give a candidate space violated the paper's First Amendment right to decide what to publish. Clearly, print media had more freedom of expression than did broadcasting.

▲ The current precedent for indecency is based on a complaint about comedian George Carlin's sketch about the "seven dirty words" that could not be aired. © paul liebhardt/Getty Images

Dirty Words, Indecent Speech, and Hefty Fines

Like the Supreme Court's rulings in the *Red Lion* and *Miami Herald* cases, regulators' actions regarding indecency in broadcasting reflected the idea that broadcasters had less freedom of expression than did print media. In theory, communication law says that the government cannot censor (prohibit before the fact) broadcast content. However, the government may punish broadcasters *after* the fact for **indecency**.

Concerns over indecent broadcast programming cropped up in 1937, when the FCC scolded NBC for airing a sketch featuring sultry comedian-actress Mae West. After the sketch, which West peppered with sexual innuendos, the networks banned her from further radio appearances for "indecent" speech. Since then, the FCC has periodically fined or reprimanded stations for indecent programming, especially during times when children might be listening. For example, after an FCC investigation in the 1970s, several stations lost their licenses or were fined for broadcasting *topless radio*, which featured deejays and callers discussing intimate sexual subjects in the afternoon. (Topless radio would reemerge in the 1980s, this time with doctors and therapists, rather than deejays, offering intimate counsel to listeners.)

The current precedent for regulating broadcast indecency stems from a complaint to the FCC that came in 1973. In the middle of the afternoon, WBAI, a nonprofit Pacifica network station in New York, aired George Carlin's famous comedy sketch about the "seven dirty words" that can't be said on TV. A man riding in a car with his fifteen-year-old son heard the program and complained to the FCC, which sent WBAI a letter of reprimand. Although no fine was issued, the station challenged the warning on principle—and won its case in court. The FCC promptly appealed to the Supreme Court. Though no court had legally defined indecency (which remains undefined today), the Supreme Court sided with the FCC in the 1978 *FCC v. Pacifica Foundation* case. The decision upheld the FCC's authority to require broadcasters to air adult programming only at times when children are not likely to be listening. The FCC banned indecent programs from most stations between 6:00 A.M. and 10:00 P.M.

Political Broadcasts and Equal Opportunity

In addition to indecency rules, another law affecting broadcasting but not the print media is **Section 315** of the Communications Act of 1934. This section mandates that during elections, broadcast stations must provide equal opportunities and response time for qualified political candidates. In other words, if broadcasters give or sell time to one candidate, they must give or sell the same opportunity to others. Local broadcasters and networks have fought this law for years, claiming that because no similar rule applies to newspapers or magazines, the law violates their First Amendment right to control content. Many stations decided to avoid political programming entirely, ironically reversing the rule's original intention. The TV networks managed to get the law amended in 1959 to exempt newscasts, press conferences, and other events—such as political debates—that qualify as news. For instance, if a senator running for office appears in a news story, opposing candidates cannot invoke Section 315 and demand free time.

Supporters of the equal opportunity law in broadcasting argue that it enables lesser-known candidates representing views counter to those of the Democratic and Republican parties to add their perspectives to political dialogue. It also gives less-wealthy candidates a more affordable channel than newspaper and magazine ads for getting their message out to the public.

The Demise of the Fairness Doctrine

Considered an important corollary to Section 315, the **Fairness Doctrine** was to controversial issues what Section 315 is to political speech. Initiated in 1949, this FCC rule required stations to air programs about controversial issues affecting their communities and to provide competing points of view during those programs. Broadcasters again protested that the print media did not have similar requirements. And, like before, many stations simply avoided airing controversial issues. The Fairness Doctrine ended with little public debate in 1987 after a federal court ruled that it was merely a regulation, not an extension of Section 315 law. The end of the Fairness Doctrine opened up the floodgates to partisan talk radio, since there was no longer a requirement that stations needed to air competing points of view. Rush Limbaugh, still talk radio's biggest star, took his show nationwide in 1988 (see Chapter 6).

Since 1987, however, support for reviving the Fairness Doctrine has surfaced periodically. Its advocates argue that broadcasting is fundamentally different from—and more pervasive than—print media. Thus, it should be more accountable to the public interest.

Communication Policy and the Internet

Many have looked to the Internet as the one true venue for unlimited free speech under the First Amendment because it is not regulated by the government, is not subject to the Communications Act of 1934, and has done little in terms of self-regulation. The Internet's global expansion is comparable to that of the early days of broadcasting, when economic and technological growth outweighed laws and regulations. At that time, noncommercial experiments by amateurs and engineering students provided a testing ground that commercial interests later exploited for profit.

Public conversations about the Internet have not typically revolved around ownership. Instead, the debates have focused on First Amendment issues, such as civility and pornography. However, as we watch the rapid expansion of the Internet, an important question confronts us: Will the Internet continue to develop as a democratic medium? In late 2010, the FCC created net neutrality rules for wired broadband providers (such as Verizon, Comcast, AT&T, and Charter, who control nearly all broadband access in the United States through DSL and cable modem service), requiring that they provide the same access to all Internet services and content (see Chapter 9, pages 278–279). The FCC's net neutrality rules were rejected by federal courts twice. The courts argued that because the FCC had not defined the Internet as a utility, it could not regulate it in this manner.

However, citizens and entrepreneurs opposed an unregulated system, arguing that the cable and telephone giants have an incentive to rig their services and cause net congestion in order to force customers to pay a premium for higher speed connections. The debate generated a record four million comments to the FCC, the vast majority in favor of net neutrality.[19] In February 2015, the FCC reclassified broadband Internet as a Title II utility and voted to approve net neutrality rules. Although the FCC has said that it does not seek to control broadband prices, the big Internet service providers are still unhappy with the decision to redefine Internet connections as an essential utility to which everyone has access (like electricity or phone service). The new net neutrality rules were upheld by the U.S. Court of Appeals in 2016, enabling the FCC to enforce open Internet standards on wired and mobile networks.

However, the future of net neutrality seems uncertain at best, as President Trump named longtime net neutrality foe Ajit Pai as the new FCC chairperson. By early 2017, Pai was calling the FCC's moves to support net neutrality "a mistake."[20]

▼ In 2015, the FCC reclassified broadband Internet as a Title II utility and approved net neutrality rules. But after Ajit Pai (shown here) became the new FCC chairperson in 2017, he questioned the FCC's position, signaling that future policy changes might be forthcoming. Bill Clark/Getty Images

Media Literacy

CASE STUDY

Fouling the First Amendment: Finding Facts in the Face of Fake News

Shortly after the 2016 election, news and entertainment Web site BuzzFeed released the disturbing results of a study on Facebook traffic: Top fake news stories from fake news sites got more online engagement (shares, reactions, and comments) leading up to the election than real news stories from legitimate news operations. It wasn't always like that. In February through April 2016, users engaged with top mainstream news stories on Facebook more than twelve million times; during this same period, users engaged with top fake news stories less than three million times. In the critical period from August through Election Day, however, fake news ruled the day: Users engaged

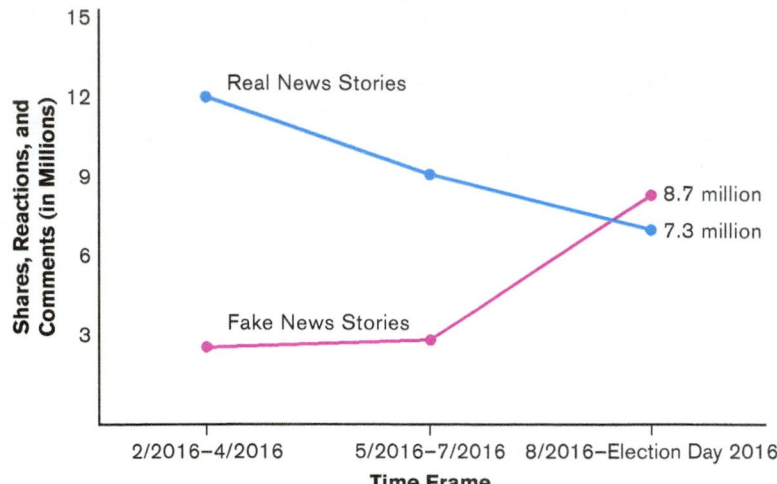

FIGURE 13.1 // TOP ELECTION STORIES: NUMBER OF FACEBOOK SHARES, REACTIONS, AND COMMENTS

Data from: Craig Silverman, "This Analysis Shows How Viral Fake Election News Stories Outperformed Real News On Facebook," BuzzFeed News, November 16, 2016, www.buzzfeed.com/craigsilverman/viral-fake-election-news-outperformed-real-news-on-facebook.

with top fake news stories 8.7 million times and with top mainstream news stories only 7.3 million times (see Figure 13.1).[1]

In the weeks and months following the 2016 election, media critics, scholars, and journalists have struggled to understand the origins and implications of fake news's dominance (see also Chapter 3). Fake news is not new. But whereas it was once mostly relegated to outlandish tabloids in grocery store checkout lines, fake news in the digital age has transformed

into an influential force affecting the highest levels of our political process.

One way we can understand the impact of fake news is to consider philosopher Jürgen Habermas's theory of the public sphere. This theory outlines how open discussion, disagreement, and debate should work so that members of a society can evaluate different ideas in order to make wise decisions on issues like public policy. According to this model, one key element of debate is that participants argue "in good faith." This means that although people may disagree on how to interpret and respond to evidence, they do not employ dishonesty to win over others to their point of view. Fake news—and those who knowingly or unknowingly share it—poisons these public sphere discussions as well as the decisions based on those debates.

If fake news is so potentially harmful to democracy and society, how is it allowed in the first place? The short answer is that it is protected under the freedom

Web Clip

YouTube.com has many videos related to fake news. One good option to search for: 'How Online Hoaxes and Fake News Played a Role in the Election' by PBS NewsHour. What role do you think fake news played in the outcome of the 2016 election? What impact might it have on future elections?

of speech guarantees of the First Amendment. It is not commercial speech attempting to sell goods and services, so being "false" is not problematic in the same way that false advertising might lead to civil and criminal action. And there is also the question of who should have the power to determine which news stories are fake and which are real, and then enforce penalties against the former. It is not difficult to imagine how this power could be abused by unscrupulous politicians looking to silence legitimate news articles that are critical of them.

For now, as with much of the Internet, fake news lives in the realm of caveat emptor, or "buyer beware." In other words, it is up to consumers to build up their media literacy and critical thinking skills so that they can avoid fake news sources and recognize credible news sources. Luckily, there are groups who are willing to help with this task.

Various library groups have provided online resources to help the public sort out the real stories from the fake, including Indiana University East and *School Library Journal*.[2] Highly regarded fact-checking and hoax-debunking sites—such as Snopes.com, Factcheck.org, Politifact.com, and the *Washington Post*'s Fact Checker—can also provide valuable help. In addition, Dr. Melissa Zimdars at Merrimack College has compiled a Google doc called "False, Misleading, Clickbait-y, and/or Satirical 'News' Sources."[3]

According to these resources, basic tips for separating fake news from real news include the following:

1. Read past the headline. Even legitimate news organizations can write poorly worded or intentionally sensational headlines.
2. Do you recognize the news outlet? If not, search for it on Google or look for it on Dr. Zimdars's list.
3. Double-check the date and time it was published. Sometimes old articles are shared again, and people mistakenly believe they are new.
4. Do you recognize the author/reporter? Conduct a Google search to see if that person exists and whether he or she has a reputation.

5. Look for links and sources, and be wary of stories that lack these elements. Follow any links that are included to see if they go somewhere reputable.
6. Look for reports on the same story in other news outlets. If it is a big story, it will almost certainly be covered elsewhere.

And of course some basic rules of critical thinking also apply. If an article elicits a powerful emotional reaction from its readers, it might be reporting on a legitimate injustice, or it might be designed to cloud your thinking with emotion. Also, the more extraordinary the claim is, the greater should be the evidence provided to back up that claim. And finally, remember that when you share something on social media, it will seem to others that you have in some way endorsed the information you are sharing—whether you have looked into the source's legitimacy or not.

APPLYING THE CRITICAL PROCESS

DESCRIPTION Visit the Facebook page of the acquaintance, friend, or relative you feel is most likely to share stories that might be fake news. Select three memes or links to articles that seem to make extraordinary or inflammatory claims.

ANALYSIS Using the six tips for separating real news from fake news, list memes or articles that should be investigated further to determine if they are credible.

INTERPRETATION Research the components of the memes/articles you identified.

EVALUATION Based on your analysis and interpretation, are these memes/articles most likely to be credible sources or fake news? What are the key factors that made you reach that decision?

ENGAGEMENT Share your findings, either with classmates or as part of a blog. By sharing your process and your findings, you may help others become more critical consumers of information on social media.

The First Amendment in a Democratic Society

Ultimately, questions about the First Amendment's implications for freedom of expression in mass media are really about democracy. And when it comes to our democracy, the news media—whether print, TV, radio, or the Internet—play a particularly important role. For most of our nation's history, citizens have counted on journalists to alert them to abuses in government and business. But today, the Fourth Estate is under siege. As discussed in the chapter opener, during and after the 2016 election, journalists dealt with historically unique challenges, as top public officials targeted the press and challenged the veracity of verifiable facts in a way not seen even during the Nixon administration. In this climate, fake news gained new life on the Internet, thanks in part to social media and the ease with which false stories could be shared (see "Media Literacy Case Study: Fouling the First Amendment: Finding Facts in the Face of Fake News" on pages 408–409).

But there are other forces that have eroded public confidence in the news media as well. For example, as newspapers, TV stations, radio stations, and Internet corporations merged into larger entertainment corporations, and as jobs in the news industry dwindled as a result of outsourcing, consolidation, and budget cuts, it has become more difficult for journalists to adequately cover and lead critical discussions about media ownership, media regulation, and business practices in general. There are fewer journalists available, and the very companies journalists work for are the prime buyers and sellers of major news-media outlets and are often participants in a political system rife with advertising money during the campaign season.

For these reasons, it has become more important than ever for citizens to share the watchdog role with journalists. Citizens not only need to think critically about the news they consume to avoid believing and sharing fake news, but also need to support local and national outlets that provide accurate and complete coverage of important ongoing topics. They also need to be aware of how media ownership can undermine even the best newsrooms—those filled with ethical and dedicated journalists. Citizen action groups like Free Press, the Media Access Project, and the Center for Digital Democracy have worked to bring media ownership issues into the mainstream. These groups remind us that the First Amendment protects not only the news media's free-speech rights but also the rights of all of us to speak out.

However, mounting concerns over who can afford access to the media go to the heart of free expression. In the wake of the 2010 *Citizens United v. Federal Election Commission* Supreme Court decision, important restrictions on big political donors disappeared. The 5–4 decision said that it was a violation of First Amendment free-speech rights for the federal government to limit corporate or union spending for TV and radio advertising, usually done through organized "Super PACs" (political action committees) that are most often sponsored by corporate interests or superrich donors. Some aspects of the current U.S. political system, then, amount to a legal pay-to-play system in which the wealthiest can wield indirect influence over elections (manipulating issues by buying lots of advertising) and more direct influence over legislation (manipulating politicians who desperately want money to pay for campaign advertising).[21] Although unpopular with a majority of Americans, this influence through campaign contributions has been defended on First Amendment grounds.

As we struggle to determine the future of converging print, electronic, and digital media, we need to take part in spirited public debates about media ownership and control, about the differences between commercial speech and free expression, and about what constitutes "speech" in the first place. As citizens, we must pay attention to who is included and excluded from opportunities not only to buy products but also to voice our views and thereby shape our nation's cultural and political landscape. To accomplish this, we need to challenge our journalists and our leaders. More important, we need to challenge ourselves to become watchdogs—critical consumers and engaged citizens—who learn from the past, care about the present, and map mass media's future.

CHAPTER ESSENTIALS

Review

- In the United States, freedom of speech and freedom of the press are protected by the First Amendment in the Bill of Rights. However, Americans have long debated what constitutes "free expression."

- Around the globe, four different models of press systems emerged in the twentieth century: the **authoritarian model**, the **state model**, the **libertarian model**, and the **social responsibility model.**

- The First Amendment prohibits censorship, which is defined as **prior restraint**—meaning that courts and governments cannot block any publication or speech before it actually occurs.

- Some forms of expression are not protected under the Constitution. These forms include sedition, **copyright** infringement, and **libel**.

- To win a libel case, public officials must prove falsehood, damages, negligence, and **actual malice**. Defenses against libel include the truth and the rule of **opinion and fair comment**—the notion that opinions are protected from libel.

- Other forms of expression not protected by the Constitution are **obscenity** and violations of the **right to privacy.**

- The First Amendment has clashed with the Sixth Amendment, which guarantees accused individuals the right to speedy and public trials by impartial juries. **Gag orders** (speech restrictions) and laws governing the use of cameras in the courtroom put restrictions on speech and other forms of expression for the sake of Sixth Amendment rights, whereas **shield laws** protect reporters from revealing confidential sources of information used in news stories.

- For the first half of the twentieth century, citizen groups and the Supreme Court failed to recognize movies as protected speech. The movie industry began regulating itself to safeguard its profits and avoid further government oversight.

- Because it uses the public airwaves, broadcasting receives fewer protections than do film and print. Although the government cannot censor broadcast content, it may punish broadcasters after the fact for **indecency.**

- **Section 315** of the Communications Act of 1934 mandates that during elections, broadcast stations must provide equal opportunities and response time for qualified political candidates. From 1949 to 1987, the **Fairness**

Doctrine—a corollary to Section 315—required stations to air programs about controversial issues affecting their communities and to provide equal time to competing points of view.

- Since the Internet is not regulated by the government, is not subject to the Communications Act of 1934, and has done little self-regulating, many consider it a true venue for free speech, though debates exist about net neutrality and what forms of expression should be allowed.

- Questions about the First Amendment's influence over freedom of expression in mass media are centered on democracy, and when it comes to our democracy, the news media play a particularly important role. As various forces have eroded public confidence in the news media, however, it has become more important than ever for citizens to share the watchdog role with journalists.

Key Terms

authoritarian model, p. 389

state model, p. 390

libertarian model, p. 390

social responsibility model, p. 390

Fourth Estate, p. 390

prior restraint, p. 391

copyright, p. 393

public domain, p. 393

libel, p. 394

slander, p. 394

actual malice, p. 395

opinion and fair comment, p. 395

obscenity, p. 396

right to privacy, p. 398

gag orders, p. 399

shield laws, p. 399

blacklisted, p. 402

indecency, p. 405

Section 315, p. 406

Fairness Doctrine, p. 406

Study Questions

1. What is the basic philosophical concept that underlies America's notion of free expression?

2. How did both the Motion Picture Production Code and the current movie-rating system come into being?

3. How does the Supreme Court view print and broadcasting as different forms of expression?

4. Why is the future of watchdog journalism in jeopardy?

14

Media Economics and the Global Marketplace

"From the start, we've always strived to do more, and to do important and meaningful things with the resources we have," Google cofounder Larry Page wrote in a 2015 letter explaining the decision to move the Google empire under a new umbrella multinational corporation called Alphabet. "We did a lot of things that seemed crazy at the time. Many of those crazy things now have over a billion users, like Google Maps, YouTube, Chrome, and Android."[1]

The move to create a new parent company for Google allowed the company to put some distance between established parts of the business and its riskier experimental ventures (sometimes called "moonshots").[2] This move was meant in part to comfort investors when those risky initiatives resulted in losses—sometimes to the tune of a billion dollars in a single quarter.[3] And while it may not please investors that initiatives like self-driving cars and balloons designed to get high-speed Internet into remote areas have yet to make money, Google wouldn't be one of the biggest companies in the world without its innovating spirit.

◀ One of Google's "moonshot" ventures is the development of a self-driving car. In 2016, the effort was split off from Google and given its own development company, Waymo. Despite the change in management organization, Waymo remains in the Google family under the umbrella corporation Alphabet. Chesnot/Getty Images

Google traces its origins to 1995, when Stanford student Sergey Brin was assigned to show prospective student Larry Page around campus. A year later, the pair were collaborating on a prototype search engine, and in 1997, they registered the domain name "Google.com"—a play on the mathematical word *googol* (the number written as a one followed by a hundred zeros). In 1998, the pair officially registered the company as an entity and hired their first employee. The company proceeded to grow at a startling pace, adding more services and features every few months.

One of those services—YouTube—has its own dizzyingly fast digital age success story. The three founders, Chad Hurley, Steve Chen, and Jawed Karim, say they got the idea for a video-sharing site during a dinner party, and on Valentine's Day 2005 they registered the trademark, name, and logo for YouTube. The first video (of Karim at the zoo) was posted on April 23, and by September the site got its first million-hit video (a Nike ad). By December, the company was getting major investment attention, and the site was more widely available after upgrading its bandwidth and servers. Google bought YouTube in October 2006, just a year and a half after the first video was posted, for $1.65 billion. Since then, YouTube has been run as a subsidiary of Google and continues to grow in popularity.

Google and YouTube exemplify the kinds of Internet-driven mass media companies of the post–digital turn. But that doesn't mean older media corporations have gone away. Some of today's biggest mass media players have long histories, which they've built on and adapted through various technological changes. These giants—such as Comcast, Time Warner, and Disney—exist and compete with relative upstarts like Amazon, Apple, Facebook, and Google. There can be big advantages to having the resources, name recognition, and established political connections that come with being a longtime member of the mass media.

For either type of company, the key to future success is investing in fresh ideas, which becomes harder to do as a company becomes more established. According to Larry Page, "As you 'age'—even when you're still a teenager like Google—you have to work hard to stay innovative."[4] Alphabet, it seems, is structured to help the company do just that.

COMPARING GOOGLE WITH OLDER MEDIA GIANTS like Disney and Comcast, we see two types of media success: one based on an idea that could have happened only in the Internet age (a need for a better search engine), and the other, legacy entertainment conglomerates that have survived years of leadership changes and power struggles to enter the twenty-first century with massive resources. Of course, not all of the mergers, takeovers, and acquisitions that have swept through the global media industries in the last twenty years have capitalized on the histories and reputations of the corporations involved. Take, for instance, the ill-timed purchase of MySpace by News Corp. in 2005. Paying $580 million for what was then the world's most popular social media site, Rupert Murdoch would watch a newcomer named Mark Zuckerberg (and his site Facebook) reduce the value of MySpace to $35 million, the price Justin Timberlake and Specific Media, Inc., paid for the service in 2011. Despite such spectacular exceptions, however, many cases of ownership convergence have provided even more economic benefit to the massive multinational corporations that dominate the current media landscape. As a consequence, we currently find ourselves enmeshed and implicated in an immense media economy characterized by consolidation of power and corporate ownership in just a few hands. This phenomenon, combined with the advent of the Internet, has made our modern media world markedly distinct from that of earlier generations—at least in economic terms. Not only has a handful of media giants—from Apple to Google—emerged, but the Internet has permanently transformed the media landscape. The Internet has dried up newspapers' classified-ad revenues; altered the way music, movies, and TV programs get distributed and exhibited; and forced almost all media businesses to rethink the content they will provide—and how they will provide it.

In this chapter, we explore the developments and tensions shaping this brave new world of mass media by:

- **examining the transition our nation has made from a manufacturing to an information economy by considering how the media industries' structures have evolved, the impact of deregulation, and the rise of media powerhouses through consolidation**

- **analyzing today's media economy, including how media organizations make money and formulate strategies within a climate of larger business trends that include the decline of labor unions, a widening wage gap, and the influence of hegemony**

- **assessing the specialization and use of synergy currently characterizing media, using the history of the Walt Disney Company as an example**

- **taking stock of the social challenges the new media economy has raised, such as subversion of antitrust laws, consumers' loss of control in the marketplace, and American culture's infiltration into other cultures**

- **evaluating the media marketplace's role in our democracy by considering such questions as whether consolidation of media hurts or helps democracy, and what impact recent media-reform movements might have on society**

The Transition to an Information Economy

In the first half of the twentieth century, the U.S. economy was built on mass production, the proliferation of manufacturing plants, and intense rivalry with businesses in other nations. By midcentury, this manufacturing-based economy began transitioning into an economy fueled by information (which new technologies made easier to generate and exchange anywhere) and by cooperation with other economies. Offices displaced factories as major work sites; centralized mass production declined in the United States and other developed nations; and American firms began outsourcing manufacturing work to developing countries, where labor was cheap and environmental standards were lax.

Mass media industries seized the opportunity to expand globally. They began marketing music, movies, television programs, and computer software overseas. And the media mergers-and-acquisitions (M&A) drive that had begun in the United States in the 1960s expanded into global media consolidation by the 1980s.

This transition from a manufacturing-based to an information-based economy had several defining points: Early regulation designed to break up monopolies in manufacturing-related industries such as oil, railroads, and steel gave way to deregulation, which ultimately catalyzed the M&A drive that created media powerhouses. These information-based corporations in turn fueled new trends in the industry (including a decline of unionized labor and a growing wage gap). Soon a new society took shape — one in which the biggest media companies defined the values that dominated culture not only in the United States but also around the globe.

How Media Industries Are Structured

Most industries that make up the media economy have one of three common structures: monopoly, oligopoly, or limited competition (see Figure 14.1).

Monopoly

A **monopoly** arises when a single firm dominates production and distribution in a particular industry—nationally or locally. For example, at the national level, AT&T ran a rare government-approved and government-regulated monopoly—the telephone business—for more than a hundred years before the government broke it up in the mid-1980s. And Microsoft dominates the worldwide market for business computer operating systems.

On the local level, monopolies have proved more plentiful, arising in any city that has only one newspaper or one cable company. The federal government has encouraged owner diversity since the 1970s by prohibiting a newspaper from operating a broadcast or cable company in the same city. But since 2003, the Federal Communications Commission (FCC) has made several efforts to relax cross-ownership rules, arguing that the Internet and cable and satellite television provide sufficient informational diversity for citizens. Media activists have countered that the large traditional media are still the dominant news media in any market, and that when they merge, it results in fewer independent media voices.

Oligopoly

In an **oligopoly**, just a few firms dominate an industry. For example, in the late 1980s, the production and distribution of the world's music was controlled by only six corporations. By 2004, after a series of acquisitions, the "big six" had been reduced to the "big four"—Time Warner (U.S.), Sony (Japan), Universal (France), and EMI (Great Britain). In late 2011, Universal purchased EMI at auction, and by 2012, three companies controlled nearly two-thirds of the recording industry market. The Internet is also changing the music game, enabling companies like Apple to gain new dominance with innovative business models such as the iTunes store. Time will tell whether the "big three" maintain their status as an oligopoly.

Firms that make up an oligopoly face little economic competition from small independent firms. However, many oligopolies choose to purchase independent companies in order to nurture the fresh ideas and products those companies generate. Without the financial backing of an oligopoly, many of those ideas and products could have a tough time making it to market.

Limited Competition

Limited competition characterizes a media market that has many producers and sellers but only a few products within a particular category.[5] For instance, hundreds of independently owned radio stations operate in the

▲ In 1911, John D. Rockefeller Sr., considered the richest man in the world, saw his powerful monopoly, Standard Oil, busted into more than thirty separate companies. Bettmann/Getty Images

United States. However, most of these commercial stations feature just a few formats—such as country, classic rock, news/talk, or contemporary hit radio. Fans of other formats—including blues, alternative country, and classical music—may not be able to find a radio station that matches their interests. Of course, as with music, the Internet is changing radio, too, enabling companies like Pandora and Spotify to offer streaming audio for a huge array of formats.

From Regulation to Deregulation

Beginning in the early twentieth century, Congress passed several acts intended to break up corporate trusts and monopolies, which often fixed prices to force competitors out of business. But later in the century, many business leaders began complaining that such regulation was restricting the flow of capital essential for funding business activities. President Jimmy Carter (1977–1981) initiated deregulation, and President Ronald Reagan (1981–1989) dramatically weakened most controls on business (e.g., environmental and worker safety rules). Many corporations in a wide range of industries flourished in this new pro-commerce climate. Deregulation also made it easier for companies to merge, to diversify, and—in industries such as the airlines, energy, communications, and financial services—to form oligopolies.[6]

In the broadcast industry, the Telecommunications Act of 1996 (under President Bill Clinton) lifted most restrictions on how many radio and TV stations one corporation could own. The act further permitted regional telephone companies to buy cable firms. In addition, cable operators regained the right to raise their rates with less oversight and to compete in the local telephone business. What prompted this shift to deregulation in the communications industry? With new cable channels, DBS, and the Internet, lawmakers no longer saw broadcasting as a scarce resource—once a major rationale for regulation as well as government funding of noncommercial and educational stations.

Not surprisingly, the 1996 act unleashed a wave of mergers in the industry, as television, radio, cable, telephone, and Internet companies fought to become the biggest corporations in their business sector and acquire new subsidiaries in other media sectors. The act also revealed legislators' growing openness to make special exemptions for communications companies. For example, despite complaints from NBC, News Corp. in 1995 received a special dispensation from the FCC and Congress that allowed it to continue owning and operating the Fox network and a number of local TV stations.

Today, regulation of the communications industry is even looser. In late 2007, the FCC relaxed its rules further when it said that a company located

FIGURE 14.1 // MEDIA INDUSTRY STRUCTURES

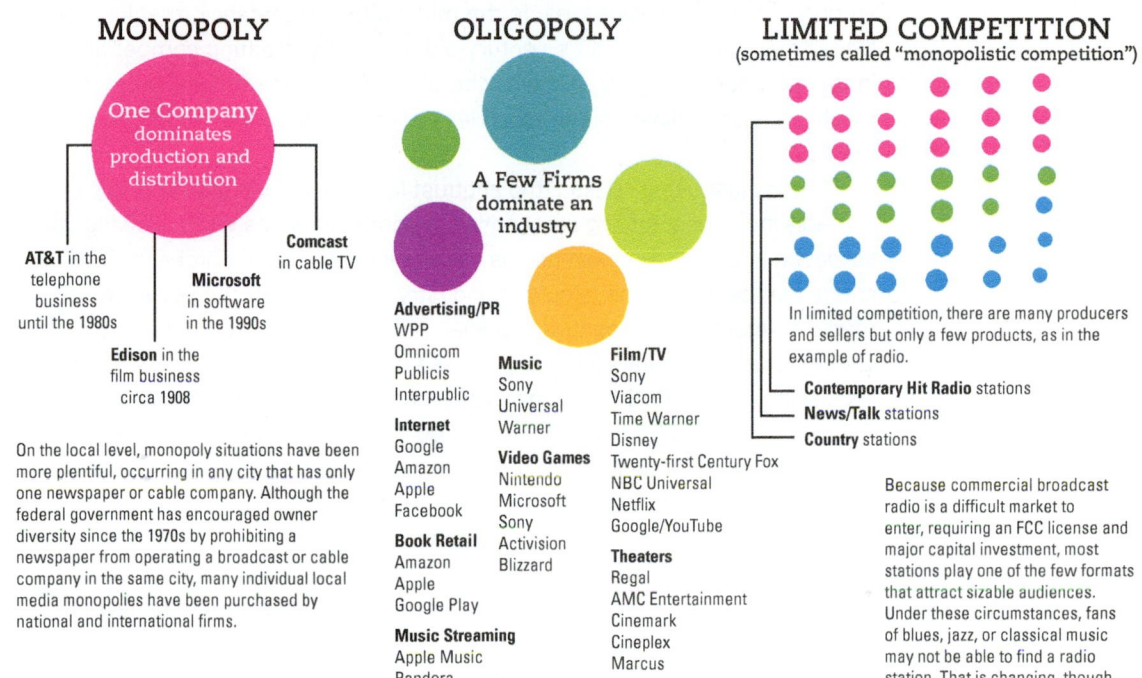

MONOPOLY

One Company dominates production and distribution

AT&T in the telephone business until the 1980s

Microsoft in software in the 1990s

Comcast in cable TV

Edison in the film business circa 1908

On the local level, monopoly situations have been more plentiful, occurring in any city that has only one newspaper or cable company. Although the federal government has encouraged owner diversity since the 1970s by prohibiting a newspaper from operating a broadcast or cable company in the same city, many individual local media monopolies have been purchased by national and international firms.

OLIGOPOLY

A Few Firms dominate an industry

Advertising/PR
WPP
Omnicom
Publicis
Interpublic

Internet
Google
Amazon
Apple
Facebook

Book Retail
Amazon
Apple
Google Play

Music Streaming
Apple Music
Pandora
Spotify

Music
Sony
Universal
Warner

Video Games
Nintendo
Microsoft
Sony
Activision
Blizzard

Film/TV
Sony
Viacom
Time Warner
Disney
Twenty-first Century Fox
NBC Universal
Netflix
Google/YouTube

Theaters
Regal
AMC Entertainment
Cinemark
Cineplex
Marcus

LIMITED COMPETITION
(sometimes called "monopolistic competition")

In limited competition, there are many producers and sellers but only a few products, as in the example of radio.

Contemporary Hit Radio stations
News/Talk stations
Country stations

Because commercial broadcast radio is a difficult market to enter, requiring an FCC license and major capital investment, most stations play one of the few formats that attract sizable audiences. Under these circumstances, fans of blues, jazz, or classical music may not be able to find a radio station. That is changing, though, with the Internet.

in a Top 20 market (ranging in size from New York to Orlando, Florida) could own one TV station and one newspaper as long as there were at least eight TV stations in that market. Previously, a company could not own a newspaper and a broadcast outlet (a TV or radio station) in the same market. In 2009, a U.S. federal court struck down the FCC's regulation limiting a cable company's holdings to not more than 30 percent of the U.S. cable market, a precursor to a wave of mergers and proposed mergers among internet service providers.

Sinclair Broadcast Group is just one corporation that took advantage of increasing deregulation, using a variety of FCC regulation waivers and loopholes to become the biggest owner of local TV stations in the United States. The company now owns and operates network-affiliated local television stations that used to compete against one another in dozens of markets, growing from 62 stations in 2004 to 173 stations by 2017.[7] Among other concerns, this type of consolidation is negatively affecting the number of media companies owned by people of color (see "The Digital Turn Case Study: Blacks Own Just Ten U.S. Television Stations. Here's Why." on pages 424–425).

The Rise of Media Powerhouses

Into the 1980s, antitrust rules attempted to ensure diversity of ownership among competing businesses. In the mid-1980s, for instance, the Justice Department broke up AT&T's century-old monopoly, creating competition in the telephone industry. But with the gradual erosion of those laws came much more consolidation and much less competition in the world of mass media.

Besides just being relaxed, the antitrust laws have been unevenly applied in media industries, forcing competition in some industries while allowing consolidation in others. For example, as the Justice Department broke up AT&T to create competition in the telephone industry, it also authorized several mass media mergers that concentrated power in the hands of a few behemoths. These included General Electric's purchase of RCA/NBC in the 1980s, Disney's acquisition of ABC for $19 billion in 1995, and Time Warner's purchase of Turner Broadcasting for $7.5 billion in 1996. In 2001, AOL acquired Time Warner for $165 billion—the largest media merger in history at the time. In 2011, cable giant Comcast purchased a majority share of NBC Universal once the deal was approved by regulatory agencies. A proposed merger between Time Warner and AT&T—valued at $85 billion—moved even closer to completion in February 2017, when new FCC chair Ajit Pai said his agency wasn't likely to review the deal.[8]

As traditional mass media corporations have grown, we've also seen the rise of new media powerhouses in the twenty-first century (see the chapter opener). Companies like Google, Amazon, and Facebook first grew to dominate their respective niches (search engines, online retail, and social media) and then branched out into new areas of the mass media. Apple and Microsoft have been around much longer but are still relatively young when compared to traditional mass media giants.

These five companies have envisioned new ways for us to experience media content: we buy content from their retail stores (e.g., the iTunes store and Amazon.com); benefit from their original content (e.g., Amazon film productions and Microsoft Office software, which is now available on mobile devices); consume content on their innovative devices (e.g., the iPad, Kindle Fire, Android mobile phone, and Xbox); and are linked to other media content (via Google search and our friends on Facebook). Imagine experiencing the mass media without using a product or service of one of these companies and you begin to understand how the digital turn—with these five companies leading the way—has transformed the mass communication environment in less than a decade.

Analyzing the Media Economy

The immense reach and heft of the mass media economy raises some complicated questions, beginning with the role government should play in regulating media ownership. Should citizens step up demands for more accountability from media? Is American culture, expressed through our mass media, hurting other cultures? And is concentration of ownership in the media damaging our democracy? To explore possible answers to these questions, we examine how media companies operate, how the Internet is transforming the media economy, the impact of different business trends, and the ways that people are persuaded to support media rules that may not be in the public's best interests.

How Media Companies Operate

Media organizations develop or distribute content, set prices, and generate profit. They are often asked to live up to society's expectations as well—that is, to operate with a sense of social responsibility in their role as mass communicators. These two main activities—maximizing profits while being socially responsible—are sometimes contradictory functions.

Maximizing Profits

Media companies make money in two main ways. The most obvious way revenue generation occurs is when consumers buy a book, song, game, movie, newspaper, magazine, or subscription—whether directly through the company or through a retailer. This monetary transaction once meant buying things like magazines or CDs in brick-and-mortar stores or through the mail. Now we buy much of our media online, often through the devices of media companies themselves (such as a Kindle).

The other way media companies generate revenue is through advertisements that support their products, such as TV and radio shows, most magazines, newspapers, and many Web sites. These media products might seem free to us, but advertisers are paying for our attention as we engage with the content. As consumers of advertising-based media, we actually have to work for the "free" content by giving our time and attention to commercial sponsors. Advertisers pay more or less depending on how many of us are being exposed to the ads and our potential buying power as an audience. Media companies similarly make money through product placement advertising in movies, television, and video games.

LaunchPad
launchpadworks.com

The Impact of Media Ownership
Media critics and professionals debate the pros and cons of media conglomerates.

Discussion: This video argues that it is the drive for bottom-line profits that leads to conglomerates. What solution(s) might you suggest to make the media system work better?

Blacks Own Just Ten U.S. Television Stations. Here's Why.

By Kristal Brent Zook

This month [May 2016], a federal district court judge in California threw out media entrepreneur Byron Allen's $20 billion lawsuit against Comcast and Time Warner Cable. The suit accused the cable giants of discriminating against black-owned media companies by creating and reserving just "a few spaces" for their channels at "the back of the bus." A judge disagreed, dismissing the seventy-one-page lawsuit in a snappy three-page decision.

But just because this particular case fell flat doesn't mean minority exclusion from broadcast and cable ownership isn't a problem. It is—a big one.

Minority owners are burdened by the legacy of racism. When the U.S. government first started giving away our airwaves in the 1930s, they were distributed exclusively to white male owners. It mostly stayed this way until the 1970s, when the FCC tried to remedy the problem by implementing a Minority Ownership Policy. The measure offered tax incentives to people seeking to sell stations to minority owners.

The policy worked. Within two years of its passage, the country went from one black-owned television station to ten. Over its total seventeen-year existence, minority ownership increased fivefold. However, it was struck down by the newly elected Republican Congress in 1995, and since then, its success has been mostly undone. In 2013, minorities owned just 6 percent of commercial television stations in the country, 6 percent of FM stations, and 11 percent of AM stations.

With a few notable exceptions (cable network Black Entertainment Television launched in 1980, and TV One followed in 1995), African American ownership remains particularly low, hovering at less than 1 percent of all television properties, and less than 2 percent of radio. Last year in fact, just two television stations were owned by black owners. (That number is up to about ten today.)

Media consolidation is at the heart of the problem. Clear Channel, for example, famously wiped out small and minority radio station owners with its buying spree, which allowed the company to snatch up as many as seven stations in a single market. According to Lauren M. Wilson—policy counsel at Free Press, a media watchdog organization— minority ownership decreases as markets become more concentrated. The proposed merger between Comcast and Time Warner Cable earlier this year was struck down by the FCC for just that reason.

But consolidation isn't the only evil at work here: Lack of diversity is compounded by historic discrimination. "The FCC has been licensing broadcasting stations for 80 years," says James Winston, president of the National Association of Black Owned Broadcasters. "During most of that time, the only people in a position to obtain them were white males." Winston explained that as technology developed from radio to television and then cable, the same white-owned companies continued to lead the pack because they could adapt to the new technology the fastest.

"African Americans and other minorities have come to the business world late, and without

▶ Web Clip
....

YouTube.com has a number of videos about media ownership. For example, search for 'Kim Keenan on Minority Media Ownership' posted by Comcast Newsmakers. How might more diverse ownership of media companies, including local radio and television stations, benefit a community?

FIGURE 14.2 // WHO OWNS COMMERCIAL BROADCASTING?

While the digital turn has created spaces inside larger social media platforms for minority voices—such as Black Twitter—traditional broadcast media overwhelmingly and disproportionately fall under white ownership.

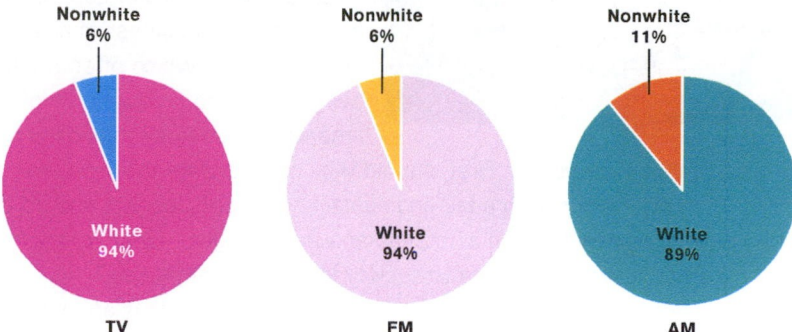

TV — Nonwhite 6% / White 94%
FM — Nonwhite 6% / White 94%
AM — Nonwhite 11% / White 89%

family-inherited wealth," he says. "We find ourselves with every disadvantage in terms of becoming successful entrepreneurs in broadcasting and in new technologies."

The FCC has done little recently to right these wrongs. After Congress tossed its Minority Ownership Policy, the FCC did not put a new strategy in place. David Honig—cofounder and president emeritus of the Multicultural Media, Telecom and Internet Council in Washington, D.C.—has represented more than seventy minority, civil rights, and religious organizations in proceedings before the FCC over the past three decades. He says that these groups come to his organization with "big business plans" for minority-focused channels but are unable to "crack the code to get in the door." Cable distributors that control

whether or not these start-ups live or die are largely white controlled. It's up to them to determine whether they want to carry, for example, the BlackEveryWoman channel.

Honig served as subcommittee chair on the FCC's Diversity Committee, which hasn't met in nearly two years; it's the only advisory committee of the agency that hasn't met for that long. The commission is expected (or, depending on who you ask, legally required by Congress) to issue reports on diversity and minority ownership every two or three years. These reports are generally late, incomplete, and unreliable.

"There are dozens of diversity proposals before the FCC gathering dust," says Honig, including new tax incentive legislation. "The FCC is doing very, very little relative to the need."

Source: Adapted from Kristal Brent Zook, "Blacks Own Just Ten U.S. Television Stations. Here's Why," Washington Post, August 17, 2015, www.washingtonpost.com/posteverything/wp/2015/08/17/blacks-own-just-10-u-s-television-stations-heres-why/.

▲ Labor activists argue that the current minimum wage is not a "living wage." As described by President Franklin D. Roosevelt in the wake of the Great Depression, a living wage means that after working a forty-hour week, a person would be able to provide necessities for a family—food, shelter, clothing, health care—and have something left over for leisure time pursuits. Scott Olson/Getty Images

Media corporations generate the most money when they can get us to buy a media product or pay for a subscription (like a cable TV package or a newspaper or magazine subscription) and thus make us the target for the advertising that comes with that media product.

Balancing Profits and the Public Good

The harshest critics of capitalism suggest that running a business is all about maximizing profits, which often means keeping wages low and production high. The resulting impact on social responsibility for media corporations is twofold. First, should they compensate the workers within their own operations with a fair and sustaining wage? Second, should they produce media content—such as stories about fair wages—that are more than just profitable and contribute to society in some positive way?

Many business executives have argued that there is an obligation in flourishing democracies to balance earning profits with serving the larger public. Recent decisions of billionaires like Warren Buffett of Berkshire Hathaway and Jeff Bezos of Amazon to buy struggling newspapers resonate with the founders' belief that a robust free press has a central role in helping democracy work well. Media corporations can also serve the public good in not only providing information necessary for democracy but also creating content that reflects the full diversity of their audience. For example, television producers in recent years have increased the diversity of their stories and representations both to make more money by attracting younger audiences and "because it's the right thing to do," as one television critic put it.[9]

How the Internet Is Changing the Game

Historically, media companies have operated in separate industries. That is, the newspaper business functioned separately from book publishing, which operated independently of radio, which worked autonomously from the film industry.

The Internet has changed all that. This medium has not only provided a whole new portal through which people can consume older media forms but also pressured virtually all older media companies to establish an online presence. Today, newspapers, magazines, book publishers, music companies, radio and TV stations, and film studios all have Web sites or mobile apps marketing digital versions and ancillaries of their products.

This development has presented new opportunities for some media organizations. For example, it enables noncommercial public broadcasters to bring in ad revenue. Public radio and TV stations, which are prohibited by FCC regulations from taking advertising, face no such prohibitions online. Many have begun raising money by posting advertisements on their Web sites.

However, the Internet has also posed new challenges for some older media companies, which must now navigate the realm of less established payment models. For instance, Internet sites like YouTube often display content from traditional broadcast and cable services; the companies selling those services lose direct-payment revenue every time someone consumes content on the Internet rather than paying for the service. But this availability may also create exposure for media companies' offerings. Traditional companies must then ask whether that new awareness translates into an increase in *paying* customers.

Business Trends in Media Industries

Consolidation and digitization are not the only trends redefining the mass media business landscape. Additional trends shaping business overall have further affected the media economy. These include the growth of flexible markets and the decline of labor unions, as well as downsizing and a growing wage gap.

Flexible Markets and the Decline of Labor Unions

In today's economy, markets are flexible—that is, business and consumer needs and preferences change continuously and quickly. Companies seeking to increase profitability alter their products, services, and production processes as needed to satisfy specialized, ever-shifting demands. Making niche products for specialized markets is expensive, and most new products fail in the marketplace. To offset their losses from product failures, companies need to score a few major successes—such as a blockbuster movie or a game-changing handheld device. Large companies with access to the most capital—such as media powerhouses—can more easily absorb losses than can small businesses with limited capital. Thus, the powerhouses stand the best chance of surviving in today's flexible markets.

To lower their costs and earn back their investments in product development, companies have begun relying heavily on cheap labor—sometimes exploiting poor workers in domestic and international sweatshops—and on quick, high-volume sales. Many U.S. companies now export manufacturing work, such as production of computers, TV sets, and DVD players, to avoid the more expensive unionized labor at home. (Today, many companies outsource even technical and customer support services for their products.) As U.S. firms have gained access to alternative sources of labor, American workers' power has decreased. Since the early 1980s, membership in labor unions has declined dramatically. Because one of the main functions of organized labor is to negotiate for better wages and employment stability and security, the drop in union membership has meant a reduction in the bargaining power of unions on behalf of workers. Many economists point to this as a major contributing factor in the exponential growth in the wage gap between workers and the people who run their companies.

The Wage Gap and Downsizing

Since the 1980s, real wages (wages adjusted for things like inflation) have stagnated for most American workers. This means that as productivity has increased, pay for many has effectively not. Consider also that the pay of chief executives of major companies grew from about twenty times the pay of the average worker in 1965 (a peak time for union membership and overall economic prosperity) to nearly three hundred times the pay of the average worker in 2015 (see Figure 14.3).[10] Chief executive officers of major media companies like CBS, Viacom, Time Warner, and Disney often show up in annual lists of the highest-paid CEOs.

Not only have wages stagnated and inequality in wages increased, but many workers have lost their jobs to downsizing as companies strive to become "more productive, more competitive, [and] more flexible."[11] Many people today scramble for paid work, often working two or three part-time and low-wage jobs. In his 2006 book *The Disposable American*, Louis Uchitelle noted unintended side effects of downsizing, including companies' difficulty in developing innovative offerings after gutting their workforces. The news media in particular has felt the pinch from this double jeopardy of downsizing and stagnant wages. Newsrooms have faced steep cuts since the 1990s, which has often meant more work for no additional pay and continued fears that workers will get a pink slip in the next round of layoffs.

The Age of Hegemony

As media corporations have grown larger, they have also been able to manage public debate and dissent about their increasing power. How? One explanation is their ability to exercise **hegemony** in our society. In hegemony, society's least powerful members are persuaded (often without realizing any persuasion has taken place) to accept the values defined by its most powerful members.

In his 1947 article "The Engineering of Consent," Edward Bernays, the father of modern public relations (see Chapter 12), expressed the core concept behind hegemony: Companies cannot get people to do what they want until the people consent to what those companies are trying to do—whether it is getting more people to smoke cigarettes or persuading more of them to go to war. To win people's consent to his clients' goals, Bernays tried to convince Americans that his clients' interests were "natural" and "common sense."

FIGURE 14.3 // CEO-TO-WORKER WAGE GAP, 1965 AND 2015

In 1965, the CEO-to-worker ratio at a major American company was 20:1—that is, the typical CEO earned twenty times the salary of the typical worker in that industry. By 2015, that ratio had climbed to 275.6:1.

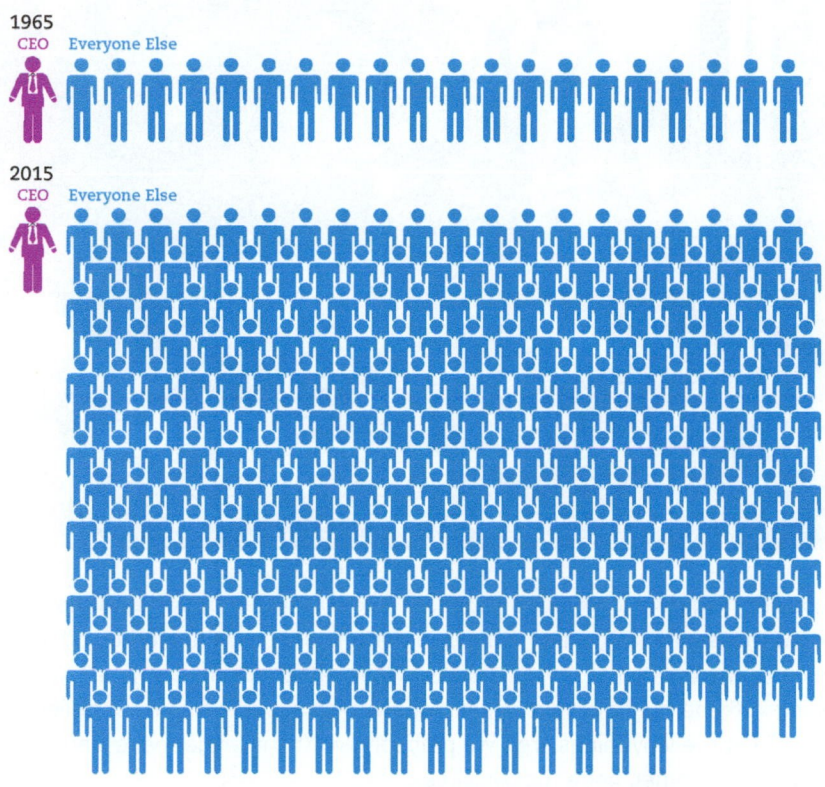

Data from: Lawrence Mishel and Jessica Schieder, "CEOs Make 276 Times More Than Typical Workers," Economic Policy Institute, August 3, 2016, www.epi.org/publication/ceos-make-276-times-more-than-typical-workers/.

Framing companies' goals in this way makes it unlikely that anyone will challenge or criticize those goals. After all, who is going to argue with common sense? Yet definitions of common sense change over time. For example, it was once common sense that the world was flat and that women and others who did not own property shouldn't be allowed to vote. When people buy uncritically into common sense, they inadvertently perpetuate the divisions that some common sense can create, and they shut out any viewpoints suggesting that these divisions are *not* natural.

The mass media—through the messages they convey in their products—play a powerful role in defining common sense and therefore setting up hegemony in society. Every time we read an article in a newspaper; read

▶ American Dream stories are distributed through our media. Early television shows in the 1950s like *The Adventures of Ozzie and Harriet* idealized the American nuclear family as central to the American Dream. © ABC/Photofest

a book or magazine; or watch a movie, TV show, or video clip on YouTube, we absorb messages suggesting what is important and how the world works. If we consume enough of these "stories," we might conclude that what we are seeing in these media products is just the way things are. And if we believe this is "just the way things are," we probably won't challenge these trends or come up with other, better possibilities.

The reason the narratives work is that they identify with a culture's dominant values. In the United States, Middle American virtues dominate our culture and include allegiances to family, honesty, hard work, religion, capitalism, health, democracy, moderation, and loyalty. These Middle American virtues are the ones that our politicians most frequently align themselves with in the political ads that tell their stories.

These virtues lie at the heart of powerful American Dream stories that for centuries have told us that if we work hard and practice such values, we will triumph and be successful. Hollywood, too, distributes these shared narratives, celebrating characters and heroes who are loyal, honest, and hardworking. Through this process, the media (and the powerful companies that control them) provide the commonsense narratives that keep the economic status quo relatively unchallenged, leaving little room for alternatives. In the end, hegemony helps explain why we sometimes support economic plans and structures that may not be in our best interest.

Specialization and Global Markets

The outsourcing and offshoring of many jobs and the breakdown of global economic borders were bolstered by trade agreements made among national governments in the mid-twentieth century. These included NAFTA (North American Free Trade Agreement) in 1994 and the WTO (World Trade Organization) in 1995. Such agreements enabled the emergence of transnational media corporations and stimulated business deals across national borders. Technology helped, too, making it possible for consumers around the world to easily swap music, TV shows, and movies on the Internet (legally and illegally). All of this has in turn accelerated the global spread of media products and cultural messages.

As globalization gathered momentum, companies began specializing to enter the new, narrow markets opening up to them in other countries. They also began seeking ways to step up their growth through synergies — opportunities to market different versions of a media product.

The Rise of Specialization and Synergy

As globalization picked up speed, several mass media—namely, the magazine, radio, and cable industries—sought to tap specialized markets in the United States and overseas, in part to counter television's mass appeal. For example, cable channels such as Nickelodeon and the Disney Channel serve the under-eighteen market, History draws older viewers, Lifetime and Bravo go after women, and BET targets young African Americans.

In addition to specialization, media companies sought to spur growth through **synergy**—the promotion and sale of different versions of a media product across a media conglomerate's various subsidiaries. An example of synergy is Time Warner's HBO cable special about "the making of" a Warner Brothers movie reviewed in *Time* magazine. Another example is Sony buying up movie studios and record labels and playing their content on its electronic devices (which are often prominently displayed in their movies). But of all the media conglomerates, the Walt Disney Company perhaps best exemplifies the power of both specialization and synergy.

Disney: A Postmodern Media Conglomerate

After Walt Disney's first cartoon company, Laugh-O-gram, went bankrupt in 1922, Disney moved to Hollywood and found his niche. He created Mickey Mouse (originally named Mortimer) for the first sound cartoons in the late

▶Released in the fall of 2013, the animated hit film *Frozen* provided a big boost for Disney. Not only did it break records at the box office, but it also boosted company profits through all of 2014 and into 2015 with *Frozen*-themed toys, DVDs, soundtracks, and a *Frozen*-themed *Disney On Ice,* which was itself poised to break records for ticket sales. © Walt Disney Pictures/Everett Collection

1920s. He later began development on the first feature-length cartoon, *Snow White and the Seven Dwarfs*, which he completed in 1937.

For much of the twentieth century, the Disney Company set the standard for popular cartoons and children's culture. Nonetheless, the studio barely broke even because cartoon projects took time (four years for *Snow White*) and commanded the company's full array of resources. Moreover, the market for the cartoon film shorts that Disney specialized in was drying up, as fewer movie theaters were showing the shorts before their feature films.

Driving to Diversify

With the demise of the cartoon film short in movie theaters, Disney expanded into other specialized areas. The company's first nature documentary short, *Seal Island,* came in 1949; its first live-action feature, *Treasure Island,* in 1950; and its first feature documentary, *The Living Desert,* in 1953. Also in 1953, Disney started Buena Vista, a distribution company. This was the first step in the studio's becoming a major player in the film industry.

Disney also counted among the first film studios to embrace television. In 1954, the company launched a long-running prime-time show, and television became an even more popular venue than theaters for displaying Disney products. Then, in 1955, the firm added another entirely new dimension to its operations: It opened its Disneyland theme park in Southern California. (Walt Disney World in Orlando, Florida, would begin operation in 1971.) Eventually, Disney's theme parks would produce the bulk of the company's revenues.

Capturing Synergies

Walt Disney's death in 1966 triggered a period of decline for the studio. But in 1984, a new management team, led by Michael Eisner, initiated a turnaround. The company's newly created Touchstone movie division reinvented the live-action/animation hybrid for adults and children in *Who Framed Roger Rabbit?* (1988). A string of hand-drawn animated hits followed, including *The Little Mermaid* (1989) and *Beauty and the Beast* (1991). By the mid-1990s, Disney

FIGURE 14.4 // EXAMPLES OF SYNERGY AT DISNEY

PROMOTE ON
ABC

PROMOTE IN
DISNEY STORES

NEW ANIMATED FEATURE,
RELEASED IN THEATERS, ON DVD,
AND ON STREAMING VIDEO

PROMOTE ON
DISNEY CHANNEL
FREEFORM

PROMOTE IN
DISNEY THEME PARKS

was well on its way to changing from a media company to a media conglomerate with its purchase of ABC and ESPN properties in 1995. At the same time, animation remained an important business and cultural touchstone for the company. In a rocky partnership with Pixar Animation Studios, Disney also distributed a series of computer-animated blockbusters—including *Toy Story* (1995) and *Finding Nemo* (2003)—and then Disney bought Pixar outright in 2006.

Since then, Disney has come to epitomize the synergistic possibilities of media consolidation (see Figure 14.4). It can produce an animated feature or regular film for theatrical release and DVD distribution. Characters and stories from blockbuster films like *The Avengers, Thor,* and the *Iron Man* franchises can become television series on ABC (Disney owns Marvel and ABC), like the program *Agents of SHIELD*, with storylines that intersect with the movies. Book versions can be released through Disney's publishing arm, Disney Publishing Worldwide, and "the-making-of" versions can appear on cable's Disney Channel or ABC Family (now called Freeform). Characters can become attractions at Disney's theme parks, which themselves have spawned lucrative Hollywood blockbusters, like the *Pirates of the Caribbean* series. Some Disney films have had as many as seventeen thousand licensed products—from clothing to toys to dog food bowls. Disney has hundreds of retail stores in malls across the U.S. And in New York City, Disney even renovated several theaters and launched versions of *Mary Poppins, The Lion King,* and *Aladdin* as successful Broadway musicals.

Expanding Globally

Building on the international appeal of its cartoon features, Disney extended its global reach by opening a successful theme park in Japan in 1983. Three years later, the company started marketing cartoons to Chinese television—attracting an estimated 300 million viewers per week. Disney also launched a magazine

Disney's Global Brand

Watch a clip from *Frozen*, one of Disney's biggest movies ever.

Discussion: What elements of *Frozen* might have contributed to its global popularity?

in Chinese. In 1997, Orbit—a Saudi-owned satellite relay station based in Rome—introduced Disney's twenty-four-hour cable channel to twenty-three countries in the Middle East and North Africa, as well as a new nationwide Disney channel in Russia in 2010. Disney also started expanding with theme parks and resorts, opening EuroDisney (now Disneyland Paris) in the 1990s, a theme park in Hong Kong in 2005, and a Disney resort in Shanghai in 2016. Disney's fifth and sixth international cruise ships will be added in 2021 and 2023.

Disney Today

Even as Disney grew into the world's No. 2 media conglomerate by the beginning of the twenty-first century, the cartoon pioneer experienced the multiple shocks of a recession, failed films and Internet ventures, and declining theme-park attendance. By 2005, Disney had fallen to No. 5 among movie studios in U.S. box-office sales—down from No. 1 in 2003. The new course for Disney was to develop (through acquisitions) new stories for movies and its other corporate offerings. In 2006, new CEO Robert Iger merged Disney and Pixar. In 2009, Disney purchased Marvel Entertainment for $4 billion, bringing Iron Man, Spider-Man, and X-Men into the Disney family; in 2012, it purchased Lucasfilm and, with it, the rights to the *Star Wars* and *Indiana Jones* movies and characters. This means that Disney now has access to whole casts of "new" characters—not just for TV programs, feature films, and animated movies but also for its multiple theme parks.

The Growth of Global Audiences

As Disney's story shows, international expansion has afforded media conglomerates key advantages, including access to profitable secondary markets and opportunities to advance and leverage technological innovations. As media technologies have become cheaper and more portable (from the original Walkman to the iPad), American media have proliferated both inside and outside U.S. boundaries.

Today, greatly facilitated by the Internet, media products flow easily into the eyes and ears of people around the world. And thanks to satellite transmission, North American and European television is now available at the global level. Cable services such as CNN and MTV have taken their national acts to the international stage, delivering their content to more than two hundred countries.

This growth of global audiences has permitted companies that lose money on products at home to profit in overseas markets. Roughly 80 percent of American movies, for instance, do not earn back their costs in U.S. theaters; they depend on foreign circulation as well as video revenue to make up for early losses. The same is true for the television industry.

Social Issues in Media Economics

Mergermania has sparked criticism in some quarters (see "Media Literacy Case Study: From Fifty to a Few: The Most Dominant Media Corporations" on pages 436–437). Some opponents lament the limits of antitrust laws. Others decry consumers' loss of control in the marketplace when just a few companies determine what messages and media content are produced. Still others warn against the infiltration of American culture and media messages into every corner of the globe.

The Limits of Antitrust Laws

Despite the intent of antitrust laws to ensure diversity of corporate ownership, companies have easily avoided these laws since the 1980s by diversifying their holdings and by forming local monopolies—especially in newspapers and cable. To accomplish this local control combined with megamedia mergers, media corporations developed well-polished and effective public relations and lobbying campaigns to get the public and lawmakers to back wave after wave of deregulation, thus weakening or stripping antitrust protections. These efforts have resulted in fewer voices in the marketplace and less competition among industry players.

Expanding through Diversification

Diversification, consolidation, and media partnerships promote oligopolies in which a few large companies control the majority of production and distribution of media content. Most media companies diversify among different media products (such as television stations and film studios), never fully dominating one particular media industry. Time Warner, for example, spreads its holdings among television programming, film, publishing, cable channels, and its Internet divisions. However, Time Warner competes directly with only a few other big companies, such as Disney, Viacom, and Twenty-first Century Fox. And Comcast, following a series of mergers, not only has become the cable and broadband company that controls the path by which so many media products are streamed into the home but also, after buying NBC Universal, controls a big portion of the media products on that path.

One prime example of a media partnership is Hulu.com, a joint venture of NBC Universal TV (Comcast), Fox Broadcasting, Disney-ABC Television, and Time Warner. Not only do these four owners of the video-streaming service offer content from the pantheon of networks they own, but they have several other "content partners" as well, including the BBC network.

From Fifty to a Few: The Most Dominant Media Corporations

When Ben Bagdikian wrote the first edition of *The Media Monopoly,* published in 1983, he warned of the chilling control wielded by the fifty elite corporations that owned most of the U.S. mass media. By the publication of the book's seventh edition in 2004, the number of corporations controlling most of America's daily newspapers, magazines, radio, television, books, and movies had dropped from fifty to five. Today, most of the leading corporations have a high profile in the United States, particularly through ownership of television networks: Time Warner (CW), Disney (ABC), Twenty-first Century Fox (Fox), CBS Corporation (CBS and CW), and Comcast-owned NBC Universal (NBC).

The creep of consolidation over the past few decades requires us to think differently about how we experience the mass media on a daily basis. Potential conflicts of interest abound. For example, should we trust how NBC News covers Comcast or how ABC News covers Disney? Should we be wary if *Time* magazine hypes a Warner Brothers film? More important, what actions can we take to ensure that the mass media function not just as successful businesses for stockholders but also as a necessary part of our democracy?

⊙ **Visit LaunchPad** to watch a video of media professionals discussing the money behind the media. How do corporations affect the media we consume and how we consume it?

Mickey Huff
Project Censored

Bedford / St. Martin's

launchpadworks.com

APPLYING THE CRITICAL PROCESS

DESCRIPTION   To help you get a better understanding of how our media landscape is changing, look at Table 14.1, which lists the Top 10 media companies for 1980, 1996, and 2014.

ANALYSIS   What patterns do you notice?

INTERPRETATION   Based on what you have discovered, what do these patterns mean? How do they reflect larger trends in the media? That is, seven of the major companies in 1980 were mostly print businesses, but in 2014, none were. Why?

EVALUATION   Although the subsidiaries of these companies often change, the charts demonstrate the wide reach of large conglomerates. Are these large media corporations good or bad for the economy? How do they affect democracy?

ENGAGEMENT   Think about how much of your daily media consumption is owned by the Top 10 corporations and about the influence they have on your news and entertainment intake. Ask two or three people around you to do the same, and compare your responses.

TABLE 14.1 // TOP 10 U.S. MEDIA COMPANIES, 1980, 1996, 2014*

1980

Rank	Company	Revenue in $Billions
1	American Broadcasting Co.	$2.204
2	CBS Inc.	2.001
3	RCA Corp.	1.521
4	Time Inc.	1.348
5	S.I. Newhouse & Sons	1.250
6	Gannett Co.	1.195
7	Times Mirror Co.	1.128
8	Hearst Corp.	1.100
9	Knight-Ridder Newspapers	1.099
10	Tribune Co.	1.048

1996

Rank	Company	Revenue in $Billions
1	Time Warner	$11.851
2	Walt Disney Co.	6.555
3	Tele-Communications Inc.	5.954
4	NBC TV (General Electric Co.)	5.230
5	CBS Corp.	4.333
6	Gannett Co.	4.214
7	News Corp.	4.005
8	Advance Publications	3.385
9	Cox Enterprises	3.075
10	Knight-Ridder	2.851

2014

Rank	Company	Revenue in $ billions
1	Comcast Corp.	$68.8
2	Google	66.0
3	Walt Disney Co.	48.8
4	DirecTV Group	33.2
5	Twenty-first Century Fox	27.7
6	Time Warner	27.4
7	Time Warner Cable	22.8
8	Dish Network	14.6
9	CBS Corp.	13.8
10	Cox Enterprises	12.2

Data from: Ad Age's 100 Leading Media Companies report, December 7, 1981; "100 Companies by Media Revenue," Advertising Age, August 18, 1997; various annual reports, 2014.

*Note: The revenue in $ Billions is based on total net U.S. media revenue and does not include nonmedia and international revenue.

This kind of economic arrangement makes it difficult for companies outside the oligopoly to compete in the marketplace. For example, an independent film production company may be unable to attract enough investors to get its movies distributed nationwide.

Building Local Monopolies

Antitrust laws aim to curb *national* monopolies, so most media monopolies today operate locally. Nearly every cable company has been granted monopoly status in its local community. These firms alone decide which channels are made available and what rates are charged. Independent voices have little opportunity or means to raise the questions that regulatory groups — such as the Justice Department and the FCC — need to hear in order to shape the laws.

The Fallout from a Free Market

Despite the concerns expressed by some critics, there has been little public debate overall about the tightening oligopoly structure of international media. Experts have identified two forces behind this vast hegemonic silence: citizens' reluctance to criticize free markets because they equate them with democracy, and the often unclear distinction between how much choice and how much control consumers have in the marketplace.

Equating Free Markets with Democracy

Throughout the Cold War period in the 1950s and 1960s, many Americans refused to criticize capitalism, which they saw as synonymous with democracy. Any complaint about capitalism was viewed as an attack on the free marketplace, and attacks on the free marketplace in turn sounded like criticism of free speech. This was in part because business owners saw their right to operate in a free marketplace as an extension of their right to buy commercial speech in the form of advertising. This line of thinking, which originated in corporate efforts to equate capitalism with democracy, still casts a shadow over American culture, making it difficult for many people to openly question the advertising-supported economic structure of the mass media.

Debating Consumer Choice versus Consumer Control

In discussing free markets, economists distinguish between *consumer control* over marketplace goods and freedom of *consumer choice*: "The former requires that consumers participate in deciding what is to be offered; the latter is satisfied if [consumers are] free to select among the options chosen for them by producers."[12] Most Americans and the citizens of other economically developed nations clearly have *choice:* options among a range of media products. Yet the choices sometimes obscure the fact that consumers have limited *control*:

power in deciding what kinds of media get created and circulated. Consumers thus have little ability to shape the messages conveyed through media products about what is important and how the world should work. Instead, they can only react to those messages.

Yet independent and alternative producers, artists, writers, and publishers have provided a ray of hope. When their work becomes even marginally popular, big media companies often capitalize on these innovations by acquiring it—which enables these works to get out to the public. Moreover, business leaders "at the top" depend on independent ideas "from below" to generate new product lines. Fortunately, a number of transnational corporations encourage the development of promising local artists.

Cultural Imperialism

The increasing dominance of American popular culture around the world has sparked heated debate in international circles. On the one hand, people in other countries seem to relish the themes of innovation and rebellion expressed in American media products, and the global spread of access to media (particularly the ease of digital documentation via mobile devices) has made it harder for political leaders to secretly repress dissident groups. On the other hand, American styles in fashion and food, as well as media fare, dominate the global market—a situation known as **cultural imperialism**. Today, numerous international observers contend that consumers in countries inundated by American-made movies, music, television, and images have even less control than American consumers. Even the Internet has a distinctively American orientation. The United States got a head start in deploying the Internet as a mass medium and has been the dominant force ever since. Although the Internet is worldwide and in many languages, the majority of the Web's content is still in English; the United States controls the top domains, including .com and .org (without the requirement of having a nation-identifying domain name, such as .jp for Japan or .fr for France); and leading global sites like Google, Facebook, Amazon, YouTube, and *Wikipedia* are all American in design.

▲ Ever since Hollywood gained an edge in film production and distribution, U.S. movies have dominated the box office in Europe, Asia, and the rest of the world. Worldwide grosses are thus more important to Hollywood than ever. Everett Collection, Inc

Defenders of American popular culture's dominance argue that a universal culture creates a *global village* and fosters communication and collaboration across national boundaries. Critics, however, point out that two-thirds of the world's population cannot afford most of the products advertised on American, Japanese, and European television. Yet they see, hear, and read about consumer abundance and middle-class values through TV and other media, including magazines and the Internet. Critics worry that the obvious disparities in economic well-being and the frustration that must surely come from not having the money to buy advertised products may lead to social unrest.

The Media Marketplace in a Democratic Society

Multinational giants are controlling more and more aspects of production and distribution of media products. This is particularly worrisome when it comes to news media: Media conglomerates that own news companies have the capacity to use those resources to promote their products and determine what news receives national coverage. When news coverage is determined by fewer decision makers, citizens cannot be certain they are receiving sufficient information with which to make decisions. That's bad news for any democracy.

Media powerhouses are also increasingly shaping the regulatory environment. Politicians in Washington, D.C., regularly accept millions of dollars from media conglomerates and their lobbying groups to finance their campaigns. Companies that provide such financial support stand a better chance of influencing regulatory decisions. Indeed, they have successfully pushed for more deregulation, which has enabled them to grow even more and come under fewer constraints. This is also bad news for our democracy, especially because the journalism subsidiaries of major media conglomerates are not completely independent of the powerful corporate and political forces on which they report. Who will tell us the news about big media and their political allies?

Despite the forces we have examined that are discouraging energetic debate about these realities, some grassroots organizations have arisen to challenge the power and reach of media behemoths. Such movements — like the National Conference for Media Reform — are typically united by geographic ties, common political backgrounds, or shared concerns about the state of the media. The Internet has also enabled media reform groups to form globally, uniting around such efforts as fostering independent media, contesting censorship, or monitoring the activities of multinational corporations.

◄ Amy Goodman is cohost of *Democracy Now!*, a radio/TV newscast airing daily on more than eight hundred public and college radio stations, satellite television, and the Internet. *Democracy Now!* argues that it maintains editorial independence by accepting funding only from listeners, viewers, and foundations, and rejecting government funding, corporate underwriting, and advertisers. MONTEMAGNI/SIPA/Newscom/Sipa Press/Brentwood California United States

This development is encouraging news: It suggests that we consumers—whether in America or elsewhere—might be willing to look more closely at the media marketplace's impact on our lives. And we may start demanding that media companies take more responsibility for fulfilling one of their key missions: making democratic life better for those of us consuming their products and absorbing their messages.

CHAPTER ESSENTIALS

Review

- By the mid-twentieth century, the United States shifted from a manufacturing-based economy to one fueled by information and cooperation with other economies, causing mass media industries to expand globally. Although early regulation was designed to break up monopolies, deregulation of the industries won out, leading to a growth in mergers and acquisitions.

- Media industries have one of three common structures: **monopoly**, **oligopoly**, or **limited competition**.

- Today's media powerhouses avoid monopoly charges by purchasing diverse types of media rather than controlling just one medium.

- Media companies make money from selling media content (e.g., physical or digital versions of books, music, films, video games, software, and apps), subscriptions to streaming content, devices on which to use that content (e.g., smartphones, tablets, e-readers, and video game consoles), and advertising.

- In addition to generating profit, media companies are often asked to operate with a sense of social responsibility in their role as mass communicators. These are sometimes contradictory functions.

- Historically, media companies have operated in separate industries; however, the Internet has changed the way people consume media. This development has presented new opportunities for some media organizations while posing challenges for some older media companies.

- Other trends that have affected the media economy include flexible markets and the decline of unionized labor, as well as downsizing and a growing wage gap.

- All these trends take place, in part, because mass media play a powerful role in establishing **hegemony**, in which a society's least powerful members are persuaded to accept the values defined by its most powerful members.

- With the rise of globalization, companies began specializing to enter the new, narrow markets in other countries. They also sought to spur growth through **synergy**.

- The Walt Disney Company is an example of a media conglomerate that has excelled at specialization and synergy. Following Disney's model, many media conglomerates look to international expansion as a way to access markets.

- Critics of mergers and media consolidation argue that antitrust laws are too limited, resulting in fewer voices in the marketplace, less competition among industry players, and loss of consumer control.

- Others warn against the infiltration of American culture and media messages into every corner of the globe—a situation known as **cultural imperialism**.

- Democracy suffers when news coverage is determined by fewer decision makers and when media powerhouses increasingly shape the regulatory environment. Grassroots organizations and the Internet have enabled media reform groups to form globally, suggesting that consumers might be willing to look more closely at the media marketplace's impact on our lives.

Key Terms

monopoly, p. 418
oligopoly, p. 419
limited competition, p. 419

hegemony, p. 428
synergy, p. 431
cultural imperialism, p. 439

Study Questions

1. How are the three basic structures of mass media organizations—monopoly, oligopoly, and limited competition—different from one another? How is the Internet changing everything?

2. Why has the federal government emphasized deregulation at a time when so many media companies are growing so large? How have media mergers changed the economics of mass media?

3. How do global and specialized markets factor into the new media economy? Using the Walt Disney Company as an example, what is the role of synergy in the current climate of media mergers?

4. What are the differences between freedom of consumer choice and consumer control over marketplace goods? What is cultural imperialism, and what does it have to do with the United States?

5. What do critics and activists fear most about the concentration of media ownership? What are some promising signs regarding the relationship between media economics and democracy?

15

Social Scientific and Cultural Approaches to Media Research

"We have no skinheads, no real KKK, no one doing anything but talking on the Internet. Well someone has to have the bravery to take it to the real world, and I guess that has to be me." These words were posted on Dylann Roof's Web site, apparently by Roof, just moments before the twenty-one-year-old went on a shooting rampage in a predominantly black church in Charleston, South Carolina, in 2015, leaving nine people dead and others wounded.[1] During his trial, after which Roof was convicted and later sentenced to death, prosecutors argued that Roof "self-radicalized" by finding and then embracing white supremacist propaganda online.[2]

Less than two years later, mass media were involved in activating people in an entirely different matter. In February 2017, Senator Elizabeth Warren was reading to the Senate chambers a copy of a letter from Coretta Scott King, widow of Civil Rights leader Martin Luther King Jr.,

◄ In 2015, a shooting massacre at a predominantly black church in Charleston by a self-professed white supremacist shocked the nation, raising fears that the killer had become self-radicalized by seeking out hate groups online. Here, South Carolina's then governor Nikki Haley is interviewed near the scene of the shooting. BRENDAN SMIALOWSKI/Getty Images

during comments regarding the confirmation of then senator Jeff Sessions, who had been nominated by President Donald Trump for U.S. attorney general. The letter, written in 1986, accused Sessions of having a racial bias against African Americans. Senate majority leader Mitch McConnell and his fellow Republican senators invoked an obscure rule to stop Warren from continuing to speak. Later asked to explain the move, McConnell told the Senate: "She was warned. She was given an explanation. Nevertheless, she persisted."[3]

Almost instantly, "Nevertheless, she persisted" became a feminist battle cry and a "weaponized meme"—a slogan with a biting underlying message tying together hundreds of pictures and other media that went viral across social media platforms.

This political activism quickly jumped from the virtual world to the real world, with the phrase appearing on products from T-shirts to coffee mugs, and inspiring hundreds of women in Minneapolis to line up for discounted tattoos of the phrase as a fund-raiser for a women's group.[4]

Whether by spreading violent hate, as in the first example, or by spreading nonviolent political activism, as in the second, media-influenced events like these have raised important questions: What power do the mass media, including social media, have over individuals and society? How to do the media contribute to the dissemination of information and opinions? And what power can we, as individuals and as a society, reclaim by using these very same media channels to make our own voices heard?

THE IDEA THAT MEDIA HAVE A SIGNIFICANT IMPACT on society has fueled the development of two types of research in the study of mass communication: social scientific and cultural studies.

Social scientific research attempts to understand, explain, and predict the impact of mass media on individuals and society. The main goal of this type of research is to define the problem with a testable hypothesis, collect data through one of various methodologies, and draw conclusions based on the data. Researchers who focus on **cultural studies** explore how people make meaning, understand reality, articulate values, and interpret their experiences through the use of cultural symbols in media. Cultural studies scholars also examine how groups such as corporate and political elites use media to circulate their messages and serve their interests. Such research focuses on daily cultural experience, examining the subtle intersections among mass communication, history, politics, and economics.

In this chapter, we look at how these two forms of media research have evolved over time by:

- **examining early media research methods, including propaganda analysis, public opinion research, social psychology studies, and marketing research**

- **assessing social scientific media research, including theories about how media influence people's behaviors and attitudes, and the benefits and limitations of such research**

- **taking stock of cultural approaches to media research, including early and contemporary cultural studies approaches and the strengths and limitations of such research**

- **considering the role of media research in our democracy and exploring how effectively such research addresses real-life problems**

Early Media Research Methods

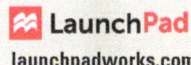

LaunchPad
launchpadworks.com

Use **LearningCurve** to review concepts from this chapter.

During most of the nineteenth century, philosophers such as Alexis de Tocqueville based their analysis of news and print media on moral and political arguments.[5] More scientific approaches to mass media research did not emerge until the late 1920s and 1930s. In 1920, Walter Lippmann's *Liberty and the News* called on journalists to operate more like scientific researchers in gathering and analyzing facts. Lippmann's next book, *Public Opinion* (1922), was the first to apply the principles of psychology to journalism. Considered by many academics to be "the founding book in American media studies,"[6] *Public Opinion* deepened Americans' understanding of the effect of media, emphasizing data collection and numerical measurement. According to media historian Daniel Czitrom, by the 1930s "an aggressively empirical spirit, stressing new and increasingly sophisticated research techniques, characterized the study of modern communication in America."[7] Czitrom traces four trends between 1930 and 1960 that contributed to the rise of modern media research: propaganda analysis, public opinion research, social psychology studies, and marketing research.

▲ Propaganda analysis researchers studied the impact of war posters and other government information campaigns to determine how audiences could be persuaded through stirring media messages about patriotism and duty. Library of Congress Prints and Photographs Division

Propaganda Analysis

Propaganda analysis was a major early focus of mass media research. After World War I, some researchers began studying how governments used propaganda to advance the war effort. They found that during the war, governments routinely relied on propaganda divisions to spread "information" to the public. Though propaganda was considered important for mobilizing public support during the war, these postwar researchers criticized it as "partisan appeal based on half-truths and devious manipulation of communication channels."[8] Harold Lasswell's 1927 study *Propaganda Technique in the World War* defined propaganda as "the control of opinion by significant symbols, . . . by stories, rumors, reports, pictures and other forms of social communication."[9]

Public Opinion Research

After the second world war, researchers went beyond the study of wartime propaganda and began examining how the mass media filter information and shape public attitudes. Social scientists explored these questions by conducting *public opinion research* through citizen surveys and polls.

Public opinion research on diverse populations has provided insight into how different groups view major national events, such as elections, and how those views affect their behavior. Journalists, however, have become increasingly dependent on polls, particularly for political insight.

Today, some critics argue that this heavy reliance on measured public opinion adversely affects Americans' participation in the political process. For example, people who read poll projections and get the sense that few others are voting for their favored candidate may not bother casting a ballot. "Why should I vote," they tell themselves, "if my vote isn't going to make a difference?" Some critics of incessant polling argue that polls mainly measure opinions on topics of interest to business, government, academics, and the mainstream news media. The public responds passively to polls, without getting anything of value in return. Professional pollsters object to **pseudo-polls**— typically call-in, online, or person-in-the-street polls that the news media use to address a "question of the day." Such polls, which do not use a random sample of the population and are therefore not representative of the population as a whole, nevertheless persist on news and entertainment Web sites, radio, and television news programs.

Social Psychology Studies

Whereas opinion polls measure public attitudes, *social psychology studies* measure the behavior, attitudes, and cognition of individuals. The Payne Fund Studies—the most influential early social psychology media studies— comprised thirteen research projects conducted by social psychologists between 1929 and 1932. Named after the private philanthropic organization that funded the research, the Payne Fund Studies were a response to a growing national concern about the effects of motion pictures on young people. The studies, which some politicians later used to attack the movie industry, linked frequent movie attendance to juvenile delinquency, promiscuity, and other problematic behaviors, arguing that movies took "emotional possession" of young filmgoers.[10]

The conclusions of this and other Payne Fund Studies contributed to the establishment of the Motion Picture Production Code, which tamed movie content from the 1930s through the 1950s (see Chapter 13). As forerunners of today's research into TV violence and aggression, the Payne Fund Studies became the model for media research, although social psychology is also used to study the mass media's relationship to body image, gender norms, political participation, and a wide range of other topics. (See Figure 15.1 on page 450 for one example of a contemporary policy that has developed from media research.)

Marketing Research

Marketing research emerged in the 1920s, when advertisers and consumer product companies began conducting surveys on consumer buying habits and other behaviors. For example, rating systems arose that measured how many people were listening to commercial radio on a given night. By the 1930s, radio networks, advertisers, large stations, and advertising agencies all subscribed to ratings services. However, compared with print media, whose circulation departments kept track of customers' names and addresses, radio listeners were more difficult to trace. The problem prompted experts to develop increasingly sophisticated market-research methods to determine

FIGURE 15.1 // TV PARENTAL GUIDELINES

The TV industry continues to study its self-imposed rating categories, promising to fine-tune them to ensure that the government keeps its distance. These standards are one example of a policy that was shaped in part by media research.

The following categories apply to programs designed solely for children:

TV-Y | All Children
This program is designed to be appropriate for all children. Whether animated or live-action, the themes and elements in this program are specifically designed for a very young audience, including children from ages 2–6. This program is not expected to frighten young children.

TV-Y7 | Directed to Older Children
This program is designed for children age 7 and above. It may be more appropriate for children who have acquired the developmental skills needed to distinguish between make-believe and reality. Themes and elements in this program may include mild fantasy violence or comedic violence, or may frighten children under the age of 7. Therefore, parents may wish to consider the suitability of this program for their very young children.

TV-Y7-FV | Directed to Older Children — Fantasy Violence
For those programs where fantasy violence may be more intense or more combative than other programs in this category, such programs will be designated **TV-Y7-FV**.

The following categories apply to programs designed for the entire audience:

TV-G | General Audience
Most parents would find this program suitable for all ages. Although this rating does not signify a program designed specifically for children, most parents may let younger children watch this program unattended. It contains little or no violence, no strong language and little or no sexual dialogue situations.

TV-PG | Parental Guidance Suggested
This program contains material that parents may find unsuitable for younger children. Many parents may want to watch it with their younger children. The theme itself may call for parental guidance and/or the program may contain one or more of the following: some suggestive dialogue (D), infrequent coarse language (L), some sexual situations (S), or moderate violence (V).

TV-14 | Parents Strongly Cautioned
This program contains some material that many parents would find unsuitable for children under 14 years of age. Parents are strongly urged to exercise greater care in monitoring this program and are cautioned against letting children under the age of 14 watch unattended. This program may contain one or more of the following: intensely suggestive dialogue (D), strong coarse language (L), intense sexual situations (S), or intense violence (V).

TV-MA | Mature Audiences Only
This program is specifically designed to be viewed by adults and therefore may be unsuitable for children under 17. This program may contain one or more of the following: crude indecent language (L), explicit sexual activity (S), or graphic violence (V).

Data from: TV Parental Guidelines Monitoring Board, www.tvguidelines.org, July 10, 2006.

consumer preferences and media use, such as direct-mail diaries, television meters, phone surveys, telemarketing, and eventually Internet tracking. In many instances, product companies paid consumers a small fee to take part in these studies. (To see how companies today track consumer habits and media use with sophisticated algorithms, see "The Digital Turn Case Study: Artificial Intelligence Gets Personal" on page 451.)

The Digital Turn

Artificial Intelligence Gets Personal

If you've used Netflix streaming, you know that the first thing you see when you log into the Web site or open the app is a list of recommended shows and movies. According to Netflix's vice president of innovation, the company is always improving the algorithm used to make these predictions with a particular goal in mind: "We should get to the point where you just turn on your Netflix app and automatically a video starts to play that you're very happy with."[1]

Netflix's attempts to predict what customers would like—a process called personalization—began when the company just used a Web site to rent out DVDs through the mail. Back then it would ask customers to rate favorites, look at what they had ordered, and base recommendations on that information.

The game has changed considerably since then thanks to the digital turn and the rise of streaming video. Although users can still rate their favorites, Netflix now collects data on what users watched, how long they watched, when they watched, and what kind of device they used to watch. This data is used to populate an interface that displays a series of rows sorted into categories of recommendations, which are based on a variety of factors. The programs Netflix thinks you will most want to watch appear to the left of each row, with their best guesses closer to the top of the screen.

Netflix has a big incentive to develop the smartest artificial intelligence (AI) possible: According to executives, this technology saves the company a billion dollars a year. For one thing, if users don't find something appealing to watch after a minute or two, they'll exit Netflix; if this happens often enough, they may unsubscribe for good, so providing accurate recommendations keeps customers tuned in. A good AI recommendation program also helps users discover more obscure titles, which boosts customer satisfaction and helps Netflix get the most value from the material it pays to keep in its catalogue.[2]

Netflix provides just one example of how data run through an algorithm dictates what you do (and don't) see on various sites. For example, online retailer Amazon estimates that a third of its sales derive from its recommendation engine;[3] what you see on your Facebook feed is determined by an algorithm; and the list of results you get from a Google search is based in part on past results and where you are physically located when you perform the search.

This move toward personalization through artificial intelligence creates concerns and questions for media critics and potential areas of study for media scholars. After all, these algorithms are created by people who work for companies with specific financial interests, which are not necessarily in line with true user preferences. For example, does Netflix have an incentive to feature its own content more prominently than other content? Does Facebook have an obligation to filter out—or at least impede—the spread of fake news? Media researchers have set out to answer questions like these in order to better understand the relationship between media, data, privacy, and audience behavior.

▶ Web Clip

YouTube.com features many videos exploring the algorithms of successful companies. For example, search for 'Why Netflix's Algorithm Is So Binge-Worthy' by NBC News. What do you see as the pros and cons of a platform like Netflix tracking your viewing activity? Do the pros outweigh the cons, or vice versa?

Social Scientific Research

Concerns about public opinion measurements, propaganda, and the impact of media on society intensified just as journalism and mass communication departments gained popularity in colleges and universities. As these forces dovetailed, media researchers looked increasingly to behavioral science as the basis for their work. Between 1930 and 1960, "who says what to whom with what effect" became the key question "defining the scope and problems of American communications research."[11] To address this question, researchers asked more specific questions, such as, If children watch a lot of TV cartoons (stimulus or cause), will this influence their behavior toward their peers (response or effect)? New social scientific models arose to measure and explain such connections—which researchers referred to as *media effects*.

Early Models of Media Effects

Between the 1930s and the 1970s, media researchers developed several paradigms about how media affect individuals' behavior. These models were known as hypodermic needle, minimal effects, and uses and gratifications. While more recent research has added nuance to these models and informed the creation of new models, these early models helped shape an important branch of mass communication research.

▼ Early media researchers concerned about Adolf Hitler's use of national radio to indoctrinate the German people in the 1930s found his international broadcasts to be failures. Because so many media messages competed with Nazi propaganda in democratic countries, Hitler's radio programs had little impact there. Bettmann/Getty Images

Hypodermic Needle

The notion that powerful media adversely affect weak audiences has been labeled the **hypodermic-needle model** or *magic bullet theory*. It suggests that the media "shoot" their effects directly into unsuspecting victims.

One of the earliest challenges to this model came from a study of Orson Welles's legendary October 30, 1938, radio broadcast of *War of the Worlds*. The broadcast presented H. G. Wells's Martian-invasion novel in the form of a news report, which frightened millions of listeners who didn't realize it was fictional (see Chapter 6). In 1940, radio researcher Hadley Cantril wrote a book-length study of the broadcast and its aftermath, titled *The Invasion from Mars: A Study in the Psychology of Panic*. Cantril argued that contrary to what the hypodermic-needle model suggested, not all listeners thought the radio program was a real news report. In fact, the relatively few listeners who thought there was an actual invasion from Mars were those who not only tuned in late and missed the disclaimer at the beginning of the broadcast but also were predisposed (because of religious beliefs) to think that the end of the world was actually near. Although social scientists have since disproved the hypodermic-needle model, many people still subscribe to it, particularly when considering the media's impact on children.

Minimal Effects

Cantril's research helped lay the groundwork for the **minimal-effects** (or *limited effects*) **model**, proposed by some media researchers. With the rise of empirical research techniques, social scientists began discovering and demonstrating that media alone do not cause people to change their attitudes and behaviors. After conducting controlled experiments and surveys, researchers argued that people generally engage in **selective exposure** and **selective retention** with regard to media. That is, people expose themselves to media messages most familiar to them, and retain messages that confirm values and attitudes they already hold. Minimal-effects researchers have argued that in most cases, mass media *reinforce* existing behaviors and attitudes rather than change them.

Indeed, Joseph Klapper, in his 1960 research study *The Effects of Mass Communication*, found that mass media influenced only those individuals who did not already hold strong views on an issue. Media, Klapper added, had a greater impact on poor and uneducated audiences. Solidifying the minimal-effects argument, Klapper concluded that strong media effects occur largely at an individual level and do not appear to have large-scale, measurable, and direct effects on society as a whole.[12]

Uses and Gratifications

The **uses and gratifications model** arose to challenge the notion that people are passive recipients of media. This model holds that people instead actively engage in using media to satisfy various emotional or intellectual needs—for example, turning on the TV in the house not only to be entertained but also to create an "electronic hearth," making the space feel more warm and alive. Researchers supporting this model use in-depth interviews to supplement survey questionnaires. Through these interviews, they study the ways in which people use media. Instead of asking, "What effects do media have on us?" these researchers ask, "Why do we use media?"

▲ The uses and gratifications model discusses media as being an "electronic hearth" that people gather around to share experiences. Here, we see people uniting in a sports bar to cheer on their favorite team. Scott Olson/Getty Images

Although the uses and gratifications model addresses the *functions* of the mass media for individuals, it does not address important questions related to the impact of the media on society. Consequently, the uses and gratifications model has never become a dominant or enduring paradigm in media research. But the rise of Internet-related media technologies has brought a resurgence of uses and gratifications research to understand why people use new media.

Conducting Social Scientific Media Research

As researchers investigated various theories about how media affect people, they also developed different approaches to conducting their research. These approaches vary depending on whether the research originates in the private or the public sector. *Private research,* sometimes called *proprietary research,* is generally conducted for a business, a corporation, or even a political campaign. It typically addresses some real-life problem or need. *Public research* usually takes place in academic and government settings. It tries to clarify, explain, or predict—in other words, to theorize about—the effects of mass media rather than to address a consumer problem.

Most media research today focuses on media's impact on human characteristics such as learning, attitudes, aggression, and voting habits. This research employs the **scientific method**, which consists of seven steps:

1. Identify the problem to be researched.
2. Review existing research and theories related to the problem.
3. Develop working hypotheses or predictions about what the study might find.
4. Determine an appropriate method or research design.
5. Collect information or relevant data.
6. Analyze results to see whether they verify the hypotheses.
7. Interpret the implications of the study.

The scientific method relies on *objectivity* (eliminating bias and judgments on the part of researchers), *reliability* (getting the same answers or outcomes from a study or measure during repeated testing), and *validity* (demonstrating that a study actually measures what it claims to measure).

A key step in using the scientific method is posing one or more **hypotheses**: tentative general statements that predict either the influence of an *independent variable* on a *dependent variable* or relationships between variables. For example, a researcher might hypothesize that frequent TV viewing among adolescents (independent variable) causes poor academic performance (dependent variable). Or a researcher might hypothesize that playing first-person-shooter video games (independent variable) is associated with aggression in children (dependent variable).

Researchers using the scientific method may employ experiments or survey research in their investigations. To supplement these approaches, researchers also use content analysis to count and document specific messages that circulate in mass media.

Experiments

Like all studies that use the scientific method, **experiments** in media research isolate some aspect of content; suggest a hypothesis; and manipulate variables to discover a particular medium's impact on people's attitudes, emotions, or behavior. To test whether a hypothesis is true, researchers expose an *experimental group*—the group under study—to selected media images or messages. To en-sure valid results, researchers also use a *control group,* which is not exposed to the selected media content and thus serves as a basis for comparison. Subjects are picked for each group through **random assignment**, meaning that each subject has an equal chance of being placed in either group.

For instance, suppose researchers wanted to test the effects of violent films on preadolescent boys. The study might take a group of ten-year-olds and randomly assign them to two groups. The experimental group then watches a violent action movie that the control group does not see. Later, both groups are exposed to a staged fight between two other boys, and researchers watch how each group responds. If the control subjects try to break up the fight but the experimental subjects do not, researchers might conclude that the violent film caused the difference in the groups' responses (see the "Bobo doll" experiment photos on page 457).

When experiments carefully account for independent variables through random assignment, they generally work well to substantiate cause-effect hypotheses. Although experiments are sometimes conducted in field settings, where people can be observed using media in their everyday environments, researchers have less control over variables in these settings. Conversely, a weakness of more carefully controlled experiments is that they are often conducted in the unnatural conditions of a laboratory environment, which can affect the behavior of the experimental subjects.

Survey Research

Through **survey research,** investigators collect and measure data taken from a group of respondents regarding their attitudes, knowledge, or behavior. Using random sampling techniques that give each potential subject an equal chance to be included in the survey, this research method draws on much larger populations than those used in experimental studies. Researchers can conduct surveys through direct mail, personal interviews, telephone calls, e-mail, and Web sites, thus accumulating large quantities of information from diverse cross sections of people. These data enable researchers to examine demographic factors along with responses to questions related to the survey topic.

Surveys offer other benefits as well. Because the randomized sample size is large, researchers can usually generalize their findings to the larger society as well as investigate populations over a long period of time. In addition, they can use the extensive government and academic survey databases now widely available to conduct **longitudinal studies**, in which they compare new studies with those conducted years earlier.

But like experiments, surveys also have several drawbacks. First, they cannot show cause-effect relationships. They can show only **correlations**— or associations—between two variables. For example, a random survey of ten-year-old boys that asks about their behavior might demonstrate that a correlation exists between acting aggressively and watching violent TV programs. But this correlation does not identify the cause and the effect. (Perhaps people who are already aggressive choose to watch violent TV programs.) Second, surveys are only as good as the wording of their questions and the answer choices they present. Thus, a poorly designed survey can produce misleading results.

Content Analysis

As social scientific media researchers developed theories about the mass media, it became increasingly important to more precisely describe the media content being studied. As a corrective, they developed a method known as **content analysis** to systematically describe various types of media content.

Content analysis involves defining terms and developing a coding scheme so that whatever is being studied—acts of violence in movies, representations of women in television commercials, the treatment of political candidates in news reports—can be accurately judged and counted. One content analysis study is conducted by GLAAD each year to count the quantity, quality, and diversity of lesbian, gay, bisexual, transgender, and queer (LGBTQ) characters on television. In 2016, GLAAD's *Where We Are on TV* report used content analysis to examine overall diversity and LGBTQ representation on prime-time scripted network TV programs, plus LGBTQ representation on cable networks and streaming services. According to the study, the overall number of "series regular" LGBTQ characters is slowly rising across all platforms, hitting an all-time high on network television at 4.8 percent. GLAAD points out that this is still proportional underrepresentation when compared to the general public, adding that there is a noticeable lack of racial diversity among the LGBTQ characters who do appear. What's more, some programs featuring LGBTQ characters continue to depict negative stereotypes of this population.[13]

Content analysis has its own limitations. For one thing, this technique does not measure the effects of various media messages on audiences or explain how those messages are presented. Moreover, problems of definition arise. For instance, how do researchers distinguish slapstick cartoon aggression from the violent murders or rapes shown during an evening police drama?

Contemporary Media Effects Theories

By the 1960s, several departments of mass communication began graduating
Ph.D.-level researchers (the first had been at the University of Iowa in 1948)
schooled in experiment and survey research techniques as well as content analysis. These researchers began developing new theories about how media affect
people. Five particularly influential contemporary theories emerged. These are
known as social learning theory, agenda-setting theory, the cultivation effect
theory, the spiral of silence theory, and the third-person effect theory.

Social Learning Theory

Some of the best-known studies suggesting a link between mass media and
behavior are the "Bobo doll" experiments, conducted on children by psychol-
ogist Albert Bandura and his colleagues at Stanford University in the 1960s.
Although many researchers criticized the use of Bobo dolls as an experimental device (since the point of playing with Bobo dolls is to hit them),
Bandura argued that the experiments demonstrated a link between violent
media programs, such as those on television, and aggressive behavior.
Bandura developed **social learning theory** (later modified and renamed
social cognitive theory), which he believed involved a four-step process:
attention (the subject must attend to the media and witness the aggressive

▼ These photos of the "Bobo
doll" experiments show that the
children who observed an adult
punching and kicking the Bobo
doll were more likely to imitate
the adult model's behavior when
returned to a room with many
toys. © Albert Bandura

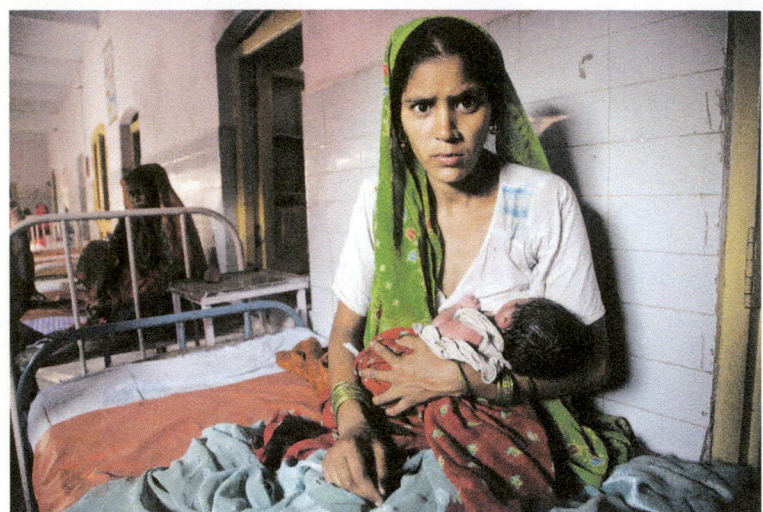

▲A consequence of agenda-setting is that the stories that don't get attention from the mass media don't make it onto the public and political agendas. Some groups try to overcome this barrier. Human Rights Watch works hard to publicize the high maternal mortality rate in rural India so that this important issue gets on the media's agenda. © Susan Meiselas/Magnum Photos

behavior), *retention* (the subject must retain the memory of what he or she saw for later retrieval), *motor reproduction* (the subject must be able to physically imitate the behavior), and *motivation* (there must be a social reward or reinforcement to encourage modeling of the behavior).

Supporters of social learning theory often cite real-life imitations of aggression depicted in media (such as the Columbine massacre) as evidence that the theory is correct. Critics argue that real-life violence actually stems from larger social problems (such as poverty or mental illness), and that the theory makes mass media the scapegoats for those larger problems.

Agenda-Setting Theory

Researchers who hold the **agenda-setting theory** believe that when mass media focus their attention on particular events or issues, they determine—that is, set the agenda for—what people discuss and what they pay attention to. Media thus do not so much tell us *what* to think as what to think *about*.

In the 1970s, Maxwell McCombs and Donald Shaw compared issues cited by undecided voters on election day with issues covered heavily by the media. Since then, researchers exploring this theory have demonstrated that the more stories the news media do on a particular subject, the more importance audiences attach to that subject. For instance, the extensive news coverage of Hurricane Katrina in fall 2005 sparked a corresponding increase in public concern about the disaster. Today, with national news coverage of the after-effects of Katrina almost nonexistent, public interest in the impact of Katrina has ebbed—even though many of the areas affected by the hurricane still lie in ruins.

The Cultivation Effect Theory

The **cultivation effect theory** holds that heavy viewing of TV leads individuals to perceive the world in ways consistent with television portrayals. The major research into this hypothesis grew from the TV violence profiles of George Gerbner and his colleagues, who attempted to make broad generalizations about the impact of televised violence. Beginning in the late 1960s, these social scientists categorized and counted different types of violent acts shown on network television. Using a methodology that combines annual content analyses of TV violence with surveys, the cultivation effect suggests that the more time individuals spend viewing television and absorbing its viewpoints, the more likely their views of social reality will be "cultivated" by the images and portrayals they see on television.[14] For example, Gerbner's studies concluded that although fewer than 1 percent of Americans are victims of violent crime in any single year, people who watch a lot of television tend to overestimate that percentage.

Some critics have charged that cultivation research has provided limited evidence to support its findings. In addition, some have argued that the cultivation effects recorded by Gerbner's studies have been minimal. When compared side by side, these critics argue, perceptions of heavy television viewers and non-viewers regarding how dangerous the world is are virtually identical.

The Spiral of Silence Theory

Developed by German communication theorist Elisabeth Noelle-Neumann in the 1970s and 1980s, the **spiral of silence theory** links mass media, social psychology, and public opinion formation. The theory proposes that those who believe that their views on controversial issues are in the minority will keep their views to themselves for fear of social isolation. The theory is based on social psychology studies, such as the classic conformity studies of Solomon Asch in 1951. In Asch's study on the effects of group pressure, he demonstrated that a test subject is more likely to give clearly wrong answers to questions about line lengths if everyone else in the room (all secret confederates of the experimenter) unanimously state an incorrect answer. Noelle-Neumann argued that this effect is exacerbated by mass media, particularly television, which can quickly and widely communicate a real or presumed majority public opinion.

Noelle-Neumann acknowledges that not everyone keeps quiet if they think they hold a minority view. In many cases, "hard-core nonconformists" exist and remain vocal even in the face of possible social isolation. These individuals can even change public opinion by continuing to voice their views.

The Third-Person Effect Theory

Identified in a 1983 study by W. Phillips Davison, the **third-person effect theory** suggests that people believe others are more affected by media messages than they are themselves. In other words, this theory posits the idea that "we" can escape the worst effects of media while still worrying about people who are younger, less educated, less informed, or otherwise less capable of guarding against media influence.

Under this theory, we might fear that other people will, for example, believe fake news, imitate violent movies, or get addicted to the Internet, while dismissing the idea that any of those things could happen to us. It has been argued that the third-person effect is instrumental in censorship, as it would allow censors to assume immunity to the negative effects of any supposedly dangerous media they must examine.

Evaluating Social Scientific Research

Media effects research has deepened our understanding of the mass media. This wealth of research exists partly because funding for studies on media's impact on young people remains popular among politicians and has drawn ready government support since the 1960s. But funding restricts the scope of some media effects research, particularly if the agendas of government agencies, businesses, or other entities do not align with researchers' interests. Moreover, because media effects research operates best in examining media's impact on individual behavior, few of these studies explore how media shape larger community and social life. Some research has begun to address these deficits, as well as to explore the impact of media technology on international communication.

Cultural Approaches to Media Research

In the 1960s, cultural approaches to media research emerged to challenge social scientific media effects theories and to compensate for those theories' limitations. In contrast to social scientific media research, the *cultural studies* mode of media research involves interpreting written and visual "texts" or artifacts as symbols that contain cultural, historical, and political meanings. For example, researchers might argue that the wave of police and crime shows that flooded the TV landscape in the mid-1960s was a response to Americans' fears about urban unrest and income disparity. A cultural approach thus offers interpretations of the stories, messages, and meanings that circulate throughout society.

Like social scientific media research, cultural studies media research has evolved in the decades since it first appeared.

Early Developments in Cultural Studies Media Research

In Europe, media studies have always favored interpretive rather than scientific approaches. Researchers there have approached the media from the perspective of literary or cultural critics rather than experimental or survey researchers.

These approaches were built on the writings of political philosophers such as Karl Marx and Antonio Gramsci, who investigated how mass media support existing hierarchies in society.

In the United States, early criticism of media effects research came from the Frankfurt School, a group of European researchers who emigrated from Germany to America to escape Nazi persecution in the 1930s. Under the leadership of Max Horkheimer, T. W. Adorno, and Leo Lowenthal, this group advocated augmenting experimental approaches with historical and cultural approaches to investigate mass media's long-range effects on audiences.

Since the time of the Frankfurt School, criticisms of the media effects tradition and its methods have continued, with calls for more interpretive studies of the rituals of mass communication. Academics who have embraced a cultural approach to media research try to understand how media and culture are tied to the actual patterns of communication in daily life. For example, in the 1970s, Stuart Hall and his colleagues studied the British print media and the police, who were dealing with an apparent rise in crime and mugging incidents. Arguing that the close relationship between the news and the police created a form of urban surveillance, the authors of *Policing the Crisis* demonstrated that the mugging phenomenon was exacerbated, and in part created, by the key institutions assigned the social tasks of reporting on crime and controlling it.[15]

Contemporary Cultural Studies Approaches

Cultural research investigates daily experiences, especially through the lenses of race, gender, class, sexuality, and imbalances of power and status in society. Such research emphasizes how some groups have been marginalized and ignored throughout history, particularly African Americans, Native Americans, Asians and Asian Americans, Arabic peoples, Latinos, Appalachians, LGBTQ individuals, immigrants, and women. Cultural studies researchers also seek to recover these lost or silenced voices. The major approaches they use are textual analysis, audience studies, and political economy studies.

Textual Analysis

Textual analysis entails a close reading and interpretation of cultural messages, including those found in books, movies, and TV programs—such as portrayals of Arab and Arab American characters in popular films.[16] Whereas social scientific research approaches media messages with the principles of modern science in mind—replicability, objectivity, and data—textual analysis looks at rituals, narratives, and meaning.

▶Media critic Jack Shaheen analyzes the cultural messages behind portrayals of Arabs and Arab Americans in film and TV, such as the Bugs Bunny cartoon shown here. From the film *Reel Bad Arabs: How Hollywood Vilifies a People*, produced and distributed by the Media Education Foundation

Although textual analysis has a long and rich history in film and literary studies, it gained new significance for mass media in the early 1970s with the work of Stuart Hall in the U.K., who theorized about how messages were sent and understood (encoded and decoded) via television, and with the publication of American Horace Newcomb's *TV: The Most Popular Art*—the first academic book to analyze television shows. Newcomb studied why certain TV programs and formats, such as the *Beverly Hillbillies, Bewitched,* and *Dragnet,* became popular. Trained as a literary scholar, Newcomb argued that content analysis and other social scientific approaches to popular media often ignored artistic traditions and social context.

Both Newcomb and Hall felt that textual analysis, which had largely focused on "important," highly regarded works of art—debates, film, poems, and books—should also be applied to popular culture. As Hall argued, things like television and popular music were important because they were what most people were using or experiencing most of the time. By the end of the 1970s, a new generation of media studies scholars, who had grown up on television and rock and roll, began studying less elite forms of culture. By shifting the focus to daily popular culture, such studies shone a spotlight on the more ordinary ways that "normal" people (not just military, political, or religious leaders) experience and interpret their daily lives through media messages (see also "Media Literacy Case Study: Terror, Torture, and TV" on pages 464–465). Researchers still examine the cultural meaning of messages in popular television, music, movies, and books consumed by those "normal" people. However, they also push that examination into post–digital turn mass media, from video games to social media to the use of smartphone technology.

Audience Studies

Audience studies differ from textual analysis in that the subject being researched is the audience for the text, not the text itself. For example, in her book *Reading the Romance: Women, Patriarchy, and Popular Literature*, Janice Radway studied a group of midwestern women who enjoyed romance novels. Using her training in literary criticism and employing interviews and questionnaires, Radway investigated the meaning of romance novels to these women. She argued that reading romance novels functions as personal time for some women. The study also suggested that these particular romance-novel fans identified with the active, independent qualities of the romantic heroines they most admired.

As a cultural study, Radway's work did not claim to be scientific, and her findings cannot be generalized to all women. Rather, Radway investigated and interpreted the relationship between reading popular fiction and ordinary life for a specific group of women.[17] Such studies help define culture as comprising both the *products* a society fashions (such as romance novels) and the *processes* that forge those products.

Political Economy Studies

A focus on the production of popular culture and the forces behind it is the topic of **political economy studies**, which examine interconnections among economic interests, political power, and ways in which that power is used. Major concerns of such studies include the increasing consolidation of media ownership. With this consolidation, the production of media content is being controlled by fewer and fewer organizations, investing those for-profit companies with more and more power to dominate public discourse. The theory is that money—not democratic expression—is now the driving force behind public communication and popular culture. Political economy studies also consider the profit motive behind certain company behaviors, such as how a company might gather data on customers (see "The Digital Turn Case Study: Artificial Intelligence Gets Personal" on page 451).

Political economy studies work best when combined with textual analysis and audience studies to provide fuller context for understanding a media product: the cultural content of the media product, the economics and politics of its production, and audiences' responses to it.

Terror, Torture, and TV

In recent years, particularly since 9/11, terrorism has commanded one of the top spots on our societal list of fears. One of the most significant media programs to feature terrorism was the fictional action drama *24*. The show had a successful eight-season run on Fox, from 2001 to 2010, and returned with a twelve-episode series in 2014 called *24: Live Another Day* and a spin-off series in 2017 called *24: Legacy.*

The series is notable for two reasons. First is the unique concept that each season of *24* covered a story lasting twenty-four hours in real time, with each of the season's twenty-four episodes documenting one hour, often with an on-screen clock marking the passage of time as Counter Terrorist Unit agent Jack Bauer (played by Kiefer Sutherland) raced to stop various terrorist actions.

Second, the series is notable for being right in the thick of the U.S. political debate on whether torture is an appropriate tactic to thwart terrorism. (Interestingly, the show was in production before the terrorist attacks of September 11, 2001.) One of the most significant legal and political debates of the early twenty-first century is whether terrorism suspects should be tortured. Those in favor of torture argue that it might yield information about other terrorists or terrorist plots. Those opposed argue that it is unethical, yields unreliable information (those being tortured may make up stories to make it stop), and puts our own citizens at risk of the same treatment by enemy states.

▲ The show *24* (shown here, with star Kiefer Sutherland at left), its limited series *24: Live Another Day,* and its spin-off *24: Legacy* often deal with weighty topics like terrorism and torture. Media researchers are interested in looking at how shows like these influence culture and society, as well as how much these shows reflect already-existing cultural norms and values. Fox Broadcasting/Photofest

By the program's fourth season in 2005, many television critics argued that *24* "normalized" torture, with its frequent portrayals of "chemical injection, electric shock and old-fashioned bone-breaking."[1] The *New York Times* asked, "Has '24' descended down a slippery slope in portraying acts of torture as normal and therefore justifiable? Is its audience, and the public more generally, also reworking the rules of war to the point where the most expedient response to terrorism is to resort to terror?"[2]

Legal writer Dahlia Lithwick suggested that "the most influential legal thinker in the development of modern American interrogation policy is . . . none other than the star of Fox television's '24,' Jack Bauer."[3] Lithwick cited a number of government

⊙ **Visit LaunchPad** to watch a clip from *24*. What messages about torture do you think this clip sends to an audience?

launchpadworks.com

officials who referred to Jack Bauer's character as inspiration for a pro-torture policy. Even the late U.S. Supreme Court justice Antonin Scalia used Jack Bauer as a reason to permit torture as an interrogation tactic: "Jack Bauer saved Los Angeles. . . . He saved hundreds of thousands of lives. . . . Are you going to convict Jack Bauer? . . . I don't think so."[4]

Most Americans, it seems, would agree. Support for using torture (or "enhanced interrogation techniques," as it is sometimes euphemistically called) rose from 45 percent of Americans in 2005 to 58 percent in 2016. Nevertheless, the report on the survey data says that most support torture only in "exceptional circumstances, such as the 'ticking time-bomb' scenario." And how often does that happen? Although it comes up quite often in a single day of 24, the Senate Select Committee on Intelligence, in its extensive 712-page 2014 study of the CIA's real-life interrogation program, "never found an example of this hypothetical ticking bomb scenario."[5]

Media researchers examine the way media "texts" like 24 influence culture and society, and how much shows like this reflect the norms and values of the culture from which they come. It's difficult to say definitively that one thing causes another (causation), yet researchers can often show that certain variables occur together with some frequency (correlation). Thus, while it may be hard to prove that a show like 24 affects societal attitudes, critical scholars might still argue that the series helped frame the debate over torture policy, creating readily accessible and understood bogeymen to reference in arguments supporting the use of torture. Scholars might also argue that by framing torture as a heroic act in the face of a ticking clock, the broader public is more likely to support a pro-torture position. Such research may draw on a textual analysis of the program, interviews with audience members, and results from public opinion surveys to support the researcher's conclusions.

APPLYING THE CRITICAL PROCESS

DESCRIPTION Do a Google search for news articles discussing the programs 24 or 24: Legacy and the use of torture. Pick three articles in a variety of publications that seem current, relevant, and detailed. Summarize each article, noting the following information: whether the article's author seemed to be troubled by the use of torture in the show; the name of the publication in which the article was published; and the sources the article cites.

ANALYSIS Put your information into chart form and note how the topic of torture is discussed. Are certain arguments or concerns more common than others? Are there patterns? Are any opposing viewpoints given?

INTERPRETATION If you identified patterns during your analysis, what might these patterns mean? Were you surprised by any of the arguments given in the articles? Did any of the articles come from a source affiliated with the show's network (Fox) or parent company (21st Century Fox), and if so, do they discuss the show differently?

EVALUATION Which of the arguments presented in the news articles seem most compelling? Why? Do you find yourself agreeing or disagreeing with articles that express concerns over the portrayal of torture in the series? Why or why not?

ENGAGEMENT Now that you have spent time reading about 24 or 24: Legacy, watch several episodes of the program. Compare your personal observations and impressions with the information you found in the articles you read, and write a blog post about your interpretation of torture's role in the original or the rebooted franchise.

Evaluating Cultural Studies Research

A major strength of cultural studies research is that researchers can more easily examine the ties between media messages and the broader social, economic, and political world, since such research is not bound by precise control variables. For instance, social scientific research on politics has generally concentrated on election polls and voting patterns. But cultural research has broadened the discussion to examine class, gender, and cultural differences among voters and the various uses of power by individuals and institutions in positions of authority.

Yet just as social scientific media research has its limits, so does cultural studies media research. Sometimes cultural studies have focused exclusively on the meanings of media programs or "texts," ignoring their effect on audiences. Some cultural studies have tried to address this deficiency by incorporating audience studies. Both social scientists and cultural studies researchers have begun to look more closely at the limitations of their work and to borrow ideas from each other to better assess media's meaning and impact.

Media Research in a Democratic Society

One charge frequently leveled at academic studies is that they don't address the everyday problems of life and thus have little practical application. To be sure, media research has built a growing knowledge base and dramatically advanced what we know about mass media's effect on individuals and societies. But the larger public has had little access to the research process, even though cultural studies research tends to identify with marginalized groups. Any scholarship is self-defeating if its complexity removes it from the daily experience of the groups it examines. Researchers themselves have even found it difficult to speak to one another because of differences in the discipline-specific language they use to analyze and report their findings.

In addition, increasing specialization in the 1970s began isolating many researchers from life outside the university. Academics were criticized as being locked away in their ivory towers, concerned with seemingly obscure matters to which the general public could not relate. However, academics across many fields moved to mitigate this isolation, becoming increasingly active in political and cultural life in the 1980s and 1990s. For example, essayist and cultural critic Barbara Ehrenreich has written frequently about labor and economic issues for such magazines as *Time* and the *Nation* and has written several books on such issues.

In recent years, public intellectuals have also encouraged discussion of the new challenges posed by media production in a digital world. Stanford University law professor Lawrence Lessig has been a leading advocate of efforts to rewrite the nation's copyright laws to enable noncommercial "amateur culture" to flourish on the Internet. He publishes his work in print and online. American University's Pat Aufderheide, longtime media critic for the alternative magazine *In These Times*, worked with independent filmmakers to develop the *Documentary Filmmakers' Statement of Best Practices in Fair Use*. The statement calls for documentary filmmakers to have reasonable access to copyrighted material for their work.

Like journalists, public intellectuals based on campuses help advance the conversations taking place in larger society. They actively circulate the most important new ideas of the day—including those related to mass media—and serve as models for how to participate in public life.

CHAPTER ESSENTIALS

Review

- Scientific approaches to mass media research did not emerge until the late 1920s and 1930s.

- Between 1930 and 1960, four trends contributed to the rise of modern media research: **propaganda analysis**, public opinion research, social psychology studies, and marketing research.

- Between the 1930s and the 1970s, **social scientific** media researchers (or *media effects* researchers) developed several models about how media affect individuals' behavior. These include the **hypodermic-needle model** (or *magic bullet theory*), the **minimal-effects** (or *limited effects*) **model**, and the **uses and gratifications model**.

- At the same time, researchers developed different approaches to conducting their research. Most social scientific media research today focuses on media's impact and employs the

scientific method, which includes the key step of posing one or more **hypotheses**. Researchers using the scientific method may conduct **experiments**, employ **survey research**, or use **content analysis** in their investigations.

- In survey research, researchers can use extensive government and academic survey databases now widely available to conduct **longitudinal studies**, in which they compare new studies with those conducted years earlier. Surveys can show only **correlations**—or associations—between two variables, not demonstrable causes and effects.

- By the 1960s, media effects researchers began developing new theories about how media affect people, including **social learning theory**, **agenda-setting theory**, the **cultivation effect theory**, the **spiral of silence theory**, and the **third-person effect theory**.

- In the 1960s, **cultural studies** approaches to media research emerged to challenge mainstream media effects theories. Early cultural studies research was built on the writings of political philosophers such as Karl Marx and Antonio Gramsci and the criticisms of media effects research from the Frankfurt School.

- Contemporary cultural studies approaches focus on research approaches, such as **textual analysis**, **audience studies**, and **political economy studies**.

- Although media research has advanced what we know about mass media's effect on individuals and society, most people do not have access to the actual research process, which makes it hard to connect scholarship to the daily experience of the groups such research examines.

- We rely on public intellectuals to help advance the conversations taking place in larger society and culture. These individuals encourage discussion of the new challenges posed by media.

Key Terms

social scientific research, p. 446

cultural studies, p. 446

propaganda analysis, p. 448

pseudo-polls, p. 449

hypodermic needle model, p. 452

minimal effects model, p. 453

selective exposure, p. 453

selective retention, p. 453

uses and gratifications model, p. 453

scientific method, p. 454

hypotheses, p. 454

experiments, p. 455

random assignment, p. 455

survey research, p. 455

longitudinal studies, p. 456

correlations, p. 456

content analysis, p. 456

social learning theory, p. 457

agenda-setting theory, p. 458

cultivation effect theory, p. 458

spiral of silence theory, p. 459

third-person effect theory, p. 459

textual analysis, p. 461

audience studies, p. 463

political economy studies, p. 463

Study Questions

1. What are ways in which the mass media might be implicated in social problems like the growth of hate groups and the spread of their messages, and how might the social scientific and cultural studies research traditions respond differently to these problems?

2. What are pseudo-polls, and what about them makes them less reliable than social scientific polls and surveys?

3. What are the main ideas behind social learning theory, agenda-setting theory, the cultivation effect theory, the spiral of silence theory, and the third-person effect theory?

4. Why did cultural studies develop in opposition to social scientific media research?

5. What role do media researchers play in public debates about the mass media?

Notes

I Mass Communication: A Critical Approach

1. Alicia Garza, "Herstory: Creation of a Movement," http://blacklivesmatter.com/herstory/; Elizabeth Day, "#BlackLivesMatter: The Birth of a New Civil Rights Movement," *Guardian*, July 19, 2015, www.theguardian .com/world/2015/jul/19/blacklivesmatter-birth-civil-rights -movement; Dayna Evans, "Black Lives Matter's Opal Tometi Explains How Words Can Change Human Behavior," *New York Magazine*, March 22, 2016, http://nymag.com /thecut/2016/03/black-lives-matter-opal-tometi.html.

2. Deron Dalton, "The Three Women behind the Black Lives Matter Movement," *Madame Noire*, May 4, 2015, http://madamenoire.com/528287/the-three-women-behind -the-black-lives-matter-movement/.

3. For a historical discussion of culture, see Lawrence Levine, *Highbrow/Lowbrow: The Emergence of Cultural Hierarchy in America* (Cambridge, Mass.: Harvard University Press, 1988).

4. For overviews of this position, see Neil Postman, *Amusing Ourselves to Death: Public Discourse in the Age of Show Business* (New York: Penguin Books, 1985), 19; and Stuart Ewen, *Captains of Consciousness: Advertising and the Social Roots of the Consumer Culture* (New York: McGraw-Hill, 1976).

5. See James W. Carey, *Communication as Culture: Essays on Media and Society* (Boston: Unwin Hyman, 1989).

6. Tasha N. Dubriwny, "Constructing Breast Cancer in the News: Betty Ford and the Evolution of the Breast Cancer Patient," *Journal of Communication Inquiry* 33, no. 2 (2009): 104–125.

7. Charles K. Atkin, Sandi W. Smith, Courtnay McFeters, and Vanessa Ferguson, "A Comprehensive Analysis of Breast Cancer News Coverage in Leading Media Outlets Focusing on Environmental Risks and Prevention," *Health Communication* 13 (January/February 2008): 3–19.

8. Brooks Barnes, "Lab Watches Web Surfers to See Which Ads Work," *New York Times*, July 26, 2009, www .nytimes.com/2009/07/27/technology/27disney.html.

9. See Jon Katz, "Rock, Rap and Movies Bring You the News," *Rolling Stone*, March 5, 1992, 33.

THE DIGITAL TURN CASE STUDY: FOMO in a Digital World, p. 13

1. Lev Grossman and Matt Vella, "iNeed?" *Time*, September 22, 2014, p. 44.

2. "Fear of Missing Out," J. Walter Thompson Intelligence, May 2011, www.jwtintelligence.com/production/FOMO _JWT_TrendReport_May2011.pdf.

3. Andrew K. Przybylski et al., "Motivational, Emotional, and Behavioral Correlates of Fear of Missing Out," *Computers in Human Behavior* 29 (2013): 1841–1848.

4. Ethan Kross et al., "Facebook Use Predicts Declines in Subjective Well-Being in Young Adults," *PLOS ONE* 8, no. 8 (2013), doi:10.1371/journal.pone.0069841.

5. Ed Diener and Robert Biswas-Diener, *Happiness: Unlocking the Mysteries of Psychological Wealth* (Malden, Mass.: Wiley-Blackwell, 2008), 51.

MEDIA LITERACY CASE STUDY: Masculinity and the Media, p. 26

1. Mark Follman, Gavin Aronsen, and Deanna Pan, "A Guide to Mass Shootings in America," *Mother Jones*, September 24, 2016, www.motherjones.com/politics/2012/07/mass -shootings-map. See also John Wihbey, "Mass Murder, Shooting Sprees and Rampage Violence: Research Roundup," October 1, 2015, http://journalistsresource.org /studies/government/criminal-justice/mass-murder -shooting-sprees-and-rampage-violence-research- roundup.

2. Jackson Katz, "Memo to Media: Manhood, Not Guns or Mental Illness, Should Be Central in Newtown Shooting," *Huffington Post*, updated February 17, 2013, www .huffingtonpost.com/jackson-katz/men-gender-gun -violence_b_2308522.html.

3. Ibid.

4. Rachel Kalish and Michael Kimmel, "Suicide by Mass Murder: Masculinity, Aggrieved Entitlement, and Rampage School Shootings," *Health Sociology Review* 19, no. 4 (2010): 451–464.

5. See Ralph Ellis and Sara Sidner, "Deadly California Rampage: Chilling Video, but No Match for Reality," CNN, May 27, 2014, www.cnn.com/2014/05/24/justice /california-shooting-deaths/.

2 Books and the Power of Print

1. BookCon, FAQs, accessed May 31, 2015, www .thebookcon.com/about/FAQs/.

2. Seth Fishman, "How to Write YA," *Publishers Weekly*, February 27, 2014, www.publishersweekly.com/pw /by-topic/childrens/childrens-authors/article/61185-how-to -write-ya.html.

3. Clare Swanson, "The Bestselling Books of 2014," *Publishers Weekly*, January 2, 2015, www .publishersweekly.com/pw/by-topic/industry-news /bookselling/article/65171-the-fault-in-our-stars-tops-print -and-digital.html.

4. Jim Milliot, "Publishing Sales Dipped in 2015," *Publishers Weekly*, July 11, 2016, www.publishersweekly.com/pw/by-topic/industry-news/financial-reporting/article/70881-publishing-sales-dipped-in-2015.html.
5. Laura M. Bell, "HelloGiggles Founder and BookCon Panelist Sophia Rossi Talks about the Love Affair between Books and the Internet," *Huffington Post*, May 28, 2015, www.huffingtonpost.com/laura-m-bell/post_9508_b_7449098.html.
6. See Elizabeth Eisenstein, *The Printing Press as an Agent of Change* (Cambridge: Cambridge University Press, 1980).
7. For a comprehensive historical overview of the publishing industry and the rise of publishing houses, see John A. Tebbel, *A History of Book Publishing in the United States*, 4 vols. (New York: R. R. Bowker, 1972–81).
8. National Association of College Stores, "Key Findings Report: Student Watch 2015–16 Academic Year," www.nacs.org/research/studentwatchfindings.aspx.
9. "Religious Books Sales Revenue in the United States from 2011 to 2015 (in Million U.S. Dollars)," www.statista.com/statistics/251467/religious-books-sales-revenue-in-the-us/.
10. Association of American Publishers, "U.S. Publishing Industry's Annual Survey Reveals Nearly $28 Billion in Revenue in 2015," July 11, 2016, http://newsroom.publishers.org/us-publishing-industrys-annual-survey-reveals-nearly-28-billion-in-revenue-in-2015/.
11. Jim Milliot, "Industry Sales Flat in 2013; Trade Dropped 2.3%," *Publishers Weekly*, June 26, 2014, www.publishersweekly.com/pw/by-topic/industry-news/financial-reporting/article/63052-industry-sales-flat-in-2013-trade-dropped-2-3.html.
12. Association of American Publishers, "U.S. Publishing Industry's Annual Survey Reveals Nearly $28 Billion in Revenue in 2015," July 11, 2016, http://newsroom.publishers.org/us-publishing-industrys-annual-survey-reveals-nearly-28-billion-in-revenue-in-2015/.
13. Steve Wasserman, "The Amazon Effect," *Nation*, May 29, 2012, www.thenation.com/article/168125/amazon-effect#.
14. "October 2015—Apple, B&N, Kobo, and Google: A Look at the Rest of the eBook Market," October 2015, http://authorearnings.com/report/october-2015-apple-bn-kobo-and-google-a-look-at-the-rest-of-the-ebook-market/.
15. "February 2016 Author Earnings Report: Amazon's Ebook, Print, and Audio Sales," February 2016, http://authorearnings.com/report/february-2016-author-earnings-report/.
16. Andrew Perrin, "Book Reading 2016," Pew Research Center, September 1, 2016, www.pewinternet.org/2016/09/01/book-reading-2016/.

THE DIGITAL TURN CASE STUDY: Self-Publishing Redefined, p. 54
1. CBS News, "Tech CEO-Turned-Erotic Romance Novelist's Double Life," May 19, 2015, www.cbsnews.com/news/tech-ceo-turned-erotica-romance-novelist-meredith-wild/.
2. Betty Kelly Sargent, "Surprising Self-Publishing Statistics," *Publishers Weekly*, July 28, 2014, www.publishersweekly.com/pw/by-topic/authors/pw-select/article/63455-surprising-self-publishing-statistics.html.
3. Author Earnings, "February 2016 Author Earnings Report: Amazon's Ebook, Print, and Audio Sales," http://authorearnings.com/report/february-2016-author-earnings-report/.
4. Alexandra Alter, "Meredith Wild, a Self-Publisher Making an Imprint," *New York Times*, January 30, 2016, www.nytimes.com/2016/01/31/business/media/meredith-wild-a-self-publisher-making-an-imprint.html?_r=0.

MEDIA LITERACY CASE STUDY: Banned Books and "Family Values," p. 56
1. Stephanie McNeal, "Liberal Groups Angry with SC Pols over Order to Teach Constitution," *FoxNews.com*, June 15, 2014, www.foxnews.com/politics/2014/06/15/liberal-groups-slam-sc-lawmakers-compromise-in-fight-over-gay-themed-reading.html; Sarah McCammon, "Books with Gay Themes Put S.C. Colleges' Funding at Risk," National Public Radio, May 9, 2014, www.npr.org/2014/05/09/310726247/gay-friendly-book-selections-put-college-funding-at-risk.

3 Newspapers to Digital Frontiers: Journalism's Journey

1. See Brooke Kroeger, *Nellie Bly: Daredevil, Reporter, Feminist* (New York: Times Books/Random House, 1994).
2. See David T. Z. Mindich, "Edwin M. Stanton, the Inverted Pyramid, and Information Control," *Journalism Monographs* 140 (August 1993).
3. Michael Schudson, *Discovering the News: A Social History of American Newspapers* (New York: Basic Books, 1978), 23.
4. Enn Raudsepp, "Reinventing Journalism Education," *Canadian Journal of Communication* 14, no. 2 (1989): 1–14.
5. Curtis D. MacDougall, *The Press and Its Problems* (Dubuque, Iowa: William C. Brown, 1964), 143, 189.
6. Walter Lippmann, *Liberty and the News* (New York: Harcourt, Brace and Howe, 1920), 92.
7. For another list and an alternative analysis of news criteria, see the Missouri Group, *News Reporting and Writing*, 12th ed. (New York: Bedford/St. Martin's, 2017), 7–9.

8. For a full discussion of the *New York Times* and mainstream journalism's treatment of the LGBTQ community and the early days of the AIDS epidemic, see Edward Alwood, *Straight News: Gays, Lesbians and the News Media* (New York: Columbia University Press, 1996); and Larry Gross, *Up from Invisibility: Lesbians, Gay Men, and the Media in America* (New York: Columbia University Press, 2001).

9. See Pew Research Center, "5 Facts about Ethnic and Gender Diversity in U.S. Newsrooms," www.pewresearch.org/fact-tank/2013/07/18/5-facts-about-ethnic-and-gender-diversity-in-u-s-newsrooms/.

10. ASNE, "ASNE Releases 2016 Diversity Survey Results," September 9, 2016, http://asne.org/content.asp?contentid=447.

11. ASNE, "2016 ASNE Diversity Survey—Methodology and Detailed Tables," http://asne.org/files/Updated%20ASNE%20Diversity%20Survey%20Methodology%20and%20Tables.pdf.

12. U.S. Census Bureau, "Quick Facts," accessed November 2, 2016, www.census.gov/quickfacts/table/PST045215/00.

13. Bob Papper, "RTDNA Research: Women and Minorities in Newsrooms," July 11, 2016, www.rtdna.org/article/rtdna_research_women_and_minorities_in_newsrooms.

14. Don Hewitt, interview conducted by Richard Campbell on *60 Minutes*, CBS News, New York, February 21, 1989.

15. Bureau of Labor Statistics, U.S. Department of Labor, *Occupational Outlook Handbook, 2016–17 Edition*, at www.bls.gov/ooh/media-and-communication/reporters-correspondents-and-broadcast-news-analysts.htm and www.bls.gov/ooh/media-and-communication/public-relations-specialists.htm.

16. Herbert Gans, *Deciding What's News* (New York: Pantheon, 1979), 42–48.

17. For reference and guidance on media ethics, see Clifford Christians, Mark Fackler, and Kim Rotzoll, *Media Ethics: Cases and Moral Reasoning*, 4th ed. (White Plains, N.Y.: Longman, 1995); and Thomas H. Bivins, "A Worksheet for Ethics Instruction and Exercises in Reason," *Journalism Educator* (Summer 1993): 4–16.

18. *SPJ Code of Ethics*, Society of Professional Journalists, 1996, www.spj.org/ethicscode.asp.

19. ASNE 2015 Census, Table A, http://asne.org/content.asp?contentid=129.

20. Pew Research Center, "Newspapers: Fact Sheet," *State of the News Media 2016*, June 15, 2016, www.journalism.org/2016/06/15/newspapers-fact-sheet/.

21. Ibid.

22. For a summary and links to the 2012 study, go to www.poynter.org/mediawire/top-stories/174826/survey-nprs-listeners-best-informed-fox-news-viewers-worst-informed/.

23. Katie Sanders, "Scoring the News, One Year Later," *PolitiFact,* August 26, 2015, www.politifact.com/punditfact/article/2015/aug/26/scoring-news-one-year-later/.

24. Michael O'Connell, "Fox News Nabs Historic Cable Ratings Victory," September 30, 2014, www.hollywoodreporter.com/live-feed/fox-news-nabs-historic-cable-736624.

25. Malcolm Gladwell, "The Satire Paradox," *Revisionist History* (podcast), August 17, 2016.

26. Heather L. LaMarre, Kristen D. Landreville, and Michael A. Beam, "The Irony of Satire: Political Ideology and the Motivation to See What You Want to See in *The Colbert Report*," *International Journal of Press/Politics* 14 (April 2009): 212–231.

27. Craig Silverman and Lawrence Alexander, "How Teens in the Balkans are Duping Trump Supporters with Fake News," *Buzzfeed,* November 3, 2016, www.buzzfeed.com/craigsilverman/how-macedonia-became-a-global-hub-for-pro-trump-misinfo?utm_term=.eeM09nYqBw#.rkZJEqp7PD.

28. Laura Sydell, "We Tracked Down A Fake-News Creator In The Suburbs. Here's What We Learned," *NPR,* Nov 23, 2016, www.npr.org/sections/alltechconsidered/2016/11/23/503146770/npr-finds-the-head-of-a-covert-fake-news-operation-in-the-suburbs.

29. Madeline Conway, "Accused 'Pizzagate' Shooter Faces Federal Charges," *Politico,* December 13, 2016, www.politico.com/story/2016/12/edgar-maddison-welch-pizzagate-charges-232570.

30. David Uberti, "The Real History of Fake News," Columbia *Journalism Review*, December 15, 2016, www.cjr.org/special_report/fake_news_history.php.

31. "Statements about Climate Change," *PolitiFact,* accessed November 2, 2016, www.politifact.com/subjects/climate-change/.

32. Sydney Ember, "Another Journalist Quits Las Vegas Newspaper Bought by Sheldon Adelson," *New York Times*, April 26, 2016, www.nytimes.com/2016/04/27/business/media/another-journalist-quits-las-vegas-newspaper-bought-by-sheldon-adelson.html?_r=0.

33. John Carroll, "News War, Part 3," *Frontline*, PBS, February 27, 2007, www.pbs.org/wgbh/pages/frontline/newswar/etc/script3.html.

MEDIA LITERACY CASE STUDY: Investigative Journalism: In the "Spotlight," p. 74
1. Scott Allen, "A Distinguished History of Digging Up the Truth," *Boston Globe*, June 22, 2012, www.bostonglobe .com/news/special-reports/2012/06/22/distinguished -history-digging-truth/koYXOjPVD3CfTuRBtp0ZnM/story .html.
2. Investigative Reporters and Editors, "About IRE," www .ire.org/about/.

THE DIGITAL TURN CASE STUDY: The *Huffington Post*: News Aggregation Aggravates Legacy News, p. 94
1. David Segal, "Arianna Huffington's Improbable, Insatiable Content Machine," *New York Times Magazine*, June 30, 2015, www.nytimes.com/2015/07/05/magazine/arianna -huffingtons-improbable-insatiable-content-machine .html?_r=0.
2. See "The New News," James Cameron Memorial Lecture, September 22, 2010, http://image.guardian.co.uk/ sysfiles/Media/documents/2010/09/23/DownieCameron .pdf; and Jack Shaffer, "Len Downie Calls Arianna Huffington a Parasite," *Slate*, September 23, 2010, www .slate.com/articles/news_and_politics/press_box/2010/09/ len_downie_calls_arianna_huffington_a_parasite.html.
3. Ibid.
4. Arianna Huffington, "Leonard Downie's Downer," *Guardian*, September 23, 2010, www.guardian.co.uk /commentisfree/cifamerica/2010/sep/23/huffington-post -washington-post.
5. Michael Calderone, "Arianna Huffington Will Leave the *Huffington Post* to Build Health and Wellness Site," *Huffington Post*, August 11, 2016, www .huffingtonpost.com/entry/arianna-huffington-post _us_57ac67e6e4b0ba7ed23f2989?section=&.

4 Magazines in the Age of Specialization

1. Sammye Johnson, "Promoting Easy Sex without the Intimacy: *Maxim* and *Cosmopolitan* Cover Lines and Cover Images," in *Critical Thinking about Sex, Love, and Romance in the Mass Media*, ed. Mary-Lou Galician and Debra L. Merskin (Mahwah, N.J.: Erlbaum, 2007), 55–74.
2. Jennifer Benjamin, "How Cosmo Changed the World," May 3, 2007, www.cosmopolitan.com/lifestyle/a1746 /about-us-how-cosmo-changed-the-world. See also Theodore Peterson, *Magazines in the Twentieth Century* (Urbana: University of Illinois Press, 1964), 5.
3. See Gloria Steinem, "Sex, Lies and Advertising," *Ms.*, July–August 1990, p. 18–28.
4. *Magazine Media Factbook 2016/17*, Association of Magazine Media, www.magazine.org/sites/default/files /MPA-FACTbook201617-ff.pdf.

5. Matt Drange, "Peter Thiel's War on Gawker: A Timeline," *Forbes*, June 21, 2016, www .forbes.com/sites/mattdrange/2016/06/21/ peter-thiels-war-on-gawker-a-timeline/#6dacc54d7e80.

THE DIGITAL TURN CASE STUDY: The Digital Pass-Along: Magazine Readers on Social Media, p. 125
1. MPA, "Magazine Media Readers Are Social: Key Research Findings," www.magazine.org/sites/default /files/SOCIAL-f5%20website.pdf; and "MPA Releases Benchmark Social Media Study," www.magazine.org /insights-resources/research-publications/guides-studies /new-mpa-releases-benchmark-social-media.
2. MPA, "Magazine Media Sees Audiences Shift to Mobile from Desktop/Laptop at a Rate of Nine to One," July 28, 2016, www.magazine.org/mpa/magazine -media-sees-audiences-shift-mobile-desktop /laptop-rate-nine-one.

5 Sound Recording and Popular Music

1. Mark Coleman, *Playback: From the Victrola to MP3* (Cambridge, Mass.: Da Capo Press, 2003).
2. IFPI, "IFPI Digital Music Report 2014," 2014, http:// www.ifpi.org/downloads/Digital-Music-Report- 2014.pdf.
3. Mick Jagger, quoted in Jann S. Wenner, "Jagger Remembers," *Rolling Stone*, December 14, 1995, 66.
4. See Mac Rebennack (Dr. John) with Jack Rummel, *Under a Hoodoo Moon* (New York: St. Martin's Press, 1994), 58.
5. Ken Tucker, quoted in Ed Ward, Geoffrey Stokes, and Ken Tucker, *Rock of Ages: The Rolling Stone History of Rock & Roll* (New York: Rolling Stone Press, 1986), 521.
6. See "The 'Nashville Sound' Begins," *Living in Stereo*, September 19, 2006, http://livinginstereo.com/?p=252.
7. See Michael D'Arcy and Sherry Anderson, "What Is Countrypolitan Music?" January 2001, www.michaelfitz .net/blog/countrypolitan_101/.
8. IFPI, "Digital Music Report 2016," www.ifpi.org /downloads/GMR2016.pdf.
9. Spotify, "Spotify Explained," accessed October 17, 2016, www.spotifyartists.com/spotify-explained.

MEDIA LITERACY CASE STUDY: Spotify and Online Streaming: Saving or Sinking the Music Industry?, p. 142
1. Robert Levine, "Billboard Cover: Spotify CEO Daniel Ek on Taylor Swift, His 'Freemium' Business Model, and Why He's Saving the Music Industry," *Billboard*, June 5, 2015, www.billboard.com/articles/business/6590101/daniel-ek -spotify-ceo-streaming-feature-tidal-apple-record-labels -taylor-swift.

2. Tim Ingham, "Daniel Ek on YouTube, SoundCloud, and Why He Didn't Build Spotify to Sell It," *Music Business Worldwide*, February 17, 2016, www.musicbusinessworldwide.com/daniel-ek-on-youtube-soundcloud-and-why-he-didnt-build-spotify-to-sell-it/.

THE DIGITAL TURN CASE STUDY: 360 Degrees of Music, p. 160

1. See Sara Karubian, "360-Degree Deals: An Industry Reaction to the Devaluation of Recorded Music," *Southern California Interdisciplinary Law Journal* 18, no. 395 (2009): 395–462, www-bcf.usc.edu/~idjlaw/PDF/18-2/18-2%20 Karubian.pdf.

6 Popular Radio and the Origins of Broadcasting

1. Cathy Applefield Olson, "'You Can't Stop Technology': iHeartMedia Chairman and CEO Bob Pittman Talks Radio and Tech at CES," *Billboard*, January 6, 2015, www.billboard.com/articles/business/6429515/bob-pittman-iheartmedia-ces-technology.

2. Robert Levine, "iHeart Is Aiming for Casual Music Fans with Streaming Service, Leaving the Music Nerds to Spotify and Apple," *Billboard*, September 29, 2016, www.billboard.com/articles/business/7525739/iheartmedia-streaming-service-radio-aol.

3. iHeartCommunications, Inc., Form 10-K, February 19, 2015, www.sec.gov/Archives/edgar/data/739708/0001400 89115000004/10-K.htm.

4. Olson, "'You Can't Stop Technology.'"

5. Tom Lewis, *Empire of the Air: The Men Who Made Radio* (New York: HarperCollins, 1991), 181.

6. Michael Pupin, "Objections Entered to Court's Decision," *New York Times*, June 10, 1934, p. E5.

7. For a full discussion of early broadcast history and the formation of RCA, see Eric Barnouw, *Tube of Plenty* (New York: Oxford University Press, 1982); Susan Douglas, *Inventing American Broadcasting, 1899–1922* (Baltimore: Johns Hopkins University Press, 1987); and Christopher Sterling and John Kitross, *Stay Tuned: A Concise History of American Broadcasting* (Belmont, Calif.: Wadsworth, 1990).

8. Michele Hilmes, *Radio Voices: American Broadcasting, 1922–1952* (Minneapolis: University of Minnesota Press, 1997).

9. "Amos 'n' Andy Show," Museum of Broadcast Communications, www.museum.tv/eotv/amosnandy.htm

10. NPR, "NPR Factsheet," accessed October 22, 2016, www.npr.org/about/press/NPR_Fact_Sheet.pdf.

11. StreamingRadioGuide, accessed October 22, 2016, http://streamingradioguide.com/.

12. "Podcast Consumption Surges to One in Five Americans," Inside Radio, March 7, 2016, www.insideradio.com/free /podcast-consumption-surges-to-one-in-five-americans /article_bce00ee0-e4b1-11e5-9077-9f119ab66694.html.

13. April Glaser, "Your Phone Has an FM Chip. So Why Can't You Listen to the Radio?," *Wired*, July 8, 2016, www.wired.com/2016/07/phones-fm-chips-radio-smartphone/.

14. National Association of Broadcasters, "Expand Access to Emergency Information: Unlock FM," accessed October 25, 2016, www.nab.org/advocacy/issue. asp?id=2354.

15. Nielsen, "State of the Media: Audio Today, How America Listens," February 25, 2016, www.nielsen.com /content/dam/corporate/us/en/reports-downloads/2016 -reports/state-of-the-media-audio-today-radio-2016.pdf.

16. Radio Advertising Bureau, "RAB Revenue Releases," 2015, www.rab.com/public/pr/rev-pr.cfm?search=2015 &section=press.

17. Federal Communications Commission, "Broadcast Station Totals as of September 30, 2016," https://apps.fcc .gov/edocs_public/Query.do?docTitleDesc=Broadcast +Station+Totals&parm=5.

18. Glenn Peoples, "How 'Playola' Is Infiltrating Streaming Services: Pay for Play Is 'Definitely Happening,'" *Billboard*, August 19, 2015, www.billboard.com/articles /business/6670475/playola-promotion-streaming-services; see also Robert Cookson, "Spotify Bans 'Payola' on Playlists," *Financial Times*, August 20, 2015, https://next .ft.com/content/af1728ca-4740-11e5-af2f-4d6e0e5eda22.

19. Peter DiCola, "False Premises, False Promises: A Quantitative History of Ownership Consolidation in the Radio Industry," Future of Music Coalition, December 2006, https://futureofmusic.org/article/research /false-premises-false-promises

20. "Statement of FCC Chairman William E. Kennard on Low Power FM Radio Initiative," March 27, 2000, www .fcc.gov/Speeches/Kennard/Statements/2000/stwek024 .html.

THE DIGITAL TURN CASE STUDY: Streaming Radio Becomes Mainstream, p. 188

1. Pandora, "Pandora Reports Q3 2016 Financial Results," October 25, 2016, http://press.pandora.com/file/4247784 /Index?KeyFile=36386210.

2. Hannah Karp, "Pandora Nears Deals for On-Demand Streaming," *Wall Street Journal*, August 19, 2016, www .wsj.com/articles/pandora-nears-deals-for-on-demand -streaming-1471599002.

3. iHeartRadio, "Introducing iHeartRadio All Access," September 23, 2016, http://blog.iheart.com/Pages /introducing-iheartradio-all-access.aspx.

4. "Small-Town Radio Attracts International Audience," *Feather River Bulletin*, February 29, 2012.

7 Movies and the Impact of Images

1. Douglas Gomery, *Shared Pleasures: A History of Movie Presentation in the United States* (Madison: University of Wisconsin Press, 1992), 18.

2. Douglas Gomery, *Movie History: A Survey* (Belmont, Calif.: Wadsworth, 1991), 167.

3. Motion Picture Association of America, "Theatrical Market Statistics," 2015, www.mpaa.org/wp-content /uploads/2016/04/MPAA-Theatrical-Market-Statistics-2015 _Final.pdf.

4. Matt Krantz, Mike Snider, Marco Della Cava, and Bryan Alexander, "Disney Buys Lucasfilm for $4 Billion," *USA Today*, October 30, 2012, www.usatoday.com/story/money /business/2012/10/30/disney-star-wars-lucasfilm/1669739/.

5. Julianne Pepitone, "Americans Now Watch More Online Movies Than DVDs," CNN/Money, March 22, 2012, http:// money.cnn.com/2012/03/22/technology/streaming -movie-sales/index.htm.

6. See Eric Barnouw, *Tube of Plenty: The Evolution of American Television*, rev. ed. (New York: Oxford University Press, 1982), 108–109.

MEDIA LITERACY CASE STUDY: Breaking through Hollywood's Race Barrier, p. 212

1. Douglas Gomery, *Shared Pleasures: A History of Movie Presentation in the United States* (Madison: University of Wisconsin Press, 1992), 155–170.

2. "Don Cheadle on Difficulty of Financing Miles Davis Film without White Actor," BBC, May 4, 2016, www.bbc.co.uk /programmes/p03q2p64/.

THE DIGITAL TURN CASE STUDY: Attracting an Audience in a Digital Age, p. 222

1. "Ryan Reynolds Might Have Leaked *Deadpool*'s Test Footage," YouTube video, February 10, 2016, www .youtube.com/watch?v=5Sq0_MGriXc.

2. Seb Joseph, "Movie Marketing Moves into the Digital Age," *Marketing Week*, February 25, 2014, www.marketingweek .com/2014/02/25/movie-marketing-moves-into-the-digital-age/.

3. "A Case Study in Gaining Exposure for Your Film," *The Vimeo Blog*, October 17, 2012, https://vimeo.com/blog /post/a-case-study-in-gaining-exposure-for-your-film.

8 Television, Cable, and Specialization in Visual Culture

1. Jacob Stolworthy, "*Stranger Things* Bigger Hit for Neflix Than *House of Cards*, *Daredevil*, and *Narcos*," *Independent*, August 15, 2016, www.independent.co.uk/arts -entertainment/tv/news/stranger-things-bigger-hit-for-netflix -than-shows-including-house-of-cards-daredevil-and -narcos-a7191971.html.

2. Tim Mulkerin, "4 Times the Budget Constraints of 'Stranger Things' Actually Made the Show Better," *Business Insider*, August 1, 2016, www.businessinsider .com/stranger-things-budget-2016-7/#the-show-was -originally-set-in-a-different-town-1. See also Sam Adams, "'Stranger Things': How Netflix's Retro Hit Resurrects the Eighties," *Rolling Stone*, July 21, 2016, www.rollingstone .com/tv/features/stranger-things-how-netflixs-hit -resurrects-the-1980s-w429804.

3. Katerina Eva Matsa, "Network News: Fact Sheet," Pew Research Center, June 15, 2016, www.journalism .org/2016/06/15/network-news-fact-sheet/.

4. See Horace Newcomb, *TV: The Most Popular Art* (Garden City, N.Y.: Anchor Books, 1974), 31, 39.

5. Michael Schneider, "These Are the 100 Most-Watched TV Shows of the 2015-16 Season: Winners and Losers," *IndieWire*, May 31, 2016, www.indiewire.com/2016/05 /most-watched-tv-show-2015–2016-season-game-of -thrones-the-walking-dead-football-1201682396/.

6. "Just the Facts: Consumer Choice Explodes, 1992–2012," National Cable & Telecommunications Association, www.ncta.com/statistic/statistic/Consumer -Choice-Explodes.aspx. See also "Industry Data," NCTA—the Internet and Television Association, accessed December 11, 2016, www.ncta.com/industry-data.

7. *United States v. Midwest Video Corp.*, 440 U.S. 689 (1979).

8. Aaron Pressman, "The Average Cable TV Bill Has Hit a New All-Time Record," *Fortune*, September 23, 2016, http://fortune.com/2016/09/23/average-cable-tv-bill/.

MEDIA LITERACY CASE STUDY: Race, Gender, and Sexual Orientation in TV Programming, p. 242

1. Larry Gross, *Up from Invisibility: Lesbians, Gay Men, and the Media in America* (New York: Columbia University Press, 2001). See also Liesbet Van Zoonen, *Feminist Media Studies* (Thousand Oaks, Calif.: Sage, 1994) and Angela McRobbie, *The Uses of Cultural Studies* (Thousand Oaks, Calif.: Sage, 2005).

2. Edward Alwood, *Straight News: Gays, Lesbians and the News Media* (New York: Columbia University Press, 1996). See also Gaye Tuchman, *Making News: A Study in the Construction of Reality* (New York: Free Press, 1978).

THE DIGITAL TURN CASE STUDY: Bingeing Purges Traditional Viewing Habits, p. 251

1. "Statistics and Facts about Binge-Watching in the U.S," *Statista*, accessed November 28, 2016, www.statista.com /topics/2508/binge-watching-in-the-us/.

2. "Netflix Declares Binge Watching Is the New Normal," PR Newswire, December 13, 2013, www.prnewswire.com/news-releases/netflix-declares-binge-watching-is-the-new-normal-235713431.html.

9 The Internet and New Technologies:
The Media Converge

1. Scott Horsley, "Marco Rubio Warns GOP on WikiLeaks: 'Tomorrow, It Could Be Us,'" *National Public Radio*, October 19, 2016, www.npr.org/2016/10/19/498529403/marco-rubio-warns-gop-on-wikileaks-tomorrow-it-could-be-us.

2. Michael B. Kelly, "Edward Snowden's Relationship with WikiLeaks Should Worry Everyone," *Business Insider*, January 4, 2014, www.businessinsider.com/edward-snowden-and-wikileaks-2014-1.

3. Zeynep Tufekci, "WikiLeaks Isn't Whistleblowing," *New York Times*, November 4, 2016, www.nytimes.com/2016/11/05/opinion/what-were-missing-while-we-obsess-over-john-podestas-email.html?_r=0.

4. "Broadband vs. Dial-Up Adoption over Time," Pew Research Internet Project, September 2013, www.pewinternet.org/data-trend/internet-use/connection-type/.

5. "Desktop Search Engine Market Share," NetMarketShare, October 2016 to December 2016, www.netmarketshare.com/search-engine-market-share.aspx?qprid=4&qpcustomd=0&qptimeframe=M.

6. Andreas Kaplan and Michael Haenlein, "Users of the World, Unite! The Challenges and Opportunities of Social Media," *Business Horizons* 53, no. 1 (2010): 59–68.

7. Chris Anderson and Michael Wolff, "The Web Is Dead. Long Live the Internet," *Wired*, August 17, 2010, www.wired.com/magazine/2010/08/ff_webrip. See also Charles Arthur, "Walled Gardens Look Rosy for Facebook, Apple—and Would-Be Censors," *Guardian*, April 17, 2012, www.guardian.co.uk/technology/2012/apr/17/walled-gardens-facebook-apple-censors.

8. "Twitter Usage/Company Facts," Twitter, updated June 30, 2016, https://about.twitter.com/company.

9. *Wikipedia*, s.v. "*Wikipedia* Seigenthaler Biography Incident," last modified January 23, 2017, http://en.wikipedia.org/wiki/Wikipedia_Seigenthaler_biography_incident.

10. Carrie Mihalcik, "Petition to Make Clinton President Largest in Change.org History," *CNET*, December 1, 2016, www.cnet.com/news/hillary-clinton-president-change-org-donald-trump-electoral-college/.

11. Tim Berners-Lee, James Hendler, and Ora Lassila, "The Semantic Web," *Scientific American*, May 17, 2001, https://www.scientificamerican.com/article/the-semantic-web/.

12. Eli Blumenthal and Elizabeth Weise, "Hacked Home Devices Caused Massive Internet Outage," *USA Today*, October 21, 2016, www.usatoday.com/story/tech/2016/10/21/cyber-attack-takes-down-east-coast-netflix-spotify-twitter/92507806/.

13. Brian Solomon, "Google Passed Apple as the World's Most Valuable Company (Again)," *Forbes*, May 12, 2016, www.forbes.com/sites/briansolomon/2016/05/12/google-passed-apple-as-the-worlds-most-valuable-company-again/#17fe0eb968fc. See also Associated Press, "Exxon Surpasses Apple as Most Valuable Company," January 13, 2017, *Beaumont Enterprise*, www.beaumontenterprise.com/news/article/Exxon-surpasses-Apple-as-most-valuable-company-4224406.php.

14. Paresh Dave, Daniel Miller, and Meg James, "Apple Now Taking Film and TV Pitches," *Chicago Tribune*, January 12, 2017, www.chicagotribune.com/bluesky/technology/la-fi-tn-apple-hollywood-20170112-story.html.

15. "IAB Internet Advertising Revenue Report: 2015 Full Year Results," *Interactive Advertising* Bureau, April 21, 2016, www.iab.com/wp-content/uploads/2016/04/IAB_Internet_Advertising_Revenue_Report_FY_2015-final.pdf, p. 4.

16. Federal Trade Commission, *Privacy Online: Fair Information Practices in the Electronic Marketplace: A Report to Congress*, May 2000, www.ftc.gov/sites/default/files/documents/reports/privacy-online-fair-information-practices-electronic-marketplace-federal-trade-commission-report/privacy2000text.pdf.

17. Mark Zuckerberg, "Our Commitment to the Facebook Community," *Facebook*, November 29, 2011, https://www.facebook.com/notes/facebook/our-commitment-to-the-facebook-community/10150378701937131.

18. "IAB Internet Advertising Revenue Report: 2015 Full Year Results," p. 7.

19. Federal Trade Commission, *Privacy Online*.

MEDIA LITERACY CASE STUDY: Net Neutrality, p. 278

1. Rebecca R. Ruiz, "F.C.C. Sets Net Neutrality Rules," March 12, 2015, *New York Times*, http://www.nytimes.com/2015/03/13/technology/fcc-releases-net-neutrality-rules.html.

2. Federal Communications Commision, "Fact Sheet: Chairman Wheeler Proposes New Rules for Protecting the Open Internet," accessed May 9, 2015, https://apps.fcc.gov/edocs_public/attachmatch/DOC-331869A1.pdf.

3. Nick Russo, Danielle Kehl, Robert Morgus, and Sarah Morris, "The Cost of Connectivity 2014: Data and Analysis on Broadband Offerings in 24 Cities around the World," Open Technology Institute, October 30, 2014, www.newamerica.org/oti/the-cost-of-connectivity-2014.

4. James O'Toole, "Chattanooga's Super-Fast Publicly Owned Internet," CNN Money, May 20, 2014, http://money.cnn.com/2014/05/20/technology/innovation/chattanooga-internet; Cedar Falls Utilities, accessed January 10, 2015, www.cfu.net/cybernet/default.aspx.

THE DIGITAL TURN CASE STUDY: Activism, Hacktivism, and Anonymous, p. 288
1. Joseph Ax, "Hacker Who Highlighted Notorious Ohio Rape Case Pleads Guilty," Reuters, November 23, 2016, www.reuters.com/article/us-ohio-rape-cyber-idUSKBN13I2J2.
2. David Kushner, "Anonymous vs. Steubenville," November 27, 2013, *Rolling Stone*, www.rollingstone.com/culture/news/anonymous-vs-steubenville-20131127.
3. Chris Landers, "Serious Business: Anonymous Takes on Scientology (and Doesn't Afraid of Anything)," *Baltimore City Paper*, April 2, 2008.
4. David Kushner, "Anonymous vs. Steubenville."

10 Digital Gaming and the Media Playground

1. Madeline Berg, "The Highest-Paid YouTube Stars 2016: PewDiePie Remains No. 1 with $15 Million," *Forbes*, December 5, 2016, www.forbes.com/sites/maddieberg/2016/12/05/the-highest-paid-youtube-stars-2016-pewdiepie-remains-no-1-with-15-million/#73fec3f86b0f.
2. Felix Kjellberg, "Let's Talk about Money," YouTube video, posted July 7, 2015, www.youtube.com/watch?v=zn0y3Opb8Wk.
3. Maeve Duggan, "Gaming and Gamers," Pew Research Center, December 15, 2015, www.pewinternet.org/2015/12/15/gaming-and-gamers/.
4. Erkki Huhtamo, "Slots of Fun, Slots of Trouble: An Archaeology of Arcade Gaming," in *Handbook of Computer Game Studies*, ed. Joost Raessens and Jeffrey Goldstein (Cambridge, Mass.: MIT Press, 2005), 6–7.
5. Ibid., 9–10.
6. Seth Porges, "11 Things You Didn't Know about Pinball History," *Popular Mechanics*, September 1, 2009, www.popularmechanics.com/technology/g284/4328211-new.
7. "Magnavox Odyssey," PONG-Story, accessed April 6, 2015, www.pong-story.com/odyssey.htm.
8. Eddie Makuch, "Here's How Many PS Plus Subscribers There Are," GameSpot, June 29, 2016, www.gamespot.com/articles/heres-how-many-ps-plus-subscribers-there-are/1100-6441361/.
9. "Video Game Console Sales Worldwide for Products Total Lifespan as of June 2016 (in Million Units)," Statista, accessed February 5, 2017, www.statista.com/statistics/268966/total-number-of-game-consoles-sold-worldwide-by-console-type/.
10. "Nintendo Co., Ltd., Consolidated Sales Transition by Region," Nintendo, www.nintendo.co.jp/ir/library/historical_data/pdf/consolidated_sales_e1606.pdf.
11. Associated Press, "Sony to Stop Selling PlayStation Portable by End of Year," *Time*, June 3, 2014, http://web.archive.org/web/20140603143428/http://time.com/2816781/sony-to-stop-selling-playstation-portable-by-end-of-year/.
12. Brian Ashcraft, "Japan, Where the PS Vita Won't Die," Kotaku, January 28, 2016, http://kotaku.com/japan-where-the-ps-vita-wont-die-1755647191.
13. "Number of Smartphones Sold to End Users Worldwide from 2007 to 2015 (in Million Units)," Statista, accessed February 5, 2017, www.statista.com/statistics/263437/global-smartphone-sales-to-end-users-since-2007/.
14. Fantasy Sports Trade Association, "Industry Demographics," accessed February 5, 2017, http://fsta.org/research/industry-demographics/.
15. "Number of World of Warcraft Subscribers from 1st Quarter 2005 to 3rd Quarter 2015 (in Millions)," Statista, accessed February 5, 2017, www.statista.com/statistics/276601/number-of-world-of-warcraft-subscribers-by-quarter/.
16. Henry Jenkins, "Interactive Audiences? The 'Collective Intelligence' of Media Fans," in *The New Media Book*, ed. Dan Harries (London: British Film Institute, 2002).
17. Douglas A. Gentile et al., "Pathological Video Game Use among Youths: A Two-Year Longitudinal Study," *Pediatrics* 127, no. 2 (2011), doi:10.1542/peds.2010-1353.
18. Florian Rehbein and Dirk Baier, "Family-, Media-, and School-Related Risk Factors of Video Game Addiction: A 5-Year Longitudinal Study," *Journal of Media Psychology: Theories, Methods and Application* 25, no. 3 (2013): 118–128.
19. "South Korean Couple Starved Child While Raising 'Virtual Baby,'" *CNN World*, March 5, 2010, www.cnn.com/2010/WORLD/asiapcf/03/05/korea.baby.starved/.
20. Entertainment Software Association, "2016 Sales, Demographic and Usage Data: Essential Facts about the Computer and Video Game Industry," http://essentialfacts.theesa.com/Essential-Facts-2016.pdf, p. 2.
21. Ibid., p. 13; "The Global Games Market Reaches $99.6 Billion in 2016, Mobile Generating 37%," Newzoo, April 21, 2016, https://newzoo.com/insights/articles/global-games-market-reaches-99-6-billion-2016-mobile-generating-37/.
22. Ian Hamilton, "Blizzard's World of Warcraft Revenue Down," *Orange County Register*, November 8, 2010, www.ocregister.com/articles/blizzard-543767-world-warcraft.html.

23. "IGA Worldwide," YouTube video, posted April 8, 2009, www.youtube.com/watch?v=dGKum-lo9V8.

24. Mansoor Mithaiwala, "Video Games That Cost More to Make Than Hollywood Blockbuster Films," *Looper*, accessed February 5, 2017, www.looper.com/35410 /video-games-cost-make-hollywood-blockbuster-films/.

25. "John Madden Net Worth," CelebrityNetworth.com, accessed April 5, 2012, www.celebritynetworth.com /richest-athletes/nfl/john-madden-net-worth.

26. "ESRB Ratings Guide," Entertainment Software Rating Board, accessed April 8, 2015, www.esrb.org/ratings /ratings_guide.jsp.

27. Evan Narcisse, "Supreme Court: 'Video Games Qualify for First Amendment Protection,'" *Time*, June 27, 2011, http://techland.time.com/2011/06/27/supreme-court-video -games-qualify-for-first-amendment-protection.

28. Ibid.

29. Todd VanDerWerff, "#Gamergate: Here's Why Everybody in the Video Game World Is Fighting," *Vox*, October 13, 2014, www.vox.com/2014/9/6/6111065/gamergate-explained -everybody-fighting.

30. Angela McRobbie, *The Uses of Cultural Studies* (Thousand Oaks: Sage, 2005).

THE DIGITAL TURN CASE STUDY: Fighting the Dark Side of Gaming Culture: Anita Sarkeesian and Feminist Frequency, p. 306

1. Anita Sarkeesian, "It's Game Over for 'Gamers': Anita Sarkeesian on Video Games' Great Future," *New York Times*, October 28, 2014, www.nytimes.com/2014/10/29 /opinion/anita-sarkeesian-on-video-games-great-future .html?_r=0.

2. Todd VanDerWerff, "#Gamergate: Here's Why Everybody in the Video Game World Is Fighting," *Vox*, October 13, 2014, www.vox.com/2014/9/6/6111065 /gamergate-explained-everybody-fighting.

3. Jen Yamato, "Anita Sarkeesian on Life after Gamergate: 'I Want to Be a Human Again,'" *Daily Beast*, September 23, 2016, www.thedailybeast.com/articles/2016/09/23/anita -sarkeesian-on-life-after-gamergate-i-want-to-be-a-human -again.html.

MEDIA LITERACY CASE STUDY: Writing about Games, p. 316

1. Todd VanDerWerff, "#Gamergate: Here's Why Everybody in the Video Game World Is Fighting," *Vox*, October 13, 2014, www.vox.com/2014/9/6/6111065 /gamergate-explained-everybody-fighting.

2. "Bow, Nigger," always_black.com, September 22, 2004, www.alwaysblack.com/blackbox/bownigger.html.

3. Kieron Gillen, "The New Games Journalism," *Kieron Gillen's Workblog*, March 23, 2004, http://gillen.cream.org /wordpress_html/assorted-essays/the-new-games -journalism.

II Advertising and Commercial Culture

1. Linda Holmes, "Rest Your Greatness: 6 Key Moments with DJ Khaled," *National Public Radio*, January 17, 2017, www.npr.org/sections/monkeysee/2017/01/17/510230324 /rest-your-greatness-six-key-moments-with-dj-khaled.

2. Max Chafkin and Sarah Frier, "How Snapchat Built a Business by Confusing Olds," *Bloomberg Businessweek*, March 3, 2016, www.bloomberg.com/features/2016-how -snapchat-built-a-business/.

3. *Advertising Age Marketing Fact Pack 2017*, 14, 16.

4. Ibid., p. 1.

5. Randall Rothenberg, Where the Suckers Moon: An Advertising Story (New York: Alfred A. Knopf, 1994), 20.

6. *Advertising Age Marketing Fact Pack 2017*, 14.

7. See Bettina Fabos, "The Commercialized Web: Challenges for Libraries and Democracy," *Library Trends* 53, no. 4 (Spring 2005): 519–523.

8. "Google's Ad Revenue from 2001 to 2016 (in Billion U.S. Dollars)," Statista, accessed February 5, 2017, www.statista .com/statistics/266249/advertising-revenue-of-google/.

9. *Advertising Age Marketing Fact Pack 2017*, 20, 24.

10. "Facebook's Advertising Revenue Worldwide from 2009 to 2016 (in Million U.S. Dollars)," Statista, accessed February 5, 2017, www.statista.com/statistics/271258 /facebooks-advertising-revenue-worldwide/.

11. *Advertising Age Marketing Fact Pack 2017*, 16.

12. See Michael Schudson, *Advertising: The Uneasy Persuasion* (New York: Basic Books, 1984), 36–43; and Andrew Robertson, *The Lessons of Failure* (London: MacDonald, 1974).

13. *Advertising Age Marketing Fact Pack 2017*, 12.

14. Alix Spiegel, "Selling Sickness: How Drug Ads Changed Healthcare," National Public Radio, October 13, 2009, www.npr.org/templates/story/story.php?storyid=113675737.

15. Jason Millman, "It's True: Drug Companies Are Bombarding Your TV with More Ads Than Ever," *Washington Post*, March 23, 2015, www.washingtonpost. com/news/wonk/wp/2015/03/23/yes-drug-companies -are-bombarding-your-tv-with-more-ads-than-ever/?utm _term=.1ffecb80be78.

16. Center for Responsive Politics, "The Money behind the Elections," OpenSecrets.org, accessed September 2014, www.opensecrets.org/bigpicture.

17. Anu Narayanswamy, Darla Cameron, and Matea Gold, "Money Raised as of November 28th," *Washington Post*, December 9, 2016, www.washingtonpost.com/graphics /politics/2016-election/campaign-finance/.

18. Ashley Balcerzak, "Update: Federal Elections to Cost Just under $7 Billion, CRP Forecasts," Center

for Responsive Politics, November 2, 2016, www
.opensecrets.org/news/2016/11/update-federal-elections
-to-cost-just-under-7-billion-crp-forecasts/.

19. Nicholas Confessore and Karen Yourish, "$2 Billion Worth
of Free Media for Donald Trump," *New York Times*, March
15, 2016, www.nytimes.com/2016/03/16/upshot/measuring-
donald-trumps-mammoth-advantage-in-free-media.html?r
egister=google&smprod=nytcore-iphone&smid=nytcore-
iphone-share&_r=1&mtrref=undefined.

20. Michael Hiltzik, "Les Moonves, CBS, and Trump: Is
TV's Business Model Killing Democracy?" *LA Times*,
March 15, 2016, www.latimes.com/business/hiltzik/la
-fi-hiltzik-trump-moonves-snap-htmlstory.html.

**MEDIA LITERACY CASE STUDY: Idiots and Objects:
Stereotyping in Advertising, p. 342**

1. Gene Demby, "That Cute Cheerios Ad with the Interracial
Family Is Back," National Public Radio, January 30, 2014,
www.npr.org/blogs/codeswitch/2014/01/30/268930004/
that-cute-cheerios-ad-with-the-interracial-family-is-back.

12 Public Relations and Framing the Message

1. Tre'vell Anderson, "With a 'Furious' Opening, 'Fate'
Debuts with Global Box Office Record," *Los Angeles
Times,* April 16, 2017, www.latimes.com/entertainment/
movies/la-et-mn-box-office-fate-of-the-furious-20170416-
story.html.

2. Jeremy Kay, "Fast & Furious 7: 'Paul Walker's the Star
of Our Film, and He Should Be Celebrated,'" *Guardian*,
April 3, 2015, www.theguardian.com/film/filmblog/2015
/apr/03/fast-and-furious-7-paul-walker-universal-marketing
-campaign.

3. Matthew J. Culligan and Dolph Greene, *Getting Back
to the Basics of Public Relations and Publicity* (New York:
Crown Publishers, 1982), 100.

4. PRSA, "PR by the Numbers—2012," http://media.prsa
.org/events/PR-by-the-Numbers.htm.

5. Marvin N. Olasky, "The Development of Corporate
Public Relations, 1850–1930," *Journalism Monographs* 102
(April 1987): 15.

6. Michael Schudson, *Discovering the News: A Social
History of American Newspapers* (New York: Basic Books,
1978), 136.

7. "Lobbying: Overview," OpenSecrets.org, accessed
February 4, 2017, www.opensecrets.org/lobby/.

8. Philip Shenon, "3 Partners Quit Firm Handling Saudis'
P.R.," *New York Times*, December 6, 2002, www.nytimes
.com/2002/12/06/international/middleeast/06SAUD.
html?ex=1040199544&ei=1&en=c061b2d98376e7ba.

9. PRSA Statement on 'Alternative Facts'," January 24, 2017,
http://media.prsa.org/news-releases/prsa-opinions-and
-commentary/prsa-makes-statement-on-alternative-facts.htm.

10. Video of "Eisenhower Answers America" commercials
available online at www.c-span.org/video/?188176-1
/eisenhower-answers-america.

**THE DIGITAL TURN CASE STUDY: Military PR in
the Digital Age, p. 367**

1. Erik Ortiz, "String of Social Media Scandals Plagues
Military," *NBC News,* February 17, 2014, www.nbcnews
.com/news/military/string-social-media-scandals-plagues
-military-n40501.

2. Cori E. Dauber, *YouTube War: Fighting in a World of
Cameras in Every Cell Phone and Photoshop on Every
Computer*, Strategic Studies Institute, U.S. Army War
College, November 2009, www.strategicstudiesinstitute
.army.mil/pdffiles/pub951.pdf.

**MEDIA LITERACY CASE STUDY: The NFL's
Concussion Crisis, p. 370**

1. Brent Schrotenboer, "NFL Takes Aim at $25 Billion, but
at What Price?" *USA Today*, February 5, 2014,
www.usatoday.com/story/sports/nfl/super/2014/01/30
/super-bowl-nfl-revenue-denver-broncos-seattle
-seahawks/5061197/.

2. Mark Fainaru-Wada and Steve Fainaru, *League of Denial:
The NFL, Concussions, and the Battle for Truth* (New York:
Crown, 2013), 6.

13 Legal Controls and Freedom of Expression

1. Philip Bump, "President Trump Is Now Speculating That
the Media Is Covering Up Terrorist Attacks," *Washington
Post*, Feb 6, 2017, www.washingtonpost.com/news
/politics/wp/2017/02/06/president-trump-is-now
-speculating-that-the-media-is-covering-up-terrorist
-attacks/?utm_term=.f155a0d72f73.

2. Philip Rucker, John Wagner, and Greg Miller, "Trump,
in CIA Visit, Attacks Media for Coverage of His Inaugural
Crowds," *Washington Post*, January 21, 2017, www
.washingtonpost.com/politics/trump-in-cia-visit-attacks
-media-for-coverage-of-his-inaugural-crowds/2017/01/21
/f4574dca-e019-11e6-ad42-f3375f271c9c_story
.html?utm_term=.5d451b1fba0c.

3. Barney Henderson, David Lawlor, and Louise Burke,
"Donald Trump Attacks Alleged Russian Dossier as 'Fake
News' and Slams Buzzfeed and CNN at Press Conference,"
Telegraph, January 12, 2017, www.telegraph.co.uk
/news/2017/01/11/donald-trump-kremlin-blast-fabricated
-report-russian-ties-asfbi/.

4. Aaron Blake, "Kellyanne Conway's 'Bowling Green
Massacre' Wasn't a Slip of the Tongue. She Has Said It
Before," *Washington Post*, February 6, 2017, www
.washingtonpost.com/news/the-fix/wp/2017/02/06

/kellyanne-conways-bowling-green-massacre-wasnt-a-slip
-of-the-tongue-shes-said-it-before/?utm_term=.340b6eb9a3f6.

5. Sabrina Siddiqui, "Trump Press Ban: BBC, CNN and
Guardian Denied Access to Briefing," *Guardian*, February
25, 2017, www.theguardian.com/us-news/2017/feb/24
/media-blocked-white-house-briefing-sean-spicer; Sydney
Ember, "Can Libel Laws Be Changed under Trump?"
New York Times, November 13, 2016, www.nytimes
.com/2016/11/14/business/media/can-libel-laws-be
-changed-under-trump.html.

6. Max Greenwood, "Trump Tweets: The Media Is the
'Enemy of the American People.'" *Hill*, February 17, 2017,
http://thehill.com/homenews/administration/320168
-trump-the-media-is-the-enemy-of-the-american-people.

7. Steve Adler, "Covering Trump the Reuters Way,"
Reuters, January 31, 2017, www.reuters.com/article
/rpb-adlertrump-idUSKBN15F276.

8. Mike Cavender, "A Free Flow of Information No
Longer," RTDNA, January 24, 2017, www.rtdna.org
/article/a_free_flow_of_information_no_longer.

9. Corky Siemaszko, "George W. Bush: Free Press
'Indispensable to Democracy,'" *NBC News*, February 27,
2017, www.nbcnews.com/news/us-news/george-w-bush
-free-press-indispensable-democracy-n726141.

10. See Douglas M. Fraleigh and Joseph S. Tuman,
Freedom of Speech in the Marketplace of Ideas (New York:
St. Martin's Press, 1998), 77.

11. Fred Siebert, Theodore Peterson, and Wilbur Schramm,
Four Theories of the Press (Urbana: University of Illinois
Press, 1956).

12. Hugo Black, quoted in *New York Times Co. v. United
States*, 403 U.S. 713 (1971), www.law.cornell.edu/supct
/html/historics/USSC_CR_0403_0713_ZC.html.

13. Sameepa Shetty, "Julian Assange and Daniel Ellsberg
Mount Snowden Defense," *Fortune*, June 20, 2013, http://
fortune.com/2013/06/20/julian-assange-and-daniel
-ellsberg-mount-snowden-defense/.

14. Robert Warren, quoted in *United States v. Progressive,
Inc.*, 467 F. Supp. 990 (W.D. Wis. 1979), www.bc.edu
/bc_org/avp/cas/comm/free_speech/progressive.html.

15. See Edward W. Knappman, ed., *Great American Trials:
From Salem Witchcraft to Rodney King* (Detroit, Mich.:
Visible Ink Press, 1994), 517–519.

16. "Live Blogging and Tweeting from Court," Digital Media
Law Project, accessed March 8, 2017, www.dmlp.org
/legal-guide/live-blogging-and-tweeting-from-court.

17. L. David Russell, Christopher C. Chiou, and Sean D.
Nelson, "Litigation in Twitter Nation: When You Can and
Can't Tweet In #Court," *Law.com*, February 6, 2017,
www.law.com/sites/almstaff/2017/02/06/litigation-in-twitter
-nation-when-you-can-and-cant-tweet-in-court/?slreturn
=20170113023426.

18. *Mutual Film Corp. v. Industrial Communication of Ohio*,
236 U.S. 230 (1915).

19. Brooks Boliek, "Sorry, Ms. Jackson: FCC Hits New
Record," *Politico*, September 10, 2014, http://www.politico
.com/story/2014/09/fcc-net-neutrality-record-110818.html.

20. Seth Fiegerman, "New FCC Chairman Wants to Fix
Net Neutrality `Mistake,'" CNN, February 28, 2017, http://
money.cnn.com/2017/02/28/technology/fcc-net-neutrality/.

21. Allan J. Lichtman, "Who Rules America?" *Hill*, August 12,
2014, http://thehill.com/blogs/pundits-blog/civil-rights
/214857-who-rules-america.

**THE DIGITAL TURN CASE STUDY: Is "Sexting"
Pornography?, p. 397**

1. Richard Wortley and Stephen Smallbone, "Child
Pornography on the Internet," U.S. Department of Justice,
May 2006, www.popcenter.org/problems/pdfs/ChildPorn.
pdf.

2. Amanda Lenhart, "Teens and Sexting," Pew Internet &
American Life Project, December 15, 2009, http://pewresearch
.org/pubs/1440/teens-sexting-text-messages.

3. Sameer Hinduja and Justin W. Patchin, "State Sexting
Laws," Cyberbullying Research Center, July 2015, http://
cyberbullying.org/state-sexting-laws.pdf.

**MEDIA LITERACY CASE STUDY: Fouling the First
Amendment: Finding Facts in the Face
of Fake News, p. 408**

1. Craig Silverman, "This Analysis Shows How Viral Fake
Election News Stories Outperformed Real News on
Facebook," BuzzFeed, November 16, 2016, https:
//www.buzzfeed.com/craigsilverman/viral-fake-election
-news-outperformed-real-news-on-facebook?utm_term
=.af725RwKnr#.igW0XqaYZj.

2. See "Fake News: Home," Indiana University East Library
Guide, accessed March 11, 2017, http://iue.libguides
.com/fakenews/index. See also Joyce Valenza, "Truth,
Truthiness, Triangulation: A News Literacy Toolkit for a
'Post-Truth' World," *School Library Journal*, November 26,
2016, http://blogs.slj.com/neverendingsearch/2016/11/26/
truth-truthiness-triangulation-and-the-librarian-way-a-news-
literacy-toolkit-for-a-post-truth-world/.

3. Melissa Zimdars, "False, Misleading, Clickbait-y, and/or
Satirical 'News' Sources," 2016, https://docs.google.com
/document/d/10eA5-mCZLSS4MQY5QGb5ewC3VAL6pLk
T53V_81ZyitM/preview.

14 Media Economics and the Global Marketplace

1. Larry Page, "G Is for Google," August 10, 2015, full text
of letter in "Google's Larry Page Explains the New Alphabet,"
CNET, www.cnet.com/news/googles-larry-page-explains
-the-new-alphabet/.

2. Conor Dougherty, "Google to Reorganize as Alphabet to Keep Its Lead as an Innovator," *New York Times*, August 10, 2015, www.nytimes.com/2015/08/11/technology /google-alphabet-restructuring.html?smid=pl-share&_r=0.
3. Seth Fiegerman, "Google's Moonshots Lost $1 Billion Last Quarter," CNN, January 26, 2017, http://money.cnn .com/2017/01/26/technology/google-earnings-q4/.
4. Dougherty, "Google to Reorganize as Alphabet."
5. Douglas Gomery, "The Centrality of Media Economics," in *Defining Media Studies*, ed. Mark R. Levy and Michael Gurevitch (New York: Oxford University Press, 1994), 202.
6. David Harvey, *The Condition of Postmodernity: An Enquiry into the Origins of Cultural Change* (Oxford: Basil Blackwell, 1989), 171.
7. Katerina Eva Matsa, "The Acquisition Binge in Local TV," Pew Research Center, May 12, 2014, www.pewresearch .org/fact-tank/2014/05/12/the-acquisition-binge-in-local-tv/. See also "About" page, Sinclair Broadcast Group, accessed March 11, 2017, http://sbgi.net/#About.
8. Harper Neidig, "FCC Chair Doesn't Expect to Review AT&T–Time Warner Merger," *Hill*, February 27, 2017, http://thehill.com/policy/technology/321351-fcc-chair -doesnt-expect-to-review-att-time-warner-merger.
9. Wesley Morris and James Poniewozik, "Why 'Diverse TV' Matters: It's Better TV. Discuss," *New York Times*, February 10, 2016, www.nytimes.com/2016/02/14/arts /television/smaller-screens-truer-colors.html.
10. Lawrence Mishel and Jessica Schieder, "CEOs Make 276 Times More Than Typical Workers," Economic Policy Institute, August 3, 2016, www.epi.org/publication /ceos-make-276-times-more-than-typical-workers/.
11. Thomas Geoghegan, "How Pink Slips Hurt More Than Workers," *New York Times*, March 29, 2006, p. B8.
12. Edward Herman, "Democratic Media," *Z Papers* (January–March 1992): 23.

15 Social Scientific and Cultural Approaches to Media Research

1. Mark Potok, "Carnage in Charleston," *Intelligence Report*, October 27, 2015, www.splcenter.org /fighting-hate/intelligence-report/2015/carnage-charleston.
2. Mark Berman, "Prosecutors Say Dylann Roof 'Self-Radicalized' Online, Wrote Another Manifesto in Jail," *Washington Post*, August 22, 2016, www.washingtonpost .com/news/post-nation/wp/2016/08/22/prosecutors -say-accused-charleston-church-gunman-self-radicalized -online/?utm_term=.29a5d98c75f9.
3. Amy B. Wang, "'Nevertheless, She Persisted' Becomes New Battle Cry After McConnell Silences Elizabeth Warren," *Washington Post*, February 8, 2017, www.washingtonpost.com/news/the-fix/wp/2017/02/08 /nevertheless-she-persisted-becomes-new-battle -cry-after-mcconnell-silences-elizabeth-warren /?utm_term=.288234177419.
4. Tracy Mumford, "'She Persisted': Woman Pack Mpls. Tattoo Shop for Solidarity in Ink," *Minnesota Public Radio*, Feb 22, 2017, www.mprnews.org/story/2017/02/22 /she-persisted-tattoos.
5. Steve Fore, "Lost in Translation: The Social Uses of Mass Communications Research," *Afterimage* 20 (April 1993): 10.
6. James Carey, *Communication as Culture: Essays on Media and Society* (Boston: Unwin Hyman, 1989), 75.
7. Daniel Czitrom, *Media and the American Mind: From Morse to McLuhan* (Chapel Hill: University of North Carolina Press, 1982), 122–125.
8. Ibid., 123.
9. Harold Lasswell, *Propaganda Technique in the World War* (New York: Alfred A. Knopf, 1927), 9.
10. See W. W. Charters, *Motion Pictures and Youth: A Summary* (New York: Macmillan, 1934); and Garth Jowett, *Film: The Democratic Art* (Boston: Little, Brown, 1976), 220–229.
11. Czitrom, *Media and the American Mind*, 132; see also Harold Lasswell, "The Structure and Function of Communication in Society," in *The Communication of Ideas*, ed. Lyman Bryson (New York: Harper and Brothers, 1948), 37–51.
12. See Joseph Klapper, *The Effects of Mass Communication* (New York: Free Press, 1960).
13. *Where We Are on TV, '16–'17*, GLAAD, www.glaad .org/whereweareontv16.
14. See Nancy Signorielli and Michael Morgan, *Cultivation Analysis: New Directions in Media Effects Research* (Newbury Park, Calif.: Sage, 1990).
15. See Stuart Hall et al., *Policing the Crisis: Mugging, the State, and Law and Order* (London: Macmillan, 1978).
16. See Jack G. Shaheen, *Reel Bad Arabs: How Hollywood Vilifies a People* (Northampton, Mass.: Interlink Publishing Group, 2001).
17. See Janice Radway, *Reading the Romance: Women, Patriarchy, and Popular Literature* (Chapel Hill: University of North Carolina Press, 1984).

THE DIGITAL TURN CASE STUDY: Artificial Intelligence Gets Personal, p. 451

1. Gus Lubin, "How Netflix Will Someday Know Exactly What You Want to Watch as Soon as You Turn Your TV On," *Business Insider*, September 21, 2016, www .businessinsider.com/how-netflix-recommendations -work-2016-9.
2. Adam Levy, "How Netflix's AI Saves It $1 Billion Every Year," Motley Fool, June 19, 2016, www.fool.com

/investing/2016/06/19/how-netflixs-ai-saves-it-1-billion
-every-year.aspx.

3. Shabana Arora, "Recommendation Engines: How
Amazon and Netflix Are Winning the Personalization
Battle," MarTech Advisor, June 28, 2016, www
.martechadvisor.com/articles/customer-experience
/recommendation-engines-how-amazon-and-netflix-are
-winning-the-personalization-battle/.

MEDIA LITERACY CASE STUDY: Terror, Torture,
and TV, p. 464

1. Adam Green, "Normalizing Torture on *24*," *New York
Times*, May 22, 2005, www.nytimes.com/2005/05/22/
arts/television/normalizing-torture-on-24.html.

2. Ibid.

3. Dahlia Lithwick, "Lithwick: How Jack Bauer Shaped U.S.
Torture Policy," *Newsweek*, July 25, 2008, http://www
.newsweek.com/lithwick-how-jack-bauer-shaped-ustorture
-policy-93159.

4. "Scalia and Torture," *Atlantic*, June 19, 2007, http://
www.theatlantic.com/daily-dish/archive/2007/06/
scalia-and-torture/227548/.

5. Rupert Stone, "Trump Might Be 'Fine' with Torture,
but Most Americans Aren't," Al Jazeera America,
February 22, 2016, http://america.aljazeera.com
/opinions/2016/2/trump-might-be-fine-with-torture-but
-most-americans-arent.html.

Glossary

A&R (artist & repertoire) agents talent scouts of the music business who discover, develop, and sometimes manage performers.

access channels in cable television, a tier of nonbroadcast channels dedicated to local education, government, and the public.

account executives in advertising, client liaisons responsible for bringing in new business and managing the accounts of established clients.

account reviews in advertising, the process of evaluating or reinvigorating an ad campaign, which results in either renewing the contract with the original ad agency or hiring a new agency.

acquisitions editors in the book industry, editors who seek out and sign authors to contracts.

actual malice in libel law, a reckless disregard for the truth, such as when a reporter or an editor knows that a statement is false and prints or airs it anyway.

ad impressions in advertising, how often ads are seen

adult contemporary (AC) one of the oldest and most popular radio music formats, typically featuring a mix of news, talk, oldies, and soft rock.

affiliate stations radio or TV stations that, though independently owned, sign a contract to be part of a network and receive money to carry the network's programs; in exchange, the network reserves time slots, which it sells to national advertisers.

agenda-setting theory a media-research argument that says that when the mass media pay attention to particular events or issues, they determine—that is, set the agenda for—the major topics of discussion for individuals and society.

album-oriented rock (AOR) the radio music format that features album cuts from mainstream rock bands.

alternative rock nonmainstream rock music, which includes many types of experimental music.

AM (amplitude modulation) a type of radio and sound transmission that stresses the volume or height of radio waves; this type of modulation was sufficient for radio content such as talk, but not ideal for music.

analog in television, standard broadcast signals made of radio waves (replaced by digital standards in 2009)

analog recording a recording that is made by capturing the fluctuations of the original sound waves and storing those signals on record grooves or magnetic tape—analogous to the actual sound.

analysis the second step in the critical process, it involves discovering significant patterns that emerge from the description stage.

anthology drama a popular form of early TV programming that brought live dramatic theater to television; influenced by stage plays, anthologies offered new teleplays, casts, directors, writers, and sets from week to week.

arcade an establishment gathering multiple coin-operated games together in a single location.

ARPAnet the original Internet, designed by the U.S. Defense Department's Advanced Research Projects Agency (ARPA).

association principle in advertising, a persuasive technique that associates a product with some cultural value or image that has a positive connotation but may have little connection to the actual product.

astroturf lobbying phony grassroots public affairs campaigns engineered by public relations firms; coined by U.S. Senator Lloyd Bentsen of Texas (named after AstroTurf, the artificial grass athletic field surface).

Atari a video game development company that released Pong, the first big-hit arcade game, and established the home-video game market through a deal with Sears.

audience studies cultural studies research that focuses on how people use and interpret cultural content. Also known as *reader-response research*.

audiotape lightweight magnetized strands of ribbon that make possible sound editing and multiple-track mixing; instrumentals or vocals can be recorded at one studio and later mixed onto a master recording in another studio.

authoritarian model a model for journalism and speech that tolerates little criticism of government or public dissent; it holds that the general public needs guidance from an elite and educated ruling class.

avatar an identity created by an Internet user in order to participate in a form of online entertainment, such as *World of Warcraft* or *Second Life*.

bandwagon effect an advertising strategy that incorporates exaggerated claims that everyone is using a particular product, so you should, too.

barter in TV, giving a program to a local station in exchange for a split in the advertising revenue.

basic cable in cable programming, a tier of channels composed of local broadcast signals, nonbroadcast access channels (for local government, education, and general public use), a few regional PBS stations, and a variety of popular channels downlinked from communication satellites.

Big Six the six major Hollywood studios that currently rule the commercial film business: Warner Brothers, Paramount, Twentieth Century Fox, Universal, Columbia Pictures, and Disney.

blacklisted when the film industry began to self-regulate in the 1920s, and actors and movie extras with minor police records or involvement in scandals were put on a list of people who would subsequently not be hired by any movie studio.

block booking an early tactic of movie studios to control exhibition involving pressuring theater operators to accept marginal films with no stars in order to get access to films with the most popular stars.

blocking broadband providers prohibiting access to legal content and services.

block printing a printing technique developed by early Chinese printers, who hand-carved characters and illustrations into a block of wood, applied ink to the block, and then printed copies on multiple sheets of paper.

blogs sites that contain articles in chronological journal-like form, often with reader comments and links to other articles on the Web (from the term *Web log*).

blues originally a kind of black folk music, this music emerged as a distinct category in the early 1900s; it was influenced by African American spirituals, ballads, and work songs in the rural South, and by urban guitar and vocal solos from the 1930s and 1940s.

book challenge a formal complaint to have a book removed from a public or school library's collection.

boutique agencies in advertising, small regional ad agencies that offer personalized services.

broadband data transmission over a fiber-optic cable — a signaling method that handles a wide range of frequencies.

broadcasting the transmission of radio waves or TV signals to a broad public audience.

catfishing the practice of pretending to be another person, even a person of a different gender, to trick someone into having an online relationship.

cathode ray tube (CRT) a key component of early television and computer screens that allowed the display of images.

CATV (community antenna television) early cable systems that originated where mountains or tall buildings blocked TV signals; because of early technical and regulatory limits, CATV contained only twelve channels.

celluloid a transparent and pliable film that can hold a coating of chemicals sensitive to light.

chapter shows in television production, situation comedies or dramatic programs whose narrative structure includes self-contained stories that feature a problem, a series of conflicts, and a resolution from week to week (for contrast, see **serial programs**).

cinema verité French term for *truth film*, a documentary style that records fragments of everyday life unobtrusively; it often features a rough, grainy look and shaky, handheld camera work.

citizen journalism a grassroots movement wherein activist amateurs and concerned citizens, not professional journalists, use Internet tools like blogs to disseminate news and information.

click-throughs in online advertising, how often users land briefly on a site before clicking through to the next site.

codex an early type of book in which paperlike sheets were cut and sewed together along the edge, then bound with thin pieces of wood and covered with leather.

collective intelligence video game tips and cheats shared by players of the games, usually online.

commercial speech any print or broadcast expression for which a fee is charged to the organization or individual buying time or space in the mass media.

common carrier a communication or transportation business, such as a phone company or a taxi service, that is required by law to offer service on a first-come, first-served basis to whoever can pay the rate; such companies do not get involved in content.

compact discs (CDs) playback-only storage discs for music that incorporate pure and very precise digital techniques, thus eliminating noise during recording and playback.

conflict of interest considered unethical, a compromising situation in which a journalist stands to benefit personally from the news report he or she produces.

consensus narrative cultural products that become popular and command wide attention, providing shared cultural experiences.

console a device used specifically to play video games.

contemporary hit radio (CHR) originally called Top 40 radio, this radio format encompasses everything from hip-hop to children's songs; it appeals to many teens and young adults.

content analysis in social science research, a method for systematically studying and coding media texts and programs.

content communities online communities that exist for the sharing of all types of content, from text to photos and videos.

cookies information profiles about a user that are usually automatically accepted by the Web browser and stored on the user's own computer hard drive.

copy editors the people in magazine, newspaper, and book publishing who attend to specific problems in writing such as style, content, and length.

copyright the legal right of authors and producers to own and control the use of their published or unpublished writing, music, and lyrics; TV programs and movies; or graphic art designs.

Corporation for Public Broadcasting (CPB) a private, nonprofit corporation created by Congress in 1967 to funnel federal funds to nonprofit radio and public television.

correlation an observed association between two variables.

country claiming the largest number of radio stations in the United States, this radio format includes such subdivisions as old-time, progressive, country-rock, western swing, and country-gospel.

cover music songs recorded or performed by musicians who did not originally write or perform the music; in the 1950s, cover music was an attempt by white producers and artists to capitalize on popular songs by blacks.

critical process the process whereby a media-literate person or student studying mass communication employs the techniques of description, analysis, interpretation, evaluation, and engagement.

cultivation effect theory in media research, the idea that heavy television viewing leads individuals to perceive reality in ways that are consistent with the portrayals they see on television.

cultural imperialism the phenomenon of American culture (e.g., media, fashion, and food) dominating the global market and shaping the cultures and identities of other nations.

cultural studies in media research, the approaches that try to understand how the media and culture are tied to the actual patterns of communication used in daily life; these studies focus on how people make meanings, apprehend reality, and order experience through the use of stories and symbols.

data mining the unethical gathering of data by online purveyors of content and merchandise.

deadheading the practice in the early twentieth century of giving reporters free rail passes as bribes for favorable stories.

deficit financing in television, the process whereby a TV production company leases its programs to a network for a license fee that is actually less than the cost of production; the company hopes to recoup this loss later in rerun syndication.

demographic editions national magazines whose advertising is tailored to subscribers and readers according to occupation, class, and zip-code address.

demographics in market research, the gathering and analysis of audience members' age, gender, income, ethnicity, and education—characteristics to better target messages to particular audiences.

description the first step in the critical process, it involves paying close attention, taking notes, and researching the cultural product to be studied.

design managers publishing industry personnel who work on the look of a book, making decisions about type style, paper, cover design, and layout.

desktop publishing a computer technology that enables an aspiring publisher/editor to inexpensively write, design, lay out, and even print a small newsletter or magazine.

developmental editors in book publishing, the editors who provide authors with feedback, make suggestions for improvements, and obtain advice from knowledgeable members of the academic community.

development budget the money spent designing, coding, scoring, and testing a video game.

digital communication images, texts, and sounds that use pulses of electric current or flashes of laser lights and are converted (or encoded) into electronic signals represented as varied combinations of binary numbers, usually ones and zeros; these signals are then reassembled (decoded) as a precise reproduction of a TV picture, a magazine article, or a telephone voice.

digital divide the socioeconomic disparity between those who do and those who do not have access to digital technology and media, such as the Internet.

digital recording music recorded and played back by laser beam rather than by needle or magnetic tape.

digital turn the shift in media use and consumption resulting from the emergence of the Internet as a mass medium, which enables an array of media to converge and be easily shared.

digital video the production format that is replacing celluloid film and revolutionizing filmmaking because the cameras are more portable and production costs are much less expensive.

digital video recorder (DVR) a device that enables users to find and record specific television shows (and movies) and store them in a computer memory to be played back at a later time or recorded onto a DVD.

digitization a process through which information in analog form (such as text or picures) is translated into binary code – a series of ones and zeros that can be encoded in software and transmitted between computers.

dime novels sometimes identified as pulp fiction, these cheaply produced and low-priced novels were popular in the United States beginning in the 1860s.

direct broadcast satellites (DBS) satellite-based services that for a monthly fee downlink hundreds of satellite channels and services; they began distributing video programming directly to households in 1994.

documentary movie or TV news genre that documents reality by recording actual characters and settings.

e-book a digital book read on a computer or electronic reading device.

e-commerce electronic commerce, or commercial activity, on the Web.

electromagnetic waves invisible electronic impulses similar to visible light; electricity, magnetism, light, broadcast signals, and heat are part of such waves, which radiate in space at the speed of light, about 186,000 miles per second.

electronic publisher a communication business, such as a broadcaster or a cable TV company, that is entitled to choose what channels or content to carry.

e-mail electronic mail messages sent by the Internet; developed by computer engineer Ray Tomlinson in 1971.

engagement the fifth step in the critical process, it involves actively working to create a media world that best serves democracy.

Entertainment Software Rating Board the video game industry's self-regulating system, designed to inform parents of sexual and violent content that might not be suitable for younger players.

episodic series a narrative form well suited to television because main characters appear every week, sets and locales remain the same, and technical crews stay with the program; episodic series feature new adventures each week, but a handful of characters *emerge* with whom viewers can regularly identify (see also **chapter shows** and **serial programs**).

ethnocentrism an underlying value held by many U.S. journalists and citizens, it involves judging other countries and cultures according to how they live up to or imitate American practices and ideals.

evaluation the fourth step in the critical process, it involves arriving at a judgment about whether a cultural product is good, bad, or mediocre; this requires subordinating one's personal taste to the critical assessment resulting from the first three stages (description, analysis, and interpretation).

evergreens in TV syndication, popular, lucrative, and enduring network reruns, such as the *Andy Griffith Show* or *I Love Lucy*.

evergreen subscriptions magazine subscriptions that automatically renew on subscribers' credit cards.

experiments in regard to the mass media, research that isolates some aspect of content, suggests a hypothesis, and manipulates variables to discover a particular text's or medium's impact on attitudes, emotions, or behavior.

Fairness Doctrine repealed in 1987, this FCC rule required broadcast stations to both air and engage in controversial-issue programs that affected their communities and, when offering such programming, to provide competing points of view.

famous-person testimonial an advertising strategy that associates a product with the endorsement of a well-known person.

feature syndicates commercial outlets or brokers, such as Universal Uclick and Tribune Media Services, that contract with newspapers to provide work from well-known political writers, editorial cartoonists, comic-strip artists, and self-help columnists.

Federal Communications Act of 1934 the far-reaching act that established the FCC and the federal regulatory structure for U.S. broadcasting.

Federal Communications Commission (FCC) an independent U.S. government agency charged with regulating interstate and international communications by radio, television, wire, satellite, and cable.

Federal Radio Commission (FRC) established in 1927 to oversee radio licenses and negotiate channel problems.

fiber-optic cable thin glass bundles capable of transmitting thousands of messages converted to shooting pulses of light along cable wires; these bundles can carry broadcast channels, telephone signals, and all sorts of digital codes.

fin-syn (Financial Interest and Syndication Rules) FCC rules that prohibited the major networks from running their own syndication companies or from charging production companies additional fees after shows had completed their prime-time runs; most fin-syn rules were rescinded in the mid-1990s.

first-run syndication in television, the process whereby new programs are specifically produced for sale in syndication markets rather than for network television.

flipper bumper an addition to the pinball machine that transformed the game from one of chance into a challenging game of skill, touch, and timing.

FM (frequency modulation) a type of radio and sound transmission that offers static-free reception and greater fidelity and clarity than AM radio by accentuating the pitch or distance between radio waves.

focus group a common research method in psychographic analysis in which a moderator leads a small-group discussion about a product or an issue, usually with six to twelve people.

folk music music performed by untrained musicians and passed down through oral traditions; it encompasses a wide range of music, from Appalachian fiddle tunes to the accordion-led zydeco of Louisiana.

format radio the concept of radio stations developing and playing specific styles (or formats) geared to listeners' age, race, or gender; in format radio, management, rather than deejays, controls programming choices.

Fourth Estate the notion that the press operates as an unofficial branch of government, monitoring the legislative, judicial, and executive branches for abuses of power.

fringe time in broadcast television, the time slot either immediately before the evening's prime-time schedule (called *early fringe*) or immediately following the local evening news or the network's late-night talk shows (called *late fringe*).

gag orders legal restrictions prohibiting the press from releasing preliminary information that might prejudice jury selection.

gangster rap a style of rap music that depicts the hardships of urban life and sometimes glorifies the violent style of street gangs.

general-interest magazine a type of magazine that addresses a wide variety of topics and is aimed at a broad national audience.

genres narrative categories in which conventions regarding similar characters, scenes, structures, and themes recur in combination.

grunge rock music that takes the spirit of punk and infuses it with more attention to melody.

HD radio a digital technology that enables AM and FM radio broadcasters to multicast two to three additional compressed digital signals within their traditional analog frequency.

hegemony the acceptance of the dominant values in a culture by those who are subordinate to those who hold economic and political power.

hidden-fear appeal an advertising strategy that plays on a sense of insecurity, trying to persuade consumers that only a specific product can offer relief.

high culture a symbolic expression that has come to mean "good taste"; often supported by wealthy patrons and corporate donors, it is associated with fine art (such as ballet, the symphony, painting, and classical literature), which is available primarily in theaters or museums.

hip-hop music that combines spoken street dialect with cuts (or samples) from older records and bears the influences of social politics, male boasting, and comic lyrics carried forward from blues, R&B, soul, and rock and roll.

Hollywood Ten the nine screenwriters and one film director subpoenaed by the House Un-American Activities Committee (HUAC) who were sent to prison in the late 1940s for refusing to discuss their memberships or to identify communist sympathizers.

HTML (HyperText Markup Language) the written code that creates Web pages and links; a language all computers can read.

human-interest stories news accounts that focus on the trials and tribulations of the human condition, often featuring ordinary individuals facing extraordinary challenges.

hypodermic-needle model an early model in mass communication research that attempted to explain media effects by arguing that the media shoot their powerful effects directly into unsuspecting or weak audiences; sometimes called the *magic bullet theory*.

hypotheses in social science research, tentative general statements that predict a relationship between a dependent variable and an independent variable.

illuminated manuscripts books from the Middle Ages that featured decorative, colorful designs and illustrations on each page.

indecency the government may punish broadcasters for indecency or profanity after the fact; over the years, a handful of radio stations have had their licenses suspended or denied due to indecent programming.

indie rock independent-minded rock music, usually distributed by smaller labels.

indies independent music and film production houses that work outside industry oligopolies; they often produce less mainstream music and film.

individualism an underlying value held by most U.S. journalists and citizens, it favors individual rights and responsibilities over group needs or institutional mandates.

infotainment a type of television program that packages human-interest and celebrity stories in TV news style.

instant messaging (IM) a Web feature that enables users to chat with buddies in real time via pop-up windows assigned to each conversation.

intellectual properties the material in video games — stories, characters, personalities, music, etc. — that requires licensing agreements.

Internet the vast central network of high-speed digital lines designed to link and carry computer information worldwide.

Internet radio online radio stations that either "stream" simulcast versions of on-air radio broadcasts over the Web or are created exclusively for the Internet.

Internet service provider (ISP) a company that provides Internet access to homes and businesses for a fee.

interpretation the third step in the critical process, it asks and answers the "What does that mean?" and "So what?" questions about one's findings.

interpretive journalism a type of journalism that involves analyzing and explaining key issues or events and placing them in a broader historical or social context.

inverted pyramid a style of journalism in which news reports begin with the most dramatic or newsworthy information—answering *who*, *what*, *where*, and *when* (and less frequently *why* or *how*) questions at the top of the story—and then tail off with less significant details.

irritation advertising an advertising strategy that tries to create product-name recognition by being annoying or obnoxious.

jazz an improvisational and mostly instrumental musical form that absorbs and integrates a diverse body of musical styles, including African rhythms, blues, big band, and gospel.

kinescope before the days of videotape, a 1950s technique for preserving television broadcasts by using a film camera to record a live TV show off a studio monitor.

kinetograph an early movie camera developed by Thomas Edison's assistant in the 1890s.

kinetoscope an early film projection system that served as a kind of peep show in which viewers looked through a hole and saw images moving on a tiny plate.

libel in media law, the defamation of character in written or broadcast expression.

libertarian model a model for journalism and speech that encourages vigorous government criticism and supports the highest degree of freedom for individual speech and news operations.

limited competition in media economics, a market with many producers and sellers but only a few differentiable products within a particular category; sometimes called *monopolistic competition*.

linotype a technology introduced in the nineteenth century that enabled printers to set type mechanically using a typewriter-style keyboard.

lobbying in government public relations, the process of attempting to influence the voting of lawmakers to support a client's or an organization's best interests.

lobbyists professionals who seek to influence the voting of lawmakers to support a client's or organization's best interests.

longitudinal studies a term used for research studies that are conducted over long periods of time, or the practice of comparing new studies with those conducted years earlier; these studies often rely on large government and academic survey databases.

low (popular) culture a symbolic expression allegedly aligned with the questionable tastes of the "masses," who enjoy the commercial "junk" circulated by the mass media, such as soap operas, rock music, talk radio, comic books, and monster truck pulls.

low-power FM (LPFM) a class of noncommercial radio stations approved by the FCC in 2000 to give voice to local groups lacking access to the public airwaves; the 10-watt and 100-watt stations broadcast to a small, community-based area.

magalogs a combination of a glossy magazine and retail catalogue that is often used to market goods or services to customers or employees.

magazine a nondaily periodical that comprises a collection of articles, stories, and ads.

malware malicious software that hackers sneak onto computers, tablets, smartphones, and high-tech household applicances.

manuscript culture a period during the Middle Ages when priests and monks advanced the art of bookmaking.

market research in advertising and public relations agencies, the department that uses social science techniques to assess the behaviors and attitudes of consumers toward particular products before any ads are created.

mass communication the process of designing and delivering cultural messages and stories to diverse audiences through media channels as old as the book and as new as the Internet.

mass customization the process whereby product companies and content providers customize a Web page, print ad, or other media form for an individual consumer.

massively multiplayer online role-playing game (MMORPG) an online fantasy game set in a virtual world in which users develop avatars of their own design and interact with other players.

mass market paperbacks low-priced paperback books sold mostly on racks in drugstores, supermarkets, and airports, as well as in bookstores.

mass media the cultural industries—the channels of communication—that produce songs, novels, news, movies, online services, and other cultural products and distribute them to a large number of people.

media buyers in advertising, the individuals who choose and purchase the types of media that are best suited to carry a client's ads and reach the targeted audience.

media convergence the first definition involves the technological merging of content across different media channels; the second definition describes a business model that consolidates various media holdings under one corporate umbrella.

media literacy an understanding of the mass communication process through the development of critical-thinking tools—description, analysis, interpretation, evaluation, engagement—that enable a person to become more engaged as a citizen and more discerning as a consumer of mass media products.

mega-agencies in advertising, large firms or holding companies that are formed by merging several individual agencies and that maintain worldwide regional offices; they provide both advertising and public relations services and operate in-house radio and TV production studios.

megaplexes movie theater facilities with fourteen or more screens.

microprocessors miniature circuits that process and store electronic signals, integrating thousands of electronic components into thin strands of silicon along which binary codes travel.

minimal-effects model a mass communication research model based on tightly controlled experiments and survey findings; it argues that the mass media have limited effects on audiences, reinforcing existing behaviors and attitudes rather than changing them. Also called the *limited effects* model.

modern era period from the Industrial Revolution to the twentieth century that was characterized by working efficiently, celebrating individuals, believing in a rational order, and reaching tradition and embracing progress.

monopoly in media economics, an organizational structure that occurs when a single firm dominates production and distribution in a particular industry, either nationally or locally.

Morse code a system of sending electrical impulses from a transmitter through a cable to a reception point; developed in the 1840s by the American inventor Samuel Morse.

movie palaces ornate, lavish single-screen movie theaters that emerged in the 1910s in the United States.

MP3 short for MPEG-1 Layer 3, an advanced type of audio compression that reduces file size, enabling audio to be easily distributed over the Internet.

muckrakers reporters who used a style of early-twentieth-century investigative journalism that emphasized a willingness to crawl around in society's muck to uncover a story.

multiple-system operators (MSOs) large corporations that own numerous cable television systems.

multiplexes contemporary movie theaters that exhibit many movies at the same time on multiple screens.

must-carry rules rules established by the FCC requiring all cable operators to assign channels to and carry all local TV broadcasts on their systems, thereby ensuring that local network affiliates, independent stations (those not carrying network programs), and public television channels would benefit from cable's clearer reception.

narrative films movies that tell a story, with dramatic action and conflict emerging mainly from individual characters.

narrowcasting any specialized electronic programming or media channel aimed at niche viewer groups.

National Public Radio (NPR) noncommercial radio established in 1967 by the U.S. Congress to provide an alternative to commercial radio.

net neutrality the principle that every web site and every user—whether a multinational corporation or you—has the right to the same Internet network speed and access.

network a broadcast process that links, through special phone lines or satellite transmissions, groups of radio or TV stations that share programming produced at a central location.

network era the period in television history, roughly from the mid-1950s to the late 1970s, that refers to the dominance of the Big Three networks—ABC, CBS, and NBC—over programming and prime-time viewing habits; the era began eroding with a decline in viewing and with the development of VCRs, cable, and new TV networks.

news the process of gathering information and making narrative reports—edited by individuals in a news organization—that create selected frames of reference and help the public make sense of prominent people, important events, and unusual happenings in everyday life.

news and talk radio the second most popular format in the nation, this format is dominated by news programs and talk shows.

newshole the space left over in a newspaper for news content after all the ads are placed.

newspaper chains large companies that own several papers throughout the country.

newsreels weekly ten-minute magazine-style compilations of filmed news events from around the world organized in a sequence of short reports; prominent in movie theaters between the 1920s and the 1950s.

newsworthy the often unstated criteria that journalists use to determine which events and issues should become news reports, including timeliness, proximity, conflict, prominence, human interest, consequence, usefulness, novelty, and deviance.

nickelodeons the first small makeshift movie theaters, which were often converted cigar stores, pawnshops, or restaurants redecorated to mimic vaudeville theaters.

objective journalism a modern style of journalism that distinguishes factual reports from opinion columns; reporters strive to remain neutral toward the issue or event they cover, searching out competing points of view among the sources for a story.

obscenity expression that is not protected as speech if these three legal tests are all met: (1) the average person, applying contemporary community standards, would find that the material as a whole appeals to prurient interest; (2) the material depicts or describes sexual conduct in a patently offensive way; (3) the material, as a whole, lacks serious literary, artistic, political, or scientific value.

off-network syndication in television, the process whereby older programs that no longer run during prime time are made available for reruns to local stations, cable operators, online services, and foreign markets.

offset lithography a technology that enabled books to be printed from photographic plates rather than metal casts, reducing the cost of color and illustrations and eventually permitting computers to perform type-setting.

oligopoly in media economics, an organizational structure in which a few firms control most of an industry's production and distribution resources.

online fantasy sports games where players assemble teams of real-life athletes and use actual sports results to determine scores.

online piracy the illegal uploading, downloading, or streaming of copyrighted material, such as music or movies.

open-source software noncommercial software shared freely and developed collectively on the Internet.

opinion and fair comment a defense against libel which states that libel applies only to intentional misstatements of factual information rather than opinion, and which therefore protects said opinion.

opt-in policies controversial Web site policies related to personal data gathering; Web sites must gain explicit permission from online consumers before they can collect users' personal data.

Pacifica Foundation a radio broadcasting foundation established in Berkeley, California, by journalist and World War II pacifist Lewis Hill; he established KPFA, the first nonprofit community radio station, in 1949.

paid prioritization favoring some Internet traffic over other lawful traffic in exchange for payment, thereby creating a "fast lane" for those who pay and a "slow lane" for all others.

paperback books books made with less expensive paper covers, introduced in the United States in the mid-1800s.

papyrus one of the first substances to hold written language and symbols; obtained from plant reeds found along the Nile River.

Paramount decision the 1948 Supreme Court decision that ended vertical integration in the film industry by forcing the studios to divest themselves of their theaters.

parchment treated animal skin that replaced papyrus as an early pre-paper substance on which to document written language.

partisan press an early dominant style of American journalism distinguished by opinion newspapers, which generally argued one political point of view or pushed the plan of the particular party that subsidized the paper.

pass-along readership the total number of people who come into contact with a single copy of a magazine.

payola the unethical (and often illegal) practice of record promoters paying deejays or radio programmers to favor particular songs over others.

pay-per-view (PPV) a cable-television service that allows customers to select a particular movie for a fee, or to pay $25 to $40 for a special one-time event.

paywall an arrangement restricting Web site access to paid subscribers.

penny arcade an early version of the modern video arcade, with multiple coin-operated mechanical games gathered together in a single location.

penny papers (also *penny press*) refers to newspapers that, because of technological innovations in printing, were able to drop their price to one cent beginning in the 1830s, thereby making papers affordable to working and emerging middle classes and enabling newspapers to become a genuine mass medium.

phishing an Internet scam that begins with phony e-mail messages that pretend to be from an official site and request that customers send their credit card numbers, passwords, and other personal information to update the account.

photojournalism the use of photos to document events and people's lives.

pinball machine a mechanical game where players score points by manipulating the path of a metal ball on a playfield in a glass-covered case, and an early ancestor of today's electronic games.

plain-folks pitch an advertising strategy that associates a product with simplicity and the common person.

podcasting enables listeners to download audio program files from the Internet for playback on computers or digital music players.

political advertising the use of ad techniques to promote a candidate's image and persuade the public to adopt a particular viewpoint.

political economy studies an area of academic study that specifically examines interconnections among economic interests, political power, and how that power is used.

pop music popular music that appeals either to a wide cross section of the public or to sizable subdivisions within the larger public based on age, region, or ethnic background; the word *pop* has also been used as a label to distinguish popular music from classical music.

populism a political idea that attempts to appeal to ordinary people by setting up a conflict between "the people" and "the elite."

portal an entry point to the Internet, such as a search engine.

postmodern period a contemporary historical era spanning the 1960s to the present; its social values include celebrating populism, questioning authority, and embracing technology.

premium channels in cable programming, a tier of channels that subscribers can order at an additional monthly fee over their basic cable service; these may include movie channels and interactive services.

press agents the earliest type of public relations practitioner, who sought to advance a client's image through media exposure.

press releases in public relations, announcements—written in the style of a news report—that give new information about an individual, a company, or an organization and pitch a story idea to the news media.

prime time in television programming, the hours between 7 and 11 P.M. (or 7 and 10 P.M. in the Midwest), when networks have traditionally drawn their largest audiences and charged their highest advertising rates.

printing press a fifteenth-century invention whose movable metallic type technology spawned modern mass communication by creating the first method for mass production; it reduced the size and cost of books, made them the first mass medium affordable to less-affluent people, and provided the impetus for the Industrial Revolution, assembly-line production, modern capitalism, and the rise of consumer culture.

prior restraint the legal definition of censorship in the United States, which prohibits courts and governments from blocking any publication or speech before it actually occurs.

product placement the advertising practice of strategically placing products in movies, TV shows, comic books, and video games so the products appear as part of a story's set environment.

professional books technical books that target various occupational groups and are not intended for the general consumer market.

Progressive Era the period of political and social reform lasting roughly from the 1890s to the 1920s that inspired many Americans—and mass media—to break with tradition and embrace change.

propaganda in advertising and public relations, a communication strategy that tries to manipulate public opinion to gain support for a special issue, program, or policy, such as a nation's war effort.

propaganda analysis the study of propaganda's effectiveness in influencing and mobilizing public opinion.

pseudo-events in public relations, any circumstance or event created solely for the purpose of obtaining coverage in the media.

pseudo-polls typically call-in, online, or person-in-the-street polls that don't use random samples and whose results thus don't represent the population as a whole.

psychographics in market research, the study of audience or consumer attitudes, beliefs, interests, and motivations.

Public Broadcasting Act of 1967 the act by the U.S. Congress that established the Corporation for Public Broadcasting, which oversees the Public Broadcasting Service (PBS) and National Public Radio (NPR).

Public Broadcasting Service (PBS) the noncommercial television network established in 1967 as an alternative to commercial television.

public domain the end of the copyright period for a cultural or scientific work, at which point the public may begin to access it for free.

publicity in public relations, the positive and negative messages that spread controlled and uncontrolled information about a person, a corporation, an issue, or a policy in various media.

public relations the total communication strategy conducted by a person, a government, or an organization attempting to reach and persuade its audiences to adopt a point of view.

public service announcements (PSAs) reports or announcements, carried free by radio and TV stations, that promote government programs, educational projects, voluntary agencies, or social reform.

pulp fiction a term used to describe many late-nineteenth-century popular paperbacks and dime novels, which were constructed of cheap machine-made pulp material.

punk rock rock music that challenges the orthodoxy and commercialism of the recording business; it is characterized by loud, unpolished qualities, a jackhammer beat, primal vocal screams, crude aggression, and defiant or comic lyrics.

radio wireless transmission of voice and music.

Radio Act of 1912 the first radio legislation passed by Congress, it addressed the problem of amateur radio operators increasingly cramming the airwaves. This act required all radio stations on land or at sea to be licensed and assigned special call letters.

Radio Act of 1927 the second radio legislation passed by Congress; in an attempt to restore order to the airwaves, it stated that licensees did not own their channels but could license them as long as they operated in order to serve the "public interest, convenience, or necessity."

Radio Corporation of America (RCA) a company developed during World War I that was designed, with government approval, to pool radio patents; the formation of RCA gave the United States almost total control over the emerging mass medium of broadcasting.

radio waves a portion of the electromagnetic wave spectrum that was harnessed so that signals could be sent from a transmission point and obtained at a reception point.

random assignment a social science research method for assigning research subjects; it ensures that every subject has an equal chance of being placed in either the experimental group or the control group.

rating in TV audience measurement, a statistical estimate expressed as a percentage of households tuned to a program in the local or national market being sampled.

reference books dictionaries, encyclopedias, atlases, and other reference manuals related to particular professions or trades.

regional editions national magazines whose content is tailored to the interests of different geographic areas.

responsible capitalism an underlying value held by many U.S. journalists and citizens, it assumes that businesspeople compete with one another not primarily to maximize profits but to increase prosperity for all.

rhythm and blues (R&B) music that merged urban blues with big-band sounds.

right to privacy addresses a person's right to be left alone, without his or her name, image, or daily activities becoming public property.

rockabilly music that mixed bluegrass and country influences with those of black folk music and early amplified blues.

rock and roll music that mixed the vocal and instrumental traditions of popular music; it merged the black influences of urban blues, gospel, and R&B with the white influences of country, folk, and pop vocals.

rotation in format radio programming, the practice of playing the most popular or best-selling songs many times throughout the day.

satellite radio pay radio services that deliver various radio formats nationally via satellite.

saturation advertising the strategy of inundating a variety of print and visual media with ads aimed at target audiences.

scientific method a widely used research method that studies phenomena in systematic stages; it includes identifying the research problem, reviewing existing research, developing working hypotheses, determining appropriate research design, collecting information, analyzing results to see if the hypotheses have been verified, and interpreting the implications of the study.

search engines computer programs that allow users to enter key words or queries to find related sites on the Internet.

Section 315 part of the 1934 Communications Act; it mandates that during elections, broadcast stations must provide equal opportunities and response time for qualified political candidates.

selective exposure the phenomenon whereby audiences seek messages and meanings that correspond to their preexisting beliefs and values.

selective retention the phenomenon whereby audiences remember or retain messages and meanings that correspond to their preexisting beliefs and values.

serial programs radio or TV programs, such as soap operas, that feature continuing story lines from day to day or week to week (see **chapter shows**).

share in TV audience measurement, a statistical estimate of the percentage of homes tuned to a certain program, compared with those simply using their sets at the time of a sample.

shield laws laws protecting the confidentiality of key interview subjects and reporters' rights not to reveal the sources of controversial information used in news stories.

situation comedy (sitcom) a type of comedy series that features a recurring cast and set as well as several narrative scenes; each episode establishes a situation, complicates it, develops increasing confusion among its characters, and then resolves the complications.

sketch comedy short television comedy skits that are usually segments of TV variety shows; sometimes known as *vaudeo*, the marriage of vaudeville and video.

slander in law, spoken language that defames a person's character.

small-town pastoralism an underlying value held by many U.S. journalists and citizens, it favors the small over the large and the rural over the urban.

snob-appeal approach an advertising strategy that attempts to convince consumers that using a product will enable them to maintain or elevate their social status.

social learning theory a theory within media effects research that suggests a link between the mass media and behavior; later modified and renamed *social cognitive theory*.

social networking sites Internet Web sites that allow users to create personal profiles, upload photos, create lists of favorite things, and post messages to connect with old friends and to meet new ones.

social responsibility model a model for journalism and speech, influenced by the libertarian model, that encourages the free flow of information to citizens so they can make wise decisions regarding political and social issues.

social scientific research the mainstream tradition in mass communication research, it attempts to understand, explain, and predict the impact—or effects—of the mass media on individuals and society.

soul music that mixes gospel, blues, and urban and southern black styles with slower, more emotional, and melancholic lyrics.

space brokers in the days before modern advertising, individuals who purchased space in newspapers and sold it to various merchants.

spam a computer term referring to unsolicited e-mail.

Spanish-language radio one of radio's fastest-growing formats, concentrated mostly in large Hispanic markets such as Miami, New York, Chicago, Las Vegas, California, Arizona, New Mexico, and Texas.

spiral of silence a theory that links the mass media, social psychology, and the formation of public opinion; it proposes that people who find their views on controversial issues in the minority tend to keep these views silent.

split-run editions editions of national magazines that tailor ads to different geographic areas.

spyware software with hidden codes that enable commercial firms to "spy" on users and gain access to their computers.

state model a model for journalism and speech that places control in the hands of an enlightened government, which speaks for ordinary citizens and workers in order to serve the common goals of the state.

stereo the recording of two separate channels or tracks of sound.

storyboard in advertising, a blueprint or roughly drawn comic-strip version of a proposed advertisement.

studio system an early film production system that constituted a sort of assembly-line process for moviemaking; major film studios controlled not only actors but also directors, editors, writers, and other employees, all of whom worked under exclusive contracts.

subliminal advertising a 1950s term that refers to hidden or disguised print and visual messages that allegedly register on the subconscious, creating false needs and seducing people into buying products.

subsidiary rights in the book industry, selling the rights to a book for use in other media forms, such as a mass market paperback, a CD-ROM, or the basis for a movie screenplay.

supermarket tabloids newspapers that feature bizarre human-interest stories, gruesome murder tales, violent accident accounts, unexplained phenomena stories, and malicious celebrity gossip.

superstations local independent TV stations, such as WTBS in Atlanta or WGN in Chicago, that have uplinked their signals onto a communication satellite to make themselves available nationwide.

survey research in social science research, a method of collecting and measuring data taken from a group of respondents.

syndication leasing TV stations the exclusive right to air older TV series.

synergy in media economics, the promotion and sale of a product (and all its versions) throughout the various subsidiaries of a media conglomerate.

talkies movies with sound, beginning in 1927.

targeted advertising ads targeted to a consumer based on information that various Web sites have gathered about that individual.

Telecommunications Act of 1996 the sweeping update of telecommunications law that brought cable fully under federal oversight and led to a wave of media consolidation.

telegraph invented in the 1840s, it sent electrical impulses through a cable from a transmitter to a reception point, transmitting Morse code.

textbooks books made for the el-hi (elementary and high school) and college markets.

textual analysis in media research, a method for closely and critically examining and interpreting the meanings of culture, including architecture, fashion, books, movies, and TV programs.

third-person effect theory theory suggesting that people believe others are more affected by media messages than they are themselves.

throttling intentionally impairing or degrading Internet performance based on content or source.

time shifting the process whereby television viewers record shows and watch them later, when it is convenient for them.

Top 40 format the first radio format, in which stations played the forty most popular hits in a given week as measured by record sales.

trade books the most visible book industry segment, featuring hardbound and paperback books aimed at general readers and sold at bookstores and other retail outlets.

trade publications specialty magazines that supply information relevant to specific manufacturing trades, professional fields, and business sectors.

transistor invented by Bell Laboratories in 1947, this tiny technology, which receives and amplifies radio signals, made portable radios possible.

TV newsmagazine a TV news program format, pioneered by CBS's *60 Minutes* in the late 1960s, that features multiple segments in an hour-long episode, usually ranging from a celebrity or political feature story to a hard-hitting investigative report.

university press the segment of the book industry that publishes scholarly books in specialized areas.

urban contemporary one of radio's more popular formats, primarily targeting African American listeners in urban areas with dance, R&B, and hip-hop music.

uses and gratifications model a mass communication research model, usually employing in-depth interviews and survey questionnaires, that argues that people use the media to satisfy various emotional desires or intellectual needs.

Values and Lifestyles (VALS) a market-research strategy that divides consumers into types and measures psychological factors, including how consumers think and feel about products and how they achieve (or do not achieve) the lifestyles to which they aspire.

vellum a handmade paper made from treated animal skin, used in the Gutenberg Bibles.

vertical integration in media economics, the phenomenon of controlling a mass media industry at its three essential levels: production, distribution, and exhibition; the term is most frequently used in reference to the film industry.

videocassette recorders (VCRs) recorders that use a half-inch video format known as VHS (video home system), which enables viewers to record and play back programs from television or to watch movies rented from video stores.

video news release (VNR) in public relations, the visual counterpart to a press release; it pitches a story idea to the TV news media by mimicking the style of a broadcast news report.

video-on-demand (VOD) cable television technology that enables viewers to instantly order programming, such as movies, to be digitally delivered to their sets.

video subscription services a term referring to cable and video-on-demand providers, introduced to include streaming-only companies like Hulu and Netflix.

viral marketing short videos or other content that marketers hope will quickly gain widespread attention as users share it with friends online, or by word of mouth.

vitascope a large-screen movie projection system developed by Thomas Edison.

Web browsers information-search services, such as Firefox and Microsoft's Internet Explorer, that offer detailed organizational maps to the Internet.

webzines magazines that publish on the Internet.

Wi-Fi a standard for short-distance wireless networking, enabling users of notebook computers and other devices to connect to the Internet in cafés, hotels, airports, and parks.

wikis Internet Web sites that are capable of being edited by any user; the most famous of these sites is Wikipedia.

Wireless Ship Act the 1910 mandate that all major U.S. seagoing ships carrying more than fifty passengers and traveling more than two hundred miles off the coast be equipped with wireless equipment with a one-hundred-mile range.

wireless telegraphy the forerunner of radio, a form of voiceless point-to-point communication; it preceded the voice and sound transmissions of one-to-many mass communication that became known as *broadcasting*.

wireless telephony early experiments in wireless voice and music transmissions, which later developed into modern radio.

wire services commercial organizations, such as the Associated Press, that share news stories and information by relaying them around the country and the world, originally via telegraph and now via satellite transmission.

World Wide Web (WWW) a data-linking system for organizing and standardizing information on the Internet; the WWW enables computer-accessed information to associate with—or link to—other information, no matter where it is on the internet.

yellow journalism a newspaper style or era that peaked in the 1890s; it emphasized high-interest stories, sensational crime news, large headlines, and serious reports that exposed corruption, particularly in business and government.

zines self-published magazines produced on person computer programs or on the Internet.

Index

Video Program for *Media Essentials*

Media Essentials doesn't just teach convergence—it also practices convergence, converging print and video with LaunchPad and a variety of recommended Web clips.

LaunchPad Videos with Quizzing

LaunchPad for *Media Essentials* includes a full e-Book as well as a library of video clips that complement text material. Here's a list of all the LaunchPad videos featured in the book by chapter, each of which is accompanied by assignable critical thinking questions that report to the gradebook.

Recommended Web Clips

There are many interesting and informative videos available on the Web. Listed below are recommended third party videos included in a number of case study boxes throughout the text. Each clip is paired with an accompanying discussion question, which makes these prompts especially useful for in-class or small group discussion.